The Statutes At Large Of Pennsylvania From 1682 To 1801 (Volume X) 1779-1781

James T. Mitchell, Henry Flanders

Alpha Editions

This Edition Published in 2021

ISBN: 9789354508257

Design and Setting By
Alpha Editions
www.alphaedis.com
Email – info@alphaedis.com

As per information held with us this book is in Public Domain.
This book is a reproduction of an important historical work. Alpha Editions
uses the best technology to reproduce historical work in the same manner
it was first published to preserve its original nature. Any marks or number
seen are left intentionally to preserve its true form.

PREFATORY NOTE.

The notes and index have been prepared under the supervision of the Commission by Harry S. Ambler, Jr., Esquire.

THE STATUTES AT LARGE OF PENNSYLVANIA.

Laws enacted in the first sitting of the fourth General Assembly of the Commonwealth of Pennsylvania, which met at Philadelphia, on Monday, the twenty-fifth day of October, in the year of our Lord 1779.

CHAPTER DCCCLXVII.

AN ACT FOR REGULATING CHIMNEY SWEEPERS WITHIN THE CITY OF PHILADELPHIA, THE DISTRICT OF SOUTHWARK AND THE TOWNSHIP OF THE NORTHERN LIBERTIES OF THE CITY OF PHILADELPHIA.

(Section 1, P. L.) Whereas the houses and estates of the inhabitants of the city of Philadelphia, the district of Southwark and the township of the Northern Liberties of the city of Philadelphia are frequently dangered by chimneys taking fire and blazing out at the top, and great complaints have been made for want of a proper regulation among those, who undertake the sweeping of chimneys:

For remedy whereof:

[Section I.] (Section II, P. L.) Be it enacted and it is hereby enacted by the Representatives of the Freemen of the Commonwealth of Pennsylvania in General Assembly met, and by the authority of the same, That no person or persons, from and after the tenth day of December next, shall follow the business or occupation of a chimney sweeper, either by himself, his servants, negroes or others within the city of Philadelphia, the district of Southwark or the township of the Northern Liberties aforesaid without having first made application to the officer hereinafter directed to be appointed, and having registered his or their name or names and the name or names of his or their servants, negroes, or other persons aforesaid, with a number affixed to each and every such name, in a book by the said officer to be kept for that purpose, and without procuring and receiving from the said officer a certificate of every such registry, containing the number and name of every person so entered, under the penalty of fifteen pounds for every day he shall follow by himself, or cause to be followed by his servants, negroes or others, the said business, which said certificates the said officer is hereby enjoined and required to make out under his hand and to deliver to the person or persons who shall apply for the same, and for every such registry and certificate he shall receive the sum of three pounds and no more.

[Section II.] (Section III, P. L.) And be it further enacted by the authority aforesaid, That every person following the business aforesaid, within the said city, district and liberties, shall (if he follows the employment himself) wear (or if he employs his servants, negroes or others) cause to be worn, on the front of their caps, in full view, without any concealment, the same figures and numbers respectively as shall be so as aforesaid entered in the said book, and contained in his or their respective certificates, and none other, in large figures, not less than two inches in length, to be made of strong, durable tin or copper; and that all and every person and persons who shall follow the said business or employment, by him or themselves, or by his or their servants, negroes or others, not having the said number fixed on his or their cap and caps, and the cap and caps of his and their servants, negroes and other persons aforesaid, according to the directions aforesaid, or when fixed, shall wilfully deface or conceal the same, or shall neglect to keep them plain and visible, shall, for each and every such offense forfeit and pay the sum of fifteen pounds for every day he or they shall follow the said employment, not wearing the said number as aforesaid.

[Section III.] (Section IV, P. L.) And be it further enacted by the authority aforesaid, That if any person or persons, undertaking the business or occupation aforesaid shall not within forty-eight hours after application to him or them made by any of the inhabitants of the said city, district or Northern Liberties, sweep or cause to be swept, such chimney or chimneys as he or they shall be required to sweep, every such person or persons so offending shall forfeit and pay the sum of fifteen pounds.

[Section IV.] (Section V, P. L.) And be it further enacted by the authority aforesaid, That every chimney sweeper shall have and receive for every chimney by him swept within the city of Philadelphia, and for every chimney by him swept in the district and liberties aforesaid not more than one mile distant from the northern and southern boundaries of the said city a sum not exceeding forty-five shillings.

[Section V.] (Section VI, P. L.) And be it further enacted by the authority aforesaid, That if the chimney of any person or persons within the said city, district or liberties shall take fire and blaze out at the top, the same not having been swept within the space of one calendar month next before the time of taking such fire, every such [person or] persons shall forfeit and pay the sum of fifteen pounds, and if any chimney shall take fire and blaze out at the top, the same having been swept within one calendar month from the time of such taking fire, the person who swept the same, either by himself, his servants or negroes, shall forfeit and pay the sum of fifteen pounds.

[Section VI.] (Section VII, P. L.) And be it further enacted by the authority aforesaid, That every person who shall follow the business or occupation of a chimney sweeper, either by himself, his servants, negroes or others within the said city of Philadelphia, the district of Southwark or the township of the Northern Liberties, shall pay unto the officer hereinafter directed to be appointed the sum of ten shillings for every working day from and after the publication hereof until the first day of April next ensuing, and thereafter from the first day of October till the first day of April in each and every year during the continuance of this act for his care and trouble in the execution thereof.

(Section VIII, P. L.) And to the end that the regulations by this act prescribed may be executed:

[Section VII.] Be it enacted by the authority aforesaid, That any three of the justices of the peace of the said city and county, together with the wardens of the said city shall appoint the officer for registering and granting certificates to chimney sweepers, and for collecting of the said fines and forfeitures, who is hereby strictly required to do and perform the several duties of the said office enjoined by this act.

[Section VIII.] (Section IX, P. L.) And be it further enacted by the authority aforesaid, That it shall and may be lawful for the justices of the peace for the city and county of Philadelphia, or any three or more of them, in open court of quarter sessions or at any other time to regulate, lessen or increase and fix the prices for sweeping of chimneys in such manner as to them shall appear just, and under their hands from time to time to publish the same in one or more of the newspapers, so that all concerned may govern themselves accordingly, anything in this act in that respect contained to the contrary in anywise notwithstanding.

[Section IX.] (Section X, P. L.) And be it further enacted by the authority aforesaid, That all and every the penalties and forfeitures imposed by virtue of this act shall be paid one-half thereof to the use of the officer aforesaid, and the other half thereof to the overseers of the poor of the said city, district or township where the offense shall be committed for the use of the poor thereof, to be sued for in the name of the officer, and recovered before any justice of the peace for the said city and county, who is hereby authorized to hear, try and determine the same.

(Section XI, P. L.) Provided always, That nothing in this act shall extend or be construed to [extend to] a greater distance than one mile from without the bounds of the city of Philadelphia.

[Section X.] (Section XII, P. L.) And be it enacted by the authority aforesaid, That so much of the act of general assembly passed in the year one thousand seven hundred and twenty-one, entitled "An act for preventing accidents that may happen by fire," [1] and of the act of general assembly passed in the year one thousand seven hundred and fifty-one, entitled "An act for the more effectual preventing accidents which may happen by fire, and for suppressing idleness, drunkenness and other debaucheries," [2] as relates to the firing of chimneys within the said city, and one other act of general assembly passed the twenty-first day of March, one thousand seven hundred and seventy-two, entitled "An act for regulating chimney sweepers within the city of Philadelphia, the district of Southwark and the township of the Northern Liberties," [3] shall be and are hereby declared to be repealed.

[Section XI.] (Section XIII, P. L.) And be it further enacted by the authority aforesaid, That this act shall continue and be in force for and during the term of seven years next ensuing, and from thence to the end of the next sitting of the general assembly and no longer.

Passed November 25, 1779. Recorded L. B. No. 1, p. 311, etc. See the note to the Act of Assembly passed March 21, 1772, Chapter 648, and the Acts of Assembly passed March 8, 1780, Chapter 888; September 29, 1787, Chapter 1318.

CHAPTER DCCCLXVIII.

AN ACT FOR RAISING THE SUM OF TWO MILLIONS FIVE HUNDRED THOUSAND DOLLARS MONTHLY DURING EIGHT MONTHS IN THE YEAR ONE THOUSAND SEVEN HUNDRED AND EIGHTY FOR THE SUPPLY OF THE TREASURY OF THE UNITED STATES OF AMERICA AND THE TREASURY OF THIS STATE.

(Section 1, P. L.) Whereas the honorable Congress, by an act of their body dated the fourth day of October last, did call upon the several states to raise, in such manner as each state may judge expedient, [sufficient sums] to enable the said states to pay into the continental treasury, or to the order of Congress, on or before the first day of February next, and on or before the

---

[1] Passed August 26, 1721, Chapter 245.
[2] Passed February 9, 1751, Chapter 388.
[3] Passed March 21, 1772, Chapter 648.

first day of each succeeding month until the first day of September next, inclusive, their respective proportions of fifteen millions of dollars:

(Section II, P. L.) And whereas the proportion of this state for the present is set at two millions three hundred thousand dollars, and it is highly proper that the good people of this commonwealth should exert themselves in furnishing this necessary supply:

(Section III, P. L.) And whereas it is expedient that the tax which will be proper for raising the moneys aforesaid be grafted upon the returns made or to be made for the tax now levying in this state by virtue of an act, entitled "An act for raising the additional sum of five millions seven hundred thousand dollars in the year one thousand seven hundred and seventy-nine,"[1] whereby much expense and trouble and also much time will be saved, and yet the payment thereof be sufficiently equal:

(Section IV, P. L.) And whereas it is necessary that the treasury of this state be also supplied:

[Section I.] Be it therefore enacted and it is hereby enacted by the Representatives of the Freemen of the Commonwealth of Pennsylvania in General Assembly met, and by the authority of the same, That in the month of January next, and so in every succeeding month after, for and during eight months ending on the thirty-first day of August next, there shall be charged upon and collected of every person in this state who is or shall be rated, assessed and charged in any of the counties of this state with any part of the said sum of five millions seven hundred thousand dollars, or for the tax on ready money by virtue of the act aforesaid, or who was or ought to be liable to and chargeable therewith, a sum of money amounting to one-half part of the whole amount of the tax, which such person was or is or ought to be chargeable with and liable to pay as aforesaid.

[Section II.] (Section VI, P. L.) And be it further enacted by the authority aforesaid, That the commissioners of the several and respective counties of this state, shall cause to be written and made out, fair duplicates of the names and surnames and sums of money chargeable by virtue of this act, monthly as

---

[1] Passed October 10, 1779, Chapter 866.

aforesaid, of and on all persons within their respective counties, and shall deliver a counterpart thereof with proper warrants and directions to the collector of the county, and the said collector shall proceed to collect the same in the manner and within the time hereinbefore specified and shall pay at the end of every month the same without delay to the treasurer of the proper county, and the treasurers of the several counties of this state shall immediately after they receive the moneys by virtue of this act, or any part thereof, transmit and pay the same to the treasurer of this state, to be by him paid over to the amount of eighteen millions four hundred thousand dollars to the treasurer of the United States, or to the order of Congress for the support of the federal army and navy, the state treasurer retaining in his hands the residue of the tax imposed by this act for the use of this state subject to the disposal of the house of assembly.

[Section III.] (Section VII, P. L.) And be it further enacted by the authority aforesaid, That the commissioners of the several counties of this state shall have and exercise like authority to enforce the collection and payment of the said tax and that like fines and penalties shall be incurred by delinquent commissioners, collectors and county treasurers, to be imposed and levied on such delinquents in like manner and by like process as are directed in like cases in and by the act before mentioned, and that all necessary powers for the effectual and timely raising, collecting and bringing into the treasury of this state the said sum of two millions five hundred thousand dollars by monthly payments as aforesaid, and like reward for the services done in execution of this act shall be exercised and used as were authorized, given and directed to be exercised and used in the execution of the act of assembly herein before mentioned, or of an act of assmbly, entitled "An act for raising the supplies for the year one thousand seven hundred and seventy-nine,"[1] in similar cases and for like purposes.

[Section IV.] (Section VIII, P. L.) Provided always, and be it further enacted by the authority aforesaid, That if by reason of any unavoidable delay the sums hereby directed to be levied,

---

[1]Passed April 3, 1779, Chapter 840.

collected and paid shall not be levied, collected and paid in the several months herein before provided according to the intent of this act, that in such case the same shall be levied, collected and paid as soon after as may be and applied in the manner herein before mentioned and directed.

(Section IX, P. L.) Provided also, That if any person liable to pay the monthly assessment aforesaid shall be disposed to advance the sums he or she is liable to pay in any other month or months, than the monthly tax demanded of him or her, the collector, upon tender thereof shall be obliged to receive and give a discharge for the same.

<small>Passed November 25, 1779. See the note to the Act of Assembly passed April 3, 1779, Chapter 840; and the Act of Assembly passed June 1, 1780, Chapter 912.</small>

CHAPTER DCCCLXIX.

AN ACT MORE EFFECTUALLY TO PREVENT COUNTERFEITING THE CONTINENTAL LOAN OFFICE CERTIFICATES, THE CONTINENTAL LOAN OFFICE BILLS OF EXCHANGE AND THE PAPER MONEY OF THE UNITED STATES OF AMERICA, OR ANY OF THEM.

(Section I, P. L.) Whereas the want of a sufficient quantity of gold and silver to answer the purposes of commerce, the exigencies of government, and to carry on the present just and necessary war against the King of Great Britain, induced the Congress of the United Colonies and now States of America, and also the assemblies, congresses and conventions of the several thirteen Colonies and now States of America, to emit and circulate certain paper bills of credit to pass in payments for limited periods, the counterfeiting of which, or the uttering the same so counterfeited as and for true, good and genuine bills, knowing the same to be so counterfeited, hath usually been made felonies in these United States respectively:

(Section II, P. L.) And whereas by an act, entitled "An act for making the continental bills of credit and the bills of credit emitted by resolves of the late assemblies, legal tender and for other purposes therein mentioned,"[1] the counterfeiting of such paper bills of credit, or uttering any of them so counterfeited, knowing them to be such, which were issued before the twenty-eighth day of January in the year one thousand seven hundred and seventy-seven, are made felonies of death without benefit of clergy; and the counterfeiting the bills of credit of this commonwealth made and issued by virtue of an act, entitled "An act for emitting the sum of two hundred thousand pounds in bills of credit for the defense of this state, and providing a fund for sinking the same by a tax on all estates, real and personal, and on all taxables within the same,"[2] or emitted and made current by the resolves of the late assemblies of Pennsylvania, or the uttering such bills, knowing them to be counterfeit as aforesaid, is by the said act made a felony of death but not ousting the benefit of clergy:

(Section III, P. L.) And whereas the counterfeiting the certificates of the continental loan offices, or any of the bills of credit emitted by the resolves of the Congress of the United States, or selling, giving in payment or otherwise uttering or distributing any of the said counterfeit certificates or bills of credit, knowing them to be such is by an act, entitled "An act for punishing the counterfeiting the continental loan office certificates and lottery tickets,"[3] made a felony of death, not ousting clergy; and the counterfeiting any of the said paper bills of credit, or continental loan office certificates, or uttering any of them, knowing the same to be so counterfeited, which have issued since the twenty-fifth day of May, one thousand seven hundred and seventy-eight, and also the counterfeiting or uttering as aforesaid any of the continental loan office bills of exchange is punishable only by the common law:

(Section IV, P. L.) And whereas it is just and right that offenses and crimes of equal enormity and guilt should receive the like punishments and it highly interests each of the United States by all means in their power to provide against the debasing of their medium of commerce:

---

[1] Passed January 29, 1777, Chapter 738.
[2] Passed March 20, 1777, Chapter 752.
[3] Passed March 20, 1777, Chapter 753.

[Section I.] (Section V, P. L.) Be it therefore enacted and it is hereby enacted by the Representatives of the Freemen of the Commonwealth of Pennsylvania in General Assembly met, and by the authority of the same, That from and after the publication of this act, if any person or persons shall, within this state or elsewhere, prepare, engrave, stamp, forge or print, or cause or procure to be prepared, engraved, stamped, forged or printed, the counterfeit resemblance of any paper bills of credit issued, emitted or made by the Congress of the United States of America or by the assemblies, congresses, conventions or other legislative authority of this, or of any other of the said states, or which shall be issued, emitted or made by them respectively, on or before the first day of January now next ensuing, or of any of the certificates of the several continental loan offices or continental loan office bills of exchange, issued or made or which shall at any time hereafter be issued or made, or shall counterfeit or sign the name or names of the signers of any true bills or loan office certificates or continental loan office bills of exchange to such counterfeit paper, with an intention that such counterfeit paper shall be passed in payments or received as genuine and good bills, certificates or bills of exchange, whether the same be so passed or received or not, or if any person or persons shall, in this state pass, pay or tender in payment any such counterfeit money or certificates or bills of exchange, or deliver the same to any other person or persons with an intention that they be passed, paid or received as and for good and genuine, knowing the [same] to be forged or counterfeited, every such person, being thereof lawfully convicted or attainted, in any court of oyer and terminer within this state by verdict of a jury, or confession of the party offending, or being indicted thereof shall stand mute, or not directly answer to the indictment, or shall peremptorily challenge more than the number of twenty persons legally returned to be of the jury for the trial of such offender, shall be adjudged a felon, and shall suffer death without benefit of clergy. And if any person or persons shall counterfeit any of the said bills of credit, loan office certificates or bills of exchange, by altering the denomination thereof with design to increase the value of such bills, certificates or bills of exchange, or shall utter such bills, certificates, or bills of exchange, knowing them to be so counterfeited or altered as aforesaid, and shall be therefore legally convicted in any court of record in this state, such person or persons shall be sentenced to the pillory and have both his or her ears cut off and nailed to the pillory, and be publicly whipped on his or her bare back with thirty-nine lashes well laid on; and, moreover, every such offender shall forfeit the sum of two thousand pounds, lawful money of Pennsylvania, to be levied on his or her lands and tenements, goods and chattels, the one moiety to the use of the state and the other moiety to the discoverer, and the offender shall pay to the party grieved double the value of the damages thereby sustained, together with the costs and charges of prosecution, and in case the offender hath not sufficient to satisfy the discoverer for his or her damages and charges and to pay the forfeiture aforesaid in such case the offender shall, by order of the court, where he or she shall be convicted, be sold as a servant, for any term not exceeding seven years for satisfaction.

[Section II.] (Section VI, P. L.) And be it further enacted by the authority aforesaid, That if any person or persons shall, within this state, prepare or make any paper of the similitude or likeness of the paper prepared or made for and used by the Congress of the United States of America, or the person or persons employed by them for the purpose of striking their paper bills of credit, continental loan office certificates or continental bills of exchange upon, and on which the same are or shall be struck, printed or made; or if any person or persons shall, within this state prepare or make any paper of the similitude or likeness of the paper prepared or made for and used by the legislative authority of this state for the purpose of striking their paper money upon, and on which the same is or shall be printed and made, and shall give, sell, deliver or otherwise employ or willingly suffer the same to be taken by or delivered or otherwise disposed of to any person or persons whomsoever, except to Congress or to the legislature of this state, or of some other of the United States or to their order or the order of some person or persons authorized by them respectively; he, she or they, being legally convicted thereof in any court of record in this state shall be imprisoned at the discretion of the court and moreover shall forfeit all his, her or their goods and chattels and one moiety of the lands to the use of this commonwealth.

[Section III.] (Section VII, P. L.) And be it enacted by the authority aforesaid, That if any person or persons shall take and prosecute any of the hereinbefore mentioned felons to conviction within this state, upon every such conviction and procuring a certificate thereof under the hands of the judges before whom the conviction shall be, or either of them, which the said judges are hereby directed and required to give, such person or persons shall receive of the treasurer of this commonwealth the sum of one hundred pounds lawful money of this state, which the said treasurer is hereby directed and required to pay out of the public money in his hands, and the same shall be allowed to him at the settlement of his accounts.

Passed November 26, 1779. See the notes to the ordinance of the First Constitutional Convention, passed August 1, 1776, Chapter 723, and the Act of Assembly passed January 29, 1777, Chapter 738.

CHAPTER DCCCLXX.

AN ACT FOR THE EFFECTUAL SUPPRESSION OF PUBLIC AUCTIONS AND VENDUES; AND TO PROHIBIT MALE PERSONS, CAPABLE OF BEARING ARMS FROM BEING PEDDLERS OR HAWKERS.

(Section I, P. L.) Whereas the practice of selling goods and merchandises by public auction or vendue in the present embarrassed state of commerce occasioned by the war now carrying on between the United States of America and Great Britain hath been made use of as a device for enhancing the prices of commodities and of depreciating the bills of credit of this state and of the United States of America:

(Section II, P. L.) And whereas the restrictions and prohibitions heretofore laid upon sales by public auction or vendue have not proved effectual:

For remedy whereof:

[Section I.] (Section III, P. L.) Be it enacted [and it is hereby enacted] by the Representatives of the Freemen of the Commonwealth of Pennsylvania in General Assembly met, and by the authority of the same, That from and after the publication of this act no goods, wares or merchandises, or other property whatsoever (except as is hereinafter excepted) shall be offered or exposed to sale, or sold by public auction, vendue or outcry in any place within the territories of this commonwealth by any person or persons whatsoever.

[Section II.] (Section IV, P. L.) And be it further enacted by the authority aforesaid, That if any person or persons shall, contrary to the directions of this act, offer or expose to sale, or shall sell by public auction, vendue or outcry within this commonwealth, any goods, wares or merchandises or property (except as is hereinafter excepted) he, she or they so offending shall forfeit and pay for every such offense a sum of money equal to the value of the goods, wares or merchandises and other property so offered or exposed to sale, or so sold by public auction, vendue or outcry, to be recovered by action of debt, or by indictment, by any person who will sue or prosecute for the same, the one-half part thereof to the use of the person so suing or prosecuting, and the other half part thereof to the use of the overseers of the poor of the city or place where the offense shall be committed.

(Section V, P. L.) Provided always, That this act shall not be construed to extend to sales at public auction or vendue, which shall be made by any sheriff or other officer in the execution of his office, who is not specially restricted by this act; nor to sales by public auction or vendue holden by executors or administrators of any real or personal estate which were bona fide of their respective testators or intestates; nor to the sale of lands, houses and other real estate, nor to the sale of the household goods (which have been in wear and use), horses, cattle and live stock being the bona fide property of resident housekeepers actually removing from any township or district of this state to another, or out of the state.

(Section VI, P. L.) Provided nevertheless, That all sales by public auction, vendue or outcry permitted by this act which shall be holden or made within the city of Philadelphia, or within two miles of the court house in High street, in the said city, other than the sales by sheriffs and other officers, executors and administrators as aforesaid, shall be holden and made in the manner hereinafter limited and directed and not otherwise.

(Section VII, P. L.) And although a monopoly of the sale of goods by public auction or vendue, in time of peace and order as the same was heretofore established in the city of Philadelphia, might be an unjustifiable limitation of private right and productive of inconvenience, yet for the more effectual attainment of the purposes of this act within the city of Philadelphia and the vicinity of the same, it is necessary that a sole auctioneer be established in the said city during the continuance of the restraint introduced by this act:

[Section III.] (Section VIII, P. L.) Be it therefore enacted by the authority aforesaid, That the sale by public auction, vendue or outcry within the said city and within two miles of the said court house from and after the publication of this act of all lands and other real estate and of all other property permitted by this act to be sold by public auction, vendue or outcry other than the sales by sheriffs and other officers, executors and administrators as aforesaid shall be performed by an officer who shall be appointed and commissioned for that purpose by the supreme executive council and who shall be styled The Auctioneer of the City of Philadelphia; and if any person or persons other than the said auctioneer, his deputy or assisttants shall in the said city or within two miles of the said courthouse offer or expose to sale, or shall sell by public auction, vendue or outcry any lands, houses or other property, permitted by this act to be sold by public auction, vendue or outcry as aforesaid, he, she or they so offending shall forfeit and pay for every offense a sum of money equal to the value of the lands, houses, goods or other property so offered or exposed to sale or so sold by public auction, vendue or outcry, to be recovered by action of debt, or by indictment in like manner and to like use as in the case of persons who shall sell by public vendue any goods by this act prohibited to be so sold as aforesaid.

[Section IV.] (Section IX, P. L.) And be it further enacted by the authority aforesaid, That it shall be the duty of the said auctioneer to enquire diligently after all offenses against this act which shall be committed within his jurisdiction as above described, and to inform against the offenders, and to recover the penalties directed and provided by this act, but not exclusive of any other person who will sue or prosecute for the same; and the said auctioneer shall, before he enters upon the duties of his said office become bound with two sufficient sureties unto the president of the supreme executive council of this state in the sum of twenty thousand pounds, conditioned for the faithful performance of the duties required of him, and for the honest and just satisfaction and payment of his employers and every of them, and besides the usual attestations required of the officers of this state by law, shall take an oath that he will, to the best of his skill and abilities, faithfully perform and execute the duties required of him by this act.

[Section V.] (Section X, P. L.) And be it further enacted by the authority aforesaid, That the recompense of the said auctioneer for selling at public auction, collecting the money and paying over the same, without loss or waste shall be as follows: For household goods, cattle and live stock, five per centum; for horses, two and a half per centum, and for ships, houses and lands an half per centum.

(Section XI, P. L.) And whereas the sale by public auction or vendue of goods taken as prize upon water and condemned in the court of admiralty has been found very prejudicial to the credit of the paper money of the United States, emitted by the honorable Congress, by affording frequent and easy opportunities of gratifying private avarice and advancing and heightening the nominal value of commodities:

For remedy whereof:

[Section VI.] (Section XII, P. L.) Be it enacted by the authority aforesaid, That during the continuance of this act the marshal of the court of admiralty of this state shall not sell any goods, wares or merchandises or other property by public auction or vendue, saving and excepting the ships or other vessels taken and condemned as prize, which vessels he shall put up with and sell together with their tackle, furniture and cannon, and not separately; and saving, also, such goods really perishable in their nature or greatly damaged so as not to be kept without further injury till the trial of the capture be finished, the same to be reported to the judge of the court of admiralty of this state upon the oaths of judicious and indifferent persons appointed to view the same, under like penalties and forfeitures, to be recovered in like manner and to like use as the forfeitures hereinbefore mentioned and directed.

[Section VII.] (Section XIII, P. L.) And be it further enacted by the authority aforesaid, That the said marshal shall make out an exact inventory of the prizes taken upon water and condemned in the court of admiralty and shall have them appraised by three or more sworn appraisers, to be appointed by the said judge, at the true value thereof in current money; which inventory and appraisement in which the distribution hereinafter directed shall be distinguished, shall be filed with the register of the said court of admiralty; and, in case no appeal be entered in due time or in case there shall be execution of the decree of the said court, upon security being entered in double the value, the same (except ships and vessels and such perishable and damaged goods as aforesaid) shall be divided and distributed by the said marshal in equal and fair shares and proportions, to the agent of the owners of the ship of war, if any there be, of the one part, and to the agent of the captain or commander, mariners and other persons entitled, by being present at the seizure of such prize, on the other part; or, if two or more ships of war shall have right to such prize, then into two general divisions, one for each, to be subdivided between the owners and crew of both of the said ships as aforesaid, where such divisions and subdivisions shall be proper and just, but into no further or less parts or shares. And in case it shall so happen that the nature of the property to be distributed as aforesaid shall not admit of a division and distribution perfectly equal, then the right to the same in kind shall be determined by lot and the unavoidable difference therein shall be equalized and paid in money by the party receiving such goods, to the other party, and the like mode of distribution shall take place in case of recapture unless the former owner shall forthwith pay down the salvage in current money. And the said marshal is, by virtue of this act, enabled to retain in his hands a sufficiency of the goods or property condemned to secure to him in all such cases of distribution as aforesaid the [payment of the] costs of suit and other reasonable charges by him expended for the securing and distributing the said captures.

[Section VIII.] (Section XIV, P. L.) And be it further enacted by the authority aforesaid, That the said marshal, for all goods so distributed, shall be entitled to a fee of one-fourth per centum and no more. And the said appraisers shall be allowed and paid a reasonable reward for each day which they shall be employed therein, to be ascertained by the said judge, the said allowance to be defrayed out of the said captures.

[Section IX.] (Section XV, P. L.) And be it further enacted by the authority aforesaid, That if any printer or other person, during the continuance of this act shall print, write or publish any advertisement of the sale of any goods or property not warranted or allowed by this act, he or she so offending shall forfeit and pay the sum of five hundred pounds, one-half part thereof to the person who shall sue for the same, and the other half part thereof to the use of the overseers of the poor of the city or place where the offense shall be committed, which sum shall be recoverable in a summary way before any justice of the peace of the proper city or county, in the manner in which demands not exceeding fifty pounds are recoverable with costs of suit.

[Section X.] (Section XVI, P. L.) And be it further enacted by the authority aforesaid, If any male person capable of bearing arms in the militia shall, during the continuance of this act by virtue of any license or otherwise, travel or go about as a peddler or hawker within this state, the person so offending shall forfeit the goods which he shall carry about with him for sale, or shall offer to sale, and any commissioned officer of the militia or constable may, and he is hereby enjoined to seize and prosecute the same to condemnation, if, under the value of fifty pounds before any justice of the peace of the county in a summary way, if above the value of fifty pounds in the court of common pleas of the same county, to be distributed, the one-half to the said officer or constable, and the other half to the overseers of the poor, for the use of the poor of the township or place where the offense was committed, otherwise such offender shall forfeit the sum of five hundred pounds to be recovered by action of debt or by indictment and applied to the same use as the penalties and forfeitures imposed by this act on persons who shall sell goods by public vendue, contrary to this act, are directed to be recovered and applied as aforesaid.

[Section XI.] (Section XVII, P. L.) And be it further enacted by the authority aforesaid, That an act of general assembly, entitled "An act for regulating peddlers, vendues, &c.,"[1] passed on the fourteenth day of February, which was in the year of our Lord one thousand seven hundred and twenty-nine, so far as the same relates to public vendues, and also so much of the said act as relates to peddlers and hawkers as is by this act altered or amended, and no more thereof is hereby repealed.

[Section XII.] (Section XXIII, P. L.) And be it further enacted by the authority aforesaid, That one other act of general assembly, entitled "An act to prohibit the sale of goods by public vendue, and to regulate hawkers and peddlers within this state,"[2] passed on the nineteenth day of June, which was in the year of our Lord one thousand seven hundred and seventy-seven, is also repealed.

[Section XIII.] (Section XIX, P. L.) And be it further enacted by the authority aforesaid, That this act shall continue and be in force until the termination and end of the present war between the United States of America and Great Britain, and no longer.

Passed November 26, 1779. See the notes to the Acts of Assembly passed February 14, 1729-30, Chapter 308; June 19, 1777, Chapter 761; and the Acts of Assembly passed March 2, 1780, Chapter 883; March 8, 1780, Chapter 887; September 22, 1780, Chapter 915; September 23, 1780, Chapter 919; April 13, 1782, Chapter 975; December 9, 1783, Chapter 1063; March 30, 1784, Chapter 1090.

---

[1] Passed February 14, 1729, Chapter 308.
[2] Passed June 19, 1777, Chapter 761.

CHAPTER DCCCLXXI.

AN ACT TO CONFIRM THE ESTATES AND INTERESTS OF THE COLLEGE, ACADEMY AND CHARITABLE SCHOOL OF THE CITY OF PHILADELPHIA, AND TO AMEND AND ALTER THE CHARTERS THEREOF CONFORMABLY TO THE REVOLUTION AND TO THE CONSTITUTION AND GOVERNMENT OF THIS COMMONWEALTH, AND TO ERECT THE SAME INTO AN UNIVERSITY.

(Section I, P. L.) Whereas the education of youth has ever been found to be of the most essential consequence as well to the good government of states and the peace and welfare of society as to the profit and ornament of individuals, insomuch that from the experience of all ages it appears that seminaries of learning, when properly conducted, have been public blessings to mankind and that on the contrary, when in the hands of dangerous and disaffected men, they have troubled the peace of society, shaken the government and often caused tumult, sedition and bloodshed:

(Section II, P. L.) And whereas the college, academy and charitable school of the city of Philadelphia, were at first founded on a plan of free and unlimited catholicism but it appears that the trustees thereof, by a vote or by-law of their board bearing date the fourteenth day of June, in the year of our Lord one thousand seven hundred and sixty-four, have departed from the plan of the original founders and narrowed the foundation of the said institution:

[Section I.] (Section III, P. L.) Be it therefore enacted and it is hereby enacted by the Representatives of the Freemen of the Commonwealth of Pennsylvania in General Assembly met and by the authority of the same, That the charter of the said seminary granted by the late proprietaries of Pennsylvania, bearing date the thirtieth day of July, in the year of our Lord one thousand seven hundred and fifty-three, whereby certain persons were incorporated by the name, style and title of The Trustees of the Academy and Charitable School in the Province of Pennsylvania, and the additional charter granted by the same proprietaries bearing date on the fourteenth day of May, in the year of our Lord one thousand seven hundred and fifty-five, by which the trustees of the same academy and charitable school were again incorporated by the name, style and title of The Trustees of the College, Academy and Charitable School of the City of Philadelphia in the Province of Pennsylvania, together with all and singular the rights, powers and privileges, emoluments and advantages and also all the estates, claims and demands to the same corporation belonging discharged from the afore recited vote or by-law of the said trustees, confining and narrowing the true and original plan of the said institution, which vote or by-law and all others contrary to the true design and spirit of the said charter, are hereby declared to be void, be and they are in and by this act, ratified and confirmed to and for the use and benefit of the same seminary forever.

(Section IV, P. L.) And to the end that the trustees hereinafter named and appointed, may be the better enabled to effectuate the pious and praiseworthy designs of the founders, benefactors and contributors of the said college, academy and charitable school of Philadelphia:

[Section II.] (Section V, P. L.) Be it further enacted by the authority [aforesaid], That it shall and may be lawful for the supreme executive council of this state to reserve such and so many of the confiscated estates yet unsold and unappropriated as to them shall appear necessary in order to create a certain fund for the maintenance of the provost, vice-provost, masters and assistants, and to uphold and preserve the charitable school of the said university.

(Section VI, P. L.) Provided always, That the yearly income of such estates so reserved and appropriated to the use of the said university do not exceed the sum of fifteen hundred pounds, computing wheat at the rate of ten shillings per bushel.

(Section VII, P. L.) And provided also, That such reservation be from time to time laid before the general assembly of this state for their approbation and confirmation.

[Section III.] (Section VIII, P. L.) Provided always, and be it enacted by the authority aforesaid, That the ratifying and confirming the said charter or anything herein contained shall not extend or be construed to extend to the confirming or establishing any of the said trustees in the said charter named or deriving by any election or pretended election or appointment by, from or under them or any of them, nor to any provost, vice-provost, professor or other minister or officer of the said seminary, other than such as are hereby or may hereafter be appointed, the said board and the faculty being hereby dissolved and vacated, nor shall the same extend to such parts of the charter, as in and by this act are or may be abrogated, annulled, altered or supplied.

[Section IV.] (Section IX, P. L.) And be it further enacted by the authority aforesaid, That from and after the passing of this act the superintendence and trust, together with all and singular the powers, authorities and estates, real, personal and mixed, of the said college, academy and charitable school shall pass to, devolve upon and be vested in the president of the supreme executive council of this commonwealth, the vice-president of the same council, the speaker of the general assembly, the chief justice of the supreme court of judicature, the judge of admiralty and the attorney-general for the time being, in virtue of their several offices; and the senior minister in standing of the Episcopal churches and congregations, and the senior minister in standing of the Presbyterians churches, and the senior minister in standing of the Baptist churches, and the senior minister in standing of the Lutheran churches, and the senior minister in standing in the German Calvinist churches, and the senior minister in standing in the Roman churches, whose churches or houses of public worship are or shall be in the city of Philadelphia, or within two miles of the old court-house in High street, in the said city, together with the Honorable Benjamin Franklin, doctor of laws, minister plenipotentiary from the United States of America to his most Christian Majesty, the Honorable William Shippen, Frederick Muhlenberg and James Searle, Esquires, delegates in the Congress of the said United States for Pennsylvania, the Honorable William Augustus Atlee, Esquire, and the Honorable John Evans, Esquire, justices of the supreme court of judicature, Timothy Matlack, Esquire, secretary of the supreme executive council of this state, David Rittenhouse, Esquire, treasurer of this state, Jonathan Bayard Smith, Esquire, Samuel Morris, Senior, Esquire, George Bryan, Esquire, Thomas Bond, doctor of physic, and James Hutchinson, doctor of physic, which said civil officers, ministers of the gospel and others herein mentioned and appointed, for and during their continuance in the said office and stations, respectively, their abode in this state and lawful capacity to act, and their successors forever hereafter shall be, remain and continue the trustees aforesaid by the name, style and title of The Trustees of the University of the State of Pennsylvania, and shall from henceforth have, hold, use, exercise and enjoy all the powers, authorities and advantages of the estates, rights, claims and demands of the trustees appointed by or in pursuance of the charters of the said corporation, or either of them, instead of the said trustees appointed by or deriving under the said charter or pretending so to do in trust nevertheless for the proper use of the said university forever.

(Section X, P. L.) Provided always, That if any trustee of the said university shall take any charge or office under the said trustees, other than that of treasurer, his place shall thereby be vacated, and in the case of a minister of the gospel taking such charge or office, or neglecting to qualify according to the directions of this act within one month after personal notice given of his coming to such trust, the next minister in seniority of the same denomination shall succeed him, such seniority to be accounted from the time of settlement of such person as minister of a congregation in or near the said city.

(Section XI, P. L.) Provided also, That in case the choice of a new trustee in the room and stead of any of the persons last named, or their successors, shall be disallowed by the house of assembly within six months, the trustees shall be obliged to make choice of some other person.

[Section V.] (Section XII. P. L.) And be it further enacted by the authority aforesaid, That instead of the oath or affirmation and declaration which were enjoined and required to be taken and made by the second or additional charter hereinbefore referred to of the said corporation by the trustees, provost, vice-provost and professors of the said college, academy and charitable school, which oath or affirmation and declaration being totally inconsistent with the independence and constitution of this commonwealth are hereby abrogated and repealed, the said trustees hereinbefore appointed, and their successors and the provost, vice-provost and professors and every of them hereafter to be appointed in such manner and form as herein is directed and required before he or they enter upon the duties of their trust or office shall, before two justices of the peace of the city of Philadelphia or of some county of this state, take and subscribe the oath or affirmation prescribed by the fortieth section of the constitution of this commonwealth to be taken by the officers of this state, and also the oath or affirmation of allegiance directed to be taken by the same officers in and by the seventh and eighth sections of an act of assembly made and passed the fifth day of December, in the year of our Lord one thousand seven hundred and seventy-eight, entitled "A further supplement to the act, entitled 'An act for the further security of the government,'"[1] and shall also take an oath or affirmation for the faithful discharge of their trust or office aforesaid.

[Section VI.] (Section XIII, P. L.) And be it further enacted by the authority aforesaid, That all and every the clause and clauses in the said charters wherein and whereby the trustees of the said college, academy and charitable school are directed and enjoined to make their rules, ordinances and statutes not repugnant to the laws in force in the kingdom of Great Britain, nor to the laws in force in the province of Pennsylvania, be and they are hereby annulled, repealed and made void and the trustees herein and hereby appointed are required and enjoined to review the rules, ordinances and statutes heretofore made by the former trustees of the said seminary which, so far as they are repugnant to the constitution and laws of this state are hereby repealed, and to frame the same, if necessary, and all rules, ordinances and statutes hereafter to be made, consistent with the constitution and laws of this commonwealth.

---

[1] December 5, 1778, Chapter 822.

[Section VII.] (Section XIV, P. L.) And be it further enacted by the authority aforesaid, That the business of the said corporation shall and may be transacted, performed and determined by the major vote of a meeting of seven at least of the trustees appointed by this act and their successors duly notified and called, other than the choice of new trustees, the nominating and constituting or the dismissing of the future provost, vice-provost or professors, or any of them, or the alienation or leasing of real estates for more than seven years, or any extraordinary and new expenditure of the income or other personal estate of the said corporation or the altering any salary or the granting degrees to the scholars of the said university or to other persons or to the making any ordinances, statute or by-law, which several enumerated acts and doings may be transacted and performed by a majority of at least eleven of the said trustees duly notified and convened as aforesaid and not otherwise.

[Section VIII.] (Section XV, P. L.) And be it further enacted by the authority aforesaid, That the clause in the first charter of the said corporation whereby the trustees thereof were limited to be inhabitants of Pennsylvania, residing within five miles of the academy and school aforesaid although license was given in the said charter to set up the same at any place within the said province which the said trustees should judge to be most convenient, so far as the same clause limits the appointment of trustees to persons residing within five miles of the said academy and school, be and the same is hereby annulled, repealed and made void.

[Section IX.] (Section XVI, P. L.) And be it further enacted by the authority aforesaid, That the trustees herein before appointed and their successors shall and may ask, demand, sue for, recover and receive all evidences, mortgages, specialties, deeds and instruments, and all papers, books of account and record and the library, philisophical apparatus and seals of the said corporation, and all debts, dues and demands to the same owing, belonging, accruing or appertaining. And in case any person or persons having the custody of the said library, apparatus, mortgages, specialties, deeds or instruments, or other papers, books or records of the said corporation, or having possession of the real estate of the said corporation or any part thereof shall refuse to deliver up the same, when demanded, it shall and may be lawful for the trustees of the said college to summon any person so refusing before any two justices of the peace of the city or the county where the said real estate lies, or the detainer of any of the records or other articles aforesaid resides, who are hereby authorized and empowered to enquire into the said complaint, in a summary way and give judgment therein as to them shall seem meet according to the merits and justice of the case, and if such judgment be given against the detainer of any of the said deeds, specialties, mortgages or other articles before enumerated and such detainer shall still refuse to deliver the same, it shall and may be lawful for the said justices, and they are hereby required to commit such refuser to prison, there to remain without bail or mainprise, until the said judgment be complied with. And in the case of real estate the said justices shall carry such judgment into execution by issuing a writ of possession, to the sheriff of the county, in the same manner as they are authorized to do by an act of assembly, entitled "An act for the sale of goods distrained for rent, and to secure such goods to the person distraining the same, for the better security of rents and for other purposes therein mentioned,"[1] in case of tenants holding over their terms: Provided always, That if either of the said parties shall demand a jury to be summoned to try the said matter in dispute, the said justice shall cause a jury forthwith to come before them thereupon in the same manner as juries are had in the case of tenants holding over their terms as aforesaid; and the said justices shall give judgment pursuant to the verdict of such jury and proceed to the execution thereof as is herein and hereby directed.

[Section X.] (Section XVII, P. L.) And be it further enacted by the authority aforesaid, That the civil officers, ministers of the gospel and other persons by this act constituted and appointed trustees of the said university, and their successors duly chosen, nominated and appointed be one community,

---
[1] Passed March 21, 1772, Chapter 645.

body politic and corporate to have perpetual succession and continuance forever by the name, style and title as aforesaid and that by the said name they shall be capable and able in law to sue and be sued, have and make a common seal and the same at their pleasure to break and alter, to make rules and statutes and to do everything necessary and needful for the good government and perfect establishment of the said university and the provost, vice-provost and professors hereafter to be appointed and constituted by the trustees aforesaid shall be named, styled and entitled the provost, vice-provost and professors of the same university and the name, style and title of the body or faculty composed of the said provost, vice-provost and professors, shall be "The Provost, Vice-provost and Professors of the University of the State of Pennsylvania."

[Section XI.] (Section XVIII, P. L.) And be it further enacted by the authority aforesaid, That the said trustees shall at all times when required submit the books, accounts and economy of the said corporation to the free examination of visitors to be appointed from time to time by the representatives of the freemen of this commonwealth in general assembly met.

[Section XII.] (Section XIX, P. L.) And be it further enacted by the authority aforesaid, That the trustees appointed by this act, or a majority of them, shall meet in the hall of the university aforesaid in the forenoon on the first Wednesday in December next, and after being duly qualified as this act prescribes proceed to the execution of their trust.

Passed November 27, 1779. See the notes to the Acts of Asembly passed March 16, 1780, Chapter 895; September 22, 1785, Chapter 1195; March 6, 1789, Chapter 1393; September 30, 1791, Chapter 1598.

CHAPTER DCCCLXXII.

AN ACT TO REPEAL PART OF AN ACT, ENTITLED "AN ACT FOR MAKING MORE EQUAL THE BURDEN OF THE PUBLIC DEFENSE AND FOR FILLING THE QUOTA OF TROOPS TO BE RAISED IN THIS STATE,"[1] AND TO CONTINUE FOR A LONGER TIME THE ACT, ENTITLED "AN ACT TO EMPOWER THE SUPREME EXECUTIVE COUNCIL AND JUSTICES OF THE SUPREME COURT TO APPREHEND SUSPECTED PERSONS, AND INCREASE THE FINES TO WHICH PERSONS ARE LIABLE FOR NEGLECTING TO PERFORM THEIR TOUR OF MILITIA DUTY."[2]

(Section I, P. L.) Whereas in and by the act first above mentioned a double tax was annually imposed upon all the estates, real and personal, of every person not subject to nor performing military duty by the militia law of this state, which is found by experience to be burdensome and inconvenient:

[Section I.] (Section II, P. L.) Be it therefore enacted and it is hereby enacted by the Representatives of the Freemen of the Commonwealth of Pennsylvania in General Assembly met.and by the authority of the same, That so much of the said act as imposes double taxes upon any person or persons whatsoever be and is hereby repealed and made void, anything in the said act to the contrary notwithstanding.

(Section III, P. L.) And whereas an act passed the last session of the late assembly, entitled "An act to empower the supreme executive council and justices of the supreme court to apprehend suspected persons and to increase the fines to which persons are liable for neglecting to perform their tour of militia duty,"[2] will expire at the end of the present session of this Assembly, and it is necessary that the same should be continued for a longer time:

[Section II.] (Section IV, P. L.) Be it therefore further enacted by the authority aforesaid, That the said act, entitled "An act to empower the supreme executive council and justices

---

[1] Passed December 26, 1777, Chapter 773.
[2] Passed October 10, 1779, Chapter 865.

of the supreme court to apprehend suspected persons, and to increase the fines to which persons are liable for neglecting to perform their tour of militia duty,"[1] be and the same is hereby declared to be in full force and virtue for and during the space of six months from the publication of this act unless the war between the United States of America and Great Britain shall sooner cease, and no longer.

Passed November 27, 1779. See the notes to the Acts of Assembly passed December 26, 1777, Chapter 773; October 10, 1779, Chapter 865.

CHAPTER DCCCLXXIII.

A SUPPLEMENT TO AN ACT ENTITLED "AN ACT FOR THE RELIEF OF THE POOR."[2]

(Section I, P. L.) Whereas the rate of assessment directed by the act of assembly, entitled "An act for the relief of the poor,"[2] passed on the twenty-ninth day of March, in the year of our Lord one thousand seven hundred and seventy-one, not exceeding three pence in the pound on all estates real and personal, and six shillings per head on every freeman not otherwise rated for his estate within the several counties of this state is found to be very inadequate to the support of the poor of the said counties, districts and townships and the frequent repetition thereof would be very inconvenient to the overseers of the poor and very troublesome to the inhabitants:

For remedy whereof:

[Section I.] (Section II, P. L.) Be it enacted, and it is hereby enacted by the Representatives of the Freemen of the Commonwealth of Pennsylvania in General Assembly met and by the authority of the same, That it shall and may be lawful for any two of the justices of the peace of any county, district or township, upon complaint of the overseers of the poor, that a sum of money is wanted or likely to be wanted for the support

---

[1] Passed October 10, 1779, Chapter 865.
[2] Passed March 29, 1771, Chapter 635.

of the poor, to issue their warrants under their hands and seals directed to the overseers of the poor of the said county, district or township, requiring them forthwith to levy, collect and raise by an equal assessment upon the clear yearly value as they shall reasonably estimate the same of all real and personal estates within the said county, districts or townships, respectively, a rate or tax not exceeding seven shillings and sixpence in the pound, upon all taxables and a sum not exceeding six pounds per head, nor less than three pounds on all freemen not otherwise rated for such tax for the relief of the poor, and the said rate shall be repeated, as often as the said justices and overseers shall find the same necessary.

[Section II.] (Section III, P. L.) And be it further enacted by the authority aforesaid, That the said-recited act for the relief of the poor passed the twenty-ninth day of March, in the year of our Lord one thousand seven hundred and seventy-one, except so much as is hereinbefore altered and repealed, shall continue, be and remain and is hereby declared to be in full force and effect.

Passed November 27, 1779. See the note to the Act of Assembly passed March 9, 1771, Chapter 635. The Act in the text was repealed by the Act of Assembly passed March 25, 1782, Chapter 9u_.

CHAPTER DCCCLXXIV.

AN ACT FOR VESTING THE ESTATES OF THE LATE PROPRIETARIES OF PENNSYLVANIA IN THIS COMMONWEALTH.

(Section I, P. L.) Whereas the charter from Charles the Second, heretofore king of England, to William Penn, under which the late province, now state of Pennsylvania, was first begun to be settled, was granted and held for the great ends of enlarging the bounds of human society and the cultivation and promotion of religion and learning; and the rights of property and powers of government thereby vested in the said William Penn and his heirs were stipulated to be used and enjoyed as well for the benefit of the settlers as for his own particular emolument, agreeable to the terms of the said charter and of certain conditions and concessions entered into between them:

(Section II, P. L.) And whereas the claims heretofore made by the late proprietaries to the whole of the soil contained within the bounds of the said charter, and in consequence thereof the reservation of quit-rents and purchase money upon all the grants of lands within the said limits, cannot longer consist with the safety, liberty and happiness of the good people of this commonwealth, who, at the expense of much blood and treasure have bravely rescued themselves and their possessions from the tyranny of Great Britain, and are now defending themselves from the inroads of the savages:

(Section III, P. L.) And whereas the safety and happiness of the people is the fundamental law of society, and it has been the practice and usage of states most celebrated for freedom and wisdom to control and abolish all claims of power and interest inconsistent with their safety and welfare; and it being the right and duty of the representatives of the people to assume the direction and management of such interest and property as belongs to the community, or was designed for their advantage:

(Section IV, P. L.) And whereas it has become necessary that speedy and effectual measures should be taken in the premises on account of the great expenses of the war, and the rapid progress of the neighboring states in locating and settling the lands heretofore uncultivated, by which multitudes of inhabitants are daily emigrating from this state:

[Section I.] (Section V, P. L.) Be it therefore enacted and it is hereby enacted by the Representatives of the Freemen of the Commonwealth of Pennsylvania in General Assembly met and by the authority of the same, That all and every the estate, right, title, interest, property, claim and demand of the heirs and devisees, grantees or others claiming as proprietaries of Pennsylvania, whereof they or either of them stood seized, or to which they or any of them were entitled, or which to them were deemed to belong on the fourth day of July, in the year of our Lord one thousand seven hundred and seventy-six, of,

1779]   *The Statutes at Large of Pennsylvania.*   35

in or to the soil and land contained within the limits of the said late province, now state, of Pennsylvania, or any part thereof, together with the royalties, franchises, lordships and all other the hereditaments and premises comprised, mentioned and granted in the same charter or letters patent of the said King Charles the Second (except as hereinafter excepted), shall be and they are hereby vested in the commonwealth of Pennsylvania for the use and benefit of the citizens thereof, freed and discharged and absolutely acquitted, exempted and indemnified of, from and against all estates, uses, trusts, entails, reversions, remainders, limitations, charges, encumbrances, titles, claims and demands whatsoever from, by or under the said charter or letters patent or otherwise, as fully, clearly and entirely as if the said charter or letters patent, and the estates, interests, hereditaments and premises therein comprised, mentioned and granted and all other the estate, right and title of the said proprietaries of, in and to the same premises were herein transcribed and repeated.

[Section II.] (Section VI, P. L.) And be it further enacted by the authority aforesaid, That the said soil and lands, hereditaments and premises and every part and parcel thereof (except as herein is excepted) from and after the date hereof shall be subject to such disposal, alienation, conveyance, division and appropriation as to this or any future legislature of this commonwealth shall from time to time seem meet and expedient in pursuance of such law or laws as shall for that purpose hereafter be made and provided.

[Section III.] (Section VII, P. L.) Provided always and be it enacted by the authority aforesaid, That all and every the rights, titles, estates, claims and demands which were granted by or derived from the said proprietaries, their officers or others by them duly commissioned, authorized and appointed or otherwise, or to which any person or persons other than the said proprietaries were or are entitled either in law or equity by virtue of any deed, patent, warrant or survey, of, in or to any part or portion of the lands comprised and contained within the limits of this state, or by virtue of any location filed in the land office at any time or times before the said fourth day of July in the year of our Lord one thousand seven hundred and seventy-six, shall be and they are hereby confirmed, ratified and established forever, according to such estate or estates, right or interests, and under such limitations and uses as in and by the several and respective grants and conveyances thereof are directed and appointed.

[Section IV.] (Section VIII, P. L.) Provided also, and be it enacted by the authority aforesaid, That all and every the private estates, lands and hereditaments of any of the said proprietaries whereof they are now possessed, or to which they are now entitled in their private several rights or capacity by devise, purchase or descent, and likewise all the lands called and known by the name of The Proprietary Tenths or Manors, which were duly surveyed and returned into the land office on or before the fourth day of July, in the year of our Lord one thousand seven hundred and seventy-six, together with the quit or other rents and arrearages of rents reserved out of the said proprietary tenths or manors, or any part or parts thereof, which have been sold, be confirmed, ratified and established forever according to such estate or estates therein, and under such limitations, uses and trusts as in and by the several and respective reservations, grants and conveyances thereof are directed and appointed.

[Section V.] (Section IX, P. L.) And be it further enacted by the authority aforesaid, That all and every the quit-rents which at any time or times heretofore have been reserved in and by any warrant, patent or other conveyance of lands or other hereditaments from, by or under the said proprietaries, their officers or others by them commissioned and appointed, and all and every the dues and arrearages of quit-rents and arrearages of purchase moneys for lands not within the tenths or manors aforesaid or which at any time or times heretofore have been deemed or taken to be due and in arrear, other than the quit or other rents reserved within the proprietary tenths or manors before mentioned shall from henceforth cease and determine and the same lands and other hereditaments shall be held free and discharged therefrom and from the payment thereof forever.

[Section VI.] (Section X, P. L.) Provided always and be it further enacted by the authority aforesaid, That in order to preserve equality among the purchasers of land under the said late proprietaries, the said arrears of purchase money, other than for lands within the said tenths and manors shall be accounted to be due and payable to the commonwealth.

[Section VII.] (Section XI, P. L.) And be it further enacted by the authority aforesaid, That all and every law or laws, act or acts of assembly heretofore made and enacted by the legislature of the province of Pennsylvania, or such parts and clauses thereof by which any right, title or claim, power or authority is or are given or granted, ratified or established in the said proprietaries, or any of them, their, or any of their officers or servants, of, in or to any of the estates, lands or other hereditaments herein and hereby vested and confirmed or meant to be hereby vested and confirmed in this commonwealth for the use and benefit of the citizens thereof, or of, in or to the quit-rents and purchase money and arrearages thereof, or of, in or to any portion thereof, herein and hereby released, discharged and abolished, or meant so to be, be and they are hereby annulled, revoked and repealed.

(Section XII, P. L.) And whereas the freemen of this commonwealth being desirous to manifest not only a regard to their own safety and happiness, but their liberality also and remembrance of the enterprising spirit which distinguished the founder of Pennsylvania, and mindful of the expectations and dependence of his descendants on the propriety thereof, and also that sundry marriage settlements and testamentary dispositions have been made thereupon, which will be wholly defeated and the parties exposed to great disappointment and loss if no provision be made therein:

[Section VIII.] (Section XIII, P. L.) Be it therefore enacted by the authority aforesaid, That the sum of one hundred and thirty thousand pounds sterling money of Great Britain be paid out of the treasury of this state to the devisees and legatees of Thomas Penn and Richard Penn, late proprietaries of Pennsylvania respectively and to the widow and relict of the said Thomas Penn, in such proportions as shall hereafter by the legislature be deemed equitable and just upon a full investigation of their respective claims.

(Section XIV, P. L.) Provided always that no part of the said sum of one hundred and thirty thousand pounds sterling shall be paid within less than one year after the termination of the present war with Great Britain and that no more than twenty thousand pounds sterling, nor less than fifteen thousand pounds sterling thereof shall be paid or payable in any one year until the whole sum be fully paid and discharged; and the first annual payment thereof be made at the expiration of one year after the termination of the said war.

(Section XV, P. L..) And whereas divers persons who have acted under the said late proprietaries, or any of them, as secretaries of the land office, receiver of purchase money, rents or other income, surveyor-general, surveyors of land, or otherwise, or being the heirs or representatives of such persons, are possessed of divers books, surveys, returns of survey, certificates, orders, or other documents, instruments, records or writings, or seals to the said propriety belonging or appertaining, or which have been usually lodged and kept in the several and respective offices of secretary of the land office, receiver-general, and surveyor-general, may neglect or refuse to deliver up the same, undiminished, to the supreme executive council of this state, as is proper and necessary upon the passing of this act:

[Section IX.] (Section XVI, P. L.) Be it therefore enacted by the authority aforesaid, That if any person or persons whatsoever who now is, or are, or hereafter shall be possessed of any of the said books, surveys, returns of survey, certificates, orders or other documents, instruments, records, writings or seals and shall, after demand thereof in writing, made by the president or vice-president of the supreme executive council of this state for one month after such demand, refuse or neglect to deliver up the same to the person or persons empowered by the said president or vice-president to receive the same, such person or persons so refusing shall forfeit and pay to the use of the commonwealth any sum not exceeding five hundred thousand pounds upon being convicted by indictment in any court of oyer and terminer; and moreover if such person or persons after such conviction persist in such refusal, such person or persons shall be sentenced to imprisonment until he or they deliver the books, surveys or other hereinbefore mentioned articles by such person or persons withheld as aforesaid.

>Passed November 27, 1779. See the Acts of Assembly passed April 1, 1784, Chapter 1094; February 10, 1785, Chapter 1130; March 16, 1785, Chapter 1137; March 28, 1787, Chapter 1284; April 9, 1794, Chapter 1562; April 3, 1794, Chapter 1727; March 23, 1797, Chapter 1934.

CHAPTER DCCCLXXV.

AN ACT FOR THE BETTER SUPPORT OF CERTAIN OFFICERS OF THIS STATE AND FOR ASCERTAINING THE SPECIFIC FINES AND PENALTIES WHICH THEY MAY INCUR BY NEGLECT OF DUTY.

(Section I, P. L.) Whereas the fees of the officers of this commonwealth who are hereafter mentioned as now regulated by law are by the great rise of the prices of the necessaries of life, become very inadequate to their expenses whilst they attend the public business, which, if it be not remedied must force the said officers to abandon their employments or introduce great exaction or extortion to the manifest enfeebling of the public authority and oppression of private persons:

(Section II, P. L.) And whereas the specific fines and penalties to which the said officers are severally and respectively liable for neglect of duty, are generally become uncertain and insufficient:

For remedy whereof:

[Section I.] (Section III, P. L.) Be it enacted and it is hereby enacted by the Representatives of the Freemen of the Commonwealth of Pennsylvania in General Assembly met, and by the authority of the same, That the fees of the said officers shall be estimated and paid according to the price of good merchantable wheat, in manner following, That is to say, the said fees as they were regulated by law or practice under the late government of Pennsylvania before the first day of July which was in the year of our Lord one thousand seven hundred and seventy-six, shall, from and after the publication of this act, be satisfied in good merchantable wheat accounting and allowing that a bushel of such wheat, weighing at least sixty pounds, was formerly sold in times of war and difficulty for ten shillings.

[Section II.] (Section IV, P. L.) Provided always, and be it further enacted by the authority aforesaid, That for the ease and conveniency of the person or persons by whom such fee or fees shall be payable, as well as the said officers such person or persons liable to pay the same may tender payment thereof in any lawful money of this state or of the United States of America in a sum proportioned and equal to the value and price of such wheat, as the same from time to time shall be estimated and declared by the representatives of the freemen of this state in general assembly met.

[Section III.] (Section V, P. L.) And be it further enacted by the authority aforesaid, That payment of fees, in wheat in manner aforesaid, shall extend to the fees of the judge, register and marshal of the court of admiralty; the secretary of the supreme executive council, who is hereby granted such and the same fees as were formerly allowed in the province of Pennsylvania to the governor's secretary and clerk of the council; the attorney-general, the master of the rolls, the prothonotary of the supreme court, the sheriff and coroner of each county; the justices of the peace of the orphan's court, and of the common pleas of each county; and the clerks of the general quarter sessions, orphans' court and common pleas of each county, and of the general quarter sessions of the city of Philadelphia; the register for the probate of wills and for granting administrations in each county, who shall be entitled to like fees, as were formerly due to the register-general of the province of Pennsylvania; the recorder of deeds, attorneys at law, the persons who shall be summoned to appear as jurors and as witnesses, the constables and the crier of every court, and the naval officer, who is hereby granted equal and like fees as were formerly allowed and due to the naval officer under the late government of Pennsylvania; the notaries public, the inspector of flour, of beef and pork and of shad and herring; the collectors of excise, the supervisors of the highways, the commissioners and assessors of the public taxes, the regulators of party walls and partition fences in the city of Philadelphia and elsewhere; the officers for regulating weights and measures, the commissioners for paving the streets and the wardens of the watch of the city of Philadelphia; the health officer, and the officer for enforcing the laws against importing convicts and impotent persons, and his interpreter and the assisting physicians; the inspectors of staves and heading and of timber, boards and planks; the measurers of wheat and other corn, and of salt in the city of Philadelphia, and the representatives in general assembly and their clerk; and the wages and mileage of the members of the supreme executive council other than the president and vice-president shall be the same as the wages and mileage of the members of assembly as the same were estabtablished by the laws of the late government of Pennsylvania and since revived by an act of this commonwealth: Provided always, That nothing in this act contained shall extend to any fees which are rated by the pound or the hundred pounds.

(Section VI, P. L.) Provided also, That the fees of the judge of admiralty, including his fee for a final decree in the case of a ship or vessel under the burden of one hundred tons shall be twenty-five bushels of good, merchantable wheat; and in the case of a ship or a vessel above the burden of one hundred tons shall be forty bushels of such wheat, payable, however, in money as in the case of the officers aforesaid.

[Section IV.] (Section VII, P. L.) And be it further enacted by the authority aforesaid, That the several specific fines to which any of the officers, or the persons summoned on juries as aforesaid, were liable before the fourth day of July, in the year of our Lord one thousand seven hundred and seventy-six, be liable and which they shall incur for any offense or neglect of duty, shall be computed and satisfied in wheat, as in the case of fees as aforesaid and tendered, paid or levied in money according to the price of such wheat from time to time, as it shall be estimated and declared by the representatives of the freemen of the commonwealth of Pennsylvania in general assembly met as aforesaid.

> Passed November 27, 1779. See the notes to the Acts of Assembly passed May 28, 1715, Chapter 206; August 22, 1752, Chapter 398, and the Acts of Assembly passed February 28, 1780, Chapter 879; March 1, 1780, Chapter 882; March 8, 1780, Chapter 888; March 17, 1780, Chapter 897; March 18, 1780, Chapter 899; June 21, 1781, Chapter 945.

Laws enacted in the Second Sitting of the Fourth General Assembly of the Commonwealth of Pennsylvania, which commenced at Philadelphia, on Wednesday, the nineteenth day of January, in the year of our Lord 1780.

CHAPTER DCCCLXXVI.

AN ACT FOR LAYING AN EMBARGO ON THE EXPORTATION OF PROVISIONS FROM THIS STATE BY SEA FOR A LIMITED TIME.

(Section I, P. L.) Whereas the last harvest of wheat and other grain, in this and the neighboring states hath not proved so abundant as it was supposed, and it is highly necessary that the exportation of victuals and provisions from this state by sea should be prohibited for a limited time in order to retain a sufficiency within the same for the sustentation of the inhabitants and for the armies and fleets of the United States of America and their allies:

[Section I.] (Section II, P. L.) Be it therefore enacted and it is hereby enacted by the Representatives of the Freemen of the Commonwealth of Pennsylvania in General Assembly met, and by the authority of the same, That an embargo be and hereby is laid on the exportation by sea, of wheat, rye, barley, oats, spelts and Indian corn, and on all meal and flour made of wheat, rye, barley, oats, spelts or Indian corn, and on bread, rice, beef, pork, bacon and live stock, and on all other victuals and provisions for the food of man, and the exportation thereof by sea from and after the publication of this act, is hereby prohibited and forbidden until the first day of September next.

(Section III, P. L.) Provided always, That this act shall not be construed to restrain the lading upon any ship of war or other vessel which shall actually be in one of the ports of the state such quantities of provisions as may be necessary for the stores only of such ship or vessel for the cruise or voyage of such ship or vessel; nor to the transportation by sea, or exportation of any victuals or provisions for the use of the armies or ships of the United States of America or their allies, such transportation or exportation being first certified to the supreme executive council of this commonwealth, and the license of the said council obtained for the same.

(Section IV, P. L.) Provided also, That if any time before the first day of September next, the continuance of the embargo laid by this act shall appear to be unnecessary or in case the neighboring and adjoining states shall not concur in an equal restriction upon the exportation of provisions the supreme executive council by proclamation may suspend the said embargo.

[Section II.] (Section V, P. L.) And be it further enacted by the authority aforesaid, That if any wheat, rye, barley, oats, spelts or Indian corn, or any meal or flour made of wheat, rye, barley, oats, spelts or Indian corn; or any bread, rice, beef, pork, bacon, live stock or other victuals or provisions whatsoever for the food of man, except as hereinbefore is excepted, shall be shipped or laden from and after the publication of this act on any ship or vessel within this state with design to export the same by sea contrary to the intent and meaning of this act, it shall and may be lawful for the naval officer, and he is hereby enjoined and required, on proper information, or it shall and may be lawful for any other person to enter on board any such ship or vessel and to seize all such wheat, rye, barley, oats, spelts and Indian corn and meal or flour, bread, rice, beef, pork, bacon, live stock and other victuals and provisions, together with the ship or vessel in which the same shall be found and her tackle, apparel and furniture, and all such victuals and provisions so shipped and laden contrary to this act, and the ship or vessel in which the same shall be so found, together with her tackle, apparel and furniture shall be forfeited; one-third part thereof to the use of the state, one-third part thereof to the use of the said naval officer or other person who shall seize the same and the other third part thereof to the use of the informer.

[Section III.] (Section VI, P. L.) Provided always, and it is hereby enacted by the authority aforesaid, That no claim for any ship or vessel or provisions seized, or pretended to be seized, in pursuance of this act shall be admitted unless security be first entered for the payment of all costs in case such seizure be condemned; and that no suit or action against the officer or person or persons making such seizure or his or their assistants shall lie unless such suit or action be brought within three months after cause shall be given.

> Passed February 28, 1780. See the notes to the Acts of Assembly passed January 2, 1778, Chapter 779; November 17, 1778, Chapter 817; and the Acts of Assembly passed September 22, 1780, Chapter 917; December 22, 1780, Chapter 922; February 27, 1781, Chapter 928; June 7, 1781, Chapter 943. Recorded L. B. No. 1, p. 328, &c.

CHAPTER DCCCLXXVII.

AN ACT FOR THE PRESERVATION OF BUILDINGS ERECTED UPON THE LANDS OF DIVERS INHABITANTS OF THIS COMMONWEALTH, FOR THE USE OF THE UNITED STATES, AND VESTING SUCH LAND WITH THE BUILDINGS, IN THE UNITED STATES DURING THE PRESENT WAR AND TO PUNISH PERSONS FOR WASTE OR TRESPASSES MADE, OR COMMITTED THEREON, AND FOR OTHER PURPOSES THEREIN MENTIONED.

(Section I, P. L.) Whereas, in the unsettled state of public affairs during the war with Great Britain the necessities of the United Colonies or States induced their officers to take possession of the lands of divers persons, inhabitants of this commonwealth, for public use, and have, at the public expense, erected thereon barracks, hospitals, stables, storehouses and other buildings:

(Section II, P. L.) And whereas, the honorable the Congress of the United States of America, by their resolve dated the twenty-third of July last, have recommended that suitable provision be made by a law for preserving the same buildings and for punishing those who shall seize upon or injure the same, and in some instances vest the ground on which such buildings are erected in the United States:

[Section I.] (Section III, P. L.) Be it therefore enacted and it is hereby enacted by the Representatives of the Freemen of the Commonwealth of Pennsylvania in General Assembly met and by the authority of the same, That all and every the buildings aforesaid, with so much of the land adjoining as may be necessary for the purpose for which such buildings were erected be vested in the United States during the war, and that the said United States be fully authorized and empowered to sue and maintain any action or actions at law against all and every person or persons who shall commit any waste or trespass thereon within this commonwealth.

[Section II.] (Section IV, P. L.) Provided always, and be it enacted by the authority aforesaid, That nothing in this act shall extend to the justifying any entry made, or possession taken of the lands or real estate of any person or persons within this commonwealth, without the consent of the owner, from and after the first day of January, in the year of our Lord one thousand seven hundred and seventy-nine, or to vest the same land so entered upon or possessed since that time in the said United States.

[Section III.] (Section V, P. L.) And be it further enacted by the authority aforesaid, That whensoever in any case it shall or may be found convenient or proper to remove any of the said buildings which are removable, the United States, or their officers duly appointed, shall and may be fully authorized so to do, whether the same buildings were erected before the said first of January, one thousand seven hundred and seventy nine or since, and that in all cases where the same building shall be so removed, all title, interest and property of the said United States of, in and to the lands whereon the said buildings shall have been erected shall from thenceforth cease and determine.

[Section IV.] (Section VI, P. L.) And be it further enacted by the authority aforesaid, That in all cases where the title of the lands are in and by this act vested in the United States during the war, the original owner or owners of the land, or the tenant or tenants, shall receive from the United States a reasonable rent for the same, according to the valuation of the said lands, exclusive of the same buildings, to be appraised by three indifferent appraisers, on oath or affirmation, one of whom shall be chosen by the United States, or their officer, one by the said owner or owners, and a third by the two so as aforesaid chosen; and that in case of the refusal of the United States, or their officer, to choose, the owner or owners shall and may, after full notice given, apply to the nearest justice of the peace of this state to choose a proper person on the part of the said United States, who is hereby empowered and enjoined so to do, and the two persons so chosen shall choose a third.

[Section V.] (Section VII, P. L.) And be it further enacted by the authority aforesaid, That from and after the termination of the present war with Great Britain, it shall and may be lawful to and for the United States, or their officers, duly authorized, in all cases where the said buildings are no longer necessary or where the owner will not agree to proper terms for continuing the same buildings, to remove the same, or pull down and remove the materials, and the same to sell and dispose of or to sell the same buildings as they then stand to the owner or owners of the land or any other person or persons, according as to them shall seem most advantageous.

[Section VI.] (Section VIII, P. L.) And be it further enacted by the authority aforesaid, That the United States of America, by the name aforesaid, shall be able and capable, within this commonwealth, now and at all times hereafter to purchase, take and hold lands, houses, hereditaments and real estates for the purpose of erecting and maintaining necessary public buildings thereon, by the gift, grant, bargain, sale, release, enfeoffment, alienation or devise, of all or any person or persons whatsoever able and capable to make the same, and that the same shall be and remain subject to the disposition and appropriation of the honorable Congress of the United States of America, according to such estate and estates therein as in and by the grant or conveyance thereof shall or may be specified and contained.

Passed February 28, 1780. See the Acts of Assembly passed September 14, 1789, Chapter 1431; September 28, 1789, Chapter 1452; April 15, 1795, Chapter 1828; February 1, 1796, Chapter 1869; March 23, 1796, Chapter 1885. Recorded L. B. No. 1, p. 329, &c.

CHAPTER DCCCLXXVIII.

AN ACT FOR VESTING THE STATE HOUSE IN THE CITY OF PHILADELPHIA; THE HOUSE IN HIGH STREET IN THE SAID CITY APPROPRIATED TO THE USE OF THE PRESIDENT OF THE SUPREME EXECUTIVE COUNCIL FOR THE TIME BEING, THE PROVINCE ISLAND AND GREAT MUD ISLAND, THE MILITARY BARRACKS IN THE NORTHERN LIBERTIES OF THE CITY OF PHILADELPHIA, AND IN THE NORTHERN PART OF THE BOROUGH OF LANCASTER, THE PUBLIC STOREHOUSE AND THE MAGAZINE FOR SECURING GUNPOWDER IN THE SAID BOROUGH, THE SEVERAL COURT HOUSES, GAOLS, PRISONS AND WORKHOUSES OF THE SEVERAL COUNTIES OF THIS STATE, AND ALL OTHER REAL ESTATE BELONGING TO THE PUBLIC IN THE COMMONWEALTH.

(Section I, P. L.) Whereas, on account of the difficulty of securing in a proper manner the real estate of the public in the late province, now state of Pennsylvania, the same was vested in feoffees or trustees or in bodies politic and corporate:

And whereas, the persons enfeoffed of the same may have, in some cases, all died and it may be difficult to ascertain the person to whom the estate so vested hath descended, if suits in the law should be necessary for the conservation of the said real estate:

For remedy whereof and to place the same on a uniform, convenient and permanent footing:

[Section I.] (Section II, P. L.) Be it enacted and it is hereby enacted by the Representatives of the Freemen of the Commonwealth of Pennsylvania, in General Assembly met, and by the authority of the same, That the state house, in the city of Philadelphia, together with the adjoining lot and piece of ground thereunto appertaining, bounded by Chestnut street on the north, Fifth street from the river Delaware on the east, Sixth street from the said river on the west, and Walnut street on the south, as the same are now vested in Samuel Rhoads and Edward Penington, and the house and lots situate on High street, Minor street and Sixth street, in the said city, late the estate of Joseph Galloway, Esquire, appropriated and appointed for the use of the president of the supreme executive council by an act, entitled "An act for vesting the house and lots therein described in trustees for the use of the president of the supreme executive council of this state for the time being,"[1] passed on the eighteenth day of March last, and the island called the Province island, situate on the south side of the mouth of the river Schuylkill, adjoining to the river Delaware, within the township of Kingsessing and county of Philadelphia, and heretofore known by the name of Fisher's island, containing about three hundred and forty-two acres, as the same was held in trust by Joseph Harvey, Thomas Tatnel, Joseph Trotter, James Morris and Oswald Peel and afterwards conveyed by the said Joseph Trotter, the survivor of the said trustees, to Joseph Fox, Samuel Rhoads, Joseph Galloway, John Baynton, Edward Penington, Charles Humphreys and Michael Hillegas, and the island in the river Delaware named Great Mud island, or Deep Water island, situate southward of the Province island, as the same was held by Joseph Galloway, and by him sold for a fortress to the public, who paid him the full consideration thereof, but had no transfer of the said island made by said Joseph Galloway; yet by his attainder it is become the estate of the public, the military barracks situate between Second and Third streets continued in the Northern Liberties of the city of Philadelphia, together with the lots and pieces of land thereunto belonging and appertaining, as the same was purchased of Anthony Wilkinson and John Jennings and wife for the purpose of erecting the said barracks at the cost of the late province, now state of Pennsylvania, and as the same are now vested in the heirs of Joseph Fox, deceased, and the military barracks in the north part of the borough of Lancaster, in the county of Lancaster, together with the lot of land thereunto appertaining as the same are now held by James Webb in trust for the public, the public storehouse situate on the western side and near the north end of Queen street, in the said borough, and the magazine for securing gunpowder in the said borough lying eastward of the

---

[1] Passed March 18, 1779, Chapter 829.

said storehouse, and the new gaol and workhouse of the city and county of Philadelphia, on Walnut street and Sixth street, in the city of Philadelphia, as the same is now vested in the commissioners of the city and county of Philadelphia, and their successors who held the same as a body politic and corporate for that purpose and all and singular the court houses, gaols, prisons and workhouses, together with the lots of land whereon they severally stand, or which are appurtenant to them of and in the several counties of this state, as they now are or heretofore have been vested in any feoffees or trustees or in any bodies politic and corporate for the several use of the said counties, respectively, and also all other real estate to the good people of this commonwealth, or of any county thereof in their public and collective capacity belonging or to their use or interest for them vested and conveyed, shall be and hereby are vested in the commonwealth, freed and discharged and absolutely acquitted, exempted and exonerated of and from and against all claims and demands of the said feoffees or trustees or bodies politic and corporate or of the survivors and survivor of such feoffees and trustees and every of them and of the heirs of such survivors and survivor forever, subject, however, to the several uses, intents, trusts, dispositions and direction for which the same have been heretofore respectively appointed and limited, and to none other, saving and always reserving to every person and persons, bodies politic and corporate, his and their heirs, successors other than the said feoffees and trustees, all such estates, right, title and interest, of, in, to and out of the premises vested in trust as aforesaid as they, every or any of them had before the passing of this act or could or might have had or enjoyed in case this act had not been made or passed.

(Section III, P. L.) Provided always, That nothing in this act shall extend to vest in the commonwealth the old temporary prison, situate on the eastern side of the main cross street in the town of Bedford, nor to vest in the commonwealth the old gaol and workhouse nor the land thereunto appertaining, fronting on the south side of High street and extending along Third street from Delaware, in the city of Philadelphia, as

1780]   *The Statutes at Large of Pennsylvania.*   51

the same was holden by Joshua Carpenter, in trust for the use of the city and county of Philadelphia:

[Section II.] But it is hereby enacted by the authority aforesaid, That the supreme executive council may and shall sell and convey the said old gaol and workhouse in the city of Philadelphia to the private use of the purchaser by deed or deeds under the great seal, signed by the president or vice-president of the said council for the sole benefit and advantage notwithstanding of the said city and county.

(Section IV, P. L.) And provided also, That the representatives of the freemen of this commonwealth in general assembly met shall and may, from time to time, by their vote appoint trustees to take upon them the care and management of the island called the Province island, together with its appurtenances, and to receive the rents, issues and profits thereof, and to account for the same and to make leases, in like manner and under like restrictions as the feoffees or trustees of the said island, heretofore vested with the estate thereof might or could do.

[Section III.] (Section V, P. L.) And be it further enacted by the authority aforesaid, That so much of an act of assembly of the late province of Pennsylvania, entitled "An act for vesting the Province island and the buildings thereon erected, and to be erected, in trustees for providing an hospital for such sick passengers as shall be imported into this province, and to prevent the spreading of infectious distempers,"[1] passed on the third day of February, which was in the year of our Lord one thousand seven hundred and forty-three; and so much of another act of assembly of the said late province, entitled "An act for vesting the state house and other public buildings, with the lots of ground whereon the same are erected, together with other lots situate in the city of Philadelphia in trustees for the uses therein particularly mentioned,"[2] passed on the twentieth day of February, which was in the year of our Lord one thousand seven hundred and thirty-six, and so much of another act of assembly of the said late province, entitled "An

---
[1] Passed February 3, 1743, Chapter 357.
[2] Passed February 30, 1736, Chapter 343.

act for erecting a new gaol, workhouse and house of correction in the city of Philadelphia,"[1] passed on the twenty-sixth day of February, which was in the year of our Lord one thousand seven hundred and seventy-three; and so much of another act of assembly of the said late province, entitled "An act to enable Jeremiah Langhorne, William Biles, Joseph Kirkbride, Junior, Thomas Watson, practitioner in physic, and Abraham Chapman to build a new court house and prison in the county of Bucks,"[2] passed on the twentieth day of March, Anno Domini one thousand seven hundred and twenty-five, and so much of the several acts of assembly of the said late province by which the counties of Lancaster, York, Cumberland, Berks, Northampton, Bedford, Northumberland and Westmoreland were erected and established, and so much of an act of assembly of this commonwealth, entitled "An act for vesting the house and lots therein described in trustees for the use of the president of the supreme executive council of this state for the time being," passed on the eighteenth day of March last, and of any other act of assembly, which is hereby altered or supplied by or is repugnant to the provisions and directions of this act is hereby repealed and made void.

Passed February 28, 1780. See the Acts of Assembly passed March 18, 1782, Chapter 959; April 1, 1784, Chapter 1097; April 8, 1785, Chapter 1165; April 2, 1790, Chapter 1507; September 30, 1791; Chapter 1589; April 15, 1795, Chapter 1838. Recorded L. B. No. 1 page 330, &c.

CHAPTER DCCCLXXIX.

AN ACT FOR ERECTING AN HIGH COURT OF ERRORS AND APPEALS.

(Section I, P. L.) Whereas by the laws of the late province, now state, of Pennsylvania a very expensive, difficult and precarious remedy was provided for parties injured by erroneous judgments, sentences and decrees given or pronounced therein,

---

[1] Passed February 26, 1763, Chapter 674.
[2] Passed March 20, 1725, Chapter 283.

by establishing an appeal from the final judgment, sentence or decree of any court within the said province to the king of Great Britain in council, or to such court or courts as by the said King, his heirs and successors should be appointed in Britain to hear and judge of appeals from the plantations, in many cases to the denial and in all to the great obstruction of justice:

(Section II, P. L.) And whereas the good people of this commonwealth, by their happy deliverance from their late dependent condition, and by becoming free and sovereign are released from this badge of slavery and have acquired the transcendent benefit of having justice administered to them at home and at moderate costs and charges:

(Section III, P. L.) And whereas it is requisite that the good people of this commonwealth, who have adopted the common law of England, should enjoy the full benefit thereof by the erection of a competent jurisdiction within this state for the hearing, determining and judging in the last instance upon complaints of error at common law; and also that a competent court of appeals should be provided within the same for reviewing, reconsidering and correcting the sentences and decrees of the court of admiralty other than in cases of capture upon the water in time of war from the enemies of the United States of America, and likewise the decrees and sentences of the several registers of wills and for granting administrations:

[Section I.] (Section IV, P. L.) Be it therefore enacted and it is hereby enacted by the Representatives of the Freemen of the Commonwealth of Pennsylvania in General Assembly met, and by the authority of the same, That when any final judgment shall be hereafter given [in the supreme court] in any suit or action, real, personal or mixed, or when any final decree or sentence shall be pronounced in the court of admiralty of this commonwealth other than in cases of capture as aforesaid, or when any final decree or sentence shall be pronounced by any register of wills and for granting administrations, the party or parties, his, her and their heirs, executors or administrators, against whom such judgment, decree or sentence shall be given, may sue forth, in the case of a complaint of error in the supreme court, a writ of error, according to the course of the common law, but not otherwise, under the less seal of the commonwealth, directed to the chief justice or other justice or justices of the said court, commanding him or them to cause the record, and all other things concerning the judgment complained of to be brought before the court hereinafter mentioned and constituted. And in case of an appeal brought from a definitive sentence or decree of the court of admiralty, or of any register of wills and for granting administrations, the appellant or appellants shall be allowed and shall have his, her or their appeal to the said court.

[Section II.] (Section V, P. L.) And be it further enacted by the authority aforesaid, That the president of the supreme executive council, the judges of the supreme court, the judge of the admiralty for the time being, together with three persons of known integrity and ability to be appointed and commissioned for seven years and removeable from office in the same manner as the justices of the supreme court now are, be and they are hereby constituted a court of record, by the name, style and title of the high court of errors and appeals; and the said high court of errors and appeals, or any four or more of them, shall have power and authority to examine all such errors as shall be assigned or found, in or upon any such judgment given in the supreme court, and thereupon to affirm or reverse the same judgment as the course of the common law and justice shall require, other than for errors to be assigned for want of form, in any writ, return, plaint, bill, declaration or other pleading, process, verdict or proceeding whatsoever; and that after the said judgment shall be affirmed or reversed the record and proceedings and all things concerning the same shall be remitted into the said supreme court, to the end that such further proceedings may be had thereupon as well for execution as otherwise as to justice shall appertain, and the said court of errors and appeals shall receive, hear and decide all such appeals from the court of admiralty, and the registers of wills and for granting administrations as aforesaid.

(Section VI, P. L.) Provided always, That such of the justices of the supreme court, and no other, or the judge of admiralty, as the case may be, who shall have heard and determined any of the causes removed or brought by writ of error or by appeal into the said court of errors and appeals shall be excluded from sitting again judicially on the hearing of the same cause or controversy in the said court of errors and appeals. And to the end that writs of error may not be brought or appeals allowed as aforesaid for matters of small and frivolous value or for mere delay:

[Section III.] (Section VII, P. L.) Be it enacted by the authority aforesaid, That no such writ of error shall be granted nor any appeal be allowed as aforesaid, until the party or parties in error, appellant or appellants, his, her or their agent or attorney in fact shall file an affidavit or affirmation with the clerk of the said court attesting that the matter in controversy exceeds the value of four hundred bushels of wheat; and the plaintiff or plaintiffs in error or the appellant or appellants shall enter into a recognizance to the defendant or defendants in error or to the appellee or appellees, with two sufficient sureties in double the sum or double the value in dispute, conditioned to prosecute his, her or their writ of error or appeal with effect in the said court of errors and appeals; which said recognizance shall be taken in the proper court or before the register for the probate of wills and granting letters of administration, if the appeal is from his sentence, and subscribed by one of the judges or by the said register, and if the judgment or decree shall be thereupon affirmed or if the plaintiff or plaintiffs in error or appellant or appellants shall fail to prosecute his, her or their suit with effect, then to satisfy the condemnation money, together with damages, or otherwise abide the judgment in error or the decree in appeal, with double costs, but if the said judgment or decree shall be reversed, each party shall pay his, her and their own costs in the said court of errors and appeals. And until such security shall be given, the power, authority or proceedings of the said supreme court, court of admiralty or register, respectively, shall not be suspended.

[Section IV.] (Section VIII, P. L.) And be it further enacted by the authority aforesaid, That upon the hearing of any cause litigated before the register of wills and for granting of administrations, the depositions of the several witnesses, examined therein shall be taken in writing, and made part of the proceeding in the cause; upon which the said court of errors and appeals may reverse the decree of the said register for any error arising either in fact or law or affirm the same according to the merits and justice of the case.

[Section V.] (Section IX, P. L.) Provided always, and be it further enacted by the authority aforesaid, That if the said register, upon a dispute upon fact[s] arising before him, shall send an issue into the court of common pleas of the county to try the said facts, which he shall do at the request of either party, and a verdict establishing the said facts be returned, the said facts shall not be re-examined on appeal; and that no appeal from the decree of the said register concerning the validity of a will or the right to administer shall stay the proceedings or prejudice the acts of any executor or adminstrator pending the same, provided the executor shall give sufficient security for the faithful execution of the will and testament to the register; but in case of refusal the said register is hereby directed to grant letters of administration during the dispute which shall suspend the power of such executor during that time.

[Section VI.] (Section X, P. L.) And be it further enacted by the authority aforesaid, That it shall be lawful for any party or parties who have heretofore appealed in any cause from the supreme court of the late province of Pennsylvania to the King of Great Britain in council, and upon which no judgment was had before the fourth day of July, in the year of our Lord one thousand seven hundred and seventy-six, to bring a new writ of error according to the common law and not otherwise before the said court of errors and appeals, and the said court is hereby empowered and enjoined to proceed therein to judgment, as in other causes made cognizable in said court by this act; provided security be first given and an affidavit or affirmation attesting that the value of the matter in dispute exceeds the sum in like case hereinbefore limited, be filed as aforesaid.

[Section VII.] (Section XI, P. L.) And be it further enacted

1780] *The Statutes at Large of Pennsylvania.* 57

by the authority aforesaid, That the said court of errors and appeals shall sit in the city of Philadelphia at least twice in every year; that is to say, on the sixth day of April and twentieth day of September, and if either of the said days should happen to be on a Sunday then on the next day following, and if there be any causes depending before the said court shall have power to adjourn from time to time and to require and compel the attendance of sheriffs, coroners, constables and other ministerial officers as fully as any court of justice in this commonwealth can or may do; and the said court of errors and appeals may appoint a suitable person to be their clerk and register, and ascertain and allow reasonable and moderate fees to such clerk and register and to any other officer employed by the said court.

[Section VIII.] (Section XII, P. L.) Provided always and be it further enacted by the authority aforesaid, That no fine or common recovery, nor any judgment in any real, personal or mixed action, nor any appeal from the court of admiralty or register of wills and for granting administrations shall be avoided or reversed for any defect or error therein, unless the writ of error be commenced or the appeal brought and prosecuted with effect within twenty years after such fines levied, common recovery suffered, judgment signed or entered of record or decree be pronounced.

(Section XIII, P. L.) Provided nevertheless, That if any person who is or shall be entitled to any such writ of error, or appeal, as aforesaid, shall at the time of such title accrued, be within the age of twenty-one years, covert, non compos mentis, in prison or out of the limits of the United States of America, that then such person, his or her heirs, executors or administrators, notwithstanding the said twenty years be expired shall and may bring his, her and their writ of error or appeal for the reversing of any such fine, recovery or judgment so as the same be done within five years after his or her full age, discoverture, coming to sound mind, enlargement out of prison or return into some one of the United States of America but not afterwards nor otherwise.

[Section IX.] (Section XIV, P. L.) And be it further enacted by the authority aforesaid, That the said judge of admiralty and every of the three persons to be appointed and associated with the president of the supreme executive council and judges of the supreme court, as judges of the said court of errors and appeals shall be entitled to the value of two bushels of wheat for each day they shall attend upon the business of the said court, to be estimated and paid according to the directions of the act, entitled "An act for the better support of certain officers of this state, and for ascertaining the specific fines and penalties which they may incur by neglect of duty,"[1] by an order on the state treasurer drawn in council and signed by the president or vice-president.

> Passed February 28, 1780. See the note to the Act of Assembly passed May 22, 1722, Chapter 255; and the act of Assembly passed September 19, 1785, Chapter 1187. The Act in the text was repealed by the Act of Assembly passed April 13, 1791, Chapter 1575. Recorded L. B. No. 1, p. 332, &c.

CHAPTER DCCCLXXX.

AN ACT FOR THE MORE EFFECTUAL SUPPLY AND HONORABLE REWARD OF THE PENNSYLVANIA TROOPS IN THE SERVICE OF THE UNITED STATES OF AMERICA.

(Section I, P. L.) Whereas the honorable the Congress of the United States did, on the fifteenth day of May, Anno Domini one thousand seven hundred and seventy-eight, resolve and provide in the words and manner following, viz.: "That all military officers commissioned by Congress, who now are, or hereafter may be, in the service of the United States, and shall continue therein during the war and do not now hold any office of profit, under the said states, or any of them, shall, after the conclusion of the war, be entitled to receive annually, for the term of seven years, if they shall live so long, one-half of the present pay of such officer, provided that no general officer of the cavalry, artillery or infantry shall be entitled

---

[1] Passed November 27, 1779, Chapter 875.

to receive more than the one-half part of the pay of a colonel of such corps, respectively, and provided that this resolution shall not extend to any officer in the service of the United States unless he shall have taken the oath of allegiance to and shall actually reside within some one of the United States." And whereas the military commissioned officers in the federal army of the United States belonging to this state have not only distinguished themselves in the field by their courage and bravery, but have exhibited extraordinary proofs of patriotism, disinterestedness and sacrifice of private considerations to the public good.

(Section II, P. L.) And whereas the continuance of the war and the signal services and sufferings of the said troops since the passing the above resolve have made it highly proper to enlarge and extend the benefits thereof. And the legislature of this state, being desirous to manifest a just sense of the important services which have been rendered by the said officers and soldiers, and in future to supply them with such necessaries as may enable them to support and perform the duties of their several stations with cheerfulness and alacrity:

[Section I.] (Section III, P. L.) Be it enacted and it is hereby enacted by the Representatives of the Freemen of the Commonwealth of Pennsylvania in General Assembly met, and by the authority of the same, That the half pay aforesaid, so far as it respects the military commissioned officers of this state in the service of the United States, shall be continued to the said officers and every of them surviving the said term of seven years, and who shall be entitled and admitted to the same in pursuance of the said resolves, for and during the lives of such officers and officer, and that the rules following shall be duly observed in the application and payment thereof, that is to say:

First. That no person shall have or receive any part of the same who was a minor under the age of eighteen years when the regiment or company in which he served shall be reduced.

Secondly. That no person shall have or receive the said half pay or any part thereof but such as have done actual service in some regiment or company.

Thirdly. That the said half pay nor any part thereof shall

[not] be allowed to any person by virtue of any warrant or appointment except to such persons as would have been otherwise entitled to receive the same as reduced officers or to such brevet officers as are hereafter mentioned.

Fourthly. That the same shall not be allowed or extended to the officers of any new raised corps, or of any troops who have been enlisted for a shorter term than the continuance of the present war.

Fifthly. That the same shall not be allowed to any officer who shall not have taken the oath or oaths of allegiance which now are or hereafter may be required of the other subjects of this state, and also reside in some one of the United States.

[Section II.] (Section IV, P. L.) And be it further enacted by the authority aforesaid, That from and after the publication of this act the widows of such commissioned military officers as have fallen in battle or died in actual service or captivity, and whose husbands, if they had lived, would have been entitled to such half pay, and those who may hereafter become the widows of officers so falling in battle or dying in actual service or captivity during the continuance of the present war shall be entitled to the half of the pay which their husbands were respectively entitled to whilst in said service, during their widowhood and no longer.

[Section III.] (Section V, P. L.) And be it further enacted by the authority aforesaid, That on the petition of any of the said widows to the orphans' court in any county of this state the said court shall, in a summary way, inquire into the claim of such widow to the half pay allowed by this act, and the said court, on receiving satisfactory proof of the marriage and that the husband of the said widow would, if he had lived, have been entitled to half pay under this act, which proof shall be by a certificate under the hand and seal of the colonel or other commanding officer of the regiment, battalion or company to which the deceased last belonged, setting forth the commission which he last held and the regiment, battalion or company in which he last served, and also the time and place of his death, such certificate to be attested under the hands of two witnesses; or, in the case of the widow of such commanding officer, from the officer next in command. And the said petitioner shall produce also to the court the commission under which such claim shall be made or at least a certificate from the honorable the board of war of the United States that such commission had issued; whereupon, if the said court shall be satisfied of the justice of such claim it shall proceed to ascertain the same by way of annuity, and make an order on the county treasurer for the payment of such annuity, either quarterly or annually, as to the said court shall seem meet according to the true intent and meaning of this act, and the said treasurer shall advance and pay the said annuity as it becomes due out of any moneys belonging to the state, which he may have in his hands and shall be allowed the same in passing his accounts.

[Section IV.] (Section VI. P. L.) And be it further enacted by the authority aforesaid, That the said orphans' court shall once in three months in every year examine the record of such annuities, and send an authentic list of the names of the said widows and sums to which they are respectively entitled to the county treasurer, distinguishing therein the names of such annuitants as have died or been married again, and the clerk of the said court, once in every year, or oftener if required, shall transmit a copy of such list to the secretary of the supreme executive council of this state.

[Section V.] (Section VII, P. L.) And be it further enacted by the authority aforesaid, That all lands which have been or may hereafter be granted within this state to any officers or soldiers of the line of this state by virtue of any resolution of Congress or law of this state as a reward for their services shall be and are hereby exempted from taxation for and during the life of such officer or soldier, respectively, unless the same shall be transferred or aliened to any other person.

[Section VI.] (Section VIII, P. L.) And be it further enacted by the authority aforesaid, That every major-general, brigadier-general, colonel, lieutenant-colonel, major, captain, lieutenant, ensign, chaplain, surgeon and surgeon's mate belonging to the troops of Pennsylvania and engaged to serve during the present war shall, during his continuance in actual service, be furnished with one complete suit of regimental uniform clothes once in every year and no more, and that the supreme executive council shall from time to time purchase and procure the same at the charge of this commonwealth out of any of the unappropriated moneys in the state treasury, the said suit of clothes to consist of the following articles, viz.: One hat, one coat, one waistcoat, two pair of breeches, three pair of stockings, thread or worsted, three pair of shoes, three shirts, three stocks.

(Section IX, P. L.) And whereas the officers and soldiers of the troops of this state in the army of the United States of America, enlisted for and during the continuance of the present war and serving in the field have been greatly distressed by the excessive advance in the prices of divers necessaries and accomodations not included in the ration of provisions furnished to them by the public, and also by the difficulty of procuring them at places distant from the place of manufacture or importation:

(Section X, P. L.) And whereas the assembly of this state did heretofore, by sundry resolves, authorize and empower the supreme executive council of this state to draw upon the state treasurer from time to time for any sums of money which they should judge necessary to relieve in some measure the necessities of the officers and soldiers belonging to this state and serving in the army of the United States, and to appoint commissaries to purchase rum, sugar, coffee, tea, chocolate, tobacco and hard soap and such other articles as to the said council might appear necessary and suitable for the comfort of the said troops, under such regulations and restrictions as are set forth and expressed in the said resolves:

(Section XI, P. L.) And whereas the council in the execution of the said resolves did direct that the distribution and issue of the said enumerated articles should not exceed the ratio or proportion following, That is to say, for each ration of provisions to which each officer and soldier as aforesaid shall be respectively entitled by the acts of Congress, one pint of rum, half a pound of sugar, a quarter of a pound of coffee, one ounce of tea, half a pound of chocolate and one-quarter of a pound of tobacco, once in every week, and the same having been found by experience to be beneficial and satisfactory:

[Section VII.] (Section XII, P. L.) Be it enacted by the authority aforesaid, That the purchase and supply of the said enumerated articles shall be and are hereby continued for the benefit of the said officers and soldiers of this state during their actual service in the army of the United States, and that the said articles shall be distributed and issued to them in the proportions above set forth and at the following prices, to wit, rum, or spirits, by the gallon, five shillings; muscovado sugar, three shillings and nine pence per pound; tea, at twelve shillings per pound; hard soap, at one shilling and three pence per pound; tobacco, at nine pence per pound, or under such other rules and regulations as the president or vice-president in council may and shall, from time to time, direct, and that the supreme executive council shall defray the expense of procuring the said articles, and the distribution thereof from time to time out of such moneys as are or may be in the state treasury not specially appropriated.

(Section XIII, P. L.) Provided, That no officer or soldier shall be deemed entitled thereto unless while on actual duty in camp or garrison or march, and that no issues be made thereof at any time under the name or character of back rations.

(Section XIV, P. L.) Provided also, That no officer shall be deemed entitled to a proportion of the said clothing or stores for more than one commission, nor any officer of this state holding or appointed to any rank by brevet unless when so appointed and distinguished by the honorable Congress for extraordinary merit and so signified in his commission; in which case and the same being duly made known to the supreme executive council, such brevet officer shall be empowered by special order of council to receive like privileges and benefits as other officers in the line.

[Section VIII.] (Section XV, P. L.) And be it further enacted by the authority aforesaid, That the officers, seamen and marines employed in the service of this state, and who were in actual service on the thirteenth day of March last and shall continue therein to the end of the present war or till honorably discharged shall be entitled to the allowances and benefits hereinbefore granted to the military officers and soldiers, respectively of the Pennsylvania troops as to half pay and clothing and to like supply and distribution of the articles above enumerated, subject to the same limitations and conditions; the half pay of the said officers of the navy to commence at the expiration of the present war or their discharge.

[Section IX.] (Section XVI, P. L.) Be it also enacted by the authority aforesaid, That the widows of any of the said officers of the said navy who now are or have been in actual service and have been killed or died in such service shall be entitled to half pay in the same manner and under the same limitations and conditions as the widows of officers in the land service hereinbefore mentioned.

(Section XVII, P. L.) And whereas, it may often happen that officers in both the sea and land service may be killed or die therein having a child or children and no wife, or such widow may remarry or die, in which case the said children may become destitute:

[Section X.] (Section XIII, P. L.) Be it therefore enacted by the authority aforesaid, That in such case the said orphans' court shall and it is hereby empowered to nominate one or more suitable persons to be guardians of the said child or children and to order and direct the half pay to which the father would have been entitled to be paid to such guardian or guardians for such time and in such manner as to the said court shall seem meet, so as the same be not longer than such child or children respectively attains the age of fourteen years, and in like manner in case of the death or marriage of any officer's widow having a child or children, to transfer and set over the half pay by her enjoyed to the use and benefit of such child or children, not exceeding the term aforesaid.

[Section XI.] (Section XX, P. L.) And be it further enacted by the authority aforesaid, That all the officers and soldiers who have been or shall be regularly transferred from any of the regiments forming the line of this state into the invalid regiment and such transfer duly certified by the commanding officer thereof to the president or vice-president in council, shall be and they are hereby entitled to all the benefits, privilges and advantages which are by this act granted to any officers or soldiers belonging to this state. And in order that the persons for whom the benefits and advantages aforesaid are intended may be clearly ascertained and determined.

[Section XII.] (Section XX, P. L.) Be it enacted by the authority aforesaid, That they are the officers and soldiers of the line of this state in the federal army consisting of eleven regiments of infantry, and the regiment of artillery, commanded by Colonel Thomas Proctor, including the companies of artillery now or late commanded by the Captains Porter, Lee, Jones and Coren, the invalids aforesaid, the Pennsylvania officers and soldiers in the several corps of guards, light dragoons, artillery and infantry other than the artificers who are no part of the eighty-eight battalions originally apportioned on the states and who are or shall be considered by the honorable Congress as part of the quota of this state and accepted as such by the president or vice-president in council, and the naval officers above mentioned.

(Section XXI, P. L.) Provided always, That no officer or soldier of the army shall be admitted to the benefits and advantages aforesaid, unless he be ascertained to belong to the quota of this state in the manner and form directed and prescribed in and by an act of Congress of the fifteenth day of March last, and accepted by the president or vice-president in council as aforesaid, nor shall any such officer or soldier be entitled to the continuance of the same unless it shall appear by returns to be made every three months or oftener by the commanding officer of the division, brigade or separate command under whom such officer or soldier shall serve, that such person shall continue in the federal army, nor unless such officer or soldier shall be certified to be commissioned and enlisted for and during the present war.

(Section XXII, P. L.) And whereas the public service may hereafter require further arrangements, regulations and alterations to be made of the regiments in the line of the state and of the officers who may compose the same or be entitled to the benefits of this act.

[Section XIII.] (Section XXIII, P. L.) Be it therefore enacted by the authority aforesaid, That if any person entitled to the emoluments, privileges and benefits by this act allowed and granted shall refuse to conform to such arrangements, regulations and alterations as may be hereafter made by the honorable the Congress of these United States or by the supreme executive council of this state in concurrence with the commander-in-chief of the armies of the United States, it shall and may be lawful, and the president or vice-president in council are hereby authorized, to retain and withhold the said benefits and advantages hereby given from any such regiment, troop, company, officer or persons so refusing for and during such refusal, anything hereinbefore contained to the contrary notwithstanding.

[Section XIV.] (Section XXIV, P. L.) Be it also enacted by the authority aforesaid, That if any difficulty or doubt should arise concerning the persons entitled to the benefits and advantages granted by this act other than the widows and children aforesaid the same shall be adjudged and finally determined by the supreme executive council of this state.

Passed March 1, 1780. See the Acts of Assembly passed December 18, 1780, Chapter 920; December 23, 1780, Chapter 926; April 10, 1781, Chapter 941; June 25, 1781, Chapter 946; September 29, 1781, Chapter 951; October 1, 1781, Chapter 955; April 13, 1782, Chapter 971; January 31, 1783, Chapter 1002; March 12, 1783, Chapter 1007; March 21, 1783; Chapter 1024; September 23, 1783, Chapter 1042; March 16, 1785, Chapter 1137; March 24, 1785, Chapter 1139; March 25, 1785, Chapter 1143; April 8, 1785, Chapter 1166; (the three Acts of Assembly passed) September 22, 1785, Chapters 1191, 1192, 1194; March 8, 1786, Chapter 1210; March 25, 1786, Chapter 1219; March 10, 1787, Chapter 1271; September 11, 1787, Chapter 1306; September 13, 1788, Chapter 1352; November 20, 1789, Chapter 1466; March 27, 1790, Chapter 1493; September 30, 1791, Chapter 1592; April 6, 1792; Chapter 1592; April 6, 1792, Chapter 1637; April 10, 1792, Chapter 1644; April 5, 1793, Chapter 1671; April 11, 1793, Chapter 1696; April 17, 1795, Chapter 1855; February 14, 1797, Chapter 1917; March 20, 1797, Chapter 1928; April 9, 1799, Chapter 2068; April 11, 1799; Chapter 2081; February 23, 1801, Chapter 2194. Recorded L. B. No. 1, p. 335, &c.

CHAPTED DCCCLXXXI.

AN ACT FOR THE GRADUAL ABOLITION OF SLAVERY.

(Section I, P. L.) When we contemplate our abhorrence of that condition to which the arms and tyranny of Great Britain were exerted to reduce us, when we look back on the variety of dangers to which we have been exposed, and how miraculously our wants in many instances have been supplied and our deliverances wrought, when even hope and human fortitude have become unequal to the conflict, we are unavoidably led to a serious and grateful sense of the manifold blessings which we have undeservedly received from the hand of that Being from whom every good and perfect gift cometh. Impressed with these ideas, we conceive that it is our duty, and we rejoice that it is in our power, to extend a portion of that freedom to others, which hath been extended to us, and a release from that state of thraldom, to which we ourselves were tyrannically doomed, and from which we have now every prospect of being delivered. It is not for us to enquire why, in the creation of mankind, the inhabitants of the several parts of the earth were distinguished by a difference in feature or complexion. It is sufficient to know that all are the work of an Almighty Hand. We find in the distribution of the human species that the most fertile as well as the most barren parts of the earth are inhabited by men of complexions different from ours and from each other, from whence we may reasonably, as well as religiously infer, that He, who placed them in their various situations, hath extended equally His care and protection to all, and that it becometh not us to counteract His mercies:

We esteem it a peculiar blessing granted to us, that we are enabled this day to add one more step to universal civilization by removing as much as possible the sorrows of those who have lived in undeserved bondage, and from which by the assumed authority of the Kings of Britain, no effectual legal relief could be obtained. Weaned by a long course of experience from those narrow prejudices and partialities we had imbibed, we find our hearts enlarged with kindness and benevolence towards men of all conditions and nations, and we conceive ourselves at this particular period extraordinarily called upon, by the blessings which we have received, to manifest the sincerity of our profession and to give substantial proof of our gratitude:

(Section II, P. L.) And whereas the condition of those persons who have heretofore been denominated negro and mulatto slaves, has been attended with circumstances which not only deprived them of the common blessings that they were by nature entitled to, but has cast them into the deepest afflictions by an unnatural separation and sale of husband and wife from each other, and from their children, an injury the greatness of which can only be conceived by supposing that we were in the same unhappy case. In justice, therefore, to persons so unhappily circumstanced, and who, having no prospect before them whereon they may rest their sorrows and their hopes, have no reasonable inducement to render that service to society which they otherwise might, and also in grateful commemoration of our own happy deliverance from that state of unconditional submission to which we were doomed by the tyranny of Britain:

[Section I.] (Section III, P. L.) Be it enacted and it is hereby enacted by the Representatives of the Freemen of the Commonwealth of Pennsylvania in General Assembly met, and by the authority of the same, That all persons, as well negroes and mulattoes as others who shall be born within this state, from and after the passing of this act, shall not be deemed and considered as servants for life or slaves; and that all servitude for life or slavery of children in consequence of the slavery of their mothers, in the case of all children born within this state from and after the passing of this act as aforesaid, shall be and hereby is utterly taken away, extinguished and forever abolished.

[Section II.] (Section IV, P. L.) Provided always, and be it further enacted by the authority aforesaid, That every negro and mulatto child born within this state after the passing of this act as aforesaid who would in case this act had not been made, have been born a servant for years or life or a slave, shall be deemed to be and shall be, by virtue of this act the servant of such person or his or her assigns who would in such case have been entitled to the service of such child until such child shall attain unto the age of twenty-eight years, in the manner and on the conditions whereon servants bound by indenture for four years are or may be retained and holden, and shall be liable to like correction and punishment, and entitled to like relief in case he or she be evilly treated by his or her master or mistress, and to like freedom dues and other privileges as servants bound by indenture for four years are or may be entitled unless the person to whom the service of any such child shall belong shall abandon his or her claim to the same, in which case the overseers of the poor of the city, township or district, respectively where such child shall be so abandoned, shall [by indenture] bind out every child so abandoned as an apprentice for a time not exceeding the age hereinbefore limited for the service of such children.

[Section III.] (Section V, P. L.) And be it further enacted by the authority aforesaid, That every person who is or shall be the owner of any negro or mulatto slave or servant for life or till the age of thirty-one years, now within this state, or his lawful attorney shall, on or before the said first day of November next, deliver, or cause to be delivered, in writing to the clerk of the peace of the county or to the clerk of the court of record of the city of Philadelphia, in which he or she shall respectively inhabit, the name and surname and occupation or profession of such owner and the name of the county and township, district or ward wherein he or she resideth, and also the name and names of any such slave and slaves and servant and servants for life or till the age of thirty-one years, together with their ages and sexes severally and respectively set forth and annexed, by such person owned or statedly employed and then being within this state, in order to ascertain and distinguish the slaves and servants for life and years till the age of thirty-one years, within this state who shall be such on the said first day of November next, from all other persons, which particulars shall by said clerk of the sessions and clerk of said city court be entered in books to be provided for that purpose by the said clerks; and that no negro or mulatto now within this state shall, from and after the said first day of November, be deemed a slave or servant for life or till the age of thirty-one years unless his or her name shall be entered as aforesaid on such record except such negro and mulatto slaves and servants as are hereinafter excepted; the said clerk to be entitled to a fee of two dollars for each slave or servant so entered as aforesaid from the treasurer of the county, to be allowed to him in his accounts.

(Section VI, P. L.) Provided always, That any person in whom the ownership or right to the service of any negro or mulatto shall be vested at the passing of this act, other than such as are hereinbefore excepted, his or her heirs, executors, administrators and assigns, and all and every of them severally shall be liable to the overseers of the poor of the city, township or district to which any such negro or mulatto shall become chargeable, for such necessary expense, with costs of suit thereon, as such overseers may be put to through the neglect of the owner, master or mistress of such negro or mulatto, notwithstanding the name and other descriptions of such negro or mulatto shall not be entered and recorded as aforesaid; unless his or her master or owner shall, before such slave or servant attain his or her twenty-eighth year, execute and record in the proper county, a deed or instrument securing to such slave or servant his or her freedom.

[Section IV.] (Section VII, P. L.) And be it further enacted by the authority aforesaid, That the offenses and crimes of negroes and mulattoes as well slaves and servants and [sic] [as] freemen, shall be inquired of, adjudged, corrected and punished in like manner as the offenses and crimes of the other inhabitants of this state are and shall be enquired of, adjudged, corrected and punished, and not otherwise, except that a slave shall not be admitted to bear witness against a freeman.

[Section V.] (Section VIII, P. L.) And be it further enacted by the authority aforesaid, That in all cases wherein sentence of death shall be pronounced against a slave, the jury before whom he or she shall be tried shall appraise and declare the value of such slave, and in case such sentence be executed, the court shall make an order on the state treasurer, payable to the owner for the same and for the costs of prosecution, but in case of a remission or mitigation for the costs only.

[Section VI.] (Section IX, P. L.) And be it further enacted by the authority aforesaid, That the reward for taking up runaway and absconding negro and mulatto slaves and servants and the penalties for enticing away, dealing with or harboring, concealing or employing negro and mulatto slaves and servants shall be the same, and shall be recovered in like manner as in case of servants bound for four years.

[Section VII.] (Section X, P. L.) And be it further enacted by the authority aforesaid, That no man or woman of any nation or color, except the negroes or mulattoes who shall be registered as aforesaid shall at any time hereafter be deemed, adjudged or holden, within the territories of this commonwealth, as slaves or servants for life, but as free men and free women, and except the domestic slaves attending upon delegates in Congress from the other American states, foreign ministers and consuls, and persons passing through or sojourning in this state, and not becoming resident therein; and seamen employed in ships, not belonging to any inhabitant of this state nor employed in any ship owned by any such inhabitant: [Provided such domestic slaves be not aliened or sold to any inhabitant] nor (except in the case of members of Congress, foreign ministers and consuls) retained in this state longer than six months.

[Section VIII.] (Section XI, P. L.) Provided always, and be it further enacted by the authority aforesaid, That this act, nor anything in it contained, shall not give any relief or shelter to any absconding or runaway negro or mulatto slave or servant, who has absented himself or shall absent himself from his or her owner, master or mistress, residing in any other state or country, but such owner, master or mistress, shall have like right and aid to demand, claim and take away his slave or servant as he might have had in case this act had not been made. And that all negro and mulatto slaves now owned, and heretofore resident in this state, who have absented themselves or been clandestinely carried away, or who may be employed abroad as seamen, and have not returned or been brought back to their owners, masters or mistresses, before the passing of this act may, within five years be registered as effectually as is ordered by this act concerning those who are now within this state, on producing such slave before any two justices of the peace, and satisfying the said justices by due proof of the former residence, absconding, taking away or absence of such slave as aforesaid; who, thereupon, shall direct and order the said slave to be entered on the record as aforesaid.

(Section XII, P. L.) And whereas attempts may be made to evade this act by introducing into this state negroes and mulattoes bound by covenant to serve for long and unreasonable terms of years, if the same be not prevented:

[Section IX.] (Section XIII, P. L.) Be it therefore enacted by the authority aforesaid, That no covenant of personal servitude or apprenticeship whatsoever shall be valid or binding on a negro or mulatto for a longer term than seven years, unless such servant or apprentice were at the commencement of such servitude or apprenticeship under the age of twenty-one years; in which case such negro or mulatto may be holden as a servant or apprentice respectively according to the covenant, as the case shall be until he or she shall attain the age of twenty-eight years, but no longer.

[Section X.] (Section XIV, P. L.) And be it further enacted by the authority aforesaid, That an act of assembly of the province of Pennsylvania, passed in the year one thousand seven hundred and five, entitled "An act for the trial of negroes,"[1] and another act of assembly of the said province, passed in the year one thousand seven hundred and twenty-five, entitled "An act for the better regulating of negroes in this province,"[2] and another act of assembly of the said province passed in the year one thousand seven hundred and sixty-

---

[1] Passed January 12, 1705-06, Chapter 143.
[2] Passed March 5, 1725-26, Chapter 292.

one, entitled "An act for laying a duty on negro and mulatto slaves imported into this province,"[1] and also another act of assembly of the said province, passed in the year one thousand seven hundred and seventy-three, entitled "An act for making perpetual an act for laying a duty on negro and mulatto slaves imported into this province and for laying an additional duty on said slaves,"[2] shall be and are hereby repealed, annulled and made void.

>Passed March 1, 1780. See the Acts of Assembly passed October 1, 1781, Chapter 953; March 29, 1788, Chapter 1345; December 8, 1789, Chapter 1476. Recorded L. B. No. 1, p. 339, &c.

CHAPTER DCCCLXXXII.

AN ACT TO COMPEL THE SETTLEMENT OF THE PUBLIC ACCOUNTS.

(Section I, P. L.) Whereas in the course of the present contest between the inhabitants of the United States of America and Great Britain very large and great expenditures and advances of public money have been made by the good people of Pennsylvania in the common cause:

(Section II, P. L.) And whereas many of the persons to whom such advances of money have been made, regardless of the public welfare, as well as of their own credit and character, have refused or neglected and do still refuse or neglect to exhibit their accounts and vouchers and to settle their accounts notwithstanding the opportunity which has been given and the repeated calls which have been made upon such defaulters by the auditors appointed and authorized in [and] by an act of assembly of this commonwealth, entitled "An act for settling the accounts of the late committee and council of safety,"[3] passed on the second day of September, which was in the year of our Lord one thousand seven hundred and seventy-eight;

---
[1] Passed March 14, 1761, Chapter 467.
[2] Passed February 26, 1773, Chapter 681.
[3] Passed September 2, 1778, Chapter 806.

and a supplement to the said act, passed on the fifth day of December following, and a further supplement to the said act,[1] passed on the thirty-first day of March last, whereby the said auditors were also authorized to audit, adjust and settle the accounts of the late navy board and board of war of this state, and such other accounts as may be intimately connected with the same:

(Section III, P. L.) And whereas divers of the said defaulters who ought to have attended upon and accounted with the committees of account of the assemblies of this commonwealth, or one of the said committees, though such persons [have] been frequently called on by the committee of accounts for the time being to appear before such committee and to exhibit their accounts and vouchers, in order that their several accounts might be adjusted and settled, have refused or neglected to appear before the said committee or to exhibit their accounts and vouchers and have their several accounts settled as aforesaid:

(Section IV, P. L.) And whereas it is highly necessary as well for ascertaining and settling the account of the expenditures made as aforesaid by Pennsylvania, before the revolution, and since, at the request and for the account of the honorable Congress of the United States of America, as the accounts of the special exertions of Pennsylvania in the common cause, in order to satisfy the good people of this state of the proper and just application of the public treasure, and of the necessity of submitting to the heavy taxes which have been laid upon them. In order, therefore, to compel the defaulters aforesaid, and every of them and all others to whom the public moneys of Pennsylvania may have been advanced, either before the revolution or since, or who may be otherwise possessed thereof and who ought to account for the same to appear before the auditors appointed or to be appointed by or in pursuance of this act to attend the said auditors and produce their accounts and vouchers, and settle their said accounts, and pay over to the treasurer of this state the balances which may be respectively due to the commonwealth from such defaulters:

---

[1] Passed December 5, 1778, Chapter 824.

1780]   *The Statutes at Large of Pennsylvania.*   75

[Section I.] (Section V, P. L.) Be it enacted and it is hereby enacted by the Representatives of the Freemen of the Commonwealth of Pennsylvania in General Assembly met, and by the authority of the same, That Joseph Dean, John Purviance and Samuel Miles, of the city and county of Philadelphia, Esquires, are hereby appointed auditors with full power to collect, audit, liquidate, adjust and settle the accounts of the late committee of safety and of the council of safety of Pennsylvania, who ceased to act in the month of March, which was in the year of our Lord one thousand seven hundred and seventy-seven, and all others which ought to have been settled before the auditors appointed by or in pursuance of the acts aforesaid, and have not been finally settled and adjusted, and the accounts of such defaulters as aforesaid, who were accountable before the committee of accounts of any former house of assembly, and the accounts of all such persons who have been or may be entrusted with or have or may become possessed of the moneys, goods or effects of this commonwealth, and are or shall be accountable for the same, except as hereafter excepted, and shall fail so to settle their several accounts and in any case wherein it shall appear that a balance of moneys shall be due by any such person or persons to this commonwealth, the said auditors, or any two of them, shall direct that payment thereof be made to the treasurer of this state, and the certificate of the said auditors, or any two of them, shall be conclusive evidence in an action of debt at the suit of the commonwealth against any person or persons of the sums of money which such person or persons owe or may be indebted to the commonwealth and no set off or deduction from the same shall be admitted; and in case any person or persons, his, her or their heirs, executors or administrators to whom the moneys of this state have been advanced, or to whose hands such moneys have or may come, and who are or may be accountable for the same before the said auditors shall upon the final settlement of his, her, or their accounts satisfy the said auditors, or any two of them, that there is a balance of money due to such person or persons from the commonwealth, the said auditors shall make an order for the same on the said treasurer, payable to the person or persons entitled to receive the same, which order the said treasurer is hereby directed to pay.

[Section II.] (Section VI, P. L.) And be it further enacted by the authority aforesaid, That the said auditors, or any two of them, are hereby directed and empowered to open an office in the city of Philadelphia for the purpose of regularly receiving, auditing and settling the said accounts and may hire and employ skilful accountants or clerks to assist them in the business hereby committed to them, and allow to such accountants and clerks suitable compensations for their services, and the said auditors shall give public notice of their appointment and of the place where the said office shall be kept by advertisements inserted in some newspaper printed in the said city and by like advertisements to be read in the courts of general quarter sessions of the peace, to be held for said city and the several counties of the state, requiring all persons who ought to account before the said auditors to attend at the said office or elsewhere as is hereinafter provided, and produce their accounts and vouchers and other evidence necessary to support and ascertain the same, and that all such defaulters do attend the said auditors and comply with the directions of this act under the pains and disabilities therein provided, and the justices of the peace in the said several courts of general quarter sessions shall cause this act to be read aloud in the said courts in order that the same may be more generally known.

[Section III.] (Section VII, P. L.) And be it further enacted by the authority aforesaid, That the said auditors shall be and are hereby authorized to purchase and prepare proper and sufficient books in which they shall enter all accounts by them settled, therein carefully distinguishing and separating all such accounts and charges as are the proper accounts and charges of this state, from such as belong to the account of the United States of America, or any of them, and to call upon the former auditors of accounts as aforesaid for the several books, papers and records belonging to the said office.

[Section IV.] (Section VIII, P. L.) And be it further enacted by the authority aforesaid, That if it shall appear to the supreme executive council of this state to be useful for the advancement of this necessary business and the ease of persons accountable before the said auditors who reside at a great distance from the said city, the said council may direct the said auditors to give their attendance at one or more place [sic] within this state on the western side of the river Susquehanna, and at two or more several places other than the said city eastward of the said river for such length of time as shall be judged suitable for the purpose of receiving, adjusting and settling the accounts of such persons who dwell remote from the said city, due notice of the same being first given by advertisement in some newspaper printed in the said city, and in the courts of general quarter sessions as aforesaid. And the better to enable the said auditors to obtain a full and certain knowledge of the accounts directed to be settled by them as aforesaid, and to make a speedy as well as a just settlement thereof:

[Section V.] (Section IX, P. L.) Be it further enacted by the authority aforesaid, That it shall and may be lawful for the said auditors, or any two of them, as often as there shall be occasion, to call before them by subpoena or summons, and in case of contempt to issue a writ of attachment in order to compel the appearance of any person or persons, who is or may be accountable before the said auditors by virtue of this act, or who the said auditors may reasonably suppose is or are capable of giving evidence or information concerning the said accounts, or any of them, and the said auditors, or any two of them, are hereby authorized to examine upon oath or affirmation any person as a witness respecting any such account, which oath or affirmation the said auditors, or any of them, is hereby empowered to administer; and in case any person or persons on whom such subpoena or summons shall be served, being accountable before the said auditors, shall refuse to appear, as in such writ shall be expressed and directed, or having appeared before the said auditors, shall refuse or neglect to exhibit his, her or their accounts, and attend the settlement thereof or, being summoned as a witness, shall neglect or refuse to appear before the said auditors at the time and place appointed in and by such subpoena or summons, and shall make default thereupon, or having appeared as aforesaid, shall refuse to make a full disclosure of his, her or their knowledge in the matter depending before the said auditors, the said auditors, or any two of them, may award an attachment and commit such delinquent or delinquents to the common gaol of the county, there to be holden till such person or persons shall submit to the said auditors, and comply with the directions of this act; and all persons who shall be summoned as witnesses by the said auditors, and every sheriff, coroner or other officer to whom they shall direct their precepts or writs as aforesaid, shall be allowed like fees for their attendance and services as witnesses summoned to appear in the inferior courts of justice and sheriffs, corners and other officers are entitled to in such courts; such costs, together with such further charges accruing, to be levied on the several delinquents by the said auditors, or any two of them, by warrant in like manner as small debts are recoverable.

[Section VI.] (Section X, P. L.) Provided always, and be it further enacted by the authority aforesaid, That if upon any subpoena or summons requiring the attendance of any person or persons before the said auditors as aforesaid, a return be made that such person is not to be found within the proper county, that the said auditors, or any two of them, may issue an attachment and proceed thereon as aforesaid as if such subpoena or summons had been duly served.

[Section VII.] (Section XI, P. L.) And be it further enacted by the authority aforesaid, That if any person or persons who by virtue of this act are or shall be accountable before the said auditors for any sum or sums of money which have been or may be advanced to such person or persons, or for any moneys, goods, chattels or effects, which have or may come to the hands or possession of such person or persons, shall, for three months after the service of such subpoena or summons as aforesaid, or three months after demand made in the general quarter sessions of the peace of the city or county where such person or persons last abode, for such person or persons to appear before the said auditors and exhibit and settle his accounts as aforesaid, refuse or neglect to obey such subpoena, summons or demand, and comply with the directions of this act, that such person and persons so refusing and neglecting shall be liable to an action of debt or other action at the suit of the commonwealth for the whole of the sum and sums of money, goods, chattels and effects belonging to the public which he ought to account for as aforesaid before the said auditors, and shall be forever barred of setting off any charge or expenditure thereout and from recovering any satisfaction for any services done for the public, unless the said auditors, or any two of them, shall, before the said term of three months be expired, certify in behalf of such person or persons that it is reasonable that further time be allowed to such person or persons for exhibting and settling his, her or their accounts, in which case, upon sufficient security being entered by the party or parties in whose behalf such certificate shall be made for the whole money or other property unaccounted for by such person or persons, the supreme executive council may by an entry on their journal allow of further time as aforesaid.

[Section VIII.] (Section XII, P. L.) And be it further enacted by the authority aforesaid, That the said auditors shall be and hereby are authorized to draw on the treasurer of this state for such moneys as may be necessary to purchase books, paper, quills and ink, and for office rent and for the salaries of their clerk or clerks and other necessary charges and expenses. And in case any of the persons who are hereby appointed auditors as aforesaid shall refuse or neglect to act as such, or in case any vacancy shall happen in the said board of auditors by death or otherwise, that then and in such case the supreme executive council of this state in the recess of the assembly shall fill up the same; otherwise the same shall be filled by vote of the assembly as often as the same shall be necessary. And each of the said auditors shall be entitled to and receive for his services in the execution of this act the value of two bushels of wheat as the same from time to time shall be declared by the assembly in pursuance of an act, entitled "An act for the better support of certain officers of this state, and for ascertaining the specific fines and penalties which they may incur by neglect of duty,"[1] for each day he shall at-

---

[1] Passed November 27, 1779, Chapter 875.

tend on and be employed in auditing and adjusting the accounts aforesaid, or such other recompense as the assembly shall direct, and the supreme executive council may draw orders on the treasurer of this state, payable to the said auditors severally, for the moneys hereby allowed to them.

(Section XIII, P. L.) Provided that nothing herein contained shall prevent the settlement of the following accounts before the committee of accounts appointed annually by the house of assembly, to wit, the settlement of the accounts of the state treasurer, the general loan office, light-house rates, duties on slaves, collectors of excise, Province island and other public estates, county commissioners and treasurers and the incidental charges of the house of general assembly.

[Section IX.] (Section XIV, P. L.) And be it further enacted by the authority aforesaid, That the aforesaid act of assembly, entitled "An act for settling the accounts of the late committee and council of safety,"[1] with the supplement and further supplement thereto and the act, entitled "An act to compel certain persons intrusted with public moneys by or for the use of this commonwealth to account for the same, and to pay such parts thereof as they shall be chargeable with into the state treasury,"[2] passed the second day of April, one thousand seven hundred and seventy-nine, are hereby repealed and made void.

[Section X.] (Section XV, P. L.) Provided nevertheless and be it further enacted by the authority aforesaid, That this repeal shall not extend to or affect any settlement of accounts made by the auditors or commissioners appointed by or in pursuance of the said acts so repealed, or any of them, but that the same shall be as sufficient and of like effect as if the same were made and settled in pursuance of this act.

<small>Passed March 1, 1780. See the Act of Assembly passed May 30, 1780, Chapter 909. The Act in the text was repealed by the Act of Assembly passed April 13, 1782, Chapter 970. Recorded L. B. No. 1, p. 342, &c.</small>

---

[1] Ante Chapters 806, 824, 825.
[2] Chapter 838.

CHAPTER DCCCLXXXIII.

AN ACT TO ALTER AND AMEND AN ACT OF ASSEMBLY ENTITLED "AN ACT FOR THE EFFECTUAL SUPPRESSION OF PUBLIC AUCTIONS AND VENDUES, AND TO PROHIBIT MALE PERSONS CAPABLE OF BEARING ARMS FROM BEING HAWKERS AND PEDDLERS," SO FAR AS TO ALLOW THE SALE BY PUBLIC AUCTION OF GOODS DAMAGED OR SHIPWRECKED.

(Section I, P. L.) Whereas in the act of assembly, entitled "An act for the effectual suppression of public auctions and vendues and to prohibit male persons capable of bearing arms from being hawkers and peddlers,"[1] passed on the twenty-sixth day of November last, no provision was made for the sale by public auction of damaged goods or goods saved out of ships or vessels wrecked or which, for the satisfaction of insurers and others, it may be proper and reasonable should be sold after that manner:

[Section I.] (Section II, P. L.) Be it therefore enacted and it is hereby enacted by the Representatives of the Freemen of the Commonwealth of Pennsylvania in General Assembly met and by the authority of the same, That from and after the publication of this act, all goods and merchandise which shall really and bona fide be damaged and in a perishable condition, or which shall be saved out of any ship or vessel cast away or wrecked or so circumstanced by distress of storms or otherwise that the cargo or lading thereof ought to be sold for the account of [the] insurers, and anchors and cables taken up at sea or in the river or bay of Delaware and which ought to be sold to ascertain the salvage due thereupon to the person or persons who may take up the same, may be sold at public auction or vendue the said act notwithstanding, subject, however, to the rules and restrictions therein prescribed as to the sale by public auction or vendue of goods and merchandise thereby permitted to be sold by public auction or vendue.

---

[1] Passed November 26, 1779, Chapter 870.

[Section II.] (Section III, P. L.) Provided always and be it further enacted by the authority aforesaid, That before the auctioneer of the city of Philadelphia shall proceed to sell by public auction or vendue any goods or merchandise by virtue of this act, he shall be furnished with the license of the president or vice-president in council authorizing such sale in which the goods and merchandize thereby permitted to be sold as aforesaid shall be specified and particularized, such license to be grounded on the report on oath or affirmation of three judicious and indifferent men who, being appointed by the said president or vice-president in council for that purpose, shall have carefully enquired of and viewed the said goods and merchandise and found them to come within the intent and benefit of this act.

Passed March 2, 1780. See the note to the Act of Assembly passed November 26, 1779, Chapter 870. Recorded L. B. No. 1, p. 346, &c.

CHAPTER DCCCLXXXIV.

AN ACT FOR CONFIRMING AND AMENDING THE CHARTER OF THE GERMAN LUTHERAN CONGREGATION IN AND NEAR THE CITY OF PHILADELPHIA IN THE STATE OF PENNSYLVANIA.

(Section I, P. L.) Whereas the members of the corporation called and known by the name of "The Rector, Vestrymen and Church-Wardens of the German Lutheran Congregation in and near the city of Philadelphia, in the Province of Pennsylvania," by their petition have shown that in the year of our Lord one thousand seven hundred and sixty-five, by the charter of the then proprietaries, Thomas Penn and Richard Penn, they were incorporated by the name, style and title aforesaid. That the first Monday in the year of our Lord one thousand seven hundred and seventy-eight was the day on which an election should have been held of the officers of the said corporation, at which time the enemy were in possession of this city and most of the petitioners dispersed in the country so that no election could be had. That, by reason thereof and for other causes therein set forth, doubts and uneasiness have arisen respecting their charter rights, for removing whereof they have prayed for a law to incorporate and secure to them their rights and privileges:

(Section II, P. L.) And whereas it is manifested to be the desire of the said congregation that sundry amendments and alterations should be made in their former constitution, which being just and reasonable are hereinafter set forth and contained:

[Section I.] (Section III, P. L.) Be it therefore enacted and it is hereby enacted by the Representatives of the Freemen of the Commonwealth of Pennsylvania in General Assembly met, and by the authority of the same, That the said corporation be confirmed and established as a body corporate and politic in law and in fact, to have continuance forever by the name, style and title of "The Ministers, Vestrymen and Church-Wardens of the German Lutheran Congregation in and near the city of Philadelphia, in the State of Pennsylvania," and the said corporation is hereby vested, confirmed and established in all and singular the estates, rights, privileges and immunities which to them in and by the said charter were given and granted, or in consequence thereof to them of right belong and appertain or ought so to do, subject only to the alterations and amendments herein specified and contained.

[Section II.] (Section IV, P. L.) And be it further enacted by the authority aforesaid, That such and so many of the fundamental articles of the said congregation mentioned and referred to in the said charter as are not altered or repealed in and by this act and are not repugnant to the laws of this commonwealth shall be, remain and continue forever valid and effectual unless the same be altered by the consent of two-third parts in number of the members of the said congregation qualified to vote at elections according to the purport and meaning of the said charter and this act.

[Section III.]. (Section V, P. L.) And be it further enacted by the authority aforesaid, That the proviso or clause in the said charter which requires that the by-laws, rules and ordinances of the said corporation be not repugnant to the laws of Great Britain or the laws then in force in the province of Pennsylvania be and is hereby annulled, repealed and made void.

[Section IV.] (Section VI, P. L.) And be it further enacted by the authority aforesaid, That the Reverend Henry Melchior Muhlenberg, the Reverend John Christopher Kuntze and the Reverend Justus Henry Christian Helmuth, the present ministers; Henry Keppele, Adam Weber, Adam Krebs, David Schaffer, Andrew Boshardt, Daniel Grub, Philip Alberti, Andrew Burkhardt, Michael Shubart, Frederick Hagner, George Godfrey Woelper and Balthaser Fleischer, the present vestrymen; George Seitz, Frederick Hailer, George Heidel, Jacob Eckfeld, Michael Fuchs, Michael Immel, George Forbach, Daniel Draiss and George Daum, the present church-wardens and their successors duly elected and appointed in such manner and form as hereinafter is directed and required, be and they are hereby confirmed, constituted and appointed to be and forever remain the members of the said corporation; that the name and office of rector be discontinued and abolished and that every of the ministers of the said congregation for the time being have a seat and vote in the vestry.

[Section V.] (Section VII, P. L.) And be it further enacted by the authority aforesaid, That the said corporation shall at all times hereafter consist of the ministers of the said congregation, duly chosen from time to time (the number of whom may be either increased or diminished according to the circumstances or desire of the said congregation), and of twelve vestrymen and nine church-wardens; and that the first named six persons of the present vestrymen, That is to say, Henry Keppele, Adam Weber, Adam Krebs, David Schaffer, Andrew Boshardt and Daniel Grub, shall be, remain and continue during their respective lives or so long as they shall continue to behave themselves conformably to the said fundamental articles of the congregation, and that one-third part in number of the remaining six vestrymen, being the two first named of the said remaining six vestrymen and one-third part in number of the church-wardens, being the three first named of the said church-wardens, shall cease and discontinue and their appointment determine on the sixth day of January, which will be in the year of our Lord one thousand seven hundred and eighty-one, at which time a new election shall be had and held of an equal number in their stead and place, by a majority of the members qualified to vote and elect according to the purport, true intent and meaning of the said charter and of this act, and on the sixth day of January, which will be in the year of our Lord one thousand and seven hundred and eighty-two, the second third part in number of the said remaining six vestrymen and of the church-wardens shall in like manner cease and discontinue and their appointment determine, and a new election be had and held in like manner of an equal number in their place and stead and on the sixth day of January, which will be in the year of our Lord one thousand seven hundred and eighty-three the last third part in number of the said remaining six vestrymen and of the church-wardens aforesaid shall cease and discontinue and their appointment determine and a new election be had and held of an equal number in their place and stead in like manner, and that in the same manner and by the like mode of rotation one-third part in number of the vestrymen other than the six first named aforesaid and of the church wardens shall cease and discontinue, and their appointments determine and a new election of the said third part be had and held in manner aforesaid on the sixth day of January in every year forever (unless when the sixth day of January in any year shall happen to be on a Sunday, in which case the election shall be held on the day next following), so that no person or persons other than the six first named vestrymen appointed for life as aforesaid shall continue to be a vestryman or church-warden for any longer time than three years without being re-elected, but that the members of the said congregation qualified to vote as aforesaid shall and may be at liberty to re-elect any one or more of the vestrymen and church-wardens whose times shall expire on the day of the said annual election whenever and so often as they shall think fit.

[Section VI.] (Section VIII, P. L.) And be it further enacted by the authority aforesaid, That whenever any vacancy shall happen by the death, refusal to serve or removal from office of any one or more of the vestrymen or church-wardens, the said corporation shall have power at their discretion to appoint the time and place for electing others in their stead, whereof they shall give public notice to the congregation on the preceding Sunday and that at the time and place so appointed, some fit person or persons shall be elected in the place and stead of him or them so dying, refusing or being removed as aforesaid, and that the person or persons so elected shall be, remain and continue in office so long as the person or persons in whose place or stead he or they shall have been so elected would or might have continued; excepting the person or persons who may happen to be elected as immediate successors of the said six first named vestrymen, who shall continue in office for three years from the next preceding annual election; yet so that if in any year there shall happen to be more than four vestrymen chosen by reason of the death or the removal from office of any one or more of the said first named six vestrymen, that then and in that case the person or persons over and above the number of four who shall be so elected to succeed any one or more of the vestrymen aforesaid, shall be, remain and continue in office so long and no longer as may be necessary in order that not more than four (being the third part of the whole number of vestrymen) may go out of office at any one annual election, and that after the deaths of the present six first named vestrymen one-third part in number of the vestrymen and of the church-wardens may go out in rotation in every year.

[Section VII.] (Section IX, P. L.) And be it further enacted by the authority aforesaid, That no person or persons shall be entitled to vote at elections who is not of the age of eighteen years and otherwise qualified agreeably to the fundamental articles aforesaid, and that all elections shall be held by ballot and that fairly and freely, without confining or restraining the electors in their choice, so that no person or persons shall be entitled to a right of nominating or appointing any person or persons to be chosen, but that every one of the electors shall be entitled equally with another to nominate or elect whomsoever he will, any rule, by-law, ordinance or article of the said congregation in anywise notwithstanding.

[Section VIII.] (Section X, P. L.) Provided always and be it enacted by the authority aforesaid, That no person or persons shall or may be eligible as a member of the said corporation or to be an officer of the said congregation, who is not a member of the same, qualified to vote as aforesaid, excepting the ministers who may from time to time be chosen to officiate in the said congregation.

[Section IX.] (Section XI, P. L.) And be it further enacted by the authority aforesaid, That the members of the said corporation, at their first meeting after each annual election, shall and may elect by ballot from among their own number a president and a secretary, and that the senior minister or any one of the vestrymen or church-wardens shall be eligible to the office of president, and in case the senior minister shall at any time happen to be chosen to the said office, that in his absence the next eldest minister present shall, for the time, be president in his stead; and that the said corporation shall and may, at the said first meeting after each annual election, choose also a treasurer, who shall be elected from among such members of the said congregation as are not members of the said corporation; that the president shall be empowered and required to call a meeting of the said corporation when and so often as he shall find it to be necessary or shall be requested so to do by any three members thereof, and that the said corporation and their successors, or a majority of two-third parts in number of them met and convened upon due notice given (which two-thirds shall be a quorum) from time to time be authorized and empowered to make by-laws, rules and ordinances and to do everything needful for the support and government of the said congregation: Provided always, That the said by-laws, rules and ordinances be not repugnant to the laws of this commonwealth and that the same be duly entered and registered in the books of record of the said congregation.

[Section X.] (Section XII, P. L.) And be it further enacted by the authority aforesaid, That the said corporation shall and may be empowered at any time hereafter to build one more church or place of public worship in addition to the two already built and that the clear yearly value of the messuages, houses, lands, tenements, rents, annuities and other hereditaments and real estate of the said corporation shall and may be of any amount not exceeding the value of one thousand bushels of good merchantable wheat for each and every of the said churches or places of public worship; the said yearly value or amount to be taken and computed exclusive of the moneys arising from the letting of the pews of the said churches or for opening the ground for burials in the church yards belonging to them and also exclusive of the voluntary contributions of the members for the support of the ministers duly officiating to the said congregation; which yearly income of the said real estate ascertained and limited as aforesaid, shall be disposed of by the said corporation for the purposes mentioned in and by the said charter of incorporation.

Passed March 3, 1780. See the Act of Assembly passed February 14, 1789, Chapter 1390. Recorded L. B. No. 1, p. 346, &c.

CHAPTER DCCCLXXXV.

AN ACT FOR RE-ESTABLISHING THE CHARTER OF THE SECOND PRESBYTERIAN CHURCH IN THE CITY OF PHILADELPHIA AND FOR OTHER PURPOSES THEREIN MENTIONED.

(Section I, P. L.) Whereas the second Presbyterian congregation in the city of Philadelphia, by their petition, have shown that by their charter of incorporation bearing date the twenty-fourth day of August, in the year of our Lord one thousand seven hundred and seventy-two, granted by the honorable Richard Penn, Esquire, then being lieutenant-governor of Pennsylvania, twenty-four persons therein named, members of the said congregation, and their successors were nominated, ordained and appointed to be the trustees of the Second Presbyterian church, in the city of Philadelphia, one-third whereof in number were to be displaced annually on the first day of January and a like number of others by the said congregation chosen in their stead, and thirteen of the said twenty-four to be a quorum, able and capable to do business:

(Section II, P. L.) And whereas the said congregation have further shown that by reason of many of their members having withdrawn themselves from their places of residence in the city on the prospect of the enemy's approach and by reason of the enemy having since been in actual possession of the city and of their church, the said annual elections were prevented from being held, so that no more than eight trustees remain, by which means there cannot be a quorum capable of doing any business, and have further shown that by experience they find that their having so large a quorum as thirteen renders it at all times very difficult to procure a board for doing business, and also that in and by the said charter it is provided that the clear yearly value of the real estate of the said corporation shall not exceed the sum of three hundred pounds sterling, money of Great Britain, for each house of public worship erected, or to be erected by the said corporation, which sum is inadequate to the pious and humane purposes intended and have, therefore, prayed that the twenty-four persons last elected to be the trustees aforesaid may, by a law, be reinstated and continued in the said trust until, in due course, others may be elected in their stead and that a smaller quorum may be established and enabled to do business and also that they may [be] enabled to hold estates to a greater amount than in and by the said charter is provided:

[Section 1.] (Section III, P. L.) Be it therefore enacted and it is hereby enacted by the Representatives of the Freemen of the Commonwealth of Pennsylvania in General Assembly met, and by the authority of the same, That the aforesaid charter of incorporation be continued and confirmed to the said congregation, the aforesaid preventions notwithstanding, and that Joseph Reed, Thomas Bourne, Andrew Hodge, Gunning Bedford, John Baird, Hugh Hodge, William Faulkner, William Smith, Isaac Snowden, Daniel Goodman, Benjamin Harbeson, Nathan Cook, William Geddis, Jared Ingersoll, William Hollinshead, James Hunter, Samuel McClean, James

Robeson, Abraham Dubois, Hugh Lenox, Jonathan B. Smith, Thomas Nevill, William McIlhenney and Joseph Eastburne, last elected to be trustees as aforesaid, be and they are hereby declared to be the present trustees of the said church by the name, style and title of "The Trustees of the Second Presbyterian Church, in the City of Philadelphia," with all and singular the powers, privileges and immunities which in and by the said charter of incorporation to the trustees of the same church are given and granted, and that they be and continue to be trustees as aforesaid until they shall be severally replaced by new elections, That is to say, that the third part in number who are first above named shall be replaced by an election of other persons or re-election of the same on the first Monday of May next, the third part who are next named shall be in the same manner replaced on the first Monday of May then after next following, and the third part last named shall in the same manner be replaced on the first Monday of May next after that following and that the elections be in like manner held thenceforth annually on the first Monday of May forever.

[Section II.] (Section IV, P. L.) And be it further enacted by the authority aforesaid, That from and after the publication of this act any nine or more of the said trustees be a quorum, able and capable to act and do business in like manner as any thirteen or more of them were made a quorum, with power to act and do business in and by the said charter of incorporation.

[Section III,] (Section V, P. L.) And be it further enacted by the authority aforesaid, That the said corporation be enabled and empowered to have and to hold messuages, houses, lands and tenements, rents, annuities and other hereditaments and real estates not exceeding the clear yearly value of one thousand bushels of good merchantable wheat for each house of public worship erected and hereafter to be erected, with a society regularly constituted, agreeable to the tenor, true intent and meaning of the said charter and with the exclusions and reservations therein expressed.

Passed March 3, 1780. See the Act of Assembly passed March 28, 1787, Chapter 1290. Recorded L. B. No. 1, p. 349, &c.

CHAPTER DCCCLXXXVI.

AN ACT FOR INCORPORATING THE SOCIETY FORMED FOR THE RELIEF OF POOR, AGED AND INFIRM MASTERS OF SHIPS, THEIR WIDOWS AND CHILDREN.

(Section I, P. L.) Whereas by an act of general assembly passed the twenty-fourth day of February, in the year of our Lord one thousand seven hundred and seventy, entitled "An act for incorporating the society formed for the relief of poor, aged and infirm masters of ships, their widows and children,"[1] it was enacted that each and every person who had subscribed certain articles of agreement bearing date the seventh day of October in the year of our Lord one thousand seven hundred and sixty-five, made and executed for the purpose of raising a fund to be appropriated towards the relief and support of poor, aged and infirm masters of ships, their widows and children, and all others who should afterwards become contributors to the said society, upon the terms in the said act specified, should be a body politic and corporate in law to all intents and purpose as by the said act more fully doth appear:

(Section II, P. L.) And whereas it has hitherto been experienced that much benefit hath accrued from the benevolence of the said society to the relief of individuals and to the public from thus encouraging an increase of skilfull mariners:

(Section III, P. L.) And whereas the late revolution requires that considerable alterations should be made in the said act to enable the said society to prosecute their benevolent and useful designs:

[Section I.] (Section IV, P. L.) Be it therefore enacted and it is hereby enacted by the Representatives of the Freemen of the Commonwealth of Pennsylvania in General Assembly met, and by the authority of the same, That all and every person and persons who have heretofore subscribed certain

---
[1] Chapter 609.

articles of agreement bearing date the seventh day of October, in the year of our Lord one thousand seven hundred and sixty-five, made and executed for the purposes aforesaid, and each and every one who shall hereafter pay and contribute any sum of money not less than three pounds and the further sum of twelve shillings annually to the treasurer hereinafter mentioned, to and for the uses and purposes in this act specified, shall be, and they are hereby declared to be, members of the said society, and are hereby made a body politic and corporate in law to all intents and purposes, and shall have perpetual succession, and may sue and be sued, plead and be impleaded, by the name of The Society for the Relief of Poor and Distressed Masters of Ships, their Widows and Children, in all courts of judicature within this commonwealth, and by that name shall and may purchase any lands, tenements and estates and also receive and take any lands, tenements or hereditaments not exceeding the yearly value of three thousand bushels of wheat of the gift, alienation or devise, and any goods and chattels of the bequest of any person or persons whatsoever, and shall and may lend on interest any sum or sums of money belonging to the said contributors to such person or persons, bodies politic or corporate, as may be willing to borrow the same, in the manner and on such real or other securities as they shall think proper and sufficient, and the said corporation are hereby empowered to have and use one common seal in all their affairs.

[Section II.] (Section V, P. L.) And be it further enacted by the authority aforesaid, That all and every deed, conveyance, mortgage, bond, bill or other securities for moneys lent, which have been heretofore taken in the name of the treasurer heretofore appointed by the said contributors, shall and may be sued for and recovered in the name of "The Society for the Relief of Poor and Distressed Masters of Ships, their Widows and Children," in as full, ample and effectual a manner as if the said deeds, conveyances, mortgages, bonds, bills and other securities had been and were taken in that name, anything in the said securities to the contrary notwithstanding.

(Section VI, P. L.) And whereas the said contributors did,

on the first Monday in January, in the present year, of our Lord one thousand seven hundred and eighty, in pursuance of the said act elect Samuel Mifflin, William Hysham, James Craig, George Ord, Nathaniel Falconer, Joseph Blewer, John Woods, William Brown, Henry Dougherty, William Alibone, John Hazelwood and Leeson Simmons to be managers for the ensuing year:

[Section III.] (Section VII, P. L.) Be it therefore enacted by the authority aforesaid, That the said Samuel Mifflin, William Hysham, James Craig, George Ord, Nathaniel Falconer, Joseph Blewer, John Woods, William Brown, Henry Dougherty, William Alibone, John Hazelwood and Leeson Simmons shall be and continue managers of the said society until the first Monday in January next after the publication of this act, and until others shall be chosen in their room, which said managers, and all other managers hereafter to be chosen by virtue of this act, or a majority of them, being persons capable of electing and being elected members of assembly within this state, are hereby authorized and empowered to provide a seal for the said society and to change or alter the same, if they shall see occasion, and also to take in, place out, secure and improve the stock, and to dispose of the interest, profits and produce thereof, together with the yearly payments of twelve shillings which shall be made after the said first Monday in January in the present year one thousand seven hundred and eighty, for and towards the relief and support of poor, aged and infirm masters of ships, their widows and children and for and towards no other use, intent and purpose whatsoever, and that all the moneys which were placed out on interest and did belong to the said society on the said first Monday in January, one thousand seven hundred and eighty, together with all future subscriptions, donations, gifts, bequests and devices, shall be adjudged and deemed capital stock, unless the same shall be otherwise declared by such donations, gifts, bequests or devices, [and] shall be from time to time laid out in the purchase of real or landed property, or placed out on good security as aforesaid, and not otherwise disposed of by the said managers.

[Section IV.] (Section VIII, P. L.) Provided always, and be

it further enacted by the authority aforesaid, That the said several sums of three pounds contribution and annual payments of twelve shillings shall be estimated and deemed to be at and after the rate of ten shillings for a bushel of good merchantable wheat weighing sixty pounds, and that the sums in current money necessary to be contributed and paid in order to procure admission as a member into the said society and the annual payment aforesaid shall be regulated and adjusted from time to time by by-laws of the said corporation made for that purpose.

[Section V.] (Section IX, P. L.) And be it further enacted by the authority aforesaid, That there shall be a general meeting of the contributors on the first Mondays in January, April, July and October in every year, and the managers, or a majority of them, are hereby also authorized and empowered to call special meetings when and as often as they shall judge necessary so to do, of which they shall give notice in one or more of the public newspapers published in the city of Philadelphia at least one week before such special meeting, at all which general and special meetings the contributors shall and may, and they are hereby authorized and empowered to consider, treat and determine of and concerning all and every the matters and things relating to the prudent management and good order of the said society, and to make and ordain all such rules, orders and by-laws as shall be useful and necessary for that purpose, and generally for the well ordering all other matters and things concerning the estate, goods, chattels, lands, tenements and revenue thereof, all which by-laws, rules and orders shall be inviolably observed by all concerned.

(Section X, P. L.) Provided always, That the said by-laws, rules and orders be not repugnant to the laws of this commonwealth, and shall be agreed to by a majority of the contributors present at such meeting.

[Section VI.] (Section XI, P. L.) And be it enacted by the authority aforesaid, That at the said general meeting on the first Monday in January yearly and every year, the said contributors who shall be present shall choose by tickets in writing twelve persons out of their own body to be the managers and one other person to be the treasurer for the ensuing year; and that the managers of the preceding year shall appoint two of their own body, with three other contributors who are not managers, to be judges of the election, who shall, under their hands or the hands of a major part of them, report the names of the persons duly elected managers and treasurer, respectively, for the ensuing year to the general meeting; and when the said election shall be finished and the report so made, the contributors present may proceed to business, and not before.

[Section VII.] (Section XII, P. L.) And be it further enacted by the authority aforesaid, That Joseph Stiles, of the city of Philadelphia, shall be treasurer to the said society for the present year, and shall continue in his said office until the first Monday in January next ensuing the publication of this act and until another shall be chosen in his stead; which treasurer, and [all] other treasurers to be elected by virtue of this act shall have the custody of the cash, securities and deeds belonging to the said society, and shall from time to time pay and deliver the same and every of them to such person or persons as the managers, or a majority of them, shall by their orders direct and appoint, which said orders shall be good vouchers to indemnify him, and the said treasurer shall, and he is hereby required to give sufficient releases and acquittances of and for all sums of money which he shall receive on any mortgage, bond, bill or other security, and within one month after request to acknowledge the same on record, if such payment shall be on mortgage, under the penalty of forfeiting any sum of money not exceeding the mortgage money, to be recovered in any court of record within this commonwealth by bill, plaint or information, and shall also keep regular and fair books of accounts of all cash, securities, deeds, writing and other things and effects by him received, paid or delivered as aforesaid, and that such treasurer, before he enters upon the duties of his office, shall give such security to the said corporation in the name aforesaid, for the due and faithful discharge of this trust, and for accounting for and delivering up to his successor in the said office all such moneys, securities, deeds, writings and effects as shall have come to his hands or custody, and which shall not have been paid or delivered upon discharge of any mortgage as aforesaid, or by order of the managers as aforesaid, as the said managers or a majority of them shall direct and require, which security the said managers are hereby enjoined and required to see duly given and executed and recorded in the office for recording of deeds for the county of Philadelphia, before any such treasurer so elected shall enter upon his said office, and before he shall receive any of the said cash, securities, deeds, writings and other effects aforesaid.

[Section VIII.] (Section XIII, P. L.) And be it further enacted by the authority aforesaid, That the said managers shall meet when and where and as often as they shall think proper, and, being a majority at least, shall and may enter upon, order, direct and dispatch all such matters and things as shall properly come before them, and such their proceedings shall be good and valid in all the affairs of the society aforesaid done and performed in pursuance of this act, or that shall be committed to their management by the contributors aforesaid from time to time at their general or special meetings.

[Section IX.] (Section XIV, P. L.) And be it further enacted by the authority aforesaid, That the said managers shall keep fair and exact minutes of all their transactions and proceedings and a true and fair list of all donations, subscriptions and payments, which shall from time to time be made to and for the uses and purposes in this act mentioned, and shall yearly and every year publish the same, together with an account of moneys expended, in some of the newspapers printed in the city of Philadelphia, and shall at all times, when required, submit the books, minutes, accounts, affairs and economy of the said society to the inspection and free examination of such committee of assembly as may from time to time be appointed for inspecting and examining the same.

[Section X.]. (Section XV, P. L.) And be it further enacted by the authority aforesaid, That from and after the publication of this act the aforesaid act passed the twenty-fourth day of February, in the year of our Lord one thousand seven hundred and seventy, shall be and it is hereby repealed and made void.

> Passed March 4, 1780. See the note to the Act of Assembly passed February 24, 1770, Chapter 609; and the Act of Assembly passed March 7, 1797, Chapter 1925. Recorded L. B. No. 1, p. 350, &c.

CHAPTER DCCCLXXXVII.

AN ACT FOR REGULATING AND ESTABLISHING ADMIRALITY JURISDICTION.

(Section I, P. L.) Whereas it is necessary that due provision be made for the trial and determination of offenses, crimes, controversies and suits within the cognizance of the maritime law and not inquirable at common law:

[Section I.]. (Section II, P. L.) Be it therefore enacted and it is hereby enacted by the Representatives of the Freemen of the Commonwealth of Pennsylvania in General Assembly met, and by the authority of the same, That a person of known integrity and ability shall be appointed and commissioned by the supreme executive council of this commonwealth for and during the term of seven years, in case he shall so long behave well, by the name and style of a judge of the admiralty, which judge shall hold a court of admiralty and therein have cognizance of all controversies, suits and pleas of maritime jurisdiction, not cognizable at the common law; offenses and crimes, other than contempts against the said court only excepted, and thereupon shall pass sentence and decree according as the maritime law, the law of nations, and the laws of this commonwealth shall require.

[Section II.] (Section III, P. L.) Provided always, and be it further enacted by the authority aforesaid, That in all cases of prize, capture or re-capture upon the water from enemies, or by way of reprisal, or from pirates, the same shall be tried, adjudged and determined, as well as to the question whether prize or not, as to the claims of the parties interested or pretending to be interested in the same, by the law of nations and the acts and ordinances of the honorable the Congress of the United States of America, before the said judge, by witnesses according to the course of the civil law. And in all such cases of prize, capture, re-capture and seizure upon the water aforesaid, an appeal from the final decree of the said judge of admiralty shall lie and be allowed to such judges or court as the said Congress have appointed or may appoint for the hearing and determining of such appeals; such appeals to be brought and conducted in the manner and within the time directed and limited in and by the acts and ordinances aforesaid, security being first given in such sum of money as the said judge of admiralty shall deem sufficient, to prosecute such appeal to effect.

[Section III.] (Section IV, P. L.) And be it further enacted by the authority aforesaid, That the captain or commander of any ship or vessel of war, or prize master or other person having charge of any capture or re-capture, or other property seized upon the water as aforesaid who shall conduct or bring the same into port shall immediately deliver the same, without diminution, to the marshal of the said court of admiralty; and within three days after the arrival of such prize as aforesaid, shall exhibit, or cause to be exhibted, a libel, or bill in writing before the said judge, therein setting forth, in ample and particular manner the time and other circumstances of the seizing and taking the same, and of the service or employment that the ship or vessel so seized was in, at the time when such ship or vessel was taken or seized and the parties aiding therein to the best of his knowledge, and shall also, without delay or diminution, deliver, or cause to be delivered, to the register of the said court of admirality upon the oath or affirmation of such person all books, documents, commissions, parchments, papers and other writings appertaining to or found on board any such ship or vessel, in order that the said judge may have the benefit of any evidence which may arise therefrom in forming his sentence.

[Section IV.] (Section V, P. L.) And be it further enacted

by the authority aforesaid, That if any person shall neglect or refuse to deliver up any such capture or seizure as aforesaid to the marshal of the said court of admiralty, or shall embezzle or keep back any part of [any] such capture, or shall withhold, embezzle or destroy any books, documents, commissions, papers, parchments or other writings appertaining to or found on board of any ship or vessel seized as a prize as aforesaid, such person so offending shall be liable to attachment and to fine or to fine and imprisonment at the discretion of the said judge as a contemner of the said court of admiralty, and, moreover, shall forfeit to the use of the commonwealth, all such offender's share or part of such capture, to be recovered by indictment; and the said judge shall, by order, stay, during the prosecution such share or part in the hands of the marshal, to the end that the same may be secured upon the conviction of such offender and paid to the treasurer of this state.

[Section V.] (Section VI, P. L.) And be it further enacted by the authority aforesaid, That immediately after any such libel, as aforesaid, shall be exhibited before the said judge, he shall direct the register of the said court of admiralty to give notice in some public newspaper to be published in the city of Philadelphia, of the day appointed for the trial of such prize, and the said register shall insert therein, if known, the name, size or burden and other description of the vessel so taken and brought into port and also the name and surname of the late master or commander of the same and of the port or place from whence such ship or vessel last sailed, and of the port or place for which such ship or vessel was destined, and in case of a recapture, he shall set forth by what ship or other vessel the same was first taken, to the end that all persons concerned may appear and show cause (if any there be) wherefore such capture or re-capture, goods, merchandise or other property should not be condemned and adjudged to the libellants.

(Section VII, P. L.) Provided always, That if it be made appear to the satisfaction of the said judge, that the cargo of any such ship or vessel seized as prize as aforesaid is damaged or consists of goods which in their nature are so perishable as not to be kept till the trial be finished without great loss, that then and in such case the said judge shall nominate and appoint three judicious and indifferent persons of the city or county where the said goods may be, who shall carefully inspect and appraise the same, and report the condition thereof and deliver the said appraisement and report supported and attested by their oaths and affirmations to the said judge, whereupon the said judge, may order the marshal of the said court immediately to sell by public auction such part of said cargo as appears to the said judge to be likely to perish or be greatly endamaged by keeping as aforesaid. And the said marshall, having sold the same accordingly, shall retain the moneys thence arising in his hands till the trial be finished, except the charges upon such prize, together with the charges attending upon such inspection and appraisement, which shall be ascertained by the said judge.

[Section VI.] (Section VIII, P. L.) And be it further enacted by the authority aforesaid, That the execution of the decree of the said judge, in any case of capture, recapture or prize taken upon the water, from which an appeal to the said judges or court of appeal shall be entered, shall not be suspended or delayed by reason of such appeal, in case the party or parties appellant shall enter sufficient security, to be approved by the said judge in at least double the value of the prize or other subject of controversy, the same value to be estimated and appraised at the price at which the said prize might then be sold, for current money, for which purpose the said judge shall appoint three skillful and indifferent appraisers, who shall exactly number, measure or weigh the several articles of which such prize shall consist, and return a particular inventory and appraisement of the same, attested by the oaths or affirmations of the said appraisers, to the register of the said court, to be filed in his office, and the stipulation or security so given and entered in case of an appeal as aforesaid shall be considered and shall have effect as a statute staple, and may be sued for and recovered by original writ to be issued out of the supreme court or other court of record, at the election of the party who shall have a right to institute such suit.

[Section VII.] (Section IX, P. L.) And be it further enacted by the authority aforesaid, That in case the said judge, upon the evidence produced to him, shall pronounce sentence of condemnation against any such ship or vessel or goods, merchandise or other property, captured or taken as prize, or recaptured or seized by way of reprisal, or from a pirate, he shall order the same to be immediately sold by public auction, to the best and highest bidder for the benefit of the captors, unless in the case of re-capture the former owner or owners in ten days after such sentence be pronounced, pay down the full salvage, together with all such costs and charges as shall be awarded thereupon. And the said marshal shall keep fair and exact accounts of the sales of all ships and other vessels, goods, merchandise and other property which shall be condemned in the said court of admiralty and sold by the said marshal as aforesaid, as soon afterwards as may be such account of sales shall be filed in the office of the register of the said court of admiralty, for the inspection and use of all persons who may be interested therein.

(Section X, P. L.) Provided always, That no negro or mulatto taken as prize upon the water shall be in any case exposed to public sale, but being appraised as is hereinbefore directed in other cases, shall be delivered to the captors or others having right to the same, at the appraised value, and if necessary by lot, and the value thereof equalized in money or goods to be delivered to the other party or parties entitled to share therein.

(Section XI, P. L.) Provided also, That nothing in this act contained which may contradict or interfere with the directions of an act assembly of this commonwealth, entitled "An act for the effectual suppression of public auctions and vendues, and to prohibit male persons capable or bearing arms from being peddlers and hawkers,"[1] passed on the twenty-sixth day of November last, shall have effect or be in force for and during the continuance of the said-recited act.

---

[1] Chapter 870.

(Section XII, P. L.) And whereas, sometimes seamen and others proceed to sea in ships and vessels of war without appointing agents to take and manage their several shares of the captures or prizes seized and taken upon the water by the ships or vessels to which they respectively belong. And whereas, such seamen and others may be absent, and owners, or part owners, of such ships and vessels of war may also be absent and have no agent or agents to take their shares or parts of such prizes when the marshal of the said court of admiralty may be ready to distribute such prizes as he is directed by this act:

[Section VIII.] (Section XIII, P. L.) Be it therefore enacted by the authority aforesaid, That whensoever the said marshal shall be ready to distribute any prize as aforesaid upon an advertisement of the same in some public newspaper in the city of Philadelphia, if an agent or agents duly authorized by the owner, seaman or other person for whom no agent shall appear and every of them, having a right to share therein, by being on board such ship or vessel at the time of capture or otherwise, shall not appear and make known his or their authority to act as an agent or agents for such absent persons, that in such case the said judge shall appoint and authorize some proper person or persons to be the agent or agents for any absent owner, seaman or other person for whom no agent shall appear for three days after such advertisement shall be published. And the agent or agents so to be appointed by the said judge, with any other persons properly entitled and authorized, whether in their own right or as agents (if such there be), shall take the said prize from the said marshal, as directed by this act and shall sell by private sale or otherwise dispose of the same, for the best advantage of the person or persons interested therein, and shall be accountable to them and every of them severally as if such agent or agents had been appointed by such owner, seaman or other person, and every agent who shall be appointed by the said judge, shall become bound to the commonwealth, with two different sureties, in a suitable sum, to be ascertained by the said judge, conditioned that he will truly account for and satisfy the person or persons for whom he shall be appointed agent; and the said obligation shall be as available to such owner, seaman or other person as bonds given by sheriffs are to the parties injured by their misconduct.

[Section IX.] (Section XIV, P. L.) And be it further enacted by the authority aforesaid, That all unclaimed parts or shares in any prizes taken upon the water and condemned in the court of admiralty of this state remaining in the hands of any agent or agents shall, after the end of one year, be reckoned from the beginning of the distribution of any prize, which have been or shall be taken from the enemy, be vested in the contributors to the Pennsylvania Hospital, and shall be accounted for and paid to the use of the said corporation, the owners of such ship or vessel being previously satisfied for any advance they shall have made to any seaman or marine, subject, however, to the demand of the person who was entitled thereto, if made within three years after the condemnation of the prize.

[Section X.] (Section XV, P. L.) And be it further enacted by the authority aforesaid, That any ships or vessels, goods or other property taken [as] prize or re-taken belonging to foreigners, whether allies of the United States of America or neutrals, which have come, or may come, to the possession of the said marshal and who shall have no attorney-in-fact or agent duly authorized to take and receive from the said marshal such ships or other vessels or other property that the same, unless in case they be of a very perishable nature and too bulky to keep without great charges, shall remain in the custody of the said marshal, without sale for three months at least after the trial of the same shall be finished and the owners thereof and their said ships or other vessels, goods or other property shall be liable to the charges and expenses which may accrue by such delay or sale.

[Section XI.] (Section XVI, P. L.) And be it further enacted by the authority aforesaid, That the supreme executive council shall appoint and commission, for and during the pleasure of the said council, an able and upright person to be register of the said court of admiralty, and that the examinations of all witnesses in any of the causes which may come before the said court of admiralty, being taken by the said register, and attested before the said judge, shall be filed in the office of the said register, such examinations to be taken ex parte after reasonable notice to the adverse party; and the attestations of the said register shall on all proper occasions be received as evidence in all courts of justice and elsewhere.

[Section XII.] (Section XVII, P. L.) And be it further enacted by the authority aforesaid, That the supreme executive council shall appoint and commission, for and during their pleasure, a person of skill and good reputation to be the marshal of the said court of admiralty, who, before he enters on his office, shall become bound to the president of the said council for the time being with two or more sureties to be approved by the said council in the value of forty thousand bushels of good merchantable wheat, each bushel thereof to weigh at least sixty pounds, which bond or obligation shall be drawn in like manner, with like condition and liable to like suit and use, and shall be recorded, as bonds entered into by sheriffs and their sureties ought to be by the laws of this commonwealth.

(Section XVIII, P. L.) And whereas the trial of pirates and other sea felons in the late British colonies, now the United States of America, hath been heretofore without a jury, and in a method much conformed to the civil law, the exercise of which jurisdiction in criminal cases was contrary to the spirit of the common law, although the legislature of England had, by a statute passed in the reign of King Henry the Eighth, entitled "For Pirates," relieved the subjects within the realm from this grievance:

(Section XIX, P. L.) And whereas the constitution of this state provideth that in all prosecutions for criminal offenses no man can be found guilty without the unanimous consent of a jury:

[Section XIII.] (Section XX, P. L.) Be it therefore enacted by the authority aforesaid, That all traitors, pirates, felons and criminals who shall offend upon the sea or within the admiralty jurisdiction, shall be enquired of, tried and judged by grand and petit juries, according to the course of the common law, in like manner as if the treason or felony or crime were committed within one of the counties of this state. And the justices of the supreme court, or any two of them, and the judge of admiralty, are hereby constituted justices of oyer and terminer, and shall hold a court of oyer and terminer in the city of Philadelphia for the hearing and trying such offenders. And the said judge of admiralty, in the absence of the chief justice of the supreme court, shall preside in such court of oyer and terminer, and if any person, upon being arraigned before the said court of oyer and terminer, shall stand mute or shall not make direct answers such person shall be deemed to have pleaded not guilty and the trial shall proceed accordingly.

[Section XIV.] (Section XXI, P. L.) And be it enacted by the authority aforesaid, That if any person shall be feloniously stricken or poisoned at sea or out of this state, and shall die of the same in this state, the offenders and their aiders and abettors may be indicted, tried and adjudged for such felony in the court of oyer and terminer of this state where such person shall die before the ordinary justices of oyer and terminer and general gaol delivery, and if any person shall be feloniously stricken or poisoned in this state and shall die of the same at sea or out of Pennsylvania, the offenders and their aiders and abettors may be indicted, tried and adjudged for such felony before the court of oyer and terminer constituted by this act for the trial of crimes committed at sea.

[Section XV.] (Section XXII, P. L.) And be it further enacted by the authority aforesaid, That all and every the proceedings of the court of admiralty of this commonwealth shall be liable to the prohibition of the supreme court of judicature in like manner and with like effect as the prohibition of the court of king's bench in England in like case.

[Section XVI.] (Section XXIII, P. L.) And be it further enacted by the authority aforesaid, That an act of assembly, entitled "An act for establishing a court of admiralty,"[1] passed on the ninth day of September, which was in the year of our Lord one thousand seven hundred and seventy-eight, is hereby repealed, annulled and made void. Provided always, That the repeal of the said act shall not extend to stop or prevent the

---

[1] Passed September 9, 1778, Chapter 811.

hearing or trial of any cause depending in the court of admiralty, or before the said commissioner of oyer and terminer, but the same may be proceeded on as by the said act is directed before the judge appointed and commissioned in pursuance of this act, the repeal thereof notwithstanding.

> Passed March 8, 1780. See the Acts of Asembly passed September 22, 1780, Chapter 915; March 28, 1787, Chapter 1281; September 29, 1787, Chapter 1322; December 7, 1789, Chapter 1474. By the Constitution of the United States, Article III, Section II,(I) the judicial power of the United States is declared to extend to all cases of admiralty and maritime jurisdictions. Recorded L. B. No. 1, p. 353, &c.

CHAPTER DCCCLXXXVIII.

AN ACT TO RESTORE AND ASCERTAIN THE VALUE OF DIVERS FINES, PENALTIES AND FORFEITURES HEREINAFTER MENTIONED, WHICH MAY BE INCURRED BY THE BREACH OF CERTAIN ACTS OF ASSEMBLY OF THIS COMMONWEALTH.

(Section I, P. L.) Whereas divers fines, penalties and forfeitures which are limited not to exceed certain sums, and the specific fines, penalties and forfeitures, which were heretofore as well before the revolution as since provided, directed and established in and by certain acts of assembly still in force, in order to secure the observance of the same have, by reason of the great variation and rise in the prices of commodities become generally uncertain and very inadequate to the purposes for which they were intended and ordained, whereby many good and wholesome laws have been enervated and have lost their proper vigor and effect, to the great injury of the sober and quiet citizens and to the dishonor of the commonwealth:

For remedy whereof:

[Section I.] (Section II, P. L.) Be it enacted and it is hereby enacted by the Representatives of the Freemen of the Commonwealth of Pennsylvania in General Assembly met, and by the authority of the same, That the several and respective fines, penalties and forfeitures aforesaid in all cases where the same are expressed and set in money, which shall be incurred by, imposed on or recovered against any person or persons in any court of record or in a summary way before any justice of the peace or otherwise, as well at the suit of the party grieved, and in an action qui tam as at the suit of the commonwealth, shall be estimated, computed, levied and satisfied after the manner by which the fees of certain officers of this state are or ought to be estimated, computed, levied and satisfied, in pursuance of an act of assembly of this commonwealth, entitled "An act for the better support of certain officers of this state, and for ascertaining the specific fines and penalties which they may incur by neglect of duty,"[1] passed on the twenty-seventh day of November last, subject, however, to the rules and directions following, That is to say: every such fine, penalty of forfeiture which shall be incurred, imposed or recovered as aforesaid, by virtue of any act of assembly which was made in the late province of Pennsylvania and has been revived since the revolution, and re-enacted by the legislature of this commonwealth shall be estimated as aforesaid as set in money of the value of good merchantable wheat, at the price of ten shillings per bushel. The fines and penalties aforesaid directed and ordained in and by an act of assembly of this commonwealth passed on the twentieth day of February, Anno Domini one thousand seven hundred and seventy-seven, entitled "An act to discourage desertion, and to punish all such as shall harbor or conceal deserters,"[2] shall be estimated as aforesaid, as set in money of the value of good merchantable wheat at the price of ten shillings per bushel. The fines and penalties aforesaid directed and ordained in and by an act of assembly of this commonwealth passed on the fourteenth day of June, Anno Domini one thousand seven hundred and seventy-seven, entitled "A supplement to the act, entitled 'An act for amending the several acts of assembly for electing members of assembly,' "[3] shall be estimated, as aforesaid, as set in money of the price of good merchantable wheat at twelve shillings per bushel. The pen-

---
[1] Chapter 875.
[2] Chapter 744.
[3] Chapter 757.

alty of fifty pounds directed to be imposed on any person not belonging to the regiments of this state for enlisting soldiers within the same by an act passed on the second day of January, Anno Domini one thousand seven hundred and seventy-eight, entitled "An act to prevent the imprisonment of soldiers for small sums and also to prevent the enlistment of soldiers within the bounds of the commonwealth of Pennsylvania by the officers of other states until the quota of this state shall be completed,"[1] shall be estimated as aforesaid as set in money of the price of good merchantable wheat at fifteen shillings per bushel. The penalty of twenty pounds directed to be imposed on judges of election neglecting to give notice of their election to persons chosen to serve in the supreme executive council or general assembly by an act passed on the twenty-third day of March, Anno Domini one thousand seven hundred and seventy-eight, entitled "A further supplement to an act, entitled 'An act for amending the several acts for electing members of assembly,'"[2] shall be estimated as aforesaid, as set in money of the price of good merchantable wheat at twenty shillings per bushel. The forfeiture of one hundred pounds, to be imposed on the master of a ship or vessel for not exhibiting a manifest of the cargo of such ship or vessel by an act passed on the tenth day of September, Anno Domini one thousand seven hundred and seventy-eight, entitled "An act for regulating navigation and trade in this state,"[3] shall be estimated as aforesaid as set in money of the price of good merchantable wheat at thirty shillings per bushel. The specific forfeitures of money to be incurred for the offenses forbidden in and by an act passed on the thirtieth day of March, Anno Domini one thousand seven hundred and seventy-nine, entitled "An act for the suppression of vice and immorality,"[4] shall be estimated as aforesaid as set in money of the price of good merchantable wheat at thirty shillings per bushel. And the forfeitures upon chimney sweepers and housekeepers offending against the act of assembly passed on the twenty-fifth day of

---

[1] Chapter 777.
[2] Chapter 790.
[3] Chapter 815.
[4] Chapter 833.

November last, entitled "An act for regulating chimney sweepers within the city of Philadelphia, the district of Southwark and the township of the Northern Liberties of the city of Philadelphia,"[1] shall be estimated as aforesaid, as set in money, of the price of good merchantable wheat at one hundred shillings per bushel.

[Section II.] (Section III, P. L.) And be it further enacted by the authority aforesaid, That so much of an act of assembly passed on the thirtieth day of September, Anno Domini one thousand seven hundred and seventy-nine, entitled "A supplement to an act, entitled 'An act for regulating, pitching, paving and cleansing the highways, streets, lanes and alleys and for regulating, making and amending the water courses and common sewers within the inhabited and settled parts of the city of Philadelphia, for raising of money to defray the expenses thereof, and for other purposes therein mentioned,'"[2] and so much of another act of assembly passed on the same day, entitled "An act to continue an act, entitled 'An act for opening and better amending and keeping in repair the public roads and highways in this province,"[3] as relate to fines and forfeitures shall be and hereby are repealed and made void.

(Section IV, P. L.) And whereas by the invasion of this state by the enemy in the years one thousand seven hundred and seventy-seven and one thousand seven hundred and seventy-eight the trustees of the loan office of this state became separated and dispersed, and discharges of mortgages were made by one trustee only:

[Section III.] (Section V, P. L.) Be it therefore enacted by the authority aforesaid, That all and every discharge or discharges of any mortgage or mortgages which have been made by one trustee as aforesaid, or which shall hereafter be made by one trustee to be appointed by the house of assembly shall be taken and held to be good and valid, anything in any law to the contrary notwithstanding.

Passed March 8, 1780. See the Act of Assembly passed June 21, 1781, Chapter 945. Recorded L. B. No. 1, p. 358, &c.

---

[1] Chapter 867.
[2] Chapter 849.
[3] Chapter 850.

CHAPTER DCCCLXXXIX.

AN ACT FOR THE AMENDMENT OF THE LAW RELATIVE TO THE PUNISHMENT OF TREASONS, ROBBERIES, MISPRISIONS OF TREASON AND OTHER OFFENSES.

(Section I, P. L.) Whereas in and by the act of assembly, entitled "An act for the advancement of justice and the more certain administration thereof,"[1] made and passed the thirty-first day of May, in the year of our Lord one thousand seven hundred and eighteen, the punishment of death is inflicted in the case of robbery upon such only as commit the same on or near the highway, so that no adequate provision seems to have been made for punishing the most atrocious robberies if the same be committed elsewhere:

[Section I.] (Section II, P. L.) Be it therefore enacted and it is hereby enacted by the Representatives of the Freemen of the Commonwealth of Pennsylvania in General Assembly met, and by the authority of the same, That from and after the passing of this act, if any person or persons shall commit robbery, which robbery is done by assaulting another, putting him in fear and taking from his person money or other goods to any value whatsoever, whether the same robbery be committed on or near the highway or elsewhere in any place or places whatsoever within this commonwealth, he or they so offending his or their counsellors, aiders, comforters and abettors, being thereof duly convicted or attainted, or being indicted and standing mute, or challenging peremptorily above the number of twenty persons returned to serve of the jury, shall suffer as felons without benefit of clergy, in like manner as by the laws of this commonwealth is provided in the case of robbers on or near the highway.

(Section III, P. L.) And whereas the forfeiture of goods and chattels, in the case of manslaughter, is rarely exacted, and

---

[1] Chapter 236.

the burning in the hand of such felons in more heinous and aggravated instances of this kind of homicide which may approach nearly to murder is too light and inadequate a punishment. To the end, therefore, that the lives of the citizens of this commonwealth may be guarded and preserved from danger:

[Section II.] (Section IV, P. L.) Be it enacted by the authority aforesaid, That in all cases of convictions of manslaughter other than by stabbing, as described in the act of assembly hereinbefore mentioned, the said forfeiture shall be removed and hereafter no more incurred; but instead thereof the court shall give judgment against such offender of imprisonment for any time not exceeding two years, and of fine at the discretion of the court, and, moreover, shall sentence such offender to find security for his good behavior during life. And in order for the punishment by banishment of offenders whose lives might be spared, and at the same time whose wicked conduct and example may render it highly dangerous that they should remain and enjoy the benefits of this free state, and to lessen sanguinary punishments:

[Section III.] (Section V, P. L.) Be it enacted by the authority aforesaid, That it shall and may be lawful to and for the president or vice-president and council of this commonwealth, upon the prayer of any person or persons under sentence of death for treason or felony to grant to such person or persons a pardon so far as respects his, her or their lives, consonant with the limitations of the constitution on condition that such person or persons shall, within a limited time, depart from this state to foreign parts beyond the sea, and that he or they shall not return into this state or any of the United States of America; and that if any person or persons so pardoned on the condition aforesaid shall break the same condition by not departing within the said time or by returning again into this state or any of the United States aforesaid, the same pardon shall be void, and such person or persons not departing or returning as aforesaid shall suffer death according to the sentence which had been before pronounced against them.

(Section IV.] (Section VI, P. L.) And be it further enacted

by the authority aforesaid, That no attainder of treason to be had from and after the end of the present war between the United States of America and Great Britain, and the acknowledgement of the independency of the said United States by the King of Great Britain shall extend to the disinheriting of any heir, nor to the prejudice of any person or persons other than the offender. And in order to the detecting and punishing in some measure persons accused of treason or misprisons of treason by one witness and at the same time to avoid confounding very different degrees of guilt in the same punishment and for removing doubts concerning the legality thereof:

[Section V.] (Section VII, P. L.) Be it enacted and declared by the authority aforesaid, That in all cases where any charge is made upon oath or affirmation against any person or persons of facts amounting to treason or misprison of treason it shall and may be lawful for the attorney-general, with the leave of the court, to proceed against and charge such person or persons with a misdemeanor and give in evidence any act or acts of treason or misprison of treason, by one witness on the trial, or other proper and legal testimony and such person or persons, upon conviction, shall suffer as in cases of misdemeanor.

Passed March 8, 1780. See the notes to the Acts of Assembly passed May 31, 1718, Chapter 236; February 11, 1777, Chapter 740. The Act in the text was repealed by the Act of Assembly passed March 31, 1860, P. L. 427, sec. 79. Recorded L. B. No. 1, p. 359, &c.

CHAPTER DCCCXC.

AN ACT TO INCREASE THE PUNISHMENTS OF HORSE STEALING.

(Section I, P. L.) Whereas the punishments heretofore provided against the crime of horse stealing have not proved sufficient to deter evil-minded persons from the commission thereof:

For remedy whereof:

[Section I.] (Section II, P. L.) Be it enacted and it is hereby enacted by the Representatives of the Freemen of the Commonwealth of Pennsylvania in General Assembly met, and by the authority of the same, That if any person or persons, from and after the passing of this act, shall feloniously take and carry away, any horse, mare or gelding of the property of any other person or persons or of the United States of America, and shall be thereof convicted, every such person or persons so offending for the first offense shall stand in the pillory for one hour, and shall be publicly whipped on his, her or their [bare] backs with thirty-nine lashes, well laid on, and at the same time shall have his, her or their ears cut off and nailed to the pillory, and for the second offense shall be whipped and pilloried in like manner and be branded on the forehead in a plain and visible manner with the letters H. T.

(Section III, P. L.) And whereas persons who have heretofore committed the offense of horse stealing have often escaped from justice by reason of the insufficiency of the bail taken for their appearance to answer for the same:

[Section II.] (Section IV, P. L.) Be it therefore enacted by the authority aforesaid, That from and after the publication of this act, no person or persons, who shall be charged with the stealing of any horse, mare or gelding on the direct testimony of one witness, or who shall be taken with such horse, mare or gelding in his or her possession shall be admitted to bail otherwise than by one or more justices of the supreme court.

[Section III.] (Section V, P. L.) And be it further enacted by the authority aforesaid, That so much of an act of assembly of the late province of Pennsylvania, entitled "An act for the advancement of justice and more certain administration thereof,"[1] and of the supplement thereto, as are contradictory to this act, and no more thereof, are repealed and made void.

Passed March 10, 1780. See the note to the Act of Assembly Passed May 31, 1718, Chapter 236. The Act in the text was repealed by the Act of Assembly passed March 31, 1860, P. L. 427, sec. 79. Recorded L. B. No. 1, p. 360, &c.

---

[1] Passed May 31, 1718, Chapter 236.

CHAPTER DCCCXCI.

AN ACT FOR THE RELIEF OF THE SUFFERING INHABITANTS OF THE COUNTIES OF NORTHAMPTON, BEDFORD, NORTHUMBERLAND AND WESTMORELAND.

(Section I, P. L.) Whereas, by the repeated depredations and incursions of the savage enemy great numbers of the inhabitants of the said counties have been driven from their habitations and otherwise much distressed and rendered unable to pay their respective proportions of the public taxes:

[Section I.] (Section II, P. L.) Be it therefore enacted and it is hereby enacted by the Representatives of the Freemen of the Commonwealth of Pennsylvania in General Assembly met, and by the authority of the same, That it shall and may be lawful for the commissioners and assessors of the said several counties, and they are hereby enjoined and required, in all cases within their respective counties, where the inhabitants have deserted their habitations, and no proper return or valuation of property can be had in the way pointed out in the laws now in force for that purpose, to obtain such account of such property, by applying to the books or rolls containing the last return of property, or such other ways or means as to them shall seem most just and reasonable, and shall thereupon proceed to value, quota and levy the same, as nearly in just proportion to other parts of the said county as may be.

[Section II.] (Section III, P. L.) And be it further enacted by the authority aforesaid, That the said commissioners and assessors, or a majority of them, are hereby authorized and required to exonerate and discharge such of their taxable inhabitants as shall make sufficient proofs, or for or in behalf of whom sufficient proofs shall be made to the said commissioners and assessors respectively, of their having been driven off and dispossessed of their settlements, or otherwise disabled by the enemy to pay their respective taxes, from the payment of the several sums or such part thereof as they shall deem just and reasonable, with which they may or ought to have been charged, as well of their respective quotas of the tax of four millions of dollars, imposed by an act passed the third day of April, one thousand seven hundred and seventy-nine, and their quotas of the tax of five millions seven hundred thousand dollars, granted and directed to be raised by an act passed the tenth day of October, in the year of our Lord one thousand seven hundred and seventy-nine, as their respective quotas of a sum of money directed to be raised by a monthly tax according to an act for that purpose passed the twenty-fifth day of November, one thousand seven hundred and seventy-nine, which remission or mitigation shall only be made in favor of those, who have bona fide suffered by the incursions of the enemy, and in such proportions as their several losses of property justly demand.

[Section III.] (Section IV, P. L.) And be it further enacted by the authority aforesaid, That the commissioners and assessors of the said counties of Northampton, Bedford, Northumberland and Westmoreland, respectively, shall transmit to the general assembly a list of the names of the persons so exonerated, stating the particular sum so remitted to each particular person, that the deficiencies which may arise in raising the quotas of the said counties by reason hereof shall be paid and made good out of the state taxes which shall be levied and raised hereafter.

Passed March 20, 1780. Recorded L. B. No. 1, p. 361, &c.

CHAPTER DCCCXCII.

AN ACT TO REVIVE AN ACT ENTITLED "AN ACT TO PREVENT THE TRESPASSING UPON THE UNENCLOSED GROUNDS, LYING IN THE TOWNSHIPS OF PASSYUNK, MOYAMENSING, NORTHERN LIBERTIES AND GERMANTOWN IN THE COUNTY OF PHILADELPHIA," AND TO EXTEND THE SAID ACT TO THE ADJOINING TOWNSHIP OF BRISTOL IN THE SAME COUNTY, AND TO PREVENT SWINE FROM RUNNING AT LARGE WITHIN THE SAID TOWNSHIPS FOR A LIMITED TIME.

(Section I, P. L.) Whereas an act of assembly, entitled "An act to prevent the trespassing upon the unenclosed grounds lying in the townships of Passyunk, Moyamensing, Northern Liberties and Germantown, in the county of Philadelphia,"[1] passed on the fifth day of April last, hath been found to be a necessary and beneficial law for the landholders and inhabitants of the said districts:

(Section II, P. L.) And whereas by reason of the scarcity of proper timber in or near the said townships, suitable to renew the fences which were destroyed by the enemy, and for want of laborers to set up the same the difficulties which occasioned the said act are not yet entirely surmounted, and as it is reasonable that the provisions thereby made should be extended to the adjoining township of Bristol, in the said county of Philadelphia, as the landholders and inhabitants of the township last named, labor under like inconveniences. And whereas the said act expired by its own limitation on the first day of December last:

[Section I.] (Section III, P. L.) Be it therefore enacted and it is hereby enacted by the Representatives of the Freemen of the Commonwealth of Pennsylvania in General Assembly met, and by the authority of the same, That from and after the publication of this act, the said act and every part thereof, the clause of limitation only excepted, shall be and hereby is revived and extended to the said township of Bristol and shall continue and be in force until the first day of December next.

[Section II.] (Section IV, P. L.) Provided always and be it further enacted by the authority aforesaid, That instead of the penalty of twenty shillings by the said act directed to be levied for every beast suffered to run at large contrary to the directions thereof there shall be levied for and during the continuance of this act the penalty of ten pounds.

[Section III.] (Section V, P. L.) And be it further enacted by the authority aforesaid, That for and during the continuance of this act it shall not be lawful for any swine, hogs, shoats or pigs to go at large within any of the said townships, whether yoked and ringed or not; but if any such be found at large within the same every such swine, hog, shoat and pig shall be forfeited, one-half part thereof to him that shall seize the same

---

[1] Chapter 842.

and the other half part to the overseers of the poor of the place where the same shall happen, for the use of the poor of such township, or if by the overseers of the poor then wholly to the use of the poor.

[Section IV.] (Section VI, P. L.) Provided nevertheless, and be it enacted by the authority aforesaid, That if any person shall think him or herself aggrieved by the seizure of any such swine, hog, shoat or pig, as aforesaid, he may appeal to any justice of the peace of the said county who is hereby empowered to hear and finally determine the same; and if thereupon the said seizure be confirmed by such justice, the person so appealing, shall further, forfeit the sum of forty shillings to the use of the poor of the township where such seizure shall be made, such sum of forty shillings being deposited with such justice before he proceed to hear the said appeal and upon such confirmation delivered to the overseers of the poor, but otherwise returned to the appellant.

[Section V.] (Section VII, P. L.) Provided also, That nothing in this act shall extend to any part of the township of Germantown which lies northwestward of Livezey's lane and a line extended in the direction of the said lane to the northeasterly line of the said township.

Passed March 13, 1780. See the note to the Act of Assembly passed April 5, 1779, Chapter 842; and the Act of Assembly passed April 2, 1781, Chapter 934. Recorded L. B. No. 1, p. 362, &c.

CHAPTER DCCCXCIII.

AN ACT OF FREE AND GENERAL PARDON AND INDEMNITY FOR THE OFFENSES THEREIN MENTIONED.

(Section I, P. L.) Whereas divers unhappy disputes have heretofore subsisted between some of the subjects of this state within the city of Philadelphia, which, by mutual misunderstandings, did, on the fourth day of October last, occasion a tumult and breach of the public peace within the said city, wherein sundry persons were unhappily killed in and near the house of James Wilson, Esquire, in Walnut street, within the said city, for which the several parties concerned therein stand bound by recognizance to answer in due course of law:

(Section II, P. L.) And whereas since the said tumult a cordial quietude has taken place, and as the rigorous prosecution of justice in all cases is not expedient, inasmuch as it may tend to perpetuate enmity and discord between the citizens of the same state, when union and harmony are so necessary against the common enemy; and it being also recommended by the supreme executive council of the state as a measure of public benefit to pass an act of indemnity and general pardon for the said offenses:

[Section I.] (Section III, P. L.) Be it enacted and it is hereby enacted by the Representatives of the Freemen of the Commonwealth of Pennsylvania in General Assembly met, and by the authority of the same, That all and every the person and persons, party and parties engaged in the said tumult and breach of the peace or who stand charged therewith or with any offense arising therefrom which is punishable by the laws of this commonwealth, by whatsoever name or names they are called or known, be and shall and they are hereby pardoned, released, indemnified and discharged to all intents and purposes whatsoever.

[Section II.] (Section IV, P. L.) Be it also enacted by the authority aforesaid, That this free pardon, indemnity and oblivion, by the general words, clauses and sentences before recited, shall be reputed, deemed, adjudged and expounded in all courts and elsewhere, most beneficial and available to all and singular the subjects, persons and parties before mentioned, and to every of them without any ambiguity, question or delay to be made, pleaded or objected by this commonwealth, the attorney-general thereof, or any person or persons acting under the authority thereof in their behalf. And also that this act shall be deemed, adjudged and taken to be a public act and shall be judicially taken notice of as such by all judges, justices and other persons whomsoever without specially pleading the same.

> Passed March 13, 1780. See the Acts of Assembly passed April 15, 1782, Chapter 979; March 28, 1785, Chapter 1147; March 17, 1786, Chapter 1213. Recorded L. B. No. 1, p. 363, &c.

CHAPTER DCCCXCIV.

AN ACT FOR INCORPORATING THE AMERICAN PHILOSOPHICAL SOCIETY HELD AT PHILADELPHIA FOR PROMOTING USEFUL KNOWLEDGE.

(Section I, P. L.) Whereas the cultivation of useful knowledge and the advancement of the liberal arts and sciences in any country have the most direct tendency towards the improvement of agriculture, the enlargement of trade, the ease and comfort of life, the ornament of society and the increase and happiness of mankind:

(Section II, P. L.) And whereas this country of North America, which the goodness of Providence hath given us to inherit, from the vastness of its extent, the variety of its climate, the fertility of its soil, the yet unexplored treasures of its bowels, the multitude of its rivers, lakes, bays, inlets and other conveniences of navigation, offers to these United States one of the richest subjects of cultivation ever presented to any people upon earth:

(Section III, P. L.) And whereas the experience of ages shows that improvements of a public nature are best carried on by societies of liberal and ingenious men, uniting their labors, without regard to nation, sect or party in one grand pursuit, alike interesting to all, whereby mutual prejudices are worn off, a humane and philosophical spirit is cherished, and youth are stimulated to a laudable diligence and emulation in the pursuit of wisdom:

(Section IV, P. L.) And whereas, upon these principles divers public-spirited gentlemen of Pennsylvania and other American states did heretofore unite themselves, under certain regulations, into one voluntary society, by the name of "The American Philosophical Society, held at Philadelphia, for promoting useful knowledge," and by their successful labors and investigations, to the great credit of America, have extended their reputation so far that men of the first eminence in the republic of letters in the most civilized nations of Europe have done honor to their publications and desired to be enrolled among their members:

(Section V, P. L.) And whereas, the said society, after having been long interrupted in their laudable pursuits by the calamities of war and the distresses of our country, have found means to revive their design, in hopes of being able to prosecute the same with their former success, and of being further encouraged therein by the public, for which purpose they have prayed us, "the Representatives of the Freemen of the Commonwealth of Pennsylvania," that they may be created one body politic and corporate forever, with such powers, privileges and immunities as may be necessary for answering the valuable purposes which the said society had originally in view:

Wherefore, in order to encourage the said society in the prosecution and advancement of all useful branches of knowledge, for the benefit of their country and mankind:

[Section I.] (Section VI, P. L.) Be it enacted and it is hereby enacted by the Representatives of the Freemen of the Commonwealth of Pennsylvania in General Assembly met, and by the authority of the same, That the members of the said American Philosophical Society, heretofore voluntary associated for promoting useful knowledge, and such other persons as have been duly elected members and officers of the same, agreeably to the fundamental laws and regulations of the said society comprised in twelve sections prefixed to their first volume of transactions, published in Philadelphia by William and Thomas Bradford, in the year of our Lord one thousand seven hundred and seventy-one, and who shall in all respect conform themselves to the said laws and regulations, and such other laws, regulations and ordinances, as shall hereafter be duly made and enacted by the said society according to the tenor hereof, be and forever hereafter shall be, one body corporate and politic in deed, by the name and style of "The American Philosophical Society, held at Philadelphia, for promoting useful knowledge," and by the same name they are hereby constituted and confirmed one body corporate and politic, to have perpetual succession, and by the same name they and their successors are hereby declared and made able and capable in law, to have, hold, receive and enjoy lands, tenements, rents, franchises, hereditaments, gifts and bequests of what nature soever, in fee simple or for term of life, lives, years or otherwise, and also to give, grant, let, sell, alien or assign the same lands, tenements, hereditaments, goods, chattels and premises, according to the nature of the respective gifts, grants and bequests made to them the said society, and of their estate therein. Provided, that the amount of the clear yearly value of such real estate do not exceed the value of ten thousand bushels of good merchantable wheat.

[Section II.] (Section VII, P. L.) And be it further enacted by the authority aforesaid, That the said society be and shall be forever hereafter able and capable in law to sue and be sued, plead and be impleaded, answer and be answered unto, defend and be defended in all or any of the courts or other places, and before any judges, justices and other person or persons, in all manner of actions, suits, complaints, pleas, causes and matters, of what nature or kind soever, within this commonwealth; and that it shall and may be lawful to and for the said society, forever hereafter to have and use one common seal in their affairs, and the same at their will and pleasure to break, change, alter and renew.

[Section III.] (Section VIII, P. L.) And be it further enacted by the authority aforesaid, That for the well governing the said society, and ordering their affairs, they shall have the following officers, That is to say, one patron, who shall be his excellency the president of the supreme executive council of this commonwealth for the time being, and likewise one president, three vice-presidents, four secretaries, three curators, one treasurer, together with a council of twelve members, and that on the first Friday of January next, between the hours of two and five in the afternoon, as many of the members of the said society as shall have paid up their arrears due to the society, and shall declare their willingness to conform to the laws, regulations and ordinances of the society then duly in force, according to the tenor hereof, by subscribing the same, and who shall attend in the hall or place of meeting of said society within the time aforesaid, shall choose by ballot, agreeable to the fundamental laws and regulations hereinbefore referred to, one president, three vice-president, four secretaries, three curators and one treasurer, and at the same time and place the members met and qualified as aforesaid shall, in like manner choose four members for the council, to hold their offices for one year, four more members for the council, to hold their offices for two years, and four more members for the council, to hold their offices for three years. And on the first Friday in January, which shall be in the year of our Lord one thousand seven hundred and eighty-two, and so likewise on the first Friday of January yearly and every year thereafter, between the hours of two and five in the afternoon, the members of the said society met and qualified as aforesaid shall choose one president, three vice-presidents, four secretaries, three curators and one treasurer, to hold their respective offices for one year, and four councilmen, to hold their offices for three years: Provided, That no person residing within the United States shall be capable of being president, vice-president, secretary, curator, treasurer or member of the council or of electing to any of the said offices who is not capable of electing and being elected to civil offices within the state in which he resides.

(Section IX, P. L.) Provided also, That nothing herein contained shall be considered as intended to exclude any of the said officers or counsellors, whose times shall be expired, from being re-elected, according to the pleasure of the said society, and of the day, hours and place of all such elections due notice shall be given by the secretaries, or some one of them, in one or more of the public newspapers of this state, agreeable to the said fundamental laws and regulations before referred to.

[Section IV.] (Section X, P. L.) And be it further enacted by the authority aforesaid, That the officers and council of the said society shall be capable of exercising such power for the well governing and ordering the affairs of the society, and of holding such occasional meetings for that purpose as shall be described, fixed and determined by the statutes, laws, regulations and ordinances of the said society hereafter to be made.

(Section XI, P. L.) Provided always, That no statute, law, regulation or ordinance shall ever be made or passed by the said society or be binding upon the members thereof, or any of them, unless the same hath been duly proposed and fairly drawn up in writing at one stated meeting of the society, and enacted or passed at a subsequent meeting at least the space of fourteen days after the former meeting, and upon due notice in some of the public newspapers that the enacting of statutes and laws, or the making and passing ordinances and regulations will be part of the business of such meeting; nor shall any statute, law, regulation or ordinance be then or at any time enacted or passed unless thirteen members of the said society, or such greater number of members as may be afterwards fixed by the rules of the society, be present, besides such quorum of the officers and council as the laws of the society, for the time being, may require, and unless the same be voted by two-thirds of the whole body then present; all which statutes, laws, ordinance and regulations so as aforesaid duly made, enacted and passed, shall be binding on every member of the said society, and be from time to time inviolably observed, according to the tenor and effect thereof: Provided, They be not repugnant or contrary to the laws of this commonwealth for the time being in force and effect.

(Section XII, P. L.) And whereas nations truly civilized (however unhappily at variance on other accounts) will never wage war with the arts and sciences and the common interests of humanity:

[Section V.] (Section XIII, P. L.) Be it further enacted by the authority aforesaid, That it shall and may be lawful for the said society, by their proper officers, at all times, whether in peace or war, to correspond with learned societies, as well as individual learned men, of any nation or country, upon matters merely belonging to the business of the said society, such as the mutual communication of their discoveries and proceedings in philosophy and science, the procuring books, apparatus, natural curiosities and such other articles and intelligence as are usually exchanged between learned bodies, for furthering their common pursuits.

(Section XIV, P. L.) Provided always, That such correspondence of the said society be at all times open to the inspection of the supreme executive council of this commonwealth.

Passed March 15, 1780. See the notes to the Acts of Assembly passed March 29, 1779, Chapter 832; November 27, 1779, Chapter 871. Recorded L. B. No. 1, p. 363, &c.

CHAPTER DCCCXCV.

AN ACT TO CURE A DEFECT IN AN ACT OF ASSEMBLY ENTITLED "AN ACT TO CONFIRM THE ESTATES AND INTERESTS OF THE COLLEGE, ACADEMY, AND CHARITABLE SCHOOL OF THE CITY OF PHILADELPHIA AND TO ALTER AND AMEND THE CHARTERS THEREOF CONFORMABLY TO THE REVOLUTION, AND THE CONSTITUTION OF THIS COMMONWEALTH; AND TO ERECT THE SAME INTO AN UNIVERSITY;" AND ALSO AN ERROR IN THE DATE OF ANOTHER ACT OF ASSEMBLY ENTITLED "A SUPPLEMENT TO AN ACT ENTITLED AN ACT FOR THE ATTAINDER OF DIVERS TRAITORS IF THEY RENDER NOT THEMSELVES BY A CERTAIN DAY AND FOR VESTING THEIR ESTATES IN THIS COMMONWEALTH AND FOR MORE EFFECTUALLY DISCOVERING THE SAME, AND FOR ASCERTAINING [AND SATISFYING] THE LAWFUL DEBTS AND CLAIMS THEREUPON.

(Section I, P. L.) Whereas in an act of assembly passed on the twenty-seventh day of November last, entitled "An act to confirm the estates and interests of the college, academy and charitable school of the city of Philadelphia, and to amend and alter the charters thereof conformably to the revolution and the constitution of this commonwealth, and to erect the same into an university,"[1] the word college was, through mistake inserted in the sixteenth section thereof, instead of the word university, by reason whereof the authority intended to

[1] Chapter 871.

be vested in two justices of the peace by said act to proceed in a summary way against persons refusing to deliver up to the trustees of the said university, upon demand the library, apparatus, mortgages, specialties, deeds or instruments or other papers or books of record or real estate of the said university in custody or possession of such persons so refusing, may be disputed and prove insufficient for the purposes designed by the legislature:

For remedy whereof:

[Section I.] (Section II, P. L.) Be it enacted and it is hereby enacted by the Representatives of the Freemen of the Commonwealth of Pennsylvania in General Assembly met, and by the authority of the same, That the said act shall be construed and taken for the benefit and relief of the trustees of the said university as fully as if the said university was named in the said sixteenth paragraph in the stead and place of the word college, and the said justices shall proceed accordingly.

(Section III, P. L.) And whereas an error in form hath been discovered in the date of an act of assembly, entitled "A supplement to an act, entitled 'An act for the attainder of divers traitors, if they render not themselves by a certain day and for vesting their estates in the commonwealth, and for more effectually discovering the same, and for ascertaining and satisfying the lawful debts and claims thereon,"[1] by writing the word April at the foot of the record of the said act, instead of the word March, which, by the minutes of the general assembly, recourse being thereunto had, appears to be the month wherein the said law was enacted, and advantage may perhaps be taken from the error last mentioned to weaken or elude the operation of the last-recited act:

For remedy whereof:

[Section II.] (Section IV, P. L.) Be it further enacted by the authority aforesaid, That the last-recited act shall have the same and equal effect and operation as if the word March had been written at the foot of the said record, in the place where the word April has been erroneously written as aforesaid. And that all sales, transfers, leases, acts and proceedings what-

---

[1] Chapter 830.

soever had, made, suffered or done under the said act of assembly shall be deemed as valid and effectual in the law to all intents and purposes as if the said error or mistake had not been made.

Passed March 16, 1780. Recorded L. B. No. 1, p. 365, &c.

CHAPTER DCCCXCVI.

AN ACT TO PREVENT TRESPASSES AND WASTE FROM BEING COMMITTED UPON THE LANDS OF ABSENT PERSONS, AND UPON VACANT AND UNAPPROPRIATED LANDS.

(Section I, P. L.) Whereas divers disorderly persons have, of late entered upon the lands of persons residing beyond the sea or without the bounds of this state, and upon lands out of the possession of any particular person, and upon lands reputed to be vacant or unappropriated under pretence of certain claims and rights or otherwise and have committed great trespasses and waste thereon by felling of timber:

(Section II, P. L.) And whereas it is likely that some of the lands aforesaid are the proper estate of the commonwealth, and those belonging to absent persons ought in this time of war, when intercourse with Europe and other foreign countries is much interrupted, to be preserved from the trespasses and waste aforesaid:

[Section I.] (Section III, P. L.) Be it therefore enacted and it is hereby enacted by the Representatives of the Freemen of the Commonwealth of Pennsylvania in General Assembly met, and by the authority of the same, That if any person or persons whatsoever under pretense of any claim or right derived from the late proprietaries or without any title shall enter upon the lands of any person or persons residing beyond seas, or without the bounds of this state or upon lands out of the possession of any particular person or upon lands which are vacant or unappropriated, or reputed to be vacant or unappropriated and shall commit any trespass or waste thereon, every person so offending, his or her aiders and abettors shall not only be liable to the owner or owners of such land or to the commonwealth for treble damages as tenants committing waste for such trespass and waste but, moreover, shall be guilty of a misdemeanor and upon conviction thereof shall be fined and imprisoned at the discretion of the court [of quarter sessions or other court] wherein such conviction shall be had.

[Section II.] (Section IV, P. L.) And be it further enacted by the authority aforesaid, That for and during the continuance of this act no surveyor or other person shall presume to measure, survey or locate any right or claim to land as aforesaid unless he be authorized so to do by the special license of the president or vice-president in council under the less seal, who, upon due proof of the equity thereof, may grant the same, and every survey, location or appropriation of land made without such license be first obtained, and unless a return of the survey thereupon made shall be made into the office of the secretary of the supreme executive council within six months after the same shall be made shall be utterly null and void.

(Section V. P. L.) And in order to correct as far as may be the mischiefs which may have arisen or may arise to the commonwealth by clandestine surveys and undue appropriations of vacant or waste lands made since the fourth day of July, which was in the year of our Lord one thousand seven hundred and seventy-six:

[Section III.] (Section VI, P. L.) Be it enacted by the authority aforesaid, That no survey or appropriation of vacant or unappropriated lands which has been made within this state since the fourth day of July, which was in the year of our Lord one thousand seven hundred and seventy-six, shall be available in law or equity or shall be considered as vesting any estate in such land unless the date and other particulars of the same, together with a clear description of the right or claim upon which it was made shall be entered in the office of the secretary of the supreme executive council within the times hereinafter limited; That is to say, in case such survey has been made in the counties of Bedford, Northumberland or Westmoreland before the first day of January next, and in case such survey has been made in any other county before the first day of November next.

[Section IV.] (Section VII, P. L.) Provided always, and be it further enacted by the authority aforesaid, That such entry in the office of the said secretary shall not give and [sic] [any] relief or benefit to any person to which he or she was not entitled before the passing of this act.

[Section V.] (Section VIII, P. L.) And be it further enacted by the authority aforesaid, That this act shall continue and be in force for and during nine months and from thence to the end of the next session of the general asembly and no longer.

Passed March 17, 1780. Recorded L. B. No. 1, p. 366, &c.

CHAPTER DCCCXCVII.

AN ACT TO RENDER THE REVENUE ARISING FROM THE EXCISE ON WINE AND SPIRITS AND ON LICENSES TO BE GRANTED TO PUBLIC HOUSES EFFECTIVE AND EQUAL TO THE PUBLIC NECESSITIES.

(Section I, P. L.) Whereas, in and by an act of assembly of the late province of Pennsylvania, passed in the year of our Lord one thousand seven hundred and fifty-six it was directed that an excise should be levied, collected and paid throughout the said province for the purposes therein mentioned, for all rum, brandy and other spirits sold, drawn, shared or bartered by any person or persons whatsoever, in any quantity under seventy gallons and for all wines sold, drawn, shared or bartered by any person or persons whatsoever under the quantity of one hogshead; such quantities to be delivered at one time and to one person at anytime from and after the first day of October, which was in the year of our Lord one thousand seven hundred and fifty-six, for and during the space of ten years then next following, and for so long after as should be necessary to answer the purposes for which the said excise was appropriated, at the rate of four pence per gallon and so proportionably for a greater or less quantity, and divers regulations were made, powers given and officers appointed in order to bring the revenue thereby to arise into the treasury.

(Section II, P. L.) And whereas, the excise aforesaid was afterwards altered, additional regulations concerning the same made, and further powers given for the more effectual collecting thereof for and during ten years from the tenth day of April, which was in the year of our Lord one thousand seven hundred and seventy-two, by an act, entitled "An act for the support of the government of this province and making the excise on wine, rum, brandy and other spirits more equal, and preventing frauds in the collecting and paying of the excise," [1] passed in the said late province on the first day of March, in the year of our Lord one thousand seven hundred and seventy-two, for the purpose of sinking and discharging certain bills of credit of the value of twenty-five thousand pounds emitted by virtue of the said act.

(Section III, P. L.) And whereas the said excise was afterwards charged with the redemption of the further sum of twenty-two thousand pounds emitted in bills of credit by virtue of an act of assembly, entitled "An act for the support of the government of this province and payment of public debts." [2]

(Section IV, P. L.) And whereas the residue of the said bills of credit, which were still current on the twenty-fifth day of May, in the year of our Lord one thousand seven hundred and seventy-eight, were called in and provided for in and by an act of this commonwealth, entitled "An act for the calling in of the bills of credit issued by the legislative authority of Pennsylvania under the sanction and authority of the crown of Great Britain and for other purposes therein mentioned," [3] and a supplement to the same whereby the said revenue of excise is now disengaged.

(Section V, P. L.) And whereas the ordinary support of government, the contingent expenses thereof and divers other calls at this time of war require considerable sums of money, and it

---

[1] Chapter 656.
[2] Passed September 30, 1775, Chapter 715.
[3] Passed March 23, 1778, Chapter 791.

would be very distressing to the people of this state now laboring under heavy taxes on their estates, real and personal, to increase their burdens of that kind.

[Section I.] (Section VI, P. L.) Be it therefore enacted and it is hereby enacted by the Representatives of the Freemen of the Commonwealth of Pennsylvania in General Assembly met, and by the authority of the same, That the said revenue of excise, shall be levied, collected and paid into the treasury of this state, during the remainder of the last-mentioned term of ten years for the purposes aforesaid. And in order to render the said revenue of excise effective, and in some measure proportioned to the great rise in the prices of wine and spirits and the necessities of the state:

[Section II.] (Section VII, P. L.) Be it further enacted by the authority aforesaid, That from and after the first day of May, next, the said excise of four pence per gallon and the sum of three pounds per annum, being the lowest rate at which any retailer of wine or spirits is allowed by the said acts of assembly to compound for the same shall be deemd to be money of the value of ten shillings for a bushel of wheat and estimated, collected, satisfied and paid in the manner after which the fees of certain officers are directed to be estimated, satisfied and paid in and by an act of assembly, entitled "An act for the better support of certain officers of this state and for ascertaining the specific fines and penalties which they may incur by neglect of duty."[1]

(Section VIII, P. L.) And whereas the great profits and advantages of late gained by the keepers of inns, taverns, ale houses and retailers of wine, rum, and other spirits will easily admit that the public income arising from licenses to be granted to such persons may be augmented to a rate in some degree proportioned to the increased prices of goods, merchandise and tavern charges, in order to answer the salaries necessary to be given to public officers:

[Section III.] (Section IX, P. L.) Be it therefore enacted by the authority aforesaid, That from and after the ninth day of August next the money directed to be paid for such licenses by

---

[1] Passed November 27, 1779, Chapter 875.

the act of assembly of the late province of Pennsylvania, entitled "An act that no public house or inn within this province shall be kept without license,"[1] and the security directed to be given by tavern keepers and others in one hundred pounds before such licenses be issued," shall be taken in a [sum] equivalent to the augmented price of such license and shall be deemed to be money of the value of ten shillings for a bushel of wheat and estimated, collected, satisfied and paid in like manner as the fees of certain officers as aforesaid.

[Section IV.] (Section X, P. L.) And be it further enacted by the authority aforesaid, That an act of assembly of this commonwealth, entitled "An act to increase the fees on tavern licenses, the fines on tippling houses and the rates of excise,"[2] passed on the fifteenth day of March, which was in the year of our Lord one thousand seven hundred and seventy-nine, and everything therein contained (saving the treble rates thereby laid upon tavern licenses which shall continue till the said ninth day of August next) shall from and after the said first day of May next be repealed and made void.

Passed March 17, 1780. See the notes to the Acts of Assembly passed February 28, 1710-11, Chapter 172; August 26, 1721, Chapter 244; September 21, 1756, Chapter 412; March 21, 1772, Chapter 656; and the Acts of Assembly passed April 6, 1781, Chapter 938; March 19, 1783, Chapter 1016; March 20, 1783, Chapter 1018; December 9, 1783. Chapter 1861; April 5, 1785, Chapter 1161; September 25, 1786, Chapter 1248; September 21, 1791, Chapter 1582; (the two Acts of Assembly passed) April 22, 1794, Chapters 1758, 1763. Recorded L. B. No. 1, p. 367, &c.

CHAPTER DCCCXCVIII.

AN ACT TO GRANT TO HENRY GUEST AN EXCLUSIVE RIGHT FOR THE TERM OF FIVE YEARS OF MAKING OIL AND BLUBBER FROM MATERIALS OF HIS OWN DISCOVERY.

(Section I, P. L.) Whereas, the encouragement of arts, manufactures and commerce has always in all civilized and well-im-

---

[1] See Acts of February 28, 1710-11, Chapter 172, and August 26, 1721, Chapter 244.
[2] Chapter 825.

proved countries been held as one of the duties of government, and that to provide suitable recompense for those who, by their own expense, ingenuity or dint of application have made new and useful discoveries is not only consistent with justice and generosity but with true policy:

(Section II, P. L.) And whereas, Henry Guest, now of the town of New Brunswick, in the state of New Jersey, has, by petition of [sic] [to] this house set forth that by long study and frequent as well as expensive experiments [sic] [he has] discovered a method hitherto unpracticed and unknown of making an oil commonly known by the name of Currier's Oil and Blubber from certain materials found within these United States, or parts thereof, and has prayed us to grant to him an exclusive right for the term of five years of making and manufacturing oil and blubber from the materials by him so discovered:

[Section I.] (Section III, P. L.) Be it therefore enacted and it is hereby enacted by the Representatives of the Freemen of the Commonwealth of Pennsylvania in General Assembly met, and by the authority of the same, That from and after the time at which the aforesaid Henry Guest shall erect a manufactory in this state, and produce oil and blubber therein for sale from the materials he has discovered, provided the same be done within the space of eight months from the time of passing this act, that he shall be and he is hereby invested, as a reward for his discovery and for the purpose of promoting useful manufactories in this state, with the sole and exclusive right, for the term of five years, of manufacturing oil and blubber from the materials he has discovered.

[Section II.] (Section IV, P. L.) And be it enacted by the authority aforesaid, That if any person or persons within this state shall, during the aforesaid term of five years, make use of the same kind of materials for the purpose of manufacturing any oil or blubber for sale, that it shall and may be lawful for the said Henry Guest, his heirs, executors or administrators, to sue for and recover for his, her or their use one-half the value of all the oil and blubber made for sale by such person or persons in the manufacturing or making of which he, she or they shall make use of any of the materials by him discovered and used in the manufacturing of oil and blubber as aforesaid.

(Section V, P. L.) And in order to prevent any disputes or uncertainties arising as to the identity of the materials discovered and used in the making of oil and blubber by the aforesaid Henry Guest, be it known and it is hereby declared that before the passing of this act he, the said Henry Guest, hath lodged in the clerk's office of this House, sealed up and endorsed by himself and the clerk, a particular account and description of the materials by him invented or discovered for the purpose of making therefrom oil and blubber.

[Section III.] (Section VI, P. L.) And be it further enacted by the authority aforesaid, That before or as soon as he, the said Henry Guest begins to manufacture the aforesaid oil and blubber in this state he shall put up in his said manufactory or manufactories a printed account in English and German of the said materials by him discovered or invented and used in the making oil and blubber, subject to the inspection of all persons, in order that no person may unknowingly offend and that all after the expiration of the term of five years may be enabled to prosecute the said manufactures to their own advantage.

Passed March 17, 1780. Recorded L. B. No. 1, p. 369, &c.

CHAPTER DCCCXCIX.

AN ACT FOR THE EFFECTUAL RECOVERING AND SECURING THE FINES, FORFEITURES AND OTHER MONEYS, DUE OR BELONGING TO THE COMMONWEALTH FOR THE USE OF THE SAME.

(Section I, P. L.) To the end that all fines, forfeitures, issues, amerciaments, fees and moneys which, by the constitution and laws were designed and ought to be applied towards defraying the necessary charges of supporting government and the administration of justice within this commonwealth, may be duly estreated, levied and paid into the public treasury, and go to the uses intended:

[Section I.] (Section II, P. L.) Be it enacted and it is hereby enacted by the Representatives of the Freemen of the Commonwealth of Pennsylvania in General Assembly met, and by the authority of the same, That all fines, issues, amerciaments, forfeited recognizances, sum and sums of money to be paid in lieu and satisfaction of them, and all other forfeitures which, from and after the publication of this act, shall be set, imposed, lost or forfeited in the supreme court or in any of the courts of common pleas, courts of general quarter sessions of the peace and gaol delivery, or before any special commissioners of oyer and terminer, in any county of this state, or before any justices or justice of the peace, shall by the justices, prothonotaries, clerks and sheriffs, respectively, be certified and estreated in and into the supreme court, to be held in Philadelphia on the tenth day of April next, expressing the cause of the loss, the court, the nature of the writ and names of the parties betwixt whom the said issues and amerciaments are lost, and from whom the said moneys were received or are still due. And that all fines, issues, amerciaments, forfeited recognizances, sum and sums of money to be paid in lieu or satisfaction of them, or any of them, and all other forfeitures whatsoever arising in the said courts, and due to the state, from and after the tenth day of April next in every year, to the twenty-fourth day of September in every year, shall be and are hereby ordained and required to be certified and estreated in and into the supreme court at Philadelphia, the last day of every September term in every year; and from the beginning of every September term there in every year to the beginning of April term there in every year, on the last day of every April term in every year, on pain that very officer and minister aforesaid who by this or any other law of this commonwealth ought to make certificates or estreats of any of the said fines, issues, amerciaments, forfeitures or moneys, making default of offending therein, and being thereof legally convicted on indictment or information in the said court, shall be fined at the discretion of the said court for the use of the state, and on further pain in case of a conviction for a second default or offense of a like nature, of being displaced and removed from office by the justices of the said supreme court.

[Section II.] (Section III, P. L.) And be it further enacted by the authority aforesaid, That the clerk of the city court in Philadelphia, and every of the clerks of the peace within this commonwealth, shall make and deliver, yearly, to the sheriff of the respective city or county where the sessions of the peace is or shall be kept, within ten days after the first day of November in every year, a true and perfect estreat or schedule of all fines, issues, amerciaments, forfeited recognizances, sum and sums of money and other forfeitures whatsoever which shall happen to be imposed, set, lost or forfeited in any of the said sessions of the peace, respectively, which shall be held before the said first day of November, by or upon any person or persons whatsoever; and shall also yearly and every year, on or before the tenth day of April, make out and deliver to the prothonotary of the supreme court a true and perfect duplicate certificate, and estreat of all the schedules so delivered to the said respective sheriffs, that so they or their opposals in the said supreme court may be charged with the money levied and received by them, respectively, upon such schedules delivered as aforesaid, on pain that every person and persons offending herein, and being thereof legally convicted in manner aforesaid shall be fined in any sum at the discretion of the said court for the use of the state; and on further pain, in case of a conviction for a second default or offense of the like nature, of being displaced and removed from office by the justices of the said supreme court.

[Section III.] (Section IV, P. L.) And be it further enacted by the authority aforesaid, That the justices of the supreme court may and shall award process for levying, as well of such fines, forfeitures, issues and amerciaments as shall be estreated into the same, as of all the fines, forfeitures, issues and amerciaments which shall be lost, taxed and set there, and not paid to the uses they shall be appropriated to.

[Section IV.] (Section V, P. L.) And be it further enacted

by the authority aforesaid, That all clerks and prothonotaries of the said courts, clerks of the peace and others to whom it belongs to make return of estreats into the said supreme court, shall deliver in all and every such estreat and estreats upon their oaths or affirmation to be administered by one or more of the judges of the same court, or any two justices of the peace to the effect following, That is to say: "You shall declare that these estreats now by you delivered are truly and carefully made up and examined, and that all fines, issues, amerciaments, recognizances and forfeitures which were set, lost, imposed or forfeited and in right and due course of law ought to be estreated in the supreme court of Pennsylvania, are, to the best of your knowledge and understanding, herein contained; and that in the same estreats are also contained and expressed all such fines and amerciaments as have been paid into the court from which the said estreats are made, without any wilful or fraudulent discharge, omission, misnomer or defect whatsoever."

[Section V.] (Section VI, P. L.) And be it further enacted by the authority aforesaid, That no justice, officer or minister of or belonging to any of the said courts, nor any prothonotary or clerk of the said supreme or other court, clerk of the peace, nor any officer or minister under them, or any of them, nor other person or persons whatsoever, do or shall spare, take off, discharge or wittingly or willingly conceal any indictment, fine, issue, amerciament, forfeited recognizance or other forfeiture whatsoever, exhibited, set, imposed, lost or forfeited in any of the courts above mentioned, or before any of the judges, justices or commissioners of or belonging to the same; or any sum or sums of money paid, or to be paid to any officer or officers, in lieu or satisfaction of any fine or forfeiture, unless it be by rule or order of court, where such indictment, fine, issue, amerciament, forfeited recognizances or other forfeiture whatsoever is or shall be exhibited, set, imposed, lost or forfeited; nor shall any of the justices, officers or ministers aforesaid, or any other willingly or wittingly mis-certify or estreat in or into any of the said supreme courts, any fine, issue, amerciament, forfeited recognizance or other forfeiture whatsoever, whereby the process of the said supreme court for the levying thereof may be made invalid and of none effect. But every such justice, officer and minister and all and every other person and persons offending herein shall, for every such offense, forfeit and pay treble the value of such fine, issue, amerciament, forfeited recognizance, sum or sums of money or other forfeiture so spared, taken off, discharged, concealed, not certified or estreated or miscertified as aforesaid, the one moiety thereof to the use of the state, and the other moiety to such person or persons as will sue for the same, to be recovered with costs in any court of record within this commonwealth by action of debt, bill or information, wherein no essoin, protection or wager of law or more than one imparlance shall be allowed.

[Section VI]. (Section VII, P. L.) And be it further enacted by the authority aforesaid, That the justices of the supreme court, or any two of them, shall view all the said estreats and cause their prothonotary or clerk to enroll them in the same court; and shall hear and determine all complaints brought before them concerning immoderate fines, issues or amerciaments estreated as aforesaid, and give relief to the party grieved, according to justice and their legal discretion.

[Section VII.] (Section VIII, P. L.) And be it enacted by the authority aforesaid, That the justices of the supreme court may and shall nominate and appoint an officer, to be styled "The Clerk of the Estreats," whose duty shall be to keep a fair and true account of all fines, issues, amerciaments, forfeited recognizances, sum and sums of money paid in lieu and satisfaction of them, and all other forfeitures, also of all fees and license money belonging to this commonwealth to be taken from the schedules or estreats thereof, delivered by the respective sheriffs to the prothonotary of said court from time to time or otherwise; to ascertain the amount of the same annually in each county, and charge the same to the proper persons; to put the aforesaid recognizances in process under the direction of the supreme court, and to do and perform all such other matters and things as the said court shall think necessary for the effectual securing the fines and moneys aforesaid to the use of the commonwealth.

[Section VIII.] (Section IX, P. L.) And be it further enacted by the authority aforesaid, That all and every the said fines, sums of money or other forfeitures which from henceforth shall be levied or received for the use of the state according to the directions and intent of this act shall be paid by the sheriff or other officer or minister who levied or received the same to such person as shall by the general assembly from time to time be appointed treasurer of this commonwealth, who shall keep a fair and true account of the same in a book to be by him provided for that purpose, and shall, from time to time lay an account thereof before the said general assembly; and the said treasurer shall receive for his trouble in receiving and paying over such moneys so by him received, three and a half per centum and the said clerk of the estreats shall receive for his trouble one and a half per centum on all moneys so as aforesaid paid into the treasury.

[Section IX.] (Section X. P. L.) And be it further enacted by the authority aforesaid, That the secretary of the supreme executive council, or his deputies, for delivering out licenses within the several counties of this state, respectively, shall keep a true and just account of all fees and license money which have been heretofore payable to the governor or his deputies for the support of government, and by the constitution of this commonwealth are directed to be paid into the public treasury, expressing the time when, the persons' names to whom any license has been granted and where they inhabit; also the names of the person or persons from whom any such fees or license money have been received, the time when received, and for what service; and shall certify the same to the justices of the supreme court on the first day of the September term at Philadelphia in every year, and shall pay the same, or cause the same to be paid [to the treasurer of this commonwealth for the time being] within ten days after, on pain of forfeiting and paying any sum that the said court in their discretion may think just and proper, the one moiety thereof to the use of the state and the other moiety to him or them that will sue for the same, to be recovered with costs as aforesaid.

[Section X.] (Section XI, P. L.) And be it further enacted

by the authority aforesaid, That the act, entitled "An act for the better recovery of fines and forfeitures due to the governor and government of this province,"[1] passed the twenty-eighth day of May, in the year of our Lord one thousand seven hundred and fifteen, be and the same is hereby repealed and made null and void.

> Passed March 18, 1780. See the note to the Act of Assembly passed May 28, 1715, Chapter 206. The Act in the text was repealed by the Act of Assembly passed December 9, 1783, Chapter 1062. Recorded L. B. No. 1, p. 369, &c.

CHAPTER CM.

AN ACT DIRECTING THE APPORTIONING AND ASSESSING OF COUNTY RATES AND LEVIES; POOR RATES; THE TAXES TO BE LAYED FOR THE OPENING, AMENDING AND REPAIRING OF ROADS AND HIGHWAYS; THE TAXES TO BE LAYED FOR SUPPORTING THE NIGHTLY WATCH, THE LAMPS AND PUMPS, AND FOR PITCHING, PAVING AND CLEANSING THE STREETS, LANES AND ALLEYS AND FOR REGULATING, MAKING AND AMENDING THE WATERCOURSES AND COMMON SEWERS IN THE CITY OF PHILADELPHIA, CONFORMABLY TO THE STATE TAXES ON TAXABLE PERSONS, AND ON ESTATES REAL AND PERSONAL; FOR EXPLAINING AND AMENDING THE ACTS PASSED IN THE YEAR ONE THOUSAND SEVEN HUNDRED AND SEVENTY-NINE, FOR ASSESSING AND LEVYING THE SAID STATE TAXES; AND FOR INCREASING THE RECOMPENSE OF COUNTY COMMISSIONERS AND ASSESSORS.

(Section I, P. L.) Whereas, in and by divers acts of assembly, county rates and levies, poor rates, taxes necessary to be levied for the opening, amending and repairing of roads and highways, and the taxes for supporting the nightly watch, lamps and pumps, and for pitching, paving and cleansing the streets, lanes and alleys, and regulating, making and amending the water courses and common sewers, in the city of Philadelphia, various modes of assessment are directed within the several counties, townships and districts and within the city of Philadelphia respectively:

---

[1] Chapter 206.

(Section II, P. L.) And whereas the making of the said assessments as is directed in and by the several acts of assembly aforesaid, hath been found to be very tedious and expensive, and the same has now become needless in most of the counties of this state by the present manner of assessing the state taxes upon taxable persons and estates real and personal, and it would save much time and trouble if the county, city, township and district rates and taxes aforesaid were assessed conformably to the state taxes:

[Section I.] (Section III, P. L.) Be it therefore enacted and it is hereby enacted by the Representatives of the Freemen of the Commonwealth of Pennsylvania in General Assembly met, and by the authority of the same, That from and after the passing of this act all county, city, township and district taxes hereinbefore numerated thereafter to be laid and assessed on the taxable persons and estates, real and personal, within any county, the city of Philadelphia, or any township or district, shall be apportioned and assessed according to the last state tax laid in the particular county and not otherwise.

[Section II.] (Section IV, P. L.) Provided always, and be it further enacted by the authority aforesaid, That nothing herein contained shall extend to any state tax on ready money, nor to debar any person who may think him or herself aggrieved by anything done by virtue of this act of any appeal to which he or she was otherwise entitled, nor to alter the mode of collecting any of the rates, levies or taxes aforesaid, nor to alter the mode of taxation in any county in which a state tax has not been made within twelve months before the laying of such county, city, township or district rate or tax.

[Section III.] (Section V, P. L.) And be it further enacted by the authority aforesaid, That if upon appeal concerning any rate or tax aforesaid it shall appear that any real estate hath been transferred from the person or persons charged for the same in the last state tax, and before the laying of such county, city, township or district rate or tax, so appealed against, the commissioners of the county, justices of the peace, wardens of the watch or commissioners for paving the streets of the city of Philadelphia, as the case may be, shall transfer to the name of the purchaser thereof, and charge such purchaser in the duplicate with the rate or tax assessed upon such estate.

(Section VI, P. L.) And whereas, it will not be reasonable that county assessors, in laying the county tax, and the assessors of the city of Philadelphia, in laying of city taxes according to the direction of this act should be paid as heretofore:

[Section IV.] (Section VII, P. L.) Be it therefore enacted by the authority aforesaid, That the said assessors shall, in executing this act, be entitled to like recompense as is hereinafter allowed to county assessors and no other.

(Section VIII, P. L.) And whereas divers owners of lands whereon improvements have been made, and on tenements, may not reside in the county or district where such lands or tenements are situate, whereby it may be difficult to collect the taxes assessed on such real estate in pursuance of the acts of assembly passed in the year one thousand seven hundred and seventy-nine authorizing the laying and assessing and levying of state taxes:

For remedy whereof:

[Section V.] (Section IX, P. L.) Be it enacted by the authority aforesaid, That the tenant or tenants, or other person residing on or occupying such real estate, his, her and their goods and chattels, as well as the lands, goods and chattels of the owner or owners thereof shall be liable to be distrained for to satisfy the said taxes, or any of them; and in case the tenant or tenants or other person or persons residing on or occupying such real estate hath or have paid or shall pay any tax laid thereon by virtue of any of the said acts, or hath or have been or shall be distrained to satisfy such tax, such tenant or tenants may retain the same out of the rent by him, or her or them payable for such real estate, to the landlord; or the said tenant or tenants or other occupier or occupiers of such estate shall recover the same with costs of suit of the owner of such estate, by action of debt, if under fifty pounds, in a summary way, in like manner as small debts are recoverable; but if the same exceed fifty pounds in any court of common pleas.

(Section X, P. L.) Provided always, That nothing in this act shall in any manner alter any contract heretofore made between any landlord and tenant concerning the payment of taxes; nor to repeal or alter the directions of the act of assembly, entitled "An act for raising the additional sum of five millions seven hundred thousand dollars in the year one thousand seven hundred and seventy-nine,"[1] passed on the tenth day of October last, obliging tenants holding under a lease whereby the rent had been reserved in current money to pay over and above the said rent all taxes on his holding.

(Section XI, P. L.) And whereas the recompense at present allowed to county commissioners and assessors is found to be unequal to their expense and labor:

Wherefore:

[Section V.] (Section XII, P. L.) Be it enacted by the authority aforesaid, That henceforth the recompense of the said commissioners and assessors shall be ten shillings per diem, of money at ten shillings for a bushel of wheat, and shall be estimated and satisfied in like manner as the recompense and fees of county commissioners and assessors were estimated and satisfied before the passing of this act.

Passed March 18, 1870. See the notes to the Acts of Assembly passed March 20, 1724-25, Chapter 284; September 15, 1756, Chapter 411; February 18, 1769, Chapter 594; the two Acts of Assembly passed March 9, 1771, Chapters 635, 636; March 21, 1772, Chapter 653. Recorded L. B. No. 1, p. 372, &c.

CHAPTER CMI.

AN ACT TO ENABLE WILLIAM CLINGAN, THOMAS BULL, JOHN KINKEAD, ROGER KIRK, JOHN SELLERS, JOHN WILSON AND JOSEPH DAVIS TO BUILD A NEW COURT HOUSE AND PRISON IN THE COUNTY OF CHESTER, AND SELL THE OLD COURT HOUSE AND PRISON IN THE BOROUGH OF CHESTER.

(Section I, P. L.) Whereas, it has been represented to this house that the holding of courts of general quarter sessions of the peace, common pleas, nisi prius, oyer and terminer and

---

[1] Chapter 866.

general gaol delivery for the county of Chester, in the borough of Chester, is very inconvenient and burdensome to a great part of the inhabitants of the said county, as the situation of said borough is at an extreme corner of said county; and that it would be very commodious and much for the advantage of the inhabitants in general if the several courts were held at a more central part of the said county:

[Section I.] (Section II, P. L.) Be it therefore enacted and it is hereby enacted by the Representatives of the Freemen of the Commonwealth of Pennsylvania in General Asembly met, and by the authority of the same, That it shall and may be lawful to and for the said William Clingan, Thomas Bull, John Kinkead, Roger Kirk, John Sellers, John Wilson and Joseph Davis, or any four or more of them, to purchase and take assurance to them and their heirs of a piece of land situate in some convenient place of the said county in trust and for the use of the said county and thereon to build and erect [or cause to be built and erected] a court house and prison, sufficient to accommodate the public service of the said county, and for the ease and convenience of the said inhabitants.

[Section II.] (Section III, P. L.) And be it enacted by the authority aforesaid, That when the said court house and prison shall be erected as aforesaid, that from thenceforth the several courts of general quarter sessions, common pleas, nisi prius, oyer and terminer and general gaol delivery for the said county shall be holden and kept at the said court house, when the same is built and erected in the place so to be provided as aforesaid.

[Section III.] (Section IV, P. L.) And be it further enacted by the authority aforesaid, That it shall and may be lawful that the said William Clingan, Thomas Bull, John Kinkead, Roger Kirk, John Sellers, John Wilson and Joseph Davis, or any four or more of them, shall have full power to expose to sale by public vendue to the highest bidder, the old court house, prison and work house, with all and singular the appurtenances and hereditaments thereunto belonging, situate in the borough of Chester aforesaid, and to give assurances to the heirs and assigns of the purchaser or purchasers forever; and the moneys therefrom arising shall be appropriated towards paying for the lands to be purchased and the new court house and prison to be built in the said place so as aforesaid to be provided.

[Section IV.] (Section V, P. L.) And be it further enacted by the authority aforesaid, That for the defraying the remainder of the expenses and charge of purchasing the land, building and erecting the said court house and prison, it shall and may be lawful for the commissioners and assessors of said county, or a majority of them, to assess and levy so much money as the said trustees, or any four of them, shall judge necessary for paying the remainder aforesaid, of purchasing the land and finishing the said court house and prison, and they are hereby required so to do.

Passed March 20, 1780. See the Acts of Assembly passed March 22, 1784, Chapter 1081; March 30, 1785, Chapter 1152; March 18, 1786, Chapter 1215; September 25, 1786, Chapter 1247; September 26, 1789, Chapter 1443; March 12, 1800, Chapter 2125. Recorded L. B. No. 1, p. 373, &c.

CHAPTER CMII.

AN ACT FOR THE REGULATION OF THE MILITIA OF THE COMMONWEALTH OF PENNSYLVANIA.

(Section I, P. L.) Whereas a militia law founded upon just and equitable principles hath been ever regarded as the best security of liberty, and the most effectual means of drawing forth and exerting the natural strength of a state:

(Section II, P. L.) And whereas a well regulated militia is the only safe and constitutional method of defending a free state, as the necessity of keeping up a standing army, especially in times of peace, is thereby superceded:

(Section III, P. L.) And whereas the militia law of this commonwealth enacted by the general assembly the seventeenth day of March, one thousand seven hundred and seventy-seven, from a change of circumstances and other causes, hath become insufficient to answer the purposes aforesaid, which renders it highly necessary that a new law should be enacted:

Therefore:

[Section I.] (Section IV, P. L.) Be it enacted and it is hereby enacted by the Representatives of the Freemen of the Commonwealth of Pennsylvania in General Assembly met, and by the authority of the same, That the president in council or, in his absence, the vice-president in council, of this commonwealth shall appoint and commissionate one reputable freeholder in the city of Philadelphia, and one in each county within this state to serve as lieutenants of the militia for the said city and counties respectively; and, also, any number of persons not exceeding two for the said city, and in the several counties any number not exceeding the number of battalions now or to be hereafter formed, to serve as sub-lieutenants in the said city and counties respectively, who, besides the powers which are given him and them by this act, shall have the title and rank which the president in council or, in his absence, the vice-president in council shall confer, which said lieutenant or, in his absence or incapacity, two or more sub-lieutenants shall have full power and authority to do and perform all and singular the duties required of the said lieutenants by this act.

[Section II.] (Section V, P. L.) And be it enacted by the authority aforesaid, That the lieutenants and sub-lieutenants, before they enter upon the execution of their offices, respectively, shall give bond to the treasurer of the county in which they severally reside, in the name of the president or commander-in-chief of the state, with one sufficient surety in the sum of twenty thousand pounds, conditioned for the faithful accounting for and paying all the moneys which shall come to their hands by virtue of this act when thereunto lawfully required. And that the public bonds given or to be given by the treasurer of the state or county treasurers for the due discharge of their respective offices shall be deemed to extend to the faithful performance of the trust hereby committed to them respectively.

[Section III.] (Section VI, P. L.) And be it further enacted by the authority aforesaid, That the said lieutenant or sub-lieutenants (once in every year) shall issue his or their warrants to the captain or commanding officer for the time being of each company of the several battalions in the said city and counties respectively, or to some other suitable person, commanding him, in the name of the commonwealth, to deliver to him or them, the said lieutenant or sub-lieutenants, within ten days from and after the date of the said warrants (unless the lieutenant or sub-lieutenants shall judge a longer time to be necessary, which he or they are hereby empowered to grant) on oath or affirmation, which any of them is hereby empowered to administer, a true and exact list of the names and surnames of each and every male white person inhabiting or residing within his township, borough, ward or district, between the ages of eighteen and fifty-three (delegates in Congress, members of the supreme executive council, members of the general assembly, judges of the supreme court, attorney-general for the state, the judges of the admiralty, treasurer of the state, sheriffs, gaolers and keepers of workhouses, ministers of the gospel of every denomination, professors and teachers in the university, postmasters and postriders belonging to the general post-office, menial servants of ambassadors or ministers and consuls from foreign courts and of delegates in Congress from other states registered with the secretary of the supreme executive council of this state and servants purchased bona fide and for a valuable consideration only excepted).

[Section IV.] (Section VII, P. L.) And be it further enacted by the authority aforesaid, That the lieutenant and sub-lieutenants aforesaid shall, within five days after they shall receive the lists aforesaid, if they see cause, alter the present divisions of the city and counties respectively and divide them into new districts, each district to contain not less than four hundred and forty nor more than one thousand, officers and privates included, at the discretion of the said lieutenants and sub-lieutenants, and then sub-divide the said districts into eight parts as nearly equal as may be, paying due regard in each division to the convenience of the inhabitants: Provided always, That two-thirds of the lieutenants met for the above purpose agree to such division, and that each person be annexed to the numerical class to which he formerly belonged.

[Section V.] (Section VIII, P. L.) And be it further enacted by the authority aforesaid, That the militia of the Northern Liberties of the city of Philadelphia, the district of Southwark and the township of Moyamensing and Passyunk be and they hereby are united to the city of Philadelphia, to act in conjunction with the militia of the said city, and distinct from the rest of the county of Philadelphia, that they draw lots for rank in battalion and be joined in brigade and act in every other matter that respects the militia law as if they were inhabitants of the said city, and to be under the direction of the lieutenant and sub-lieutenants of the city.

[Section VI.] (Section IX, P. L.) And be it further enacted by the authority aforesaid, That the lieutenant and sub-lieutenants of the city of Philadelphia and districts annexed, shall, out of the several battalions of the said city and districts annexed, take such a number as will compose eight companies to form one battalion of artillery, to be officered and arrayed as follows, that is to say, one lieutenant-colonel, one major, eight captains, eight captain lieutenants, eight first lieutenants, sixteen second lieutenants, the senior to bear the standard and the junior to do the duty of conductor; paymaster, adjutant and quartermaster to be taken from the line; one surgeon, one sergeant major, fife major, drum major, eight clerks, thirty-two sergeants, forty-eight bombadiers, forty-eight gunners, eight drummers, eight fifers and four hundred matrosses, and both the officers and privates of the said battalion shall be subject to the same fines and penalties for any omission of duty as the infantry: Provided, nevertheless, That the persons composing the artillery heretofore formed may be permitted to continue as a part of the said battalion of artillery and the officers shall be elected in the same manner as is directed by this act for the election of officers of the infantry.

[Section VII.] (Section X, P. L.) And be it further enacted by the authority aforesaid, That the several captains of the artillery battalion shall determine their rank by lot, and be numbered from one to eight in numerical order, and be subject to be drawn forth into actual service in rotation by companies, according to their number in rank, number one in rank with the first class of the militia and so on, until all shall take their tour, or otherwise as the commander-in-chief of the militia shall direct.

(Section XI, P. L.) And whereas it is expedient to embody such a number of light horse as will be useful when the militia is called into actual service:

Therefore:

[Section VIII.] (Section XII, P. L.) Be it further enacted by the authority aforesaid, That each of the lieutenants of the several counties of this state may form a corps of light horse not to exceed six privates for each battalion of infantry in each county, to be taken distributively out of each, in case volunteers offer; otherwise, at large throughout the county. And the light horse shall be officered as light horse usually are, and shall be subject to appear upon muster days, and shall turn out in classes as other militia; and in case any person who shall be admitted into the said light horse shall fail of providing himself with a suitable horse, weapons and furniture, such person shall be liable to be called out and serve in the foot militia.

[Section IX.] (Section XIII, P. L.) And be it further enacted by the authority aforesaid, That the troop of light horse in the city of Philadelphia shall be limited to the number of fifty, exclusive of officers, the vacancies thereof to be filled in the manner heretofore practiced; and the said troops shall be liable to appear on muster days, and to be called out into service as other militia, and the light horse of this state, when in actual service, shall be subject to the same rules and regulations as the foot militia and to like fines and penalties for neglect of meeting on muster days or turning out on their tour when thereunto called, such fines and penalties to be appropriated as the fines and penalties for like offenses in other cases.

[Section X.] (Section XIV, P. L.) And be it further enacted by the authority aforesaid, That if any light horseman shall be elected or appointed a commissioned officer in any battalion

1780]   *The Statutes at Large of Pennsylvania.*   149

of infantry of his proper city or county, and on notice given him in writing by the lieutenant shall accept thereof, his place in the said light horse shall be vacated and any light horseman who shall be absent more than four months from his city or county shall vacate his place in the troop to which he belonged.

[Section XI.] (Section XV, P. L.) And be it further enacted by the authority aforesaid, That the lieutenant or sub-lieutenant shall appraise the horse of each person serving as a light horseman, immediately before every time of going into actual service, and enter the same in a book, and in case such horse shall be killed or die in actual service or be taken by the enemy, otherwise than by neglect he shall be paid the value of such appraisement by an order to be drawn by the lieutenant or any two sub-lieutenants on the militia fund in the hands of the treasurer for that purpose.

[Section XII.] (Section XVI, P. L.) And be it further enacted by the authority aforesaid, That the said lieutenants shall give public notice by advertisements at ten or more of the most public places in the said districts respectively, of the said divisions being made, and appointing a certain day for each district, not less that [sic] [than] ten days after the said notice, and requiring the male white inhabitants between the ages aforesaid residing in the said divisions respectively to meet at a certain place as near the centre of the said division as may be, and then and there, between the hours of ten in the morning and six in the afternoon of the said day, to elect, by ballot, two field officers, That is to say, one lieutenant, colonel and one major, and the inhabitants of the said sub-divisions respectively shall elect by ballot, as aforesaid, on the same or some other day as soon as convenient, one captain, one lieutenant and one ensign, previous to which said election the said inhabitants shall elect two freeholders to preside as judges thereof, and all and each of these officers respectively shall be such persons as have taken the oath of allegiance and abjuration agreeable to the laws of this state; and each captain shall appoint a suitable person for clerk in his company; and the said lieutenant or sub-lieutenant shall attend and superintend each and every of the said battalion elections, and shall cause the lieutenant-colonels so elected in the city and counties respectively to meet together as soon as may be, and cast lots for rank of the battalions and the rank of the officers in each battalion shall be determined by the lot drawn by their respective lieutenant-colonels, and the captains so elected in the sub-divisions shall meet and cast lots for their rank in the battalion to which they belong, and the rank of the sub-altern officers in each company shall be determined by the lot drawn by their respective captains. And the said lieutenants shall, within ten days, or as soon as may be, having regard to their local situation, transmit proper certificates to the president of the supreme executive council of the names of the persons so as aforesaid elected, and their rank, both of battalion and companies in the several battalions, in order that commissions may be forthwith granted to them agreeable to the said certificates, and elections for officers in the light horse shall be made in like manner as elections for officers in the infantry.

[Section XIII.] (Section XVII, P. L.) And be it further enacted by the authority aforesaid, That if any battalion, troop or company shall neglect or refuse to elect their officers as aforesaid, then, in such case, it shall and may be lawful for the lieutenant, with the advice and consent of two or more of the sub-lieutenants of the city of Philadelphia, and of such county where such neglect or refusal shall be, to nominate one reputable person to the supreme executive council in the room of each officer so neglected to be chosen, and the said council, approving thereof, shall commission the said person, which shall be as effectual to all intents and purposes as if the said officers had been elected as before directed, and the said lieutenant shall, as soon as may be, acquaint the parties so neglecting or refusing with the appointments so as aforesaid made. And the said several and respective officers elected or appointed as aforesaid shall serve respectively as officers of the militia for the space of three years, at the end of which time the lieutenant of the city and counties respectively, in the manner hereinbefore directed, shall cause a new election to be held in the said city and counties respectively, but nothing herein contained shall be construed to render any of the former officers incapable of being re-elected.

[Section XIV.] (Section XVIII, P. L.) And be it further enacted by the authority aforesaid, That the commissioned officers of each company shall appoint three sergeants, three corporals, one drummer and fifer for their respective companies, and all persons who have heretofore been officers in the militia under the late law, if not re-elected, shall deliver up their arms, accoutrements, drums, fifes and colors if paid for by the public, to the lieutenant or sub-lieutenant of the city or county aforesaid; and the lieutenant of the city of Philadelphia and the lieutenant of the counties respectively are hereby authorized to purchase such drums, fifes and colors as may be afterwards wanted to supply the companies in the city and counties respectively.

[Section XV.] (Section XIX, P. L.) And be it further enacted by the authority aforesaid, That the field officers of each battalion in this state shall constitute and appoint, in their respective battalion, one chaplain, one quartermaster, one surgeon, one adjutant, one quartermaster sergeant, one sergeant major, one drum and fife major; and the lieutenants and sub-lieutenants of the city and counties respectively shall, at their discretion, furnish and procure proper carriages for the battalion or drafts of the militia when it shall be necessary.

[Section XVI.] (Section XX, P. L.) And be it further enacted by the authority aforesaid, That the lieutenant or sub-lieutenants of the city and counties respectively shall pay such wages as shall be necessary to one adjutant, one quartermaster sergeant and one drummer and fifer for every day that the service may require them, out of the moneys arising from fines, on the said adjutant, quartermaster sergeant, drummer and fifer producing a certificate of the service so performed from the commanding officer of the said battalion or company.

(Section XXI, P. L.) And whereas the sums allowed by the late militia law for a drummer and fifer have been insufficient and many officers have been obliged to pay considerably more:

[Section XVII.] (Section XXII, P. L.) Be it therefore enacted by the authority aforesaid, That the lieutenants shall and hereby are required to pay unto such captains or commanding officers of companies such reasonable sums as they have expended for drummers and fifers on their producing an account of such costs properly certified.

[Section XVIII.] (Section XXIII, P. L.) And be it further enacted by the authority aforesaid, That the commissioned officers of each company of militia shall nominate and appoint one discreet person who shall be called the almoner, residing in the district or sub-division out of which their company is formed, provided such almoner is above the age of fifty-three years, to take proper care of the families of such poor militiamen, within their respective districts, as are in actual service in their own turn and to grant them such support as their necessities may require, provided such support do not exceed half the price of daily labor as the same shall be ascertained as hereinafter is directed, and the said officers of the company, or any two of them, shall make out a certificate of their nomination and appointment, directed to the lieutenant of the city or lieutenant or sub-lieutenants of the county to which the company belongeth; which certificates shall enable the said almoner thereby appointed to draw from time to time on the said lieutenant or sub-lieutenant for such sum or sums of money as shall be necessary for the purpose aforesaid, and he shall render an account of the moneys by him drawn to the said lieutenants.

[Section XIX.] (Section XXIV, P. L.) And be it further enacted by the authority aforesaid, That every sub-lieutenant of the said city and several counties shall, once in every three months, render an account to his proper lieutenant of all moneys received by him and of his expenditures by virtue of this act, and settle and pay to him the balance of the same, and the lieutenant of the said city and each county respectively shall make out complete accounts of all the moneys received by him and of his expenditures and return the same to the supreme executive council once in every six months, and each lieutenant and sub-lieutenant is hereby empowered to employ one clerk the better to complete the same, and on failure of accounting as aforesaid each lieutenant and sub-lieutenant shall forfeit and pay for every such neglect the sum of ten thousand pounds, to be applied as other fines are directed to be applied by this act.

[Section XX.] (Section XXV, P. L.) And be it further enacted by the authority aforesaid, That the precedence of the officers of the city of Philadelphia and of the several counties in this commonwealth shall be determined as follows, That is to say, when the commissions are of equal rank and date the officers of the city of Philadelphia and districts annexed shall take rank or precedence of all other officers of equal rank in this state and next to them the officers of the county of Philadelphia and so on, according to the seniority of the counties respectively.

[Section XXI.] (Section XXVI, P. L.) And be it further enacted by the authority aforesaid, That the whole of the militia so enrolled as aforesaid shall be subject to be exercised in companies under their respective officers as followeth, That is to say, in the city of Philadelphia and districts annexed in companies on the two last Mondays in the month of April and in battalion on the two first Mondays in the month of May; and the first battalion shall muster in battalion on the third Monday in May, the second battalion on the Tuesday following, the third battalion on the Wednesday, and so on till the whole number of battalions shall have mustered according to their numerical rank on any or every day of the week (Saturday and Sunday excepted) until the whole number of battalions shall have mustered in the aforesaid manner; and on the day following, should it not happen to be Saturday or Sunday, the whole number of battalions belonging to the city of Philadelphia and districts annexed shall meet in brigade and the militia of the city of Philadelphia and districts annexed shall meet to exercise in companies the two last Mondays in the month of August and in battalion on the two first Mondays in the month of September, and the first battalion on the second Monday in the month of October, the second battalion on the Tuesday following, and the third battalion on the Wednesday and so on until the whole number of battalions according to their rank have mustered, except as before excepted. And then, on the day following (with the foregoing exceptions) the whole battalions shall meet in brigade. And in each and every county in the following manner, That is to say, in companies the two last Mondays in the month of April, and the two first Mondays in the month of May, and shall begin their mustering in battalion in the following manner to wit, the first battalion shall meet in battalion on the third Monday of the said month, the second battalion on the Tuesday following, the third battalion on the Wednesday, and so on according to the rank of battalions in the aforesaid manner mustering each day in the week (Saturday and Sunday excepted) and until the whole number of battalions belonging to each county shall have mustered in this manner; and in companies the two first Mondays in the month of October, and the two first Mondays in the month of November; and the first battalion in battalion on the third Monday in the month of November, the second battalion on the Tuesday following, the third battalion on the Wednesday and in this manner until the whole number of battalions belonging to each county according to their ranks severally shall have mustered on any day it may happen (except on a Saturday or Sunday as before excepted). And on each of the said days every militiaman so enrolled shall duly attend with his arms and accoutrements in good order; and a sergeant, or the clerk of each company, shall, at the end of one hour after the time appointed for the meeting of the company or battalion, call over the muster roll of the company, noting those who are absent and on that day shall make return in writing to the captain or commanding officer then present of such absentees, and all persons so absent at the time of calling over the roll or who shall depart from the parade before duly discharged shall be liable to the fines hereafter mentioned.

[Section XXII.] (Section XXVII, P. L.) And be it further enacted by the authority aforesaid, That if any commissioned officer shall neglect or refuse to attend on any of the days appointed for exercise in companies as aforesaid (unless prevented by sickness or some other unavoidable accident) such commissioned officer shall forfeit and pay the price of three days' labor; and any non-commissioned officer or private and all enrolled persons so refusing or neglecting (except as before excepted) shall forfeit and pay the price of one and a half days' labor, and on a brigade or battalion day a field officer shall forfeit and pay the price of six days' labor, and a commissioned officer under that rank the price of four days' labor, and a non-commissioned officer or private and all enrolled persons refusing to meet and exercise the price of two days' labor (excepting as before excepted), the said prices to be ascertained as hereafter directed. The names and surnames of all which person so incurring the said fines and penalties (except such as may have paid the same into the hands of the captain or commanding officer of the company) shall be duly returned by the captain or commanding officer of each company under his hand, together with such fines as he has received to the lieutenant-colonels or commanding officers of the battalions respectively on each field day, which said lieutenant-colonel or commanding officer of battalion shall, on receipt of such fines and returns, forthwith transmit the same to the lieutenant or one of the sub-lieutenants of the county; and also a duplicate thereof to the treasurer of the county, and the said lieutenant or sub-lieutenant shall immediately after the said returns are respectively made to him cause the same to be recovered by issuing his warrant to the sheriff, constable or other fit person that he can procure to levy the aforesaid fines by distress and sale of the offender's goods and chattels, together with five per centum for collecting where no distress is necessary to be made, and seven and a half per centum in case of distress and sale, in full for his trouble for levying, selling and collecting (unless the offender show cause of absence by sickness or otherwise, and can produce a certificate from the captain or commanding officer of the company, who may give such certificate if he verily believes the offender ought to be excused from paying the said fines), but if no such goods and chattels can be found, then to seize and take the body of such offender, and commit him to the common gaol or some other place of close confinement for the space of ten days for each fine, unless he sooner pay the same. And the lieutenant shall twice in each year transmit the said fines, when collected, into the hands of the county treasurer, who shall pay the same into the hands of the state treasurer, to be kept as a fund, subject to such drafts as may be made upon him from time to time by the lieutenant or at least two sub-lieutenants for the use of the militia of that county. But if the funds of any county, by the generality of their turning out, should be insufficient to answer the drafts for the support of persons serving or suffering in the militia, in that case the executive council shall be empowered to draw on the funds of such other counties whose surplus may be most enabled to bear it.

[Section XXIII.] (Section XXVIII, P. L.) And be it further enacted by the authority aforesaid, That the treasurer of each county and the state treasurer shall keep all the moneys arising from fines by the militia law separate from all other moneys, and keep separate books to enter the same for the purposes hereinafter mentioned.

[Section XXIV.] (Section XXIX, P. L.) And be it enacted by the authority aforesaid, That whenever it may be necessary to call into actual service any part of the militia, in case of a rebellion or invasion of this or any of the adjoining states, then it shall and may be lawful for the president or vice-president in council to order into actual service such part of the militia, by classes, of the city of Philadelphia or any of the county or counties as the exigency may require: Provided, That the part so called doth not exceed four classes of the militia of the county or counties so called out: And provided also, That such counties shall not be again called upon to furnish any more militia until an equal number of classes of the militia of the other counties respectively be first called, unless the danger of an invasion from Indians or others should make it necessary to keep in reserve the militia of such county or counties for their own immediate defense.

(Section XXX, P. L.) And to the end that the militia, when called by classes, shall be properly officered, the following order is hereby directed and enjoined, That is to say:

For the first draft, the captain of the first company, the lieutenant of the second and the ensign of the fourth.

Second draft, the captain of the second company, the lieutenant of the first and the ensign of the third.

Third draft, the captain of the third company, the lieutenant of the fourth and the ensign of the second.

Fourth draft, the fourth captain, the lieutenant of the third company and the ensign of the first.

Fifth draft, the fifth captain, the lieutenant of the sixth company and the ensign of the eighth.

Sixth draft, the sixth captain, the lieutenant of the fifth company and the ensign of the seventh.

Seventh draft, the captain of the seventh company, the lieutenant of the eighth and the ensign of the sixth.

Eighth draft, the captain of the eighth company, the lieutenant of the seventh and the ensign of the fifth.

Non-commissioned officers to take tour of duty with the commissioned officers.

And the field officers of battalions in the city of Philadelphia and in each county of this state shall be divided in like manner, and each class to be considered as a detachment from different corps liable to serve two months and no longer, and to be relieved by the class next in numerical order, the relief to arrive at least two days before the expiration of the term of the class to be relieved, but nothing herein contained shall prevent the supreme executive council from employing or calling out part of any class or any company or companies, battalion or battalions without respect to this rule whenever the exigency is too sudden to allow the assembling of the scattered militia which compose the particular classes and the service of the persons so called out, shall be accounted as part of their tour of duty and the militia in actual service shall receive the same pay and rations as continental troops, their pay to commence two days before marching, and receive pay and rations at the rate of fifteen miles per day on their return home.

(Section XXXI, P. L.) And whereas the militia, when called into actual service, are not entitled to any bounty, such as clothing at the public expense and, therefore, their reward is not equal to that of the regular troops:

[Section XXV.] (Section XXXII, P. L.) Be it therefore enacted by the authority aforesaid, That when the militia, or any detachment thereof, are called out on duty each non-commissioned officer and private shall receive such a sum as, including the continental pay, will amount to the price of common labor for the time of service given, to be drawn from the treasury by the paymasters of the militia from time to time appointed; and the officers, whose duty it may be are hereby required to make out separate pay rolls of the said bounty and that all commissioned officers shall, over and above the pay established from time [to time] by the honorable Congress, receive the same bounty which a private shall receive.

[Section XXVI.] (Section XXXIII, P. L.) And be it further enacted by the authority aforesaid, That at each quarter sessions of the peace of the city and in the several counties throughout the state the price of common labor then current in the said city and counties respectively shall be inquired into and ascertained, and the justices, or a majority of them, attending the said courts are hereby required to fix and determine what is the average price of common labor at that time by the day, which price so determined by the said justices shall be considered as a rate by which all fines shall be determined for neglects or omissions of militia duty during and from that time to the end of the next quarter sessions of the peace, and the said justices are hereby required to make out a certificate of the price so determined for the lieutenants of the said city and counties respectively under their hands and seals.

[Section XXVII.] (Section XXXIV, P. L.) And be it further enacted by the authority aforesaid, That when any class or classes of the militia shall be called to perform any tour of duty, the lieutenant or sub-lieutenants shall cause each and every person so called to be notified of such call at least three days before the time of assembling the said militia by a written or printed notice being delivered to him personally or left at his house or usual place of abode by some officer or other fit person employed for that purpose by the commanding officer of said company, and any person refusing or neglecting to perform such tour of duty shall pay, for each and every day he shall so neglect or refuse the price of one day's labor, and in case he shall be possessed of such estate as is hereinafter mentioned, shall pay such additional sum as by this act is further directed.

[Section XXVIII.] (Section XXXV, P. L.) And be it further enacted by the authority aforesaid, That the master or mistress of any apprentice and the father or mother of any minor liable to serve in the militia who shall refuse or neglect to attend as aforesaid, such minor being in the service of his father or mother, master or mistress, they shall be respectively accountable for the fine or fines so incurred by such minor or apprentice.

[Section XXIX.] (Section XXXVI, P. L.) And be it further enacted by the authority aforesaid, That no mariner or seaman shall be subject to the fines and penalties of this act for not performing militia duties if such mariner or seaman is in actual employ by being shipped for a voyage or absent at sea.

[Section XXX.] (Section XXXVII, P. L.) And be it further enacted by the authority aforesaid, That the militia of this state whilst in the actual service of the United States shall be subject to the same rules and regulations as the federal army: Provided, That upon any transgression or offense of a militiaman, whether officer or private, against the rules and regulations of the federal army the cause shall be tried and determined by a court martial of the militia of this state, and that it shall be in the power of the president of the supreme executive council, or in case of his absence, of the commanding officer of the militia to mitigate, suspend or pardon any punishment to which any militiaman may be sentenced by a general court-martial.

[Section XXXI.] (Section XXXVIII, P. L.) And be it further enacted by the authority aforesaid, That if any delinquent shall neglect or refuse to pay the fine for an omission of performing his tour of militia duty, within five days after the appeal [hereinafter mentioned] it shall and may be lawful for the lieutenant or any sub-lieutenant to issue his warrant to the sheriff, or any constable or other fit person that he can procure, to levy the said fine, by distress and sale of the offender's goods and chattels, lands and tenements, together with seven and a half per centum and the charges of keeping the distress, in full for his trouble for levying, selling and collectting; which said distress and sale shall be made according to the directions of the law for levying and selling goods and chattels distrained for rent; but if no such goods and chattels, lands and tenements can be found, then to seize and take the body of such offender and commit him to the common gaol or some other place of close confinement for the space of four months, unless he sooner pays the said fine, and no process shall issue to stay the execution of such warrant unless in case of the seizure of real estates.

(Section XXXIX, P. L.) Provided always, That if any person shall think himself aggrieved in the seizure of his lands and tenements he may enter an appeal before the justices to the next court of common pleas for said county, and on the party giving sufficient security within six days next after any lands and tenements shall be seized or distrained as aforesaid to prosecute such appeal with effect, the justices shall receive the same and stay further process, and the said justices shall return every such appeal on the first day of the next term, and the court shall direct a trial by a jury of the country as in cases of debt, whose verdict shall be final and conclusive; and, except in extraordinary cases, of which the court shall judge, all such appeals shall be tried at the term to which such returns shall be made.

(Section XL, P. L.) Provided also, That in case real estate be sold as aforesaid, such sale shall be made by the sheriff of the county, who shall make a sufficient deed for the same and put the purchaser into possession thereof.

[Section XXXII.] (Section XLI, P. L.) And be it further enacted by the authority aforesaid, That no militiaman shall withdraw himself from the company to which he belongs under the penalty of the value of twenty days' labor, to be sued for and recovered by the commanding officer of the company from which he shall so withdraw himself before any justice of the peace by action of debt: Provided nevertheless, That persons removing out of the bounds of one battalion or company to another, shall apply to the commanding officer of the company to which he did belong who shall give him a discharge, certifying the class to which he belongs, and whether he hath served his tour of duty or not, which certificate the said militiaman shall produce to the captain or commanding officer of the company in whose bounds he next settles within ten days after his settlement under penalty of the value of thirty days' labor to be recovered and applied as aforesaid; and the captain or commanding officer is hereby required to enroll him in the class specified in the said certificate.

[Section XXXIII.] (Section XLII, P. L.) And be it enacted by the authority aforesaid, That in all cases of doubt respecting the age of any person enrolled or intended to be enrolled in the militia, the party questioned shall prove his age to the satisfaction of the officers of the company within the bounds of which he may reside, or a majority of them.

(Section XLIII, P. L.) And whereas it is just and reasonable that those who have considerable property should pay for the protection of that property when they do not give their service in facing danger in the field or bearing any of the necessary fatigues attending a military life; and to compel all persons to give their personal service or some equivalent therefore in some proportion to such property:

[Section XXXIV.] (Section XLIV, P. L.) Be it therefore enacted by the authority aforesaid, That all and every person and persons who are in and by this act required to perform a tour of duty, and have an estate shall pay for neglecting to perform the said tour of duty, in addition to the fine of the price of one day's labor as aforesaid the sum of fifteen shillings in every hundred pounds on all his rateable property and occupation in the manner directed to be ascertained by an act of assembly passed the third day of April, one thousand seven hundred and seventy-nine, entitled "An act to raise the supplies for the year one thousand seven hundred and seventy-nine,"[1] and as may be directed to be taken by every yearly or other state tax in future.

(Section XLV, P. L.) And in order that the lieutenant of each county may have the amount of the whole estate of each person

---

[1] Chapter 840.

residing in said county, although the said estate or estates may be situate in some other county or counties, that he, the said lieutenant, may be able, where the case requires it, to levy for the interest on the whole wheresoever lying within this state:

[Section XXXV.] (Section XLVI, P. L.) Be it further enacted by the authority aforesaid, That the assessors of each and every county finding any kind of taxable estate within said county belonging to persons resident in some other county within the state shall and are hereby required to make out a list of the amount of the valuation of such estate or estates, placing the same opposite the name of such proprietor, and once in every year send such lists to the lieutenant of the county where the owner of such estate may reside.

[Section XXXVI.] (Section XLVII, P. L.) And be it further enacted by the authority aforesaid, That the lieutenant of the city of Philadelphia and of the several counties of this state shall have and receive the value of one and an half bushels of wheat per day, and the sub-lieutenants for the said city and counties shall have and receive the value of one and a quarter bushels of wheat per day each, as the same shall be declared from time to time by the general assembly, for their trouble, and for every day in which they shall be employed in doing and performing the respective duties required by this act, which said sum or sums shall be respectively paid unto them out of the fines incurred by this act.

[Section XXXVII.] (Section XLVIII, P. L.) And be it further enacted by the authority aforesaid, That it shall and may be lawful for any person called to do a tour of militia duty to find a sufficient substitute, having been previously classed at least six months in the company or battalion to which the person belongs who hires such substitute: Provided always, That persons serving by substitute as aforesaid, if said substitute shall be called in his own turn into actual service before the term expires which he was to serve for his employer, that then the person procuring such substitute shall march in the said substitute's turn or be liable to pay his fine for neglect, which fine is to be recovered as other fines for neglect of serving are by this act directed to be recovered and that sons who are not subject to the militia law may be admitted as substitutes for their fathers, and that each substitute be approved of by the lieutenant or sub-lieutenant.

[Section XXXVIII.] (Section XLIX, P. L.) And be it further enacted by the authority aforesaid, That the lieutenant or one of the sub-lieutenants shall, within ten and not less than five days after the marching of any part of the militia, call to his assistance two freeholders, one of whom shall be a justice of the peace, to sit at the most convenient place for the inhabitants of their respective districts (notice having been given of such place in the written or printed summons of every militiaman), and shall there hear and determine all appeals that may be made by the persons thinking themselves aggrieved by anything done in pursuance of this act, and they are hereby authorized and required to grant such relief to such appellant as to them shall appear just and reasonable in consideration of such inability of body as in the opinion of the court renders him incapable of performing military duty, and each of the said freeholders, before they shall sit on the said appeal, shall take the following oath or affirmation, viz.: "That he will hear and impartially determine on the cases of appeal that may be laid before him agreeable to law and according to the best of his knowledge," which oath or affirmation the said justice, lieutenant or sub-lieutenant is hereby empowered and required to administer, and the said justice and freeholder shall have and receive from the said lieutenant the value of one bushel of wheat each for every day they sit on the said appeals, and the said lieutenant and justice of the peace shall each keep a separate record of the proceedings of such court of appeals.

[Section XXXIX.] (Section L, P. L.) And be it further enacted by the authority aforesaid, That if any person or persons shall knowingly sell, buy, take or exchange, conceal or otherwise receive any arms, accoutrements, colors or drums belonging to this state or the United States on any account or pretense whatsoever, the person so offending, being convicted thereof before one or more justice or justices of the peace of the city or county where such offense shall be committed, shall forfeit and pay for every such offense treble the value of such arms or accoutrements, to be ascertained by the said justice or justices and levied by distress and sale of the offender's goods and chattels by the justice or justices before whom such offender shall be convicted, returning the overplus, if any, on demand, to such offender, and for want of such distress shall commit such offender to the common gaol of the county, there to remain without bail or mainprise for any term not exceeding three months, unless such money shall be sooner paid; and in every case the proof of the property shall be made by the possessor of such arms or accoutrements.

[Section XL.] (Section LI, P. L.) And be it further enacted by the authority aforesaid, That no person, not being a subject of this state or any of the United States, who already has deserted or shall hereafter desert from the enemy in the course of the present war, shall be enrolled in any company of militia of this state during the present contest or be subject to any fine or penalty for not serving as by this act is required of others.

[Section XLI.] (Section LII, P. L.) And be it enacted by the authority aforesaid, That no civil process shall be served on any commissioned, non-commissioned officer or private at any regimental review or training of any company, or while going to or returning from the place of such review or training.

[Section XLII.] (Section LIII, P. L.) And be it enacted by the authority aforesaid, That all moneys passing into the treasury by virtue of the directions of this act shall be appropriated as a fund for the benefit and relief of such officers and privates of the militia of this state as are or shall be wounded and disabled in service, and of the widows and children of such as have or shall fall in battle or otherwise loose their lives in the service of the state, and shall not be considered as a revenue for any other purpose than that of supporting the necessary officers for carrying this law into effect, equipping and furnishing the militia with every necessary apparatus for the defense and security of the state, the surplus, if any, to be appropriated in such manner and to such uses as the assembly shall from time to time direct and appoint.

[Section XLIII.] (Section LIV, P. L.) And be it further enacted by the authority aforesaid, That if any commissioned officer, non-commissioned officer or private militiaman of this state who has lost or may hereafter lose a limb in any engagement in the service of the state, or in the service of the United States of America, or be so disabled as to render him incapable of getting a livelihood, he shall receive during life or the continuance of such disability a pension adequate to the necessity of such disabled officer or private militiaman by the judgment of the orphans' court of the county where such disabled officer or private militiaman shall dwell or reside. And every officer or private disabled as aforesaid shall, before he be legally entitled to the pension above mentioned, produce a certificate, upon oath, from the commanding officer who was in the same engagement in which he was wounded, or from the officer next in command, or the surgeon that attended him, and upon such disabled officer, non-commissioned officer or private militiaman's producing such certificate as aforesaid to the orphans' court of the county where such disabled officer, non-commissioned officer or private militiaman shall dwell or reside, the said court is hereby enjoined and required, if they are satisfied of the truth thereof, to give every such officer or private an order on the lieutenant of the said city or county for such sums of money from time to time as to them shall appear just and necessary, provided such sums of money do not exceed the half pay and rations of such officer or private. And the said lieutenant is hereby enjoined and required to accept and pay the said order to such officer or private. And the said lieutenant shall draw on the state treasurer as often as he shall have occasion for such sum or sums of money as he shall make appear to the president and council to be necessary for carrying this proviso into execution.

[Section XLIV.] (Section LV, P. L.) And be it enacted by the authority aforesaid, That if any officer, non-commissioned officer or private militiaman residing in this state, having a family, has been killed, shall be killed or shall die of his wounds received in the service of this or the United States, a certificate from the commanding or other officer next in rank who was in the same engagement in which he was killed or wounded and died of his wounds, being produced to the orphans' court, and also a certificate from the overseers of the poor and two other reputable freeholders of the township, borough, ward or district where the family of such deceased officer or private militiaman shall dwell or reside at that time, setting forth the particular circumstances of such family, the age or ages of the child or children and the necessity of granting them some support, the said orphans' court, when possessed of the certificates aforesaid, is hereby authorized to give orders upon the lieutenant of the city or county for such sum of money as they may think just and necessary for the support of such family from time to time.

(Section LVI, P. L.) Provided always, That the sum of money aforesaid does not exceed the half pay and rations that such officer, non-commissioned officer or private was entitled to at the time of his death.

[Section XLV.] (Section LVII, P. L.) And be it further enacted by the authority aforesaid, That if any field or other commissioned officer, at any regimental review or on any other occasion when the battalion or company to which he may belong, or in which he holds a command is paraded in arms, shall appear, misbehave or demean himself in an unofficerlike manner, he shall, for such offense, be cashiered or punished by fine at he discretion of a general court martial as the case may require in any sum not exceeding the price of six days' labor; and if any non-commissioned officer or private shall, on any occasion of parading the company to which he belongs, appear with his arms and accoutrements in an unfit condition, or be found drunk or shall disobey orders or use any reproachful or abusive language to his officers, or any of them, or shall quarrel himself or promote any quarrel among his fellow soldiers he shall be disarmed and put under guard by order of the commanding officer present until the company is dismissed, and shall be fined in any sum not exceeding the price of ten days' labor nor less than one day's labor.

[Section XLVI.] (Section LVIII, P. L.) And be it further enacted by the authority aforesaid, That if the lieutenant-colonel or commanding officer of any battalion shall neglect or refuse to give orders for assembling his battalion at the times appointed by this law or at the direction of the lieutenant or sub-lieutenant of the city or any county when the said lieutenant or sub-lieutenant is thereto commanded by the president or vice-president in council, or in case of an invasion of the city or county to which such battalion belongs, he shall be cashiered and punished by fine at the discretion of a general court-maritial; and if a commissioned officer of any company shall, on any occasion neglect or refuse to give orders for assembling the company to which he belongs, or any part thereof, at the direction of the lieutenant-colonel or commanding officer of the battalion to which such company belongs he shall be cashiered and punished by fine at the discretion of a regimental court-martial and a non-commissioned officer offending in such case shall be fined in any sum not exceeding the price of ten days' labor.

[Section XLVII.] (Section LIX, P. L.) And be it further enacted by the authority aforesaid, That if any captain or commanding officer of a company shall refuse or neglect to make out a list of the persons noticed to perform any tour of duty and send or convey the same to the lieutenant-colonel or commanding officer of the battalion to which such company may belong for such neglect or refusal he shall be cashiered or fined at the discretion of a regimental court-martial.

[Section XLVIII.] (Section LX, P. L.) And be it further enacted by the authority aforesaid, That the following rules and regulations shall be those by which the militia shall be governed.

1st. Every general court-martial shall consist of thirteen members, all of whom shall be commissioned officers and of such rank as the case may require, and these thirteen shall choose a president out of their number, who shall be a field officer.

2d. Every regimental court-martial shall be composed of five members, all commissioned officers, who are to choose one of their members as president not under the rank of a captain.

3d. In any court-martial not less than two-thirds of the members must agree in every sentence for inflicting any punishment, otherwise the person charged shall be acquitted.

4th. The president of each and every court-martial, whether general or regimental, shall require all witnesses in order to the trial of offenders to declare on oath or affirmation that the evidence they shall give is the truth, the whole truth and nothing but the truth, and the members of all such courts shall take an oath or affirmation, which the president is required to administer to the other members and the next in rank is required to administer to him that they will give judgment with impartiality.

5th. All members of any militia called as witnesses in any case before a court-martial who shall refuse to attend and give evidence shall be censured or fined at the discretion of the court.

6th. No officer or private man being charged with transgressing these rules shall be suffered to do duty in the battalion, company or troop to which he belongs until he has had his trial by a court-martial, and every person so charged shall be tried as soon as a court-martial can be conveniently assembled.

7th. If any officer or private man shall think himself injured by his lieutenant-colonel or the commanding officer of the battalion and shall, upon due application made to him, be refused redress, he may complain to the lieutenant of the county, who shall summon a general court-martial that justice may [be] done.

8th. If an inferior officer or private man shall think himself injured by his captain or other superior officer in the battalion, troop or company to which he belongs, he may complain to the commanding officer of the battalion who shall summon a regimental court-martial for the doing justice according to the nature of the case.

9th. No penalty shall be inflicted at the discretion of the court-martial other than degrading, cashiering or fining.

10th. The commanding officer of the militia for the time being shall have full power of pardoning or mitigating any censures or penalties ordered to be inflicted on any private or non-commissioned officer for the breach of any of these articles by a general court-martial, and every offender convicted as aforesaid by any regimental court-martial, may be pardoned, or have the penalty mitigated by the lieutenant-colonel or commanding officer of the battalion, excepting only where such censures or penalties are directed as satisfaction for injuries received by one officer or private man from another, but in case of officers such sentence to be approved by the commander-in-chief or the nearest general officer of the militia, who are respectively empowered to pardon or mitigate such sentence or disapprove the same.

11th. The militia, on the days of exercise, may be detained under arms on duty in the field any time not exceeding six hours, provided they are not kept above three hours under arms at any one time without allowing them a proper time to refresh themselves.

12th. No company or battalion shall meet at a tavern on any of the days of exercise, nor shall march to any tavern before they are discharged; and any person who shall bring any kind of spiritous liquor to such place of training shall forfeit such liquors so brought for the use of the poor belonging to the township where such offender lives.

13th. All fines that shall be incurred by any breach of these rules shall be paid into the hands of the clerk of the company to which the offenders belong, but if a field officer, to the clerk of that company whose captain has the first rank in the battalion, within three weeks after they become due; but in case of neglect or refusal to pay any of the said fines, then in such case, upon application made by the clerk to whom such fine or fines ought to have been paid, it shall and may be lawful for any one justice of the peace of the county, if the fine does not exceed fifty pounds, or two justices if above that sum, by warrant under his or their hands and seals to levy such fine or fines respectively on the offender's goods and chattels, and otherwise proceed in recovering the same as is by law directed, and when recovered the said justice or justices are required to pay such fines into the hands of the clerk who applied for recovery and shall be applied as other fines before directed.

[Section XLIX.] (Section LXI, P. L.) And be it further enacted by the authority aforesaid, That in any case wherein any person is by this act called to do or perform anything in execution thereof, or otherwise, and no special recompense is herein provided for such service, such person shall be satisfied for the same at the discretion of the lieutenant, taking to his assistance two sub-lieutenants of the city or county respectively.

[Section L.] (Section LXII, P. L.) And be it further enacted by the authority aforesaid, That in any case wherein the person who shall be authorized to collect any fine due by virtue of this act shall need assistance in levying the same, such collector, on application to any captain or inferior officer of the militia of the place where such fine shall be due, shall be assisted therein by a sufficient party of militia of the neighborhood ordered on such duty by such captain or other officer, and if such captain or other officer or any of the party by such captain or other officer ordered on such duty refuse or neglect to perform the said duty, such captain or other officer shall forfeit and pay the sum of fifty pounds, and if any non-commissioned officer or private be delinquent therein he shall forfeit and pay the sum of twenty-five pounds, to be recovered with costs of suit as demands for fifty pounds are by law recoverable, to be applied as other fines levied by virtue of this act.

[Section LI.] (Section LXIII, P. L.) And be it further enacted by the authority aforesaid, That in case any militiaman shall desert when he is out on a tour of duty the commanding officer of the battalion or detachment from which he deserts shall, as soon as possible, give notice thereof to the lieutenant of the city or county or sub-lieutenant of the district from which he came who, if he does not see proper to send him back shall subject him to the payment of such fine as he would have paid if he had not gone out on such tour.

[Section LII.] (Section LXIV, P. L.) And be it further enacted by the authority aforesaid, That if any suit or suits shall be brought or commenced against any person or persons for anything done in pursuance of this act, the action shall be laid in the county where the causes of such action did arise and not elsewhere, and the defendant or defendants in such action or actions to be brought may plead the general issue, and give this act and the special matter in evidence; and if the jury shall find for the defendants in such action or actions, or if the plaintiff or plaintiffs shall be non-suited or discontinue his or their action or actions after the defendant or defendants shall have appeared, or if upon demurrer judgment shall be given against the plaintiff or plaintiffs the defendant or defendants shall have treble costs and have the like remedy for the same as any defendant or defendants had or have in other cases to recover costs by law.

[Section LIII.] (Section LXV, P. L.) And be it further enacted by the authority aforesaid, That all and every the fines and forfeitures by this act made payable and the mode of recovery not hereinbefore particularly pointed out shall be recovered by the lieutenant of each county and of the city of Philadelphia by summons or warrant and execution from under the hand and seal of a justice of the peace in the neighborhood where the person charged resides, directed to any constable of the city or county, requiring him to levy the same on the goods and chattels of the delinquent, and the same cause to be appraised by two freeholders, and after being publicly advertised seven days make sale thereof, and after payment of the fine or forfeiture to the lieutenant, together with costs and charges, pay the overplus, if any, to the owner, and if goods and chattels sufficient to discharge the same cannot be found, that then the justice granting such precept shall certify the proceedings had thereon to the prothonotary of the county court of common pleas, who is thereupon required to issue a fieri facias directed to the sheriff of said county for levying the fines and forfeitures aforesaid, together with the costs on the lands or tenements of such delinquent.

[Section LIV.] (Section LXVI, P. L.) Provided always, and be it enacted by the authority aforesaid, That if any person or persons shall think him or themselves aggrieved by the judgment of the justice aforesaid in any suit of fifty pounds or upwards, he or they may appeal before the justice aforesaid, and on the party's giving security within six days next after any such judgment to prosecute such appeal in the court of common pleas of the county with effect, the justice shall receive the same and stay further process, and the said justice shall return every such appeal on the first day of the next term, and the court shall direct a trial by jury, as in other cases of debt, whose verdict shall be final and conclusive; and all such appeals shall be tried at the term to which such returns shall be made, any law, custom or usage to the contrary notwithstanding.

[Section LV.] (Section LXVII, P. L.) And be it further enacted and declared, That the act entitled "An act to regulate the militia of the commonwealth of Pennsylvania,"[1] passed on the seventeenth day of March, Anno Domini one thousand seven hundred and seventy-seven; also, the supplement to the said act passed the nineteenth day of June, Anno Domini one thousand seven hundred and seventy-seven;[2] also, a further supplement to the said act passed on the thirtieth day of December, Anno Domini one thousand seven hundred and seventy-three;[3] also, a further supplement to the said act passed on the fifth day of April, Anno Domini one thousand seven hundred and seventy-nine;[4] also, such parts of an act, entitled "An act to empower the supreme executive council and justices of the supreme court to apprehend suspected persons and to increase the fine to which persons are liable for neglecting to do their tour of militia duty,"[5] as relates to the fining the militia for not performing a tour of duty and the pay of the lieutenants are hereby repealed and made void.

[Section LVI.] (Section LXVIII, P. L.) Provided always, That nothing in this act contained shall be deemed to repeal, alter or dispense with the powers, authorities or duties of the present lieutenants and sub-lieutenants of the city and counties aforesaid, or of any other officer or person under the militia laws that have been in force in this state immediately before the passing of this act until their respective offices are supplied and filled by new appointments in virtue of this act which

---

[1] Chapter 750.
[2] Chapter 760.
[3] Chapter 781.
[4] Chapter 843.
[5] Chapter 865.

said present lieutenants and sub-lieutenants or other proper officers are hereby authorized required and enjoined to collect or cause to be collected all [such] fines and forfeitures as have been or shall be incurred during the continuance of their respective commissions and pay in the same agreeable to this law, or the late laws aforesaid on or before the first day of July next. But in case the president or vice-president and council shall approve of the discontinuing to act or resignation of the said present lieutenants and sub-lieutenants or any of them and not otherwise it shall be lawful for such officer and he is hereby required to deliver to his successor in office an account on oath of all the moneys uncollected and outstanding on account of fines and forfeitures aforesaid, who is in such case empowered and required to collect the same.

> Passed March 20, 1780. See the Acts of Assembly passed May 26, 1780, Chapter 908; September 22, 1780, Chapter 916; March 21, 1783, Chapter 1022; September 22, 1783, Chapter 1038; December 9, 1783, Chapter 1061; September 29, 1787, Chapter 1319; March 22, 1788, Chapter 1339; November 19, 1788, Chapter 1383; March 27, 1789; Chapter 1416; March 3, 1790, Chapter 1483; March 27, 1790, Chapter 1493; April 5, 1790, Chapter 1513 (repealed by the Act of Assembly passed) April 11, 1793, Chapter 1696. Recorded L. B. No. 1, p. 374, &c.

CHAPTER CMIII.

AN ACT TO DISCONTINUE A ROAD CALLED PALMER'S LANE IN THE TOWNSHIP OF THE NORTHERN LIBERTIES IN THE COUNTY OF PHILADELPHIA AND NEAR TO THE LOWER FALLS OF SCHUYLKILL.

(Section I, P. L.) Whereas it has been represented to us on the petition of John Redman of the city of Philadelphia, practitioner in physic, and Nathaniel Falconer, of the same place, mariner, that in the year one thousand seven hundred and twenty-three, four, a road was laid out from the market place in Germantown, in the county of Philadelphia, to Robert Roberts' ferry, on the river Schuylkill, which entered the lands then owned by William Palmer, and since by the said John Redman and Nathaniel Falconer, at the northwest end of the same, and from thence running south and by east fifty-two perches, then south twelve degrees west, twelve perches, then south thirty-six degrees west, twenty perches, then south sixty-one degrees west twenty perches, then south thirty-two degrees west, twenty-eight perches, making in the whole one hundred and thirty-two perches in length:

(Section II, P. L.) And whereas another road was laid out in the year one thousand seven hundred and sixty, on the petition of divers inhabitants of Germantown and Blockley township, in the said county of Philadelhia, forty feet wide, extending from the place where the aforesaid road enters the lands then owned by William Palmer and since by John Redman and Nathaniel Falconer aforesaid, running by several courses one hundred and thirty-three perches and an half in length, at which distance it enters the Wissahickon road, leading either to the city of Philadelphia or to the falls of Schuylkill:

(Section III, P. L.) And whereas, it has been further represented to us by the aforesaid John Redman and Nathaniel Falconer that the supervisors of the highways neglect or refuse to keep the first mentioned of the above said two roads in repair, alleging that it is but of little public use, whereby the owners of the lands through which it passes are frequently obliged to repair it at their own expense to prevent their lands being cut and injured by such carriages as may at times pass through the same:

(Section IV, P. L.) And whereas, the unnecessary multiplying of roads not only tends to increase the expenses of the highways, but is likewise a waste of land which might otherwise be employed to the raising of produce:

[Section I.] (Section V, P. L.) Be it therefore enacted and it is hereby enacted by the Representatives of the Freemen of the Commonwealth of Pennsylvania in General Assembly met, and by the authority of the same, That from and after the publication of this act the first mentioned of the two above said roads be discontinued and abolished.

Passed March 20, 1780.

CHAPTER CMIV.

AN ACT TO REPEAL DIVERS ACTS OF ASSEMBLY OF THIS COMMONWEALTH HEREIN AFTER MENTIONED, FOR PREVENTING FORESTALLING AND REGRATING, AND FOR THE ENCOURAGEMENT OF FAIR DEALING; AND AN ACT ENTITLED "AN ACT TO PERMIT THE MAKING OF WHISKEY AND OTHER SPIRITS FROM RYE, BARLEY, OR THE MALT MADE THEREOF, UNDER CERTAIN RESTRICTIONS THEREIN MENTIONED; AND TO PROHIBIT THE DISTILLING ANY WHISKEY OR OTHER SPIRITS FROM ANY OTHER GRAIN, MEAL, MALT OR FLOUR."

(Section I, P. L.) Whereas the operation of an act of assembly of this commonwealth passed on the second day of January, which was in the year of our Lord one thousand seven hundred and seventy-eight, entitled "An act to prevent forestalling and regrating and to encourage fair dealing,"[1] and a supplement and further supplement to the same act, passed on the first day of April and tenth day of September following;[2] and another act of assembly, entitled "An act for the more effectually preventing engrossing and forestalling, for the encouragement of commerce and the fair trader and for other purposes therein mentioned,"[3] passed on the eighth day of October last, and another act of assembly, entitled "An act to permit the making of whiskey and other spirits from rye, barley and the malt made thereof under certain restrictions therein mentioned, and to prohibit the distilling any whiskey or other spirits from any other grain, meal, malt or flour,"[4] passed on the eighth day of October last, have not been found to answer the good purposes for which they were made, and have produced some inconveniences, so that it appears to be of no public advantage that they should continue in force:

[Section I.] (Section II, P. L.) Be it therefore enacted and

---
[1] Chapter 779.
[2] Chapter 797.
[3] Chapter 859.
[4] Chapter 856.

it is hereby enacted by the Representatives of the Freemen of the Commonwealth of Pennsylvania in General Assembly met, and by the authority of the same, That the said-recited acts and every clause, matter and thing therein contained be and the same are hereby repealed and made void.

Passed March 22, 1780.

CHAPTER CMV.

AN ACT FOR PROCURING A SUPPLY OF PROVISIONS AND OTHER NECESSARIES FOR THE USE OF THE ARMY.

(Section I, P. L.) Whereas the honorable the Congress of these United States have resolved that this state be called on to procure, within the present year, the following articles for the use of the army, viz.: Forty thousand barrels of flour, two hundred thousand bushels of Indian corn or other short forage equivalent, one thousand seven hundred tons of hay, fourteen thousand one hundred and eighty-nine bushels of salt and twenty-four thousand four hundred and twenty-three gallons of rum:

In order, therefore, to comply with the said requisition:

[Section I.] (Section II, P. L.) Be it enacted and it is hereby enacted by the Representatives of the Freemen of the Commonwealth of Pennsylvania in General Assembly met, and by the authority of the same, That for the purpose of carrying this act into effect there be appointed one commissioner of purchases in the city of Philadelphia and one in each county of this state by the president or vice-president in council, the persons so appointed to be resident in the city or county for which they are respectively appointed.

[Section II.] (Section III, P. L.) And be it further enacted by the authority aforesaid, That each and every of the said commissioners before they enter upon the execution of their trust shall give such security for the faithful performance thereof as the said council shall think proper and take the following oath or affirmation (which may be administered by any justice of the peace in the city or county for which the said commissioners shall be respectively appointed), to wit: I, A. B., do swear (or affirm) that I will diligently and faithfully, without favor, affection or partiality, execute the duty and trust reposed in me by an act of the general assembly of this commonwealth, entitled "An act for procuring a supply of provisions and other necessaries for the use of the army."

[Section III.] (Section IV, P. L.) And be it further enacted by the authority aforesaid, That the said commissioners shall severally, in the city and each of the counties for which they are respectively appointed, be authorized and required to purchase all the wheat and wheat flour and other articles above enumerated which can be procured within the said city and several counties [respectively] for which they [are] chosen, and not elsewhere, at such price or prices as shall be ascertained and fixed in the manner which is hereinafter directed and appointed. And in case a sufficient quantity of wheat or other articles so required cannot be procured by purchase, that then and in that case any or either of the said commissioners having knowledge or cause to apprehend that any wheat or flour, rye, Indian corn or other necessaries so required are withheld from sale or public market, may and is hereby required to apply to the next justice of the peace and lodge such information with him, who, thereupon, is hereby authorized and required to issue his warrant, under his hand and seal, directed to the constable of the said township or district and two reputable freeholders, who shall, upon the receipt thereof proceed with the said commissioner to where such flour, grain or other stores is supposed to be and there to demand of the owner or other person having care thereof to admit such officer, freeholders and commissioners to view the same, and on his neglect or refusal so to do, it shall and may be lawful for the said constable, freeholders and commissioner, with such assistance as may be necessary, to break open, in the day time, any house, barn, outhouse, mill or storehouse, or other houses where such grain or flour may be suspected to be, and seize and take into their possession all such wheat and wheat flour and other articles as above, whether found in the hands of millers, merchants, traders, farmers or others, leaving to the farmers as much as may be sufficient to support their families until the first day of August next after such seizure, and one-third of what shall be found in their possession over and above the same quantity and to all others sufficient only for the support of their families during the time aforesaid: Provided always, That no person or persons be allowed to retain the said one-third part over and above what is necessary for the support of his or their family unless the same be of his own raising or growth, and in case any debate shall arise as to what ought to be detained by the owner it shall be settled as the price is hereinafter directed to be.

(Section V, P. L.) Provided nevertheless, That if any or either of the said commissioners in pursuance of this act shall seize any wheat or other necessaries required by this act in the hands or possession of any tenant, being bona fide the rent reserved for said land and due in wheat or other grain to the landlord, then and in that case it shall and may be lawful for the said tenant to pay or tender in payment to the said landlord or to his attorney all moneys so received for such wheat or other grain from said commissioner, such payment so made or tendered to be made shall be deemed good and available in law against all further suit or suits or other proceedings of the said landlord for or in recovery of any such rent or any part thereof, any law, custom or usage to the contrary notwithstanding.

[Section IV.] (Section VI, P. L.) And be it further enacted by the authority aforesaid, That the said commissioners and each of them within the city or county for which they are respectively appointed be authorized and required to hire, or, if need be, to seize, any mill or mills for grinding the said wheat and to hire or seize as aforesaid any storehouses for the safe keeping the said wheat and flour, and to hire or, if need be, to impress any horses and carriages, boats and other vessels for transporting the same and to hire persons and procure materials for making sacks, barrels or other proper casks or boxes for the containing or transporting the same; to hire fit persons for threshing out the wheat or other grain above mentioned, if it may be necessary, and in general to do all and everything which may be needful for the procuring, collecting and transporting the said wheat and flour and other above enumerated articles to such place or places as are hereinafter directed, and it shall and may be lawful for the said commissioners to seize and take all wheat, rye and flour that has been bought by quartermasters, commissaries, forage masters or their deputies or persons acting under them, and which is now lying in any mill or storehouse, paying them the money they have advanced thereon or assuming the payment to the persons of whom the said quartermasters or commissaries bought the same, provided they have not paid them, unless the said commissary shall, upon application made to him by the commissioner, render an account of the quantity of wheat, rye, flour or any other grain by him purchased and lying in said storehouse or mills and give sufficient assurance under his hand that the said wheat, rye and flour or other grain shall be in twenty days deposited in a proper magazine for the use of the army.

[Section V.] (Section VII, P. L.) And be it further enacted by the authority aforesaid, That the price of such articles shall be ascertained and fixed by the said commissioner and party or, in case they cannot agree, by and with the assistance of such reputable third person not interested immediately in the price as may be appointed for that purpose by the next justice of the peace, and such price so fixed shall be paid in ready money or lawfully tendered before such wheat or flour or other articles as above so bought or seized shall be removed; and the said commissioners respectively shall take receipts in a proper book for that purpose for all moneys so paid, mentioning the quantity of such article or articles so bought or seized and the price of the same and the name of the person from whom bought or seized in words at length.

[Section VI.] (Section VIII, P. L.) And be it further enacted by the authority aforesaid, That the said wheat and flour and the shorts and bran and other enumerated articles, when collected by the said commissioners, or any of them, shall be transported and delivered by them in such quantities and proportions and at such times and places as by the supreme executive council of this commonwealth shall from time [to time] be ordered and required so that the same may be conveyed and deposited in such place or places within his state as the commander-in-chief shall appoint and direct, and the commissioners shall employ proper wagons and carriages for transporting the said grain or flour, paying the wagoner or owner thereof by the hundred weight or bushel per mile, they finding their own forage or paying the commissioner for any forage he may from time to time supply them with in order to enable them to transport said grain or flour.

[Section VII.] (Section IX, P. L.) And be it further enacted by the authority aforesaid, That each and every of the said commissioners shall cease and desist from purchasing and collecting wheat and flour and other articles by virtue of this act whenever they shall be ordered so to do by the supreme executive council, and the said council shall superintend the said purchase so as from time to time to direct, limit, restrain, dismiss or supercede the said commissioners of purchase, or any of them, as shall in their discretion best promote the public service and that the said commissioners and every of them be enjoined and required to make monthly returns to the said council of their proceedings and of the quantities of wheat and flour and other articles procured by them in pursuance of this act and shall settle their accounts annually and finally with the committee of accounts of the general assembly.

[Section VIII.] (Section X, P. L.) And be it further enacted by the authority aforesaid, That any commissioner as aforesaid who shall, after purchasing the articles, or any of them, directed to be purchased by this act, clandestinely dispose of or sell or barter the same, or any part thereof, or shall deal on his own account, or on the account of any other person in any of the articles which he shall be directed to purchase by virtue of this act, or shall deal in any other article or make any purchase whatever (otherwise than as herein directed) with the money he may be intrusted with by virtue of this act or shall lend out the same, each commissioner so offending shall, on conviction thereof, by proof of one or more witnesses before any court of quarter sessions, forfeit and pay double the value of the article so dealt in or the sum so lent as aforesaid.

[Section IX.] (Section XI, P. L.) And be it further enacted by the authority aforesaid, That the state treasurer, when he issues any of the money emitted by the act of this session for emitting money, to the commissioners agreeable to the orders of the supreme executive council shall number each half sheet on the margin and sign his name in words at length thereto, and each commissioner, at the settlement of his accounts, in case he has not paid the whole away in purchases, shall return the money remaining in his hands in the very identical sheets or half sheets he received under the penalty of forfeiting double the sum so remaining, to be recovered by action of debt.

[Section X.] (Section XII, P. L.) And be it further enacted by the authority aforesaid, That the said commissioners, for their trouble and expense, exclusive of all costs for seizure, threshing, carting, boating, storage and grinding, shall be allowed two shillings for every barrel of flour, for every hundred bushels of short forage, fifteen shillings; for every ton of hay, seven shillings and six pence; for every hundred bushels of salt, fifteen shillings, and five shillings for every hundred gallons of rum or other spirits, and for all moneys expended in the employment of wagons, boats or carriages in transporting the same, two and a half per centum.

[Section XI.] (Section XIII, P. L.) And be it further enacted by the authority aforesaid, That all justices, sheriffs and other civil officers be and they are hereby enjoined and required to aid and assist the said commissioners and every of them to carry this law and the intention thereof into full and speedy effect.

[Section XII.] (Section XIV, P. L.) And be it further enacted by the authority aforesaid, That during the continuance of this act no quartermaster, forage master, commissary or any of their deputies or assistants or other officer on the staff of Congress be suffered or allowed to purchase any wheat or wheat flour or other of the above articles except for their own private consumption within this state, upon pain of forfeiting the value of the wheat or wheat flour or other article so by him or them purchased, and that any or either of them offending herein shall and may be indicted in any court of quarter sessions of the peace in the said city [or] any county of this state, and, being convicted thereof, shall be adjudged to forfeit and pay to the amount of the value of the said article or articles so by him or them purchased, one-half to the use of the informer and the other half to the use of this commonwealth, on the trial of which indictment the said informer shall be received and admitted as a witness.

Passed March 23, 1780. See the note to the Act of Assembly passed January 2, 1778, Chapter 782.

CHAPTER CMVI.

AN ACT FURTHER TO CONTINUE SUCH PARTS OF AN ACT ENTITLED "AN ACT TO EMPOWER THE SUPREME EXECUTIVE COUNCIL AND JUSTICES OF THE SUPREME COURT TO APPREHEND SUSPECTED PERSONS, AND TO INCREASE THE FINES TO WHICH PERSONS ARE LIABLE FOR NEGLECTING TO PERFORM THEIR TOUR OF MILITIA DUTY," AS RELATES TO THE APPREHENDING OF SUSPECTED PERSONS."[1]

(Section I, P. L.) Whereas the act, entitled "An act to empower the supreme executive council and justices of the supreme court to apprehend supected persons, and to increase the fines to which persons are liable for neglecting to perform their tour of militia duty," passed the tenth day of October last, was, by another act passed on the twenty-seventh day of November last, continued for six months beyond the first limitation thereof, and the said extended term will shortly expired; and the powers and authorities by the said act given have been found useful, and it is proper the same be further extended:

[Section I.] (Section II, P. L.) Be it therefore enacted and it is hereby enacted by the Representatives of the Freemen of the Commonwealth of Pennsylvania in General Assembly met, and by the authority of the same, That the said act, as far as

[1] Passed October 10, 1779, Chapter 865.

it relates to the apprehending of suspected persons shall be and the same hereby is continued for six months from and after the twenty-seventh day of April next, unless the war between the United States of America and Great Britain shall sooner cease.

Passed March 24, 1780. See the note to the Act of Assembly passed October 10, 1779, Chapter 865.

CHAPTER CMVII.

AN ACT FOR STRIKING THE SUM OF ONE HUNDRED THOUSAND POUNDS IN BILLS OF CREDIT FOR THE PRESENT SUPPORT OF THE ARMY, AND FOR ESTABLISHING A FUND FOR THE CERTAIN REDEMPTION OF THE SAME AND FOR OTHER PURPOSES THEREIN MENTIONED.

(Section I, P. L.) Whereas every motive and consideration which can interest the citizen and patriot do call upon the representatives of the freemen of this commonwealth to find efficacious and certain means of procuring and providing an immediate supply of provisions and other articles for the support of the army:

(Section II, P. L.) And whereas, as well for this purpose as for supplying the good people of Pennsylvania with a medium of commerce and exchange of commodities of a stable and solid nature from the want of which they already suffer; and if the same be not remedied may soon be involved in great difficulties:

(Section III, P. L.) And whereas, in the embarrassments of trade occasioned by the present war it is not to be expected that sufficient quantities of gold and silver money can be procured or retained in this state for the purposes of private dealing or public purchases, and this commonwealth is possessed of a very considerable real estate which may and part of which ought to be considered and pledged as a fund [of credit], for relieving the public necessities and supplying the treasury at this important crisis:

[Section I.] (Section IV, P. L.) Be it therefore enacted and it is hereby enacted by the Representatives of the Freemen of the Commonwealth of Pennsylvania in General Assembly met, and by the authority of the same, That bills of credit to the value of one hundred thousand pounds shall be prepared and printed on good strong paper, under the care and direction of Michael Shubart, John Biddle, Paul Cox and Isaac Snowden, of the city of Philadelphia, gentlemen, the cost and expense whereof shall be paid by the treasurer of this commonwealth out of any unappropriated moneys in his hands, and the said bills of credit shall be prepared and made in the manner and form following, that is to say:

Pennsylvania.

This bill of ———— shillings, with annual interest at five per centum shall be redeemed first June, one thousand seven hundred and eighty-four in silver dollars at seven shillings and six pence each, by the sale of land according to act of assembly of twenty-fifth of March, one thousand seven hundred and eighty, dated ———————— April, 1780.

And the said bills shall have the state arms as an escutcheon in the margin thereof, with such other devices as the said Michael Shubart, John Biddle, Paul Cox and Isaac Snowden shall think proper in order to prevent counterfeits, and to distinguish their several and respective denominations, each of which bills shall be of the several and respective denominations following, and no other, that is to say:

Eight thousand six hundred and ninety-six of the said bills the sum of five shillings each.

Eight thousand six hundred and ninety-six of the said bills the sum of ten shillings each.

Eight thousand six hundred and ninety-six of the said bills the sum of fifteen shillings each.

Eight thousand six hundred and ninety-six of the said bills the sum of twenty shillings each.

Eight thousand six hundred and ninety-six of the said bills the sum of thirty shillings each.

Eight thousand six hundred and ninety-four of the said bills the sum of forty shillings each.

Eight thousand six hundred and ninety-six of the said bills the sum of fifty shillings each.

Eight thousand six hundred and ninety-six of the said bills the sum of sixty shillings each.

And the said Michael Shubart, John Biddle, Paul Cox and Isaac Snowden shall use their best care, attention and diligence during the printing of the said bills, that the number and amount thereof according to the said several denominations be not exceeded nor any clandestine or fraudulent practices used by the printer, his servants or others.

(Section V, P. L.) And for perfecting the said bills according to the true intent and meaning of this act:

[Section II.] Be it enacted by the authority aforesaid, That the said bills shall be signed by two of the persons hereafter named, that is to say: Daniel Wister, Levi Budd, Philip Boehm, Robert Cather, Jedediah Snowden, William Lawrence Blair, Elias Lewis Treachel, John Miller, Joseph Watkins, John Knox, Nathan Jones and William Thorne, who are hereby nominated and appointed signers thereof, and who shall, before they receive or sign any of them, take an oath or affirmation to the effect following: "That they shall well and truly sign and number all the bills of credit that shall come to their hands for that purpose, according to the directions of this act and the same so signed and numbered will re-deliver or cause to be re-delivered unto the said Michael Shubart, John Biddle, Paul Cox and Isaac Snowden, or any of them, pursuant to the directions of this act."

(Section VI, P. L.) And to avoid the danger of embezzlement or misapplication of any of the said bills of credit:

[Section III.] Be it further enacted by the authority aforesaid, That the said Michael Shubart, John Biddle, Paul Cox and Isaac Snowden, after the said bills shall be printed, shall deliver from time to time so many of them to the signers aforesaid, to be signed and numbered by parcels as they shall judge proper, for which the said signers, or some of them, shall give their receipts; that is to say, that not more than three thousand pounds of the said bills shall remain in the hands of any two of such signers at the same time, and so, from time to time, till the whole of the said bills be signed; of all which bills of credit so delivered to be signed and numbered as aforesaid a true account shall be kept by the signers who, upon re-delivery of each or any parcel of the said bills by them signed and numbered, shall have the receipt of the said Michael Shubart, John Biddle, Paul Cox or Isaac Snowden, to charge them before any committee of assembly appointed to inquire into the same.

(Section VII, P. L.) And each of the said signers shall have ten shillings for every thousand of the said bills by them signed and numbered, and no more, and the said Michael Shubart, John Biddle, Paul Cox and Isaac Snowden shall severally receive ten shillings per diem for every day they shall be employed in the said business, and the treasurer of this state shall, for receiving and paying, have and receive ten shillings per hundred pounds for his care and trouble, to be paid out of the moneys struck by virtue of this act.

[Section IV.] (Section VIII, P. L.) And be it enacted by the authority aforesaid, That the bills of credit hereby directed to be prepared and made, as fast as the same shall be signed, numbered and perfected as aforesaid shall be delivered to the said treasurer by the said Michael Shubart, John Biddle, Paul Cox and Isaac Snowden, or any of them, who shall give his receipt or receipts for the same and shall issue and pay the same according to the drafts of the president or vice-president in council for the purposes hereinafter mentioned.

(Section IX, P. L.) And in order that the holders of the bills of credit to be struck and emitted by virtue of this act, which bills are hereby declared to be at the rate of seven shillings and six pence for a milled dollar of the Spanish colonies in America weighing seventeen pennyweights and six grains, may have the fullest and most perfect assurance that the same bills shall be redeemed, together with an annual interest of five per centum on or before the first day of June, one thousand seven hundred and eighty-four, at the full price at which they are delivered out in pursuance of this act, without any deduction or delay.

[Section V.] (Section X, P. L.) Be it enacted by the authority aforesaid, That, together with the guarantee of the

1780] *The Statutes at Large of Pennsylvania.* 187

honor and faith of Pennsylvania, which is hereby given, so much and such part of the lots and lands lying and being within the city of Philadelphia belonging to the commonwealth and the tract of lany known by the name of the Province island, situate in the township of Kingsessing, in the county of Philadelphia, shall be, and hereby are pledged and declared to be the fund out of which the bills of credit aforesaid to the amount of one hundred thousand pounds and the interest aforesaid shall be redeemed and cancelled, within the term aforesaid.

[Section VI.] (Sevtion XI, P. L.) And be it further enacted by the authority aforesaid, That for this purpose within the term aforesaid, the president or vice-president in council, shall expose to public sale and sell such and so many of the said lots and lands in the said city, and the said island except the hospital erected on the said island and six acres of land thereto appurtenant and adjacent, and on payment of the purchase money shall make good and effectual grants for the same under the great seal in fee simple to the purchasers thereof without other reservation than one acorn out of each grant, if demanded. And the said president or vice-president in council shall receive in payment for such real estate so sold as aforesaid the bills of credit issued by virtue of this act, or such Spanish milled dollars as aforesaid, or an equal sum in gold or silver, and no other money whatever, and with the gold and silver so received shall redeem the said bills of credit, and all of them which shall be brought in within nine months after the same shall be called in by public notice published, and continued for and during four weeks in the public newspapers of this and the adjoining states.

[Section VII.] (Section XII, P. L.) And be it further enacted by the authority aforesaid, That the said bills of credit shall be and hereby are appropriated towards procuring, purchasing and collecting wheat, flour and other goods directed to be purchased in and by an act of this session of assembly, entitled "An act for procuring a supply of provisions and other necessaries for the use of the army,"[1] and for such other uses and purposes as shall be necessary for the support of the army.

---

[1] Passed March 23, 1780, Chapter 905.

(Section XIII, P. L.) And whereas it has been the earnest desire of the good people of Pennsylvania that all possible justice should be done to the possessors of the bills of credit which have been issued by the honorable Congress, and to the public creditors who have advanced great sums of money on loan but the attainment thereof has not been within the reach of any particular state.

[Section VIII.] (Section XIV, P. L.) It is therefore declared by the representatives aforesaid on behalf of Pennsylvania, that this state will most cheerfully concur in and adopt such reasonable and salutary measures as may be proposed by Congress and adopted by the several states for the funding and redemption of its full proportion and share of the bills of credit and loan office certificates which have been issued by Congress.

(Section XV, P. L.) And whereas, the honorable the Congress by their act of the twenty-fifth day of February last, have determined to leave in the treasury of the several states two-third parts of the taxes by them called for to be raised monthly for eight months, in the year one thousand seven hundred and eighty, in order to enable the said states to purchase certain supplies of provisions and other goods, apportioned on and requested of the said states respectively for the public service, and the money arising thereon amounting to near twelve millions of dollars will not be necessary for that purpose, in case such supplies can be otherwise procured.

[Section IX.] (Section XVI, P. L.) Be it therefore enacted by the authority aforesaid, That the bills of credit of the United States of America, which shall come into the hands of the treasurer of this state in payment of the said two-thirds of the state taxes to be levied monthly for eight months in the year one thousand seven hundred and eighty, and bills of credit issued by Congress equal to the amount of the two-thirds of such taxes shall not be again issued, but shall be detained in the said treasurer's hands subject to the directions of the house of assembly.

[Section X.] (Section XVI, P. L.) And be it further enacted by the authority aforesaid, That from and after the publication of this act, if any person or persons shall, within this state or elsewhere, prepare, engrave, stamp, forge or print the counterfeit resemblance of any paper bills of credit which shall be issued, emitted and made in virtue of this act, or shall counterfeit or sign the name or names of the signer or signers of the said bills of credit to such counterfeit bills of credit with an intention that such counterfeit bills of credit shall be passed in payments, or received as genuine and good bills, whether the same be so passed or received or not; or if any person or persons shall in this state pass, pay or tender in payment any such counterfeit money, or deliver the same to any other person or persons with an intention that they be passed, paid or received as and for good and genuine, knowing the same to be forged or counterfeited, every such person being thereof legally convicted or attainted in any court of oyer and terminer within this state by verdict of a jury or confession of the party offending, or being indicted thereof shall stand mute or not directly answer to the indictment, or shall peremptorily challenge more than the number of twenty persons legally returned to be the jury for the trial of such offender, shall be adjudged a felon, and shall suffer death without benefit of clergy. And if any person or persons shall countereit any of the said bills of credit by altering the denomination thereof with design to increase the value of such bills or shall utter such bills knowing them to be so counterfeited or altered as aforesaid, and shall be thereof legally convicted in any court of record in this State, such person or persons shall be sentenced to the pillory, and have both his or her ears cut off and nailed to the pillory, and be publicly whipped on his or her bare back with thirty-nine lashes well laid on, and moreover every such offender shall forfeit the sum of two thousand pounds, lawful money of Pennsylvania to be levied on his or her lands and tenements, goods and chattels, the one moiety to the use of the state, and the other moiety to the discoverer; and the offender shall pay to the party grieved double the value of the damages thereby sustained, together with the costs and charges of prosecution; and in case the offender hath not sufficient to satisfy the discoverer for his or her damages and charges, and to pay the forfeiture aforesaid, in such case the offender shall, by order of the court where he or she shall be convicted, be sold as a servant for any term not exceeding seven years for satisfaction.

> Passed March 25, 1780. See the note to the Act of Assembly passed March 5, 1725-26, Chapter 289, and the Acts of Assembly passed December 23, 1780, Chapter 924; April 10, 1781, Chapter 942; June 25, 1781, Chapter 948.

Laws enacted in the third sitting of the fourth General Assembly of the commonwealth of Pennsylvania, which commenced at Philadelphia on Wednesday, the tenth day of May, in the year of our Lord 1780.

CHAPTER CMVIII.

AN ACT FOR THE GREATER EASE OF THE MILITIA AND THE MORE SPEEDY AND EFFECTUAL DEFENCE OF THIS STATE.

(Section I, P. L.) Whereas it hath been found by experience that frequent calls of the militia hath proved very inconvenient to the good people of this state, and especially in seed time and harvest, when their utmost exertion is requisite for the cultivating of their lands and gathering in the produce thereof:

For remedy whereof and that a body of men may be raised and equipped for the defense of this state:

[Section I.] (Section II, P. L.) Be it enacted and it is hereby enacted by the Representatives of the Freemen of the Commonwealth of Pennsylvania in General Assembly met, and by the authority of the same, That each and every company of militia within this state shall, on or before the fifteenth day of June next, provide or hire one able-bodied man not less than eighteen or more than forty-five years of age to be formed into a corps for the above purpose, which shall be known and distinguished by the name of the Pennsylvania Volunteers.

(Section III, P. L.) Provided always, That no deserter from the British army or from the army or navy of the United States or any wagoner actually engaged for any time in the service of said states shall be enlisted or shall pass muster in the said corps of which requisites and exceptions the lieutenant or sub-lieutenant of the city, county or districts for which such volunteer shall be procured shall be judge.

(Section IV, P. L.) And that the terms and continuance of enlistment may be fully known and understood:

[Section II.] Be it further enacted by the authority aforesaid, That every person engaged in said service shall sign an enlistment in the following terms, viz.: "I, A. B., having engaged to serve as a Pennsylvania Volunteer for the ———— company of the ———— battalion of militia, of the county of ————, in the state of Pennsylvania, do hereby engage to be true and faithful in the said service until the fifteenth day of January next, unless sooner discharged, and to be obedient to the authority of said state and my superior officers, according to the rules and discipline of war and the establishment of the corps in which I am now entered," which said enlistment signed by two witnesses shall be transmitted by the captain or commanding officer of such company to the lieutenant or sub-lieutenant within whose jurisdiction such company may be within two days next thereafter, who within three days after the receipt thereof shall transmit a certified copy of such enlistment to the commanding officer of that part of the said corps raised within his jurisdiction and shall also transmit therewith an order to said officer to rendezvous his men so enlisted with all possible expedition at a certain day and place, that they may pass muster and proceed on service.

[Section III.] (Section V, P. L.) And be it further enacted by the authority aforesaid, That if any taxable person enrolled in any company of militia within this tate or any other taxable inhabitant residing within the limits of the said company shall neglect or refuse to pay into the hands of the commanding officer of the company a proportionable share of the sum necessary to hire and procure such volunteer, then the lieutenant of said company and two freeholders chosen for that purpose by a majority of the same shall assess and levy a proportionable part of said sum on such person or person so refusing having due regard to the ability of each person as well officer as private. And the lieutenant or sub-lieutenant of the city or county, where such person or persons may reside shall issue his warrant and cause the same to be levied as the militia fines and penalties are levied and collected.

[Section IV.] (Section VI, P. L.) And be it further enacted by the authority aforesaid, That if any company of militia of this state shall neglect or refuse to furnish such volunteer, the captain or commanding officer thereof shall and he is hereby authorized and required to hire or furnish a volunteer as above for such company and with the assistance of two freeholders assess and levy the hire of such volunteer with the expense and charges of levying and collecting the same on all taxable inhabitants residing within the limits of said company; and in case the captain or commanding officer of any such company refuse or neglect so to do, or if any company should be without such officer, then the lieutenant or sub-lieutenant, where the same shall happen shall, with all convenient speed, hire or procure such volunteer and annex him to his respective corps and shall charge the whole expense of procuring such volunteer on said company, and shall cause the same to be levied and collected as other fines and penalties are directed to be by the militia law of this state.

[Section V.] (Section VII, P. L.) And be it further enacted by the authority aforesaid, That the president or vice-president in council is hereby authorized and empowered to organize and form the said volunteers into one or more regiments or corps, as in his discretion he shall think necessary, and arm and equip them with the public arms of this state and appoint and commission such and so many officers from each county as such establishment may require; which said officers, non-commissioned officers and privates shall receive the same pay and rations as the troops for the time aforesaid shall receive in the federal army.

[Section VI.] (Section VIII, P. L.) And be it further enacted by the authority aforesaid, That the several captains or commanding officers of the companies of militia shall notify their respective companies to meet on or before the fifteenth day of June next, to carry the said act as far as it concerns them into execution, and every person neglecting or refusing shall be liable to the same fines and penalties as is directed for non-attendance on muster days by the militia law of this state.

[Section VII.] (Section IX, P. L.) And be it further enacted by the authority aforesaid, That if any person so engaging as a volunteer and being required by the lieutenant or sub-lieutenant of the city or of any county of this state to march to the place of rendezvous shall neglect or refuse so to do, or shall withdraw himself or desert from the said service, or sell or embezzle the arms or accoutrements or any part of them provided for him as aforesaid, such volunteer shall be subject to such punishments as are inflicted for the like offenses in the federal army, the trial to be had as is directed by the militia law of this state.

[Section VIII.] (Section X, P. L.) And be it further enacted by the authority aforesaid, That if any lieutenant or sub-lieutenant of the city or any county of this state shall neglect or refuse to do the duties of him or them herein required, they shall be fined for every such offense at the discretion of the president or vice-president in council. And if any captain or lieutenant or commanding officer of any company or any person appointed to assess or collect the charge of hire of any of the said volunteers neglect or refuse to do the duties required of them according to the directions of this act they shall be fined by the lieutenant or sub-lieutenant of the city or county where the offense shall happen as collectors of the public state tax are or may be on neglect or refusal to do the duties of them required.

[Section IX.] (Section XI, P. L.) And be it further enacted by the authority aforesaid, That the president or vice-president in council is hereby authorized to issue such orders to the commissioners of purchase, or other person in any county of this state as may be necessary for the proper subsistence of said troops while continued in service.

[Section X.] (Section XII, P. L.) And be it further enacted by the authority aforesaid, That all persons engaged in this corps of Pennsylvania volunteers shall be exempted from being charged with or paying any state or other tax levied during the time of their service as above.

(Section XIII, P. L.) Provided always, That nothing herein contained shall be construed or understood to prevent the reduction or discharge of the said volunteers by the president or vice-president in council at any time before the expiration of the term of enlistment.

(Section XIV, P. L.) Whereas, since the third reading of this act fresh information of the increasing dangers and distresses which the inhabitants of the frontier counties are exposed to from the incursions of the Indians has been laid before this assembly, from which there is reason to conclude that one man to be raised from each company of militia as provided for in the former part of this act will not be sufficient to answer the good purposes expected therefrom; therefore,

[Section XI.] (Section XV, P. L.) Be it further enacted by the authority aforesaid, That one other volunteer be hired by each company of militia within this state in addition to the one already directed to be raised, at the time and place and in the manner as is hereinbefore directed; and that all and every part of this act shall be construed to extend to the said additional volunteers as fully as if this act had above directed that each and every company of the militia within this state should provide or hire two able-bodied men.

Passed May 26, 1780. See the note to the Act of Assembly passed March 20, 1780, Chapter 902; and the Act of Assembly passed September 29, 1787, Chapter 1319. Recorded L. B. No. 1, p. 390, &c.

CHAPTER CMIX.

A SUPPLEMENT TO AN ACT ENTITLED "AN ACT TO COMPEL THE SETTLEMENT OF THE PUBLIC ACCOUNTS,"[1] AND FOR OTHER PURPOSES THEREIN MENTIONED.

(Section I, P. L.) Whereas, by the act, entitled "An act to compel the settlement of the public accounts,"[1] passed on the first day of March last, it is enacted "That in any case wherein it shall appear that a balance of moneys shall be due by any person or persons to this commonwealth the said auditors, or any two of them, shall direct that payment thereof be made to the treasurer of this state; and the certificates of the said auditors, or any two of them, shall be conclusive evidence in an action of debt, at the suit of the commonwealth, against any person or persons of the sums of money which such person

[1] Passed March 1, 1780, Chapter 882.

or persons owe or may be indebted to the commonwealth, and no setoff or deduction from the same shall be admitted," by which manner of recovering such balance of moneys due to this commonwealth great delays may be occasioned:

Therefore:

[Section I.] (Section II, P. L.) Be it enacted and it is hereby enacted by the Representatives of the Freemen of the Commonwealth of Pennsylvania in General Assembly met, and by the authority of the same, That where a balance of moneys shall be due by any person or persons to this commonwealth the auditors appointed by the above-mentioned act, or any two of them, shall grant execution thereupon directed to the sheriff of the city or county where the defendant or person from whom a balance of such moneys shall be due to this state shall be or reside or where such person or persons, lands or tenements shall lie, commanding the said sheriff to levy the said debt or balance due and costs on the defendant's goods and chattels, lands and tenements, who, by virtue thereof, shall expose the same to sale by public vendue, returning the overplus, if any, to the defendant and for want of such sufficient distress to take the body of the said defendant and him safely to keep in the common gaol of the city or county where such defendant shall be found until the said sum of money, with costs, be paid.

(Section III, P. L.) And whereas, the fines imposed by law on delinquent collectors of public taxes have been found to be insufficient and the collectors of fines incurred by the non-performance of militia duties are not subject to any penalty for neglects or omissions:

Therefore:

[Section II.] (Section IV, P. L.) Be it enacted by the authority aforesaid, That if any person appointed or to be appointed collector of any state, county or other public tax imposed by any law of this state now in force shall, after notice of his appointment, refuse or neglect to do and perform the duties required of him by such law, then and in such case the commissioners and assessors of the city or county where such neglect or refusal shall happen, or a majority of them, shall fine such delinquent collector in any sum not less than five hundred pounds nor more than one thousand pounds, to be recovered and applied as other fines are directed by the law under which such collector doth act, and the said commissioners and assessors shall appoint other collectors in the room and stead of such delinquents.

(Section V, P. L.) And whereas, the present allowance of two dollars for every hundred pounds which was allowed the county treasurers by an act of assembly, entitled "An act for raising the additional sum of five millions seven hundred thousand dollars for the current year one thousand seven hundred and seventy-nine,"[1] passed the tenth day of October, one thousand seven hundred and seventy-nine is not sufficient for their services and risk:

(Section VI, P. L.) And whereas the exigencies of the times require their making more frequent payments into the state treasury and it is just and proper to enable them better to bear the expenses of traveling:

[Section III.] (Section VII, P. L.) Be it enacted by the authority aforesaid, That they shall and are hereby allowed two dollars in addition to their former allowance made by the act, entitled "An act for raising the additional sum of five millions seven hundred thousand dollars for the current year, one thousand seven hundred and seventy-nine,"[1] and the same allowance of two dollars in every one hundred pounds is hereby given to them for receiving and paying all the moneys collected by the monthly taxes now ordered to be levied and collected.

And to encourage the collectors to be very diligent and spend the whole of their time in that service:

[Section IV.] (Section VIII, P. L.) Be it enacted by the authority aforesaid, That the collectors of the five millions seven hundred thousand dollars tax and all the monthly taxes be allowed the further sum of six pence in the pound in addition to that already allowed.

[Section V.] (Section IX, P. L.) And be it further enacted by the authority aforesaid, That if any person whose duty it may be to collect the fines incurred by the neglect or non-performance of militia duties as required by the militia law of this state shall refuse or neglect to do and perform all or any

---
[1] Chapter 866.

of the duties required by the said law or shall refuse or neglect to settle his duplicate and pay the moneys due to the lieutenant or sub-lieutenants agreeably to the direction of his warrant within ten days after being required by the said lieutenant or sub-lieutenants, then and in such case the lieutenant or sub-lieutenant of the city or county where such neglect or refusal shall happen with the assistance of two justices of the peace of the said city or county shall fine such delinquent collector in any sum not less than five hundred pounds nor more than one thousand pounds, to be recovered and applied in the same manner as other fines are directed to be recovered and applied by the said law.

(Section X, P. L.) And whereas the collecting of the taxes already laid or to be hereafter assessed or laid on account of the want of a sufficient quantity of cash among the poorer people of this state and such as live at great distances from market may greatly distress such people:

Therefore:

[Section VI.](Section XI, P. L.) Be it enacted by the authority aforesaid, That the commissioners of purchases for this state shall, for their respective city or counties, appoint a mill or other fit place or places in each township or district of this state, with a suitable person at such mill or place, to receive wheat flour and other supplies for the army, and also give notice to the treasurer of each county in writing of the name of the person and place or places so appointed.

[Section VII.] (Section XII, P. L.) And be it further enacted by the authority aforesaid, That such of the inhabitants of this state as shall carry their wheat flour or other supplies for the army to the said mill or other place so appointed and sell the same to the commissioner of purchases or to the person aforesaid duly appointed by such commissioner his receipt shall be received by the collector of such township or district in discharge of the public taxes hereafter to be paid.

[Section VIII.] (Section XIII, P. L.) And be it further enacted by the authority aforesaid, That notes or certificates which remain unpaid signed by the commissary general of purchases or quartermaster general or by their agents or persons appointed by them to purchase articles or supplies for the army of the United States shall be received by the collectors of the several townships and districts of this state in the payment of any state or continental tax due to the first day of March last from the persons in whose names they have been given and the county treasurers shall receive the same in such payment as aforesaid from such collector. Provided, the persons paying in the said notes or certificates indorse the same to the collectors who receive them and also take an oath or affirmation before a magistrate that they have been obtained for the value and the articles therein expressed and delivered for the use of the United States and for which no payment hath been made, which oath or affirmation shall be indorsed on each note or certificate.

[Section IX.] (Section XIV, P. L.) And be it further enacted by the authority aforesaid, That if any such note or certificate held by any person shall exceed the amount of the taxes due from such person at the time they are paid in, the collector of the said tax shall give his receipt to the person paying in such note or certificate for the surplusage thereof, and the said receipt shall be a discharge for so much of his further state taxes as the same with interest at six per centum until discounted shall amount to.

(Section XV, P. L.) Provided always, That such receipt correspond with the entry which shall be made thereof in the said treasurer's books, who is hereby enjoined and required, on receiving such notes or certificates from the said collectors, to keep a fair and true record of all such sums as they may contain over and above the amount of the tax charged against such person in whose favor they have been received, noting also the name of such person and shall discount the amount of such surplus, with the interest thereon, to the collector of the next or other subsequent [state] tax in whose tax roll such person shall be charged.

[Section X.] (Section XIV, P. L.) And be it further enacted by the authority aforesaid, That the state treasurer shall receive such notes and certificates so endorsed as above from the county treasurers and shall deliver them to the principal of the respective departments from whom payment is due, or to their agents in the city of Philadelphia, and shall take receipts from the said principals or from their agents, making their principals accountable for the amount of the notes or certificates paid in as aforesaid, with the interest thereon allowed and due, and shall lodge the same with the board of treasury that this state may have proper credit for the same.

> Passed May 30, 1780. See the note to the Act of Assembly passed March 1, 1780, Chapter 882. The Act in the text was repealed by the Act of Assembly passed April 13, 1782, Chapter 970. Recorded L. B. No. 1, p. 391, &c.

CHAPTER CMX.

A FURTHER SUPPLEMENT TO AN ACT ENTITLED "AN ACT FOR REGULATING AND CONTINUING THE NIGHTLY WATCH, ENLIGHTENING THE STREETS, LANES AND ALLEYS IN THE CITY OF PHILADELPHIA AND FOR OTHER PURPOSES THEREIN MENTIONED;[1] AND TO AN ACT WHICH IS A SUPPLEMENT THERETO,[2] PASSED IN THE YEAR OF OUR LORD ONE THOUSAND SEVEN HUNDRED AND SEVENTY-SIX.

(Section I, P. L.) Whereas, by an act as a further supplement to the aforesaid acts of general assembly, passed the fifth day of April, in the year of our Lord, one thousand seven hundred and seventy-nine, by reason of the increase of watchmen and workmen's wages, excessive high price of oil and materials, it was found expedient and necessary that further provision should be made to enable the wardens and assessors of the city of Philadelphia to raise and levy an additional tax not exceeding six pence in the pound on the inhabitants and on all the estates, real and personal, and to authorize their treasurer to receive the rents and income of the market houses, ferries, wharves and public landing places, within the bounds and limits of the said city, to the end the difficulties under which the wardens then labored might be in some measure removed

---

[1] Passed March 9, 1771, Chapter 636.
[2] Passed April 6, 1776, Chapter 719.

and the nightly watch so necessary might be kept up and continued; and as the said recited act expires with the present sitting of the general assembly the same difficulties would again occur:

For remedy whereof:

[Section I.] (Section II, P. L.) Be it enacted and it is hereby enacted by the Representatives of the Freemen of the Commonwealth of Pennsylvania in General Assembly met and by the authority of the same, That from and after the passing of this act it shall and may be lawful for the wardens of the said city to let or demise the market houses, ferries, wharves and public landing places, and they with the assessors of the said city, to raise and levy an additional rate not exceeding sixpence in the pound on the inhabitants and on all estates real and personal and taxables within the city of Philadelphia, to be levied and collected in the same manner, by the same persons and for the same uses as directed in and by two several acts of general assembly, the one passed the ninth day of March, in the year of our Lord one thousand seven hundred and seventy-one, and the other passed the sixth day of April, in the year of our Lord one thousand seven hundred and seventy-six, for regulating and continuing the nightly watch, enlightening the streets, lanes and alleys of the city of Philadelphia and for other purposes therein mentioned, over and above the rates and sums of money thereby authorized to be raised, levied and collected; and to authorize their treasurer to receive the rents of the market houses, ferries, wharves and public landing places and all other the income, fines, forfeitures and emoluments which were formerly received by the treasurer or the mayor and commonalty of the city of Philadelphia.

[Section II.] (Section III, P. L.) And be it enacted by the authority aforesaid, That the clerk of the market for the time being shall collect the rents of the market houses, stalls and stands in the market places as they become due quarterly, and in arrear, and after deducting the costs and charges of repair (to be allowed of by the said wardens) and his accustomed fees for collecting shall pay the overplus, together with the moneys already collected for rent and in his hands to the treasurer of the wardens and assessors for the time being (whose receipt, which he is hereby required to give, shall be a sufficient discharge for any sum of money so paid), under such penalty as the city court of the city of Philadelphia shall judge proper to inflict.

[Section III.] (Section IV, P. L.) And be it further enacted by the authority aforesaid, That the owners and occupiers of the several ferries, wharves and public landing places within the said city shall, from time to time, pay their respective rents as they become due to the treasurer of the wardens and assessors of the city of Philadelphia for the time being (whose receipt, which he is hereby required to give, shall be a sufficient discharge to him or them for the sum of money so paid), under the penalty of treble the amount of the said rents for every neglect or refusal.

[Section IV.] (Section V, P. L.) And be it further enacted by the authority aforesaid, That every other person who shall have or receive or get into his custody or possession any moneys in virtue of this act and neglect or refuse to pay the same to the treasurer of the wardens and assessors within ten days such person shall for every neglect or refusal, forfeit and pay after the same shall come into his custody or possession, every treble the amount of such suum or sums of money so by him collected and received, and the said treasurer is hereby required to give receipts for the moneys so by him received, whose receipt shall be a sufficient discharge to the persons paying the same.

[Section V.] (Section VI, P. L.) And be it further enacted by the authority aforesaid, That the moneys which shall be received by the treasurer of the wardens and assessors aforesaid by virtue of this act and the act to which this is a supplement, shall be disposed of by the wardens, or a majority of them, and applied to the same uses and purposes as mentioned and specified in an act of general assembly passed the ninth day of March, in the year of our Lord one thousand seven hundred and seventy-one, entitled "An act for regulating and continuing the nightly watch, enlightening the streets, lanes and alleys of the city of Philadelphia, and for other purposes therein mentioned." [1]

---

[1] Ante.

[Section VI.] (Section VII, P. L.) And be it further enacted by the authority aforesaid, That the wardens of the city of Philadelphia for the time being are hereby empowered to purchase a lot of ground on the north side of Sassafras street, adjoining the public wharf at the end of the said street on the river Delaware, in the said city, and to take a deed or deeds for the same in their names as wardens for the use of the city of Philadelphia, to be annexed to and made use of as a public wharf at the end of the said street for such estate and estates, term or time as the same can or may be legally granted and conveyed.

[Section VII.] (Section VIII, P. L.) Provided always and be it enacted by the authority aforesaid, That nothing in this act shall extend or be construed to extend to the estate and interest formerly held by the corporation of the city of Philadelphia, usually called the middle ferry on Schuylkill, for the space of one year from the first day of May, one thousand seven hundred and eighty, to the first day of May, one thousand seven hundred and eighty-one, unless the wardens of the said city shall undertake and engage with the president or vice-president in council to keep and maintain, at their own expense, the bridge now erected over Schuylkill in good repair for the passage of men, horses and carriages during the said term.

[Section IX, P. L.] And provided also, That nothing herein contained shall extend to the annulling or making void any contract or engagement made by the authority of the supreme executive council with the quartermaster general of the United States for the passage of men, horses or carriages in the immediate service of the United States.

Passed May 30, 1780. See the note to the Act of Assembly passed March 9, 1771, Chapter 636. Recorded L. B. No. 1, p. 393, &c.

CHAPTER CMXI.

AN ACT TO SUSPEND THE OPERATION FOR A LIMITED TIME OF THE SEVERAL LAWS OF THIS COMMONWEALTH FOR MAKING THE BILLS OF CREDIT OF THE UNITED STATES A LEGAL TENDER IN THE PAYMENT OF DEBTS EQUAL TO GOLD AND SILVER.[1]

(Section I, P. L.) Whereas, certain of the bills of credit emitted by the honorable the Congress of the United Colonies or States of America have hitherto been by the laws of this state a legal tender in the payment of all debts, dues and contracts equal to gold and silver: And whereas, the total repeal of the said acts or the further continuance of the said bills as a legal tender equal to gold and silver might, in the present situation of affairs, be attended with many and great inconveniences:

For remedy whereof and until some mode more suited to the interest and circumstances of the parties concerned be devised:

[Section I.] (Section II, P. L.) Be it enacted and it is hereby enacted by the Representatives of the Freemen of the Commonwealth of Pennsylvania in General Assembly met, and by the authority of the same, That from and after the passing of this act so much of the several acts of assembly of this state as make the said bills of credit a legal tender equal to gold and silver shall be and they are hereby suspended for and during the space of three months, and from thence until the end of the next sitting of the general assembly.

[Section II.] (Section III, P. L.) Provided always, That this act, nor anything herein contained, shall extend or be construed to extend to any debt, contract, bargain or agreement had, made or entered into since the first day of November, one thousand seven hundred and seventy-nine, or to any debt or demand whereupon any distress [may] be made or upon which any action or suit shall be commenced in any court of law within this state, or to any sheriff, attorney in law or fact,

---

[1] See Act of January 29, 1777, Chapter 738.

executor, guardian or other person having received money by legal authority in right of another, but that it shall and may be lawful to make payment in all such cases as might have been done before the passing this act.

<small>Passed May 31, 1780. See the notes to the Act of Assembly passed March 5, 1725-26, Chapter 289; January 29, 1777, Chapter 738; and the Acts of Assembly passed June 1, 1780, Chapter 912; September 22, 1780, Chapter 918; December 22, 1780, Chapter 923; June 21, 1781, Chapter 945. Recorded L. B. No. 1, p. 394, &c.</small>

CHAPTER CMXII.

AN ACT FOR FUNDING AND REDEEMING THE BILLS OF CREDIT OF THE UNITED STATES OF AMERICA AND FOR PROVIDING MEANS TO BRING THE PRESENT WAR TO A HAPPY CONCLUSION.

(Section I, P. L.) Whereas the honorable the Congress of the United States of America, by their act of the eighteenth day of March last, have resolved and recommended to the several states in the words following, That is to say: These United States having been driven into this just and necessary war at a time when no regular [civil] governments were established of sufficient energy to enforce the collection of taxes or to provide funds for the redemption of such bills of credit as their necessities obliged them to issue, and before the powers of Europe were sufficiently convinced of the justice of their cause or of the probable event of the controversy to afford them aid or credit, in consequence of which their bills increasing in quantity beyond the sum necessary for the purpose of a circulating medium and wanting at the same time specific funds to rest on for their redemption, they have seen them daily sink in value, notwithstanding every effort that has been made to support the same, insomuch that they are now passed by common consent in most parts of these United States at least thirty-nine fortieths below their nominal value, and still remain in a state of depreciation, whereby the community suffers great injustice, the public finances are deranged and the necessary dispositions for the defense of the country are much impeded and perplexed; and as effectually to remedy these evils for which [purpose] the United States are now become competent, their independence being well assured, their civil governments established and vigorous and the spirit of their citizens ardent for exertions, it is necessary speedily to reduce the quantity of the paper medium in circulation and to establish and appropriate funds that shall ensure the punctual redemption of the bills:

Therefore:

Resolved, That the several states continue to bring into the continental treasury, by taxes or otherwise, their full quotas of fifteen million of dollars monthly, as assigned them by the resolution of the seventh day of October, one thousand seven hundred and seventy-nine, a clause in the resolve of the twenty-third day of February last for relinquishing two-thirds of the said quotas to the contrary notwithstanding; and that the states be forthwith called on to make provision for continuing to bring into the said treasury their like quotas monthly to the month of April, one thousand seven hundred and eighty-one, inclusive:

That silver and gold be receivable in payment of the said quotas at the rate of one Spanish milled dollar in lieu of forty dollars of the bills now in circulation.

That the said bills as paid in, except for the months of January and February past, which may be necessary for the discharge of past contracts, be not reissued but destroyed.

That as fast as the said bills shall be brought in to be destroyed and funds shall be established as hereafter mentioned for other bills, other bills be issued not to exceed on any account one-twentieth part of the nominal sum of the bills brought in to be destroyed.

That the bills which shall be issued be redeemable in specie within six years after the present, and bear an interest at the rate of five per centum per annum, to be paid also in specie at the redemption of the bills or the election of the holder annually at the respective continental loan offices in sterling bills of exchange drawn by the United States on their commissioners in Europe at four shillings and six pence sterling per dollar.

That the said new bills issue on the funds of individual states for that purpose established, and to be signed by persons appointed by them, and that the faith of the United States be also pledged for the payment of the said bills in case any state on whose funds they shall be emitted should, by the events of war, be rendered incapable to redeem them, which undertaking of the United States and that of drawing bills of exchange for payment of interest as aforesaid shall be endorsed on the bills to be emitted and signed by a commissioner to be appointed by Congress for that purpose.

That the face of the bills to be emitted read as follows, viz.:

The possessor of this bill shall be paid ——————— Spanish milled dollars by the thirty-first day of December, one thousand seven hundred and eighty-six, with interest in like money at the rate of five per centum per annum by the state of ——————, according to an act of the legislature of the said state of the ————— day of —————, one thousand seven hundred and eighty.

And the indorsement shall be as follows, viz.:

The United States ensure the payment of the within bill and will draw bills of exchange for the interest annually if demanded, according to a resolution of Congress of the eighteenth day of March, one thousand seven hundred and eighty.

That the said new bills shall be struck under the direction of the board of treasury in due proportion for each state according to their said monthly quotas and lodged in the continental loan offices in the respective states where the commissioners to be appointed by Congress, in conjunction with such persons as the respective states appoint, shall attend the signing of the said bills, which shall be completed no faster than in the aforesaid proportion of one to twenty of the other bills brought in to be destroyed and which shall be lodged for that purpose in the said loan offices.

That as the said new bills are signed and completed the states, respectively, on whose funds they issue receive six-tenths of them, and that the remainder be subject to the orders of the United States and credited to the states on whose funds they are issued, the accounts whereof shall be adjusted agreeably to the resolution of the sixth day of October, one thousand seven hundred and seventy-nine.

That the said new bills be receivable in payment of the said monthly quotas at the same rate as aforesaid of specie, the interest thereon to be computed to the respective states to the day the payment becomes due.

That the respective states be charged with such parts of the interest on their said bills as shall be paid by the United States in bills of exchange and the accounts thereof shall be adjusted agreeably to the resolution aforesaid of the sixth of October, one thousand seven hundred and seventy-nine.

That whenever interest on the bills to be emitted shall be paid prior to their redemption, such bills shall be thereupon exchanged for others of the like tenor, to bear date from the expiration of the year for which such interest is paid.

That the several states be called upon to provide funds for their quotas of the said new bills to be so productive as to sink or redeem one-sixth part of them annually after the first day of January next.

That nothing in the foregoing resolutions shall be construed to ascertain the proportions of the expense incurred by the war which each state, on a final adjustment, ought to be charged with, or to exclude the claims of any state to have the prices at which different states have furnished supplies for the army hereafter taking in[to] consideration and equitably adjusted.

That the foregoing resolutions, with a letter from the president, be dispatched to the executive of the several states, and that they be requested to call their assemblies, if not already convened, as speedily as possible, to take them into immediate consideration to establish ample and certain funds for the purposes therein mentioned, and to take every other measure necessary to carry the same into full and vigorous effect, and that they transmit their acts for that purpose to Congress without delay.

(Section II, P. L.) And whereas the depreciation of the currency of the United States now in circulation and the speculation which has taken place in consequence thereof has opened a door to numerous frauds and may operate to the general injury of virtue and morality to the great dishonor of the state unless timely prevented:

(Section III, P. L.) And whereas the prospect of an appreciation, unless regulated on just and equitable principles, might likewise be followed by a train of evils as pernicious as those we have already experienced and not only encourage but enable such persons as have obtained large sums for small value to derive an undue advantage therefrom, and it being the duty of government to prevent, as far as possible, the evils and dangers of a fluctuating medium of commerce and to fix and establish the value of such medium in such manner that security and confidence may be again introduced into commerce and order and economy into the public expenditures:

(Section IV, P. L.) And whereas the evils and inconveniences hitherto attending the depreciation of the currency of the United States, have in a great measure been balanced by a real reduction and discharge of a very great part of the national debt, insomuch that it would now be a manifest public injustice as well as a burden intolerable to be borne to tax the good people of this state or of the United States to pay that part of the public debt over again which by a kind of common consent has been discharged by the said depreciation; and as we are fully convinced that in case the measures recommended by Congress in their act of the eighteenth day of March last to the several states shall be adopted by them, the public credit will be established upon just and permanent principles it is, therefore, incumbent on us to provide for the execution thereof so far as the same concerns this state:

[Section I. (Section V, P. L.) Be it, therefore, enacted and it is hereby enacted by the Representatives of the Freemen of the Commonwealth of Pennsylvania in General Assembly met, and by the authority of the same, That the monthly taxes on estates, real and personal, and on taxable persons which are directed to be quotaed, assessed and levied throughout the several counties of this state in and by an act of assembly, entitled "An act for raising the sum of two millions five hundred thousand dollars monthly during eight months in the year one thousand seven hundred and eighty, for the supply of the treasury of the United States of America and the treasury of this state,"[1] passed on the twenty-sixth day of November last, shall be continued from the end of the said eight months for so long time as shall be necessary, together with the said monthly taxes already directed as aforesaid to redeem the said bills of credit of the United States of America now in circulation to the amount of twenty-five millions of dollars; and that gold and silver and the new bills of credit hereinafter mentioned be received in payment of the said monthly taxes after the rate of one milled dollar in lieu of forty of the said bills of credit of the United States of America now in circulation, and that the bills of credit last mentioned when received in taxes (except as to the taxes of the month of January and February last) be not again issued, but kept in the hands of the treasurer of this state, to be cancelled and destroyed and that other and new bills redeemable in specie within six years after the present year, bearing a yearly interest of five per centum, payable also in specie at the time of redemption, or at the option of the holder, annually, in sterling bills of exchange after the rate of four shillings and six pence sterling per dollar, shall be emitted in the manner and to the amount, if the same shall be necessary, recommended by the honorable Congress in their act aforesaid.

[Section II.] (Section VI, P. L.) And it is hereby declared by the authority aforesaid, That this house will, as soon as convenient, provide adequate funds for redeeming and cancelling the eighth part of the said new bills of credit amounting to one million two hundred and fifty thousand dollars of the value of four shillings and six pence sterling each, or of so many thereof as may be issued in manner aforesaid, together with the interest thereon to accrue as aforesaid.

[Section III.] Provided always, and be it enacted by the authority aforesaid, That nothing in this act shall extend to establish or continue beyond the [tax for the] month of August

---

[1] Chapter 866.

next the apportionment and applotment of the said monthly taxes according to the assessment thereof within any township, district or ward made by virtue of an act of assembly, entitled "An act for raising the additional sum of five millions seven hundred thousand dollars in the year one thousand seven hundred and seventy-nine,"[1] but the same shall be re-assessed within such townships, districts and wards on new returns of persons and estates, to be directed and made for that purpose, in the manner and under the penalties directed and provided in and by the act of assembly last recited, without altering the quotas of the several counties, or any of them, in order to levy the taxes by this act authorized to be raised and collected for the month of September and the months following in an equal and just manner.

(Section VIII, P. L.) Provided also, That the tax on money directed to be levied by said act be discontinued and cease.

(Section IX, P. L.) And for perfecting the said bills according to the true intent and meaning of this act:

[Section IV.] Be it enacted by the authority aforesaid, That the said bills to be emitted in the manner aforesaid shall be signed by two of the persons hereafter named, That is to say: Michael Shubart, Daniel Wister, Levi Budd, Philip Boehm, Robert Cather, Jedediah Snowden, William Lawrence Blair, John Miller, John Knox and Nathan Jones, who are hereby nominated and appointed signers thereof, and who shall, before they receive or sign any of them, take an oath or affirmation to the effect following: That they shall attend and well and truly sign and number all such bills as shall be deemed the proportion for this state, agreeable to the above resolve, and each of the said signers shall have ten shillings for every thousand of the said bills by them signed and numbered and no more.

[Section V.] (Section X, P. L.) And be it further enacted by the authority aforesaid, That from and after the publication of this act if any person or persons shall, within this state or elsewhere, prepare, engrave, stamp, forge or print the counterfeit resemblance of any paper bills of credit which shall be issued, emitted and made in virtue of this act or shall counter-

---

[1] Passed October 19, 1779, Chapter 866.

feit or sign the name or names of the signer or signers of the said bills of credit to such counterfeit bills of credit, with an intention that such counterfeit bills of credit shall be passed in payment or received as genuine and good bills, whether the same be so passed or received or not, or if any person or persons shall, in this state, pass, pay or tender in payment any such counterfeit money or deliver the same to any person or persons with an intention that they be passed, paid or received as and for good and genuine, knowing the same to be forged or counterfeited, every such person being thereof legally convicted or attainted in any court of oyer and terminer within this state by a verdict of a jury [or] confession of the party offending or being indicted thereof shall stand mute or not directly answer to the indictment, or shall peremptorily challenge more than the number of twenty persons legally returned to be of the jury for the trial of such offender, shall be adjudged a felon and shall suffer death without benefit of clergy; and if any person or persons shall counterfeit any of the said bills of credit by altering the denomination thereof with design to increase the value of such bills, or shall utter such bills knowing them to be so counterfeited or altered as aforesaid, and shall be thereof convicted in any court of record in this state, such person or persons shall be sentenced to the pillory, and have both his or her ears cut off and nailed to the pillory and be publicly whipped on his or her bare back with thirty-nine lashes well laid on; and, moreover, every such offender shall forfeit the sum of two thousand pounds lawful money of Pennsylvania, to be levied on his or her lands and tenements, goods and chattles, the one moiety to the use of this state and the other moiety to the discoverer, and the offender shall pay to the party aggrieved double the value of the damages thereby sustained, together with costs and charges of prosecution. And in case the offender hath not sufficient to satisfy the discoverer for his or her damages and charges and to pay the forfeiture aforesaid in such case the offender shall, by order of the court where he or she shall be convicted, be sold as a servant for any term not exceeding seven years for satisfaction.

[Section VI.] (Section XI, P. L.) And be it further enacted by the authority aforesaid, That this act and everything therein contained so far as respects the new bills of credit to be emitted by Congress for the redemption of the present currency of the United States shall be suspended until a majority of the states shall adopt the above act or resolves of Congress of the eighteenth day of March last.

[Section VII.] (Section XII, P. L.) And be it further enacted by the authority aforesaid, That so much of the thirteenth section of an act, entitled "An act for making the continental bills of credit and the bills of credit emitted by the resolves of the late assembly legal tender and for other purposes therein mentioned,"[1] passed the twenty-ninth day of January, one thousand seven hundred and seventy-seven, as prohibits the asking or taking a less price in gold or silver than in the said bills of credit; and also, the eighth section of the act, entitled "An act for the regulation of the markets of the city of Philadelphia, and for other purposes therein mentioned,"[2] passed the fifth day of April, one thousand seven hundred and seventy-nine, forbidding the buying, selling or renting, or offering to buy, sell or rent with or for hard money, are hereby repealed and made void; and that from and after the passing of this act all contracts whatever hereafter made shall take effect and be payable according to the special nature of such contract, any law heretofore to the contrary notwithstanding.

(Section XIII, P. L.) And whereas, it has been recommended to the legislature of the different states by the honorable Congress of the United States by their resolve of the twenty-seventh day of May instant, to pass laws for the punishment of such persons as shall encourage desertions from the fleets and armies of any foreign power who shall prosecute the war in America in conjunction with these United States, and for recovering such deserters as shall conceal themselves among the inhabitants:

(Section XIV, P. L.) And whereas this house entertain the highest sense of gratitude for the generous assistance afforded these United States by our illustratrious allies and esteem it

---

[1] Chapter 738.
[2] Chapter 845.

their duty and interest to afford every assistance and support to any power who shall prosecute the war in America in conjunction with these United States:

Therefore:

[Section VIII.] (Section XV, P. L.) Be it enacted by the authority aforesaid, That any person or persons who shall promote or encourage desertion or harbor or conceal any deserter from the fleets or armies of any power who shall prosecute the war in America in conjunction with these states, shall be subject to the like fines and penalties as are by the laws now in being of this commonwealth inflicted on persons for promoting or encouraging desertion or harboring or concealing deserters from the army of the United States.

[Section IX.] (Section XVI, P. L.) And be it further enacted by the authority aforesaid, That any person or persons who shall apprehend and secure any deserter from any of the fleets or armies of any power who shall, in conjunction with these states, prosecute the war in America, shall be entitled to the like reward as is allowed to persons apprehending and securing deserters from the army of the United States.

Passed June 1, 1780. See the notes to the Acts of Assembly passed March 5, 1725-26, Chapter 289; December 19, 1780, Chapter 921; June 21, 1781, Chapter 945; January 31, 1783, Chapter 1003; March 17, 1786, Chapter 1212; March 22, 1788, Chapter 1340; November 22, 1788, Chapter 1384. Recorded L. B. No. 1, p. 394, &c.

CHAPTER CMXIII.

AN ACT FOR PROCURING AN IMMEDIATE SUPPLY OF PROVISIONS FOR THE FEDERAL ARMY, IN ITS PRESENT EXIGENCY.

(Section I, P. L.) Whereas, the resolutions of the honorable Congress of the United States lately passed for the supply of the federal army, have not yet been fully executed, and it is indispensably necessary that extraordinary exertions should be made at this time without regard to specific quantities or

1780]   *The Statutes at Large of Pennsylvania.*   215

specific articles as required by Congress; this state, therefore, ever desirous to manifest its zeal in the common cause, being now specially called upon by the honorable Congress to furnish a supply of meat, hath resolved to comply therewith to the utmost of its ability:

To this end, therefore:

[Section I.] (Section II, P. L.) Be it enacted and it is hereby enacted by the Representatives of the Freemen of the Commonwealth of Pennsylvania in General Assembly met, and by the authority of the same, That it shall and may be lawful for the president or vice-president in council from time to time to appoint such and so many diligent, honest inhabitants of this state as they shall deem necessary as commissioners to procure meat at the most reasonable rates for the army, and the said commissioners shall severally transport the same to such place or places within this state as the supreme executive council shall direct, there to be delivered to the commissary general of purchases for the army, his deputies or agents, taking from the said commissary or agent his certificate therefor, expressing particularly the number, quantity and quality of the same, together with his receipt for the value thereof as paid by the said commissioner, which account, together with the charges thereon, the said commissioner shall deliver to the commissary on oath or affirmation if required.

[Section II.] (Section III, P. L.) Be it also enacted, That all cattle, sheep or salted provisions shall be subject to be seized by the commissioners appointed by virtue of this act, or either of them, his or their deputies or agents, to and for the use of the said army, the person taking and seizing the same paying therefor at such rates as shall be fixed by two indifferent freeholders of the neighborhood, one to be appointed by the commissioner or his deputy or agent, and the other by the owner of such cattle, sheep or salted provisions and in case such owner shall refuse to appoint such appraiser, then the said commissioner, his agent or deputy shall and he is hereby authorized and empowered to fix the price and pay the same, or give a certificate therefor as is hereafter mentioned.

(Section IV, P. L.) Provided always, That if any person

whose cattle, sheep or meat shall be so seized or taken, shall make oath or affirmation that such cattle, sheep or salted provisions are necessary for the private use of the possessor and his family or for sale by retail as a butcher [or for the necessary use of the master and mariners of any ship or vessel outward bound] then and in such case, upon a true copy of the said oath or affirmation being served on the person so seizing the said cattle, sheep or salted provisions, the same shall be discharged from such seizure.

[Section III.] (Section V, P. L.) Be it also enacted by the authority aforesaid, That the said persons so appointed shall severally at least once in every month make returns to the president or vice-president in council of the quantities of meat by them respectively purchased or seized, the price paid for the same and of the quantities delivered to the commissary general, his deputies or assistants, specifying the names of the persons to whom the same were respectively delivered, the prices thereof and the place or places where the said meat was procured, under the penalty of forfeiting his commission or allowance for the said service.

And to the intent that both purchaser and seller may be assured of the price and certainty of payment for all cattle, sheep or salted provisions procured by virtue of this act:

[Section IV.] (Section VI, P. L.) Be it enacted by the authority aforesaid, That all voluntary sellers of the said enumerated articles to the said persons so appointed, shall be entitled to the current prices therefor; the said sale and price to be certified by the said purchaser under his hand, which said certificate shall be and is hereby declared to be good and effectual in the payment of all state taxes for the money therein expressed, and the several collectors of taxes within this state are hereby enjoined and required to receive the said crtificates in payment.

(Section VII, P. L.) Provided always, That such certificate be not transferrable to any other person, but available only to the person whose name shall be expressed therein, and if the amount of such certificate shall exceed the tax for which it shall be tendered in payment, then the collector, upon such person producing the same shall indorse the allowance made thereupon as so much of the said certificate paid and shall keep an exact register of the names of the persons and the amount of the sums so indorsed in credit as aforesaid, a copy whereof he shall deliver to the county treasurer as his voucher, but if the said certificate shall not exceed the tax demanded the collector shall take up the same, crediting the tax as aforesaid and returning such certificate to the county treasurer.

[Section V.] (Section VIII, P. L.) Be it also enacted by the authority aforesaid, That the faith and honor of the state be and it is hereby pledged for the faithful and just payment of such of the said certificates as shall not be paid in for taxes as aforesaid, together with lawful interest thereon at the rate of six per centum, on or before the first day of March next.

(Section IX, P. L.) And whereas, the spirited exertions of individuals in such an exigency deserve the utmost encouragement, and there is reason to believe that many faithful friends to their country will, if duly secured against loss or damage (as it is reasonable they should be) furnish the said persons so appointed with cattle, sheep or salted provisions procured by their personal credit and influence.

[Section VI.] (Section X, P. L.) Be it, therefore, enacted, That any person so delivering to the person so appointed any number of cattle not less than five or sheep not less than twenty, shall be entitled to an order on the president or vice-president in council for the full amount of the price thereof, together with all reasonable charges attending the said service as the same shall be settled by the commissioners.

[Section VII.] (Section XI, P. L.) Be it also enacted by the authority aforesaid, That if any person or persons shall oppose the persons appointed by virtue of this act in the execution of the several duties herein assigned them, such person or persons shall be and they are hereby declared, on conviction in due course of law, to be liable to the penalty of two thousand pounds, to be levied on their goods and chattels, lands and tenements or, in case no such effects can be found, to imprisonment without bail or mainprise for the space of six months, and also to such pains and penalties as are by law inflicted in case of resistance to any sheriff or known officer in the execution of their offices respectively.

[Section VIII.] (Section XII, P. L.) Be it also enacted, That it shall and may be lawful for the president or vice-president in council to make such allowance as may be necessary to the officers in and by this act appointed; and in case of any doubt or difficulty arising in the execution thereof the same shall be referred to the supreme executive council, whose determination in all matters not specially provided for herein shall be directory and conclusive.

[Section IX.] (Section XIII, P. L.) Be it also enacted, That it shall and may be lawful for the president or vice-president in council, by proclamation, to suspend the several powers and authorities herein granted if the circumstances of the federal army shall, in their judgment, admit thereof.

[Section X.] (Section XIV, P. L.) Be it also enacted, That this act shall be and remain in full force and virtue, unless suspended as aforesaid, until the end of the next sitting of the general assembly, and no longer.

Passed June 1, 1780. See the note to the Act of Assembly passed January 2, 1778, Chapter 782, and the Act of Assembly passed December 4, 1789, Chapter 1470. Recorded L. B. No. 1, p. 397, &c.

Laws enacted in the fourth sitting of the fourth General Assembly of the Commonwealth of Pennsylvania which commenced at Philadelphia on Friday, the first day of September, in the year of our Lord 1780.

CHAPTER CMXIV.

AN ACT TO REMEDY THE INCONVENIENCES OF HOLDING THE ANNUAL ELECTIONS IN THE FOURTH DISTRICT OF THE COUNTY OF CUMBERLAND AND THE SECOND DISTRICT IN THE COUNTY OF BEDFORD AT THE PLACES HERETOFORE APPOINTED BY THE LAWS OF THIS COMMONWEALTH.

(Section I, P. L.) Whereas, it has been found very inconvenient for the freemen of the fourth district of Cumberland county to attend the annual election at the house of James Purdy, in Farmanaugh township, as by an act, entitled "A supplement to an act, entitled 'An act for amending the several acts for electing members of assembly,' "[1] passed the fourteenth day of June, one thousand seven hundred and seventy-seven, is directed:

For remedy whereof:

[Section I.] (Section II, P. L.) Be it enacted and it is hereby enacted by the Representatives of the Freemen of the Commonwealth of Pennsylvania in General Assembly met, and by the authority of the same, That henceforth the freemen of the fourth district of the said county shall meet on the day by the constitution of this commonwealth appointed for such election at the house of Thomas Wilson, in the township of Millford, and then and there elect members of general assembly and other elective officers for said county, and make return thereof according to the laws heretofore made and provided.

(Section III, P. L.) And whereas, it is very inconvenient for

---

[1] Chapter 757.

the freemen of the townships of Air and Bethel, in the county of Bedford, to attend the annual election at the house of John Burd, in the second district of said county, as by the above-recited act is directed:

Therefore:

[Section II.] (Section IV, P. L.) Be it enacted by the authority aforesaid, That henceforth the said townships of Air and Bethel shall be a fifth district of the said county of Bedford for the purpose of such annual election, and that the freemen of the said townships shall hereafter meet on the day appointed by the constitution of this commonwealth for such election at the house of William Hart, in the said township of Bethel, and then and there elect members of general assembly and other elective officers for said county according to the said constitution and the laws in such case made and provided, and a return of such elections shall be made in the same manner as the laws of this commonwealth direct for other districts, anything in the above-recited act to the contrary in any wise notwithstanding.

Passed September 20, 1780. See the note to the Act of Assembly passed June 14, 1777, Chapter 757. Recorded L. B. No. 1, p. 399, &c.

CHAPTER CMXV.

A SUPPLEMENT TO THE ACT ENTITLED "AN ACT FOR REGULATING AND ESTABLISHING ADMIRALTY JURISDICTION." [1]

(Section I, P. L.) Whereas by the act of assembly, entitled "An act for regulating and establishing admiralty jurisdiction," [1] passed the eighth day of March last, no provision is made for the trial of capital and criminal offenses committed at sea previous to the passing of the said act, and it is reasonable that the same mode [of trial] should be adopted for offenders of this kind before the said time as since and it is necessary that all such offenders should be duly punished:

---

[1] Chapter 887.

[Section I.] (Section II, P. L.) Be it therefore enacted and it is hereby enacted by the Representatives of the Freemen of the Commonwealth of Pennsylvania in General Assembly met and by the authority of the same, That all traitors, pirates, felons and criminals who have offended upon the seas or within the admiralty jurisdiction on or before the said eighth day of March last may and shall be inquired of, tried, adjudged and punished in the same manner, at any admiralty sessions to be held for the trial of such offenses as if the same had been committed since the aforesaid day; and if any person or persons happen to be indicted for any such offense done or hereafter to be done upon the seas, or in any other place within the admiralty jurisdiction, or as accessaries before or after the fact, either on the land or upon the seas, by a grand jury [for] the city or county of Philadelphia or for either of them, before the judges, or any two of them, of the court of admiralty sessions mentioned in the act to which this is a supplement, that then such order, process, judgment and execution shall be used, had, done and made to and against every such person and persons so being indicted, as against traitors, felons, murderers and other criminals, for treason, felony, robbery, murder, manslaughter or other like offense done upon the land within the said city or county as by the laws of this commonwealth is accustomed; and the trial of such offense or offenses, if it be denied by the offender or offenders, shall be had by twelve lawful men of the said city and county of Philadelphia, or either of them; and such as shall be convicted of any such offense or offenses, by verdict, confession or otherwise in the said court, shall have and suffer such pains of death, losses of lands, goods and chattels and other punishment as if they had been convicted and attainted of any treasons, felonies, robberies or other the said offenses done upon the land, and shall be utterly excluded the benefit of clergy where the same is taken away or not admitted for such like offense committed within the body of a county or on land.

[Section II.] (Section III, P. L.) And be it further enacted by the authority aforesaid, That if any of the subjects of this state or any of the United States of America shall commit any piracy or robbery or any act of hostility against other the subjects of this state or of any of the other United States of America, upon the sea, under color of any commission from any foreign prince or state, or pretence of authority from any person whatsoever, such offender and offenders and every of them shall be deemed, adjudged and taken to be pirates, felons and robbers, and they and every of them being duly convicted thereof, according to the act of assembly above recited for regulating and establishing admiralty jurisdiction or this act, shall have and suffer such punishment and forfeitures as pirates, felons and robbers upon the seas ought to have and suffer.

[Section III.] (Section IV, P. L.) And be it further enacted by the authority aforesaid, That if any commander or master of any ship or any seaman or mariner shall, in any place where the admiralty hath jurisdiction, betray his trust and turn pirate, enemy or traitor and piratically and feloniously run away with his or their ship or ships, or any barge, boat, ordinance, ammunition, goods or merchandises or yield them up voluntarily to any pirate, enemy or traitor, or bring any seducing message from either of them, or consult, combine or confederate with, or attempt or endeavor to corrupt any commander, master, officer or mariner to yield up or run away with any ship, goods or merchandise or turn pirate, or go over to pirates or enemies; or if any person shall lay violent hands on his commander, whereby to hinder him from fighting in defense of his ship and goods committed to his trust or shall confine his master or make or endeavor to make a revolt in his ship, he shall be adjudged [to be] a pirate, felon and robber, and being convicted thereof as aforesaid shall have and suffer such pains of death, loss of lands, goods and chattels as pirates, felons and robbers upon the seas ought to have and suffer.

(Section V, P. L.) And whereas, complaint has been made that many soldiers have deserted from the armies of the United States of America and entered on board private armed ships, and when in foreign ports have deserted them, whereby the states have been greatly injured in the loss of soldiers and subjects:

[Section IV.] (Section VI, P. L.) Be it therefore enacted

by the authority aforesaid, That every captain, master or other officer belonging to any vessel who shall receive or entertain any deserter, knowing him to be such, shall forfeit and pay to this commonwealth the sum of ten thousand pounds, to be recovered by seizure of his or their goods and chattels, or of moneys in the hands of the marshal or agents, or where a sufficient sum of money cannot be obtained through the above means then and in that case to suffer one year's imprisonment without bail or mainprise.

[Section V.] (Section VII, P. L.) And be it further enacted by the authority aforesaid, That all shares of prizes and wages to which deserters from the armies of the United States of America who have or shall enter on board any private ship of war or other vessel that are or may hereafter be entitled to, shall be confiscated and forfeited to the use of this commonwealth and applied for the recruiting the line of this state in the federal army, and all wills and powers, letters of attorney, deeds of sale and every other species of conveyance executed by such deserters, either before the sailing of such vessels or at any time after their return, sending prizes into any port of this state, before the marshal of the admiralty court has given notice of his being fully prepared [fully] to pay shares of prizes to persons entitled to receive them shall be null and void; and if, after the publication of this act the marshal of the admiralty court or any agent shall advance goods or money to any person discovered to be a deserter before the marshal shall have given notice that he is ready to fully pay all shares of prizes, such advance shall be at the risk and loss of the person advancing it.

[Section VI.] (Section VIII, P. L.) And be it further enacted by the authority aforesaid, That his excellency the president or honorable vice-president and executive council of this state be authorized to appoint an agent and proper persons under him to visit all vessels in the ports of this state on board of which it may be suspected deserters are entered or engaged, and there demand of the senior officer on board the roll of his crew, and that each man, when his name is called over, shall be shown to the person or persons authorized as above, and all such as are claimed as deserters shall be delivered up, and in case the officer immediately commanding on board any vessel shall refuse to produce his roll, show the men or deliver up such as shall be claimed as deserters, he shall forfeit and pay the sum of ten thousand pounds, to be recovered by an action to be brought for that purpose, or suffer one year's imprisonment, which penalty shall also be incurred by every person obstructing such search, and it shall be the proper business of the above-mentioned agent to give notice to the marshal of all deserters by him or the persons under him discovered, and claim and receive their shares of prizes and wages and pay the same unto the state treasurer.

(Section IX, P. L.) And whereas, it is found by experience inexpedient to continue the eleventh section in the act to which this is a supplement any longer in force:

[Section VII.] (Section X, P. L.) Be it enacted by the authority aforesaid, That the said section "providing that nothing in the said act contained, which might contradict or interfere with the directions of an act of assembly of this commonwealth, entitled 'An act for the effectual suppression of public auctions and vendues, and to prohibit male persons capable of bearing arms from being peddlers and hawkers,'[1] passed on the twenty-sixth day of November last, should have effect or be in force for and during the continuance of the said-recited act," be and the same is hereby repealed and made void, and all prizes and property condemned by the judge of the admiralty in pursuance of the directions of the said act, except negroes and mulattoes, may and shall be sold at public auction by the marshal of the said court of admiralty to the highest bidder for the same, which sale shall commence within twelve days after such condemnation, on giving six days' previous notice thereof, as well in hand bills as in one or more of the public newspapers of the city of Philadelphia, and the said sale shall be continued without unnecessary intermission until the whole are sold; and the net proceeds thereof be distributed as by the said act is prescribed, which distribution shall by him be made within twenty days after such sale is completed, under the

---

[1] Passed November 26, 1779, Chapter 870.

penalty of twenty per centum for the sum so neglected to be paid, to be recovered in an action brought for the same. Provided always, That persons legally authorized shall appear and make demand thereof agreeable to the mode prescribed by the act to which this is a supplement.

[Section VIII.] (Section XI, P. L.) And be it further enacted by the authority aforesaid, That in case any vessels, goods, wares or merchandise so as aforesaid sold by the marshal shall not be paid for by the purchaser within three days after the sale thereof, that then the said marshall shall or may again expose such vessels, goods, wares or merchandise to public auction for the account of the captors, and having disposed of them for money, shall and may recover against the first purchaser all loss whatsoever which may arise on such second sale, together with costs, damages and charges, in any court of common pleas within this commonwealth.

[Section IX.] (Section XII, P. L.) And be it further enacted by the authority aforesaid, That all other parts of the act of assembly before recited, and to which this is a supplement, not hereby altered or supplied, shall remain, continue and be in full force and virtue.

<small>Passed September 22, 1780. See the note to the Act of Assembly passed March 8, 1780, Chapter 887, and the Act of Assembly passed March 28, 1787, Chapter 1281. Recorded L. B. No. 1, p. 399, &c.</small>

CHAPTER CMXVI.

A SUPPLEMENT TO THE ACT ENTITLED "AN ACT FOR THE REGULATION OF THE MILITIA OF THE COMMONWEALTH OF PENNSYLVANIA." [1]

(Section I, P. L.) Whereas, the mode of determining the bounty of the militia while in actual service by the justices of the several courts of quarter sessions, as directed by the act above mentioned, has been found on experience inconvenient

---

[1] Passed March 20, 1780, Chapter 902.

and unequal, inasmuch as persons rendering the same services, bearing equal hardships and exposed to equal danger are partially and unequally compensated, thereby creating discontents and distinctions prejudicial to this important and necessary service:

For remedy whereof:

[Section I.] (Section II, P. L.) Be it enacted and it is hereby enacted by the Representatives of the Freemen of the Commonwealth of Pennsylvania in General Assembly met, and by the authority of the same, That the average price of common labor by the day in the city of Philadelphia and counties of this state, respectively, shall be inquired into, ascertained and fixed by the representatives of the freemen of the commonwealth of Pennsylvania in general assembly met, which price so fixed and determined shall be the rate by which all fines and penalties for neglect of militia duty and the bounty of the militia shall be estimated and determined, during and from that time to the end of the next sitting of general assembly, and so from time to time at every succeeding session.

(Section III, P. L.) Provided always, That this act or anything herein contained shall not be construed to alter, mitigate or discharge any fine or penalty already accrued or which may hereafter accrue before the said rate shall be determined and fixed by the general assembly as aforesaid, but that all and singular the powers and authority of the quarter sessions as given by the said act shall continue until the said rate shall be fixed by the general assembly, and no longer.

(Section IV, P. L.) And whereas sundry former lieutenants and sub-lieutenants who have acted under the late militia law have refused or neglected to deliver up the duplicates, books and papers belonging to their offices, whereby the fines and penalties accrued for former delinquencies still remain uncollected to the great discouragement of those who have rendered their personal service in time of danger and to the injury of the public:

For remedy whereof:

[Section II.] (Section V, P. L.) Be it enacted by the authority aforesaid, That if any persons who may have acted in the office of lieutenant or sub-lieutenant of the city of Philadelphia or any of the counties of this state shall, upon the resignation of his office, or being legally superceded therein, refuse to deliver [up] to his successor in office or to any person who is or shall be appointed by the president or vice-president in council to receive the same, all and singular the books, duplicates, returns or other papers belonging to or [in use] in the said office, demand being first made thereof in writing, he or they so offending shall forfeit the sum of ten thousand pounds and the necessary costs of prosecution for every such refusal, to be recovered by his said successor in office or other person duly authorized as aforesaid upon indictment, bill, plaint or information or by action of debt in any court of record within this state, to be applied as other militia fines are directed by the law to which this is a supplement, and in case of a second refusal such person shall suffer as well the said penalty as the further punishment of six months' imprisonment without bail or mainprise, and the justices of the court where such penalty shall be recovered shall order the said commitment accordingly.

[Section III.] (Section VI, P. L.) And be it further enacted by the authority aforesaid, That so much and such parts of the law to which this is a supplement as are by this act altered and amended be and are hereby repealed and declared null and void.

Passed September 22, 1780. See the note to the Act of Assembly passed March 20, 1780, Chapter 902. The Act in the text was repealed by the Act of Assembly passed March 21, 1783, Chapter 1022. Recorded L. B. No. 1, p. 401, &c.

CHAPTER CMXVII.

AN ACT TO REVIVE AND CONTINUE FOR A FURTHER LIMITED TIME THE ACT FOR LAYING AN EMBARGO ON THE EXPORTATION OF PROVISIONS FROM THIS STATE BY SEA, FOR A LIMITED TIME.

(Section I, P. L.) Whereas, an act, entitled "An act for laying an embargo on the exportation of provisions from this state, by sea, for a limited time," [1] passed on the twenty-eighth day of February, Anno Domini one thousand seven hundred and eighty, is expired by its own limitation, and it being expedient to continue the same to a further time:

Therefore:

[Section I.] (Section II, P. L.) Be it enacted and it is hereby enacted by the Representatives of the Freemen of the Commonwealth of Pennsylvania in General Assembly met, and by the authority of the same, That the said act, and every clause, proviso and thing therein contained, save the clause limiting the continuance thereof, shall be and the same is hereby continued for six months, and from thence to the end of the next sitting of the general assembly.

> Passed September 22, 1780. See the note to the Act of Assembly passed February 28, 1780, Chapter 876; and the Act of Assembly passed December 22, 1780, Chapter 922. The Act in the text was repealed by the Act of Assembly passed February 27, 1781, Chapter 928. Recorded L. B. No. 1, p. 402, &c.

CHAPTER CMXVIII

AN ACT TO CONTINUE FOR A LONGER TIME THE ACT ENTITLED "AN ACT TO SUSPEND THE OPERATION FOR A LIMITED TIME OF THE SEVERAL LAWS OF THIS COMMONWEALTH FOR MAKING THE BILLS OF CREDIT OF THE UNITED STATES A LEGAL TENDER IN THE PAYMENT OF DEBTS EQUAL TO GOLD AND SILVER." [2]

(Section I, P. L.) Whereas the above-recited act would expire with the ending of this present session of assembly, and it is just and necessary that the same should be continued, until the value of the said currency can be fixed at some certain standard, and a proper mode established which will make the advantages equal to both debtor and creditor:

Therefore:

[Section I.] (Section II, P. L.) Be it enacted and it is hereby enacted by the Representatives of the Freemen of the Common-

---

[1] Chapter 876.
[2] Chapter 911.

wealth of Pennsylvania in General Assembly met, and by the authority of the same, That the act, entitled "An act to suspend the operation for a limited time of the several laws of this commonwealth for making the bills of credit of the United States a legal tender in the payment of debts equal to gold and silver,"[1] passed the thirty-first day of May, one thousand seven hundred and eighty, be and is hereby continued in full force until the end of the next sitting of the general assembly, and no longer.

> Passed September 22, 1780. See the note to the Act of Assembly passed May 31, 1780, Chapter 911; and the Act of Assembly passed June 21, 1781, Chapter 945. Recorded L. B. No. 1, p. 402, &c.

CHAPTER CMXIX.

AN ACT TO ALTER AND AMEND AN ACT ENTITLED "AN ACT FOR THE EFFECTUAL SUPPRESSION OF PUBLIC AUCTION AND VENDUES AND PROHIBIT MALE PERSONS CAPABLE OF BEARING ARMS FROM BEING HAWKERS AND PEDDLERS."[2]

(Section I, P. L.) Whereas it appears to be necessary in the present situation of the trade and commerce of this state that the sale of goods at public vendue should be enlarged and extended:

[Section I.] (Section II, P. L.) Be it therefore enacted and it is hereby enacted by the Representatives of the Freemen of the Commonwealth of Pennsylvania in General Assembly met, and by the authority of the same, That from and after the publication of this act it shall and may be lawful for the president or vice-president in council to appoint and license three auctioneers, one for the city of Philadelphia, one for the Northern Liberties and one for the district of Southwark, who shall continue for and during the will and pleasure of the said president and council, and shall give bond to the president and his successors, with two sufficient sureties in the sum of twenty thou-

---
[1] Chapter 911.
[2] Passed November 26, 1779, Chapter 870.

sand pounds, for the faithful discharge of their duties, and for well and truly performing the terms and payments in and by this act directed and required.

[Section II.] (Section III, P. L.) And be it further enacted by the authority aforesaid, That the said auctioneers and no other shall, from and after the publication of this act, have full power and authority to set up and expose to sale by public outcry and vendue, all and any houses, lands, goods, wares and merchandises and property whatsoever, negroes and mulatto slaves excepted, rendering and paying to the state treasurer for the use of the commonwealth one per centum of the gross amount of the sales so by him or them made as aforesaid, in manner following, That is to say: That each and every of the said auctioneers shall, once in every three month[s], render an account upon oath to the said treasurer (which oath he is hereby empowered to administer and is directed to file the said account with the said oath in his office) of all the effects and property by him or them sold at any time before the said time of rendering the same account and since his last settlement, and shall then immediately pay to the same treasurer the full amount of the said one pound in the hundred pounds upon the same account; and upon any failure in rendering the same account upon oath, or of payment of the said sum of one per centum, any auctioneer so failing or neglecting shall be discharged from his place and the said bond put immediately in suit. And if any person or persons other than the said auctioneers shall be found selling or disposing of any lands, tenements, goods, wares, merchandises or property whatsoever within the city of Philadelphia, the Northern Liberties or the district of Southwark, except as hereinafter is excepted by way of vendue or auction such person or persons so offending and being thereof legally convict[ed] shall, for every such offense, forfeit the sum of twenty thousand pounds to the use of the poor of the city, liberties or district where such offense shall be committed. And, moreover, it shall and may be lawful for any justice of the peace of the said city, liberties or district, respectively, upon his own view or on the testimony and information of one or more creditable witnesses to him given of any persons selling any lands, tenements, goods, wares, merchandise or other property whatever by way of vendue or auction as aforesaid, except as by this act is excepted, within the said city, district or liberties to cause such person or persons so offending to [be] apprehended and may oblige him, her or them to find sureties for his, her or their good behavior and appearance at the next court of quarter sessions of the peace to be held for the said city, liberties or districts, respectively.

[Section III.] And it is further declared, That if the party so bound over, shall, during the continuance of his, her and their recognizances, presume again to sell or expose to sale by way of vendue as aforesaid any lands, tenements, goods, wares, merchandise or other property whatsoever within the said city, liberties or district, such selling or exposing to sale shall be deemed and is hereby declared to be a breach of the said recognizance.

[Section IV.] (Section IV, P. L.) Provided always, and it is hereby further enacted, That nothing herein contained shall extend or be construed to extend to hinder any lawful executor or executors, administrator or administrators, to expose to sale by way of public auction, vendue or otherwise, any lands, tenements, goods or chattels of their respective testators or intestates or to hinder any sheriff, constable, lieutenant or sub-lieutenant or other officer to sell and dispose of by way of vendue any lands, tenements, goods or chattels taken in execution and liable to be sold by order of law, or to hinder any person or persons from selling or exposing to sale by way of vendue any goods or chattels of any kind whatsoever taken and distrained for rent in arrear, but that all and every [such] person or persons may do therein as they might have done, any [prohibition] in this or any former law contained to the contrary notwithstanding.

(Section V, P. L.) And whereas the crime of horse stealing is become so frequent in this and the neighboring states as to render every precaution and remedy necessary and proper:

[Section V.] (Section VI, P. L.) Be it therefore enacted by the authority aforesaid, That each and every of the said auctioneers shall keep a register of the horses, mares [or] geldings by them respectively exposed to sale, in their respective offices, wherein shall, before sale, be inserted the color, size and principal marks, natural and artificial, of every horse, mare or gelding by him exposed to sale, and the age, as the intended vendor shall declare it, the name or names of the persons offering the same for sale, and after the sale the name of the person to whom the same is sold, which said register is hereby declared to be so far a public record as that every person shall be entitled to a view thereof and a copy, if demanded, paying for such inspection the sum of two dollars and for such copy the sum of six dollars, and shall be read in evidence on any trial respecting the property of such horse, mare or gelding.

[Section VI.] (Section VII, P. L.) And be it further enacted by the authority aforesaid, That no sale of any stolen horse, mare or gelding by virtue of this act shall be deemed a public sale in market overt, so as to change the property thereof.

[Section VII.] (Section VIII, P. L.) And be it further enacted by the authority aforesaid, That no vendue shall be held by the said auctioneers, or any of them, out of the city or district for which he or they shall be appointed, and that their fees or recompense for selling at public auction, collecting the money and paying over the same without loss or waste shall be as follows: For household goods, cattle and live stock, five per centum; for horses, two and a half per centum; for ships, houses and lands an half per centum; for rum, sugar, tea, coffee and all other groceries, two and a half per centum; for European and American manufactures, in such lots or proportions as are usually sold in wholesale stores, five per centum.

Passed September 23, 1780. See the note to the Act of Assembly passed November 26, 1779, Chapter 870; and the Acts of Assembly passed April 13, 1782, Chapter 975; December 9, 1783, Chapter 1063. Recorded L. B. No. 1, p. 402, &c.

Laws of the First Sitting of the Fifth General Assembly of the Commonwealth of Pennsylvania, which met at Philadelphia on Tuesday, the twenty-third day of October, in the year 1780.

CHAPTER CMXX.

AN ACT TO SETTLE AND ADJUST THE ACCOUNTS OF THE TROOPS OF THIS STATE IN THE SERVICE OF THE UNITED STATES; AND FOR OTHER PURPOSES THEREIN MENTIONED.

(Section I, P. L.) Whereas, from a variety of causes, the United States have not been able to comply with their engagements heretofore made to the officers and private men of the Pennsylvania line, which hath occasioned great injury to those troops, to whose virtuous exertions America is much indebted:

[Section I.] (Section II, P. L.) Be it therefore enacted and it is hereby enacted by the Representatives of the Freemen of the Commonwealth of Pennsylvania, in General Assembly met, and by the authority of the same, That the supreme executive council be and they are hereby authorized and directed to appoint three auditors to settle the depreciation of the pay accounts of all the officers and private men of the Pennsylvania line from the first day of January, one thousand seven hundred and seventy-seven, to the first day of August, one thousand seven hundred and eighty, and the said auditors, or any two of them, are hereby empowered and directed to estimate in specie all sums of continental money received by the said officers and private men on account of their pay within the period aforesaid agreeable to a scale of depreciation hereinafter mentioned and contained.

[Section II.] (Section III, P. L.) And be it further enacted by the authority aforesaid, That the said auditors, or any two of them, are hereby empowered and directed to give to the officers and private men to whom pay on such settlement as aforesaid shall be found due, certificates specifying the sums due in specie, which certificates shall be received and considered as equal to specie, in payment of the estates hereinafter mentioned and directed to be sold.

[Section III.] (Section IV, P. L.) And be it further enacted by the authority aforesaid, That all confiscated estates not already sold or appropriated to public use shall, on the first day of July next, or as soon after as may be convenient, be disposed of at public sale for the highest price, which sale the supreme executive council are hereby directed to order the agents for confiscated estates to make, giving due notice thereof, and the said agents are hereby directed to receive in payment for the estates which they shall sell as aforesaid, specie or bills of credit of this state equivalent thereto, or the certificates aforesaid, which sales shall be made upon the same terms of payment as have heretofore been directed in the sale of other confiscated estates.

[Section IV.] (Section V, P. L.) And be it further enacted by the authority aforesaid, That in order to prevent the certificates of the private men of the line aforesaid from being counterfeited, or becoming objects of speculation, no transfer or assignment of the same shall be good and valid in law, unless attested by the officer commanding the regiment to which said privates shall belong.

[Section V.] (Section VI, P. L.) And be it further enacted by the authority aforesaid, That in case the possessor or possessors of the said certificates shall think proper to purchase unlocated lands belonging to this state with the same, then and in such case it shall and may be lawful for the commissioners or other proper officers of the land office, so soon as the said office shall be opened by law, and they are hereby directed to receive the said certificates so unpaid equal in value to specie in payment for the lands so purchased from the said land office, which lands purchased with and paid for in the certificates aforesaid are to be rated and granted at the same price at which unlocated lands shall or may be rated and granted to any person or persons tendering gold or silver or currency equivalent thereto.

[Section VI.] (Section VII, P. L.) And be it further enacted by the authority aforesaid, That the said auditors shall, in like manner, settle and adjust the accounts of all officers and private men of the line aforesaid who have fallen or died in the service during the said period; and their widows and children shall be entitled to such certificates and to all the benefits and advantages hereby granted to the officers and private men now in the said line.

[Section VII.] (Section VIII, P. L.) And be it further enacted by the authority aforesaid, That the officers and private men of the state navy now in actual service shall and are hereby declared to be equally entitled to all benefits and allowances extended to the Pennsylvania line by this act, and all officers and soldiers of this state taken prisoners in the actual service of this or the United States shall likewise be considered as being within the intent and meaning of this act so far as to be entitled to all the benefits and advantages hereby granted and extended to the officers and privates of the Pennsylvania line aforesaid.

[Section VIII.] (Section IX, P. L.) And be it further enacted by the authority aforesaid, That the auditors aforesaid previous to their entering on the duties required of them by this act, shall severally take the following oath or affirmation, to wit:

"I, A. B., do swear or affirm (as the case may be) that I will well and truly perform all and singular the duties required of me by the act, entitled 'An act to settle and adjust the accounts of the troops of this state (meaning Pennsylvania) in the service of the United States and for other purposes therein mentioned,' to the best of my knowledge and abilities, without partiality or respect to any person or persons whatsoever."

And the auditors aforesaid are hereby fully authorized and directed to settle the aforesaid accounts upon oath or affirmation, which oath or affirmation shall be by them administered.

[Section IX.] (Section X, P. L.) And be it further enacted by the authority aforesaid, That this or any future assembly, notwithstanding the provision made as aforesaid, may or shall, if they think proper, call in all such certificates given and not redeemed as aforesaid and pay off the same in specie or other current money equivalent.

[Section X.] (Section XI, P. L.) And be it further enacted by the authority aforesaid, That in case any of the confiscated estates above mentioned shall be sold and paid for in specie or other current money, then the agents aforesaid shall pay the said moneys so received to the treasurer of this state, which he is hereby directed to reserve for redeeming the certificates aforesaid, which shall remain unpaid in such manner as the general assembly shall order and direct. And all certificates received by the agents aforesaid and commissioners of the land office by virtue of this act shall be by them delivered to the treasurer aforesaid, who is hereby directed to keep the same, to be cancelled and destroyed in such maner as the general assembly shall order and direct.

[Section XI.] (Section XII, P. L.) And be it further enacted by the authority aforesaid, That the following scale of depreciation shall be the rule by which the said auditors shall be governed in the settlement aforesaid:

One Thousand Seven Hundred and Seventy-seven.

January, one and a half.
February, one and a half.
March, two.
April, two and a half.
May, two and a half.
June, two and a half.
July, three.
August, three.
September, three.
October, three,
November, three.
December, four.

One Thousand Seven Hundred and Seventy-Eight.

January, four.
February, five.

March, five.
April, six.
May, five.
June, four.
July, four.
August, five.
September, five.
October, five.
November, six.
December, six.

One Thousand Seven Hundred and Seventy-nine.

January, eight.
February, ten.
March, ten and a half.
April, seventeen.
May, twenty-four.
June, twenty.
July, nineteen.
August, twenty.
September, twenty-four.
October, thirty.
November, thirty-eight and an half.
December, forty-one and an half.

One Thousand Seven Hundred and Eighty.

January, forty and an half.
February, forty-seven and an half.
March, sixty-one and an half.
April, sixty-one and an half.
May, fifty-nine.
June, sixty-one and an half.
July, sixty-four and an half.

[Section XII.] (Section XIII, P. L.) And be it further enacted by the authority aforesaid, That the auditors aforesaid shall be entitled to receive the same pay and allowance as the auditors of this state appointed by the legislature for the settlement of the public accounts.

[Section XIII.] (Section XIV, P. L.) And be it further enacted by the authority aforesaid, That printed certificates shall be provided by direction of the supreme executive council in such manner and form as they shall judge necessary and proper and delivered to the auditors aforesaid, to be by them applied to the uses and purposes hereinbefore directed.

> Passed December 18, 1780. See the Acts of Assembly passed April 10, 1781, Chapter 941; October 1, 1781, Chapter 955; March 12, 1783, Chapter 1007; March 21, 1783, Chapter 1024; March 25, 1786, Chapter 1219. Recorded L. B. No. 1, p. 404, &c.

CHAPTER CMXXI.

A SUPPLEMENT TO AN ACT ENTITLED "AN ACT FOR FUNDING AND REDEEMING THE BILLS OF CREDIT OF THE UNITED STATES OF AMERICA AND FOR PROVIDING MEANS TO BRING THE PRESENT WAR TO AN HAPPY CONCLUSION." [1]

(Section I, P. L.) Whereas it is the duty of the representatives of the freemen of this state to provide adequate funds for redeeming and cancelling the eighth part of the new bills of credit emitted or to be emitted by Congress in consequence of their act of the eighteenth day of March last, amounting to one million two hundred and fifty thousand dollars of the value of four shillings and six pence sterling each, or so many thereof as may be issued, together with the interest thereon, to accrue as mentioned in the act to which this act is a supplement:

Therefore:

[Section I.] (Section II, P. L.) Be it enacted and it is hereby enacted by the Representatives of the Freemen of the Commonwealth of Pennsylvania in General Assembly met, and by the authority of the same, That the sum of ninety-three thousand six hundred and forty pounds ten shillings shall be raised, levied and paid in each and every [of] the next [six] succeeding years on the persons and estates of the inhabitants of the

---

[1] Passed June 1, 1780, Chapter 912.

city of Philadelphia and the several counties of this state in the proportion and manner following: That is to say, the city and county of Philadelphia, thirty-one thousand and twenty-three pounds fifteen shillings; the county of Bucks, six thousand one hundred and thirty-five pounds fifteen shillings; the county of Chester, nine thousand eighteen hundred and forty-nine pounds fifteen shillings; the county of Lancaster, thirteen thousand three hundred and thirty pounds seventeen shillings and six pence; the county of York, seven thousand four hundred and twenty-eight pounds; the county of Cumberland, six thousand nine hundred and eighty pounds twelve shillings and six pence; the county of Berks, six thousand seven hundred and four pounds twelve shillings and six pence; the county of Northampton, three thousand eight hundred and fifty-nine pounds ten shillings; the county of Bedford, two thousand one hundred and fifteen pounds fifteen shillings; the county of Northumberland, three thousand five hundred and ninety-eight pounds two shillings and six pence, and the county of Westmoreland two thousand six hundred and thirteen pounds fifteen shillings, amounting in the whole to five hundred and sixty-one thousand eight hundred and forty-three pounds, to be cancelled and destroyed at such times as the general assembly of this state shall hereafter direct.

[Section II.] (Section III, P. L.) And be it enacted by the authority aforesaid, That the act, entitled "An act to raise the supplies for the year one thousand seven hundred and seventy-nine,"[1] passed on the third day of April, in the year of our Lord one thousand seven hundred and seventy-nine, and the act, entitled "An act for raising the additional sum of five millions seven hundred thousand dollars for the current year one thousand seven hundred and seventy-nine,"[2] passed the tenth day of October, in said year, and every clause and thing in the said acts contained shall be in force and shall be extended and applied to the raising, levying, collecting and paying the taxes or sums of money hereby directed to be levied and paid as fully as if said acts were herein inserted except only where the former

---

[1] Passed April 3, 1779, Chapter 840.
[2] Passed October 10, 1779, Chapter 866.

is amended, supplied or altered by the latter or either of the said acts are amended, supplied or altered by this act.

[Section III.] (Section IV, P. L.) And be it further enacted by the authority aforesaid, That every single freeman who, at the time of assessing any tax required by this act, is of the age of twenty-one years or upwards and has been out of his apprenticeship or servitude for the space of six months, shall be assessed any sum not exceeding three pounds nor less than one pound by the township, ward or district assessors and two freeholders, anything in the acts above mentioned to the contrary in anywise notwithstanding.

(Section V, P. L.) And whereas, divers owners of lands whereon improvements have been made and of tenements may not reside in the county or district where such lands or tenements are situate, whereby it may be difficult to collect the taxes assessed on such real estate:

For remedy whereof:

[Section IV.] (Section VI, P. L.) Be it enacted by the authority aforesaid, That the tenant or tenants or other person residing on or occupying such real estate, his, her and their goods and chattels, as well as the lands, goods and chattels of the owner or owners thereof, shall be liable to be distrained to satisfy the said taxes, or any of them. And in case the tenant or tenants or other person or persons residing on or occupying such real estate shall pay any tax laid thereon by virtue of this act, or shall be distrained to satisfy such tax, such tenant or tenants may retain the same out of the rent by him, her or them payable for such estate to the landlord; or the said tenant or tenants or other occupier or occupiers of such estate shall recover the same, with costs of suit, of the owner of such estate by action of debt, if under five pounds in a summary way in like manner as small debts are recoverable, but if the same exceed five pounds in any court of common pleas.

(Section VII, P. L.) Provided always, That nothing in the foregoing section shall in any manner alter any contract made between [any] landlord and tenant concerning the payment of taxes.

[Section V.] (Section VIII, P. L.) And be it enacted by the authority aforesaid, That the eighteenth section of the act, entitled "An act for raising the additional sum of five millions seven hundred thousand dollars for the current year one thousand seven hundred and seventy-nine,"[1] passed on the tenth day of October, in said year, obliging tenants holding under leases made before the first day of January, one thousand seven hundred and seventy-seven, whereby the rent has been reserved in current money, to pay over and above said rent all taxes on his holding, shall not be extended to the paying the taxes herein directed to be levied and paid.

[Section VI.] (Section IX, P. L.) And be it enacted by the authority aforesaid, That the office and duty of city and county assessors shall hereafter cease and the commissioners of the city and counties of this state shall do and perform the several duties heretofore done and performed by the said city and county assessors, any law of this commonwealth to the contrary in anywise notwithstanding.

[Section VII.] (Section X, P. L.) And be it further enacted by the authority aforesaid, That the time the commissioners shall meet in the city and counties of this state to issue their warrants in pursuance of this act to the ward, district and township assessors shall be on the first Tuesday in August annually.

(Section XI, P. L.) And whereas, it is highly necessary that the bills of credit emitted or that shall hereafter be emitted by Congress, according to their act of the eighteenth day of March last, as the quota of this state, should be made legal tender in all payments whatsoever:

[Section VIII.] (Section XII, P. L.) Be it therefore enacted by the authority aforesaid, That the said bills emitted or issued as the quota of this state in manner aforesaid shall hereafter be current money in this state and legal tender to all intents and purposes whatsoever according to the sums mentioned or expressed in the said bills: That is to say, every dollar of the said bills shall be of the value of one Spanish milled silver dollar, weighing seventeen pennyweight and six

---

[1] Passed October 10, 1779, Chapter 866.

grains, and eight dollars of the said bills shall be equal in value to one gold half johannes of Portugal weighing nine pennyweight, and in the like proportion for all other gold or silver coin; and every tender and payment in the said new bills is hereby declared to be good to all intents and purposes whatsoever, any contract, agreement or bargain between parties to the contrary in anywise notwithstanding.

[Section IX.] (Section XIII, P. L.) And be it enacted by the authority aforesaid, That if any person or persons, bodies politic and corporate from and after the passing of this act shall refuse to receive any of the said bills of credit, when tendered in payment of any debt or demand whatsoever, provided the whole of such debt or demand be so tendered, such person or persons, bodies politic and corporate so refusing shall be forever barred from suing for or recovering the same before any judge or in any court of this state.

[Section X.] (Section XIV, P. L.) And be it enacted by the authority aforesaid, That if any person whatsoever shall, after the passing of this act, refuse to take and receive any of the bills of credit aforesaid in payment for any live stock necessary of life, commodity, manufacture, article or goods whatsoever, which he or she shall sell or expose to sale, or offer the same for a less price or smaller sum of money to be paid in gold or silver than in the bills of credit emitted as aforesaid, or [that] shall give or receive a greater nominal sum of said new bills of credit for a less in gold or silver, every such person, being thereof legally convicted in any court of general quarter sessions of the peace in this state, shall, for the first offense, forfeit and pay double the value of the article or articles so sold or exposed to sale, one moiety thereof to the person or persons giving information of the same and prosecuting the offender to conviction, and the other moiety for the use of the poor of the city, district or township where the offense shall be committed; and for the second offense shall suffer imprisonment during the present war and forfeit to the commonwealth one-half of his or her lands and tenements, goods and chattels.

[Section XI.] (Section XV, P. L.) And be it further enacted by the authority aforesaid, That the party giving information as aforesaid shall be admitted as a competent witness in all cases on the trial of offenders against this act, any law, custom or usage to the contrary in anywise notwithstanding.

> Passed December 19, 1780. See the note to the Act of Assembly passed June 1, 1780, Chapter 912, and the Acts of Assembly passed June 21, 1781, Chapter 945; June 25, 1781, Chapter 948; January 31, 1783, Chapter 1003; March 25, 1785, Chapter 1140; March 18, 1786, Chapter 1214. Recorded L. B. No. 1, p. 406, &c.

CHAPTER CMXXII.

AN ACT TO PERMIT THE EXPORTATION OF FLOUR OF WHEAT FROM THIS STATE BY SEA UNDER CERTAIN LIMITATIONS AND RESTRICTIONS.

(Section I, P. L.) Whereas prohibitions on the exportation of provisions must ever be injurious to this country except in years of scarcity, and as this cause of the late embargoes is in some measure removed by the greater plenty wherewith it hath pleased Providence to bless the land, and as the ability of this state to furnish its quota of supplies for carrying on a just and necessary war depends materially on the freedom of trade:

And whereas, by an act of assembly passed on the twenty-eighth day of February last, entitled "An act for laying an embargo on the exportation of provisions from this state by sea for a limited time,"[1] the exportation from this state by sea of all provisions for the food of man, was, from and after the publication thereof until the first day of September following, forbidden under the penalties and forfeitures in the said act provided and contained:

And whereas, the said act having expired by its own limitation was, by another act of assembly, passed on the twenty-second day of September last, revived and continued for and during the term of six months and from thence to the end of the next sitting of the general assembly:

---

[1] Passed February 28, 1780, Chapter 876.

[Section I.] (Section II, P. L.) Be it therefore enacted and it is hereby enacted by the Representatives of the Freemen of the Commonwealth of Pennsylvania in General Assembly met, and by the authority of the same, That it shall and may be lawful, during the continuance of the said embargo, the said-recited acts notwithstanding, to lade and export by sea, out of this state, flour of wheat, the same being first inspected and found to be good and merchantable and packed according to law, in the manner and upon the conditions and under the regulations hereinafter provided and set forth, and not otherwise. That is to say: In every ship or other vessel, truly and bona fide armed, fitted and provided with six or more carriage guns and suitable ammunition for the same, each of the said guns to be of such caliber as to be capable of discharging an iron ball weighing at least three pounds avoirdupois, and the said vessel to be manned with twenty seamen and other persons of the age of eighteen years or more each, for and during the intended voyage, who shall be actually hired and employed for the defense and service of such vessel, any quantity of such flour not exceeding four hundred hundreds weight of one hundred and twelve pounds to the hundred. In every ship or other vessel truly and bona fide fitted and provided with ten or more carriage guns and suitable ammunition for the same, each of the said carriage guns to be of such caliber as to be capable of receiving and discharging an iron ball weighing at least four pounds avoirdupois, the said vessel to be manned with thirty seamen and other persons of the age of eighteen years or more, actually hired and employed for the defense and service of such vessel, for and during the intended voyage, any quantity of such flour not exceeding one thousand hundreds weight as aforesaid. In every ship and other vessel truly and bona fide armed, fitted and provided with fourteen or more carriage guns and suitable ammunition for the same, each of the said guns to be of such caliber as to be capable of receiving and discharging an iron ball weighing at least four pounds avoirdupois, the said vessel to be manned with not less than forty seamen and other persons of the age of eighteen years or more, actually hired and employed in the defense and service of such vessel, for and during the intended voyage, any quantity of flour that such vessel can reasonably lade and carry.

[Section II.] (Section III, P. L.) And be it further enacted by the authority aforesaid, That no flour designed for exportation in pursuance of this act shall be laden on board of any ship or vessel before the master of such ship or vessel shall deliver to the naval officer of the port of Philadelphia a memorial in writing, therein expressing and setting forth such design, the name and kind of vessel, her size [or] tonnage, the name and names of the owner or owners, and the place of their several abodes, the number and size of the carriage guns with which such vessel is or is intended to be armed and fitted, and the number of seamen and others as aforesaid that he will hire and employ during the intended voyage, together with the quantity of flour he is desirous to lade, and requesting the said naval officer to grant his permit for the lading thereof; in which said memorial whatever respects number shall be expressed in words at length, and not in figures; whereupon, the said naval officer having first taken a bond to the commonwealth from the said master and two sufficient resident sureties, each obligee bound severally as well as jointly, for at least double the value of such flour designed to be shipped as aforesaid, conditioned for the true and faithful compliance of said master and the owners of such vessel, with the several requisites, regulations and limitations of this act, the said naval officer shall grant a permit for the lading of such quantity of flour as is in such case allowed by this act.

(Section IV, P. L.) Provided always, That no permit shall be available for lading of any flour in pursuance of this act unless the same shall be shipped in the proper vessel and within forty days after the date of such permit, nor unless such lading be in the day time and at some unenclosed wharf within the city of Philadelphia. Provided also, That no suit shall be brought on any bond taken as aforesaid unless within two years after the date.

[Section III.] (Section V, P. L.) And be it further enacted by the authority aforesaid, That in any suit which may be brought on any bond taken as aforesaid by the naval officer, the burden of the proof shall lie upon the obligees or obligee, defendants or defendant in such suit and not upon the state; and it shall be sufficient on the part of the commonwealth, in order to recover in such action to allege any proper matter for that purpose without proving the same.

(Section VI, P. L.) And whereas, it is the intent and meaning of the legislature that the shipping of flour in pursuance of this act shall not distress the public service or intercept proper supplies for the army; and it is reasonable that those who partake of the advantages herein given should make some recompense for the same:

[Section IV.] (Section VII, P. L.) Be it therefore enacted by the authority aforesaid, That before any ship or vessel on which any flour shall be laden in pursuance of this act, shall be cleared out the master of such ship or vessel shall produce to the said naval officer a certificate, to be filed by the said naval officer, from the proper [officer] to be appointed by the president and council for that purpose, acknowledging the receipt, or, in case the same shall not be accepted, the tender of a quantity of good merchantable flour of wheat for the use of the public equal to one-third part [of] the quantity of flour laden in such vessel, the same to be paid for at the market price, at the time of delivery. Provided, That the supreme executive council shall be and hereby is vested with power to take off the first above-mentioned restriction when it appears to them that the quota of flour desired by Congress of this state is provided or for other reasons by them deemed sufficient.

[Section V.] (Section VIII, P. L.) Provided also, and be it further enacted by the authority aforesaid, That nothing in this act shall be construed to discharge the master of any ship or other vessel lading flour in pursuance of this act from exhibiting and delivering to the said naval officer a fair and true manifest of the lading of such ship or other vessel, or from attesting to the same, or from giving bond for the due lading thereof or any other requisite of the act of assembly, entitled "An act for the regulation of navigation and trade in this state,"[1] passed on the tenth day of September, one thousand seven hundred and seventy-eight.

---

[1] Passed September 10, 1778, Chapter 813.

[Section VI.] And it is hereby further enacted, That if such master shall neglect to perform the said requisites, such neglect shall be a forfeiture of the bond taken from him and his sureties before he was permitted to lade flour in pursuance of this act.

[Section VII.] (Section IX, P. L.) And be it further enacted by the authority aforesaid, That the fines, penalties and forfeitures provided for offenses against this act and the act first herein recited for laying an embargo and reviving and continuing the same, shall be imposed and levied on all persons and ships and their lading, this act notwithstanding, unless it shall be made appear to the satisfaction of the court and jury that the conditions, regulations and limitations of this act have been fully complied with.

[Section VIII.] Lastly, it is declared that nothing in this act is intended to restrain or limit the power given by the constitution to the president and council to lay embargoes whenever they think proper.

Passed December 22, 1780. See the note to the Act of Assembly passed February 28, 1780, Chapter 876; and the Acts of Assembly passed February 27, 1781, Chapter 928; June 7, 1781, Chapter 943. Recorded L. B. No. 1, p. 407, &c.

CHAPTER CMXXIII.

AN ACT TO REVIVE AND AMEND AN ACT ENTITLED "AN ACT TO SUSPEND THE OPERATION FOR A LIMITED TIME OF THE SEVERAL LAWS OF THIS COMMONWEALTH FOR MAKING THE BILLS OF CREDIT OF THE UNITED STATES A LEGAL TENDER IN THE PAYMENT OF DEBTS EQUAL TO GOLD AND SILVER."[1]

(Section I, P. L.) Whereas the above-recited act, entitled "An act to suspend the operation for a limited time of the several laws of this commonwealth for making the bills of credit of the United States a legal tender in the payment of debts equal to gold and silver,"[1] passed the thirty-first day of May last past,

[1] Passed May 31, 1780, Chapter 911.

would have expired by its own limitation at the end of the [last session of] assembly, but the same was continued by an act passed the twenty-second day of September last, until the end of the present session of assembly, and it is just and necessary that the same should be continued until the value of the said currency can be fixed at some certain standard, and a proper mode established, which will make the advantages equal to both debtor and creditor:

[Section I.] (Section II, P. L.) Be it therefore enacted and it is hereby enacted by the Representatives of the Freemen of the Commonwealth of Pennsylvania in General Assembly met, and by the authority of the same, That the said act, entitled "An act to suspend the operation for a limited time of the several laws of this commonwealth for making the bills of credit of the United States a legal tender in the payment of debts equal to gold and silver,"[1] passed the thirty-first day of May, one thousand seven hundred and eighty, and every article, matter and thing therein contained (except the clause limiting the time of its continuance) is hereby revived and continued and declared to be in full force, except where the same is hereby altered or amended.

[Section II.] (Sction III, P. L.) Provided always nevertheless, That where any person or persons are about to remove out of this state and refuse to give security to their creditor or creditors, or where any person or persons refuse to appear without process, and put in special bail to the plaintiff's action for the debt or cause for which he complains, or where any tenant or tenants have committed or shall commit any waste or destruction in the houses or lands or hold possession against the will of the landlord after the expiration of the lease, in all such cases it shall and may be lawful for such landlords or creditors to make distresses or bring suits as the case may require for their rents, debts or demands, and the enacting clause of the first-mentioned act suspending the operation of the several laws of this commonwealth for making the bills of credit of the United States a legal tender in the payment of debts equal to gold and silver, revived and continued by this act, shall be extended to such landlords and creditors in as full and ample a manner as if no such distress had been made or suit brought, anything in the proviso to the first-mentioned act revived and amended by this act, or in this act contained to the contrary thereof in anywise notwithstanding.

> Passed December 22, 1780. See the note to the Act of Assembly passed May 31, 1780, Chapter 911; and the Act of Assembly passed June 21, 1781, Chapter 945. Recorded L. B. No. 1, p. 409, &c.

CHAPTER CMXXIV.

A SUPPLEMENT TO AN ACT ENTITLED "AN ACT FOR STRIKING THE SUM OF ONE HUNDRED THOUSAND POUNDS IN BILLS OF CREDIT FOR THE PRESENT SUPPORT OF THE ARMY AND FOR ESTABLISHING A FUND FOR THE REDEMPTION OF THE SAME AND FOR OTHER PURPOSES THEREIN MENTIONED."[1]

(Section I, P. L.) Whereas, it is necessary that the bills of credit emitted and made current by the act, entitled "An act for striking the sum of one hundred thousand pounds in bills of credit for the present support of the army and for establishing a fund for the redemption of the same and for other purposes therein mentioned,"[1] be made a legal tender in all cases whatsover:

[Section I.] (Section II, P. L.) Be it therefore enacted and it is hereby enacted by the Representatives of the Freemen of the Commonwealth of Pennsylvania in General Assembly met, and by the authority of the same, That the bills of credit emitted by the act aforesaid be and are hereby declared to be legal tender to all intents and purposes whatsoever, and shall be taken and received in payment in all bargains, contracts, purchases, agreements, dealings, debts, dues and demands according to the sum specified in the said bills, to be taken and received at the rate or value of fifteen shillings for every two dollars and so in proportion for a larger or less sum and of equal value in the payment of such bargain, contract, purchase,

---
[1] Passed March 25, 1870, Chapter 907.

agreement, dealing, debt, due and demand whatsoever with two Spanish milled dollars, each weighing seventeen pennyweight and six grains, and sixty shillings of the emission aforesaid shall be taken and received at the rate of or equal in value to one gold half johannes of Portugal weighing nine pennyweight, and in like proportion for all other gold or silver coin, any contract, agreement or bargain between parties to the contrary in anywise notwithstanding.

[Section II.] (Section III, P. L.) And be it further enacted by the authority aforesaid, That if any person or persons, bodies politic and corporate from and after the publication of this act shall refuse to receive any of the said bills of credit, when tendered in payment of any debt, bargain, contract or demand whatsoever, provided the whole of the said debt, or demand be so tendered, such person or persons, bodies politic and corporate so refusing shall be forever barred from suing for and recovering the same from any judge or in any court of this state.

[Section III.] (Section IV, P. L.) And be it further enacted by the authority aforesaid, That if any person whatsoever shall, after the passing of this act, refuse to take and receive any of the bills of credit aforesaid, in payment for any live stock, necessary of life, commodity, manufacture, article or goods whatsoever which he or she shall sell, or expose to sale or offer the same for a less price or smaller sum of money to be paid in gold or silver than in the bills of credit emitted as aforesaid, or that shall give or receive a greater nominal sum of said bills of credit for less in gold or silver, every such person being thereof legally convicted in any court of general quarter sessions of the peace in this state, shall, for the first offense, forfeit and pay double the value of the article or articles so sold or exposed to sale, one moiety thereof to the person or persons giving information of the same and prosecuting the offender to conviction, and the other moiety for the use of the poor of the city, district or township where the offense shall be committed, and for the second offense shall suffer imprisonment during the present war and forfeit to the commonwealth one-half of his or her lands, tenements goods and chattels.

[Section IV.] (Section V, P. L.) And be it further enacted by the authority aforesaid, That the party giving information as aforesaid shall be admitted a competent witness on the trial of offenders against this act, any law, custom or usage to the contrary in anywise notwithstanding.

[Section V.] (Section VI, P. L.) And be it further enacted by the authority aforesaid, That so much of the bills of credit aforesaid as have been received by the lieutenants and sublieutenants of the city of Philadelphia and the several counties of this state, the collectors of taxes or other public dues, county treasurers and all public agents for or on account of any tax, public due, militia fine or forfeiture whatever shall, in the settlement of the accounts of the said officers and agents respectively be estimated and paid at the same rate at which the said bills were received by them respectively.

[Section VI.] (Section VII, P. L.) And be it further enacted by the authority aforesaid, That the rate of exchange between continental currency and the bills of credit hereby made legal tender shall be and hereby is declared to be seventy-five of the former for one of the latter, which rate of exchange shall continue to the first day of February next, and the supreme executive council are [hereby] empowered and required from and after the said first day of February to publish in the several English and German newspapers printed in the city of Philadelphia, in the first week in every month the then rate of exchange between specie and continental money which exchange so published in each month shall be the exchange between continental money and the state money hereby made a legal tender.

Passed December 23, 1780. See the note to the Act of Assembly passed March 25, 1780, Chapter 907. Recorded L. B. No. 1, p. 410, &c.

CHAPTER CMXXV.

AN ACT FOR AN IMPOST ON GOODS, WARES AND MERCHANDISE IMPORTED INTO THIS STATE.

(Section I, P. L.) Whereas, in and by an act of assembly of this commonwealth, entitled "An act for the regulation of navigation and trade in this state," [1] passed on the tenth day of September, which was in the year of our Lord one thousand seven hundred and seventy-eight, among other things it was enacted and directed "That the master of any ship or other vessel, except ships or vessels of war, privateers and their prizes, arriving at any port of this state shall, within forty-eight hours after such arrival, repair to the naval office in the city of Philadelphia, and there exhibit and deliver to the naval officer of this state a true manifest, signed by the said master, of all the goods, wares and merchandise, laden and imported in such ship or vessel, setting forth the packages, marks and number thereof, and the nature and quantity of their contents, in number, weight and measure, as they are commonly counted, estimated and sold, and also his own name and surname, the name and burden of his ship or vessel, the names and abode of the owner or owners thereof, the country, port or place where the said cargo was shipped, together with such documents as are usually furnished in such place of lading, to masters of vessels sailing from thence with goods, wares and merchandise."

(Section II, P. L.) And whereas, it is necessary at this time for the public service that further and other funds besides the taxes on estates, real and personal, should be established.

(Section III, P. L.) And whereas, considerable sums may be levied by a small impost on goods and merchandise imported into this state, without burdening commerce:

[Section I.] (Section IV, P. L.) Be it therefore enacted and it is hereby enacted by the Representatives of the Freemen of the Commonwealth of Pennsylvania in General Assembly

---

[1] Passed September 10, 1778, Chapter 925.

met, and by the authority of the same, That from and after the first day of February next, there shall be raised, collected and paid the duties hereinafter set forth and particularized, upon all goods, wares and merchandise, except as hereinafter excepted. That is to say, upon every gallon of rum, brandy and other spirituous liquors, two pence. Upon every gallon of Maderia wine, four pence. Upon all other wines, two pence. Upon all wines in bottles, six pence per dozen. Upon every hundred weight of unrefined sugar, one shilling. Upon every hundred weight of loaf sugar, one shilling and six pence. Upon every gallon of molasses, one penny. Upon every hundred weight of coffee, one shilling. Upon every hundred weight of cocoa, one shilling. Upon every pound of green tea, six pence. Upon every pound of bohea and other tea, one penny. Upon all other goods and merchandise, one per centum upon the value thereof, to be estimated and fixed by the importer or his agent.

[Section II.] (Section V, P. L.) And be it further enacted by the authority aforesaid, That if the naval officer, in behalf of the commonwealth, shall tender to the importer the sum of money at which any specific quantity of goods, imported into this state shall be valued as aforesaid, together with ten per centum over and above such sum, the property of the said goods, together with the casks and other packages wherein they shall be contained, shall, thereupon vest in the commonwealth, and the importer shall be liable for all freight and other charges which shall have accrued upon the same previous to the landing; and a permit shall be granted for the landing of such goods for the use of the state, and the commonwealth, if necessary, may sue for and recover the possession of such goods, for which tender shall be made as aforesaid, by action of detinue, trover and conversion, or replevin as may be thought best.

[Section III.] (Section VI, P. L.) And be it further enacted by the authority aforesaid, That the said naval officer shall, upon due entry of any goods, wares and merchandise, imported as aforesaid, and upon payment of, or securing the duties imposed by this act, by a sufficient bond, payable within one month after the date of such bond, to the commonwealth, and not otherwise, grant a permit for the landing thereof.

(Section VII, P. L.) Provided always, That if the master of any ship or other vessel shall not, upon delivering his manifest to the said naval officer as aforesaid, pay or secure as is hereinbefore directed the duties by this act imposed upon the goods, wares and merchandise of which he shall make report, that each particular importer may pay or secure in manner aforesaid, the duties imposed and payable on his own property, and such importer shall thereupon be entitled to a permit for the landing of the same.

(Section VIII, P. L.) Provided also, That if any goods, wares and merchandise imported into this state, and which shall be liable to any duty by virtue of this act, shall remain in any ship or other vessel after ten days, to be reckoned from the arrival of such ship or vessel without the said duty being paid or secured as aforesaid, it shall and may be lawful for the master of the ship or vessel in which such goods remain and who shall not be willing to pay or secure the duties thereon, to deliver the same to the said naval officer, to be warehoused or otherwise secured and kept at the charge and risk of the owner thereof; and such delivery shall exonerate the said master. And the said naval officer shall keep all goods, wares and merchandise so delivered to him, other than perishable goods for and during the term of three months, after which, being first appraised, they may be sold at auction by the naval officer upon the order of the president and council, and the money thence arising after the said duty and all charges shall be deducted shall be lodged with the state treasurer for the use of the owner.

[Section IV.] (Section IX, P. L.) And be it further enacted by the authority aforesaid, That if the master of any ship or vessel, or other person, shall unload or discharge out of any ship or vessel, being in the river Delaware or any branch thereof, any goods, wares or merchandise, with intent to land the same within this state, before entry, and without having obtained a permit for so doing, or if any person shall be aiding and assisting in landing or in conveying or housing the same, every such person so offending shall forfeit and pay any sum not exceeding five hundred pounds, and all goods, wares and merchandise so landed, or the value thereof, shall be forfeited and the goods shall be seized by the [said] naval officer or his deputy.

[Section V.] (Section X, P. L.) And be it further enacted by the authority aforesaid, That the said naval officer or his deputy and assistants shall have full power and authority, by virtue of this act, to enter any ship or vessel, and into any house or other place where he shall have reason to suspect that any goods, wares or merchandise liable to the said duty shall be concealed, and therein to search for the same and to do all other things which shall be necessary to secure the said duties, or to seize and secure any goods, wares or merchandise which he shall suppose to be forfeited. And in case of refusal or opposition, having first obtained from the justices of the supreme court, or any two of them, or in their absence from any two justices of the peace of the proper city or county, a writ of assistance, shall break open doors and remove obstacles and do and perform every and all other things which by this act he is authorized to do.

(Section XI, P. L.) Provided always, That no search of any dwelling shall be made in manner aforesaid until due cause of suspicion hath been shown to the satisfaction of a justice of the supreme court or of a justice of the peace, as in the case of stolen goods, nor before sun rise nor after sun setting.

[Section VI.] (Section XII, P. L.) And be it further enacted by the authority aforesaid, That all masters of vessels and other persons trading and plying in the Delaware and coming into any port or place within this state, having on board any ship, sloop, shallop or other vessel any of the goods liable to pay the duties imposed by this act, shall and they are hereby required and enjoined to observe and comply with the directions of this act, under like pains, penalties and forfeitures as in the case of ships and other vessels arriving from beyond sea. Provided, That no river vessel shall be hereby obliged to pay any greater fee than two shillings for exhibiting a manifest of any goods liable to the said duty.

(Section XIII, P. L.) And whereas, the penalties imposed by the act hereinbefore recited will be hereafter insufficient to enforce the exhibiting of manifests by masters of ships arriving in the ports of this state:

[Section VII.] (Section XIV, P. L.) Be it therefore enacted by the authority aforesaid, That if any master of any ship or vessel, arriving in any port of this state, shall neglect or refuse to exhibit the manifest of his cargo by the said-recited act enjoined, in the manner and within the time therein prescribed, every such master so offending shall forfeit and pay the sum of one thousand pounds.

[Section VIII.] (Section XV, P. L.) And be it further enacted by the authority aforesaid, That the several fines, penalties and forfeitures which shall be incurred by any offense against this act, or against the act aforesaid, may be prosecuted and recovered, if the same shall be under the value or sum of fifty pounds, before any two justices of the proper county, with appeal to the quarter sessions, where the same shall be finally determined, as in the case of fines, penalties and forfeitures inflicted by the excise laws of this state, and no certiorari shall lie in such case; but if the same shall exceed the value or sum of fifty pounds, then in the proper county court of common pleas, or in the supreme court, at the election of the prosecutor, and shall be distributed one moiety thereof to the prosecutor and the other moiety to the commonwealth; and in every prosecution against goods seized, as forfeited by virtue of this act, the onus probandi shall lie upon the claimant, and not upon the prosecutor, and no claim for the same shall be admitted before security be entered for the costs of suit.

[Section IX.] (Section XVI, P. L.) Provided always, and be it further enacted by the authority aforesaid, That if the said naval officer or any other person shall be sued or prosecuted for anything done in pursuance of this act, he may plead the general issue and give this act and the special matter in evidence for his justification, and if, upon trial thereof, a verdict shall be given or upon demurrer judgment shall go for the defendant, or if the plaintiff or prosecutor shall become nonsuit, or discontinue or fail of prosecution the defendant shall recover treble costs of suit.

(Section XVII, P. L.) Provided also, That no suit for anything done in pursuance of this act shall be brought unless such suit be commenced within one year next after the injury or pretended injury shall be done or committed.

[Section X.] (Section XVII, P. L.) And be it further enacted by the authority aforesaid, That the said naval officer shall keep fair, distinct and true accounts of all his doings relative to the premises, and shall, once in every month, pay over to the treasurer of the state all moneys belonging to the commonwealth which shall come to his hands, and shall submit all his books and papers at all times to the inspection of the president and council, or of such person as they shall authorize for that purpose; and shall, once in every year, or oftener if required, settle his accounts with the auditors of the public accounts, or otherwise, as the general assembly for the time being shall direct. And the said naval officer, for his reward in executing this act, shall be entitled to an half per centum on the whole of the moneys by him received and paid, and two shillings from the party executing any bond for each bond he shall take as aforesaid, and to no other satisfaction.

[Section XI.] (Section XIX, P. L.) And be it further enacted, That the said duties shall be payable in gold or silver, as the same was taken in payments and passed current in the late province of Pennsylvania, on the first day of January, which was in the year of our Lord one thousand seven hundred and seventy-five, or other current money equivalent; and all fines and penalties and other moneys in this act mentioned shall be deemed, accounted, levied, satisfied and paid accordingly.

[Section XII.] (Section XX, P. L.) And be it further enacted by the authority aforesaid, That the said naval officer shall give bond to the commonwealth with two sufficient sureties in the sum of ten thousand pounds of gold and silver money aforesaid, or other money equivalent, conditioned for the due and faithful performance of, as well the duties required of him by this act, as of those enjoined upon him by the act of assembly hereinbefore recited. And the sureties offered by the said naval officer shall be subject to the approbation of the president and council, and the bond given by him shall be recorded and filed in the office of the secretary of the supreme executive council. And the naval officer may appoint a deputy or deputies, for whom he shall be answerable.

(Section XXI, P. L.) Provided always, That nothing in this act shall give any authority to demand or collect any impost or duty on common salt, saltpetre, gun-powder, lead or shot, or on prize goods or on goods, wares and merchandise of the growth, product or manufacture of the United States of America, or any of them.

(Section XXII, P. L.) And whereas, it is just and necessary that the repayment of any loan or loans which have been or may be negotiated in consequence of certain resolutions of the late assembly, passed the twenty-ninth day of May last, should be provided for and secured:

[Section XIII.] (Section XXIII, P. L.) Be it therefore enacted by the authority aforesaid, That so much of the said duties as may amount to the loan or loans negotiated as aforesaid shall be reserved and set apart in the hands of the state treasurer subject to the orders of the supreme executive council, for the express purpose of discharging the full amount of the said loan or loans, together with the interest which may accrue thereon, according to the terms upon which the said loan or loans have been or shall be procured.

>Passed December 23, 1780. See the note to the Act of Assembly passed September 10, 1778, Chapter 815; and the Acts of Assembly passed April 5, 1781, Chapter 937; April 9, 1782, Chapter 965; November 22, 1782, Chapter 998; March 20, 1783, Chapter 1018; September 17, 1783, Chapter 1032; September 25, 1783, Chapter 1051; November 18, 1783, Chapter 1058; March 15, 1784, Chapter 1076; March 16, 1785, Chapter 1137; April 2, 1785, Chapter 1157; September 20, 1785, Chapter 1188; December 24, 1785, Chapter 1198 (the two Acts of Assembly passed)April 8, 1786, Chapters 1226, 1227; September 26, 1786, Chapter 1254; March 15, 1787, Chapter 1276; September 17, 1788, Chapter 1354; September 29, 1789, Chapter 1454. The power of laying duties or imposts on imports or exports was surrendered to the United States, by the Constitution of the United States, Article I, Section X. Recorded L. B. No. 1, p. 410, &c.

CHAPTER CMXXVI.

AN ACT TO COMPLETE THE QUOTA OF THE FEDERAL ARMY ASSIGNED TO THIS STATE.

(Section I, P. L.) Whereas, the practice of enlisting soldiers for short terms, has been attended with great inconvenience and danger to this and the United States in creating a necessity of frequently calling forth the militia, at a very heavy expense, and waste of important time, and by reducing the forces in the field at critical periods to a number vastly inadequate to the service, for the prevention of which in future the legislature conceive it to be absolutely necessary to raise, with all possible expedition, a sufficient number of troops to complete the quota of the army required of this state by the honorable the Congress, to serve during the present war with Great Britain and have therefore agreed, That:

[Section I.] (Section II, P. L.) It be enacted and it is hereby enacted by the Representatives of the Freemen of the Commonwealth of Pennsylvania in General Assembly met, and by the authority of the same, That there shall, with all convenient speed, be enlisted within this state two thousand seven hundred able-bodied men to serve during the present war with Great Britain, who shall be raised and procured by or at the expense of the inhabitants of the city of Philadelphia and the several counties of this state in number and according to the proportions following, to wit, by the city [and county] of Philadelphia, eight hundred and ninety-five. The county of Bucks, one hundred and seventy-seven. The county of Chester, two hundred and eighty-four. The county of Lancaster, three hundred and eighty-four. The county of York, two hundred and fourteen. The county of Cumberland, two hundred and two. The county of Berks, one hundred and ninety-three. The county of Northampton, one hundred and twelve. The county of Bedford, sixty-one. The county of Northumberland, seventy-five, and the county of Westmoreland, one hundred and three.

[Section II.] (Section III, P. L.) And be it further enacted by the authority aforesaid, That the commissioners of the city and several counties of this state, respectively, or any two of them, shall direct the assessors of the several townships, wards and districts in the said city and counties, respectively, to meet at the times and places hereinafter mentioned: That is to say, in the city and counties of Philadelphia, Bucks, Chester, Lancaster, Berks and Northampton on or before the twenty-second day of January next; and in the counties of York, Cumberland, Bedford, Northumberland and Westmoreland, on or before the first day of February next, at the usual places of holding courts in the said city and counties, respectively, or at such other place or places where the said commissioners shall think most convenient, and shall then and there, in conjunction with the said assessors, proceed to class the taxable persons and property within the said city and counties, respectively, in such manner that the said property, together with a proportionable sum on all taxable single freemen shall be divided into as many equal parts as the said quota of men, which the said city or counties, respectively, are by this act required to enlist, shall consist of, paying due regard to the ease and convenience of the inhabitants by including those who reside near to each other within the same class; and shall transmit to the several classes, by persons by them to be appointed for that service, an order in writing, under the hands of the said commissioners, or any two of them, with a duplicate annexed, containing the names of each and every person composing the same, requiring each of the said classes to enlist during the war, and deliver to the proper officer one able-bodied recruit within fifteen days thereafter.

[Section III.] (Section IV, P. L.) And be it further enacted by the authority aforesaid, That every class which shall deliver a soldier who was enlisted during the present war, and hath deserted the service, to the officer appointed as aforesaid, shall be excused from furnishing a recruit as above required.

(Section V, P. L.) Provided always, That nothing herein contained shall authorize any person or persons to enlist any deserter from the British army, or from the navy of the United

States, as a recruit for the class to which he belongs or for any other.

[Section IV.] (Section VI, P. L.) And be it further enacted by the authority aforesaid, That if any class or classes shall neglect or refuse to enlist one able-bodied recruit as aforesaid, within the time limited and directed, or to make return thereof to the assessor of the proper township, ward or district, it shall and may be lawful for the said commissioners, or any two of them, and the assessor of such ward, district or township, where such neglect or refusal shall happen, to proceed and levy on each class so neglecting or refusing a tax not exceeding fifteen pounds specie, or other current money equivalent, on the persons severally composing such class or classes, in equal proportions, according to the last public tax levied therein, which they are hereby enjoined and directed to do within two days after such neglect or refusal, and shall cause the same to be levied, collected and paid in the manner at present in force and practice with respect to other taxes.

[Section V.] (Section VII, P. L.) And be it further enacted by the authority aforesaid, That where any class or person therein shall furnish such recruit, and any dispute may arise about the sum or sums of money which any person or persons therein should or ought to pay towards the enlistment of such recruit, or shall neglect or refuse to pay their proportion thereof the same shall be adjusted, collected and paid in the manner directed in the foregoing clause for the levying, collecting and paying the expenses of enlistment in cases where the classes have neglected or refused.

[Section VI.] (Section VIII, P. L.) And be it further enacted by the authority aforesaid, That the supreme executive council be and they are hereby authorized and empowered to appoint an officer or officers for the purpose of recruiting and taking all recruits in charge that shall be enlisted in pursuance of this act, and make such drafts on the treasurer of the state for the filling up the aforesaid quota of troops in the city of Philadelphia and the several counties as by them from time to time shall be judged necessary, in favor of such officer or officers to be by them appointed for the service aforesaid, so as the sums drawn for do not exceed the penalties incurred by the delinquent classes.

[Section VII.] (Section IX, P. L.) And be it further enacted by the authority aforesaid, That every such recruit, enlisted for any class, shall be attested before the next or some justice of the peace, and if accepted by him, shall, by one of the said classes, be delivered to the nearest officer appointed for that purpose, who, upon the receipt of such recruit and certificate from the said justice of the peace of his having been attested as above, shall give a receipt in favor of such class for said recruit.

[Section VIII.] (Section X, P. L.) And be it further enacted by the authority aforesaid, That all moneys paid by executors, guardians or others in legal trust, in right of another, in pursuance of this act, shall be allowed in their accounts at the time of the settlement thereof.

[Section IX.] (Section XI, P. L.) And be it further enacted by the authority aforesaid, That every recruit so enlisted and entered into the army shall receive one complete suit of clothes each year, and at the end of the war two hundred acres of land and all other pay, gratuities and exemptions that other soldiers in the line of this state are or shall be entitled to.

[Section X.] (Section XII, P. L.) And be it further enacted by the authority aforesaid, That any county commissioner herein required to perform certain duties and neglecting or refusing so to do, according to the true intent and meaning of this act (except in case of sickness or removal), shall be fined by the supreme executive council of this state in any sum not exceeding five hundred pounds, and any assessor, collector or other person required in pursuance of this act to perform any duty and neglecting or refusing to perform the same (except as above excepted) shall be fined in any sum not exceeding one hundred pounds, by the commissioners of the city or any of the counties of this state, or any two of them, where the offense may happen, who shall appoint another or others in their stead.

(Section XIII, P. L.) And whereas, it may happen that a part or the whole of the property in some of the said classes may not have any person in the occupation or possession thereof or resident thereon to represent it:

[Section XI.] (Section XIV, P. L.) Be it therefore enacted by the authority aforesaid, That the collector of the township, ward or district wherein such property may be found shall give speedy information thereof to the commissioners of the county, who shall, without delay, publish, or cause to be published, in some of the newspapers, printed in the city of Philadelphia, for three weeks successively an account of all property so circumstanced in their said county, and of the sum or sums of money chargeable thereon, requiring the owner or owners to make payment thereof to the proper person at or before the expiration of two months from the date of such publication; and, on failure of such payment at the expiration of such term, the commissioners of the proper county, or any two of them, may, and they are hereby authorized, empowered and required to expose such property, or as much thereof as may be necessary, to pay such sum or sums of money, with reasonable costs, to sale at public auction, and, after due and public notice given of such intended sale for at least ten days, to sell the same to the highest and best bidder; and the said commissioners, or any two of them, shall convey any houses, lands or tenements so sold to the purchaser or purchasers thereof in fee simple or for such estate as the delinquent owner thereof held the same, which shall be good and valid in law; and the said commissioners, after deducting the sum or sums of money aforesaid, and the reasonable costs, shall return and pay the overplus of the consideration money, if any, to the owner or owners when thereunto required.

[Section XII.] (Section XV, P. L.) And be it further enacted by the authority aforesaid, That all tenants in possession shall be accountable for and pay any sum or sums of money charged by virtue of this act on the lands in his or her possession, and may discount the same out of his or her rent; and in case one year's rent should prove insufficient to defray the same, the said lands shall be liable for the sums charged thereon, and the same or such parts thereof as may be sufficient may be sold therefor in the manner prescribed in the foregoing clause.

[Section XIII.] (Section XVI, P. L.) And be it further enacted by the authority aforesaid, That the persons to be appointed by the commissioners of the city and several counties to transmit and deliver to the several classes, their order with the duplicate hereinbefore mentioned, shall be paid such reasonable rewards, respectively, for that service as shall be agreed for, by drafts of the said commissioners, or any two of them, on the treasurer of the proper county, who is hereby directed to answer and discharge the same out of any money in his hands belonging to such county and unappropriated.

Passed December 23, 1780. See the Acts of Assembly passed June 25, 1781, Chapter 946; September 29, 1781, Chapter 951; August 11, 1784, Chapter 1104; September 6, 1785, Chapter 1171; November 10, 1787, Chapter 1326. Recorded L. B. No. 1, p. 413, &c.

Laws enacted in the Second Sitting of the Fifth General Assembly of the Commonwealth of Pennsylvania, which commenced at Philadelphia on Tuesday, the sixth day of February, in the year of our Lord 1781.

CHAPTER CMXXVII.

AN ACT TO SUSPEND THE OPERATION OF THE SEVERAL LAWS OF THIS COMMONWEALTH MAKING THE BILLS OF CREDIT MADE CURRENT BY THE RESOLVES OF THE LATE ASSEMBLIES OF PENNSYLVANIA,[1] AND THE BILLS OF CREDIT ISSUED BY THE ASSEMBLY OF THIS STATE THE TWENTIETH DAY OF MARCH, IN THE YEAR OF OUR LORD ONE THOUSAND SEVEN HUNDRED AND SEVENTY-SEVEN, LEGAL TENDER.[2]

(Section I, P. L.) Whereas, the depreciation of the bills of credit issued by the resolves of the late assemblies of Pennsylvania and made legal tender by a law of this state, passed on the twenty-ninth day of January, one thousand seven hundred and seventy-seven, and of the bills of credit of this state issued by an act passed on the twentieth day of March, one thousand seven hundred and seventy-seven, now in circulation, and the speculation that has taken place in consequence thereof have opened a door to numerous frauds and may operate to the general injury of virtue and morality and to the great dishonor of the state unless timely prevented:

And whereas, many of the good citizens of this state have, in their petitions to this house, set forth the very mischievous and alarming consequences of continuing the same bills of credit a legal tender and praying that the laws making them a legal tender may be repealed or suspended:

[Section I.] (Section II, P. L.) Be it therefore enacted and it is hereby enacted by the Representatives of the Freemen of the

---

[1] Passed January 29, 1777, Chapter 738.
[2] Passed March 20, 1777, Chapter 752.

Commonwealth of Pennsylvania in General Assembly met, and by the authority of the same, That from and after the passing of this act so much of the several acts of assembly of this state as makes the said bills of credit a legal tender shall be and is hereby suspended, anything in the said laws to the contrary in anywise notwithstanding.

[Section II.] (Section III, P. L.) Provided always nevertheless, That this act shall not extend, or be construed to extend to any sheriff, attorney, executor, administrator, guardian or other person having received money by legal authority in right of another, but that it shall and may be lawful to make payment in all such cases as might have been done before the passing of this act, anything herein contained to the contrary notwithstanding.

(Section IV, P. L.) Provided also, That nothing in this act contained shall prevent, or be construed to prevent, the bills of credit aforesaid from being of the same value in the payment of taxes and all other debts and demands whatsoever, as the bills of credit of the United States issued before the eighteenth day of March last.

Passed February 20, 1781. See Acts of Assembly passed April 3, 1781, Chapter 935; June 21, 1781, Chapter 945. Recorded L. B. No. 1, p. 415, etc.

CHAPTER CMXXVIII.

AN ACT TO REPEAL THE ACT ENTITLED "AN ACT TO REVIVE AND CONTINUE FOR A FURTHER LIMITED TIME THE ACT FOR LAYING AN EMBARGO ON THE EXPORTATIONS OF PROVISIONS FROM THIS STATE BY SEA FOR A LIMITED TIME,"[1] AND ALSO CERTAIN PARTS OF AN ACT ENTITLED "AN ACT TO PERMIT THE EXPORTATION OF FLOUR OF WHEAT FROM THIS STATE, BY SEA UNDER CERTAIN LIMITATIONS AND RESTRICTIONS."[2]

(Section I, P. L.) Whereas, it has been found by experience that prohibitions on the exportation of the commodities of this

---

[1] Passed September 22, 1780, Chapter 917.
[2] Passed December 22, 1780, Chapter 922.

country have tended greatly to the impoverishment thereof without producing any adequate benefit to the community:

[Section I.] (Section II, P. L.) Be it therefore enacted and it is hereby enacted by the Representatives of the Freemen of the Commonwealth of Pennsylvania in General Assembly met, and by the authority of the same, That the act, entitled "An act to revive and continue for a further limited time the act for laying an embargo on the exportation of provisions from this state by sea for a limited time,"[1] passed on the twenty-second day of September last, be and the same is hereby repealed.

(Section III, P. L.) And whereas, the limitations and restrictions contained in the act, entitled "An act to permit the exportation of flour of wheat from this state by sea under certain limitations and restrictions,"[2] have been productive of mischievous consequences to this state and cannot be attended with the advantages expected by the legislature by reason of the full liberty given to commerce in a neighboring state:

[Section II.] (Section IV, P. L.) Be it therefore enacted by the authority aforesaid, That the said last mentioned act and every clause, proviso and thing therein contained, except the permission to export the flour therein mentioned, be and the same is hereby repealed, excepting also the clause obliging all persons shipping flour of wheat to offer or tender a quantity equal to one-third [part] of the quantity to be shipped unto the proper officer appointed by the president and council for that purpose as is more fully and particularly expressed in the seventh section of the said act.

Passed February 27, 1781. See the Act of Assembly passed June 7, 1781, Chapter 943. Recorded L. B. No. 1, p. 415, etc.

CHAPTER CMXXIX.

AN ACT TO DISSOLVE THE MARRIAGE OF GILES HICKS WITH HIS WIFE HESTER HICKS LATE HESTER McDANIEL.

(Section I, P. L.) Whereas, Giles Hicks, of the state of Penn-

---

[1] Passed September 22, 1780, Chapter 917.
[2] Passed December 22, 1780, Chapter 922.

sylvania, Esquire, and captain in the tenth regiment of the said state hath presented a petition to this house setting forth that in the month of November, one thousand seven hundred and seventy-six, when he was a minor of the age of fifteen years, he was seduced by the artifices of a certain Hester McDaniel and her relations to contract marriage with her contrary to the consent of his guardians and other friends: That the said Hester was at the time of the said marriage a common prostitute and hath since lived separate from the said Giles in open adultery with divers other men, by means whereof she became so diseased of the lues venerea as to be declared incurable after seven months continuance in the Pennsylvania Hospital, and praying leave to bring in a bill for the dissolution of the said marriage after due notice given:

And whereas, it appears to this house that the facts alleged in the said petition are true:

And whereas, this house did, by their resolve of the twenty-first day of November, one thousand seven hundred and eighty, give permission to the said Giles Hicks to bring in a bill to divorce him from his said wife Hester, agreeable to the prayer of his said petition, he, the said Giles Hicks, giving previous notice of his design and this permission at least three weeks in the public newspaper printed in the city of Philadelphia, entitled "The Pennsylvania Gazette and Weekly Advertiser:"

And whereas, it hath been sufficiently proved to the house that the said notice hath been given:

Therefore:

[Section I.] (Section II, P. L.) Be it enacted and it is hereby enacted by the Representatives of the Freemen of the Commonwealth of Pennsylvania in General Assembly met, and by the authority of the same, That the marriage of the said Giles Hicks with the said Hester be and is hereby declared to be dissolved and annulled to all intents and purposes whatsoever. And the said Giles Hicks and the said Hester shall be and they are hereby henceforth, respectively, declared to be separated, set free and totally discharged from their matrimonial contract and from all duties and obligations to each other as husband and wife as fully, effectually and absolutely to all intents and purposes as if they had never been joined in matrimony or by any other contract whatsoever, any law, usage or custom to the contrary notwithstanding.

[Section II.](Section III, P. L.) And be it further enacted by the authority aforesaid, That from and after the date hereof the said Giles Hicks be and he hereby is freely, fully and entirely authorized and empowered to contract matrimony and the same in due form to celebrate with any other woman in like manner as he, the said Giles, if he had [never] been married to the said Hester, lawfully might or could do.

Passed March 9, 1780. Recorded L. B. No. 1, p. 416, etc.

CHAPTER CMXXX.

A FURTHER SUPPLEMENT TO THE ACT ENTITLED "AN ACT FOR MAKING THE RIVER SCHUYLKILL NAVIGABLE AND FOR THE PRESERVATION OF THE FISH IN THE SAID RIVER."[1]

(Section I, P. L.) Whereas, several of the commissioners nominated and appointed in and by the act of assembly, passed on the twenty-sixth day of February, in the year of our Lord one thousand seven hundred and seventy-three, entitled "A supplement to the act, entitled 'An act for making the river Schuylkill navigable and for the preservation of the fish in the said river,'"[2] have, since the passing of the same, departed this life, removed from the neighborhood of the said river or engaged in other business, so that the regulations and provisions in the said act contained, to which this act is a further supplement, cannot now be properly carried into execution:

[Section I.] (Section II, P. L.) Be it therefore enacted and it is hereby enacted by the Representatives of the Freemen of the Commonwealth of Pennsylvania in General Assembly met,

---
[1] Passed March 14, 1761, Chapter 465.
[2] Passed February 26, 1773, Chapter 680.

and by the authority of the same, That David Rittenhouse, Owen Biddle, Mark Bird, Balser Gheer, Thomas Potts, David Thomas, Patrick Anderson, John Mear, Isaac Hewes, Nathan Levering, George Douglass, John Heister and Christian Steer shall be and they are hereby appointed commissioners for clearing, scouring and making the river Schuylkill navigable, and for putting in execution all and singular the purposes mentioned in the act passed the fourteenth day of March, in the year of our Lord one thousand seven hundred and sixty-one, entitled "An act for making the river Schuylkill navigable, and for the preservation of the fish in the said river,"[1] or contained in the above-recited supplement thereto; and that they, or a majority of them, or of the survivors of them, shall have, hold and exercise all and every the powers, authorities, jurisdictions, rights and privileges given and granted in and by the said-recited act to the commissioners therein appointed, and shall be subject to the same duties, to all intents and purposes, as if they had been the commissioners therein particularly appointed.

[Section II.] (Section III, P. L.) And be it further enacted by the authority aforesaid, That the surviving commissioners appointed by the said-recited act, entitled "A supplement to the act, entitled 'An act for making the river Schuylkill navigable and for the preservation of the fish in the said river,'" shall, and they are hereby enjoined and required, immediately after the passing of this act, to deliver [over] to the commissioners hereinbefore appointed all and every the sum and sums of money by them, or either of them, collected or received, and remaining in their, or either of their, hands unappropriated and unapplied to the purposes mentioned in the said-recited act, together with all books, subscriptions and other papers, vouchers and accounts and all tools and implements which have been provided for opening and cleaning the said river, and are or shall be in their or any of their custody, power or possession.

(Section IV, P. L.) And whereas, it is represented to the legislature that notwithstanding the good and wholesome regulations contained in divers acts of assembly, now in force, for the preservation of fish in the said river Schuylkill, great injury is done by a practice of driving the said river with brush nets:

For remedy whereof:

[Section III.] Be it further enacted by the authority aforesaid, That if any person or persons shall, from after the publication of this act, take any fish whatsoever with brush nets or such like devices, or shall drive the said river with such nets, or in any manner make use of the same therein, he, she or they so offending, being thereof convicted before any two justices of the peace in and for the county where he, she or they shall be apprehended (which justices are hereby authorized and empowered to hear, try and determine the same), shall forfeit for every such offense the sum of twenty pounds, one-half thereof to be paid to the overseers of the poor of the township where such offender shall reside, for the use of the poor thereof, and the other half to the informer, and likewise pay the costs of prosecution, and, moreover, it shall and may be lawful to and for any person or persons whatsoever, to remove or destroy any such brush net or other like device found in any part of the said river; and that all and every person or persons who shall assault, hinder or obstruct any person in taking, removing or destroying any of the said brush nets or other like device in any part of the river aforesaid, and shall be thereof convicted in manner aforesaid, shall forfeit and pay for every such offense fifty pounds, one moiety thereof to the use of the poor as aforesaid and the other moiety to the use of the party so obstructed or aggrieved.

[Section IV.] (Section V, P. L.) Provided always, and be it further enacted by the authority aforesaid, That no person or persons shall draw any seine or net for the purpose of catching shad in that part of the river Schuylkill between the mouth thereof and the lower falls, five miles from the city of Philadelphia, after the twentieth day of May, or between said falls and the black rock, near the mouth of French creek, after the twenty-fifth of said month, or in any part of the said Schuylkill river after the first day of June in every year, under the penalty of ten pounds for every such offense, to be recovered as aforesaid.

[Section V.] (Section VI, P. L.) And be it further enacted by the authority aforesaid, That so much of the above-recited supplementary act as relates to the appointment of commissioners shall be and the same is hereby repealed, made null and void.

> Passed March 24, 1781. See the note to the Act of Assembly passed March 14, 1761, Chapter 465; and the Act of Assembly passed March 15, 1784, Chapter 1078. Section V of the act in the text was repealed by the Act of Assembly passed March 28, 1785, Chapter 1146. Recorded L. B. No. 1, p. 417, etc.

CHAPTER CMXXXI.

AN ACT FOR ERECTING PART OF THE COUNTY OF WESTMORELAND INTO A SEPARATE COUNTY.

(Section I, P. L.) Whereas, the inhabitants of that part of Westmoreland county, which lies west of the Monongahela river, have represented to the assembly of this state the great hardships they lie under, from being so remote from the present seat of judicature and the public offices:

For remedy whereof:

[Section I.] (Section II, P. L.) Be it enacted and it is hereby enacted by the Representatives of the Freemen of the Commonwealth of Pennsylvania in General Assembly met, and by the authority of the same, That all that part of the state of Pennsylvania west of the Monongahela river and south of the Ohio, beginning at the junction of the said rivers, thence up the Monongahela river aforesaid to the line run by Mason and Dixon, thence by the said line due west to the end thereof, and from thence the same course to the end of five degrees west longitude, to be computed from the river Delaware, thence by a meridian line extended north until the same shall intersect the Ohio river, and thence by the same to the place of beginning (the said lines from the end of Mason and Dixon's line to the Ohio river to be understood as to be hereafter ascertained by commissioners now appointed or to be appointed for that purpose), shall be and the same is hereby declared to be erected into a county henceforth to be called Washington.

[Section II.] (Section III, P. L.) And be it further enacted by the authority aforesaid, That the inhabitants of the said county of Washington shall, at all times hereafter, have and enjoy all and singular the jurisdictions, powers, rights, liberties and privileges whatsoever, which the inhabitants of any other county within this state do, may or ought to enjoy by any charter of privileges, or the laws of this state, or by any other ways and means whatsoever.

[Section III.] (Section IV, P. L.) And be it further enacted by the authority aforesaid, That the trustees, or any three of them, hereinafter appointed by this act to take assurance of a piece of land, whereon to erect a court house and prison, shall, on or before the first day of July next ensuing, divide the said county into townships or districts.

[Section IV.] (Section V, P. L.) And be it further enacted by the authority aforesaid, That the inhabitants of each township or district within the said county, qualified by law to elect, shall meet at some convenient place within their respective townships or districts at the same time that the inhabitants of the several townships or districts of the other counties within this state, shall meet for like purposes and choose inspectors; and the inhabitants of the said county, qualified as aforesaid, shall (until otherwise ordered by the house of assembly) meet at the house of David Hoge, at the place called Catfishes Camp, in the aforesaid county, at the same time the inhabitants of the other counties shall meet for like purpose, and there elect two representatives to serve them in assembly, one counsellor, two fit persons for sheriffs, two fit persons for coroners and three commissioners in the same manner and under the same rules, regulations and penalties as by the constitution and laws of this state is directed in respect to other counties, which representatives so chosen shall be members of the general assembly of the commonwealth of Pennsylvania, and shall sit and act as such as fully and as freely as any of the other representatives of this state do, may, can and ought to do. And the said counsellor, when so chosen, shall sit and act, as fully and as freely as any of the other members of the supreme executive council of this state do, may, can or ought to do.

[Section V.] (Section VI, P. L.) And be it further enacted by the authority aforesaid, That the justices of the supreme court of this state shall have the like powers, jurisdictions and authorities within the said county of Washington as by law they are vested with, and entitled to, in the other counties within this state, and are hereby authorized and empowered from time to time to deliver the gaols of the said county of capital or other offenders in like manner as they are authorized to do in the other counties of the state.

[Section VI.] (Section VII, P. L.) And be it further enacted by the authority aforesaid, That the freeholders of each township or district in the county aforesaid are hereby authorized and required to meet on the fifteenth day of July next, at some proper and convenient place and elect two fit persons for justices of the peace for each township. But before the freeholders of the respective townships or districts in the said county shall proceed to the election of two fit persons for justices of the peace, they shall, on the same day and at the place appointed for the election, elect one sufficient person for inspector and two persons for assistant judges; and the said judges shall assist the said inspector in receiving and counting the votes of the electors and in preventing frauds and impositions therein; and when the elections are finished and the numbers cast up, the inspector and judges aforesaid, or a majority of them, shall forthwith transmit a certificate thereof, under their hands and seals to the president and council, and one-half the number so elected in each township or district shall be commissioned according to the constitution of this state.

[Section VII.] (Section VIII, P. L.) And be it further enacted by the authority aforesaid, That before the inspectors and judges aforesaid proceed to receive the votes of the freeholders in their respective townships or districts, they shall take an oath or affirmation to the following effect, speaking the words themselves, without any persons administering the same, to wit (if an inspector):

"I do swear, or I do solemnly, sincerely and truly declare and affirm, that I will well and faithfully [receive] and cast up [all] the freeholders' votes within my township or district qualified by law to vote as may be offered to me at this election for fit persons for justices of the peace, and I will not refuse any vote through prejudice or ill will nor receive any through favor or affection, but will behave myself as an honest inspector of this election, according to the best of my skill and judgment."

And if a judge of the election, as follows, viz.:

"I will faithfully assist the inspector of this election in performing the duties required of him by this act according to the best of my skill and judgment."

[Section VIII.] (Section IX, P. L.) And be it further enacted by the authority aforesaid, That when the persons elected for justices of the peace, as aforesaid, or that shall be appointed by the president and council, have taken the oaths or affirmations required by the laws of this commonwealth and received their commissions, as directed in the constitution of this state, the said justices, or any three of them, shall and may hold courts of general quarter sessions of the peace and gaol delivery, and county courts for holding of pleas; and shall have all and singular the powers, rights, jurisdictions and authorities, to all intents and purposes, as other justices of the courts of general quarter sessions and justices of the county courts for holding of pleas, in the other counties in this state may, can or ought to have in their respective counties; which said courts shall sit and be held for the said county of Washington on the Tuesdays next preceding Westmoreland county courts in every of the months of January, April, July and October at the house of David Hoge aforesaid in the said county of Washington, until a court house shall be built; and when the same is built and erected in the county aforesaid, the said several courts shall then be holden and kept at the said court house on the days before mentioned.

[Section IX.] (Section X, P. L.) And be it further enacted by the authority aforesaid, That it shall and may be lawful to and for James Edgar, Hugh Scott, Van Swearingham, Daniel Lite and John Armstrong, or any three of them, to take up or purchase and take assurance to them and their heirs of a piece of land situated in some convenient place in the said county to be approved of by the president and supreme executive council, in trust [and] for the use of the inhabitants of the said county, and thereupon to erect and build a court house and prison sufficient to accommodate the public service of the said county.

[Section X.] (Section XI, P. L.) And be it further enacted by the authoritiy aforesaid, That for the defraying the charges of purchasing the land and building and erecting the court house and prison aforesaid it shall and may be lawful to and for the commissioners and township assessors of the said county, or a majority of them, to assess and levy, and they are hereby required to assess and levy in the manner directed by the acts for raising county rates and levies, so much money as the said trustees, or any three of them, shall judge necessary for purchasing the land and finishing the said court house and prison.

(Section XII, P. L.) Provided always, That the sum of money to be raised do not exceed one thousand pounds current money of this state.

[Section XI.] (Section XIII, P. L.) Provided also, and be it further enacted by the authority aforesaid, That no action or suit now commenced or depending in the said county of Westmoreland against any person living within the bounds of the said county of Washington, or elsewhere, shall be stayed or discontinued by this act, or by anything herein contained, but the same actions already commenced or depending may be prosecuted and the judgment thereupon rendered as if this act had not been made, and that it shall and may be lawful to and for the justices of the said county of Westmoreland to issue any judicial process, to the sheriff of the county of Westmoreland aforesaid, for carrying on and obtaining the effect of their suits, which sheriff shall be obliged to yield obedience in executing the said writs, and to make due return thereof to the justices of the court of the said county of Westmoreland in the same manner as if the parties lived and resided within the same.

[Section XII.] (Section XIV, P. L.) And be it further enacted by the authority aforesaid, That Henry Taylor, of the said county of Washington, be and hereby is appointed collector of the excise of the same county, and is hereby authorized and empowered by himself or his sufficient deputy, duly constituted, and for whom he shall be accountable, to demand, collect, receive and recover the excise directed to be paid by any act or acts of assembly of this state, and also the arrearages thereof of and from all and every person and persons within the said county, retailing, vending or consuming any of the liquors by the said acts liable to pay the same; and also to recover and receive all and every the duties, fines and forfeitures laid or imposed or that shall become due for anything done contrary to the intent of the said acts.

[Section XIII.] (Section XV, P. L.) And be it further enacted by the authority aforesaid, That the said collector of excise for the county of Washington aforesaid, the better to enable him to recover the arrearages of excise, which shall be due before the passing of this act, shall apply to the collector of excise for the county of Westmoreland for a list (which the collector of the said county of Westmoreland is hereby enjoined and required to deliver), containing the names of each and every person in arrear for excise within the said county and how much from each of them.

[Section XIV.] (Section XVI, P. L..) And be it further enacted by the authority aforesaid, That the collector of the county of Washington aforesaid, before he enters upon the execution of his said office, is hereby required to give bond, with two sufficient sureties, to the treasurer of this state for the time being in the sum of two hundred pounds current money of the said state for the faithful discharge of his duty, and for paying all such sums of money as he shall, from time to time, receive by virtue of this act. And, further, the collector of the said county of Washington shall in all things govern himself and be subject to the same regulations, restrictions, fines and forfeitures and shall observe like rules, orders and directions as the collectors of the other counties aforesaid by the laws of this state are liable to. And the said collector, for the discharge of the duty of his office within the said county of

Washington, shall have and receive like fees, perquisites and rewards for his services enjoined by this act as the other collectors aforesaid (the collector of Philadelphia county excepted) by the acts aforesaid are entitled to for their services.

[Section XV.] And be it further enacted by the authority aforesaid, That until a sheriff and coroner shall be chosen in the county of Washington in pursuance of this act, it shall and may be lawful for the sheriff and coroner of Westmoreland to officiate and act in the discharge of their respective duties as fully and amply as they may or can do in the county of Westmoreland.

[Section XVI.] (Section XVIII, P. L.) And be it further enacted by the authority aforesaid, That before any sheriff hereafter to be appointed and commissionated for the said county of Washington shall enter upon the duties of his office he shall become bound in an obligation, with two or more sufficient sureties to be approved of by the president of this state, for the time being, in the sum of one thousand pounds and with like conditions as is directed with respect to the sheriffs of the other counties within this state, which said obligation shall be taken in the name of the commonwealth of Pennsylvania and entered upon record in the office for recording of deeds in the said county of Washington, and shall be in trust to and for the use and benefit of the person or persons who shall be injured by any breach, neglect or omission of duty in such sheriff, and may be proceeded upon in the same manner as is directed in respect to sheriff's bonds in and by the laws of this commonwealth now in force, and that the treasurer hereafter to be appointed for said county for receiving the state taxes, before he shall enter on the duties of his office, shall give security in like manner as other county treasurers are by law directed to give security, in the sum of one thousand pounds, and that the treasurer for said county, for receiving the county levies, shall, in like manner, give security in the sum of five hundred pounds.

Passed March 28, 1781. Recorded L. B. No. 1, p. 418, etc. As to section IV see the Act of Assembly passed March 31, 1784, Chapter 1093.

CHAPTER CMXXXII.

AN ACT TO PREVENT THE ATTAINDER OF DANIEL RUNDLE AND MATTHIAS ASPDEN FOR A LIMITED TIME, ON CONDITION THAT THEY RENDER THEMSELVES TO TAKE THEIR TRIAL ON OR BEFORE A CERTAIN DAY THEREIN LIMITED AND APPOINTED.

(Section I, P. L.) Whereas, his excellency the president and the honorable the supreme executive council of this commonwealth, by their proclamation under the hand of the said president and the seal of the state, bearing date the twenty-seventh day of July, in the year of our Lord one thousand seven hundred and eighty, by virtue of the powers and authorities to them given in and by an act of the general assembly, entitled "An act for the attainder of divers traitors, if they render not themselves by a certain day, and for vesting their estates in this commonwealth and for more effectually discovering the same, and for ascertaining and satisfying the lawful debts and claims thereupon,"[1] did charge and require, amongst others, Daniel Rundle and Matthias Aspden, merchants, late of the city of Philadelphia, to render themselves to some or one of the justices of the supreme court or of the justices of the peace of one of the counties within this state, on or before the first day of April then next following and also abide their legal trials, respectively, for high treason, on pain that they and each of them not rendering themselves as aforesaid and abiding the trial aforesaid, shall, from and after the said first day of April, stand and be attainted of high treason to all intents and purposes, and shall suffer such pains and penalties and undergo all such forfeitures as persons attainted of high treason ought to do:

And whereas, it is now made appear that the said Daniel Rundle and Matthias Aspden were, at the time of the said proclamation and probably still are, in Europe, that their friends have used all lawful means in their power to convey intelligence to them of their being so proclaimed as aforesaid,

---

[1] Passed March 6, 1778, Chapter 784.

but that there is very great reason to believe that the said intelligence never has reached them; and it being also shown that the said Daniel Rundle and Matthias Aspden were called to Europe about their own private affairs, and it being alleged and insisted that the said Daniel Rundle and Matthias Aspden will certainly render themselves up and stand their trial for the matters alleged against them if they can be indulged with time to a further day, and have notice of the proceedings here:

Wherefore, it has been prayed on their and each of their behalf that the aid of the legislature may be interposed to stay their attainder, for that no other power is supposed to be competent to that end, which, being just and reasonable:

[Section I.] (Section II, P. L.) Be it therefore enacted and it is hereby enacted by the Representatives of the Freemen of the Commonwealth of Pennsylvania in General Assembly met, and by the authority of the same, That further time be given to the said Daniel Rundle and Matthias Aspden, and each of them, for rendering themselves respectively to one of the justices of the supreme court, or of the peace aforesaid, and abiding their trial aforesaid for the term or space of nine months, to be computed from the day of passing this act.

[Section II.] (Section III, P. L.) And be it further enacted by the authority aforesaid, That the said Daniel Rundle and Matthias Aspden, or either of them, so as aforesaid rendering himself to one of the justices aforesaid on or before the thirty-first day of December next and abiding his trial aforesaid, he or they so rendering himself and abiding his trial, shall not become attainted or suffer the penalties or undergo the forfeitures of high treason for or on account of his not rendering himself and abiding his trial on or before the day limited and prefixed in and by the same proclamation; but, that their, and each of their, attainders be staid, and that he or they so rendering himself or themselves on or before the day hereinbefore limited and appointed and abiding his trial according to the purport, true intent and meaning of this act shall and may be and remain free and clear from all and every attainder and attainders other than such as may ensue upon a full and plain trial and the verdict of their country in due course of law, anything in the afore-recited act of attainder or proclamation in anywise notwithstanding.

[Section III.] Provided always, and be it further enacted by the authority aforesaid, That if the said Daniel Rundle and Matthias Aspden shall not render themselves, respectively, to some or one of the justices of the supreme court or of the justices of the peace of one of the counties within this state on or before the said thirty-first day of December, and also abide their legal trial for such treasons as may be alleged against them, respectively, that then and from thenceforth he or they so not rendering himself as aforesaid, or not abiding the trial aforesaid, shall stand and be adjudged and by the authority of this present act be convicted and attainted of high treason to all intents and purposes whatsoever and shall suffer and forfeit as a person attainted of high treason by law ought to suffer and forfeit, and that he or they so not rendering himself and abiding the trial aforesaid, his estate and effects shall in all things be dealt with, disposed of, regulated and conducted according to the act hereinbefore first recited, anything herein contained to the contrary notwithstanding.

Passed March 31, 1780. Recorded L. B. No. 1, p. 420, etc.

CHAPTER CMXXXIII.

AN ACT FOR VESTING THE ESTATE LATE OF HENRY HUGH FERGUSON IN ELIZABETH HIS WIFE.

(Section I, P. L.) Whereas, Henry Hugh Ferguson, late of the township of Horsham, in the county of Philadelphia, is and stands attainted of high treason, and the estate which he had in this commonwealth is forfeited:

And whereas, by the marriage of the said Henry Hugh Ferguson with his wife, Elizabeth (late Elizabeth Graeme), he became seized of an estate of freehold in a farm and tract of land commonly called Graeme Park, situated in the township and county aforesaid (of which the said Elizabeth was before and at the time of the marriage aforesaid seized in her demesne as of fee), during the joint lives of them, the said Henry Hugh Ferguson and Elizabeth, his wife:

And whereas, the said Elizabeth appears to have acted a friendly part to the cause of the United States and to be in such a peculiar situation as to deserve the protection and indulgence of this commonwealth:

[Section I.] (Section II, P. L.) Be it therefore enacted, and it is hereby enacted by the Representatives of the Freemen of the Commonwealth of Pennsylvania in General Assembly met, and by the authority of the same, That all the estate, right, title or interest which the said Henry Hugh Ferguson acquired in the aforesaid farm and tract of land, with the appurtenances, by his marriage with the said Elizabeth, shall be and are hereby vested in the said Elizabeth during her natural life, the said marriage and the attainder of the said Henry Hugh Ferguson and the forfeiture accruing to the commonwealth thereupon to the contrary hereof in anywise notwithstanding.

Passed April 2, 1781. Recorded L. B. No. 1, p. 421, etc.

CHAPTER CMXXXIV.

AN ACT TO REVIVE AN ACT ENTITLED "AN ACT TO REVIVE AN ACT TO PREVENT THE TRESPASSING UPON THE UNENCLOSED GROUNDS LYING IN THE TOWNSHIPS OF PASSYUNK, MOYAMENSING, NORTHERN LIBERTIES AND GERMANTOWN IN THE COUNTY OF PHILADELPHIA AND TO EXTEND THE SAID ACT TO THE ADJOINING TOWNSHIP OF BRISTOL IN THE SAME COUNTY, AND TO PREVENT SWINE FROM RUNNING AT LARGE WITHIN THE SAID TOWNSHIPS FOR A LIMITED TIME."[1]

(Section I, P. L.) Whereas, the act of assembly passed the third day of March, [in the year of our Lord one thousand seven hundred and eighty], to prevent the trespassing upon the unenclosed grounds lying in the townships of Passyunk, Moyamensing, Northern Liberties and Germantown, in the county

---

[1] Passed March 13, 1780, Chapter 892.

of Philadelphia, and to extend the said act to the adjoining township of Bristol, in the same county, and to prevent swine from running at large within the said townships for a limited time, hath been found a necessary and beneficial law for the landholders and inhabitants of the said district:

And whereas the said act has expired by its own limitation:

[Section I.] (Section II, P. L.) Be it therefore enacted, and it is hereby enacted by the Representatives of the Freemen of the Commonwealth of Pennsylvania in General Assembly met, and by the authority of the same, That from and after the passing of this act the said revised act and every clause, matter and thing therein contained, the clause of limitation and the fourth section directing the penalty only excepted, shall be and is hereby revived as fully as if the same was herein particularly recited, and shall continue until the first day of November next, and no longer.

[Section II.] (Section III, P. L.) Provided always, and be it further enacted by the authority aforesaid, That instead of the penalty of ten pounds by the said act directed to be levied for every beast suffered to run at large contrary to the directions thereof, there shall be levied for and during the continuance of this act the sum of twenty shillings.

Passed April 2, 1781. Recorded L. B. No. 1, p. 421, etc. See the Acts of Assembly passed April 5, 1779, Chapter 840; March 13, 1780, Chapter 892.

CHAPTER CMXXXV.

AN ACT DIRECTING THE MODE OF ADJUSTING AND SETTLING THE PAYMENT OF DEBTS AND CONTRACTS ENTERED INTO AND MADE BEWEEN THE FIRST DAY OF JANUARY, ONE THONSAND SEVEN HUNDRED AND SEVENTY-SEVEN, AND THE FIRST DAY OF MARCH, ONE THOUSAND SEVEN HUNDRED AND EIGHTY-ONE, AND FOR OTHER PURPOSES THEREIN MENTIONED.

(Section I, P. L.) Whereas, the good people of this state labor under many inconveniences for want of some rule whereby to settle and adjust the payment of debts and contracts entered into and made between the first day of January, one thousand seven hundred and seventy-seven, and the first day of March, one thousand seven hundred and eighty-one, many of which are yet due and unsatified, and it seems just and reasonable that some rule should be by law established for liquidating and adjusting the same so as to do justice as well to the debtors as creditors:

[Section I.] (Section II, P. L.) Be it therefore enacted, and it is hereby enacted by the Representatives of the Freemen of the Commonwealth of Pennsylvania in General Assembly met, and by the authority of the same, That from and after the passing of this act all debts and contracts of what nature or kind soever entered into or made within the period aforesaid now remaining due and unfulfilled for the payment of money, shall be liquidated, settled and adjusted agreeable to a scale of depreciation hereinafter mentioned and contained: That is to say, by reducing the amount of all such debts and contracts to the true value in specie at the days or times the same were incurred or entered into; and, upon payment of the said value so found in specie or other money equivalent, the debtors or contractors shall be forever discharged of and from the said debts or contracts, any law, custom or usage to the contrary in anywise notwithstanding.

[Section II.] (Section III, P. L.) And be it further enacted by the authority aforesaid, That the proviso clause in the suspension act of the thirty-first day of May, one thousand seven hundred and eighty, continued by a supplement of the twenty-second day of September, one thousand seven hundred and eighty, and also the proviso clause of the suspension act of the twentieth day of February, one thousand seven hundred and eighty-one, so far as the same takes off or restrains the enacting clause in the said laws in case of payment of any debt or demand whereupon any distress may be made or upon which any action or suit shall be commenced in any court of law within this state shall be and the same are hereby repealed, anything in the said proviso clauses to the contrary notwithstanding.

[Section III.] (Section IV, P. L.) And be it further enacted by the authority aforesaid, That in all cases between debtors and creditors for debts or demands due and payable or incurred on or before the first day of March, one thousand seven hundred and eighty-one, where the parties cannot otherwise agree, it shall and may be lawful for any court of law and for any justice of the peace (in cases of debts and demands cognizable before one justice of the peace), upon the prayer of either party, to appoint three or more auditors in presence of the parties if they will, upon reasonable notice attend, otherwise upon proof of such notice to the court or justice to appoint the said auditors, ex parte, in manner following, to wit: By naming a treble number and each of the parties to strike out one alternately until the number to be appointed only remain in nomination, and in case of non-attendance of either party, the clerk of such court or the justice of the peace to strike for the absent party; which auditors so appointed shall have full power and authority, upon notice to the parties, to meet, hear and examine the parties upon interrogatories and also such witnesses, papers and proof of the parties, as shall be to them adduced, and thereupon liquidate, adjust and settle all debts or demands and other controversies subsisting between the parties agreeable to the directions of this act where that can be done, but in cases where the act shall not apply, then to settle and adjust the same according to equity and good conscience upon due consideration had of the nature and circumstances of the case, but the said auditors shall not have any power or authority, in cases where partial payments have been made in money then current to reduce such payment. And the said auditors, where any tender has been made before the first day of March, one thousand seven hundred and eighty-one, in money current, shall not allow the creditor more than the value of his debt reduced to specie, at the time when such tender was made; and where it shall appear to the said auditors that any debtor who had willingly received bills of credit made current in payment of his debts, and was also prepared and ready to pay the sum due by him in such money, but was prevented by the creditor absconding, concealing his bonds or papers or secretly assigning them or such like evasions, in all such cases the debtor shall have the benefit of a legal tender;

and the said auditors, upon settling and adjusting all such debts or demands, shall make report to the court or justice, as the case may require, which report shall be of the same force and effect as a verdict of a jury in the case, and the court or justice shall enter judgment on such report.

[Section IV.] (Section V, P. L.) And be it further enacted by the authority aforesaid, That the following scale of depreciation shall be the rule to determine the value of the several debts, contracts and demands in this act mentioned, compared with silver and gold:

One Thousand Seven Hundred Seventy-seven.

January, one and a half.
February, one and a half.
March, two.
April, two and a half.
May, two and a half.
June, two and a half.
July, three.
August, three.
September, three.
October, three.
November, three.
December, four.

One Thousand Seven Hundred Seventy-eight.

January, four.
February, five.
March, five.
April, six.
May, five.
June, four.
July, four.
August, five.
September, five.
October, five.
November, six.
December, six.

One Thousand Seven Hundred and Seventy-nine.

January, eight.
February, ten.
March, ten and an half.
April, seventeen.
May, twenty-four.
June, twenty.
July, nineteen.
August, twenty.
September, twenty-four.
October, thirty.
November, thirty-eight and an half.
December, forty-one and an half.

One Thousand Seven Hundred and Eighty.

January, forty and an half.
February, forty-seven and an half.
March, sixty-one and an half.
April, sixty-one and an half.
May, fifty-nine.
June, sixty-one and an half.
July, sixty-four and an half.
August, seventy.
September, seventy-two.
October, seventy-three.
November, seventy-four.
December, seventy-five.

One Thousand Seven Hundred and Eighty-one.

January, seventy-five.
February, seventy-five.

[Section V.] (Section VI, P. L.) And be it further enacted by the authority aforesaid, That the act, entitled "A supplement to an act for the more easy recovery of small debts,"[1] passed on the ninth day of October, one thousand seven hundred and seventy-nine, be and the same is hereby repealed and made void.

[Section VI.] (Section VII, P. L.) And be it further enacted

---

[1] Passed October 9, 1779, Chapter 862.

by the authority aforesaid, That the act, entitled "An act for limitation of actions,"[1] passed the twenty-seventh day of March, one thousand seven hundred and thirteen, shall not run or operate during the time courts of justice were shut in this state, nor during the time of any suspension act of this state in any action or distress prohibited to be made or brought by such act, under the penalty of taking depreciated money in full payment.

Passed April 3, 1781. Recorded L. B. No. 1, p. 422, etc. See the Acts of Assembly passed February 20, 1781, Chapter 927; June 21, 1781, Chapter 945.

CHAPTER CMXXXVI.

AN ACT TO PREVENT THE EXPORTATION OF BREAD AND FLOUR NOT MERCHANTABLE, AND FOR REPEALING AT A CERTAIN TIME ALL THE LAWS HERETOFORE MADE FOR THAT PURPOSE.

(Section I, P. L.) Whereas, the regulations hitherto made for the inspection of bread and flour have not been quite effectual and a variety of laws on the same subject tend to mislead the people:

[Section I.] (Section II, P. L.) Be it therefore enacted and it is hereby enacted by the Representatives of the Freemen of the Commonwealth of Pennsylvania in General Assembly met, and by the authority of the same, That the act, entitled "An act to prevent the exportation of bread and flour not merchantable,"[2] passed the fourteenth day of October, one thousand seven hundred and thirty-three (excepting that part of it which repeals the act therein mentioned and called an act to prevent the exportation of bread and flour not merchantable), and the act, entitled "A supplement to the act, entitled 'An act to prevent the exportation of bread and flour not merchantable, and to the act which is an amendment thereof,'"[3] passed on the sixth [sic] [ninth] day of October, one thousand seven hun-

---

[1] Passed March 27, 1713, Chapter 196.
[2] Passed October 17, 1733, Chapter 332.
[3] Passed October 9, 1779, Chapter 855.

1781]   *The Statutes at Large of Pennsylvania.*   289

dred and seventy-nine, be and continue in force until the first day of October next, and that from and after that day the same acts be and the same are hereby repealed.

(Section III, P. L.) Provided always, That the millers and bolters shall be allowed until the first day of October next to sell and dispose of, for exportation, their flour in barrels of any other dimensions than those by the said acts, or any of them, prescribed.

(Section IV, P. L.) And whereas, it is the duty and interests of all governments to prevent fraud and promote the interests of just and useful commerce:

[Section II.] (Section V, P. L.) Be it therefore further enacted by the authority aforesaid, That from and after the said first day of October next all flour casks shall be made of good seasoned materials, well made and tightened with ten hoops, sufficiently nailed with four nails in each chine hoop and three nails in each upper bilge hoop, and of the following dimensions, viz.: The staves to be of the length of twenty-seven inches, but of different diameters at the heads according to their numbers, That is to say, casks, number one, shall be of the diameter of eighteen inches at the head; casks number two, sixteen inches and a half, and casks number three, fifteen inches and a half; that every miller or bolter of flour and baker of bread for transportation out of the state shall provide and have a distinguishable brand mark, which he shall cause to be entered with the clerk of the quarter sessions of the county where he doth reside, together with his name and place of abode, under the penalty of the sum of five shillings for every day during which he shall have exercised his said business of a miller, bolter or baker without such entry; for the making of which entries, the said clerk shall be entitled to the sum of one shilling each. And that every miller or bolter of flour or baker of bread shall, with his said mark, brand each and every cask of flour or bread before the same shall be removed from the place where the same was bolted or baked; and every miller or bolter shall also brand every cask of flour according to the respective diameters above specified with the said numbers one, two or three, and with the weight, respectively, under the penalty of one shilling and six pence for every barrel of flour not hooped and nailed as aforesaid, and for every cask of flour or bread so removed and not branded as aforesaid.

[Section III.] (Section V, P. L.) And be it further enacted by the authority aforesaid, That the said millers or bolters shall put in the cask number one, the full quantity or weight of two hundred and twenty-four pounds of flour; in the cask number two, the full quantity or weight of one hundred and ninety-six pounds, and in the casks number three, the full quantity or weight of one hundred and sixty-eight pounds of flour; and that if any miller or bolter shall use or pack with flour any other casks than [those] of three several sizes and dimensions aforesaid, he shall forfeit to the purchaser thereof the value or charge of such cask in his account; and that if any miller or bolter shall pack any casks of the said sizes or dimensions with a less quantity of flour than is above specified for the same, respectively. he shall forfeit the same casks and flour.

[Section IV.] (Section VI, P. L.) And be it further enacted by the authority aforesaid, That all wheat flour bolted for sale and transportation out of the state shall be made merchantable and of due fineness without any mixture of coarser and other flour.

[Section V.] (Section VII, P. L.) And be it further enacted by the authority aforesaid, That all casks wherein bread shall be packed, shall be weighed and the tare marked thereon, and if any person shall put a false or wrong tare on any cask of bread to the disadvantage of the purchaser, he or she shall forfeit for every cask so falsely tared the sum of five shillings; and the inspectors, or their deputies, respectively, upon suspicion or upon the request of the buyers, shall and are hereby required to unpack any such cask of flour or bread as aforesaid; and if there shall be a lesser quantity of flour than is above directed, or if the cask or casks wherein bread is packed shall be found to weigh more than is marked thereon, then the miller, bolter or baker, as the case may be, shall pay the charges of unpacking and repacking over and above the penalties aforesaid; but, otherwise, the said charges shall be paid by the inspector or by the purchaser if the trial be made at his request.

[Section VI.] (Section VIII, P. L.) And be it enacted by the authority aforesaid, That every baker of bread for exportation, shall deliver with the said bread an invoice of the contents thereof, with his brand mark made thereon, together with his name signed thereto, under the penalty of forty shillings for every invoice delivered contrary thereto; and if any cask or casks of bread, upon trial, be found lighter than is set down in the invoice, such baker shall forfeit the bread and casks so falsely invoiced.

[Section VII.] (Section IX, P. L.) And be it enacted by the authority aforesaid, That no cart, wain or wagon shall be made use of for the carrying or conveying of flour or bread from any mill or other place to the place of exportation or to any landing place but such as shall be provided with a good and sufficient covering; and that no flour shall be left at any landing or other place in order to be transported, except the same be put in a store or shelter sufficient to keep it dry, and that no flour or bread shall be carried or conveyed by water from any mill or landing place to the place of exportation in any open boat, flat or shallop without a good and sufficient covering or tarpauling to secure the same in case of rain.

[Section VIII.] (Section X, P. L.) And be it enacted by the authority aforesaid, That if the owner or possessor of any cart, wain or wagon, boat, flat or shallop shall cause or suffer any flour or bread to be wet or take damage for want of due care, or not being provided as aforesaid in the moving, carrying or transporting the same from any mill or other place to the place of exportation, every such person shall forfeit, for every cask of flour or bread so damaged, the sum of one shilling.

[Section IX.] (Section XI, P. L.) And be it enacted by the authority aforesaid, That no merchant or other person whatsoever shall lade or ship any flour for transportation out of this state before he, she or they shall offer the same to the view and examination of the inspector of the port from whence the same is shipped, or intended to be shipped, or his deputy, under the penalty of five shillings for every cask. And the said inspector or deputy shall search and try the same by boring the head and piercing it through with a proper instrument, in order to prove whether it be honestly and well packed, as also to enable him to judge of the goodness thereof, and shall afterwards plug up the hole. And if the said inspector shall judge the same to be merchantable, he shall brand every such cask of flour, on the quarter, with the arms of the state of Pennsylvania, in a fair and distinguishable manner, for which he shall receive one penny for each cask, and no more. But if he shall judge such flour not to be merchantable, and the possessor or owner thereof shall acquiesce under such judgment, he shall, in such case, pay to the said inspector the said sum of one penny for each and every such cask, and on his refusal or neglect, the inspector may recover the same, as debts under forty shillings are recoverable, with costs of suit; and if the possessor of any flour shall offer to transport the same out of this state, without being approved and branded in the manner hereinbefore mentioned the same flour shall be forfeited.

[Section X.] (Section XII, P. L.) And be it further enacted by the authority aforesaid, That where any dispute shall arise between any of the said inspectors or their deputies with the owner or possessor, concerning the fineness or goodness of such flour of the goodness of the materials of which the casks are made, then, upon application made by the owner or possessor of such flour, to one of the magistrates of the city or county where the dispute shall arise, the said magistrate shall issue his warrant to three indifferent and judicious persons to be triers thereof (one of them to be named by the said owner or possessor, one by the said inspector or his deputy and the third by the said magistrate), directing the said triers to view and examine the said flour and make report to him forthwith touching the condition thereof, and that if they shall find the said flour not merchantable, that they certify to him the cause thereof, and whether it be that the said flour wants due fineness, is musty, sour or the like; and if sour, whether such sourness is occasioned by the greenness of the timber whereof the casks are made, or by being brought in any open boat or shallop, or upon the deck of any other vessel without a tarpaulin or cover, or for any other and what cause, and the said magistrate shall thereupon give his judgment agreeable to the report of the said triers, or any two of them; and in case the said magistrate shall, on such report, adjudge the said flour not to be merchantable, he shall award the owner or possessor thereof to pay into the hands of the said inspector one shilling for each and every such cask so adjudged to be unmerchantable, besides reasonable costs; but in case the said flour shall be found merchantable, the inspector shall be adjudged to pay all the costs which shall have accrued, and the said officer shall thereupon brand the said flour in the manner before directed. And if it shall appear, either by the report aforesaid or otherwise, that any flour is become unmerchantable by fault of the miller, bolter or shallopman, flatman, carter or wagoner in every such case the owner of such flour shall recover against the said miller, bolter, shallopman, flatman, carter or wagoner, by default of whom or of whose servant or servants such flour shall have been injured, the damages which such owner shall have sustained, with full costs of suit.

[Section XI.] (Section XIII, P. L.) And be it further enacted by the authority aforesaid, That the masters of ships and other vessels lading flour for exportation from this state shall, in their manifests, which in pursuance of the act, entitled "An act for regulating trade and navigation in this state,"[1] they are obliged to exhibit and deliver to the naval officer thereof, expressly and distinctly declare how many barrels of flour are shipped on board of their respective vessels, and by whom each parcel thereof is shipped, to which manifest or declaration the inspector aforesaid shall have free access and liberty to take abstracts thereof, and if any master of a vessel shall refuse or neglect to make such return to the naval officer as aforesaid, he shall, over and above the penalty in the said last named act mentioned, forfeit to the said inspector the amount of his fees for trying and examing the whole cargo of flour shipped on board of his vessel.

[Section XII.] (Section XIV, P. L.) And be it further enacted by the authority aforesaid, That the said inspector, or

---

[1] Passed September 10, 1778, Chapter 815.

his deputies, shall have full power and authority by virtue of this act, and without any further or other warrant, to enter on board any ship or other vessel whatsoever lying or being in any port or place of this state, or into any mill, store or granary within the same, to search for and discover any flour intended to be transported out of this state, and if the owner or possessor thereof, or their servants or others shall deny him or them entrance or if the said inspector or his deputies shall be in anywise molested in making such discovery as aforesaid, or if such owner or possessor shall refuse to permit the said inspector or his deputy to view or examine the same, every such person so offending shall forfeit and pay the sum of ten pounds for every such offense.

[Section XIII.] (Section XV, P. L.) And be it further enacted by the authority aforesaid, That if any person or persons shall counterfeit the aforesaid brand marks, or either of them, or impress or brand the same on any cask of flour, he, she or they, being thereof legally convicted, shall, for the first offense, forfeit and pay the sum of five pounds; for the second offense, the sum of ten pounds; and for the third offense shall be committed to gaol and sentenced to the pillory, there to stand the space of two hours on a market day in any city, borough or town where the fact shall have been committed.

[Section XIV.] (Section XVI, P. L.) And be it further enacted by the authority aforesaid, That none of the said inspectors or their deputies shall, directly or indirectly, vend, barter, sell, exchange or trade in flour under the penalty of fifty pounds, to be recovered by action of debt, bill, plaint or information, by any person who will sue for the same to effect in any court of record in this state, the one-half thereof to the use of the person or person so suing, the other half to be paid to the treasurer of the state for the public use. And every person or persons so offending and thereof convicted shall be and they are hereby disabled from acting thereafter in their respective offices.

[Section XV.] (Section XVII, P. L.) And be it further enacted by the authority aforesaid, That the said inspectors be empowered to appoint deputies under them, but before any inspector or deputy shall do anything in his said office he shall take an oath or affirmation before any one justice of the peace of any county of this state, faithfully and impartially to perform his trust and duty to the best of his skill and understanding according to the directions of this present act.

[Section XVI.] (Section XVIII, P. L.) And be it further enacted by the authority aforesaid, That all and singular the fines, forfeitures and charges mentioned in this act, where the same, respectively, exceed not five pounds, shall be recovered in the same manner as other debts and demands under the said sum of five pounds are recoverable, and where the same exceed the said sum of five pounds they may be sued for and shall be recovered in any court of record in this state, by bill, plaint or information, wherein no essoin, protection or wager of law, nor more than one imparlance, shall be allowed, all which said fines and forfeitures not hereinbefore directed how to be applied shall be paid to the said inspector or his deputy, who shall keep a just and true account thereof, and shall, once in every year, at the time of appointing overseers of the poor, deliver unto the magistrates a true and exact list of all such fines and forfeitures, the one-half whereof he shall immediately pay into the hands of the overseers of the poor of the place where the forfeitures happen, and shall retain the other half to his own use. And if any of the said inspectors or deputies shall neglect or refuse to account and pay as aforesaid he shall forfeit his office.

[Section XVII.] (Section XIX, P. L.) And be it further enacted by the authority aforesaid, That Jacob Bright be and he is hereby appointed inspector for the city and county of Philadelphia; and Adam Grubb, for the county of Chester; and Joseph McElvaine, for the county of Bucks. The said inspectors to hold their offices from the publication of this act for the space of four years, and from thence until the end of the next sitting of assembly, and no longer, except they shall be re-appointed by the assembly. And if any, or either of the said inspectors shall happen to die, or by any accident or otherwise shall be rendered incapable, or shall knowlingly suffer any flour to be carried out of this state without trying every cask thereof as aforesaid, or shall neglect to keep a sufficient number of deputies to assist him in the execution of his office, whereby the possessor of such flour shall suffer any damage or delay, or shall otherwise misbehave him or themselves therein, it shall and may be lawful to and for a majority of the justices of the peace of the city of Philadelphia, or of the respective counties before mentioned, and they are hereby enjoined and required, on the conviction of the said officer of any of the said crimes, or on his death, to nominate and appoint some other fit person in his or their place or places, who shall thereupon, on taking the said oath, be the inspector until the assembly shall appoint another to be invested with the powers and subject to the duties hereinbefore mentioned.

> Passed April 5, 1781. Recorded L. B. No. 1, p. 423, etc. See the notes to the Acts of Assembly passed October 14, 1733, Chapter 332; October 6, 1779, Chapter 855, and the Acts of Assembly passed December 28, 1781, Chapter 956; March 9, 1783, Chapter 1017; September 15, 1784, Chapter 1112; September 12, 1789, Chapter 1433; September 30, 1791, Chapter 1595; April 18, 1795, Chapter 1862; March 16, 1798, Chapter 1975; March 15, 1800, Chapter 2144. Section XV of the Act in the text was repealed by the Act of Assembly passed March 31, 1860, P. L. 452.

CHAPTER CMXXXVII.

AN ACT TO VEST IN THE CONGRESS OF THE UNITED STATES, A POWER TO LEVY DUTIES OF FIVE PER CENTUM AD VALOREM, ON CERTAIN GOODS AND MERCHANDISE IMPORTED INTO THIS COMMONWEALTH, AND ON PRIZES AND PRIZE GOODS CONDEMNED IN THE COURT OF ADMIRALITY OF THIS STATE, AFTER THE FIRST DAY OF MAY, ONE THOUSAND SEVEN HUNDRED AND EIGHTY-ONE, AND FOR APPROPRIATING THE SAME.

(Section I, P. L.) Whereas, the Congress of the United States, by their act of the third day of February last, did resolve that it be recommended to the several states, as indispensably necessary, that they vest a power in Congress to levy, for the use of the United States, a duty of five per centum ad valorem, at the time and place of importation, upon all goods, wares and merchandise of foreign growth and manufacture, which might be imported into any of the said states, from any foreign port, island or plantation, after the first day of May, one thousand seven hundred and eighty-one, except arms, ammunition, clothing and other articles, imported on account of the United States, or any of them, and except wool cards and cotton cards and wire for making them, and also except salt during the war. Also, a like duty of five per centum on all prizes and prize goods condemned in the court of admiralty of any of these states, as lawful prize, that the moneys arising from the said duties be appropriated to the discharge of the principal and interest of the debts already contracted, or which might be contracted on the faith of the United States for supporting the present war that the said duties be continued until the said debts should be fully and finally discharged:

[Section I.] (Section II, P. L.) Be it therefore enacted and it is hereby enacted by the Representatives of the Freemen of the Commonwealth of Pennsylvania in General Assembly met, and by the authority of the same, That the United States in Congress assembled shall be, and they hereby are fully authorized and empowered to levy, for the use of the said states, a duty of five per cent ad valorem, at the time and place of importation upon all goods, wares and merchandise of foreign growth and manufacture which may be imported into this commonwealth from any port, island or plantation, not within any of the United States, after the first day of May, in the year one thousand seven hundred and eighty-one, except arms, ammunition, clothing and other articles imported on account of the said states, or any of them, and except wool cards and cotton cards and wire for making them, and also except salt during the war. That the said states be and they hereby are also empowered to levy, for the use aforesaid, a like duty of five per centum on all prizes and prize goods condemned by the admiralty court of this commonwealth as lawful prize:

And whereas it will conduce to the general interest that the commercial regulations throughout the said states be uniform and consistent:

[Section II.] (Section III, P. L.) Be it therefore further enacted by the authority aforesaid, That the said United States, in Congress assembled, shall be and they are hereby fully authorized to appoint one or more collector or collectors in this commonwealth, to collect the said duties according to such rules and ordinances for collecting and levying the same, as they shall judge expedient: Provided always, That such rules and ordinances be not repugnant to the constitution and laws of this state.

[Section III.] (Section IV, P. L.) And be it further enacted by the authority aforesaid, That the moneys arising from the said duties shall be and they hereby are appropriated to the discharge of the principal and interest of the debts already contracted or which may be contracted on the faith of the said United States for supporting the present war.

[Section IV.] (Section V, P. L.) And be it further enacted by the authority aforesaid, That this act shall be and continue in force until the full and final discharge of the debts hereinbefore mentioned, and no longer.

Passed April 5, 1781. Recorded L. B. No. 1, p. 426, etc. The Act in the text was repealed by the Act of Assembly passed September 23, 1783, Chapter 1039.

CHAPTER CMXXXVIII.

AN ACT FOR AMENDING AND CONTINUING AN ACT ENTITLED "AN ACT FOR THE SUPPORT OF THE GOVERNMENT OF THIS PROVINCE, MAKING THE EXCISE ON WINE, RUM, BRANDY AND OTHER SPIRITS MORE EQUAL, AND PREVENTING FRAUDS IN THE COLLECTING AND PAYING THE SAID EXCISE." [1]

(Section I, P. L.) Whereas, the act of assembly, entitled "An act for the support of the government of this province, making the excise on wine, rum, brandy and other spirits more equal, and preventing frauds in the collecting and paying the said excise," [1] passed on the twenty-first day of March, in the year of our Lord one thousand seven hundred and seventy-two, will

[1] March 21, 1772, Chapter 656.

expire on the tenth day of April which will be in the year of our Lord one thousand seven hundred eighty and two: And whereas, it is necessary for the supporting the honor of government, discharging its debts and incidental expenses and for carrying on the war against the King of Great Britain, to continue the present excise on wine, rum, brandy and other spirits and to raise additional sums of money upon the same:

[Section I.] (Section II, P. L.) Be it therefore enacted and it is hereby enacted by the Representatives of the Freemen of the Commonwealth of Pennsylvania in General Assembly met, and by the authority of the same, That so much of the act of assembly aforesaid, not altered by this act as relates to the excise on wine, rum, brandy and other spirits and the collecting and paying the same shall be continued and the same is hereby continued for the term of ten years, from and after the aforesaid tenth day of April, which will be in the year of our Lord one thousand seven hundred eighty and two.

[Section II.] (Section III, P. L.) Provided always, and be it further enacted by the authority aforesaid, That the retailers of spirits distilled from the natural products of this state, late province of Pennsylvania, shall take permits from the collector of the excise and give him security in like manner in all respects as other retailers are obliged to do, anything in the nineteenth section of the act of assembly aforesaid to the contrary notwithstanding.

[Section III.] (Section IV, P. L.) And be it further enacted by the authority aforesaid, That from and after the thirtieth day of May next, until the expiration of this act, there shall be raised, levied, collected and paid the rate, duty and sum of four pence a gallon, and so in proportion, [for] any greater or lesser quantity over and above the rate and duty imposed by the above-recited act, upon all such wine, rum, brandy and other spirits bartered, sold or consumed within this state, as are subjected to a duty by the said act, which rates, duties and sums imposed by the act amended and continued by this act, and by this act shall be paid in specie or other money equivalent and not otherwise.

[Section IV.] (Section V, P. L.) And be it further enacted

by the authority aforesaid, That the several and respective duties by this act granted and continued shall be raised, levied, collected and paid during the term and time aforesaid, by the same ways, means and methods and by such rules and directions and under such penalties and forfeitures, and with such powers in all respects, not otherwise directed by this act, as are prescribed, mentioned or expressed in the said former act, or in any other act of assembly, thereby referred unto, for and concerning the duties by the same imposed and granted, and that the same act before mentioned and the act or acts thereby referred unto as for and concerning the said duties on wine, rum, brandy and other spirits, and every article, rule, clause, matter and thing therein contained and now being in force, not otherwise altered by this act, shall be and continue in full force and effect, to all intents and purposes for raising, levying, collecting, securing and accounting for the rates, duties and impositions hereby granted, imposed and continued, respectively, and for levying and recovering the penalties and forfeitures and all other matters and things during the continuance of this act, as fully as if the same were particularly and at large repeated in the body of this present act.

[Section V.] (Section VI, P. L.) Provided always, and it is hereby enacted, That nothing in this act contained shall extend, or be construed to extend, to allow any collector of excise for any county of this state any larger or greater sum for his trouble and care in collecting and paying the additional rate, duty or excise by this act imposed than at the rate of one per centum on all sums by him to be collected and paid in virtue hereof.

[Section VI.] (Section VII. P. L.) And be it further enacted by the authority aforesaid, That the treasurer of this state for the time being shall and he is hereby enjoined and required to pay all and singular the sum and sums of money arising by this act, or the act hereby referred unto, which shall be at any time in his hands, as the general assembly shall, by act of assembly, vote or draft, direct and order and not otherwise, anything in any former act of assembly to the contrary notwithstanding.

[Section VII.] (Section VIII, P. L.) And be it further enacted by the authority aforesaid, That no other rates or duties be demanded, received or paid in this state on any wine, rum, brandy or other spirits than those imposed and made payable by this act and the act hereby amended and continued, any law, usage or custom to the contrary notwithstanding.

> Passed April 6, 1781. Recorded L. B. No. 1, p. 427, etc. See the note to the Act of Assembly passed March 21, 1772, Chapter 656, and the Act of Assembly passed March 19, 1783, Chapter 1016.

CHAPTER CMXXXIX.

AN ACT FOR EMITTING THE SUM OF FIVE HUNDRED THOUSAND POUNDS IN BILLS OF CREDIT, FOR THE SUPPORT OF THE ARMY AND FOR ESTABLISHING A FUND FOR THE REDEMPTION THEREOF AND FOR OTHER PURPOSES THEREIN MENTIONED.

(Section I, P. L.) Whereas, it is not to be expected, during the present war with Great Britain, that sufficient quantities of gold and silver money can be procured or retained in this state, for the procuring and providing sufficient supplies of provisions and other articles for the support of the army, and for the purposes of private dealings, for which purpose and for supplying the good people of this state with a medium of commerce of a stable and solid nature for want of which they already suffer:

And whereas, there are many and large arrearages and sums of money due to this state from private persons for lands heretofore granted and claimed, which ought to be pledged as a fund of credit for the relieving the public necessities and supplying the treasury at this time:

[Section I.] (Section II, P. L.) Be it therefore enacted and it is hereby enacted by the Representatives of the Freemen of the Commonwealth of Pennsylvania in General Assembly met, and by the authority of the same, That bills of credit to the value of five hundred thousand pounds shall be prepared and printed with all possible dispatch after the publication of this act on good strong paper, under the care and direction of George Gray, John Steinmetz, Henry Hill, Samuel Penrose, Henry Hayes and William Harris, the charges whereof shall be paid by the state treasurer out of the moneys so prepared and printed, which bills of credit shall be made and prepared in manner and form following, viz.:

"This bill shall pass current for ————, according to an act of general assembly of the commonwealth of Pennsylvania passed the seventh day of April, in the year one thousand seven hundred and eighty-one. Dated the ———— day of April, Anno Domini one thousand seven hundred and eighty-one."

And the said bills shall have the state arms as an escutcheon in the margin thereof, with such other devices as the said George Gray, John Steinmetz, Henry Hill, Samuel Penrose, Henry Hayes and William Harris, or a majority of them, shall think proper, in order to prevent counterfeits, and to distinguish their several and respective denominations, which bills shall be of the several and respective denominations following, and no other. That is to say:

Twenty-nine thousand and seventy-seven of the said bills, the sum of five pounds each.

Twenty-nine thousand and seventy-seven of the said bills, the sum of three pounds each.

Twenty-nine thousand and seventy-seven of the said bills, the sum of two pounds ten shillings each.

Twenty-nine thousand and seventy-seven of the said bills, the sum of two pounds each.

Twenty-nine thousand and seventy-seven of the said bills, the sum of one pound ten shillings each.

Twenty-nine thousand and seventy-seven of the said bills, the sum of one pound each.

Twenty-nine thousand and seventy-six of the said bills, the sum of fifteen shillings each.

Twenty-nine thousand and seventy-six of the said bills the sum of ten shillings each.

Forty thousand of the said bills, the sum of five shillings each.

Forty thousand of the said bills, the sum of two shillings and six pence each.

Forty thousand of the said bills, the sum of two shillings each.

Twenty thousand of the said bills, the sum of one shilling and six pence each.

Twenty thousand of the said bills, the sum of one shilling each.

Eighty thousand of the said bills, the sum of nine pence each.

Eighty thousand of the said bills, the sum of six pence each, **and**

Eighty thousand of the said bills, the sum of three pence each.

(Section III, P. L.) And the said George Gray, John Steinmetz, Henry Hill, Samuel Penrose, Henry Hayes and William Harris shall use their best care, attention and diligence during the making of the paper and printing of the said bills, that the number and amount thereof, according to the said several denominations, be not exceeded, nor any clandestine or fraudulent practices used by the paper maker or the printer, his or their servants or others.

(Section IV, P. L.) And for the perfecting the said bills according to the true intent and meaning of this act:

[Section II.] Be it enacted by the authority aforesaid, That the said bills, the denomination whereof shall be ten shillings and upwards, shall be signed by any two of the persons hereinafter mentioned, and that every of the said bills the denomination whereof shall be under ten shillings, shall be signed by any one of the persons hereinafter mentioned. That is to say: Cadwalader Morris, Samuel Meredith, James Budden, Joseph Wharton, Joseph Bullock, Samuel Caldwell, Michael Shubart, David H. Cunningham, Jacob Barge, Philip Boehm, John Purviance, Joseph Dean, John Miller, Jonathan Mifflin, Isaac Howell, Richard Bache, John Baynton, Tench Francis, David Shaffer, Senior, Thomas Pryor, Robert Knox, John Mease, Jacob S. Howell and John Patton, who are hereby nominated and appointed signers thereof, and who shall, before they receive or sign any of them, take an oath or affirmation to the effect following, viz.: That they shall well and truly sign and number all the bills of credit that shall come to their hands for that purpose according to the directions of this act, and the same so signed and numbered will re-deliver or cause to be re-delivered unto George Gray, John Steinmetz, Henry Hill, Samuel Penrose, Henry Hayes and William Harris, or any of them, pursuant to the directions of this act.

(Section V, P. L.) And to avoid the danger of embezzlement or misapplication of any of the said bills of credit:

[Section III.] Be it enacted by the authority aforesaid, That the said George Gray, John Steinmetz, Henry Hill, Samuel Penrose, Henry Hayes and William Harris, after the said bills shall be printed, shall deliver from time to time so many of them to the signers aforesaid by parcels to be signed and numbered as they shall judge proper, for which the said signers, or some one of them, shall give receipts. That is to say: That not more than three thousand pounds of the said bills shall remain in the hands of any two of them at the same time, and so, from time to time, till the whole of the said bills be signed, of all which bills of credit so delivered to be signed and numbered as aforesaid, a true account shall be kept by the signers, who, upon re-delivery of each or any parcel of the said bills by them signed and numbered shall have the receipt of the said George Gray, John Steinmetz, Henry Hill, Samuel Penrose, Henry Hayes and William Harris, or any two of them, to charge them before any committee of assembly appointed to enquire into the same; and each of the said signers shall have fifteen shillings for every thousand of the said bills by him signed and numbered, and no more; and the said George Gray, John Steinmetz, Henry Hill, Samuel Penrose, Henry Hayes and William Harris shall severally receive twenty-five shillings for every day they shall be employed in the said business, and the treasurer of this state shall, for receiving and paying, have and receive two shillings and six pence per hundred pounds for his care and trouble, to be paid out of the moneys emitted by virtue of this act.

[Section IV.] (Section VI, P. L.) And be it enacted by the authority aforesaid, That the bills of credit hereby directed to be prepared and made as fast as the same shall be signed, numbered and perfected as aforesaid, shall be delivered to the treasurer of the state by the said George Gray, John Steinmetz, Henry Hill, Samuel Penrose, Henry Hayes and William Harris, or any of them, who shall give a receipt or receipts for the same, and shall issue and pay the same according to the drafts of the general assembly or of the president or vice-president in council for public use.

[Section V.] (Section VII, P. L.) And be it further enacted by the authority aforesaid, That, together with the guarantee of the honor and faith of Pennsylvania which is hereby given, so much as shall be sufficient of the arrearages and sums of money due to this state for lands heretofore granted or claimed by virtue of warrants, locations, surveys or any other title that might be deemed good and valid, according to the law, custom or usage in force under the late government, shall be and hereby is pledged and declared to be a fund out of which the bills of credit aforesaid shall be redeemed and cancelled, within the term of five years from the passing of this act, in the manner following. That is to say: The one-fifth part thereof yearly and every year until the whole shall be redeemed and cancelled as aforesaid.

[Section VI.] (Section VIII, P. L.) And be it enacted by the authority aforesaid, That the bills of credit emitted by this act be and are hereby declared to be legal tender to all intents and purposes whatsoever, and shall be taken and received in payment in all bargains, contracts, purchases, agreements, dealings, debts, dues and demands, according to the sum specified in said bill, to be taken and received at the rate or value of fifteen shillings for every two dollars, and so in proportion for a larger or lesser sum, and of equal value, in the payment of such bargain, contract, purchase, agreement, dealing, debt, due and demand whatsoever with two Spanish milled dollars, each weighing seventeen pennyweight and six grains; and sixty shillings of the emission aforesaid shall be taken and received at the rate of or equal in value to one gold half johannes of Portugal, weighing nine pennyweight, and in the like proportion for all other gold or silver coin, any contract, agreement or bargain between parties to the contrary in anywise notwithstanding.

[Section VII.] (Section IX, P. L.) And be it enacted by the authority aforesaid, That if any person or persons, bodies politic and corporate from and after the publication of this act shall refuse to receive any of the said bills of credit, when tendered in payment of any debt, bargain, contract or demand whatsoever, provided the whole of the said debt or demand be so tendered, such person or persons, bodies politic and corporate so refusing shall be forever barred from suing for or recovering the same before any judge or in any court of this state.

[Section VIII.] (Section X, P. L.) And be it enacted by the authority aforesaid, That if any person whatsoever shall, after the passing of this act, refuse to take and receive any of the bills of credit aforesaid in payment of any live stock, necessary of life, commodity, manufacture, article or goods whatsoever which he or she shall sell or expose to sale, or offer the same for a less price or smaller sum of money to be paid in gold or silver, than in the bills of credit emitted as aforesaid, or that shall give or receive a greater nominal sum of said bills of credit for a less in gold or silver, every such [person] being thereof legally convicted, in any court of general quarter sessions of the peace in this state or before one justice of the peace in cases where the forfeiture shall not exceed five pounds) shall, for every offense, forfeit and pay the value of the article or articles so sold or exposed to sale, one moiety thereof to the person or persons giving information of the same and prosecuting the offender to conviction, and the other moiety for the use of the poor of the city, district or township where the offense shall be committed.

[Section IX.] (Section XI, P. L.) And be it further enacted by the authority aforesaid, That the party giving information as aforesaid, shall be admitted a competent witness on the trial of offenders against this act, any law, custom or usage to the contrary in anywise notwithstanding.

[Section X.] (Section XII, P. L.) And be it further enacted by the authority aforesaid, That from and after the publication of this act, if any person or persons shall, within this state or elsewhere, prepare, engrave, stamp, forge or print the counterfeit resemblance of any paper bills of credit which shall be issued, emitted and made in virtue of this act, or shall counterfeit or sign the name or names of the signers of the said bills of credit to such counterfeit bills of credit, with an intention that such counterfeit bills of credit shall be passed in payments or received as genuine and good bills, whether the same be so passed or received or not; or if any person or persons shall, in this state, pass, pay or tender in payment any such counterfeit money, or deliver the same to any other person or persons with an intention that they may be paid, passed or received as and for good and genuine, knowing the same to be forged or counterfeited, every such person being thereof legally convicted or attainted in any court of oyer and terminer within this state, by verdict of a jury or confession of the party offending, or being indicted thereof shall stand mute or not directly answer to the indictment or shall peremptorily challenge more than the number of twenty persons legally returned to be of the jury for the trial of such offender, shall be adjudged a felon and shall suffer death without benefit of clergy, and if any person or persons shall counterfeit any of the said bills of credit by altering the denomination thereof with design to increase the value of such bills, or shall utter such bills knowing them to be so counterfeited or altered as aforesaid, and shall be thereof legally convicted in any court of record in this state, such person or persons shall be sentenced to the pillory, have both his or her ears cut off and nailed to the pillory and be publicly whipped on his or her bare back with thirty-nine lashes well laid on; and, moreover, every such offender shall forfeit the sum of two thousand pounds, lawful money of Pennsylvania, to be levied on his or her lands and tenements, goods and chattels, the one moiety to the use of the state and the other moiety to the discoverer; and the offender shall pay to the party grieved double the value of the damages thereby sustained, together with costs and charges of prosecution; and in case the offender hath not sufficient to satisfy the discoverer for his or her damages and charges, and pay the forfeiture aforesaid, in such case the offender shall, by order of the court where he or she shall be convicted, be sold as a servant for any term not exceeding seven years for satisfaction.

[Section XI.] (Section XIV, P. L.) And be it further enacted by the authority aforesaid, That from and after the first day of June next, no money shall be received in taxes or other public dues in this state other than gold and silver or bills of credit by law equivalent thereto. And that the treasurer of this state be and he hereby is authorized and empowered to set apart the sum of two hundred thousand pounds of the money to be emitted in pursuance of the directions of this act for the purpose of exchanging old continental bills of credit, the commonwealth money emitted by an act passed the twentieth day of March, one thousand seven hundred and seventy-seven, and the money heretofore emitted by the resolves of the assemblies of Pennsylvania according to the rate of exchange to be declared by the president and supreme executive council agreeable to the powers vested in them by an act passed the twenty-third day of December, one thousand seven hundred and eighty. And in order to accommodate the people possessing any of the said old continental, commonwealth or resolve money in the several counties of this state, the state treasurer is hereby authorized to employ the several county treasurers in exchanging the same according to the said rates declared by the supreme executive council and under such restrictions as they may judge proper and necessary.

<small>Passed April 7, 1781. Recorded L. B. No. 1, p. 428, etc. See the Acts of Assembly passed June 25, 1781, Chapter 948; April 13, 1782, Chapter 971; April 13, 1782, Chapter 978; January 31, 1783, Chapter 1003; September 16, 1785, Chapter 1180; March 28, 1787, Chapter 1283; December 4, 1789, Chapter 1470.</small>

CHAPTER CMXL.

AN ACT FOR ESTABLISHING A LAND OFFICE, AND FOR OTHER PURPOSES THEREIN MENTIONED.

(Section I, P. L.) Whereas many of the lands in this state heretofore taken up and located under grants, warrants and other office rights before the tenth day of December, in the year of our Lord one thousand seven hundred and seventy-six, are yet unpatented and the purchase money and arrearages of purchase money thereon due, are vested in the commonwealth subject to the disposal of the legislature, and the owners and holders of such rights since the shutting up of the land office, have not had it in their power to pay in the purchase money or arrearages of purchase money and obtain patents to complete their titles to the same:

For remedy whereof:

[Section I.] (Section II, P. L.) Be it enacted and it is hereby enacted by the Representatives of the Freemen of the Commonwealth of Pennsylvania in General Assembly met, and by the authority of the same, That an office be and it is hereby erected, constituted and appointed, which shall consist of three persons or officers called or known by the names of the secretary of the land office, receiver-general and surveyor-general, which office shall be held and kept in the city of Philadelphia, or such other place as the general assembly shall, from time to time, order and direct; and that into the said office shall be removed and safely kept, all the records and papers of the former land office or board of property in the hands, custody or possession of the late secretary, surveyor-general, receiver-general or of any other person or persons intrusted with the care or management thereof, by or under the late proprietaries of the province of Pennsylvania, or of their governors or lieutenant or deputy governors and all future grants and confirmations of land shall issue from the said office in manner and form hereinafter mentioned.

[Section II.] (Section III, P. L.) And be it further enacted by the authority aforesaid, That the said secretary of the land office, the receiver-general and surveyor-general shall be appointed by the general assembly and commissioned by the president or vice-president in council and shall hold their said offices for the term of five years unless sooner removed by the representatives of the freemen of this commonwealth in general assembly met. And the said secretary of the land office, receiver-general and surveyor-general shall be entitled to receive such fees from time to time as heretofore have been allowed by law until the same shall be altered by the legislature and shall have power to appoint deputies or clerks, to assist in executing the business of their respective offices, for whose conduct they shall be responsible, and copies of records, entries and papers of the said office, duly attested by them or their lawful deputies under their hand and seal of office, shall be as good evidence as the original by law might or could be. And the surveyor-general shall have power to appoint a deputy or deputies in any county of this state, who shall have power to make and return into the land office surveys of land only in the county for which [such] deputy or deputies shall be appointed, for the conduct of which deputy or deputies the said surveyor-general shall be responsible.

[Section III.] (Section IV, P. L.) And be it further enacted by the authority aforesaid, That the secretary of the land office, surveyor-general and receiver-general shall severally, before they are empowered to act, enter into an obligation before the president of the state with one or more sufficient sureties in the sum of ten thousand pounds to the commonwealth of Pennsylvania, conditioned for the faithful discharge of their respective offices.

[Section IV.] (Section V, P. L.) And be it further enacted by the authority aforesaid, That all and every the person and persons who are, or shall be, entitled either in law or equity to any lands in this state within the limits of the Indian purchase, by virtue of any grant, warrant or location before the tenth day of December, in the year of our Lord one thousand seven hundred and seventy-six, upon which patents have not issued, shall and may, upon payment to the receiver-general of the land-office hereby established, of the purchase money and interest thereon, or the arrearages of such purchase money and interest agreed on for the said lands, together with the office fees, or if no purchase money or interest is or remains due therefor, then upon payment of the office fees be entitled to receive a patent or patents for the same as is hereafter directed, any former law, custom or usage to the contrary hereof in anywise notwithstanding. And in all cases where surveys have not yet been made or returned to the former land office on any grant, warrant or location issued before the said tenth day of December, in the year aforesaid, the owner or owners thereof, upon applying to the land office at any time within the space of one year from the passing of this act and paying down the one-third of the purchase money and interest then due on the same shall be entitled to receive an order directed to the surveyor-general to have the same surveyed and returned, and after such survey and return, on payment of the residue of the purchase money and interest in manner aforesaid, he or they shall be entitled to receive a patent and confirmation of the same in like manner.

[Section V.] (Section VI, P. L.) And be it further enacted by the authority aforesaid, That all purchase money due for lands in this state taken up or entries thereof made, by any grant, license, warrant, application or office right whatever before the said tenth day of December, in the year aforesaid, shall be paid into the receiver-general of the land office hereby established. That is to say: The one-fourth part thereof in one year after the passing of this act, one other fourth part thereof in two years after passing this act and one other fourth part thereof in three years after passing this act and the residue thereof in four years after the passing of this act. And in case of neglect or refusal of paying the aforesaid quotas of the purchase money and interest at the time herein limited for payment thereof by the space of six months, it shall and may be lawful for the commissioners of the county where the lands lie to issue their warrant to the sheriff of the said county, who is hereby enjoined and required to execute the same, commanding him, after due notice, to expose the same lands, or so much thereof as may be necessary, to discharge the sum due, with interest and costs, to sale, and transmit the [same] to the receiver-general of the land office of this state, and the said sheriff shall give the purchaser a deed for the land so by him sold upon receipt of the purchase money and interest.

(Section VII, P. L.) Provided always, That nothing herein contained shall empower any commissioner to issue his warrant, or any sheriff to sell any lands for non-payment of purchase money and interest where actual settlements have been made by the owner or owners of the lands and where the owner or owners of such lands have been drove [sic] off by the power of the enemy.

[Section VI.] (Section VIII, P. L.) And be it further enacted by the authority aforesaid, That the several officers of the land office shall meet annually and transmit to the respective county commissioners lists of the delinquents for purchase money and interest or arrearages of purchase money and interest in their respective counties, under the hand and seal of the secretary of the land office.

[Section VII.] (Section IX, P. L.) And be it further enacted by the authority aforesaid, That all lands within this state heretofore surveyed under any grant, warrant, location or other office right, shall be returned into the surveyor-general's office (if not already returned) in the space of nine months from the passing of this act; and upon application made by the owners of such lands to the surveyor and their paying or tendering him his legal fees, in such case, if the surveyor refuse or neglect to make or cause to be made returns of the said land, he shall forfeit and pay the sum of fifty pounds, the one half to the informer and one half to the use of the state, to be recovered in any court of quarter sessions in this state by indictment or information.

[Section VIII.] (Section X, P. L.) And be it further enacted by the authority aforesaid, That all patents to be granted in pursuance of this act shall be by deed poll and signed by the president or in his absence by the vice-president in council, and countersigned by the secretary of council and under the state seal, in form following, viz.:

"The supreme executive council of the commonwealth of Pennsylvania. To all to whom these presents shall come, greeting: Know ye, that in consideration of the sum of ——————, lawful money paid by A. B. into the receiver-general's office of this commonwealth, there is granted by the said commonwealth unto the said A. B. a certain tract or parcel of land, containing ———— acres, lying in the county of ———— and township of ———— (describing the particular bounds of the land and the date of the survey on which the grant issues), with its appurtenances. To have and to hold the said tract or parcel of land, with the appurtenances, unto the said A. B. and his heirs, to the use of the said A. B., his heirs and assigns forever (here insert the tenure and reservation). In witness whereof, his excellency ————, esquire, president (or, if absent, the honorable ————, esquire, vice-president) of the supreme executive council, hath hereunto set his hand and caused the state seal to be hereunto affixed the ———— of ————, in the year of our Lord 178—, and of the commonwealth the ————. Attest, ————, secretary."

Which patent shall be recorded in the rolls office of this state.

[Section IX.] (Section XI, P. L.) And be it further enacted by the authority aforesaid, That all and every of the land or lands granted in pursuance of this act shall be free and clear of all reservations and restriction as to mines, royalties, quitrents or otherwise, so that the owners thereof, respectively, shall be entitled to hold the same in absolute and unconditional property to all intents and purposes whatsoever, and to all and all manner of profits, privileges and advantages belonging to or accruing from the same, and that clear and exonerated from any charge or encumbrance whatsoever, excepting the debts of the said owner and excepting and reserving only the fifth part of all gold and silver ore for the use of this commonwealth, to be delivered at the pit's mouth, clear of all charges.

[Section X.] (Section XII, P. L.) And be it further enacted by the authority aforesaid, That nothing in this act shall extend, or be construed to extend, to give validity to any grant, warrant or location issued after the fourth day of July, in the year of our Lord one thousand seven hundred and seventy-six, for any lands or lots within ten miles of the city of Philadelphia or within three miles of any county town in this state, or to any warrant, grant or location for a greater quantity of land than five hundred acres in one tract or to any lands or lots not granted in the usual forms of the land office or to lands not within the Indian purchase, anything herein contained to the contrary in anywise notwithstanding.

<blockquote>Passed April 9, 1781. Recorded L. B. No. 1, p. 431, etc. See the Acts of Assembly passed June 25, 1781, Chapter 947; April 5, 1782, Chapter 964; April 1, 1784, Chapter 1094; April 8, 1785, Chapter 1162; September 16, 1785, Chapter 1180.</blockquote>

CHAPTER CMXLI.

AN ACT TO AMEND THE ACT ENTITLED "AN ACT FOR THE MORE EFFECTUAL SUPPLY AND HONORABLE REWARD OF THE PENNSYLVANIA TROOPS IN THE SERVICE OF THE UNITED STATES OF AMERICA,"[1] AND THE ACT ENTITLED "AN ACT TO SETTLE AND ADJUST THE ACCOUNTS OF THE TROOPS OF THIS STATE IN THE SERVICE OF THE UNITED STATES AND FOR OTHER PURPOSES THEREIN MENTIONED."[2]

(Section I, P. L.) Whereas, doubts have arisen whether the chaplains and surgeons of the Pennsylvania line are included in the act, entitled "An act to settle and adjust the accounts of the troops of this state in service of the United States, and for other purposes therein mentioned," passed the eighteenth day of December, in the year of our Lord one thousand seven hundred and eighty:[2]

And whereas, the chaplains and surgeons of the said Pennsylvania line engaged to serve during the present war have not, by the act, entitled "An act for the more effectual supply and honorable reward of the Pennsylvania troops in the service of the United States of America,"[1] the encouragement and reward their services and sufferings justly entitle them to:

[Section I.] (Section II, P. L.). Be it therefore enacted and it is hereby enacted by the Representatives of the Freemen of the Commonwealth of Pennsylvania in General Assembly met, and by the authority of the same, That the chaplains and regimental surgeons of the Pennsylvania line engaged to serve during the present war shall be, and they are hereby entitled to all the

---

[1] Passed March 1, 1780, Chapter 880.
[2] December 18, 1780, Chapter 920.

emoluments and benefits, to all intents and purposes, which the military commissioned officers in the said line are entitled to, under the act, entitled "An act to settle and adjust the accounts of the troops of this state in the service of the United States, and for other purposes therein mentioned,"[1] passed on the eighteenth day of December, in the year of our Lord one thousand seven hundred and eighty, and also shall be entitled to the half pay of a captain during life, they, the said chaplains and surgeons continuing in the service during the present war with Great Britain.

[Section II.] (Section III, P. L.) Provided always, and be it enacted by the authority aforesaid, That all commissioned officers, chaplains and surgeons of the Pennsylvania line aforesaid who are or hereafter shall be entitled to half pay shall be liable to be called into actual service by the supreme executive council of this state at any time hereafter; and if any of the commissioned officers, chaplains or surgeons of the said line shall neglect or refuse to go and continue in said service when called to it as aforesaid, such half pay shall from thence cease and determine, anything in any law of this state to the contrary in anywise notwithstanding.

[Section III.] (Section IV, P. L.) And be it enacted by the authority aforesaid, That the supreme executive council of this state may and they are hereby authorized and empowered to appoint any additional number of auditors, above the number of [three] mentioned in the act, entitled "An act to settle and adjust the account of the troops of this state in the service of the United States, and for other purposes therein mentioned," as they shall judge necessary for expediting the business to be performed by the said auditors, which additional auditors shall have all the powers and authority and the like reward for their services which are given and granted by the said act to the auditors therein mentioned.

(Section V, P. L.) And whereas, it hath been represented to this house that it is both necessary and expedient to pay off and discharge a certain proportion of the sums specified in the

---

[1] December 18, 1780, Chapter 920.

certificates lately granted to the officers and soldiers of the Pennsylvania line for their depreciation of pay:

[Section IV.] (Section VI, P. L.) Be it therefore further enacted by the authority aforesaid, That the supreme executive council be and they hereby are authorized to draw upon the treasurer of the state for such sum or sums of money as they may deem necessary, and place the same into the hands of certain commissioners to be especially appointed by them for that purpose (which they are hereby empowered to do), who shall attend at the rendezvous of the respective regiments on or before the first day of May next ensuing, and then and there pay to such officers and privates who are in actual service [and shall make]application for the same, one-third part of the sums found due on settlement and specified in the certificates aforesaid, respectively.

[Section V.] (Section VII, P. L.) And be it further enacted by the authority aforesaid, That the said commissioners are hereby authorized and directed to take up and transmit to the treasurer of this state the certificates aforesaid and to issue new certificates to the said officers and private men for their respective balances, which said new certificates shall bear lawful interest and shall be transferable in the same manner as promissory notes are by law, any former law to the contrary hereof in anywise notwithstanding.

[Section VI.] (Section VIII, P. L.) And be it further enacted by the authority aforesaid, That the certificates of such officers and soldiers as shall not apply to the commissioners aforesaid for payment shall bear lawful interest and be transferable in like manner as the new certificates hereinbefore directed to be granted, and the possessor or possessors of the same may, when he or they shall think proper, call on the treasurer of the state for a third part of the sums mentioned in the said certificates, respectively, who is hereby authorized and directed to pay the same, and the said treasurer is hereby further authorized and directed to retain the said certificates in his hands and grant new certificates for such balance as may be due in manner and form as is above directed.

[Section VII.] (Section IX, P. L.) And be it further enacted by the authority aforesaid, That the supreme executive council be and they hereby are authorized and empowered to order sale to be made of all forfeited estates appropriated by the act, entitled "An act to settle and adjust the accounts of the troops of this state in the service of the United States, and for other purposes therein mentioned,"[1] on or before the tenth day of May next ensuing and apply the money arising therefrom to the uses and purposes in the said act mentioned, anything in the fourth section thereof to the contrary notwithstanding.

Passed April 10, 1781. Recorded L. B. No. 1, p. 433, etc. See the Act of Assembly passed October 1, 1781, Chapter 955.

CHAPTER CMXLII.

AN ACT FOR THE BETTER SUPPORT OF THE PUBLIC CREDIT BY AN IMMEDIATE SALE OF THE LANDS THEREIN MENTIONED, AND FULLY SECURING THE PURCHASERS THEREOF IN THEIR TITLES, AND ALSO FOR PRESERVING THE COMMON LANDS APPURTENANT TO THE CITY OF PHILADELPHIA, AND OTHER TOWNS IN THIS STATE FROM UNWARRANTABLE ENCROACHMENT.

(Section I, P. L.) Whereas the speedy and honorable redemption of the bills of credit issued for the support of the just and necessary war in which we are now engaged, will have a happy tendency to re-establish public faith and induce well-affected individuals freely to advance their property for the purposes of government if they are secured of a true and real equivalent:

And whereas, the bills of credit of this state dated on the twenty-ninth day of April last, were funded upon the solid property of the state, consisting of the Province island and the unappropriated lots contained within the bounds of the city of Philadelphia, which said lands were, by a former act of assembly, subjected to sale, to be made by the president or vice-president in council, at any time within four years thereafter. And a speedy sale of the said island having become necessary,

[1] Ante.

the same hath been advertised at public auction to redeem the said bills of credit so far as the price thereof shall extend:

And whereas, it is manifest that a part of the said bills of credit will remain unredeemed after the said island shall be sold as aforesaid, for the redemption of which the said city lots have been solemly pledged, and it is necessary to dispose of the same in like manner so that the purchasers may be assured of a clear and indefeasible title, and thereby be induced to offer the full value thereof:

[Section I.] (Section II, P. L.) Be it therefore enacted and it is hereby enacted by the Representatives of the Freemen of the Commonwealth of Pennsylvania in General Assembly met, and by the authority of the same, That it shall and may be lawful for the president or vice-president in council, and he is hereby authorized and required, with all convenient speed, to apportion and set off such and so many of the said city lots as shall, in his judgment and discretion, be sufficient to satisfy and redeem the residue of the said bills of credit, together with the interest which shall be due thereon, and also the charges of selling the said lands and cancelling the said bills of credit remaining unredeemed after the sale of the said island, and so apportioned and set off, sell the same at public auction to the highest bidder, pursuant to the said act, entitled "An act for striking the sum of one hundred thousand pounds in bills of credit, for the present support of the army, and for establishing a fund for the certain redemption of the same, and for other purposes therein mentioned,"[1] in all cases receiving in payment for the said island and the said lots the said bills of credit issued pursuant to the said act, or Spanish milled dollars, or an equal sum in gold or silver, and no other money whatsoever.

[Section II.] (Section III, P. L.) Be it also enacted by the authority aforesaid, That each and every purchaser of the said lands hereinbefore mentioned and every part thereof, having received his deed or grant from the president or vice-president in council shall from thenceforth become seized of a sure and indefeasible estate in fee simple against all claims or demands

---

[1] Passed March 25, 1780, Chapter 907.

whatsoever and in case of any suits brought for such land or any part thereof, the grantee under this act, his or her heirs or assigns, may plead the general issue and give this act in evidence, which shall be final and conclusive to the court and jury against any claimant or demandant, in any suit to be brought at any time hereafter for the lands which shall be granted as aforesaid, or any part thereof.

(Section IV, P. L.) And whereas, it may happen that claims may be hereafter made upon some of the said lots by the descendants of the original purchasers under William Penn, esquire, or purchases under his successors, to grantees who have neglected to set out and appropriate the same in severalty, so as to be distinguished from the common lands, appurtenant to the said city:

For remedy whereof:

[Section III.] (Section V, P. L.) Be it enacted by the authority aforesaid, That in every such case the claimant, having ascertained the justice and right of his claim, agreeable to the laws of this state, as hereinafter set forth, shall be entitled to a full equivalent for the same, having due regard to situation in any other of the unappropriated lots appurtenant to the city and now vested in this commonwealth.

(Section VI, P. L.) And to the end that speedy and ample justice may be done to every such claimant, prosecuting his claim within the time hereafter limited:

[Section IV.] Be it enacted by the authority aforesaid, That in case any suit be brought, every such claimant or other claimant of any part of the lands whereof this commonwealth is possessed (lands in the counties of Bedford, Northumberland, Westmoreland and Washington only excepted), before he or she takes possession of any part of the said lots or lands so claimed, shall proceed in manner following and no other, viz.: He shall present a petition to the president or vice-president in council, setting forth, in a summary manner, the nature of his claim, and whence derived, and if, in such petition, he or she shall request a trial by a jury, the said president or vice-president in council shall, ex-officio, grant the same, by directing the attorney-general to receive a declaration in ejectment, against himself, as representing the commonwealth in such cases, wherein the premises claimed shall be particularly described and appear thereto in the supreme court only, and proceed to trial thereupon, according to the laws and practice of this state in possessory actions. And if it shall happen that judgment be obtained against the said attorney-general, on verdict or demurrer and the court award costs thereupon, the said president or vice-president in council is hereby authorized and required to cause the same to be paid, the bill being first duly taxed, together with necessary and reasonable expenses, attending the defense, out of any moneys which shall be in the hands of the treasurer of the state not otherwise specially appropriated.

[Section V.] (Section VII, P. L.) And be it further enacted by the authority aforesaid, That upon such claim being ascertained as aforesaid, or if the claimant shall not, in his or her said petition, request a trial by jury (which omission shall be deemed a full and final consent to abide the determination of the president or vice-president in council on the merits of his or her claim); and if such determination shall be in his or her favor, he or she shall then be entitled, at his own expense, to a writ, to be framed by the prothonotary of the supreme court in which the premises recovered, shall be also particularly described, directed to the sheriff of the county, commanding him to summon a jury of twelve good and lawful men, who, being duly sworn or affirmed, shall proceed to assign to [the] said claimant so much of the said unappropriated lots within this city as shall, in their judgment (having due regard to quantity and quality) be equal in value to the lots so claimed by him or her; and such writ, being duly returned to the said supreme court, such return approved by the court, and judgment thereon entered shall be conclusive in favor of the party, and a writ of possession issue thereupon.

(Section VIII, P. L.) And whereas a century hath now elapsed since the granting of the original charter of Pennsylvania, and upwards of eighty years since its actual settlement, and it being reasonable that there should be a limitation of suits and dormant claims upon the estate of the public, as well as that of individuals:

[Section VI.] (Section IX, P. L.) Be it therefore enacted by the authority aforesaid, That no person shall have or maintain any action, real, personal or mixed, against the commonwealth, represented as aforesaid or otherwise, for any lands, tenements or hereditaments, within Pennsylvania, by virtue of any grant or conveyance of the original proprietor to his or her ancestor or predecessor; or to the ancestor or predecessor of his or her grantor, unless he or she shall commence and prosecute the same within seven years after the publication of this act; or by virtue of any grant or conveyance of the subsequent proprietaries of this state (lands in the counties of Bedford, Northumberland, Westmoreland and Washington only excepted), but within ten years from the publication hereof and in default thereof all and every such claimants or claimant shall be utterly barred and excluded from any entry, right of entry, title, property and demand in or upon such lands or any suit whatsoever in law or equity for the same.

(Section X, P. L.) Provided always, That if any person or persons who is or are entitled to have, or maintain any such action, be at the time of the publication of this act, within the age of twenty-one years, feme covert, non compos mentis, imprisoned or beyond sea, other than those who have voluntarily gone to the dominions of the King of Great Britain from this or any of the United States since the fourth day of July, one thousand seven hundred and seventy-six, that then such person or persons shall be at liberty (except as before excepted), to bring the said actions, so as he or they commence the same within such times as are hereinbefore limited after his, her or their coming to or being of full age, discoverture, sound memory, at large, or returning to this state, as in the case of other persons.

(Section XI, P. L.) And whereas, divers persons pretending title or leases or permissions from the late proprietaries, or without any pretence whatsoever, have taken into possession divers lots appurtenant to the city, and to the other towns within this state, which lots were held by the said proprietaries as such, and not in their private several right and capacities:

And whereas, such possession is not only injurious to the

other citizens who are entitled to the use of said lands, as common for their cattle, but will embarrass the future sale and appropriation of the said lots for the general benefit of the state:

For remedy whereof:

[Section VII.] (Section XII, P. L.) Be it enacted by the authority aforesaid, That the care and custody of the city lots in Philadelphia shall be and is hereby vested in the wardens of the city; and the care and custody of the lots appurtenant to the town of Reading shall be and hereby is vested in Samuel Mifflin, Henry Christ and Henry Haller; and the care and custody of the lots appurtenant to the town of York, in the county of York, shall be and hereby is vested in Archibald McClean, Michael Swoope and William Scott; and the care and custody of the lots appurtenant to the town of Carlisle, in the county of Cumberland, shall be and hereby is vested in John Montgomery, Samuel Laird and James Pollock; and the care and custody of the lots appurtenant to the several towns of Easton, in the county of Northampton, Bedford, in the county of Bedford, Sunbury, in the county of Northumberland, and Hannah's town, in the county of Westmoreland, shall be and is hereby vested in the justices of the peace residing in and within two miles of the said towns, respectively, to the end that the said lots may be preserved from encroachment and private use, and for the benefit of common to the inhabitants of the said city and towns, until the same be appropriated under the authority of the legislature of the state, for building, improvement or other use. And that all such encroachments and unwarrantable enclosures within the said city and towns may be discovered and removed without delay:

[Section VIII.] (Section XIII, P. L.) Be it enacted by the authority aforesaid, That the said wardens of the city of Philadelphia, the said Samuel Mifflin, Henry Haller, Henry Christ, Archibald McClean, Michael Swoope, William Scott, John Montgomery, Samuel Laird and James Pollock, of Reading, York and Carlisle; and the said justices of [Northampton], Bedford, Northumberland and Westmoreland, respectively, or any two of them, are hereby authorized and required, on their own knowledge, or on the complaint of any two reputable freeholders made to them in writing, and in the said writing declaiming any right or pretence in themselves to said lots, or any part thereof, to summon any person possessing any of the said lots before any justice of the supreme court in the vacation, or on the circuit, to show by what warrant or authority he or she holds or possesses the said lots, or any part of them; and if the said party shall not plead title to the premises under a patent, or judgment of court or a possessory right, by virtue of an unexpired lease from the said proprietaries, or their agent duly authorized, at the same time producing such patent, judgment or lease, or an authentic record thereof, it shall and may be lawful for the said justice, at the expiration of fifteen days from the service of said summons, and he is hereby required to award the possession of said lot to the commonwealth, and issue his warrant to the sheriff of the county to abate and remove the enclosures of said lot or buildings erected thereon, as in the case of common nuisance, and open the premises as a free common of pasture to the inhabitants; upon which proceedings no writ of certiorari or other writ of removal to any superior court shall be allowed or received, so as to stay the delivery of the possession agreeable to the award of the said justice and the tenor and direction of said writ. But if the [said] judgment shall be reversed for any cause whatsoever the party shall be restored to his possession.

(Section XIV, P. L.) Provided always, That nothing herein contained shall defeat or prejudice, or be construed to the defeasance or prejudice of, any title which the party so dispossessed may have and which he may prosecute as hereinbefore directed.

[Section IX.] (Section XV, P. L.) Be it also enacted by the authority aforesaid, That if any suit or suits shall be brought against any person or persons for anything done pursuant to this act, the action shall be laid in the county where the cause of action shall arise, and not elsewhere, nor after twelve months. And the defendant or defendants in such action to be brought may plead the general issue and give this act and the special matter in evidence; and if the jury shall find for the defendant or defendants in such action or actions, or the plaintiff become non-suit, or discontinue his, her or their action or actions, after the defendant or defendants shall have appeared, or if, upon demurrer, judgment shall be given against the plaintiff or plaintiffs, the defendant or defendants shall recover treble costs, and have the like remedy for the same as any defendant or defendants had or have in other cases to recover costs by law.

[Section X.] (Section XVI, P. L.) Be it also enacted by the authority aforesaid, That if the said wardens of the city of Philadelphia, or Samuel Mifflin, Henry Christ, Henry Haller, Archibald McClean, Michael Swoope, William Scott, John Montgomery, Samuel Laird and James Pollock, of the towns of Reading, York and Carlisle, or the said justices dwelling in or near the towns of Easton, Bedford, Sunbury and Hannah's town, refuse or neglect to perform the duties herein and hereby directed, and the same shall be presented in the court of oyer and terminer or the court of general quarter sessions of the peace of the proper county, and bills of indictment in either of the said courts be found against them or any of them for such refusal or neglect, whereon they, or any of them, shall be prosecuted to conviction, they shall pay a fine of twenty pounds each for every such offense, to the use of the poor of the said city and towns, respectively, to be paid to the overseers thereof.

Passed April 10, 1781. Recorded L. B. No. 1, p. 434, etc. See the Acts of Assembly passed April 8, 1786, Chapter 1225; April 8, 1791, Chapter 1555.

Laws enacted in the Third Sitting of the Fifth General Assembly of the Commonwealth of Pennsylvania, which commenced at Philadelphia, on Thursday, the twenty-fourth day of May, A. D. 1781.

CHAPTER CMXLIII.

A SUPPLEMENT TO AN ACT ENTITLED "AN ACT TO PERMIT THE EXPORTATION OF FLOUR OF WHEAT FROM THIS STATE, BY SEA, UNDER CERTAIN LIMITATIONS AND RESTRICTIONS."[1]

(Section I, P. L.) Whereas, the limitations and restrictions contained in the sixth and seventh sections of the act, entitled "An act for laying an embargo on the exportation of provisions from this state, by sea, for a limited time,"[2] passed the twenty-eighth day of February, one thousand seven hundred and eighty, and also contained in the fourth section of an act, entitled "An act to revive and continue for a further limited time the act for laying an embargo on the exportation of provisions from this state, by sea, for a limited time,"[3] and also certain parts of an act, entitled "An act to permit the exportation of flour wheat from this state by sea under certain limitations and restrictions,"[4] passed the twenty-seventh day of February, one thousand seven hundred and eighty-one, whereby all persons shipping flour of wheat were to offer or tender a quantity equal to one-third part of the quantity to be shipped unto the proper officer appointed by the president and council for that purpose, have been found, by experience, prejudicial to the commerce of this state, and have not produced the good effects expected therefrom by the legislature:

---

[1] Passed December 22, 1780, Chapter 922.
[2] Passed February 28, 1780, Chapter 876.
[3] Passed September 22, 1780, Chapter 917.
[4] Passed February 27, 1781, Chapter 928.

[Section I.] Be it therefore enacted and it is hereby enacted by the Representatives of the Freemen of the Commonwealth of Pennsylvania in General Assembly met, and by the authority of the same, That the sixth and seventh sections of the act, entitled "An act to permit the exportation of flour of wheat from this state, by sea, under certain limitations and restrictions," and all things therein contained, compelling or obliging the shipper of wheat flour to tender or deliver to the said officer a quantity equal to one-third part of the quantity to be shipped, be and the same are hereby repealed and made null and void, anything in the fourth section of the act aforesaid, passed the said twenty-seventh day of February, one thousand seven hundred and eighty-one, to the contrary thereof in anywise notwithstanding.

Passed June 7, 1781. Recorded L. B. No. 1, p. 437, etc.

CHAPTER CMXLIV.

AN ACT TO RAISE EFFECTIVE SUPPLIES FOR THE YEAR ONE THOUSAND SEVEN HUNDRED AND EIGHTY-ONE.

(Section I, P. L.) Whereas the honorable Congress of the United States of America did, by their resolution of the fifteenth of January, one thousand seven hundred and eighty-one, demand of the several states in union such effective supplies as might enable them to carry on the war with vigor and effect:

And whereas it is the desire of the representatives of the freemen of this state to comply with the said resolution of Congress:

[Section I.] (Section II, P. L.) Be it therefore enacted and it is hereby enacted by the Representatives of the Freemen of the Commonwealth of Pennsylvania in General Assembly met and by the authority of the same, That the sum of two hundred thousand pounds shall be raised, levied, collected and paid within the current year (over and above all arrearages of taxes assessed in the old continental currency), and shall be levied, assessed and raised in the city of Philadelphia and the several counties of this state according to the method and proportion following. That is to say:

In the city [and county] of Philadelphia, the sum of sixty-six thousand two hundred and sixty pounds five shillings and eight pence.

In the county of Bucks, the sum of thirteen thousand one hundred and five pounds thirteen shillings and two pence.

In the county of Chester, the sum of twenty-one thousand and thirty-seven pounds seventeen shillings and three pence.

In the county of Lancaster, the sum of twenty-eight thousand four hundred and seventy-two pounds eight shillings and five pence.

In the county of York, the sum of fifteen thousand eight hundred and sixty-two pounds eighteen shillings.

In the county of Cumberland, the sum of fourteen thousand nine hundred and nine pounds sixteen shillings.

In the county of Berks, the sum of fourteen thousand three hundred and twenty pounds three shillings and seven pence.

In the county of Northampton, the sum of eight thousand two hundred and forty-three pounds thirteen shillings and eight pence.

In the county of Bedford the sum of four thousand five hundred and nineteen pounds seven shillings and five pence.

In the county of Northumberland, the sum of five thousand five hundred and eighty-two pounds fifteen shillings and two pence.

In the counties of Westmoreland and Washington, the sum of seven thousand six hundred and eighty-five pounds one shilling and eight pence.

[Section II.] (Section III, P. L.) And be it further enacted by the authority aforesaid, That the commissioners of the city and county of Philadelphia, and of every county in this state, or any two of them, shall meet together on or before the first Tuesday in July next, at their usual places of meeting, in the city and in their several counties, and shall then and there issue their warrants, under their hands and seals, to the township, ward or district assessors of each township, ward or district within their respective counties, requiring them, the said assessors, to make fair returns in writing on a certain day to be by them appointed, of the names and surnames of all the taxable inhabitants and single freemen within their respective townships, wards or districts, together with a fair and true return of all their estates, real and personal, made taxable by this act; in what county situated, and to whom such estates do respectively belong. And to enable the commissioners to do the strictest justice in assigning the quota of the several townships, wards and districts within the city and each county of this state, the said assessors are hereby empowered and required to administer to each taxable within their respective townships, wards or districts an oath or affirmation in the following words, viz.:

'I, A. B., do swear (or solemnly, sincerely and truly declare and affirm) that the return which I have made is to the best of my knowledge a just and true return of all my taxable property, real and personal, and in what county situated. And that I have not, directly or indirectly, parted with or disposed of any property on any condition, expressed or implied, to have the same returned to me with intention to avoid paying the tax thereupon."

And if any person or persons shall neglect or refuse to give a return of their taxable property when required as aforesaid, or shall neglect or refuse to swear or affirm to the truth of the same, every such person or persons so neglecting or refusing shall, for every such offense, forfeit and pay a sum equal to the tax at which such person or persons shall be rated by this act, to be levied and collected by the collector of the proper township by virtue of a special warrant, which the commissioners, or any two of them, are hereby empowered and required to grant, and the same shall be paid into the treasury of this commonwealth. And in order that the said tax may be levied, the assessor shall use his best endeavors according to the duty of his office to inform himself of all property so concealed or refused to be returned, and shall make return thereof, that the same may be taxed according to the true intent and meaning of this act.

[Section III.] (Section IV, P. L.) And be it further enacted by the authority aforesaid, That if any person shall neglect or refuse to make returns on oath or affirmation as aforesaid of all and every tract or parcel of land he or she shall possess within this state, to the assessor of the place where such person shall dwell or reside, all such lands so omitted shall be liable and subject to be charged with all such taxes the next or any subsequent assessment which the same lands ought to have been charged with had they been duly assessed as by this act is directed. And if any such tract or parcel of land so returned shall be situated out of the city or county where such person and assessor shall dwell, then the commissioners of the city or such county, or some one of them, shall, as soon as conveniently may be, transmit a copy of such return to the commissioners of the county where the land shall lie.

[Section IV.] (Section V, P. L.) And be it further enacted by the authority aforesaid, That any two or more of the commissioners of the respective counties shall have power and they are hereby enjoined and required to appoint assessors in case of removal by death, disability, refusal or neglect to serve of the present assessors, or where the townships neglect to elect such assessors.

[Section V.] (Section VI, P. L.) And be it further enacted by the authority aforesaid, That when the commissioners of any county shall receive the return of the assessors, as before directed, they shall forthwith proceed to quota the several townships, wards and districts in the city of Philadelphia and the several counties of this state in proportion to the quantity and quality of the property returned as aforesaid.

[Section VI.] (Section VII, P. L.) And be it further enacted by the authority aforesaid, That the commissioners of the several counties within this state, shall, within six days after the quotaing the townships, wards and districts as aforesaid, furnish the assessor of each ward, township and district with a true and fair transcript of the quota or sum of money charged upon and demanded from such township, ward or district, to which such assessor doth belong.

[Section VII.] (Section VIII, P. L.) And be it further enacted by the authority aforesaid, That the assessors of each township, ward or district within this state, with the assistance of two freeholders of the proper township, ward or district who shall and are hereby required to be appointed by the commissioners of the county for that purpose shall, within three days after the said assessors shall be come possessed of the quota or sum of money so assessed, levy and assess the same equally and impartially on all and every person and on all the estates, real and personal, within their respective townships made taxable by this act.

[Section VIII.] (Section IX, P. L.) And be it further enacted by the authority aforesaid, That the following enumerated articles shall be and are hereby made taxable and no other, viz.: The time of servitude of all bound servants above the age of fourteen years; all negro and mulatto slaves above the age of twelve years; all horses and mares above three years old; all horned cattle above three years old; plate and pleasurable carriages; all lands held by deed, warrant, location or improvement; houses and lots of ground and ground rents; all grist mills, saw mills, fulling mills, slitting mills, hemp mills, oil mills, snuff mills and paper mills; all forges, furnaces, bloomaries, distilleries, sugar houses, breweries, tan yards and ferries, and all wares and merchandise and all professions, trades and occupations.

[Section IX.] (Section X, P. L.) And be it further enacted by the authority aforesaid, That all and every the enumerated articles aforesaid shall be valued at and for so much as they would bona fide sell for, or are worth, and such a rate or rates shall be assessed or levied thereon, as will amount to the sum of money quotaed upon the city of Philadelphia and the several counties of this state.

[Section X.] (Section XI, P. L.) And be it further enacted by the authority aforesaid, That each single freeman who, at the time of assessing any tax imposed by this act, is or shall be of the age of twenty-one years or upwards and has been out of his apprenticeship six months, shall pay a sum not exceeding six pounds nor under forty-five shillings; and that all trades, professions and occupations (ministers of the gospel of all denominations and schoolmasters only excepted) shall be rated at the discretion of the township, ward or district assessors and two freeholders of the proper township, ward or district, having due regard to the profits arising from them.

(Section XII, P. L.) And whereas divers owners of lands whereon improvements have been made and of tenements may not reside in the county or district where such lands or tenements are situated, whereby it may be difficult to collect the taxes assessed on such real estate.

For remedy whereof:

[Section XI.] Be it enacted by the authority aforesaid, That the tenant or tenants, or other person residing on or occupying such real estate, his, her and their goods and chattels, as well as the lands, goods and chattels of the owner or owners thereof, shall be liable to be distrained to satisfy the said taxes, or any of them. And in case the tenant or tenants or other person or persons residing on or occupying such real estate shall pay any tax laid thereon by virtue of this act, or shall be distrained to satisfy such tax, such tenant or tenants may retain the same out of the rent by him, her or them payable for such estate; or said tenant or tenants, or other occupier or occupiers of such estate shall recover the same, with costs of suit, of the owner of such estate by action of debt; if under five pounds in a summary way, in like manner as small debts are recoverable, but if the same is above five pounds in any court of common pleas.

(Section XIII, P. L.) Provided always, That nothing in the foregoing section shall in any manner alter any contract made between any landlord and tenant concerning the payment of taxes.

[Section XII.] And be it further enacted by the authority aforesaid, That each county commissioner and township, ward, district or assistant assessor shall, respectively, before they enter on any of the duties required of them by this act, before some one justice of the peace for the proper county, make oath or affirmation as is hereinafter directed, to wit: If a county commissioner:

"I, A. B., do swear or affirm that I will well and truly cause the rates and sums of money by this act imposed to be duly and equally assessed and laid according to the rules and directions mentioned in the act, entitled 'An act to raise effective supplies for the year one thousand seven hundred and eighty-one,' to the best of my skill and knowledge, so far as relates to the duty and office of a commissioner, and herein I will spare no person for favor or affection or grieve any for hatred or ill-will." If a township, ward, district or assistant assessor, the following oath or affirmation, to wit:

"I, A. B., do swear or affirm that I will faithfully and impartially assess the quota of the township, ward or district of —————————, imposed by virtue of the act, entitled 'An act to raise effective supplies for the year one thousand seven hundred and eighty-one,' on the several persons and taxable property therein contained, to the best of my skill and understanding; that in performing the duties required of me by that act I will spare no person for favor or affection or grieve any for hatred or ill-will."

[Section XIII,] (Section XV, P. L.) And be it further enacted by the authority aforesaid, That the commissioners of any two of them, shall appoint one fit person in or for any township, ward or district to be collectors of the taxes to be raised by virtue of this act.

[Section XIV.] (Section XVI, P. L.) And be it further enacted by the authority aforesaid, That the commissioners of the proper county shall prefix in the duplicate delivered to the collector, before the delivery thereof, a warrant, under their hands and seals, authorizing and requiring the collector, after the day of appeal shall be passed ten days, to levy the sums rated on all persons who shall not, upon demand after the said appeal, forthwith satisfy the same.

[Section XV.] (Section XVII, P. L.) And be it further enacted by the authority aforesaid, That if any assessor legally chosen or any person appointed by the said commissioners to be an assessor, or assistant assessor, or collector, shall not, within two days after notice in writing of such election or appointment, make known his intention to the commissioners of the county to serve or decline the office to which such person hath been or shall be so chosen or appointed, the said commissioners shall consider such person as having refused to serve in such office, and may proceed to fine such person and appoint another in his stead, as if such person had actually refused to serve in such office.

[Section XVI.] (Section XVIII, P. L.) And be it further enacted by the authority aforesaid, That the fine on any person refusing to serve as an assessor or assistant assessor shall be any sum not exceeding fifty pounds; and the fine on any person refusing to serve as collector of any district shall be any sum not exceeding fifty pounds. And in case any assessor, or assistant assessor or collector, after taking upon him his office, shall neglect to perform his duty therein, any such delinquent shall be fined in any sum not exceeding one hundred pounds, and if any person chosen or appointed to be an assessor or appointed to be an assistant assessor or a collector, or if any other person shall detain any warrant, duplicate or other writing, necessary to the assessing or levying the said tax beyond the time when such person shall have declined or be deemed to have declined any such office, or after demand thereof made by the commissioners, or by any person authorized by them to demand the same, every such delinquent shall be fined in any sum not exceeding one hundred pounds; the said fines to be ascertained and set by the commissioners of the county, and levied as other fines are or ought to be levied by virtue of the said act.

[Section XVII.] (Section XIX, P. L.) And be it further enacted by the authority aforesaid, That in case any collector, after distress and sale by him made, shall have any overplus money remaining in his hands, such collector, first tendering the same before one witness to the owner of the goods distrained and sold, shall, upon the refusal of such owner to receive such money, pay the same to the treasurer of the county, who shall deduct therefrom one per centum and give notice thereof, in twenty days, to the commissioners of all sums so paid; and the owner thereof shall have the remainder discounted out of any future tax, and the receipt of the said treasurer shall exonerate the collector.

[Section XVIII.] (Section XX, P. L.) And be it further enacted by the authority aforesaid, That the collectors shall make out true and fair accounts in writing of every seizure by them made, with the charges, to be settled by the commissioners; which commissioners shall make the collectors such reasonable allowance for their trouble as to them shall seem right, and the said commissioners shall have full power and authority in all cases to call upon collectors who have or in future may have any overplus money in their hands and to proceed against them in such cases as the law directs in case of delinquent collectors.

[Section XIX.] (Section XXI, P. L.) And be it further enacted by the authority aforesaid, That the collectors of every district, ward or township shall pay unto the county treasurer the whole of the tax charged in his duplicate within thirty days after the day of appeal, unless he hath been obliged to make distress for any part thereof; in which case, and no other, he shall, as to the tax assessed on the parties distrained on, have ten days more, after which the commissioners of the county shall fine such delinquent collector at the rate of three pence in the pound, upon all sums charged in his duplicate which such collector shall not have paid to the said treasurer for every day he shall fail to make payment thereof as aforesaid, such fine to be recovered in manner aforesaid.

[Section XX.] (Section XXII, P. L.) And be it further enacted by the authority aforesaid, That every county treasurer of this state shall pay over all sums of money by him received by virtue of this act to the treasurer of this commonwealth within the time hereinafter limited. That is to say: The treasurer of the county of Philadelphia, within three days after he shall receive the same; the treasurer of the county of Bucks, within four days after he shall receive the same; the treasurer of the county of Chester, within four days aftr he shall receive the same; the treasurer of the county of Lancaster, within six days after he shall receive the same; the treasurer of the county of York, within seven days after he shall receive the same;

and the treasurer of the county of Cumberland shall be allowed eight days and the treasurer of the county of Berks six days. And the treasurer of the county of Northampton, seven days, and the treasurer of the county of Bedford, twelve days, and the treasurer of the counties of Westmoreland and Washington, twenty days, and the treasurer of the county of Northumberland twelve days for the like purpose.

[Section XXI.] (Section XXIII, P. L.) And be it further enacted by the authority aforesaid, That the commissioners of the several counties of this state shall cause their clerk to make out a fair transcript of the assessment of every tax laid upon the county by virtue of this act, and having signed the same, shall cause such transcript to be delivered to the treasurer of the commonwealth within thirty days after the days of appeal.

[Section XXII.](Section XXIV, P. L.) And be it further enacted by the authority aforesaid, That the commissioners of the city and several counties shall, each of them, have and receive seven shillings and six pence per day, and each of the township, ward and district assessors and assistant assessors shall have and receive five shillings per day, for each day they shall bona fide be employed in the performance of the several duties required of them by this act, and that the collectors severally employed in and for the due execution of this act shall be allowed six pence in the pound for every pound by them so collected, and no more.

[Section XXIII.] (Section XXV, P. L.) And be it further enacted by the authority aforesaid, That all sums of money to be assessed and levied by this act shall be paid and discharged in gold or silver money, at the rate of three pounds for one-half johannes of Portugal weighing nine pennyweight, and seven shillings and six pence for one Spanish milled dollar weighing seventeen pennyweight and six grains, and so in proportion for all other gold or silver money, and in no other money whatsoever. Provided always, nevertheless, That all persons who have taken the oath or affirmation of allegiance to this state, within the time and in the manner prescribed by law, shall be and are hereby authorized and permitted to pay one-half of the sums assessed upon them, respectively, in the paper bills of credit emitted in pursuance of an act passed on the seventh day of April, one thousand seven hundred and eighty-one, but the other half shall be paid in gold or silver, at the rate aforesaid.

(Section XXVI, P. L.) And whereas it is absolutely necessary that this act be put in force and executed with all convenient speed:

Therefore:

[Section XXIV.] Be it enacted by the authority aforesaid, That if any of the said commissioners shall refuse or neglect to do his or their duty in the premises, he or they so offending shall be fined by the supreme executive council of this state in any sum not exceeding five hundred pounds for every offense, which, by virtue of their warrant directed to the sheriff or coroner of the county where such offender or his estate is at the time of issuing such warrant, shall be levied by seizure of lands, distress and sale of goods or imprisonment of the body, as the case shall require.

[Section XXV.] (Section XXVII, P. L.) And be it further enacted by the authority aforesaid, That the act for raising supplies for the year one thousand seven hundred and seventy-nine, and every article, clause, matter and thing therein contained (except what is herein altered or supplied) shall be and is hereby declared to be extended to this act, and shall continue in full force and virtue till all and every sum and sums of money hereby imposed shall be raised, levied, collected and paid.

Passed June 21, 1781. Recorded L. t. No. 1, p. 438, etc. See the Acts of Assembly passed June 25, 1781, Chapter 948; September 29, 1781, Chapter 951; April 5, 1785, Chapter 1161.

CHAPTER CMXLV.

AN ACT FOR THE REPEAL OF SO MUCH OF THE LAWS OF THIS COMMONWEALTH AS MAKE THE CONTINENTAL BILLS OF CREDIT AND THE BILLS EMITTED BY THE RESOLVES OR ACTS OF THE ASSEMBLIES OF THE SAID COMMONWEALTH A LEGAL TENDER, AND FOR OTHER PURPOSES THEREIN MENTIONED.[1]

(Section I, P. L.) Whereas the honorable the Continental Congress and the different legislatures of the United States of America, struggling in support of their inborn rights and invaded liberties, have been necessitated, by reason of the scarcity of specie, to emit large sums of paper currency, by the rapid depreciation whereof the said United States have labored under great difficulties in procuring the necessary supplies for carrying on the present war:

And whereas the quantity of specie being of late considerably increased within the said United States, the said Congress have, in the most pressing manner, recommended to the different legislatures of the same states to repeal all laws making the paper bills of credit of the United States a legal tender equal to gold and silver:

In compliance with the said recommendation and for attaining the good ends and purposes thereby intended:

[Section I.] (Section II, P. L.) Be it enacted and it is hereby enacted by the Representatives of the Freemen of the Commonwealth of Pennsylvania in General Assembly met, and by the authority of the same, That so much of all and every of the laws of this commonwealth as declare the bills of credit emitted by the honorable the Continental Congress, or by the resolves of the assemblies of the late province of Pennsylvania, or by the present or late assembly or assemblies of this commonwealth, to be a legal tender in discharge of debts, contracts or demands; and so much of the said laws as impose any penalty or forfeiture upon persons refusing to accept any of the said bills of credit, in satisfaction of any debts, contracts or demands; and so much of the said laws as impose any penalty

---

[1] See Act of January 29, 1777, Chapter 738.

or forfeiture upon persons refusing to receive the said bills of credit in payment for any live stock, necessary of life, commodity, article or goods whatsoever, or upon persons offering such goods or articles for a less price or smaller sum of money to be paid in gold or silver or other current money, than in the bills of credit aforesaid; or upon persons giving or receiving a greater nominal sum of the said bills of credit for a less in gold or silver, shall be and the same is and are hereby repealed and made void.

(Section III, P. L.) Provided always, nevertheless, That the foregoing clause shall not extend or be construed to extend to repeal, alter or make void any laws or sections, or clauses of laws whereby the paper bills of credit emitted in pursuance of an act passed on the twenty-fifth day of March, one thousand seven hundred and eighty, and the paper bills of credit emitted in pursuance of the act passed on the seventh day of April, one thousand seven hundred and eighty-one, are made receivable at the same rate as gold and silver in the payment of the arrearages of purchase money due for lands or lots, sold or to be sold or conveyed by this state, forfeited estates only excepted.

(Section IV, P. L.) Provided also, That nothing in this act contained shall affect any tender made in due and legal manner, under and according to the directions of any of the said laws, or any suits, actions and judgments which have been commenced or had, or which are now depending, or which hereafter may be brought for or by reason of any tender made before the passing of this act.

[Section II.] (Section V, P. L.) And be it further enacted by the authority aforesaid, That all debts, duties, rents, annuities and other demands, granted or contracted for by any deed, will, mortgage, bond, specialty, bill of exchange, note, assumpsit or otherwise since the first day of January, one thousand seven hundred and seventy-seven, which were expressed to be paid and discharged in any foreign money, or in gold and silver money of any denomination, or in bullion or in any commodity, and which have not since been paid and satisfied or discharged shall be deemed, construed and taken to be yet due and owing from debtors to creditors, in such money or other commodity as in the said contracts were expressed, and the same may be sued for and recovered in any court of justice within this commonwealth having competent jurisdiction, in so much gold and silver money as shall be equal in value to the debt or duty, according to the terms of the contract.

(Section VI, P. L.) And whereas, most of the debts contracted before the first day of January, one thousand seven hundred and seventy-seven, are due and owing from persons who, from principles of honor and honesty, have declined paying their creditors with a depreciated [paper] currency when, by law, they might have so done, and it would be unreasonable that such debtors should be compelled to discharge their old debts in gold or silver money until it shall become more plenty and easier to be acquired:

[Section III.] (Section VII, P. L.) Be it therefore enacted by the authority aforesaid, That where any judgment already hath been or hereafter shall be entered in any court of record within this commonwealth by default, upon the confession of the party, the report of referees or the verdict of a jury or otherwise, for any sum of money contracted for, or due for rents, ground rents or annuities before the first day of January, one thousand seven hundred and seventy-seven (debt due to the state excepted), the said court is hereby authorized, if the same be not ascertained by the said confession, report or verdict, to ascertain how much of the said sum of money is due to the plaintiff for the principal sum due, and how much thereof is for interest, damages, costs and charges, and to give judgment for the whole sum, which judgment shall remain as a lien upon the real estate of the defendants, in the same manner as judgments at law bind such estate, and thereupon the said court shall award execution against the defendant for so much of the said sum only as the said interest, damages, costs and charges shall amount to, which money shall be levied, recovered and paid in gold and silver money, but no execution shall issue for the principal sum until two years after the passing of this act, or until permission shall be given for that purpose by an act of the assembly of this Commonwealth; but the defendant shall, nevertheless, pay the interest of the said principal sum yearly, as it shall grow due, and in default thereof, the plaintiff shall be entitled to writs of execution as often as there shall be occasion to recover the same.

(Section VIII, P. L.) Provided always, nevertheless, That if the defendants in any such cause shall not be at the time of rendering the said judgment, seized of a sufficient real estate within this commonwealth, in his own right to secure the said debt, and shall be about to depart from this state, without leaving such real estate, and shall refuse to give other security for the said principal sum, to the satisfaction of the said court, then, and in such case, the said court are hereby authorized and required to award execution for the whole sum contained in the said judgment, as well principal as interest, damages, costs and charges, anything herein contained to the contrary notwithstanding.

(Section IX, P. L.) And in order to prevent unnecessary suits, and to give debtors a reasonable time to prepare themselves for payment of their old debts before any suit can be brought:

[Section IV.] Be it enacted by the authority aforesaid, That no suit shall be commenced against any person (other than the subjects of his Britannic majesty) for any debt or duty contracted for before the first day of January, one thousand seven hundred and seventy-seven, under or by virtue of this act, where the sum demanded exceeds fifty pounds within less than six months from the passing of this act, unless the creditor shall have demanded from the person of the debtor, or by a [note], in writing, left at the place of his abode, satisfaction of the said debt, at least three months before bringing his suit, or unless the creditor, or some person for him, shall swear or affirm that he apprehends a danger of losing his debt by [the] delay.

[Section V.] (Section X, P. L.) And be it further enacted by the authority aforesaid, That nothing in this act contained shall extend to revive any debts or demands which were, on or before the first day of January, one thousand seven hundred and seventy-six, barred by any act for the limitation of actions then in force; and that no debt or demand which was not barred by such act for the limitation of actions on the said first day of January, one thousand seven hundred and seventy-six, shall be barred by the said act, until two years after the passing of this act, and until such time as is limited by law, according to the nature of each case.

(Section XI, P. L.) And whereas divers persons, as agents, factors, bailiffs and receivers, sheriffs, attorneys at law and in fact, executors, administrators, guardians, trustees and other persons in right of their respective offices, trusts and appointments, may have received sums of money for the use of their principals and persons interested, some of whom may have applied such moneys to their own use, others may have kept the same by them, until it depreciated to a much greater degree, and others may have placed the same out on interest for the use and benefit of their principals; and it is fit and right that justice should take place in such varied cases as nearly as may be ascertained.

[Section VI.] (Section XII, P. L.) Be it therefore enacted by the authority aforesaid, That where any agent, factor, bailiff or receiver, sheriff, attorney at law or in fact, executor, administrator, guardian, trustee or other person has, in right of his office, trust or appointment, received any sum or sums of money for the use of his or their principals or persons interested, and have applied the same to their own private use, in such case he or they shall be accountable to his or their principals or persons interested as aforesaid for so much gold and silver money as the said bills of credit, or other money, so by them received were worth at the time of such application, according to the rate of depreciation affixed to the act, entitled "An act directing the mode of adjusting and settling the payment of debts and contracts entered into and made between the first day of January, one thousand seven hundred and seventy-seven, and the first day of March, one thousand seven hundred and eighty-one, and for other purposes therein mentioned,"[1] passed the third day of April, one thousand seven hundred and eighty-one. And where any such agent, factor, bailiff, receiver, sheriff, attorney at law or in fact, executor, administrator,

---

[1] Passed April 3, 1781, Chapter 935.

guardian, trustee or other person, having received any sum or sums of money as aforesaid, shall render an account on oath or affirmation, of his manner of his disposing of the same, and of the profit or loss arising thereupon, and the principal or other person interested as aforesaid shall not be able to disprove the same, in case of loss, then and in such case such profit or loss shall go to the benefit or prejudice of the principals or persons interested as aforesaid, allowing a reasonable compensation to such agent, factor, bailiff, receiver, sheriff, attorney at law or in fact, executor, administrator, guardian, trustee or other person, for his trouble in managing the same; and if any agent, factor, bailiff, receiver, sheriff, attorney at law or in fact, executor, administrator, guardian, trustee or other such person receiving as aforesaid, shall decline to make such oath or affirmation and to render such account, it shall be presumed that he applied said moneys to his own use, and he shall be accountable therefor in the manner hereinbefore mentioned in such cases.

(Section XIII, P. L.) And whereas, by an act of assembly of this commonwealth, passed the twenty-seventh day of November, one thousand seven hundred and seventy-nine, entitled "An act for the better support of certain officers of this state, and for ascertaining the specific fines and penalties which they may incur by a neglect of duty,"[1] the fees of the said officers and the fines and penalties which they might incur by neglect of duty were regulated by the price of wheat, which has been found inconvenient and uncertain:

[Section VII.] (Section XIV, P. L.) Be it therefore enacted by the authority aforesaid, That from and after the passing of this act, all the fees due to the officers in the said act mentioned, and all the fines and penalties which they have or may incur, by a neglect of duty, shall be paid, levied, collected and received by and from them in gold and silver money, as they were regulated by law or practice, under the late government of Pennsylvania, before the first day of July, one thousand seven hundred and seventy-six, anything in the said law to the contrary notwithstanding.

---

[1] Passed November 27, 1779, Chapter 875.

(Section XV, P. L.) And whereas, by an act of assembly of this commonwealth passed the eighth day of March, one thousand seven hundred and eighty, entitled "An act to restore and ascertain divers fines, penalties and forfeitures, hereafter mentioned, which may be incurred by the breach of certain acts of assembly of this commonwealth,"[1] the said fines, penalties and forfeitures therein mentioned, were also regulated by the price of wheat, which mode has been found inconvenient, uncertain and inadequate:

[Section VIII.] Be it therefore enacted by the authority aforesaid, That all fines, penalties and forfeitures of every kind imposed by virtue of any acts of the assemblies of the late province of Pennsylvania, which are now in force, shall be levied, collected and recovered in so much gold and silver money as in the said several acts is particularly inflicted and respectively specified, and all fines, penalties and forfeitures imposed by any acts of the assembly of this commonwealth, since the revolution shall be levied, collected and recovered in so much gold and silver money as the sum specified in the respective acts for the said fines, penalties and forfeitures were worth at the several times of passing the said acts, according to the rate of depreciation aforesaid.

[Section IX.] (Section XVI, P. L.) Provided always, and be it further enacted by the authority aforesaid, That all debts or contracts which have been entered into at any time from or since the first day of March, one thousand seven hundred and eighty-one, or shall be entered into hereafter, shall be paid and discharged according to the special nature of the contract. That is to say: Contracts made for gold and silver shall be paid and discharged in the same, and contracts for paper currency of any emission shall be payable in the same emission, excepting only that contracts entered into as above for old continental currency (if any such there be) shall be liquidated and paid at specie value, which value shall be ascertained and determined by a justice of the peace or the justices of the common pleas, as the case may be, within their respective jurisdictions.

[Section X.](Section XVII, P. L.) And be it enacted by the

---

[1] Passed March 8, 1780, Chapter 888.

authority aforesaid, That nothing in this act shall be extended to prevent the receiving the bills of credit emitted in consequence of the resolution of Congress of the eighteenth of March, one thousand seven hundred and eighty, in taxes to be laid in pursuance of an act of general assembly of this state, entitled "A supplement to an act, entitled 'An act for funding and redeeming the bills of credit of the United States of America, and for providing means to bring the present war to a happy conclusion,'"[1] passed the nineteenth day of December, one thousand seven hundred and eighty.

Passed June 21, 1781. Recorded L. B. No. 1, p. 442, etc. See the Act of Assembly passed March 12, 1782, Chapter 1008.

CHAPTER CMXLVI.

AN ACT FOR RECRUITING THE PENNSYLVANIA LINE IN THE ARMY OF THE UNITED STATES.

(Section I, P. L.) Whereas, the frequent calling forth the militia of this state is attended with great expense and loss of time, to prevent which in future as much as may be:

[Section I.] (Section II, P. L.) Be it enacted and it is hereby enacted by the Representatives of the Freemen of the Commonwealth of Pennsylvania in General Assembly met, and by the authority of the same, That there shall, with all convenient speed, be enlisted within this state two thousand seven hundred able bodied men, to serve in the Pennsylvania line for the term of eighteen months from the first day of July next, who shall be raised and procured by or at the expense of the inhabitants of the city of Philadelphia and the several counties of this state, in number and according to the proportion following: That is to say: By the city and county of Philadelphia, eight hundred and ninety-five; the county of Bucks, one hundred and seventy-seven; the county of Chester, two hundred and eighty-four; the county of Lancaster, three hundred and eighty-

---

[1] Passed December 19, 1780, Chapter 921.

1781]   *The Statutes at Large of Pennsylvania*   345

four; the county of York, two hundred and fourteen; the county of Cumberland, two hundred and two; the county of Berks, one hundred and ninety-three; the county of Northampton, one hundred and twelve; the county of Bedford, sixty-one; the county of Northumberland, seventy-five, and the counties of Westmoreland and Washington, one hundred and three.

[Section II.] (Section III, P. L.) And be it enacted by the authority aforesaid, That the commissioners of the city and several counties of this state, respectively, or any two of them, shall forthwith transmit to the several classes, classed by virtue of an act of the assembly of this state, entitled "An act to complete the quota of the federal army assigned to this state," passed the twenty-third day of December, one thousand seven hundred and eighty,[1] by persons to be by them appointed for that service, an order in writing, under their hands, with a duplicate annexed, containing the names of each and every person composing such class, requiring each of the said classes to enlist for the term of eighteen months, as aforesaid, and deliver to the proper officer one able-bodied recruit within fifteen days thereafter.

[Section III.] (Section IV, P. L.) And be it enacted by the authority aforesaid, That if any class or classes shall neglect or refuse to enlist one able-bodied recruit as aforesaid, within the time limited and directed, or to make return thereof to the assessor of the proper township, ward or district, it shall and may be lawful for the said commissioners, or township, ward or district assessors, or any of them, and they are hereby authorized and required to enlist for the term aforesaid and deliver to the proper officer one able-bodied recruit in behalf of such class or classes respectively; and that it shall and may be lawful for the said commissioners, township, ward or district assessors, or either of them, where such neglect or refusal shall happen, to proceed and levy, in the manner directed by the laws now in force for levying and collecting other public taxes, on the class or classes so neglecting or refusing, the sum agreed to be paid by the said commissioners, township, ward or district assessors, or any of them, to the said recruit, and the reasonable

---

[1] Passed December 23, 1780, Chapter 926.

expenses accruing thereupon, in proper proportions, according to the last public tax levied therein, which they are hereby enjoined and directed to do within two days after such recruit shall be enlisted.

(Section V, P. L.) And whereas, it may happen that a number of the said classes may prove delinquent and recruits may not be procured immediately to supply the deficiency:

[Section IV.] (Section VI, P. L.) Be it therefore enacted by the authority aforesaid, That the commissioners of the several counties, respectively, shall provide and keep a book in which they shall enter, in numerical order, the several delinquent classes as they shall be returned to them, and shall enlist recruits for [the] said delinquent classes according to their respective numbers, and in like manner levy and collect the sums imposed upon them, respectively, by this act.

(Section VII, P. L.) And whereas great injustice may be done and unnecessary expense may be occasioned to the delinquent classes by the commissioners and assessors giving high and extravagant sums of money for recruits in their behalf:

[Section V.] (Section VIII, P. L.) Be it therefore enacted by the authority aforesaid, That each and every commissioner and assessor shall, before he enters on the duties required of him by this act, take the following oath or affirmation, viz.:

I, A. B., do swear (or solemnly, sincerely and truly declare and affirm) that in executing the duties required of me by the act, entitled "An act for recruiting the Pennsylvania line in the army of the United States," I will grieve no person or class (as therein mentioned) through hatred or ill-will, but to the best of my judgment and abilities will procure recruits or cause the same to be procured for delinquent classes on the cheapest and best terms in my power.

[Section VI.] (Section IX, P. L.) And be it enacted by the authority aforesaid, That any person who, in pursuance of this act, shall enlist and deliver to the proper officer one able-bodied recruit shall be exempted from all militia duty for and during the time of such enlistment.

[Section VII.] (Section X, P. L.) And be it enacted by the authority aforesaid, That every recruit so enlisted and entered into the Pennsylvania line, shall receive the same pay, clothing and rations as the troops of this state in the service of the United States, and also half pay during life if disabled in the service.

[Section VIII.] (Section XI, P. L.) And be it further enacted by the authority aforesaid, That where any class or person therein shall furnish such recruit in behalf of such class, and any dispute may arise about the sum or sums of money which any person [or persons] therein should or ought to pay towards the enlistment of such recruit, or shall neglect or refuse to pay their proportion thereof, the same shall be adjusted, collected and paid in the manner directed in the foregoing clause for the levying, collecting and paying the expenses of enlistment, in cases where the classes have neglected or refused.

[Section IX.] (Section XII, P. L.) And be it enacted by the authority aforesaid, That the supreme executive council and the commanding officer of the Pennsylvania line be and they are hereby authorized and empowered to appoint officers of the said line in each county, for the purpose of inspecting and taking such recruits in charge that shall be enlisted in pursuance of this act.

[Section X.] (Section XIII, P. L.) And be it further enacted by the authority aforesaid, That every recruit enlisted for any class shall be attested before the next or some justice of the peace, if accepted by the proper officer, shall, by one of the said classes, be delivered to the nearest officer appointed for that purpose, who, upon the receipt of such recruit and certificate from the said justice of the peace of his having been attested as above, shall give a receipt in favor of such class for said recruit.

[Section XI.] (Section XIV, P. L.) And be it further enacted by the authority aforesaid, That all moneys paid by executors, guardians or others, in legal trust, in right of another, in pursuance of this act, shall be allowed in their accounts at the time of the settlement thereof.

[Section XII.] (Section XV, P. L.) And be it further enacted by the authority aforesaid, That any county commissioner herein required to perform certain duties and neglecting or refusing so to do, according to the true intent and meaning of this act (except in case of sickness or removal) shall be fined by the supreme executive council of this state in any sum not exceeding five hundred pounds in specie. And any assessor, collector or other person required, in pursuance of this act, to perform any duty and neglecting or refusing to perform the same (except as above excepted), shall be fined in any sum not exceeding fifty pounds specie, by the commissioners of the city or any of the counties of this state, or any two of them, where the offense may happen, who shall appoint another or others in their stead.

And whereas, it may happen that a part or the whole of the property in some of the said classes may not have any person in the occupation or possession thereof or resident thereon to represent it:

[Section XIII.] (Section XVII, P. L.) Be it therefore enacted by the authority aforesaid, That the collector of the township, ward or district wherein such property may be found shall give speedy information thereof to the commissioners of the county, who shall, without delay, publish, or cause to be published, in some of the newspapers printed in the city of Philadelphia, for three weeks successively an account of all property so circumstanced in their said county, and of the sum or sums of money chargeable thereon, requiring the owner or owners to make payment thereof to the proper person at or before the expiration of two months from the date of such publication; and on failure of such payment at the expiration of such term, the commissioners of the proper county, or any two of them, may and they are hereby authorized, empowered and required to expose such property, or as much thereof as may be necessary, to pay such sum or sums of money, with reasonable costs, to sale at public auction and after due and public notice given of such intended sale for at least ten days, to sell the same to the highest and best bidder; and the said commissioners, or any two of them, shall convey any houses, lands or tenements so sold to the purchaser or purchasers thereof in fee simple, or for such estate as the delinquent owner thereof held the same, which shall be good and valid in law; and the said commissioners, after deducting the sum or sums of money aforesaid and the reasonable costs, shall return and pay the overplus of the consideration money, if any, to the owner or owners when thereunto required.

[Section XIV.] (Section XVIII, P. L.) And be it further enacted by the authority aforesaid, That all tenants in possession shall be accountable for and pay any sum or sums of money charged by virtue of this act on the lands in his or her possession, and may discount the same out of his or her rent; and in case one year's rent should prove insufficient to defray the same, the said lands shall be liable for the sums charged thereon, and the same, or such parts thereof as may be sufficient, may be sold therefor in the manner prescribed in the foregoing clause.

[Section XV.] (Section XIX, P. L.) And be it further enacted by the authority aforesaid, That the persons to be appointed by the commissioners of the city and several counties to transmit and deliver to the several classes their order, with the duplicate hereinbefore mentioned, shall be paid such reasonable rewards, respectively, for that service as shall be agreed for by the said commissioners.

Passed June 25, 1781. Recorded L. B. No. 1, p. 446, etc. See the Act of Assembly passed September 29, 1781, Chapter 951.

CHAPTER CMXLVII.

A SUPPLEMENT TO AN ACT ENTITLED "AN ACT FOR ESTABLISHING A LAND OFFICE AND FOR OTHER PURPOSES THEREIN MENTIONED."[1]

(Section I, P. L.) Whereas, it appears necessary to explain certain parts of the act, entitled "An act for establishing a land office and for other purposes therein mentioned,"[1] and to make some amendments thereto:

Therefore:

[Section I.] (Section II, P. L.) Be it enacted and it is hereby

---

[1] Passed April 9. 1781, Chapter 940.

enacted by the Representatives of the Freemen of the Commonwealth of Pennsylvania in General Assembly met, and by the authority of the same, That the meaning of the word location, mentioned in the fifth section of the said act, was, is, and is hereby declared to be, an application made by any person or persons for land in the office of the secretary of the late land office of Pennsylvania, and entered in the books of the said office, numbered and sent to the surveyor-general's office.

[Section II.] (Section III, P. L.) And be it further enacted by the authority aforesaid, That it shall and may be lawful to and for the president, or, in his absence, the vice-president, in council, to sign all and every warrant and warrants of acceptance, re-survey and partition as fully as the governor of the late province of Pennsylvania or commissioner of property might or could have done.

[Section III.] (Section IV, P. L.) And be it further enacted by the authority aforesaid, That the receiver-general shall, once in every month, pay into the hands of the treasurer of this commonwealth all moneys which shall come to his hands by virtue of the said act to which this is a supplement, which shall be subject to the disposal of the legislature of this state, to whom he is to account once in every year.

[Section IV.] (Section V, P. L.) And be it further enacted by the authority aforesaid, That the rate of exchange at which the receiver-general shall receive the five pounds sterling for every hundred acres of land shall and is hereby declared to be at the rate of one hundred and sixty-six and two-thirds of the currency of this state for one hundred pounds sterling.

Passed June 25, 1781. Recorded L. B. No. 1, page 449, etc.

CHAPTER CMXLVIII.

AN ACT FOR RAISING ADDITIONAL SUPPLIES FOR THE YEAR ONE THOUSAND SEVEN HUNDRED AND EIGHTY-ONE.

(Section I, P. L.) Whereas, it is become necessary that vigorous and effectual measures should be adopted to answer the present exigency of the public:

And whereas, it is the earnest desire of the representatives of the freemen of this commonwealth to restore and support th credit of the paper money of this state by all just means in their power:

[Section I.] (Section II, P. L.) Be it therefore enacted and it is hereby enacted by the Representatives of the Freemen of the Commonwealth of Pennsylvania in General Assembly met, and by the authority of the same, That the sum of eighty thousand pounds, in addition to the sums of money directed to be raised by the act, entitled "A supplement to the act, entitled 'An act for funding and redeeming the bills of credit of the United States of America, and for providing means to bring the present war to an happy conclusion,"[1] passed on the nineteenth day of December, one thousand seven hundred and eighty, and by the act, entitled "An act to raise effective supplies for the year one thousand seven hundred and eighty-one,"[2] passed the twenty-first day of June, one thousand seven hundred and eighty-one, shall be raised, levied, collected and paid into the treasury of this state within the current year, and shall be assessed and levied on the persons and estates of the inhabitants of the city and county of Philadelphia, and the several counties of this state, in the proportion and manner following, viz.:

The city and county of Philadelphia, the sum of twenty-six thousand five hundred and four pounds, three shillings.

The county of Bucks, the sum of five thousand two hundred and forty-two pounds six shillings.

---

[1] Passed December 19, 1780, Chapter 921.
[2] Passed June 21, 1781, Chapter 944.

The county of Chester, the sum of eight thousand four hundred and fifteen pounds seven shillings.

The county of Lancaster, the sum of eleven thousand three hundred and eighty-eight pounds five shillings.

The county of York, the sum of six thousand three hundred and forty-five pounds four shillings.

The county of Cumberland, the sum of five thousand nine hundred and sixty-four pounds.

The county of Berks, the sum of five thousand seven hundred and twenty-eight pounds four shillings.

The county of Northampton, the sum of three thousand two hundred and ninety-seven pounds ten shillings.

The county of Bedford, the sum of one thousand eight hundred and seven pounds sixteen shillings.

[The county of Northumberland, the sum of two thousand two hundred and thirty-three pounds three shillings.] And

The counties of Westmoreland and Washington, the sum of three thousand and seventy-four pounds two shillings.

[Section II.] (Section III, P. L.) And be it further enacted by the authority aforesaid, That the tax for raising the said sum of eighty thousand pounds shall be grafted upon and added to the tax directed to be levied and collected within the current year by the said act, entitled "A supplement to an act, entitled 'An act for funding and redeeming the bills of credit of the United States of America, and for providing means to bring the present war to an happy conclusion,"[1] and shall be assessed, levied, collected and paid in the manner and within the time and under the penalties and forfeitures therein expressed, contained and directed.

[Section III.] (Section IV, P. L.) And be it further enacted by the authority aforesaid, That the said act, entitled "A supplement to an act, entitled 'An act for funding and redeeming the bills of credit of the United States of America, and for providing means to bring the present war to an happy conclusion,'" and every clause, matter and thing therein contained shall be in force, and (so far as respects the levying, collecting and paying the said tax) shall be extended and applied to the

---

[1] Ante.

raising, levying, collecting and paying the additional sum and sums of money hereby directed to be levied and paid as fully as if the said act was herein inserted; excepting only where the same is hereby altered, amended or supplied.

[Section IV.] (Section V. P. L.) Provided always, and be it further enacted by the authority aforesaid, That the paper bills of credit emitted in pursuance of an act entitled "An act for striking the sum of one hundred thousand pounds in bills of credit for the present support of the army, and for establishing a fund for the certain redemption of the same, and for other purposes therein mentioned,"[1] passed the twenty-fifth day of March, one thousand seven hundred and eighty, and the bills of credit emitted in pursuance of the resolutions of Congress of the eighteenth of March, one thousand seven hundred and eighty; and the bills of credit emitted in pursuance of the act entitled "An act for emitting the sum of five hundred thousand pounds in bills of credit, for the support of the army, and for establishing a fund for the redemption thereof, and for other purposes therein mentioned,"[2] passed the seventh day of April, one thousand seven hundred and eighty-one, ad gold and silver at their legal value, shall be received in payment of the said taxes, and no other money whatever.

(Section VI, P. L.) And whereas it is expedient that all unnecessary expenses be prevented in the levying and collecting the aforesaid taxes; therefore,

[Section V.] Be it enacted by the authority aforesaid, That the taxes hereby directed to be assessed, levied and collected, and the taxes to be assessed, levied and collected, by virtue of the aforesaid act entitled "A supplement to an act entitled An act for funding and redeeming the bills of credit of the United States of America, and for providing means to bring the present war to an happy conclusion,"[3] shall be assessed and levied on the returns of taxable persons and property made or to be made in pursuance of the directions of the act for raising effective supplies for the year one thousand

---

[1] Passed March 25, 1780, Chapter 907.
[2] Passed April 7, 1781, Chapter 939.
[3] Ante.

seven hundred and eighty-one, passed the twenty-first day of June, one thousand seven hundred and eighty-one, anything in the aforesaid acts to the contrary notwithstanding.

Passed June 25, 1781. Recorded L. B. No. 1, page 450, etc.

Laws enacted in the Fourth Sitting of the Fifth General Assembly of the Commonwealth of Pennsylvania, which commenced at Philadelphia, on Tuesday, the fourth day of September, A. D. 1781.

CHAPTER CMXLIX.

AN ACT TO INCORPORATE THE GERMAN SOCIETY CONTRIBUTING FOR THE RELIEF OF DISTRESSED GERMANS IN THE STATE OF PENNSYLVANIA.

(Section I, P. L.) Whereas the arrival of Germans from Europe, and the numerous settlements made by them in Pennsylvania, have greatly contributed to the present wealth and strength of this state; and the means of encouraging these foreigners to come and settle among us, by removing or lessening their distresses in a new country, have, on sundry occasions, deservedly engaged the attention of the former government of this country:

(Section II. P. L.) And wheras a number of German inhabitants of the city of Philadelphia and its neighborhood by their humble petition to the general assembly of this state, have represented and shown, that some time in the year of our Lord, one thousand seven hundred and sixty-four, some of the petitioners and divers other persons, all Germans by birth or descending from Germans who had settled in this state, moved by the sufferings of their countrymen then newly arrived, formed themselves into a charitable society, under the name of "The German Society of Philadelphia, in the province of Pennsylvania," and by voluntary subscriptions and stated contributions from time to time supplied the poor, the sick and otherwise distressed Germans brought to the city of Philadelphia, and have aided and assisted such passengers as for want of acquaintance with the language and laws of the country were in danger of being oppressed. Also, that some of the petitioners aforesaid have purchased two contiguous lots in the said city of Philadelphia, in order to build thereon for the reception and accommodation of their countrymen when need shall be. Also, that they have it in view to enlarge upon and further to extend the benefit of their first institution, by applying part of the fund of money in their hands, and which hereafter they may raise, for and towards other charitable purposes, such as to teach and improve poor children, both in the English and German languages, reading and writing thereof, and to procure for them such learning and education as will best suit their genius and capacities, and enable the proper objects to receive the finishing of their studies in the university established in the said city of Philadelphia; likewise to erect a library and to do any other matter or thing which, without any prejudice to other inhabitants of this state, in charity they might do for the relief and benefit of their own countrymen; wherefore, they have humbly prayed that they might be incorporated by a law for this purpose:

[Section I.] (Section II, P. L.) Be it therefore enacted and it is hereby enacted by the Representatives of the Freemen of the Commonwealth of Pennsylvania in General Assembly met, and by the authority of the same, That Henry Keppele, president; Lewis Weiss, vice-president; Lewis Farmer and Henry Leighthouser, secretaries; Christopher Ludwick, Peter Ozeas, Andrew Burckhart, John Fritz, Peter Kraft and Melchior Steiner, overseers; Michael Shubart, treasurer; Henry Kammerer, solicitor; and William Lehman, deacon; the present officers of the said German Society, elected and chosen at the last meeting of the members of that society, on the twenty-sixth day of December last past, and their successors in the respective offices and all persons who have subscribed and hereafter shall subscribe the rules and regulations of the said society, and have continued, and shall from time to time continue to contribute towards the aforesaid charitable purposes of the said society, be, and they are hereby made and constituted a corporation and body politic in law and in fact to have continuance forever by the name, style and title of The German Society contributing for the relief of distressed Germans in the state of Pennsylvania.

[Section II.] (Section IV, P. L.) And be it further enacted by the authority aforesaid, That the said corporation and their successors, by the name, style and title aforesaid, shall forever hereafter be persons able and capable in law, as well to take, receive and hold all and all manner of lands, tenements, rents, annuities, liberties, franchises and other hereditaments which at any time or times heretofore have been granted, bargained, sold, enfeoffed, released, devised or otherwise conveyed to the said German Society, or to any person or persons for their use or in trust for them; and the same lands, tenements, rents, annuities, liberties, franchises and other hereditaments are hereby vested and established in the said corporation and their successors forever. And the said corporation and their successors are hereby declared to be seized and possessed of such estate or estates therein as in and by the respective grants, bargains, sales, enfeoffments, releases, devises or other conveyances thereof is or are declared, limited and expressed; as, also, that the said corporation and their successors, at all times hereafter, shall be capable and able to purchase, have, receive, take, hold and enjoy in fee simple, or of any other lesser estate or estates, any lands, tenements, rents, annuities, liberties, franchises or other hereditaments by the gift, grant, bargain, sale, alienation, enfeoffment, release, confirmation or devise, of any person or persons, bodies politic and corporate, capable and able to make the same, and, further, that the said corporation and their successors may take and receive any sum or sums of money and any manner and portion of goods and chattels that shall be given and bequeathed to them by any person or persons, bodies corporate and politic, capable to make a gift or bequest thereof, such money, goods and chattels to be laid out by them in a purchase or purchases of lands, tenements, messuages, houses, rents, annuites or other hereditaments, to them and their successors forever, or the moneys lent on interest or otherwise disposed of according to the articles and by-laws of the said society and the intention of the donors.

[Section III.] (Section V, P. L.) And be it further enacted

by the authority aforesaid, That at every the four quarterly meetings of the said society. That is to say: On the twenty-sixth day of December, on the twenty-fifth day of March, on the twenty-fourth day of June and the twenty-ninth day of September in every year or when either of those days shall happen to be on a Sunday, then on the day following, each and every of the members of the said society, may propose any person or persons to be ballotted for as a member of the said society or corporation, and such person or persons, so proposed and balloted for, upon being elected by two-thirds in number of the members present, by ballot as aforesaid, and signing the articles of said society, and paying the entrance money, shall, from thenceforth become a member of the said corporation, and whilst he shall, from time to time, contribute towards the purposes aforesaid, shall remain a member of the said corporation, and not otherwise, making nevertheless proper and reasonable allowance of delay for his residence in the frontiers of this state, or his being engaged in the land or sea service of this state, or any of the United States, or a prisoner war, or beyond sea on a fair trade.

[Section IV.] (Section VI, P. L.) Provided always, and be it enacted by the authority aforesaid, That the members of the said society shall not at any time hereafter be less than seventy-five in number nor more than three hundred.

[Section V.] (Section VII, P. L.) And be it further enacted by the authority aforesaid, That the said corporation and their successors, or the majority of such as shall be convened at any of the four quarterly meetings of the said society, shall be authorized and empowered and they are hereby authorized and empowered, to make rules, by-laws and ordinances, and to do everything needful for the good government and support of the affairs of the said corporation. Provided always, That the said by-laws, rules and ordinances, or any of them, be not repugnant to the laws of this commonwealth, and that all their proceedings be fairly and regularly entered in a book to be kept for that purpose, which book and all papers and other documents of the said society shall at all times be liable to the inspection of the president and vice-president of the supreme executive council, the speaker of the general assembly and chief justice of the state for the time being, and that at the general meeting of the members of the said society or corporation on the days aforesaid, they, the said members, or a majority of such as shall be present, be authorized and empowered to elect and choose by ballot, one president, one vice-president, six overseers, a treasurer, two secretaries, one solicitor and one deacon; the said officers to be inhabitants of the said city of Philadelphia, and to remain in office until the next meeting of the said corporation on the twenty-sixth day of December then next following; and in case of death, removal or refusal to serve of any one or more of the officers so chosen, his or their place so dying, removing, or being removed or refusing, shall be supplied by an election in like manner at the next quarterly meeting and the person or persons so chosen shall remain in his said office by virtue of the said election until the next December meeting aforesaid.

[Section VI.] (Section VIII, P. L.) And be it further enacted by the authority aforesaid, That the rents, interest and profits arising from the said real and personal estate of the said corporation shall, by the officers of the said corporation and their successors, chosen and appointed in such manner and form as hereinbefore is directed and required, from time to time be applied for the relief and support of the poor, distressed Germans arriving in this state from parts beyond sea, for the erecting or supporting schools and seminaries of learning, and one or more library or libraries within this state, for the better educating and instructing the children and youth of the Germans and descendants of Germans, and in building, repairing and maintaining school houses, and other houses necessary for the purposes aforesaid, for salaries to schoolmasters and teachers and for such other charitable uses as are conformable to the true design and intent of the same society.

[Section VII.] (Section IX, P. L.) Provided always, and be it enacted by the authority aforesaid, That in the disposal and application of the public moneys of the said corporation, the aforesaid president, vice-president, overseers, secretaries, treasurer, solicitor and deacon, and their successors in office, or any seven of them, the said officers, may make orders and directions, for the relief of poor and distressed persons, and supporting scholars, schoolmasters and others, coming under their notice, and that upon emergent occasions, when immediate relief is wanted, an order signed by one of the presidents, and two of the overseers, directed to the treasurer, shall be a sufficient authority for the said treasurer to discharge and pay such order. Provided also, That neither of the said officers shall at any time during the execution of his office, or afterwards, be entitled to demand, sue for or recover any pay, reward or commission for his service in any of the said offices respectively.

[Section VIII.] (Section X, P. L.) And be it further enacted by the authority aforesaid, That the said corporation and their successors shall have full power and authority to make, have and use one common seal, with such device and inscription as they shall think proper and the same to break, alter and renew at their pleasure.

(Section IX, P. L.) And be it further enacted by the authority aforesaid, That the said corporation and their successors, by the name, style and title aforesaid, shall be able and capable in law to sue and be sued, plead and be impleaded in any court or courts, before any judge or judges, justice or justices, in all and all manner of suits, complaints, pleas, causes, matters and demands of whatever kind, nature and form they may be, and all and every matter or thing therein to do, in as full and effectual a manner as any other person or persons, bodies politic and corporate within this commonwealth may or can do.

[Section X.] (Section XII, P. L.) Provided always, and be it further enacted by the authority aforesaid, That the clear yearly value or income of the messuages, houses, lands, tenements, rents, annuities or other hereditaments, and real estate of the said corporation and interest of money lent, shall not exceed the sum of two thousand and five hundred pounds, lawful money of Pennsylvania, to be taken and esteemed exclusive of the moneys arising from annual or other stated subscriptions or payments, which said moneys shall be received by the treasurer of the said corporation, and disposed of by him upon the order of the other officers, or a majority of them, in the manner hereinbefore described, pursuant to a vote or votes of the members of the said society, appropriating the same at one of their quarterly meetings.

Passed September 20, 1781. Recorded L. B. No. 1, p. 452, etc.

CHAPTER CML.

AN ACT TO MAKE MORE EFFECTUAL PROVISION FOR THE DEFENSE OF THIS STATE.

(Section I, P. L.) Whereas the intelligence received of the preparations made by the enemy at New York indicate an invasion of the state, against which it is our duty to make every provision of defense which the circumstances of this commonwealth admit, and that the executive authority of the state be furnished with sufficient powers to draw forth the resources thereof with the utmost vigor and dispatch:

[Section I.] (Section II, P. L.) Be it therefore enacted and it is hereby enacted by the Representatives of the Freemen of the Commonwealth of Pennsylvania in General Assembly met, and by the authority of the same, That the president (or vice-president) in council be and is hereby authorized to call forth such and so many wagons as shall appear to them necessary for the transportation of the necessary baggage and stores of such troops, either continental or militia; as may be called forth into actual service on this emergency, or for the transportation of the records, books and papers, or other public property, either of the United States or of this state.

[Section II.] (Section III, P. L.) And be it further enacted by the authority aforesaid, That the late wagon-masters of the several counties in this state, and their deputies (or such other persons as shall be appointed by the supreme executive council) and the constables be empowered and are hereby required to do the several duties in the premises which were enjoined by the former wagon laws of this state, and that the owners of all such wagons be entitled to receive the sum of twenty-five shillings specie per diem for a wagon and four horses with suitable gears, and the sum of fifteen shillings specie per diem for a wagon and two horses with gears as aforesaid, they, the said owners, finding the driver and necessary forage for their respective teams.

[Section III.] (Section IV, P. L.) And be it further enacted by the authority aforesaid, That in case a sufficient number of wagons cannot be procured in the manner above mentioned, the president or vice-president in council be and hereby is authorized and empowered to direct his warrant, under his hand and seal, to such persons in the city or any county in this state as shall be deemed proper, authorizing such persons to seize and impress any wagons, horses and gears, boats, sloops or shallops for the transportation of the several articles above mentioned, and in the meantime to detain all wagons, horses, boats or other vessels which any persons may endeavor to remove.

[Section IV.] (Section V, P. L.) And be it further enacted by the authority aforesaid, That the president or vice-president in council be and hereby is in like manner authorized and empowered to seize and impress arms, ammuniton and military stores and provisions and forage of all kinds whatsoever, belonging to any private person or companies, and apply them, if need be, to the public use, such seizure to be certified and the value thereof [ascertained] as nearly as possible in specie.

[Section V.] (Section VI, P. L.) And be it further enacted by the authority aforesaid, That the president or vice-president in council be in like manner authorized and empowered to billet and quarter such troops as may be called together for the special defense of the state, in this emergency, upon any public houses, or in case of their insufficiency upon private houses, having due respect to the number and convenience of families.

(Section VII, P. L.) And whereas, the usual mode of calling out the militia by classes may be attended with fatal delay to the interests and property of the good people of this state:

[Section VI.] (Section VIII, P. L.) Be it therefore further enacted by the authority aforesaid, That the president or vice-president in council be and is hereby authorized and empowered (if the designs of the enemy shall, in their judgment, make it necessary) to call forth the whole of the militia without any respect to classes, and in that case every person now serving on a tour of militia duty shall repair to [and] join his own proper battalion, orders being first received therefor, and shall be allowed for the service already done.

[Section VII.] (Section IX, P. L.) And be it further enacted by the authority aforesaid, That if any person or persons called forth by the president or vice-president in council in manner aforesaid, shall refuse or neglect to perform a tour of militia duty, the person or persons so neglecting or refusing shall be subject to the same fines and penalties as in other cases when called forth in classes, by virtue of the law for regulating the militia of this state, anything in the said law to the contrary thereof notwithstanding.

[Section VIII.] (Section X, P. L.) And be it further enacted by the authority aforesaid, That the president or vice-president in council be authorized to draw upon the treasury for such money as may be necessary in the present emergency for repairing and procuring arms and ammunition and for other contingent expenses attending the present service.

[Section IX.] (Section XI, P. L.) And be it further enacted by the authority aforesaid, That the president or vice-president in council be authorized and empowered, when occasion shall require, to impress by warrant, under hand and seal, such and so many horses and wagons, with suitable gears, as he may judge necessary for the removal of the families and property of those inhabitants of the city of Philadelphia and the Northern Liberties and the district of Southwark, who may be in actual service against the enemy, and of such other citizens and persons who, in his opinion, may be entitled to and require the same, the hire of all such wagons and horses to be paid by the persons making use thereof: Provided nevertheless, That if any horses or wagons shall be impressed by virtue hereof and no use made thereof by the citizens [or persons] for whom they may be impressed, the expense thereof shall be paid by the state treasurer, upon the order of the president or vice-president in council.

[Section X.] (Section XII, P. L.) And be it further enacted by the authority aforesaid, That this act shall be and remain in force until ten days after the meeting of the next general assembly of this commonwealth, and no longer.

Passed September 28, 1781. Recorded L. B. No. 1, p. 455, etc.

CHAPTER CMLI.

AN ACT TO ALTER AND SUPPLY AN ACT ENTITLED "AN ACT FOR RECRUITING THE PENNSYLVANIA LINE IN THE ARMY OF THE UNITED STATES." [1]

(Section I, P. L.) Whereas a number of the classes have not procured recruits according to the directions of the act, entitled "An act for recruiting the Pennsylvania line in the army of the United States," [1] which this act is intended to alter and supply, passed on the twenty-fifth day of June, one thousand seven hundred and eighty-one:

(Section II, P. L.) And whereas, it is absolutely necessary that money be procured from the delinquent classes and that the recruiting of the said line be carried on to effect in the most expeditious manner:

Therefore:

[Section I.] (Section III, P. L.) Be it enacted and it is hereby enacted by the Representatives of the Freemen of the Commonwealth of Pennsylvania in General Assembly met, and by the authority of the same, That the commissioners of the several counties within this state proceed, without delay, to levy the sum of twenty pounds specie on each of the delinquent classes within the city and the several counties, and cause the same to be collected and paid into the treasury of each county in the manner and under the pains and penalties directed in and by the act, entitled "An act to raise effective supplies for the year one thousand seven hundred and eighty-one." [2]

---

[1] Passed June 25, 1781, Chapter 946.
[2] Passed June 21, 1781, Chapter 944.

[Section II.] (Section IV, P. L.) And be it further enacted by the authority aforesaid, That all moneys brought into the treasury of each county in pursuance of this act shall be paid into the hands of the treasurer of the state by the treasurers of the several counties and remain there, subject to the orders of the supreme executive council of this state, for the sole purpose of recruiting the Pennsylvania line in the army of the United States.

[Section III.] (Section V, P. L.) And be it further enacted by the authority aforesaid, That all recruits who may or shall be enlisted in pursuance of this act shall be enlisted for a term not less than eighteen months from the date of their respective enlistments.

[Section IV.] (Section VI, P. L.) And be it further enacted by the authority aforesaid, That the supreme executive council of this state be and hereby is authorized and empowered to take such measures as to them may seem most expedient and effectual for enlisting the recruits necessary to complete the line of this state as directed by this act and the act which this act is intended to alter and supply.

[Section V.] (Section VII, P. L.) And be it further enacted by the authority aforesaid, That the act, entitled "An act for recruiting the Pennsylvania line in the army of the United States," passed the twenty-fifth day of June, one thousand seven hundred and eighty-one, and which this act is intended to alter and supply, and every clause, matter and thing contained therein, except what is herein altered or supplied shall be and continue in force and effect.

(Section VIII, P. L.) And whereas, it is absolutely necessary that some method be speedily taken more effectually to prevent desertion, Therefore,

[Section VII.] (Section IX, P. L.) Be it enacted by the authority aforesaid, That any person who shall, according to an act to discourage desertion, passed the twentieth day of February, one thousand seven hundred and seventy-seven, apprehend and deliver to the sheriff or jailor of the county a deserter from the line of this state, shall be exempted from his two next succeeding tours of militia duty, on producing the certificate of the sheriff or jailor of the county of his having delivered such deserter into his custody, to the lieutenant of the county, or such other officer or officers, whose duty it may be to superintend the appeals held on the calls of the militia when it would have been otherwise the turn of such person to have served.

Passed September 29, 1781.

CHAPTER CMLII.

AN ACT TO VEST THE TITLE OF A MESSUAGE AND LOT OF GROUND IN THE TOWN OF LISBURN IN JOHN RANKIN, ESQUIRE.

(Section I, P. L.) Whereas, John Rankin, esquire, of York county, hath presented a petition to this house, setting forth that a house and lot, in the town of Lisburn, in the county of Cumberland, was heretofore taken in execution as the estate of a certain Richard Carson, and in due form of law struck off and sold to James Rankin, and the consideration money by him paid to the sheriff; that the said Richard Carson held the possession of the said messuage and lot of ground, with the consent of the said James Rankin and afterwards paid and satisfied him for the money by him advanced to the sheriff; that the petitioner, with the knowledge and at the request of the said James Rankin, contracted verbally with the said Richard Carson for the premises, and afterwards paid him the full price agreed upon and obtained possession of the said premises. That soon after the petitioner, together with said James Rankin, went to Carlisle and employed a conveyancer to procure a sheriff's deed for the premises to the said John Rankin. That afterwards the said James Rankin joined the enemy at Philadelphia, and was thereupon attainted of high treason, previous to which the conveyancer aforesaid, had procured a sheriff's deed for the premises in the name of James Rankin, duly acknowledged in court and recorded, and thereupon prayed the house would permit him to bring in a bill to vest the title of the premises in the petitioner:

[Section I.] (Section II, P. L.) Be it therefore enacted and it is hereby enacted by the Representatives of the Freemen of the Commonwealth of Pennsylvania in General Assembly met, and by the authority of the same, That the lot of ground aforesaid, with the buildings and appurtenances, situate, lying and being in the town of Lisburn, in the county of Cumberland, containing, in front, on a street in the general plan of the said town, called Main street, one hundred and thirteen feet, and in depth on the westward side, three hundred and seventy-five feet to Yellow Breeches creek, and in depth on the eastward side two hundred and forty feet, be, and the same is hereby vested in the said John Rankin, his heirs and assigns, to be held by him, the said John Rankin, his heirs and assigns forever, subject to the same rents and conditions that the said Richard Carson formerly held the same, any law, custom or usage to the contrary thereof in anywise notwithstanding.

Passed September 29, 1781. Recorded L. B. No. 1, p. 458, etc.

CHAPTER CMLIII.

AN ACT TO GIVE RELIEF TO CERTAIN PERSONS TAKING REFUGE IN THIS STATE WITH RESPECT TO THEIR SLAVES.

(Section I, P. L.) Whereas many virtuous citizens of America and inhabitants of states that have been invaded are obliged, by the power of the enemy, to take refuge in this state:

And whereas, it is just and necessary that the property of such persons should be protected:

[Section I.] Be it therefore enacted and it is hereby enacted by the Representatives of the Freemen of the Commonwealth of Pennsylvania in General Assembly met, and by the authority of the same, That all and every person and persons, under the above description, now residing in this state, or who hereafter may be in like circumstances, shall retain, possess and hold their slaves, anything in the act for the gradual abolition of slavery passed the first day of March, one thousand seven hundred and eighty, to the contrary notwithstanding.

(Section III, P. L.) Provided always, That the owner or owners of such slaves, his or their lawful attorney, shall, in six months from the passing of this act, or in six months after their arrival in this state, as the case may be, register said slaves in manner and form directed in the fifth section of the act above mentioned for the gradual abolition of slavery. And be it further provided, That such slaves shall not be aliened or sold to any inhabitant nor retained in this state as slaves longer than six months after the conclusion of the present war with Great Britain.

[Section II.] (Section IV, P. L.) And be it also provided and declared, That nothing herein contained shall be deemed, construed or taken to enslave any person or persons who have been emancipated or freed under or by virtue of the act aforesaid.

Passed October 1, 1781. Recorded L. B. No. 1, p. 459, etc.

CHAPTER CMLIV.

AN ACT TO DISSOLVE THE MARRIAGE OF JACOB BILLMEYER WITH HIS WIFE MARY BILLMEYER LATE MARY EICHELBERGER.

(Section I, P. L.) Whereas, Jacob Billmeyer, of the town of York, in the state of Pennsylvania, conveyancer, hath presented a petition to this house, setting forth that his wife Mary, about eight years since, eloped from his bed and board, without any reasonable cause ,and ever since continued to absent herself from his bed and board; and that in the month of February, in the year of our Lord one thousand seven hundred and seventy-eight, she, the said Mary, became acquainted with a certain William Cole, with whom she intermarried and cohabited, and afterwards eloped out of this state, and hath borne a child or children to the said William Cole; and praying leave to bring in a bill for the dissolution of said marriage after due notice given:

(Section II, P. L.) And whereas, it appears to this house that the facts alleged in the said petition are true:

And whereas, this house did, by their resolve of the tenth day of March, in the year of our Lord one thousand seven hundred and eighty-one, give permission to the said Jacob Billmeyer to bring in a bill to divorce him from his said wife Mary, agreeable to the prayer of his said petition, he, the said Jacob Billmeyer, giving previous notice of his design and this permission, at least two months in the public newspaper printed in the city of Philadelphia, entitled "The Pennsylvania Gazette and Weekly Advertiser:"

And whereas, it hath been sufficiently proved to this house that the said notice hath been given:

Therefore:

[Section I.] (Section III, P. L.) Be it enacted and it is hereby enacted by the Representatives of the Freemen of the Commonwealth of Pennsylvania in General Assembly met, and by the authority of the same, That the marriage of the said Jacob Billmeyer with the said Mary be and the same is hereby declared to be dissolved and annulled to all intents, constructions and purposes whatsoever. And the said Jacob Billmeyer and the said Mary shall be, and they are, hereby henceforth, respectively declared to be separated, set free and totally discharged from their matrimonial contract and from all duties and obligations to each other as husband and wife, as fully, effectually and absolutely, to all intents and purposes, as if they had never been joined in matrimony or by any other contract whatsoever, any law, usage or custom to the contrary thereof in anywise notwithstanding.

Passed October 1, 1781. Recorded L. B. No. 1, p. 460, etc.

CHAPTER CMLV.

A SUPPLEMENT TO THE ACT ENTITLED "AN ACT TO AMEND THE ACT ENTITLED 'AN ACT FOR THE MORE EFFECTUAL SUPPLY AND HONORABLE REWARD OF THE PENNSYLVANIA TROOPS, IN THE SERVICE OF THE UNITED STATES OF AMERICA,'" AND THE ACT ENTITLED "AN ACT TO SETTLE AND ADJUST THE ACCOUNTS OF THE TROOPS OF THIS STATE, IN THE SERVICE OF THE UNITED STATES, AND FOR OTHER PURPOSES THEREIN MENTIONED."[1]

(Section I, P. L.) Whereas the United States, in Congress assembled, by their act of the thirteenth day of June, in the year of our Lord one thousand seven hundred and eighty-one, resolved and recommended to the several states in the words following. That is to say: "That it be and hereby is recommended to the several states to which the officers of the hospital and medical department now in service, respectively, belong, or of which they are or were inhabitants, to settle the accounts of the said officers for depreciation, on the principles established by the resolution of Congress of the tenth day of April, one thousand seven hundred and eighty, and to make provision for paying the balances that may be found due in the same manner with other officers of the line:"

Therefore, in compliance with the act of Congress aforesaid:

[Section I.] (Section II, P. L.) Be it enacted and it is hereby enacted by the Representatives of the Freemen of the Commonwealth of Pennsylvania in General Assembly met, and by the authority of the same, That the officers of the hospital and medical department now in the service of the United States, and who are citizens of this state, shall be and they are hereby entitled to all the emoluments and benefits, to all intents and purposes, which the military commissioned officers, chaplains and regimental surgeons of the Pennsylvania line are entitled to under the act, entitled "An act to settle and adjust the accounts of the troops of this state, in the service of the United States, and for other purposes therein mentioned,"[2] passed the eighteenth day of December, one thousand seven hundred and

---
[1] Passed April 10, 1781, Chapter 941.
[2] Passed December 18, 1780; Chapter 920.

eighty, and the act, entitled "An act to amend the act, entitled "An act for the more effectual supply and honorable reward of the Pennsylvania troops, in the service of the United States of America,"[1] passed the tenth day of April, one thousand seven hundred and eighty-one, and shall be entitled to half pay during life, they, the said officers of the hospital and medical department, now in the service of the United States, and who are or were inhabitants of this state, continuing in service during the present war with Great Britain.

(Section III, P. L.) Provided always, That every such officer of the hospital and medical department shall be liable to be called into actual service by the supreme executive council of this state, at any time thereafter, and if any of the aforesaid officers on half pay shall neglect or refuse to go and continue in said service, when called to it as aforesaid, such half pay shall, from the time of such neglect or refusal, cease and determine, anything to the contrary in any law of this state notwithstanding.

(Section IV, P. L.) And whereas, it may be difficult for the auditors appointed, or to be appointed, by the supreme executive council to ascertain the rights of the officers of the hospital and medical department who shall claim the benefits and emoluments granted by this act:

Therefore:

[Section II.] Be it enacted by the authority aforesaid, That the supreme executive council of this state shall and they are hereby authorized and empowered to hear and determine upon the respective claims of every person who may apply for the benefits and emoluments granted by this act, and to dismiss every such claim or issue an order (as the case may require), directing the auditors to settle and adjust the account or accounts of the said officer or officers without delay; and thereupon, and not otherwise, the said auditors shall proceed in the same manner as is directed respecting the military commissioned officers, chaplains, and regimental surgeons of the Pennsylvania line by the acts to which this is a supplement.

(Section VI, P. L.) And whereas, some doubts have arisen

---

[1] Ante.

whether officers and soldiers who have fallen in battle, or were taken by the enemy and were exchanged, or died in captivity before the passing of the act, entitled "An act to settle and adjust the accounts of the troops of this state in the service of the United States, and for other purposes therein mentioned,"[1] or their widows and children were entitled to the benefits of the said act.

For remedy whereof:

[Section III.] Be it therefore enacted by the authority aforesaid, That all officers and privates of this state, whether of the state regiments, flying camp or militia, made prisoners in the actual service of this or any of the United States, whensoever exchanged, or their legal representatives shall be and hereby are entitled to receive the full depreciation of their pay to the time of such exchange. And the auditors appointed, or who hereafter may be appointed, by the supreme executive council to settle the depreciation accounts are hereby authorized and required to proceed and settle their accounts in the manner directed for the adjusting and settling the accounts of the troops of this state now in service.

[Section IV.] (Section VIII, P. L.) And be it further enacted by the authority aforesaid, That the widows and children of the officers of the said regiments, known by the name of the state regiments of this state or of the flying camp of this state, who have fallen in battle or died in captivity, shall be and are hereby entitled to receive the half pay of such officers from and since the time of their death, for and during the time, in the manner and under the restrictions mentioned in the fourth, fifth, seventeenth and eighteenth sections of the act, entitled "An act for the more effectual supply and honorable reward of the Pennsylvania troops in the army of the United States of America,"[2] passed the first day of March, one thousand seven hundred and eighty, and all arrearages of pay due to said officers and depreciation on their pay accounts to be adjusted and settled as directed in the foregoing clause.

Passed October 1, 1781. Recorded L. B. No. 1, p. 460, etc. See the Act of Assembly passed March 27, 1790, Chapter 1493.

---

[1] Ante.
[2] Passed March 1, 1780, Chapter 880.

CHAPTER CMLVI.

AN ACT [1] FOR THE DEFENSE OF THE FRONTIERS OF THIS STATE AND FOR OTHER PURPOSES THEREIN MENTIONED.

(Section I, P. L.) Whereas, the repeated incursions and depredations of the savage allies of the King of Great Britain, in conjunction with his forces, have been carried on for some years past on the frontiers of this state, to the great injury of that part of Northampton county which lies beyond the mountains, and also the counties of Bedford, Northumberland, Westmoreland and Washington, and the district or township of Armagh, in Cumberland county:

(Section II, P. L.) For remedy whereof:

[Section I.] Be it enacted and it is hereby enacted by the Representatives of the Freemen of the Commonwealth of Pennsylvania in General Assembly met, and by the authority of the same, That one company in addition to the four companies already ordered to be raised by a resolve of the house of assembly of the twenty-third day of December, one thousand seven hundred and eighty, be immediately raised, completed and equipped, to serve during the present war, or until discharged, each company to consist of one captain, one lieutenant, one ensign, four sergeants, four corporals, one drummer, one fifer and sixty privates, which five companies are to be completed, paid, clothed, victualed and otherwise provided for and rewarded with lands at the end of the war as the other troops in the service of the United States and belonging to this state are and shall be under the direction of the supreme executive council of this state for the time being, for the defense of the said frontiers.

[Section II.] (Section III, P. L.) And be it further enacted by the authority aforesaid, That the supreme executive council shall appoint and commission the additional officers of said

---

[1] The original roll of this act is missing; and therefore it has been compared with the copy in the Act Books.

corps, to be taken from those of the Pennsylvania line who are now, or hereafter may be on half pay; and shall pay to the officers, or any other person enlisting any able-bodied recruit, the sum of thirty shillings as soon as he shall be attested and have passed muster; and shall, over and above the clothing, rations and other emoluments mentioned in the foregoing clause to be given to each soldier, as therein directed, pay the sum of six pounds bounty to each recruit, one-third part thereof at the time of enlistment, and the remaining two-thirds when they shall severally pass muster as aforesaid.

(Section IV, P. L.) And whereas, such incursions and depredations of the enemy are often so sudden and violent as to require the immediate exertion of the inhabitants of the said counties and frontiers, in order to put a stop to the enemy's penetrating into the said counties and district, and also to pursue, overtake, waylay and discover and otherwise annoy them in their retreat:

[Section III.] Be it therefore further enacted by the authority aforesaid, That as often as such incursions and depredations shall happen to be made, or as often as there shall be sufficient reason to apprehend such shall be the design of the enemy, that then and in such case, and in such case only, such of the inhabitants as will from time to time go in pursuit of the enemy, in order to overtake and waylay them, or to discover their tracks and approaches, shall be entitled to militia pay and rations of provisions while it shall appear they were necessarily employed in such service. Provided always, That before such pay is ordered to be made, the lieutenant of the respective county, on the oath or affirmation of one or more of the party so serving, shall certify the time and nature of the service in which he or they have been so employed and the necessity of a party or parties going on such service. And the supreme executive council are hereby authorized and empowered to draw on the treasury of this state from time to time for such sum or sums as shall be necessary for the purposes aforesaid.

[Section IV.] (Section V, P. L.) And be it further enacted by the authority aforesaid, That the forces raised, or to be raised, under and by virtue of this act, shall be subject to and bound by the same rules and regulations as the federal army of the United States.

[Section V.] (Section VI, P. L.) And be it further enacted by the authority aforesaid, That the supreme executive council be empowered, and they are hereby empowered, to order the whole or part of the said troops on any expedition which they may deem necessary against the savages or other enemies bordering on the frontiers of this state.

(Section VII, P. L.) And whereas, by such incursions and depredations, a great part of the inhabitants of the said frontiers have been driven from their habitations and otherwise much distressed and thereby rendered unable to pay the public dues:

[Section VI.] Be it therefore enacted by the authority aforesaid, That it shall and may be lawful to and for the commissioners of the said counties, respectively, or any two of them, and they are hereby enjoined and required, in all cases wherein the inhabitants have been obliged by the enemy to abandon their habitations, so that no proper return can be obtained of their property as pointed out by law, to obtain such [account] by the books or rolls of the last valuation of property, or by such other ways and means as to them shall seem just and satisfactory, and shall thereupon proceed to value and levy the same, in just proportion to the other parts of the counties, respectively, as nearly as may be.

[Section VII.] (Section VIII, P. L.) And be it further enacted by the authority aforesaid, That the said commissioners, or any two of them, are hereby authorized and required to exonerate and discharge such of the taxable inhabitants as shall make sufficient proofs or for and in behalf of whom satisfactory evidence shall appear to the said commissioners, respectively, of their having been driven off and dispossessed of their settlements or otherwise distressed by means of the enemy, from the payment of all or such part as to them shall seem just and reasonable, as well of the taxes already laid and assessed on the said inhabitants, since the first day of September, one thousand seven hundred and eighty, as the taxes which may be laid as aforesaid during the continuance of the present distressed state of the counties aforesaid.

(Section IX, P. L.) And whereas a considerable number of the said inhabitants have, with great courage and fortitude, stood their ground, on the verge of the frontiers, at the hazard of their lives, and thereby formed in some measure a barrier to the flying inhabitants and eventually prevented the enemy from penetrating into the interior parts of the state:

[Section VIII.] Be it therefore enacted by the authority aforesaid, That for the greater encouragement of such as have stood, and will hereafter so stay on their plantations, at the verge of the frontiers, at the hazard of their lives, that it shall and may be lawful for the said commissioners, in like manner as aforesaid, to exonerate and discharge from the payment of taxes, either in whole or in part, as shall seem to them just and reasonable, all such as have so stood and will hereafter in like manner stand in defense of the frontiers.

[Section IX.] (Section X, P. L.) And be it further enacted by the authority aforesaid, That the said commissioners, or any two of them, shall transmit without delay to the general assembly a list of the names of the persons so exonerated, stating the amount of the sum or sums so remitted, that the deficiencies which may arise in raising the quotas of the said counties may be made good and provided for in levying and raising the other taxes of the state.

Passed December 22, 1781. See the Act of Assembly passed January 27, 1797, Chapter 1913.

CHAPTER CMLVII.

AN ACT FOR THE SUPPORT OF GOVERNMENT, AND THE ADMINISTRATION OF JUSTICE.

(Section I, P. L.) Whereas, those who dedicate their time and abilities to the service of the public ought to receive a reasonable compensation:

[Section I.] (Section II, P. L.) Be it therefore enacted and it is hereby enacted by the Representatives of the Freemen of the Commonwealth of Pennsylvania in General Assembly met, and by the authority of the same, That the following annual salaries shall be allowed to the several officers of the state, hereinafter mentioned, to commence on the twenty-second day of June last past, and to continue for the space of one year, and until the same shall be afterwards altered by the legislature; to be paid to them severally on their receipts, or on their drafts, quarterly, on the treasurer of the state. That is to say:

To the president of the supreme executive council or commander-in-chief of the forces of this state, for the time being, the sum of twelve hundred and fifty pounds.

The vice-president, the sum of five hundred pounds.

The chief justice, the sum of nine hundred pounds.

The second justice of the supreme court, the sum of four hundred pounds.

The third and fourth justices of the supreme court, the sum of three hundred pounds each.

The attorney-general, the sum of one hundred and fifty pounds.

The secretary of the supreme executive council, being register of forfeited estates, including the expense of clerks, the sum of five hundred pounds. Provided always, That all fees appertaining to the office of said secretary of the supreme executive council shall be paid quarterly by the secretary into the hands of the state treasurer for the use of the state.

[Section II.] (Section III, P. L.) And be it further enacted by the authority aforesaid, That the following wages shall be allowed to and paid to the persons hereinafter mentioned, to wit:

To the delegates or deputies of this commonwealth in the Congress of the United States of America, for every day's attendance in the public service, each the sum of one pound ten shillings.

The members of the supreme executive council, other than the president and vice-president for every day's attendance, each the sum of seventeen shillings and six pence.

The speaker of the house of assembly, for each day's attendance, the sum of one pound two shillings and six pence.

The other members of the house of assembly, for every day's attendance, each the sum of fifteen shillings.

The clerks of the house of assembly, for every day's attendance, the sum of one pound.

The sergeant-at-arms, for every day's attendance, the sum of ten shillings.

The door-keeper of the council and the door-keeper of the house of assembly, each the sum of ten shillings for every day's attendance.

[Section III.] (Section IV, P. L.) And be it further enacted by the authority aforesaid, That every delegate in Congress and member of council shall be further allowed, towards his traveling charges, after the rate of six pence per mile, once in every three months, in coming in and going from the places where the Congress and council shall respectively sit, provided he shall so often actually visit his family; and that every member of assembly shall be further allowed, towards his traveling charges, after the same rate, once in each sitting of the house; which said wages and traveling expenses shall be paid by the treasurer of this state to the delegates representing this state in Congress, and to the members of the council and their door-keeper, on the drafts of the president or vice-president in council; and to the speaker and other members of assembly, to the clerk of the assembly, sergeant-at-arms and door-keeper, on the drafts of the speaker of the house, signed in assembly.

[Section IV.] (Section V, P. L.) And be it further enacted by the authority aforesaid, That so much of any act of assembly heretofore made as declares what salaries shall be paid to the several officers of government and what wages shall be allowed to the speaker and other members of assembly, to the delegates representing this state in Congress, to the members of council and others herein specially mentioned shall be and is hereby repealed.

Passed December 27, 1781. Recorded L. B. No. 1, p. 264. See the Acts of Assembly passed February 25, 1783, Chapter 1005. The Act in the text was repealed by Acts of Assembly passed March 25, 1785, Chapter 1142; September 17, 1785, Chapter 1185.

CHAPTER CMLVIII.

A SUPPLEMENT [1] TO THE ACT ENTITLED "AN ACT TO PREVENT THE EXPORTATION OF BREAD AND FLOUR NOT MERCHANTABLE, AND FOR REPEALING, AT A CERTAIN TIME, ALL THE LAWS HERETOFORE MADE FOR THAT PURPOSE. [1]

(Section I, P. L.) Whereas it has been found, by experience, that sundry amendments and alterations are necessary in the act, entitled "An act to prevent the exportation of bread and flour not merchantable, and for repealing, at a certain time, all the laws heretofore made for that purpose." [2]

[Section I. (Section II, P. L.) Be it therefore enacted and it is hereby enacted by the Representatives of the Freemen of the Commonwealth of Pennsylvania in General Assembly met, and by the authority of the same, That when any flour shall be offered for sale which shall, on trial (agreeable to the form mentioned and directed in the aforesaid act), be found packed in casks made of unseasoned materials, every person so offering the same for sale shall be adjudged to pay into the hands of the inspector, for each and every such cask so found, the sum of two shillings; and the owner of such flour shall have his remedy against the miller or cooper who has furnished the cask, for the damages which he may sustain.

(Section III, P. L.) And whereas the penalty of five shillings per day on bolters, millers and bakers, for not entering their respective brands with the clerk of the quarter sessions in the counties where they reside, is considered as exorbitant and severe:

[Section II.] Be it therefore enacted by the authority aforesaid, That the said penalty shall be thirty shillings for every such neglect, to be recovered as a debt under forty shillings, by any person that will sue for the same, on proof made that the said bolter, miller or baker has exercised his [said] employ-

---

[1] The original roll of this act is missing; and therefore it has been compared with the copy in the Act Books.
[2] Passed April 5, 1781, Chapter 936.

ment in manufacturing flour or bread for exportation, for one month, without having made such entry.

(Section IV, P. L.) And whereas the forfeiture of the casks and their contents, in case of deficiency of weight, is considered as too severe, since accidental deficiencies may happen, where no fraud was intended:

[Section III.] Be it therefore enacted by the authority aforesaid, That in all cases where casks of flour are found deficient in weight upon trial and examination, agreeable to the direction of the act aforesaid, the person so offering such deficient cask or casks shall forfeit, for every pound so wanting in weight, the sum of nine pence to be paid into the hands of said inspector.

(Section V, P. L.) And whereas, it has been found impracticable to brand all the casks of flour and bread offered for exportation with the arms of this state, agreeable to the directions contained in said act:

[Section IV.] Be it enacted by the authority aforesaid, That the said inspector shall stamp the said casks and the plugs (put into the holes made by the said inspector) with the letters S. P. And all casks with counterfeited stamps, as well as casks, the contents of which may have been changed after inspection, shall be liable to seizure and forfeiture, if offered for transportation out of this state.

(Section VI, P. L.) And whereas, doubts have arisen whether middlings can be exported out of this state under the aforesaid law:

[Section V.] Be it therefore enacted by the authority aforesaid, That it shall and may be lawful to export middlings; but every cask of middlings exported or offered for exportation shall, besides and exclusive of the miller's common brands, be branded by the miller with the word MIDDLINGS at length, or be liable to seizure and forfeiture.

[Section VI.] (Section VII, P. L.) And be it further enacted by the authority aforesaid, That all fines and penalties herein mentioned shall be recovered and applied in manner and form as is directed by this act, and the act to which this is a supplement.

[Section VII.] (Section VIII, P. L.) And be it further enacted by the authority aforesaid, That so much of the fifth section of the above-recited act as imposes a fine of five shillings per day on bolters and millers for the neglect therein mentioned, and the clauses of forfeiture mentioned in the sixth section, and that part of the eleventh section which enjoins the branding casks with the arms of the state shall be and they hereby are altered and repealed.

Passed December 28, 1781. See the note to the Act of Assembly passed April 5, 1781, Chapter 934.

CHAPTER CMLIX.

AN ACT FOR THE BETTER REPAIRING AND AMENDING THE BANKS, DAMS, DITCHES, SLUICES AND FLOODGATES ON STATE-ISLAND.

(Section I, P. L.) Whereas numbers of the owners of the lands and meadows on the State island (late the Province island) by their petition have prayed that a law may be passed to compel the several owners of the said island to contribute to the support and repairs of the banks, dams, ditches, sluices and floodgates thereon, suggesting that the same are much out of repair for want of some provision being made by a law for this purpose, which being right and reasonable:

[Section I.] (Section II, P. L.) Be it therefore enacted and it is hereby enacted by the Representatives of the Freemen of the Commonwealth of Pennsylvania in General Assembly met, and by the authority of the same, That William Bingham, Elijah Weed, Charles Miller, William Turnbull and John Taylor, or any three of them, be and they are hereby constituted, authorized and appointed to be managers of the said island, and John Wilcocks, treasurer, to be, remain and continue until the second Monday in January next; and that on the said second Monday in January next, and on the second Monday of January in every year forever, the owners of the said island, or as many of them as shall think fit to attend, by themselves or their representatives, shall meet together at the Coffee House, in the city of Philadelphia, or at such other convenient place as shall hereafter be appointed by the managers for the time being, or a majority of them, and then and there elect, by ballot, five managers and a treasurer for the ensuing year.

[Section II.] (Section III, P. L.) And be it enacted by the authority aforesaid, That the said managers, or any three of them, shall, from time to time, do, or cause to be done, all and every the repairs to the said banks, dams, ditches, sluices and floodgates, and open and make new ones where it may be needful: Provided always, That no new works, banks, dams, ditches, sluices or floodgates be made by the said managers, or any of them, without the approbation of at least three of the said managers, who shall be authorized to undertake such new work only in case it shall be their opinion that the same will be for the common benefit and advantage of the owners of the said meadows; and that the said managers be authorized and empowered to assess on all and every the owners of the meadows on the said island, which are liable to be overflown for want of such necessary work or repairs, in proportion to the quantity of such meadows which respectively belong to each owner, such sum or sums of money as the said managers, or a majority of them, shall from time to time deem necessary for the benefit and security of the same.

[Section III.] (Section IV, P. L.) And be it further enacted by the authority aforesaid, That if any owner or owners of any such meadows shall neglect or refuse, by the space of ten days after notice shall be given to him or them of such money or moneys being so assessed, for his proportion of the sum at any time to be raised to pay his or their said proportion of the same moneys to the treasurer for the time being, it shall and may be lawful for the said treasurer, by order of the said managers, or a majority of them, either to levy distress on the goods and effects of the said several owners, or their tenants, found on the said island, and to proceed therein in like manner as in the case distresses for rents; or to sue, commence and prosecute an action or actions of debt for the same in any court in which debts to the like amount are cognizable, and to recover the same, with costs, in his name as treasurer aforesaid.

[Section IV.] (Section V, P. L.) And be it further enacted by the authority aforesaid, That the style of the said managers shall be "The managers of State island," and the style of the said treasurer shall be "The treasurer of State island," and that by such style and name they shall be called and known in all judicial proceedings. And also that the said managers shall be empowered to require and take such security from the said treasurer as to them, or a majority of them, shall seem needful for the faithful discharge of his trust; and that the said treasurer shall pay the moneys to the order of the said managers whilst he continues in office, and, as soon as a successor shall be chosen, shall pay over the balance remaining in his hands to such successor; and that if he neglect so to do by the space of five days after he shall be thereunto required by the managers, or a majority of them, he shall forfeit the sum of one hundred pounds, to be recovered by his successor, to the use of the said owners, over and besides the balance so remaining due.

Passed March 18, 1782. Recorded L. B. No. 1, p. 467, etc. See the note to the Act of Assembly passed February 28, 1780, Chapter 878.

CHAPTER CMLX.

AN ACT FOR PREVENTING AND PUNISHING THE COUNTERFEITING OF THE COMMON SEAL, BANK BILLS AND BANK NOTES OF THE PRESIDENT, DIRECTORS AND COMPANY OF THE BANK OF NORTH AMERICA AND FOR OTHER PURPOSES THEREIN MENTIONED.

(Section I, P. L.) Whereas it is necessary to take effectual measures for preventing and punishing frauds and cheats which may be put upon the president, directors and company of the bank of North America by altering, forging or counterfeiting the common seal and the bank bills and bank notes of the said president, directors and company:

[Section I.] (Section II, P. L.) Be it therefore enacted and it is hereby enacted by the Representatives of the Freemen of the Commonwealth of Pennsylvania in General Assembly met, and by the authority of the same, That if any person or persons shall forge, counterfeit or alter the common seal of the said president, directors and company, or any bank bill or bank note, made or given out, or to be made or given out for the payment of any sum of money by or for the said president, directors and company, or shall tender in payment, utter, vend, exchange or barter any such forged, counterfeit or altered bill or note, or shall demand to have the same exchanged for ready money by the said president, directors and company or any other person or persons (knowing such bill or note so tendered, uttered, vended, exchange or bartered, or demanded to be [so] exchanged, to be forged, counterfeited or altered), with intent to defraud the said president, directors and company, or any other person or persons, bodies politic or corporate, then every such person or persons so offending, and being thereof convicted in due form of law, shall be deemed guilty of felony, and shall suffer death as a felon, without benefit of clergy.

[Section II.] (Section III, P. L.) And be it further enacted by the authority aforesaid, That if any president, director or any officer or servant of the said president, directors and company, being intrusted with any such bill or note, or any bond, deed, money or other effects, belonging to the said president, directors and company, or having any such bill or note, or any bond, deed, money or other effects, lodged or deposited with the said president, directors and company, or with such officer or servant as an officer or servant of the said president, directors and company, shall secrete, embezzle, or run away with any such bill, note, bond, deed, money or other effects, or any part of them, every [president, director,] officer or servant so offending and being thereof convicted in due form of law, shall be deemed guilty of felony, and shall suffer death as a felon, without benefit of clergy.

Passed March 18, 1782. Recorded L. B. No. 1, p. 468, etc. The Act in the text was repealed by the Act of Assembly passed September 13, 1785, Chapter 1178.

CHAPTER CMLXI.

AN ACT TO RAISE EFFECTIVE SUPPLIES FOR THE YEAR ONE THOUSAND SEVEN HUNDRED AND EIGHTY-TWO.

(Section I, P. L.) Whereas the United States of America in Congress assembled have, by their resolution of the thirtieth of October, demanded of the several states in union such effective supplies as may enable them to carry on the war with vigor and effect, and improve our late successes into a full establishment of independence and peace:

And whereas it is the desire of the representatives of the freemen of this state to comply with the said resolutions:

[Section I.] (Section II, P. L.) Therefore, be it enacted and it is hereby enacted by the Representatives of the Freemen of the Commonwealth of Pennsylvania in General Assembly met, and by the authority of the same, That the sum of four hundred and twenty thousand two hundred and ninety-seven pounds and fifteen shillings, being the quota required of this state, be raised, levied, collected and paid for the year one thousand seven hundred and eighty-two, in four equal payments, the first payment to be made on the first day of July next ensuing and the second at the expiration of three months thereafter, and so on at the end of every three months thereafter until the whole sum is paid. And the same shall be levied, assessed and raised in the city of Philadelphia and the several counties of this state according to the method and proportions following: That is to say:

For the city and county of Philadelphia, the sum of one hundred and thirty-nine thousand two hundred and forty-five pounds and four shillings.

For the county of Bucks, the sum of twenty-seven thousand five hundred and forty-one pounds and nine shillings.

For the county of Chester, the sum of forty-four thousand two hundred and ten pounds and sixteen shillings.

For the county of Lancaster, the sum of fifty-nine thousand eight hundred and thirty-four pounds and ten shillings.

For the county of York, the sum of thirty-three thousand three hundred and thirty-five pounds and fourteen shillings.

For the county of Berks the sum of thirty thousand and ninety-three pounds and thirteen shillings.

For the county of Cumberland the sum of thirty-one thousand three hundred and thirty-two pounds and fifteen shillings.

For the county of Northampton the sum of seventeen thousand three hundred and twenty-four pounds and two shillings.

For the county of Bedford, the sum of nine thousand four hundred and ninety-seven pounds and eight shillings.

For the county of Northumberland the sum of eleven thousand seven hundred and thirty-two pounds and two shillings.

For the county of Westmoreland, the sum of eight thousand and seventy-five pounds and one shilling.

And for the county of Washington, the sum of eight thousand and seventy-five pounds and one shilling.

[Section II.] (Section III, P. L.) And be it further enacted by the authority aforesaid, That the commissioners of the city and county of Philadelphia, and of every county of this state, or any two of them, shall meet together on or before Monday, the fifteenth day of April, next, at their usual place of meeting in the city and in their several counties, and then and there issue their warrants, under their hands and seals, to the township, ward or district assessors of each township, ward or district within their respective counties, requiring them, the said assessors, to notify the freemen of their several townships, wards or districts, by public advertisement, to meet and choose two freeholders of their proper district, to assist the said assessor in laying and assessing the taxes required within the present year; and also requiring the said assessors to demand of all and every taxable inhabitant, residing within their respective townships, wards or districts a full and true account of all their estate, real and personal, within this state, made taxable by this act, and in what county situate, of which the said assessors shall make fair and true returns in writing to the said commissioners on a certain day to be by the said commissioners appointed; and of the names and surnames of the said two assisting freeholders so chosen by each township, ward or district; and of all and every the taxable inhabitants and single freemen within their respective townships, wards or districts, together with their trades, professions or occupations, and offices and posts of profit. And if any person or persons shall neglect or refuse to give a return of their taxable property, when required as aforesaid, every such person or persons so neglecting or refusing shall, for every such offense, forfeit and pay a sum equal to the tax at which such person or persons shall be rated by this act, to be levied and collected by the collector of the proper township, by virtue of a special warrant which the commissioners, or any two of them, are hereby authorized and required to grant, and the same shall be paid into the treasury of this commonwealth.

(Section IV, P. L.) And in order that the taxes hereby directed to be imposed may be truly laid and levied, and for the better detecting of frauds and concealments of taxable property:

[Section III.] Be it enacted by the authority aforesaid, That it shall and may be lawful to and for the said assessors and commissioners, or any of them, or any other person authorized by the board of commissioners, and they are hereby enjoined and required to use their best endeavors to inform themselves of all taxable property concealed or refused to be returned; and for that purpose they may search all public records within their respective counties, or in the city of Philadelphia, as the case may require; and all officers having care or charge of such records are hereby enjoined and required to be aiding and assisting in such searches, and to grant to every such assessor or commissioner, or any other person authorized by the board of commissioners, free access, at all proper times, to the said public records, for the above purpose without fee or reward.

[Section IV.] (Section V, P. L.) And be it further enacted by the authority aforesaid, That if any person shall neglect or refuse to make return of all and every tract or parcel of land he or she shall possess within this state to the assessor of the place where such person shall dwell or reside, all such lands so omitted shall be liable and subject to be charged with all such taxes the next or any subsequent assessment, which the same lands ought to have been charged with had they been duly assessed as by this act is directed, together with the penalty hereinbefore mentioned for refusing or neglecting to make return of their taxable property when duly required. And if any such tract or parcel of land so returned shall be situate out of the city or county where such person and assessor shall dwell, then the commissioners of the city or such county, or some one of them, shall, as soon as conveniently may be, transmit a copy of such return to the commissioners of the county where the land shall lie.

[Section V.] (Section VI, P. L.) And be it further enacted by the authority aforesaid, That if any person shall wilfully conceal, in the returns which he or she shall make to township, district or ward assessor, any part of his or her personal property made taxable by this act, with intent to screen the same from taxation, the person so concealing shall pay fourfold taxes on all property so concealed; and the money arising thereupon, over and above the taxes which such property ought to have yielded, shall be paid to the supervisors of the highways of such township, district or ward, for and towards repairing the public roads and highways within the same; and that any of the inhabitants of such township, ward, district who shall be [a] competent witness in other cases, shall be a sufficient witness to prove such concealment.

[Section VI.] (Section VII, P. L.) And be it further enacted by the authority aforesaid, That when the commissioners of any county shall receive the return of the assessors, as before directed, they, or any two of them, shall forthwith proceed to quota the several townships, wards and districts in the city of Philadelphia, and the several counties of this state, in proportion to the quantity and quality of the property returned as aforesaid.

[Section VII.] (Section VIII, P. L.) And be it further enacted by the authority aforesaid, That the commissioners of the several counties within this state shall, within six days after quotaing the townships, wards or districts as aforesaid, furnish the assessor of each township, ward or district, with a true and fair transcript of the quota or sum of money charged upon and demanded from such township, ward or district to which such assessor doth belong. And they, the said commissioners, or any two of them, are hereby enjoined and required to appoint one or more assessors and assistant freeholders, as the case may require, in case of removal by death, disability, refusal or neglect to serve of the present assessors, or where the townships, wards or districts neglect to elect such assessor or assistant freeholders.

[Section VIII.] (Section IX, P. L.) And be it further enacted by the authority aforesaid, That the assessor of each township, ward or district, with the two assistant freeholders, of the proper township, ward or district, shall, immediately after the said assessor shall become possessed of the quota or sum of money charged as aforesaid by the commissioners, assess the same equally and impartially on all and every person and persons and on all the estates, real and personal within their respective townships, wards and districts, made taxable by this act and shall make return thereof to the said commissioners before the expiration of ten days.

[Section IX.] (Section X, P. L.) And be it enacted by the authority aforesaid, That the following enumerated articles shall be, and are hereby made taxable and no other, to wit: The time of servitude of all bound servants above the age of fourteen years; all negro and mulatto slaves above the age of twelve years; all horses, mares and horned cattle above three years old; sheep, plate, coaches, berlins, landaus, chariots, calashes, chaises, caravans, riding chairs and other carriages kept by any person for his or her own use, and for the purposes of traveling or pleasure; all lands held by deed, warrant, location or improvement; houses and lots of ground and ground-rents; all grist-mills, saw-mills, fulling-mills, slitting and rolling-mills, hemp-mills, oil-mills, snuff-mills and paper-mills; all forges, furnaces, bloomeries, distilleries, sugar-houses, malt-houses, breweries, tan-yards and ferries, wares and merchandise; and all offices and posts of profit, and all professions, trades and occupations.

[Section X.] (Section XI, P. L.) And be it further enacted by the authority aforesaid, That all and every the enumerated articles aforesaid of real and personal property shall be valued at and for so much, bona fide, as they are worth or would sell for, and such a rate or rates shall be assessed and levied thereon as will amount to the sum of money quotaed upon the city of Philadelphia and the several counties of this state.

[Section XI.] (Section XII, P. L.) And be it further enacted by the authority aforesaid, That the sums of money raised by virtue of this act in the city and county of Philadelphia, and the several counties of this state, shall not be deemed or held as the exact proportion of the said city and counties, but the same shall hereafter be correctly and finally adjusted and ascertained by the legislature of this state, according to the returns of property to be laid, by virtue of this act, before the general assembly.

[Section XII.] (Section XIII, P. L.) And be it further enacted by the authority aforesaid, That every single freeman, who, at the time of assessing any tax imposed by this act, is or shall be of the age of twenty-one years or upwards, and has been out of his apprenticeship nine months, shall pay a sum not exceeding six pounds nor under three pounds. And that all offices and posts of profit, trades, occupations and professions (that of ministers of the gospel of all denominations and schoolmasters only excepted), shall be rated at the discretion of the township, ward or district assessors, and two assistant freeholders of the proper township, ward or district, having due regard to the profits arising from them.

[Section XIII.] (Section XIV, P. L.) And be it further enacted by the authority aforesaid, That it shall be lawful for the township assessors, when taking the said return, to demand security of any single freeman or sojourner within his township, ward or district, for the amount of the largest tax of freemen or sojourners in this act mentioned, and upon his or their refusing to enter sufficient security or paying the said tax, the said assessor is hereby authorized to take the body of the said freeman or sojourner before the nearest justice, who is hereby authorized to commit him or them to the common gaol of the county, there to remain for the space of one month, or until he enters such security or pays the tax.

(Section XV, P. L.) And for the better discovery of single freemen, inmates or sojourners intended by this act to be taxed:

[Section XIV.] Be it enacted by the authority aforesaid, That every householder in this state shall, upon demand of any assessor of his or her township, ward or district, give an account of the names and occupations of such persons as shall sojourn or lodge in their respective houses, under the penalty of thirty pounds, to be recovered and applied to and for the repairs of the public highways of the said township, ward or district as aforesaid.

(Section XVI, P. L.) And whereas divers owners of lands whereon improvements have been made, and of tenements, may not reside in the county, township, ward or district where such lands or tenements are situated, whereby it may be difficult to collect the taxes assessed on such real estate:

For remedy whereof:

[Section XV.] Be it enacted and it is hereby enacted by the authority aforesaid, That the tenant or tenants, or other person residing on or occupying such real estate, his, her and their goods and chattels, as well as the lands, goods and chattels of the owner or owners thereof, shall be liable to be distrained to satisfy the said taxes, or any of them. And in case the tenant or tenants, or other person or persons residing on or occupying such real estate, shall pay any tax laid thereon by virtue of this act, such tenant or tenants may retain the same out of the rent by him, her or them payable for such estate; or the said tenant or tenants, or other occupier or occupiers of such estate shall recover the same, with costs of suit and damages, of the owner of such estate by action of debt; if under five pounds in a summary way as small debts are recoverable; but if the same is above five pounds in any court of common pleas.

(Section XVII, P. L.) Provided always, That nothing in the foregoing section shall in any manner alter any contract made between any landlord and tenant, concerning the payment of taxes.

[Section XVI.] (Section XVIII, P. L.) And be it further enacted by the authority aforesaid, That every county commissioner and every township, ward and district assessor and assistant shall, respectively, before they enter on any of the duties required of them by this act, before some one justice of the peace for the proper county, make oath or affirmation as is hereinafter directed, to wit: If a county commissioner:

"I, A. B., do swear or affirm, that I will well and truly quota the several townships, wards and districts and cause the rates and sums of money imposed by the act, entitled 'An act for raising effective supplies for the year one thousand seven hundred and eighty-two,' to be duly and equally assessed and laid, according to the rules and directions mentioned in the said act, to the best of my skill and knowledge, so far as relates to the duty of a commissioner, and herein I will spare no person for favor or affection, or grieve any for hatred or ill-will."

If a township, ward or district assessor or assistant, the following oath or affirmation, to wit:

"I, A. B., do swear or affirm, that I will faithfully and impartially assess the quota of the township, ward or district of―――― imposed by virtue of the act, entitled 'An act to raise effective supplies for the year one thousand seven hundred and eighty-two,' on the several persons and taxable property therein contained, to the best of my skill and understanding; and that in performing the duties required of me by that act, I will spare no person for favor or affection or grieve any for hatred or ill-will."

[Section XVII.] (Section XIX, P. L.) And be it further enacted by the authority aforesaid, That the county commissioners or any two of them, shall appoint a fit person (who shall be a freeholder) for or in every township, ward or district, to be collector of the taxes to be raised by virtue of this act, and shall cause fair duplicates of the assessment of every township, ward or district, to be made one part whereof shall be kept by the said commissioners of the proper county, and the other part shall be transmitted to the collector of every district, with a warrant under the hands and seals of the commissioners, or any two of them, authorizing and requiring the said collector after the day of appeal shall be passed ten days, to levy the sums rated on all persons who shall not, upon demand, after the said appeal, forthwith satisfy the same, and to acquaint them of the day of appeal, which shall be appointed by the commissioners within twenty days after the said assessments are made, but where the collector cannot meet with the party of whom demand is to be made as aforesaid, he shall leave notice in writing with some of the family, at the place of the party's last abode of such demand, signifying also the day of appeal; at which day every of the collectors shall return their several duplicates.

[Section XVIII.] (Section XX, P. L.) And be it further enacted by the authority aforesaid, That if any assessor legally chosen, or any person appointed by the said commissioners to be an assessor or an assistant or collector shall not, within two days after notice in writing of such election or appointment, make known his intention to the commissioners of the county to serve or decline the office to which such person hath been or shall be so chosen or appointed, the said commissioners or any two of them, may consider such persons as having refused to serve in such office, and may proceed to fine such person, and appoint another in his stead, as if such person had actually refused to serve in such office.

[Section XIX.] (Section XXI, P. L.) And be it further enacted by the authority aforesaid, That the fine on any person refusing to serve as an assessor or assistant shall be the sum of ten pounds; and the fine on any person refusing to serve as collector of any district shall be the sum of fifteen pounds. And in case any assessor or assistant or collector, after taking upon him his office, shall neglect to perform his duty therein, any such delinquent shall be fined in the sum of thirty pounds; and if any person chosen to be an assessor, or an assistant or collector, or if any other person shall detain any warrant, duplicate or other writing, necessary to the assessing or levying the said tax, beyond the time when such person shall have declined, or be deemed to have declined any such office, and after demand thereof made by any of the said commissioners, or by any person authorized by them to demand the same, every such delinquent shall be fined for such offense the sum of twenty-five pounds. The said fines to be levied and recovered as other fines are or ought to be levied and recovered by virtue of this act.

[Section XX.] (Section XXII.) And be it further enacted by the authority aforesaid, That if any person or persons find him or themselves aggrieved with any of the said assessments, he or they may appeal to the commissioners of the proper county, on the particular days appointed for the district.

[Section XXI.] (Section XXIII, P. L.) And be it further enacted by the authority aforesaid, That the said commissioners are hereby required to meet on the said day of appeal, where the said assessors shall also attend, whereupon the said commissioners shall strictly examine the persons appealing upon their oath or affirmations or otherwise, concerning the cause of their appeal; and upon such examination, or proof of others, they are hereby empowered to diminish or add to the person's rate or assessment, as to them shall seem just and reasonable, with power to call before them such persons, and take notice of such estates as they find are omitted in the said assessment, in order to rectify it; and if the person so omitted refuse or neglect to appear and give an account of their taxable estate, they shall pay double the sum they should or ought to have been rated at by this act. And the said commissioners shall cause their clerks to draw fair duplicates of the assessments of the said respective districts, so rectified as aforesaid, and deliver them to the collectors of the several townships, wards or districts where they belong, within ten days after the appeal.

[Section XXII.] (Section XXIV, P. L.) And be it further enacted by the authority aforesaid, That if any person or persons so rated or assessed by virtue of this act, shall refuse or neglect to pay the sum or sums so assessed within twenty days after demand made as aforesaid, it shall be lawful for the said collectors, respectively, by virtue of the aforesaid warrant, to call to their assistance, if occasion be any constable or other person, and in case of resistance to break open, in the daytime, any house, trunk, box, chest, closet, cupboard or other things, where any such offender's goods and chattels or effects are supposed to be, and make distress and sale thereof, having previously caused the same to be inventoried, appraised and advertised in three or more of the most public places within such township, ward or district, and rendering the overplus, if any be, to the owner after reasonable charges deducted; but if no distress can be found by the collector, and the party refuses or neglects to show him goods or chattels of his own forthwith to satisfy the money then due, with reasonable charges, then the collector shall take the body of every such person, and bring him to the county gaol, and deliver him to the sheriff or keeper of the said gaol, who shall detain him in close custody without bail or mainprise until payment be made or he be otherwise discharged.

(Section XXV, P. L.) Provided always, That when effects cannot be found sufficient to answer the whole sum in arrear, with charges as aforesaid, then distress shall be made for so much as the effects extend to, and the party imprisoned only for the residue thereof, with incident charges; all which charges of distress, assistance and bringing to prison shall be adjusted and settled by any two or more of the commissioners when such occasion shall happen.

[Section XXIII.] (Section XXVI, P. L.) And be it further enacted by the authority aforesaid, That the collector of every district, ward or township shall pay unto the county treasurer the whole of the tax charged in his duplicate within thirty days after the day of appeal, unless he has been obliged to make distress for any part thereof, in which case he shall, as to the tax assessed on the parties distrained on, have twenty days more, after which the commissioners of the county shall fine such deficient collector at the rate of one penny half-penny in the pound upon all sums charged in his duplicate, which such collector shall not have paid to the said treasurer for every ten days he shall fail to make payment thereof as aforesaid; such fine to be recovered in manner aforesaid.

(Section XXVIII, P. L.) Provided the said commissioners give the said collector ten days' notice of such complaint being lodged by the treasurer, that the said collector may have an opportunity of making it appear that he hath done his duty faithfully in collecting and paying in the same or give sufficient reasons for the omission, in which case the commissioners, or any two of them, shall be authorized to remit the fine.

(Section XXVIII, P. L.) And, moreover, it shall be lawful for the commissioners of the proper county, or any two of them, and they are hereby required to meet and issue out their warrant under their hands and seals to the sheriff or coroner of the proper county, requiring him to take the body and seize and secure the estate, real and personal, belonging to such delinquent, or which shall come into the hands or possessions of his heirs, executors or administrators, wherever the same can be discovered or found in this state, and make return of his proceedings therein at such time and place as the commissioners shall appoint.

[Section XXIV.] (Section XXIX.) And be it further enacted by the authority aforesaid, That the said commissioners, who shall cause the said lands and estates to be seized and secured as aforesaid, shall be and are hereby empowered to appoint a time for a general meeting of the commissioners of such county, and to cause public notice to be given where such meeting shall be appointed, ten days at least before such general meeting; and the commissioners then present at such meeting, or the majority of them, in case the money detained by such delinquent be not then paid or satisfied, shall and are hereby empowered and required to issue forth their warrants or precepts to the sheriff or coroner of the proper county, empowering and requiring him to sell and dispose of all such estate as shall be, for the cause aforesaid, seized and secured, or such part thereof as will be sufficient to satisfy deficiencies aforesaid, and all charges, and to bring the money arising by such sale to the commissioners who granted such warrants, in order to satisfy and pay in to the respective county treasurers, for the time being, the sum or sums that shall be so unpaid or detained in the hands of the said collectors or other persons, their heirs, executors or administrators, respectively, with damages for what shall be [so] unpaid, returning the overplus, if any be, to the owner, after all necessary charges deducted; and when any sale of land, tenements or hereditaments shall be made by such sheriff or coroner, respectively, pursuant to this act, the title and conveyance thereof shall be by deed, signed, sealed and delivered by the sheriff or coroner to such person or persons as shall purchase the same, in fee simple or otherwise, which shall be most absolute and available in law against the said delinquents and their heirs and assigns and all claiming under them.

(Section XXX, P. L.) And be it further enacted by the authority aforesaid, That if the owner or owners of land and other real property by this act made subject to taxation, or some person or persons for him or them do not appear, or shall neglect or refuse to pay the rates assessed thereon within thirty days after the days of the appeal, then and in every such case the said land or other real property, together with the rates assessed thereon, shall be advertised in the township and county in which such lands do lie, or in the place where such owner or owners do dwell; and the commissioners of the respective counties, or any two of them, shall and they are hereby required to give public notice thereof in some of the English and German papers for at least three months, that sale will be made of such part of the said lands as will be sufficient to discharge the taxes due for the same, and all charges accruing by reason of the refusal or non-payment thereof, and if the owner or owners of such lands or other real estate, or some person or persons in their behalf, do not appear to discharge and pay the said taxes, with all the charges as aforesaid at or before the expiration of said term, then the said commissioners of the respective counties, or any two of them, are authorized and hereby empowered to sell the said lands or other real estates, or so much thereof as aforesaid, by public vendue, to such person or persons as will appear to give most for the same, returning the overplus, if any be, to the owner or owners of such lands or their legal representatives as aforesaid, after all necessary charges deducted. And when any sale of such land or other real estate shall be made as aforesaid by the commissioners, or any two of them, pursuant to this act, the title and conveyance thereof shall be by deed, signed, sealed and delivered by the said commissioners, or any two of them, to such person or persons as shall purchase the same in fee-simple or otherwise, which shall be most absolute and available in law, against the said delinquents, and their heirs and assigns and all claiming under them.

[Section XXXI.] (Section XXXI, P. L.) And be it further enacted by the authority aforesaid, That in case any collector, sheriff or coroner, after distress and sale by him or them made, shall have any overplus money remaining in his, or any of their hands, such collector, sheriff or coroner, first tendering the same before one witness to the owner of the goods distrained and sold, shall, upon the refusal of such owner to receive such money, pay the same to the treasurer of the county, who shall deduct therefrom one per centum and give notice thereof within twenty days to the commissioners of all sums so paid; and the owner thereof shall have the remainder discounted out of any future tax; and the receipt of the said treasurer shall exonerate the collector, sheriff or coroner.

[Section XXVII.] (Section XXXII, P. L.) And be it further enacted by the authority aforesaid, That the collectors shall make out fair and true accounts, in writing, of every seizure by them made, with the charges to be settled by the commissioners, who shall make the collectors such reasonable allowance for their trouble as to them shall seem right; and the said commissioners shall have full power and authority in all cases to call upon collectors, who have, or in future have, any overplus money in their hands, and to proceed against them in such cases as the law directs in case of delinquent collectors.

[Section XXVIII.] (Section XXXIII, P. L.) And be it further enacted by the authority aforesaid, That every county treasurer of this state shall pay over all sums of money by him received by virtue of this act to the treasurer of this commonwealth, within the time hereinafter limited, and the said treasurer of the commonwealth shall keep the same subject to the drafts of the superintendent of the finances of the United States of America, and for no other purpose whatsoever. That is to say: The treasurer of the county of Philadelphia, within three days after he shall receive the same; the treasurer of the county of Bucks within four days after he shall receive the same; the treasurer of the county of Chester, within four days after he shall receive the same; the treasurer of the county of Lancaster, within six days after he shall receive the same; the treasurer of the county of York, within seven days after he shall receive the same; and the treasurer of the county of Cumberland shall be allowed eight days, and the treasurer of the county of Berks six days, and the treasurer of the county of Northampton seven days, and the treasurer of the county of Bedford twelve days, and the treasurer of the counties of Westmoreland and Washington twenty days, and the treasurer of the county of Northumberland twelve days for the like purpose.

[Section XXIX.] (Section XXXIV, P. L.) And be it further enacted by the authority aforesaid, That the commissioners of the city and several counties shall, each of them, have and receive ten shillings, and each of the township, ward and district assessors and assistant freeholders shall have and receive seven shillings and six pence per day for each day they shall bona fide be employed in the performance of the duties required of them by this act, and no other fee or reward whatsoever for their services, any law, custom or usage to the contrary in anywise notwithstanding. And that the collectors severally employed in and for the due execution of this act shall be allowed sixpence in the pound for every pound by them so collected, and no more; the said several sums so allowed to be drawn from the county treasury out of the county rates and levies, and to be finally submitted to the examination of the justices and grand jury in the same manner as other accounts against the county.

[Section XXX.] (Section XXXV, P. L.) And be it further enacted by the authority aforesaid, That all sums of money to be assessed and levied by this act shall be paid and discharged in gold or silver money, at the rate of three pounds for one-half johannes of Portugal weighing nine pennyweights, and seven shillings and six pence for one Spanish milled dollar weighing seventeen pennyweights and six grains, and so in proportion for all other gold or silver money, and in no other money whatsoever.

(Section XXXVI, P. L.) And whereas, it is absolutely necessary that this act be put in force and executed with all convenient speed:

Therefore:

[Section XXXI.] Be it enacted by the authority aforesaid, That if any of the said commissioners shall refuse or neglect to perform his or their duty in the premises, he or they so offending shall be fined by the supreme executive council of this state in any sum not exceeding five hundred pounds for every offense, which, by virtue of their warrant, directed to the sheriff or coroner of the county where such offender or his estate is, at the time of issuing such warrant, shall be levied by the seizure of land, distress and sale of goods, or imprisonment of body, as the case shall require.

[Section XXXII.] (Section XXXVII, P. L.) And be it further enacted by the authority aforesaid, That the county treasurers, respectively, for their trouble in receiving and paying all such moneys as shall come into their hands, respectively, by virtue of this act, shall be allowed seven shillings and six pence for every hundred pounds; and the treasurer of the state shall be allowed, for his trouble in receiving and paying all such moneys as shall come into his hands by virtue of this act, the sum of two shillings and six pence for every hundred pounds, and no more.

[Section XXXIII.] (Section XXXVIII, P. L.) And be it further enacted by the authority aforesaid, That the commissioners of each respective county shall, at the next meeting of assembly after the said taxes are settled and adjusted, cause to be laid before the house, a true and fair transcript of all the returns of property made taxable by this act, and the valuation of the same, together with the pound rate and the sums quotaed on each township, ward or district.

[Section XXXIV.] (Section XXXIX, P. L.) And be it further enacted by the authority aforesaid, That the commissioners of each county be and they are hereby empowered to employ suitable clerks for transacting the business required of such clerks by this act, who are to be paid for their services out of the county rates and levies.

Passed March 27, 1782. Recorder L. B. No. 1, p. 469, etc. See the Acts of Assembly passed September 31, 1783, Chapter 1003; March 20, 1783, Chapter 1018; March 21, 1783, Chapter 1021; April 5, 1785, Chapter 1161.

CHAPTER CMLXII.

AN ACT TO AMEND AN ACT, ENTITLED "AN ACT FOR THE BETTER EMPLOYMENT OF THE POOR OF THE CITY OF PHILADELPHIA, THE DISTRICT OF SOUTHWARK, THE TOWNSHIPS OF MOYAMENSING, PASSYUNK AND THE NORTHERN LIBERTIES,[1] AND TO REVIVE AND PERPETUATE AN ACT, ENTITLED "AN ACT FOR THE RELIEF OF THE POOR,"[2] AND FOR REPEALING TWO OTHER ACTS HEREIN MENTIONED.

(Section I, P. L.) Whereas, the poor within the city of Philadelphia, the district of Southwark and townships of Moyamensing and the Northern Liberties have become very burdensome and expensive to the inhabitants, and the expense thereof is like to increase:

And whereas, for remedy thereof, by employing the said poor, an act of assembly was passed on the eighth day of February, in the year one thousand seven hundred and sixty-six, in the late province of Pennsylvania, entitled "An act for the better employment of the poor of the city of Philadelphia, the district of Southwark, the townships of Moyamensing, Passyunk and the Northern Liberties,"[1] whereby all persons who should contribute the sum of ten pounds or more were incorporated by the name of "Contributors to the relief and employment of the poor in the city of Philadelphia;" and such of the said contributors as should think fit were enabled [to meet] on the second Monday in the month of May then next following, and on the second Monday in the month of May yearly, forever, at some convenient place in the said city, and then and there to choose twelve persons of their own number to be managers of the said contributions and of the buildings to be erected for the reception, employment and relief of the poor of the said city, district and townships in pursuance of the said act:

(Section II, P. L.) And whereas, by the decease of many of the contributors and the legal disability of others of the said contributors who yet survive, the choosing of the managers

---
[1] Passed February 8, 1766, Chapter 534.
[2] Passed March 9, 1771, Chapter 635.

and the burden of serving in that office has devolved upon a small number of persons, and it is now become difficult to procure a succession of managers to superintend the almshouse and the house of employment in the said city, and to provide for, employ and relieve the poor aforesaid out of the said surviving contributors, who are qualified to elect or to be elected as aforesaid:

For remedy whereof:

[Section I.] Be it enacted by the Representatives of the Freemen of the Commonwealth of Pennsylvania in General Assembly met, and by the authority of the same, That in case the contributors aforesaid shall not meet on the second Monday in May next, or in any succeeding year, in the said city, and choose twelve managers as aforesaid, or if the said contributors shall meet on the second Monday in May next, or in any future year, and having made such choice of managers as aforesaid, the persons then and there chosen, or a majority of them, shall not meet together on the third Monday of the same month, in the said city, as by the said act they were directed and enjoined, then and in such case, and upon such neglect, whether in the month of May next or in the month of May in any future year, the overseers of the poor of the said city of Philadelphia, district of Southwark and townships of Moyamensing, and the Northern Liberties, for the time being, shall become invested with all and singular the powers, authorities, rights, claims, demands, interest and estate, real, personal and mixed, which then shall be of the said corporation, in as ample a manner and for the same uses and purposes as the same are or were invested in, or ought to be exercised, possessed or enjoyed by the said corporation.

[Section II.] (Section III, P. L.) And be it further enacted by the authority aforesaid, That the said overseers of the poor for the time being, whenever the succession of the said managers shall fail as aforesaid, shall become a body politic and corporate in law, for the purpose of superintending the house of employment, and the other purposes for which the said managers were appointed and constituted as aforesaid, by the name of "The Guardians of the Poor in the City of Philadelphia," with all the powers and faculties of a body politic and corporate, and the said guardians of the poor in the city of Philadelphia may hold real estates, not exceeding the yearly value of two thousand pounds, and may take and receive any grant, gift, bequest or alienation of goods and chattels whatsoever.

[Section III.] (Section IV, P. L.) And be it further enacted by the authority aforesaid, That the said eventual corporation of the guardians of the poor in the city of Philadelphia shall half-yearly appoint six of their number to superintend the almshouse and house of employment, to exercise and perform all the authorities of the present managers of the said institution; and the said six overseers shall, during their continuation as managers as aforesaid, be exempted from all other duties of the said office of overseers, and the whole duties thereof shall be performed by the rest of the said overseers.

[Section IV.] (Section V, P. L.) And be it further enacted by the authority aforesaid, That from and after the passing of this act, any overseer of the poor of the said city, district and townships may, with the consent of any one justice of the peace, afford relief to the sudden necessity of any poor person, not exceeding the value of three pounds within three months.

[Section V.] (Section VI, P. L.) And be it further enacted by the authority aforesaid, That one-half of the overseers of the poor who shall be nominated and shall take upon themselves the duties of the said office within the said city, district and townships, on the twenty-fifth day of March next, or afterwards, as immediate successors of the present overseers of the [poor of the] said city, district and townships, shall not continue in office longer than six calendar months and the other half of the said overseers shall continue in office until the twenty-fifth day of March, one thousand seven hundred and eighty-three; and that on the twenty-fifth day of September next, or within ten days after, the justices of the peace of the city and county of Philadelphia, or any three or more of them, shall meet at the county court house in the said city, and then and there appoint and constitute successors to serve for one year, in the stead of those who shall be appointed as aforesaid for six months; and so every twenty-fifth day of March, and every twenty-fifth day of September, yearly, for and during the continuance of the act, entitled "An act for the relief of the poor," [1] the said justices shall meet at the said court-house, and shall then and there appoint and constitute one-half of the said overseers half-yearly, in order that there may be always some experienced persons in office. And if any person who shall be appointed an overseer of the poor, in pursuance of this act, shall refuse or neglect to serve in the said office, he shall be fined in like sum, and the said fine shall be levied in like manner and go to the same uses, as if such person had been appointed on the twenty-fifth day of March and had refused or neglected to serve thereupon.

(Section VII, P. L.) And whereas, divers disorderly persons, by their own lewdness, drunkenness or other evil practices, have fallen sick and become chargeable to the said city, district and townships, and have been unwilling or unable to reimburse the expenses which have been incurred in order to their cure and recovery; and it may be some relief to the inhabitants of the said city, district and townships, who have been put to great charge by such disorderly persons, and may deter such disorderly persons from returning to their former evil practices if such disorderly persons were hereafter obliged to make compensation by servitude:

[Section VI.] (Section VIII, P. L.) Be it therefore enacted by the authority aforesaid, That from and after the passing of this act, the overseers of the poor of the said city, district and townships, or any two of them, with the approbation and concurrence of any two justices of the peace of the city and county of Philadelphia, shall, and they are hereby authorized to bind out, by indenture or deed poll, any such disorderly persons to any master or mistress, and his or her assigns, who will advance and pay such consideration for such service as the said overseers shall think fit to accept for the same. Provided always, That no married man or woman nor any person of the age of forty years and upwards shall be liable to be bound by indenture or deed poll as aforesaid, and that no such binding shall be for a longer term than will be sufficient to reimburse the overseers aforesaid the expenses incurred, in behalf and on account of such person, and so as the same do not exceed in the whole the space of three years.

(Section IX, P. L.) And whereas, the act, entitled "An act for the relief of the poor,"[1] passed the ninth day of March, in the year one thousand seven hundred and seventy-one,[1] hath been found by experience to be of great public utility:

[Section VII.] (Section X, P. L.) Be it further enacted by the authority aforesaid, That the said act, and every article, clause, matter and thing therein contained, is hereby revived, re-enacted and made perpetual, except the clause limiting the continance thereof, and such other parts thereof as are hereby altered, amended and supplied or relate to the mayor, recorder and alderman of the city of Philadelphia, whose authority, jurisdiction and power, granted by the said act, shall be exercised by the justices of the peace of the said city, or any three of them, agreeable to the directions of the act passed the fourteenth day of March, in the year one thousand seven hundred and seventy-seven.[2]

[Section VIII.] (Section XI, P. L.) And be it further enacted by the authority aforesaid, That an act, entitled "An act for the better relief of the poor of the city of Philadelphia, the district of Southwark and the townships of Moyamensing, Passyunk and the Northern Liberties, in the county of Philadelphia,"[3] passed the second day of April, in the year one thousand seven hundred and seventy-nine, and also an act, entitled "An act for the relief of the poor,"[4] passed the twenty-seventh day of November, in the year one thousand seven hundred and seventy-nine, are hereby repealed and made void.

[Section IX.] (Section XII, P. L.) And be it further enacted by the authority aforesaid, That so much of the act, entitled "An act for the better employment of the poor of the city of Philadelphia, the district of Southwark, the townships of Moyamensing, Passyunk and Northern Liberties,"[5] passed the eighth day of February, in the year one thousand seven hundred and

---

[1] Passed March 9, 1771, Chapter 635.
[2] Passed March 14, 1777, Chapter 746.
[3] Passed April 2, 1779, Chapter 839.
[4] Passed November 27, 1779, Chapter 873.
[5] Passed February 8, 1766, Chapter 534.

sixty-six, as incorporates the township of Passyunk with the city of Philadelphia, the district of Southwark and the townships of Moyamensing and Northern Liberties is hereby repealed and made void.

> Passed March 25, 1782. Recorded L. B. No. 1, p. 486, etc.,See the Act of Assembly passed March 27, 1789, Chapter 1410; June 13, 1836, P. L. 541.

CHAPTER CMLXIII.

AN ACT TO INCORPORATE THE SUBSCRIBERS TO THE BANK OF NORTH AMERICA.

(Section I, P. L.) Whereas, the United States in Congress assembled, from a conviction of the support which the finances of the United States would receive from the establishment of a national bank, passed an ordinance to incorporate the subscribers for this purpose, by the name and style of "The President, Directors and Company of the Bank of North America:"

And whereas, the president and directors of the said bank have applied to this house for a similar act of incorporation, which request it is proper and reasonable to grant:

[Section I.] (Section II, P. L.) Be it therefore enacted and it is hereby enacted by the Representatives of the Freemen of the Commonwealth of Pennsylvania in General Assembly met, and by the authority of the same, That those who are, and those who shall become subscribers to the said bank, be and forever hereafter shall be a corporation and body politic to all intents and purposes, by the name and style of "The President, Directors and Company of the Bank of North America."

[Section II.] (Section III, P. L.) And be it further enacted by the authority aforesaid, That the said corporation are hereby declared and made able and capable in law to have, purchase, receive, possess, enjoy and retain lands, rents, tenements, hereditaments, goods, chattels and effects of what kind, nature or quality soever, to the amount of ten millions of Spanish silver milled dollars, and no more. And also to sell, grant, demise, alien, or dispose of the same lands, rents, tenements, hereditaments, goods, chattels and effects.

[Section III.] (Section IV, P. L.) And be it further enacted by the authority aforesaid, That the said corporation be and shall be forever hereafter able and capable in law to sue and be sued, plead and be impleaded, answer and be answered unto, defend and be defended in courts of record or any other place whatsoever, and to do and execute all and singular other matters and things, that to them shall or may appertain to do.

[Section IV.] (Section V, P. L.) And be it further enacted by the authority aforesaid, That for the well governing of the said corporation and the ordering of their affairs they shall have such officers as they shall hereafter direct or appoint: Provided nevertheless, That twelve directors, one of whom shall be the president of the corporation, be of the number of their officers.

[Section V.] (Section VI, P. L.) And be it further enacted by the authority aforesaid, That Thomas Willing be the present president, and that the said Thomas Willing and Thomas Fitzsimons, John Maxwell Nesbitt, James Wilson, Henry Hill, Samuel Osgood, Cadwallader Morris, Samuel Inglis, Samuel Meredith, William Bingham, Timothy Matlack and Andrew Caldwell be the present directors of the said corporation, and shall so continue until another president and other directors shall be chosen, according to the laws and regulations of the said corporation.

[Section VI.] (Section VII, P. L.) And be it further enacted by the authority aforesaid, That the president and directors of the said corporation shall be capable of exercising such powers for the well governing and ordering of the affairs of the said corporation and of holding such occasional meetings for that purpose as shall be described, fixed and determined by the laws, regulations and ordinances of the said corporation.

[Section VII.] (Section VIII, P. L.) And be it further enacted by the authority aforesaid, That the said corporation may make, ordain, establish and put in execution such laws, ordinances and regulations as shall seem necessary and convenient for the government of the said corporation.

(Section IX, P. L.) Provided always, That nothing hereinbefore contained shall be construed to authorize the said corporation to exercise any powers in this state repugnant to the laws or constitution thereof.

[Section VIII.] (Section X, P. L.) And be it further enacted by the authority aforesaid, That the said corporation shall have full power and authority to make, have and use a common seal, with such device and inscription as they shall think proper, and the same to break, alter and renew at their pleasure.

[Section IX.] (Section XI, P. L.) And be it further enacted by the authority aforesaid, That this act shall be construed and taken most favorably and beneficially for the said corporation.

Passed April 1, 1782. Recorded L. B. No. 1, p. 484, etc. The Act in the text was repealed by the Act of Assembly passed September 13, 1785, Chapter 1178, and was revived by the Act of Assembly passed March 17, 1787, Chapter 1278.

CHAPTER CMLXIV.

AN ACT TO VEST CERTAIN POWERS IN THE PRESIDENT OF THIS STATE, TOGETHER WITH THE OTHER OFFICERS THEREIN NAMED, AND FOR OTHER PURPOSES THEREIN MENTIONED.

(Section I, P. L.) Whereas many delays have been occasioned in transacting the business of the land office of this state by reason of doubts which remained with the different officers, touching their power of determining many controversies on caveats, which stand undetermined on the books of said office, as well as a great variety of other cases touching escheats, warrants granted to agree, rights of pre-emption, promises and other imperfect titles:

(Section II, P. L.) For remedy whereof:

[Section I.] Be it enacted by the Representatives of the Freemen of the Commonwealth of Pennsylvania in General Assembly met, and by the authority of the same, That the president or vice-president and a member of the supreme executive council, appointed by the council for that purpose, together with the secretary of the land office, the receiver-general and the surveyor-general for the time being, shall be a board of property, to hear and determine in all cases of controversy on caveats in all matters of difficulty or irregularlity, touching escheats, warrants on escheats, warrants to agree, rights of pre-emption, promises, imperfect titles or otherwise which heretofore have, or hereafter may, arise in transacting the business of the said land office. And the secretary of the land office is hereby empowered and directed to receive and enter caveats in his said office, copies whereof to be transmitted to and entered in the surveyor-general's office; and the said secretary of the land office, shall with the approbation and consent of the president or vice-president, appoint days of hearing, and shall grant citations, at the reasonable request of any party or person applying for the same, or otherwise, as the case may require, for which said services they, the said officers of the land office, shall take and receive such fees only as were customary at the former board of property.

(Section III, P. L.) Provided always nevertheless, That no determination of this board of property shall be deemed, taken or construed to extend, in any measure whatever, to the preventing either of the parties from bringing their action at the common law, either for the recovery of possession or determining damages for waste or trespass, but the courts of law shall remain open to the said parties in as full and ample manner as if no determination had ever been given.

(Section IV, P. L.) And whereas, it was enacted by the sixth and seventh sections of a law of this state, passed the ninth day of April last, entitled "An act for establishing a land office and for other purposes therein mentioned,"[1] that in cases where any office right issued before the tenth day of December, one thousand seven hundred and seventy-six, had not been executed, that the owner or owners should make application within one year, and pay a third part of the purchase money, to the receiver-general, before any survey shall be made; and that all payments for lands taken up on any office right whatever shall be made, one-fourth part in one year, another fourth part in two years, another fourth part in three years, and the residue

---

[1] Passed April 9, 1781, Chapter 940.

in four years from the passing of the said act, which respective times or periods are found, on experience and reflection, much too short for the purpose aforesaid:

[Section II.] Be it therefore enacted by the authority aforesaid, That the said respective times and periods are enlarged over and above the dates and times mentioned in said act for the space of two years.

(Section V, P. L.) And whereas, it was enacted by the ninth section of the law aforesaid, that all lands within this state, heretofore surveyed under any grant, warrant, location or other office right, shall be returned into the surveyor-general's office (if not already returned) in the space of nine months after passing the said act, which time is already expired, and it is found that very few have called on the late deputy surveyors for their drafts, or to discharge the fees due on the same, and a literal observance of the said act would involve not only the late deputy surveyors, but the owners of lands in manifest loss and inconvenience:

[Section III.] Be it therefore enacted by the authority aforesaid, That it shall and may be lawful for the surveyor-general of this state to receive returns of such surveys as shall appear to him to have been faithfully and regularly made, from the said late deputy surveyors, their heirs or legal representatives, for such further period as to him shall seem just and reasonable. And that there shall no action, loss or damage accrue to any person or persons by reason of neglect in complying with the aforesaid clause or section before the passing of this act.

(Section VI, P. L.) And whereas, the receiver-general of the land office formerly received a salary from the late proprietaries of Pennsylvania and no fees were annexed to his office. In order, therefore, for the support of the present receiver-general:

[Section IV.] Be it enacted by the authority aforesaid, That the receiver-general shall, for his trouble and expenses, have and receive fees as follows, viz.:

For every search in his office, one shilling and six pence.

For receiving, booking and giving a receipt for any sum on account, in part, two shillings and six pence.

For every copy of account, or other transcript from the books, one penny per line.

For office seal and certificate, two shillings and six pence.

For final settlement, calculation, closing the account, receiving the money, and giving a receipt, including necessary searches, seventeen shillings and six pence.

For a certificate to the supreme executive council of moneys paid previous to the execution of a patent, two shillings and six pence.

Which said fees shall be in full of all dues or demands by him to be made, in any cases whatsoever.

(Section VII, P. L.) And the aforesaid sixth, seventh and ninth sections of the law aforesaid, so far as respect the periods and times in the same respectively mentioned, and no further, are hereby altered and repealed.

> Passed April 5, 1782. Recorded L. B. No. 1, p. 482, etc. See the Acts of Assembly passed April 1, 1784, Chapter 1094; September 16, 1785, Chapter 1180; January 8, 1791, Chapter 1522.

CHAPTER CMLXV.

AN ACT FOR GUARDING AND DEFENDING THE NAVIGATION IN THE BAY AND RIVER DELAWARE, AND FOR OTHER PURPOSES THEREIN MENTIONED.

(Section I, P. L.) Whereas, the trade of this state hath of late been much annoyed by the privateers and boats of the enemy cruising in Delaware bay, and the neighborhood thereof, whereby many vessels have been captured, as well of those going out and returning from sea, as of the bay and river craft plying between the city of Philadelphia and the states of New Jersey and Delaware, to the great loss of many individuals, and the manifest injury of the trade of this commonwealth:

(Section II, P. L.) And whereas, it is expedient and necessary that an armed force should be provided and supported, to protect and facilitate commerce by guarding and defending the navigation in the said bay and river, and the neighborhood thereof, and that suitable funds should be appropriated for the expense thereof:

[Section I.] (Section III, P. L.) Be it enacted by the Representatives of the Freemen of the Commonwealth of Pennsylvania in General Assembly met, and by the authority of the same, That John Patton, Francis Gurney [and] William Allibone be appointed commissioners to purchase, or otherwise procure, equip, man and to arm, furnish, support and manage such suitable vessel or vessels, as to them shall seem proper and fitting for the protection and defense of the navigation in and near the said bay and river; which armament, or such part thereof as they shall think necessary, shall be continued and kept in service for so long a time, during the present war, as they shall think necessary or till otherwise directed by the general assembly.

[Section II.] (Section IV, P. L.) And be it further enacted by the authority aforesaid, That the said commissioners shall report to the supreme executive council every such vessel or vessels as they shall have so purchased or procured and equipped for the service aforesaid, and the supreme executive council are hereby authorized and directed to appoint and commission the proper officers for such vessel or vessels.

[Section III.] (Section V, P. L.) And be it further enacted by the authority aforesaid, That each and every of the said commissioners shall, before he enters upon the duties of his appointment, take the following oath or affirmation of office, to wit:

I, A. B., do swear or affirm that I will well and truly execute and perform the several duties enjoined and prescribed by the act, entitled "An act for guarding and defending the navigation in the bay and river Delaware, and for other purposes therein mentioned."

[Section IV.] (Section VI, P. L.) And be it further enacted by the authority aforesaid, That the said commissioners shall, as often as they shall be ordered and directed by the supreme executive council, lay before the said executive council a state of their proceedings in the execution of their office, and also an account of their receipts and expenditures, accompanied with suitable documents and vouchers.

[Section V.] (Section VII, P. L.) And be it further enacted by the authority aforesaid, That the moneys arising from the tonnage on vessels, by virtue of an act, entitled "An act appointing wardens for the port of Philadelphia, and for other purposes therein mentioned,"[1] passed the twenty-sixth day of February, in the year one thousand seven hundred and seventy-three, except so much thereof as shall be necessary for the purposes mentioned in the said act, to be ascertained from time to time by the supreme executive council, and the moneys which have arisen since the twenty-third day of March last, and which shall hereafter arise from the duties collected and to be collected by virtue of an act, entitled "An act for an impost on goods, wares and merchandise imported into this state,"[2] passed the twenty-third day of December, one thousand seven hundred and eighty, be and they are hereby declared to be appropriated for and towards a fund for defraying the expense of procuring and maintaining such armament aforesaid, and shall continue to be applied to that purpose, and to no other, any former appropriation thereof notwithstanding, for so long a time as the said commissioners shall think proper to continue such armament, or till otherwise directed by the general assembly, and until the expense thereof and the debts which shall have been contracted therefor shall be fully paid and satisfied out of the same, together with such other funds as are or shall be appropriated to that purpose.

(Section VIII, P. L.) And whereas, the funds hereinbefore mentioned may be insufficient to enable the said commissioners to raise the sum necessary to provide the said armament so speedily as may be requisite, and the merchants and traders have signified their willingness to submit to a further impost on the importation of goods for this salutary purpose:

[Section VI.] Be it enacted by the authority aforesaid, That from and after the passing of this act there shall be raised, collected and paid, upon all goods, wares and merchandise im-

---

[1] Passed February 26, 1773, Chapter 671.
[2] Passed December 23, 1780, Chapter 925.

ported into this state (except on common salt, saltpetre, gunpowder, lead, shot, prize goods brought in for condemnation and goods, wares and merchandise of the growth, produce and manufacture of any of the United States of America), in addition to and besides the duties or imposts made payable by the aforesaid act, entitled "An act for an impost on goods, wares and merchandise, imported into this state,[1] passed the twenty-third day of December, one thousand seven hundred and eighty, a further impost or duty, equal to the impost or duty in the said act mentioned and directed to be received. That is to say, upon every gallon of rum, brandy, and other spirituous liquors, two pence; upon every gallon of Madeira wine, four pence; upon every gallon of other wine, two pence, upon all wines in bottles, six pence per dozen bottles; upon every hundred weight of unrefined sugar, one shilling; upon every hundred weight of loaf sugar, one shilling and six pence; upon every gallon of molasses, one penny; upon every hundred weight of coffee, one shilling; upon every pound of green tea, six pence; upon every pound of Bohea and other tea, one penny; upon all other goods and merchandise (except as before excepted), one per centum upon the value thereof, to be ascertained as in and by the said act is mentioned and directed.

(Section IX, P. L.) And to the end that [the] additional duties hereby imposed may be duly collected and paid:

[Section VII.] Be it further enacted and declared, That all the powers and authorities, and the penalties, regulations and directions, given and expressed in and by the said act, entitled "An act for an impost on goods, wares and merchandise, imported into this state,"[1] shall be and they are hereby extended and made applicable to the collection of the further duties hereby imposed, as fully and amply to all intents and purposes as if the same was herein repeated and enumerated.

[Section VIII.] (Section X, P. L.) And be it further enacted by the authority aforesaid, That it shall and may be lawful for the said commissioners to procure on loan such sum and sums of money as they shall find necessary (not exceeding in the

---

[1] Passed December 23, 1780, Chapter 925.

whole twenty-five thousand pounds) to be repaid with interest, out of the produce of the said funds, and the commissioners are hereby authorized to draw, from time to time, as they shall find occasion out of the hands of the collectors, the moneys arising from the duties herein appropriated, and to apply the same to the repayment of the moneys so borrowed, or to such other purposes within the meaning of this act as they shall think expedient, and the collector of the said duties is hereby directed to make payment as aforesaid to the said commissioners, the directions contained in any former act or acts to the contrary notwithstanding.

(Section XI, P. L.) And in order to enable the said commissioners to borrow or procure upon loan such sum or sums of money as may be necessary for carrying into execution the service herein directed:

[Section IX.] Be it further enacted by the authority aforesaid, That all and every contract which they shall find it [necessary to make] for that purpose shall be and is declared to be hereby fully ratified and confirmed, and that the funds hereinbefore assigned shall be mortgaged and pledged for the re-payment of all such moneys so to be borrowed and expended, until the whole shall be fully paid.

(Section XII, P. L.) Provided nevertheless, That no premium or interest shall be allowed for any such moneys which shall amount to above six per centum per annum.

[Section X.] (Section XIII, P. L.) Provided also, and be it further enacted by the authority aforesaid, That the additional duties hereby imposed and laid shall continue no longer than, in conjunction with the other duties hereby appropriated, they shall produce a sufficient sum to discharge the loan hereinbefore mentioned and specified.

(Section XIV, P. L.) And whereas, it is proper to ascertain what proportion of the prize money which may arise from captures which may be made by the said armament, or any part thereof, shall be given to the officers, mariners and marines employed therein:

[Section XI.] Be it enacted by the authority aforesaid, That there shall be reserved to the use of the state one-half the net proceeds of the prize money which shall arise from captures made by the said armament, or any part thereof, of all vessels, goods and condemnable articles, except the body, tackle, apparel, furniture and appurtenaces of cruising vessels, not being merchant vessels; and that the residue of the prize money arising from such captures as are not included in the said exception, together with the whole of the net proceeds of such prizes as come within the said exception, shall be paid to the officers, mariners, marines and others employed in actual service in the said armament, in such proportions as shall, from time to time, be agreed upon by the articles of agreement made between the agents or commissioners for conducting and managing the said armament and the said officers, mariners and marines.

Passed April 9, 1782. Recorded L. B. No. 1, p. 479, etc. See the Acts of Assembly passed April 15, 1782, Chapter 984; November 22, 1782, Chapter 998. The Act in the text was repealed by the Act of Assembly passed September 17, 1783, Chapter 1032.

CHAPTER CMLXVI.

A SUPPLEMENT TO AN ACT ENTITLED "AN ACT FOR ESTABLISHING COURTS OF JUDICATURE IN THIS PROVINCE." [1]

(Section I, P. L.) Whereas, by an act of general assembly of the late province of Pennsylvania, now in force within this commonwealth, entitled "An act for establishing courts of judicature in this province," [1] it is provided "that if any defendant or defendants in any suit or action, by reason of his or their sudden departure out of this province, shall require a more speedy determination in such action or suit than can be obtained by the common or ordinary rules of proceedings in any of the courts of common pleas in this province, the justices, upon application to them made, shall grant to such defendant or defendants, special courts and shall proceed to hear and

---

[1] Passed May 22, 1722, Chapter 255.

1781]   *The Statutes at Large of Pennsylvania.*   417

determine the premises according to the course and practice of the said courts of common pleas and for the usual fees therein taken:"

(Section II, P. L.) And whereas, it is but just and reasonable that any plaintiff or plaintiffs in any suit or action who is or are about to depart out of this commonwealth should be entitled to the like speedy relief with any such defendant or defendants, more especially since the late revolution, which hath induced many foreigners to come into this commonwealth on the business of commerce and other lawful occasions, and who may have received injuries against which they cannot, by the laws now in force, obtain that speedy relief which the nature of their respective cases and the exigencies of their affairs may require:

(Section III, P. L.) For remedy whereof and for the better securing speedy and ample justice to all such person and persons:

[Section I.] Be it enacted and it is hereby enacted by the Representatives of the Freemen of the Commonwealth of Pennsylvania in General Assembly met, and by the authority of the same, That if any plaintiff or plaintiffs, defendant or defendants, in any suit or action that may at any time or times hereafter be depending in the supreme court, or in any of the courts of common pleas within this commonwealth, for debts contracted after the passing of this act, by reason of his or their sudden departure therefrom shall require a more speedy determination in such suit or action than can be obtained by the common or ordinary rules of proceedings in the said courts, the justices of the said supreme court and of the said courts of common pleas, respectively, shall, on application to them made for that purpose, and upon giving security for costs, if required, grant to such plaintiff or plaintiffs, special courts and shall, without the usual imparlances, proceed to hear and determine the premises according to the course and practice of the said courts, respectively, and for the usual and customary fees therein taken.

[Section II.] (Section IV, P. L.) And be it further enacted by the authority aforesaid, That the provision made for the speedy relief of such defendant or defendants as in and by the said-recited act is or are mentioned, in the several courts of common pleas, shall be and the same hereby is extended to all such defendant or defendants in any suit or action which shall hereafter be depending in the said supreme court of this commonwealth.

[Section III.] (Section V, P. L.) Provided always, That nothing in this act or in the said-recited act contained shall be construed, deemed or taken to bar or prevent any such plaintiff or defendant, upon reasonable cause shown from being allowed a convenient and sufficient time, under all the circumstances of his, her or their case, to procure such testimony as may be necessary for the support of his, her or their suit, action or defense.

Passed April 10, 1782. Recorded L. B. No. 1, p. 489, etc. The Act in the text was repealed by the Act of Assembly passed March 27, 1789, Chapter 1413.

CHAPTER CMLXVII.

A SUPPLEMENT TO THE ACT, ENTITLED "AN ACT FOR REGULATING NAVIGATION AND TRADE IN THIS STATE."[1]

(Section I, P. L.) Whereas, it is necessary in time of war to avoid strengthening the hands of our enemies by consuming their manufactures and encouraging and increasing their commerce, at the same time that it is expedient to promote and encourage a commercial intercourse with our allies and other nations in amity with us:

And whereas, the laws now existing have been found insufficient for these salutary purposes and in some instances inconvenient:

[Section I.] (Section II, P. L.) Be it enacted by the Representatives of the Freemen of the Commonwealth of Pennsylvania in General Assembly met, and by the authority of the same,

---

[1] Passed September 10, 1778, Chapter 815.

That during the continuance of the present war between the United States of America and Great Britain, no goods, wares or merchandise of the growth, produce or manufacture of Great Britain, or any of her dominions, except as hereinafter is excepted, shall be imported by land or water into this state, nor shall any goods, wares or merchandise of any kind whatsoever be imported into this state from Great Britain or any of her dominions, on pain of confiscation of all such goods, wares and merchandise, one-half thereof to the use of the informer or prosecutor, and the other half to the use of this commonwealth, to be recovered either by seizure of such goods in nature of an attachment and prosecution in rem, or by an action of debt against the importer for the value of such goods, wares and merchandise in any court of record in this state: Provided, That such action or prosecution be brought and commenced within six months from the time the cause shall have arisen.

(Section III, P. L.) Provided always, That goods, wares and merchandise taken as prize and coming into any port in this commonwealth for trial and condemnation, or bona fide purchased as such in any port or place within the jurisdiction of the United States, and duly certified as hereinafter is directed, and goods, wares and merchandise imported from any port or place in the dominions of France, Spain or the United Provinces or other powers at open war with Great Britain shall not be liable to confiscation, seizure or molestation by virtue of this act.

(Section IV, P. L.) And whereas, it is expedient, as well to guard against the importation of goods of the growth, manufacture or produce of Great Britain, or the dominions thereof from neutral ports and from such of the United States as have not provided sufficiently by law against the importation of British goods as to encourage and protect the importation of such goods as may be lawfully imported from such ports, that the rules necessary to be observed in such importations should be clearly ascertained and described:

[Section II.] (Section V, P. L.) Be it enacted by the authority aforesaid, That from and after the passing of this act, every captain, master or commander of any ship or vessel coming into any port in this state to enter and discharge, from any neutral port or place, shall deliver to the naval officer, together with the manifest of the cargo of such ship or vessel, a certificate or certificates respecting every shipment or parcel of the goods, wares or merchandise imported in such vessel, which certificates respectively shall contain in substance the following requisite, to wit: a list or account of the casks, bales or packages of such shipment or parcel of goods, with their respective marks and numbers and a general account of the kinds, quantity and quality of the articles contained in each cask, bale or package, and a declaration, on oath or affirmation, of the shipper or exporter of such goods, wares and merchandise, that neither the same, or any part or parcel thereof are of the growth, produce or manufacture of Great Britain, or of any dominion or territory thereunto belonging or appertaining; which oath or affirmation shall be administered by the principal officer of the customs, or by a notary public or by such other officer in the port or place of shipment as shall be authorized by the government of the country to administer oaths and affirmations and authenticate testimony of the like nature, which oath or affirmation shall be certified under the hand and official seal of such officer, and that, from and after the passing of this act as aforesaid, every captain, master or commander of any ship or vessel coming into any port in this state as aforesaid, from any other port in the United States, shall deliver to the naval officer, in like manner, such certificate or certificates as are above required for goods coming from neutral ports, save only that in case any part of the cargo of such ship or vessel shall be of the growth, produce or manufacture of Great Britain, or [of] any of her dominions, it shall be certified under the hand and seal of the principal officer of the customs or of the judge, register or marshal of the court of admiralty, either on the knowledge of such officer or on the oath or affirmation of the person shipping the goods, that such goods, wares and merchandise were taken as prize and have been legally condemned as such, or sold by order of the court of admiralty. And that all goods, wares and merchandise imported into this state from and after the time aforesaid, other than such as are hereinbefore excepted, not being accompanied by and included in such certificate or certificates as aforesaid, shall be liable to seizure and confiscation as aforesaid, as goods, wares or merchandise of the growth, produce or manufacture of Great Britain or the dominions thereof.

(Section VI, P. L.) Provided nevertheless, That if on proof of the claimant of such goods that such certificate or certificates have been obtained, and are lost or destroyed by accident or from other good cause it shall appear to the court reasonable and proper to grant further time for the recovery of such certificates or for obtaining others in their stead, it shall and may be lawful for such court, having cognizance thereof, to grant such further reasonable time as to the court shall seem proper.

[Section III.] (Section VIII, P. L.) And be it further enacted by the authority aforesaid, That so much of the act, entitled "An act for regulating navigation and trade in this state,"[1] passed the tenth of September, one thousand seven hundred and seventy-eight, as is hereby altered and amended be and the same is hereby repealed.

Passed April 10, 1782. Recorded L. B. No. 1, p. 490, etc. The Act in the text was repealed by the Act of Assembly passed September 20, 1782, Chapter 986.

CHAPTER CMLXVIII.

AN ACT FOR THE RELIEF OF JOHN AMIEL AN INSOLVENT DEBTOR, CONFINED IN THE OLD GAOL OF THE CITY AND COUNTY OF PHILADELPHIA.

(Section I, P. L.) Whereas, John Amiel, a prisoner confined in the gaol of the city and county of Philadelphia for debt, by his petition to this house, hath set forth that by reason of

---

[1] Passed September 10, 1778, Chapter 815.

misfortunes he is wholly unable to satisfy his creditors, and hath prayed that he may be discharged from further confinement; and the house having thereupon, by their committee, caused due and full inquiry to be made into the circumstances of the said John Amiel's case, and the prayer of his said petition being found reasonable and necessary:

[Section I.] (Section II, P. L.) Be it therefore enacted and it is hereby enacted by the Representatives of the Freemen of the Commonwealth of Pennsylvaina in General Assembly met, and by the authority of the same, That the county court of common pleas in and for the city and county of Philadelphia (by the process of which court the said John Amiel hath been committed) be, and they are hereby authorized and required, upon the petition of the said John Amiel, to grant [unto] him the like relief as by the laws of this state is provided and enacted for insolvent debtors, who are confined in execution for debt, not exceeding one hundred and fifty pounds to any one person:

[Section II.] (Section III, P. L.) And be it further enacted by the authority aforesaid, That the same court, upon such petition being made to them by the said John Amiel, for his discharge as aforesaid, shall thereupon proceed in all things conformably to the purport, true intent and meaning of the several acts of assembly now in force in this commonwealth for the relief of insolvent debtors not owing more than one hundred and fifty pounds to one person, as aforesaid, that their discharges be equally valid and effectual, and their proceedings equally good and binding to all intents and purposes whatsoever.

[Section III.] (Section IV, P. L.) Provided always, and be it enacted by the authority aforesaid, That if any creditor or creditors of the said John Amiel do not or shall not reside in this state at the time of such proceeding before the same court, that the service of notice of the application of the said court, or of any rule or order of the same court in the premises, on the known agent or attorney of such creditor or creditors within this state, shall be equally good and effectual as if the same notice or notices were served on such creditor or creditors in person.

<blockquote>Passed April 13, 1782. Recorded L. B. No. 1, p. 492, etc. See the Acts of Assembly passed September 13, 1785, Chapter 1179; April 19, 1794, Chapter 1756.</blockquote>

CHAPTER CMLXIX.

AN ACT FOR ERECTING THE TOWN OF CARLISLE, IN THE COUNTY OF CUMBERLAND, INTO A BOROUGH; FOR REGULATING THE BUILDINGS, PREVENTING NUISANCES, AND ENCROACHMENTS ON THE COMMONS, SQUARES, STREETS, LANES AND ALLEYS OF THE SAME, AND FOR OTHER PURPOSES THEREIN MENTIONED.

Whereas the inhabitants of the town of Carlisle have represented by their petition to the assembly that the said town has greatly improved and is yearly increasing in buildings and number of inhabitants; that a good court house and gaol and three churches or houses for public worship are erected, and that the courts of justice for the county are held there; that encroachments and nuisances have been committed in the public squares, streets, lanes, alleys and commons of said town; that contentions happen relative to partition walls and fences, and a variety of other matter to the great annoyance and inconvenience of the inhabitants:

(Section II, P. L.) And whereas it is necessary, as well for the benefit of the inhabitants of the said town as those who trade and resort there, and for the advantage of the public in general, that the encroachments, nuisances, contentions, annoyances and inconveniences in the said town and commons thereto belonging should, for the future, be prevented:

[Section I.] (Section III, P. L.) Be it enacted and it is hereby enacted by the Representatives of the Freemen of the Commonwealth of Pennsylvania in General Assembly met, and by the authority of the same, That the said town of Carlisle and commons shall be, and the same is hereby erected into a borough, which shall be called "The Borough of Carlisle" forever;

the extent of which borough is and shall be comprised within the following boundaries, to wit, beginning at a walnut corner tree of land now of Thomas Wilson's heirs, being a post at the corner of the widow McDonald's out-lots, thence by the said land of Thomas Wilson's heirs adjoining the out-lots south twenty-four degrees and one-quarter east two hundred and thirty-three perches to a post on Letort Spring, thence down the said spring the different courses thereof fifty-nine perches to a white oak at the corner of Jonathan Holme's land, thence by the same and adjoining out-lots south twenty-six degrees east one hundred and twenty perches to a post, thence by the same south sixty-one degrees east one hundred and twenty-one perches to a hickory; thence by the same south forty-one degrees east one hundred perches to a white oak stump; thence by number one, of the small tracts of land sold by the late proprietaries to the inhabitants of the town of Carlisle now in the possession or occupancy of James Davis, south forty-nine degrees west ninety perches to a black oak, thence by Charles McClure's land, south forty-nine degrees west one hundred and tweny-nine perches to a black oak, thence by the same north seventy-five degrees west twenty-one perches to a post, and south forty degrees west fifty perches to a black oak, and north seventy-five degrees and an half west one hundred and fifty-four perches to a post on Letort Spring, thence down said spring the different courses thereof forty-four perches to a post on the west side of the spring, thence by the said Charles McClure's land in right (as is said) of Baynton and Wharton south eighty-nine degrees west one hundred and fifty-nine perches and adjoining out-lots, thence by the same adjoining out-lots and commons belonging to the town north eighty-one degrees west one hundred and thirty-five perches to a post, where a hickory tree formerly stood, thence by Ephraim Blaine's land, in right of Hugh Parker, and the late proprietaries (as is said) and by John Smith's and Company's land north one hundred and eighty-one perches to a post, thence by the said John Smith's and Company's land south eighty degrees west one hundred thirty-four perches to a post, thence the same course extending by Ephraim Blaine's land twenty-six perches, thence north eight degrees east one hundred and forty-two perches and four-tenths of a perch to James Young's line, including the out-lots, thence by the said James Young's line south forty-three degrees east seventy-four perches to a hickory, and adjoining out-lots, thence by the same north eighty-three and an half east one hundred perches and two-tenths of a perch to a stone corner, thence by the same north twenty-four degrees and one-quarter west fifty-nine perches to a post, thence by the same north eighty-seven degrees east forty perches and an half to a post, thence by the same and Ross Mitchell's line north two degrees and a half west one hundred and seventy-seven perches to a post, thence along the road laid out through Ephraim Blaine's land from said Mitchell's line to said Blaine's mill north eighty-one degrees and a half west two hundred and thirty-two perches to the road leading from Carlisle town to said mill; thence along said Carlisle road south four degrees west twenty-two perches to the place of beginning, including the town of Carlisle, commons and all the out-lots.

[Section II.] (Section IV, P. L.) And be it further enacted by the authority aforesaid, That Robert Miller and Samuel Postlethwaite be and they hereby are appointed the present burgesses, and the said Robert Miller shall be called the chief burgess within the said borough, and William Irwin, William Holmes, James Pollock and Casper Cropt assistants for advising, aiding and assisting the said burgesses in the execution of the powers and authorities herein given them; and Robert Smith to be high constable, and John Heap to be town clerk, to continue burgesses, assistants, high constable and town clerk until the first day of May, one thousand seven hundred and eighty-three, and from thence until others shall be duly elected and appointed in their place as hereinafter is directed.

[Section III.] (Section V, P. L.) And be it further enacted by the authority aforesaid, That the said burgesses, freeholders and inhabitants within the borough aforesaid, and their successors forever hereafter, shall be one body corporate and politic in deed and name, and by the name of "The Burgesses and Inhabitants of the borough of Carlisle," in the county of Cumberland, one body corporate and politic in deed and name are hereby fully created, constituted and confirmed; and by the same name of "The Burgesses and Inhabitants of the borough of Carlisle," shall have a perpetual succession; and they and their successors, by the name of "The Burgesses and Inhabitants of the borough of Carlisle," shall at all times hereafter be persons able and capable in law to have, get, receive and possess lands, tenements, rents, liberties, jurisdictions, franchises and hereditaments, to them and their successors in fee simple or for term of life, lives, years or otherwise, and also goods and chattels and other things of what nature or kind soever; and also give, grant, let, sell and assign the same lands, tenements, hereditaments, goods and chattels and to do and execute all other things about the same by the name aforesaid; and they shall be forever hereafter persons able and capable in law to sue and be sued, plead and be impleaded, answer and be answered unto, defend and be defended, in all or any of the courts within this commonwealth or other places and before any judges, justices or other persons whatsoever within this commonwealth in all manner of actions, suits complaints, pleas, causes and matters whatsoever; and that it shall and may be lawful to and for the said burgesses and inhabitants of Carlisle aforesaid, and their successors forever hereafter, to have and use one common seal for the sealing of all business whatsoever touching the said corporation and the same from time to time, at their will, to change and alter.

[Section IV.] (Section VI, P. L.) And be it further enacted by the authority aforesaid, That it shall and may be lawful for the burgesses, constable, assistants and freeholders, together with such inhabitants, housekeepers, within the said borough as shall have resided therein at least for the space of one whole year next preceding any such election, as is hereinafter directed, and hire a house and ground within the said borough of the yearly value of five pounds or upwards, on the first day of May, one thousand seven hundred and eighty-three, and on that day yearly forever thereafter, unless the same shall happen to fall on Sunday, and then on the next day following, publicly to meet in some convenient place within the said borough, to be appointed by the chief constable, and then and there to nominate, elect and choose by ballot two able men of the inhabitants of the said borough to be burgesses, one to be constable and one to be town clerk, and four to be assistants within the same, for assisting the said burgesses in managing the affairs of the said borough, and in keeping peace and good order therein; which election shall be taken from time to time by the high constable of the year preceding, and the names of the person so elected shall be certified under his seal to the president of the supreme executive council, for the time being, within fifteen days next after such election; and the burgess who shall have the majority of votes shall be called the chief burgess of the said borough. But in case it shall so happen that the said freeholders and inhabitants, housekeepers aforesaid, shall neglect or refuse to choose burgesses and the other officers in manner aforesaid, that then it shall and may be lawful for the president in council to nominate, appoint and commissionate burgesses, constable, town clerk and assistants for that year, to hold and continue in their respective offices until the next time of annual election appointed as aforesaid, and so often as occasion shall require.

[Section V.] (Section VII, P. L.) And be it further enacted by the authority aforesaid, That the said burgesses for the time being shall be and are hereby empowered and authorized to be conservators of the peace within the said borough, and shall have powers by themselves and upon their own view, or in other lawful manner, to remove all nuisances in the said streets, lanes, alleys, squares and commons, within the borough aforesaid, as they shall see occasion, with power also to arrest, imprison and punish rioters and other breakers of the peace or good behavior; award process, bind to the peace or behavior, commit to prison and make calendars of the prisoners by them committed and the same to return, together with such recognizance and examination as shall be by them taken, to the next court of quarter sessions of the county of Cumberland, there to be proceeded on as occasion shall require, and to do all and singular other matters and things within the said borough as fully and effectually to all intents and purposes as justices of the peace in their respective counties may or can lawfully do.

[Section VI.] (Section VIII, P. L.) And be it further enacted by the authority aforesaid, That before any of the said burgesses, constable, town clerk or other officers shall take upon them their respective offices they shall take and subscribe such oath or affirmation of allegiance and fidelity as by the laws of the commonwealth are in such cases provided, together with the oath or affirmation for the due execution of their respective offices; and every chief burgess so elected or appointed from year to year as aforesaid shall, within ten days immediately after his election, take the oath or affirmation aforesaid, before a justice of the peace for the county aforesaid, and that on his failure to take the oaths or affirmations aforesaid, within the time aforesaid (unless disabled by sickness or other reasonable cause) another chief burgess shall, from time to time and as often as occasion shall require, be appointed in the stead of such person so failing to appear and qualify himself as aforesaid, which burgess so to be appointed by the president and council, shall and may hold and enjoy his office until the day of election next ensuing the day of his appointment; and the chief burgess having qualified himself in manner aforesaid, shall enter upon his office, and the other burgess, constable, town clerk or other officers shall and may qualify themselves for their respective offices by taking and subscribing the oaths or affirmations aforesaid, before the said chief burgess, or before one of the justices of the peace of the said county, who are hereby authorized and empowered to administer the same.

[Section VII.] (Section IX, P. L.) And be it further enacted by the authority aforesaid, That it shall and may be lawful for the burgesses, freeholders and inhabitants, housekeepers aforesaid, and their successors, to have, hold and keep, within the said borough, two markets in each week, that is to say, one market on Wednesday and one market on Saturday in every week of the year forever, in the center square of the said borouugh; and two fairs in the year, the first to begin on the thirteenth day of May, one thousand seven hundred and eighty-three, and the other of said fairs to begin on the thirteenth day of November following, each fair to continue two days, and when either of those days shall happen to fall on Sunday, then the said fairs to be keep [kept] [sic] the next day or two days following, together with free liberties, customs, profits and emoluments to the said markets and fairs belonging and in anywise appertaining forever. And that there shall be a clerk of the market of the said borough who shall have the assize of bread, wine, beer, wood and all other provisions brought for the use of the inhabitants, and who shall and may perform all things belonging to the office of a clerk of the market within the said borough; and that Samuel Laird shall be the present clerk of the market, who shall be removable, for any malfeasance in his office, by the burgesses and assistants aforesaid and another from time to time appointed and removed as they shall find necessary.

[Section VIII.] (Section X, P. L.) And be it further enacted by the authority aforesaid, That if any of the inhabitants of the said borough shall hereafter be elected to the office of burgesses, high constable, or assistants and having notice of his or their election shall refuse to undertake and execute that office to which he is chosen it shall and may be lawful for the burgesses, high constable and assistants then acting to impose such moderate fines on the person or persons so refusing, as to them shall seem meet, so always that a fine imposed on a burgess elect do not exceed the sum of ten pounds, and the fine of a high constable or assistant elect, do not exceed the sum of five pounds, each to be levied by distress and sale of the goods of the party refusing, by warrant under the hand and seal of one of the said burgesses, or by any other lawful ways or means whatsoever, for the use of the said corporation; and in any such case, it shall and may be lawful for the said inhabitants to proceed to the choice of some other fit person or persons in the stead of such who shall so refuse.

[Section IX.] (Section XI, P. L.) And be it further enacted by the authority aforesaid, That it shall and may be lawful for the said burgesses, high constable and assistants for the time being, to assemble town meetings as often as they shall find occasion, at which meetings they may make such ordinances and rules, not repugnant to or inconsistent with the laws of the commonwealth, as to the greatest part of the inhabitants shall seem necessary and convenient, for the good government of the said borough, and the same rules and orders to put in execution, and the same to revoke, alter and make anew as occasion shall require. And also to impose such rules and amercements upon breakers of the said ordinances as to the makers thereof shall be thought reasonable, to be levied as above is directed in case of fines for the use of the said borough; and also at the said meetings to mitigate or release the said fines on the submission of the parties.

[Section XII, P. L.) And for the better preventing all encroachments, nuisances, contentions, annoyances and inconveniences whatsoever, within the bounds and limits of the said borough:

[Section X.] Be it further enacted by the authority aforesaid, That where any buildings have been heretofore erected within the original plan of said borough (other than such as have been erected unjustly on the commons thereof), and shall happen to encroach on any of the said streets and alleys or squares, such buildings shall not be deemed, held or taken for nuisances or abateable as such. But (to prevent a continuance of such encroachments) after such buildings shall be decayed or require rebuilding:

[Section XI.] Be it further enacted by the authority aforesaid, That the owner of such buildings shall not at any time rebuild on the street, lane, alley or square so encroached on: And in case any person or persons shall rebuild on the said street, alley or square so encroached on, the same shall be deemed, taken and adjudged a public nuisance, and shall be abateable and punishable as such, and the person or persons so rebuilding shall forfeit and pay the sum of twenty pounds to the supervisors of the said streets, lanes, alleys and squares, to be applied towards repairing the same, being thereof first legally convicted in any county court of quarter sessions for the county of Cumberland.

(Section XIII, P. L.) And to the intent that the said streets, lanes, alleys and such others as shall be hereafter laid out, may be duly regulated, made and kept in good order:

[Section XII.] Be it enacted by the authority aforesaid, That no person or persons whatsoever shall, from and after the publication of this act, lay the foundation of any party wall or front of any building, adjoining the streets, lanes and alleys within the said borough, before they have applied to the surveyors or regulators, to be appointed by the burgesses and assistants of the said borough, who are hereby empowered, as often as there shall be occasion to appoint three discreet persons to be surveyors or regulators of the said streets, lanes and alleys, so far as the same are already laid out and built upon, and of such streets, lanes and alleys as shall hereafter from time to time be laid out and opened by the owners of the ground within the said borough respectively, which said persons so to be appointed shall direct the regulation of the said streets, lanes and alleys, and of the footway on the sides of the streets and fronting the houses and lots in the said borough with the width or breadth of such footway; and upon application made to them shall regulate and lay out the proper gutters, channels and conduits, for the carrying off the water; and shall and may enter upon the lands of any person or persons in order to set out the foundations and to regulate the walls to be built between party and party as to the breadth and thickness thereof; which foundations shall be equally laid upon the lands of the persons between whom such party wall is to be made; and the first builder shall be reimbursed one moiety of the charge of such party wall, or for so much thereof as the next builder shall have occasion to make use of, before such next builder shall any ways use or break into the said wall and the charge or value thereof shall be set by the said regulators, or any two of them.

[Section XIII.] (Section XIV, P. L.) And be it further enacted by the authority aforesaid, That if any person or persons shall begin or lay the foundation of any party wall or building, before the place be viewed and directed by the said regulators, or any two of them, or otherwise than the same shall be set out and directed by the said regulators, every such person or persons, as well employers as master-builders, shall forfeit and pay the sum of five pounds to the burgesses of the said borough for the time being, or one of them, for the public use and benefit thereof, being of the said offense first convicted in the county court of quarter sessions of the county of Cumberland.

[Section XIV.] (Section XV, P. L.) Provided always, and be it further enacted, That if either party between whom such foundation shall be laid out, shall find themselves aggrieved by the order or direction of the said regulators, he, she or they may appeal to the justices at the next court of quarter sessions to be held for the said county, who shall finally adjust and settle the same and the costs of such appeal shall be paid as the same court shall direct.

[Section XV.] (Section XVI, P. L.) And be it further enacted by the authority aforesaid, That the said regulators or surveyors attending the said [service], for their trouble, shall be paid by the party or parties concerned in such foundation or erecting such party wall, the sum of five shillings each.

[Section XVI.] (Section XVII, P. L.) And be it further enacted by the authority aforesaid, That the said surveyors or regulators, or any two of them, shall have full power to regulate partition fences within the said borough; and where the adjoining parties do improve or enclose their lots, such fences shall be made in the manner generally used, and kept in repair at the equal cost of the parties, so that the price for making exceed not fifty shillings for every hundred feet, unless the owners or possessors between whom such fence is or shall be erected do agree otherwise; and if either party between whom such partition fence is or shall be made shall neglect or refuse to pay his part or moiety for the repairing or setting up of such partition fence as aforesaid, that then the party at whose cost the same was so repaired or set up may, if above five pounds, have his action at law for the said moiety of such costs, and if five pounds or under, the same shall be determined before either of the burgesses of the said borough or any justice of the peace of the said county, as in cases of debts not exceeding five pounds.

[Section XVII.] (Section XVIII, P. L.) And be it further

enacted by the authority aforesaid, That the freeholders and others within the said borough, qualified by charter to elect burgesses and assistants shall meet together on the third Saturday in the month of March, one thousand seven hundred and eighty-three, and every year thereafter on the same [day] at the court house in the said borough, and then and there, by tickets in writing, between the hours of ten in the morning and four in the afternoon, choose two discreet and reputable freeholders of the said borough to be the supervisors of the highways, and two to be assessors, which said supervisors and assessors, when chosen and returned in writing under the hand of one of the burgesses of the said borough, into the office of the clerk of the county court of quarter sessions for the said county, shall be the assessors of the said borough, and the supervisors of the streets, lanes, alleys, roads and highways thereof, for the ensuing year; and if any supervisor or assessor so elected, or otherwise appointed by virtue of this act, shall refuse to make upon himself the said office he shall for every such offense, forfeit and pay any sum not exceeding ten pounds, to be applied towards maintaining, amending, cleansing and repairing the said streets, lanes, alleys and highways.

[Section XVIII.] (Section XIX, P. L.) And be it further enacted by the authority aforesaid, That the said supervisors of the highways shall, at least five days before the third Saturday in March yearly and every year, give public notice in writing, by affixing the same at the court house in the said borough, that the inhabitants and freeholders thereof are to meet on that day to elect assessors and supervisors for the said borough according to the directions of this act.

[Section XIX.] (Section XX, P. L.) And be it further enacted by the authority aforesaid, That it shall and may be lawful for the said supervisors, together with the assessors aforesaid for the time being, to lay a rate or rates in any one year not exceeding one shilling in the pound on the clear yearly value of the real and personal estates of all and every the freeholders and inhabitants within the said borough, to be employed for the amending, repairing and keeping clean and in good order the streets, lanes, alleys and highways aforesaid, agreeable to the true intent and meaning of this act. Provided nevertheless, That the said rate or assessment shall be laid according to the best of their skill and judgment and as near as may be to the county assessment for other purposes laid in pursuance of an act, entitled "An act for raising county rates and levies,"[1] having due regard to every man's estate within the said borough, without favor or affection to any person whomsoever. And the said supervisors and assessors, and each of them shall, before they take on themselves the duties enjoined and required by this act, take an oath or affirmation, respectively, to the effect following, that is to say: "That they will well and truly cause the rates and sums of money by this act imposed to be duly and equally assessed and laid, to the best of their skill and knowledge, and therein shall spare no person for favor or affection nor grieve any for hatred or ill-will; and that they and each of them, the said assessors and supervisors, will diligently attend and faithfully execute their said offices, respectively, during the time of their continuance therein according to the best of their abilities and judgment." Which oath or affirmation the burgesses of the said borough, or any one of them, or any justice of the peace of the said county of Cumberland are hereby empowered and required to administer and to certify the same to the clerk of the sessions of the peace of the said county, to be by him filed among the records and papers of his office.

[Section XX.] (Section XXI, P. L.) And be it further enacted by the authority aforesaid, That if any of the said supervisors or assessors, as aforesaid chosen, shall refuse or neglect to take upon him or themselves the said office respectively, or shall die or remove out of the said borough, or if the freeholders and inhabitants of the borough aforesaid shall neglect or refuse to elect or choose supervisors or assessors as is hereinbefore directed and appointed, then and in every such case it shall and may be lawful to and for the burgesses and assistants of the said borough, with one or more of the justices of the peace of the said county, and they are hereby enjoined and required to appoint another supervisor or supervisors, assessor

---

[1] Passed March 20, 1724-5, Chapter 284.

or assessors in the room and stead of every such supervisor or supervisors, assessor or assessors so refusing, dying or removing as aforesaid; which said supervisor or supervisors, assessor or assessors so appointed shall have the same powers and authorities and shall be liable to the same penalties as the supervisors or assessors so chosen by the inhabitants of the said borough in pursuance of the direction of this act; and that the supervisors and assessors shall have and receive, for their trouble in rating and assessing the said rate, three pence in every pound, and the said supervisors shall have and receive six pence in the pound for collecting the same and four shillings each for every day they shall attend in overseeing, employing and attending the workmen upon the public streets, lanes, alleys and highways within the said borough.

[Section XXI.] (Section XXII, P. L.) And be it further enacted by the authority aforesaid, That the said supervisors, before they proceed to the collecting of the said rate shall procure the same to be allowed by the burgesses of the said borough, or one of them, and one or more of the justices of the peace of the said county of Cumberland; and if any person [or persons] so rated and assessed, shall refuse to pay the sum or sums on him or them charged and shall not enter his or their appeal at the next court of general quarter sessions, that it shall and may be lawful to and for the said supervisor or supervisors (having first obtained a warrant under the hand and seal of one of the said burgesses, or one of the justices of the peace aforesaid, who are hereby empowered and required to grant such warrant) to levy the same on the goods and chattels of the person or persons so refusing, and in case such person shall not, within three days next after such distress made, pay the sum or sums on him or her assessed, together with the charges of such distress, that then the said supervisors or supervisor may proceed to the sale of the goods distrained, rendering to the owner the overplus, if any shall remain on such sale, reasonable charges being first deducted. Provided nevertheless, That if any person or persons shall find him, her or themselves aggrieved with such rate or assessment it shall be lawful for the justices of the peace at their next general quarter sessions, upon the petition of the party to take such order therein as to them shall appear just, and the same shall conclude and bind all parties; and the supervisors, in case of such appeal, shall forbear making distress until the same be determined in the quarter sessions, in the manner herein directed and appointed.

[Section XXII.] (Section XXIII, P. L.) And be it further enacted by the authority aforesaid, That the tenant or tenants, or other persons residing on or having the care of lands of persons not residing in the said borough, his, or her or their goods and chattels shall be liable to be distrained in manner aforesaid for the payment of the said tax.

[Section XXIII.] (Section XXIV, P. L.) And be it further enacted by the authority aforesaid, That where any tenant shall, before the passing of this act, have taken, on a lease for one or more years, any lands or tenements, and shall pay the said rate hereby imposed on the said lands or tenements so leased, or shall have his or her goods and chattels distrained for the same, in such case it shall and may be lawful for the said tenant or tenants, or other persons aforesaid, to deduct the tax so paid out of the rent due or to become due, or for the tenant or tenants, or other persons aforesaid, to recover the same from the owner or owners by action of debt, together with costs of suit. Provided, always, That nothing herein contained shall make void or alter any contract heretofore made between any landlord and tenant respecting the payment of the road tax, or any usage or custom in respect to the tenant's paying the said tax, now subsisting between landlord and tenant.

[Section XXIV.] (Section XXV, P. L.) And be it further enacted by the authority aforesaid, That the said supervisors shall, and they are hereby required and enjoined, as often as the said several streets, lanes, alleys and highways shall be out of repair or want cleansing, to hire and employ a sufficient number of laborers, and the necessary carts or wagons, to work upon, open, amend, repair and clean the same, and to carry off and remove any filth, mud or dirt which shall be therein, in the most effectual manner, and shall purchase all materials necessary for that purpose, and oversee the said laborers, and take care that the said streets, lanes, alleys and highways be effectually opened, amended, repaired and cleaned agreeable to the regulations so made by the said regulators according to the true intent and meaning of this act.

(Section XXVI, P. L.) And in order to enable the said supervisors the more effectually to discharge their duty:

[Section XXV.] Be it enacted by the authority aforesaid, That it shall and may be lawful for the supervisors aforesaid, or any other person or persons by his or their order and directions, to enter upon any lots or lands adjoining to or lying near the said streets, lanes, alleys and highways, and to cut or open such drains or ditches through the same as he or they shall judge necessary completely to carry off and drain the water from such streets, lanes, alleys and highways, provided the same be done with as little injury and damage as may be to the owners of such lot or land, which drains and ditches so cut and opened shall be kept open by the said supervisors, if necessary, for amending and keeping clean and in good order the said streets, lanes, alleys or highways, or any or either of them, and shall not be stopped or filled up by the owner or owners of such lot of land, or any other person or persons whatsoever under the penalty of three pounds for every such offense ,to be paid and applied for and towards keeping in good order and repair the said streets, lanes, alleys and highways.

[Section XXVI.] (Section XXVII, P. L.) And be it further enacted by the authority aforesaid, That all and every supervisor or supervisors aforesaid who shall refuse or neglect to do and perform his or their duty as directed by this act (not otherwise particularly provided for) shall be fined and pay the sum of three pounds for every such offense, to be recovered in a summary way before either of the burgesses of the said borough, or any justice of the peace of the county residing in the said borough, and to be applied towards repairing and keeping clean and in good order the said streets, lanes, alleys and highways. Provided always, That if any such supervisor or supervisors shall conceive him or themselves aggrieved by the judgment of such burgess or justice, he may appeal to the next county court of general quarter sessions, who shall, on the petition of the party, take such order therein as to them shall appear just and reasonable and the same shall be conclusive to all parties.

[Section XXVII.] (Section XXVIII, P. L.) And be it further enacted by the authority aforesaid, That the person or persons who shall have served the office of supervisor or supervisors the preceding year, shall, on the first day of May yearly, or within six days after, make up and produce to the said burgesses and assistants fair and just accounts of all such sums of money by him or them expended on the said streets, lanes, alleys and highways, and of all sums of money by him or them received by virtue of any assessments and of all fines and penalties which have come to their hands; which accounts shall be entered in a book to be provided for that purpose, and shall be attested on oath or affirmation by such supervisor or supervisors, if required by any three or more of the freeholders or inhabitants of the said borough. And the said burgesses and assistants, or any four of them, of which four a burgess shall be one, shall have full power to adjust and settle the said accounts and to allow of such charges and sums only as they shall think just and reasonable; and if there shall appear to be any money remaining in the hands of the said supervisor or supervisors, they shall, by order, in writing, signed by them, direct the same to be paid to the succeeding supervisor or supervisors; but in case the said supervisor or supervisors shall be found in advance for moneys expended and shall have carefully collected the sums of money assessed and imposed by virtue of this act, then the said burgesses and assistants shall, in like manner, order the succeeding supervisors to repay and reimburse the same as soon as a sufficient sum of money shall come to their hands; and if such supervisor or supervisors shall neglect or refuse to make up and produce fair and just accounts as aforesaid, or having made up and produced such accounts, shall neglect or refuse forthwith to pay the moneys which he or they shall be ordered as aforesaid to pay, or shall not deliver up the books wherein such accounts shall be entered to their successors, it shall and may be lawful for either of the burgesses of the said borough, or any justice of the peace, on complaint to him made by any two of the said assistants, to commit such delinquent or delinquents to the county gaol, until the same shall be done. Provided always, That if any supervisor shall think himself aggrieved by the settlement of his accounts as aforesaid, he may (having first paid over to his successor or successors the balance found in his hands) appeal to the next court of quarter sessions, who shall, on the petition of the party, take such order therein and give such relief as to them shall seem just and reasonable, and the same shall conclude and bind all parties.

[Section XXVIII.] (Section XXIX, P. L.) And be it enacted by the authority aforesaid, That the said borough of Carlisle, according to the extent, bounds and limits thereof by charter, shall henceforth be deemed and taken and is hereby declared to be one distinct district in the said county of Cumberland; and that two overseers of the poor shall be appointed, and one inspector to serve at the general election in and for the said county of Cumberland shall be elected in and for the said borough, in the same manner as they are by law directed to be appointed and chosen in and for the several townships within this commonwealth, which said overseers so nominated and inspectors so elected shall have, use and exercise all and every the powers, rights and privileges and be subject to the same penalties and forfeitures within the said borough, respectively, which are lawfully used, had and exercised and which are to be suffered by and imposed on the several overseers and inspectors of the several townships aforesaid, to all intents and purposes as if they were respectively nominated and chosen overseers of the poor, and inspector of any of the townships aforesaid in pursuance of the laws of this commonwealth in such cases made and provided.

(Section XXX, P. L.) And whereas, doubts have arisen whether, according to the laws now in force, the justices of the peace residing within the said borough, and who are chargeable with or rated to the taxes, levies or rates within the same may lawfully act in any case relating to the said borough:

[Section XXIX.] Be it therefore enacted by the authority

aforesaid, That it shall and may be lawful to and for the justices of the peace of the said borough and all and every the justice or justices of the peace of the county of Cumberland aforesaid, residing or being in the same to make, do and execute all and every act or acts, matter or matters, thing or things appertaining to their office as justice or justices of the peace, so far as the same relates to the laws for the relief, maintenance and settlement of poor persons, for passing and punishing of vagrants, for opening, amending and repairing the streets, lanes, alleys or highways, or to any other laws concerning taxes, levies or rates, notwithstanding any such justice or justices is or are rated or chargeable with the taxes, levies or rates within the same borough.

[Section XXX.] (Section XXXI, P. L.) Provided always, and be it further enacted by the authority aforesaid, That this act, or anything herein contained, shall not authorize or empower any justice or justices of the peace for or within the said borough to act in the determination of any appeal to the quarter sessions of the peace for the said county of Cumberland, from any order, matter or thing relating to the same borough, anything herein contained to the contrary in anywise notwithstanding.

(Section XXXII, P. L.) And whereas it hath frequently happened that persons, in digging cellars and building houses, have thrown the clay and dirt from their cellars and the rubbish from their buildings into the streets, lanes, alleys and highways of the said borough, and by suffering the same to remain there have rendered the said streets, lanes and alleys impassable:

[Section XXXI.] Be it therefore enacted by the authority aforesaid, That if any person or persons, in digging or making of cellars, foundations and buildings, vaults, wells, sinks, drains or other works or improvements, shall, after the publication of this act, cast or throw any dirt, earth, clay, stone or other matter into any public street, lane, alley or highway within the said borough, and shall keep or suffer such dirt, earth, clay, stone or other matter to remain upon such street, lane, alley or highway so as unnecessarily to incommode or annoy the inhabitants of the said borough, and shall not remove the same upon notice given to him, her or them for that purpose, or by order of the burgesses of the said borough, or either of them, or by the regulators aforesaid, or any two of them, every such person and persons so offending and being thereof convicted before either of the burgesses of the said borough, or any justice of the peace of the county aforesaid, shall forfeit, for every such offense, the sum of thirty shillings and shall pay the cost of removing the same.

[Section XXXII.] (Section XXXIII, P. L.) And be it further enacted by the authority aforesaid, That if any person or persons whatsoever shall cast or lay, or cause to be cast or laid, any shavings, mud, ashes, dung or other filth or annoyance on any pavement, street, lane or alley within the said borough, and shall not remove the same on notice given to him, her or them by the burgesses of the said borough, or either of them, or by the regulators aforesaid, or any two of them, every such person and persons so offending, and being thereof convicted before either of the burgesses of the said borough, or [before] any justice of the peace of the county aforesaid shall forfeit [and pay] for every such offense the sum of twenty shillings, and shall pay the cost of removing the same.

[Section XXXIII.] (Section XXXIV, P. L.) And be it further enacted by the authority aforesaid, That if any person or persons shall, after the publication of this act, cast or throw out of any cart, wagon or other carriage, any rubbish, dirt or earth in any public street, lane or alley of the said borough, save only in such parts and places as shall be appointed and agreed on by the said regulators and the supervisors aforesaid, or any three of them, every such person and persons so offending, and being thereof convicted before either of the burgesses of the said borough, or before any justice of the peace of the said county, shall forfeit for every such offense the sum of ten shillings, and shall pay the cost of removing the same.

[Section XXXIV.] (Section XXXV, P. L.) And be it further enacted by the authority aforesaid, That if any distiller, soap-boiler or tallow-chandler within the said borough shall discharge any foul or nauseous liquor from any still-house or workshop, so that such liquor shall pass into or along any of the said streets, lanes or alleys, or if any soap-boiler or tallow-chandler shall keep, collect or use, or cause to be kept, collected or used in any of the built parts of the said borough any stale, stinking or putrid fat, grease or other matter, or if any butcher shall keep at or near his slaughter-house any garbage or filth whatsoever so as to annoy any neighbor or any other person whatsoever, he, she or they so offending and being thereof convicted before the burgesses of the said borough, or either of them, or before any justice of the peace of the said county, shall forfeit and pay for every such offense the sum of thirty shillings, together with the costs of the prosecution.

[Section XXXV.] (Section XXXVI, P. L.) And be it further enacted by the authority aforesaid, That if any person or persons shall, after the publication thereof, presume to cast, carry, draw out or lay any dead carcas, or any excrement or filth from vaults, privies or necessary-houses and shall leave such carcass or filth without burying the same a sufficient depth in any unenclosed grounds within the limits of the said borough, or on or near any of the streets, lanes, alleys or highways aforesaid, every person or persons so offending, and being thereof convicted before either of the burgesses of the said borough, or before any justice of the peace of said county, shall forfeit for every such offense the sum of thirty shillings, and shall pay the cost of removing and burying such carcass, excrement or filth in such place and manner as the burgesses of the said borough, or either of them, or the said regulators or supervisors, or any two of them, shall direct or appoint.

[Section XXXVI.] (Section XXXVII, P. L.) And be it further enacted by the authority aforesaid, That if any person or person whatsoever shall wilfully stop or obstruct the passage of the waters of any of the common sewers hereafter to be made within the said borough, he or they so offending shall forfeit, for every such offense, any sum not exceeding twenty pounds, and shall pay the costs of removing such obstruction.

[Section XXXVII.] (Section XXXVIII, P. L.) And be it further enacted by the authority aforesaid, That if any person or persons shall make any pavement or footway before their houses or lots in the said borough of a greater width, or breadth, or height than allowed or directed by the surveyors or regulators to be appointed by virtue of this act, or contrary to the directions of the said regulators, or any two of them, or shall set up posts in the streets, lanes or alleys aforesaid, or any of them, otherwise than as allowed and directed by the said regulators, or any two of them, and shall refuse or neglect to take up, remove or place the same in such manner as the said regulators, or any two of them, shall direct or order, after two days' notice to him, her or them for that purpose given by order of the burgesses of the said borough, or either of them, or by order of the said regulators, or any two of them, every such person so offending and being thereof convicted before either of the burgesses of the said borough, or before any justice of the peace of the county aforesaid, shall forfeit and pay the sum of thirty shillings for every such offense; and the said regulators, or any two of them, shall and may take up, regulate, pull down, remove and replace such pavement and posts, in such manner as they shall think proper, and the costs of taking up, regulating, pulling down, removing and replacing such pavements and posts shall be paid by the party or parties so offending in the premises.

[Section XXXVIII.] (Section XXXIX, P. L.) And be it further enacted by the authority aforesaid, That if any person or persons shall hereafter make and set up, or shall cause to be made and set up, in any street of fifty feet wide or upwards within the said borough, any porch, cellar, door or step, which shall extend beyond the distance of four feet and three inches into such street, or a proportionate distance into any narrower street, and if any person or persons shall hereafter make and set up, or cause to be made and set up, any bulk, jut-window or encumbrance whatsoever whereby any passage of any street, lane or alley shall be obstructed, or shall place or cause to be placed any spout or gutter whereby the passage of any street, lane or alley shall be incommoded, every person so offending and being thereof convicted before the burgesses of the said borough, or either of them, or before any justice of the peace of the county aforesaid, shall, for every such offense, forfeit and pay the sum of thirty shillings, and shall forthwith remove the said nuisance, or cause the same to be removed; and, on failure thereof, by the space of three days next after notice to him, her or them for that purpose given, by order of the burgesses of the said borough, or by the said regulators, or any two of them, then and in that case the regulators aforesaid, or any of them, shall and may remove the same, or cause the same to be removed, and the costs and expenses attending such removal shall be paid by the party or parties so offending.

[Section XXXIX.] (Section XL, P. L.) And be it further enacted by the authority aforesaid, That the owner or owners of every house within the said borough having, at the publication hereof, any porch, cellar door or step extending into any street beyond the limits aforesaid, or having fixed or fastened to such house any bulk, jut-window or other encumbrance whatsoever shall, yearly and every year, pay to the supervisors of the said streets, lanes, alleys and highways, to be applied towards repairing and amending the same, such sum or sums of money as the said burgesses and assistants shall assess, until such porch, cellar door or step to him, her or them respectively belonging shall be reduced to the limits aforesaid, or such bulk, jut-window or other encumbrance shall be removed and taken away; and every owner or owners of any house or houses whereunto any spouts or gutters shall, at the time of the publication hereof, be so fixed or placed that the waters thereby discharged may incommode persons passing in the streets, lanes or alleys shall and they are hereby enjoined and required forthwith to remove or effectually to alter or amend the same.

[Sction XL.] (Section XLI, P. L.) And be it enacted by the authority aforesaid, That if any person or persons, after the publication of this act, shall wilfully or maliciously remove, misplace or injure any pipes or trunks already fixed or placed, or that shall be hereafter fixed or placed by direction of the burgesses and assistants of the said borough, for conveying water to, from or through any part of the said borough, or if any person or persons shall wilfully and maliciously, without the consent and direction of the burgesses and assistants aforesaid, by any ways or means whatsoever, obstruct or prevent the course of such waters in or through any such trunks, pipes or conduits, as are or shall or may be placed as aforesaid, or shall spoil or injure any cistern which shall or may be placed for the reception of such water, every person so offending and being thereof legally convicted before the burgesses of the said borough, or either of them, or before any justice of the peace for the county aforesaid, shall forfeit and pay the sum of five pounds for every such offense, and shall pay the costs of repairing and putting such trunks, pipes, conduits or cisterns in good order and repair.

(Section XLII, P. L.) And whereas, it hath been usual for the merchants and traders within the said borough to keep large quantities of gunpowder in their dwelling houses and shops, to the manifest danger of the inhabitants:

[Section XLI.] Be it therefore enacted by the authority aforesaid, That no person or persons whatsoever within the limits of said borough shall, from and after the publication of this act, keep in any house, shop, cellar, store or other place within the said borough, any more or greater quantity than twenty-five pounds weight of gunpowder, which shall be kept in the highest story of the house, at any one time, unless it be at least fifty yards from any dwelling house, under the penalty of ten pounds.

(Section XLIII, P. L.) And whereas, several persons, without right or legal authority, have built on and fenced in many parts of the said commons which, by this act, are included in and made part of the said borough, which commons ought to be not only beneficial and convenient for the inhabitants for an outlot for their cattle in the meantime, but in time to come may be appropriated for the further extention and increase of the buildings in the said borough:

[Section XLII.] Be it therefore enacted by the authority aforesaid, That all such buildings, fences or other erections whatsoever already made or erected, or which shall or may hereafter be so made or erected by any person or persons whatsoever, on any part of the said commons, shall be deemed, held and taken for nuisances, and as such may be abated, prostrated, thrown down and removed, and that it shall and may be lawful for the burgesses, assistants, regulators and supervisors aforesaid, for the time being, or the majority of them, with the consent and approbation of the chief burgess, to abate, prostrate, throw down and remove all such buildings, fences and erections, as are now erected and built, or that hereafter may be erected and built on the same commons. And in case the said burgesses, assistants, regulators and supervisors, or the majority of them as aforesaid, with the consent and approbation of the chief burgess, shall be opposed in abating, prostrating, throwing down and removing the said buildings, fences or other erections, that then it shall and may be lawful for the said burgesses, assistants, regulators and supervisors, or the majority of them as aforesaid, to call to their assistance all or any of the inhabitants of the said borough, who are hereby enjoined and required to be aiding and assisting to the burgesses, assistants, regulators and supervisors, or the majority of them, as aforesaid, in abating, prostrating, throwing down and removing all such buildings, fences and erections by this act declared nuisances as aforesaid.

[Section XLIII.] (Section XLIV, P. L.) And be it further enacted by the authority aforesaid, That if any person or persons shall, at any time after the publication of this act, presume to erect or build any buildings, fences or other erection whatsoever on the said commons, that then the said buildings, fences or other erections shall be abated, prostrated, thrown down and removed as aforesaid; and that the offender or offenders being thereof duly convicted before the said burgesses, or any one of them, shall pay a fine in the discretion of the said burgesses, or any one of them, not exceeding one hundred pounds, to be levied by distress and sale of the offender's goods as hereinbefore is directed in case of fines.

[Section XLIV.] (Section XLV, P. L.) And be it further enacted by the authority aforesaid, That if any person or persons shall dig any hole, pit or quarry on the commons aforesaid, without having first obtained leave, in writing, from the burgesses and assistants, regulators and supervisors as aforesaid, or shall neglect or refuse to fill up and level such hole, pit or quarry, after one month's notice given by the burgesses, assistants, regulators or supervisors aforesaid, or any two of them, that then the said regulators and supervisors, or any two of them, shall cause the said holes, pits or quarries to be filled up, and the party or parties so offending shall be at the charge and expense of such filling up, and, moreover, pay a fine at the discretion of the said burgess and assistants, not exceeding twenty pounds.

[Section XLV.] (Section XLVI, P. L.) And be it further enacted by the authority aforesaid, That all the penalties, fines and forfeitures hereinbefore imposed by this act, the manner of levying and recovering of which is not before directed, not exceeding the sum of five pounds, shall be recovered before one of the burgesses of the said borough, or before one of the justices of the peace of and for the said county of Cumberland, and shall be levied by warrant under the hand and seal of such burgess or justice, directed to any constable of said borough or county, who is hereby empowered and required to execute the same by distress and sale of the goods and chattels of the offender; and where goods and chattels sufficient cannot be found, then the party or parties so offending shall be committed to the common gaol of the said county, there to remain until payment made, or until discharged by due course of law; and if such penalties, fines and forfeitures shall exceed the sum of five pounds, then to be recovered by action of debt, bill, plaint or information, in any county court within this state, wherein no essoin, protection or wager of law, nor more than one imparlance shall be allowed; and all fines and forfeitures arising by this act not hereinbefore appropriated shall be paid to the supervisors of the streets, alleys and highways, to be employed in mending and repairing the same.

[Section XLVI.] (Section XLVII, P. L.) And be it enacted by the authority aforesaid, That nothing in a certain act of assembly passed in the year of our Lord one thousand seven hundred and seventy-two, entitled "An act for opening and better amending and keeping in repair the public roads and highways within this province,"[1] shall be deemed, construed or taken to extend to the public roads, streets, lanes or alleys within the said borough, or to the assessing the inhabitants thereof for the purposes therein mentioned, or to any other matter or thing to be done or performed therein; but the said act, so far as it respects or relates to said borough, and no further is hereby declared to be repealed.

[Section XLVII.] (Section XLVIII, P. L.) And be it also enacted by the authority aforesaid, That if any person or persons be sued or prosecuted for anything done in pursuance of this act he, she or they may plead the general issue and give this act and the special matter in evidence for their justification, and if the plaintiff or prosecutor become non-suit or suffer a discontinuance, or a verdict pass against him, the defendant shall have treble costs, to be recovered as in cases where costs by law are given to defendants.

<pre>Passed April 13, 1782. Recorded L. B. No. 1, p. 493, etc.
See the Acts of Assembly passed September 13, 1785, Chapter 1179; April 19, 1794, Chapter 1756.</pre>

CHAPTER CMLXX.

AN ACT FOR METHODIZING THE DEPARTMENT OF ACCOUNTS OF THIS COMMONWEALTH AND FOR THE MORE EFFECTUAL SETTLEMENT OF THE SAME.

(Section I, P. L.) Whereas, the methods heretofore practised for the settlement of the accounts of this state have, by experience, been found not to answer the good purposes intended thereby:

For remedy whereof:

[Section I.] Be it enacted by the Representatives of the Freemen of the Commonwealth of Pennsylvania in General Assembly met, and by the authority of the same, That an office shall be instituted in this commonwealth for auditing, liquidating

---

[1] Passed March 21, 1772, Chapter 653.

and adjusting all the accounts thereof, and that the same shall be established and kept at the place where the general assembly of the state shall hold their sessions, to be styled "The Comptroller-General's office," and that a person of known integrity, diligence and capacity be appointed to execute and perform the duties of said office, by the name of "The Comptroller-General," who shall be and hereby is authorized and empowered to liquidate and settle, according to law and equity, all claims against the commonwealth, for services performed, moneys advanced or articles furnished, by order of the legislative or executive powers, for the use of the same, or for any other purpose whatever; to inspect and examine all vouchers which shall be produced in support of such accounts or claims, and in all cases of doubt or difficulty to call upon witnesses, examine them on oath or affirmation, touching any charge or account which it may be probable their evidence would tend to elucidate or explain; which oath or affirmation the said comptroller-general is hereby authorized and empowered to administer; to judge of prices and charges in all cases wherein such prices or charges have not been ascertained and fixed by persons duly authorized to ascertain and fix the same, and, generally, to call upon all persons or their representatives who have been or shall be possessed of any moneys, goods or effects belonging to this state, and have not severally accounted for the same, other than and except the collectors of public taxes, and the treasurers of the different counties, and to keep fair, distinct and clear accounts of all the revenues and expenditures of the commonwealth, of every kind and nature whatsoever.

[Section II.] (Section II, P. L.) And be it further enacted by the authority aforesaid, That from and after the first day of May next, all accounts between this state and any officer of the same, and all and every other person or persons (except as before excepted) shall be rendered into the said office in the first instance, where they shall, without delay, be liquidated, adjusted and settled; and upon settlement of any such account, the same shall be transmitted, together with the vouchers thereto belonging, to the president and council, who, if satisfied with the justice of such settlement, shall, by warrant drawn on the treasurer of the state, direct the payment of any balance which may appear to be due thereupon to the party entitled to receive the same; and the president and council shall, by their secretary, return the same accounts and vouchers into the said office, together with such warrant; and the said comptroller-general shall make an entry in his books of such warrant, and having certified the same on the back thereof, shall forthwith deliver it to the party entitled to receive such balance, and shall carefully file and deposit all such accounts and vouchers in his office; and if upon any settlement a balance shall be found due to the state, the account and vouchers shall be filed in the said office, in like manner as afore-directed; and the said comptroller-general shall forthwith take the most effectual steps for the speedy recovery of the same.

(Section III, P. L.) And whereas, many accounts of long standing are still unsettled, or have not been finally closed, and large sums of money or considerable effects belonging to the commonwealth, remain in the hands of divers persons, and the same will probably be lost, if vigorous measures be not taken to compel such persons to settle their accounts, and discharge the balances which may appear to be due to the state.

[Section III.] (Section IV, P. L.) Be it therefore enacted by the authority aforesaid, That the comptroller-general shall, with all convenient speed, form abstracts or lists of the names and surnames, additions and places of abode of all persons who shall have received moneys, effects or property of this commonwealth into their hands which they have not accounted for, and of the value or amount received by each person, as well as the dates of the several transactions; for which purpose he shall be, and hereby is authorized and empowered to call for all the books and papers, accounts and vouchers, appertaining to or belonging to the state, which shall be in possession of the auditors heretofore appointed, or in the hands of any other person or persons whatever.

[Section IV.] (Section V, P. L.) And be it further enacted by the authority aforesaid, That the said comptroller-general shall, with all dispatch, direct the prothonotary of the county wherein the person or persons whose names shall be contained in such abstract be resident, or in which they had their last known abode, to issue process, commanding the sheriff or coroner of the said county to summon such person or persons to appear within three months in the comptroller's office, and there exhibit and settle their accounts, and pay all sums of money belonging to the state, of which they shall, respectively, be found possessed; whereupon such sheriff or other officer shall serve a copy of such summons upon the party or parties aforesaid, at least thirty days before the end of the term last mentioned, and shall make proper return of every such summons within twenty days after such service, to the prothonotary upon oath; and if such person or persons, whose name or names shall be contained in such summons are not found within the county, the sheriff or coroner of the same shall proceed to demand and call, in an audible public manner, upon such person or persons, in open quarter sessions of the peace, to appear as aforesaid and settle his, her or their accounts and pay over to the treasurer of the state all moneys belonging to the state which they severally possess and detain in their hands respectively.

[Section V.] (Section VI, P. L.) And be it further enacted by the authority aforesaid, That if any person or persons who shall be summoned or demanded, and called upon as aforesaid, shall refuse or neglect to exhibit their accounts as aforesaid, within three months after the service of such summons, every and all such delinquent or delinquents shall be liable to answer for and pay to the treasurer of the state the amount of the moneys or the full value of all public effects, which shall appear to the comptroller-general to have been received or come to the hands or possession of such person or persons, respectively, without any allowance, deduction or set-off whatsoever.

[Section VI.] (Section VII, P. L.) And be it further enacted by the authority aforesaid, That if any auditor or auditors, person or persons aforesaid, having in his or their possession any of the public books, [or papers], accounts or vouchers hereinbefore mentioned, shall refuse or neglect, within ten days after demand made by the said comptroller-general, to deliver up to him on oath, all and every the books, papers, accounts or vouchers aforesaid, all and every such auditor or auditors, person or persons, so offending against this act, shall be proceeded against by the comptroller, and shall forfeit and pay any sum not exceeding one thousand pounds, to the use of the state, to be recovered on conviction in any court of record within the same.

[Section VII.] (Section VIII, P. L.) And be it further enacted by the authority aforesaid, That in case any person shall be found to have a balance in his or her hands due to the state and shall, on order from the comptroller-general, refuse or neglect to pay the same as before directed, and in case any person who shall be summoned or demanded and called upon in open quarter sessions of the proper county, shall not exhibit his or her accounts and procure the same to be settled, according to the directions of this act, all and every such person shall be liable to be taken and imprisoned in any county gaol, by warrant under the hand and seal of the prothonotary of said county, or his or her goods and chattels shall be distrained and sold after thirty days from such distraining, by warrant under the hand and seal of said prothonotary, to satisfy such balance or such value or sum certified as aforesaid, together with costs and charges; and if other property cannot be found, the lands and houses of the delinquent may be taken and sold by the sheriff of the county so far as may be necessary for the purposes aforesaid, by virtue of a writ of fieri facias, to be issued by the prothonotary of the county where such real estate lieth, upon a certificate of the debt due to the state from the comptroller being filed with such prothonotary.

[Section VIII.] (Section IX, P. L.) And be it further enacted by the authority aforesaid, That the money so recovered shall be paid by the sheriff or coroner who shall receive the same into the hands of the treasurer of the state, for the use of the state, within thirty days after such recovery.

[Section IX.] (Section X, P. L.) And be it further enacted by the authority aforesaid, That no account whatever between the commonwealth and any public officer or other person whatsoever, except as before excepted, shall be deemed to be settled and the party exonerated from settling and supporting the same in the manner required by this act, until the same shall be audited, liquidated and settled in the office of the comptroller-general erected by this act, other than and except all such accounts as have been settled by auditors or commissioners heretofore appointed for the purpose or by the committees of assembly.

[Section X.] (Section XI, P. L.) Provided nevertheless, and be it further enacted by the authority aforesaid, That the said comptroller-general shall be and is hereby authorized and empowered to examine, revise and correct all and every the account or accounts settled by the auditors, commissioners or committees of assembly aforesaid, and shall report all substantial errors or omissions which he may discover to the general assembly of this commonwealth, who shall finally determine thereon, either by directing a re-settlement of such accounts with the said comptroller-general or by confirming the same.

[Section XI.] (Section XII, P. L.) Be it further enacted by the authority aforesaid, That it shall and may be lawful for the said comptroller-general, as often as there shall be occasion, to call before him, by subpoena or summons, and in case of contempt to issue a writ of attachment in order to compel the appearance of any person or persons who the said comptroller-general may reasonably suppose is or are capable of giving evidence or information concerning the said accounts, or any of them; and in case any person or persons on whom such subpoena or summons shall be served, shall refuse to appear, as in such writ shall be expressed and directed, or, having appeared, shall refuse to make a full disclosure of his, her or their knowledge in the matter depending before the said comptroller-general, the said comptroller-general may award an attachment and commit such delinquent or delinquents to the common gaol of the county, there to be holden till such person or persons shall submit to the said comptroller-general and comply with the directions of this act; and all persons who shall be summoned as witnesses by the said comptroller-general, and every sheriff, coroner or other officer to whom he shall direct his precepts or writs, shall be allowed like fees for their attendance and services as witnesses summoned to appear in the inferior courts of justice and sheriffs, coroners and other officers are entitled to in such courts, such costs, together with further charges accruing, to be levied on the several delinquents by the said comptroller-general, by warrant, in like manner as small debts are recoverable.

[Section XII.] (Section XIII, P. L.) Provided always, and be it further enacted by the authority aforesaid, That if upon any subpoena or summons requiring the attendance of any person or persons before the said comptroller-general as aforesaid, a return be made that such person is not to be found within the proper county, that the said comptroller-general may issue an attachment and proceed thereon as aforesaid, as if such subpoena or summons had been duly served.

[Section XIII.] (Section XIV, P. L.) And be it further enacted by the authority aforesaid, That the secretary of the supreme executive council shall be and he is hereby required and enjoined, once in every month, to enter in the comptroller-general's office all and every marriage and tavern or other license, noting how many of said licenses have been paid for and the sums so paid, and also what number of blank licenses have been granted either for marriages or taverns not paid for and to whom granted, and the said comptroller-general shall cause fair entries to be made of all such sums of money so received by the secretary, and also of all such licenses as have been so granted to the several prothonotaries and others and have not been paid for, and shall open an account against all such prothonotaries or other persons for the amount of such licenses, and the said prothonotaries and others, at least once in three months, shall settle their respective accounts with the comptroller-general, in which the treasurer's receipts and the blank licenses which may at such time be unused and produced to the said comptroller shall be received and accepted by him as the only sufficient vouchers in such settlement.

[Section XIV.] (Section XV, P. L.) And be it further enacted by the authority aforesaid, That the comptroller-general shall particularly attend to such parts of the accounts already settled, or that may hereafter be settled, as are properly a charge against the United States and, selecting such parts with great precision, institute an account between the United States and the commonwealth, in forming which he shall regulate himself by the resolution of Congress authorizing such charges, and by the accounts raised against the commonwealth in the books of the department of the treasury of the United States; and where any charge shall appear to him to be of a federal nature, although such charge shall not be expressly acknowledged by Congress, he shall open a separate account for the same, to be finally settled on such principles as may hereafter be established by Congress and agreed to by this commonwealth.

[Section XV.] (Section XVI, P. L.) And be it further enacted by the authority aforesaid, That the treasurer of this state shall not, from and after the first day of May next, issue or pay any of the public moneys which have come, or shall come, to his hands, without a warrant for so doing, signed by the president or vice-president in council and entered in the comptroller-general's office, such entry to be certified on such warrant by the said comptroller-general, other than and except the moneys appropriated to the use of the United States for the current year, which shall remain subject to the orders of the superintendent of the finances of the United States, and the wages and incidental expenses of the house of assembly, which shall be paid on warrants drawn by the speaker in assembly, any law, custom or usage to the contrary in anywise notwithstanding. Provided always, That such orders or warrants, drawn by the superintendent of the finances or speaker for the purposes aforesaid, be first entered and certified in the comptroller-general's office as before directed.

[Section XVI.] (Section XVII, P. L.) And be it further enacted by the authority aforesaid, That the books, papers and transactions of the office of the comptroller-general shall be open to the inspection and examination of the committees of accounts, who shall be empowered by the assembly of this state for the time being or executive council; and the said comptroller-general shall be obliged to furnish annually and at all other times a state or abstract of the public accounts, or any of them, to the legislative and supreme executive powers of the state when he shall be thereunto required by either of them.

[Section XVII.] (Section XVIII, P. L.) And be it further enacted by the authority aforesaid, That the salary of the comptroller-general shall be the sum of five hundred pounds per annum, payable in quarterly payments, by warrant drawn on the treasurer for that purpose by the president or vice-president in council.

[Section XVIII.] (Section XIX, P. L.) And be it further enacted by the authority aforesaid, That the said comptroller-general shall, before he enters on the duties of said office, give bond, with one or more sufficient sureties, in the sum of five thousand pounds to the president or vice-president in council for the faithful performance of the duties of his office, and shall likewise take and subscribe the following oath or affirmation, to wit: I do swear or affirm that I will faithfully execute the office of comptroller-general for the commonwealth of Pennsylvania, and will do equal right and justice to all men to the best of my judgment and abilities, according to law and equity.

[Section XIX.] (Section XX, P. L.) And be it further enacted by the authority aforesaid, That the act of assembly of this commonwealth, entitled "An act to compel the settlement of public accounts,"[1] passed on the first day of March, one thousand seven hundred and eighty, and a supplement to the said act,[2] passed on the thirtieth day of May in the same year, as likewise all and every act or acts of the assemblies of this commonwealth heretofore passed, for regulating or settling the accounts of the same, of every kind or nature whatsoever, shall, from and after the passing of this act, be, and the said acts are hereby repealed and declared void.

[Section XX.] (Section XXI, P. L.) And be it further enacted by the authority aforesaid, That this act shall be publicly read in every court of oyer and terminer and of the quarter sessions of the peace which shall be holden in this state be-

---
[1] Passed March 1, 1780, Chapter 882.
[2] Passed May 30, 1780, Chapter 909.

tween the first day of May and the first day of January next, during which all other business shall cease.

[Section XXI.] (Section XXII, P. L.) And be it further enacted by the authority aforesaid, That John Nicholson be and he is hereby appointed comptroller-general for the time being.

Passed April 13, 1782. Recorded L. B. No. 1, p. 508, etc. See the Acts of Assembly passed September 20, 1782, Chapter 988; February 18, 1785, Chapter 1133; April 4, 1785, Chapter 1158; March 24, 1786, Chapter 1218.

CHAPTER CMLXXI.

AN ACT FOR SETTLING AND ADJUSTING THE DEPRECIATION OF THE PAY ACCOUNTS OF SUNDRY OFFICERS, NON-COMMISSIONED OFFICERS AND PRIVATES BELONGING TO THE STATE OF PENNSYLVANIA, AGREEABLE TO THE RESOLVES OF THE UNITED STATES IN CONGRESS ASSEMBLED.

(Section I, P. L.) Whereas the United States in Congress assembled, on the tenth day of April, one thousand seven hundred and eighty, did resolve in the words following, to wit: "Resolved, That when Congress shall be furnished with proper documents to liquidate the depreciation of the continental bills of credit, they will, as soon thereafter as the state of the public finances will admit, make good to the line of the army and the independent corps thereof, the deficiency of their original pay, occasioned by such depreciation; and that the money and articles heretofore paid or furnished, or hereafter to be paid or furnished by Congress or the states, or any of them, as for pay, subsistence or to compensate for deficiencies, shall be deemed as advanced on account until such liquidation as aforesaid shall be adjusted, it being the determination of Congress that all the troops serving in the continental army shall be placed on an equal footing: Provided, That no person shall have any benefit of this resolution except such as were engaged during the war or for three years, and are now in service, or shall hereafter engage during the war."

(Section II, P. L.) And by their resolve of the twentieth of February, one thousand seven hundred and eighty-two, it is ordered and recommended to the several states in the words following, That is to say: "Resolved, That it be and hereby is recommended to the legislatures of the several states to settle and discharge, on account of the United States, the depreciation of pay of such officers in the late general hospital as are inhabitants of or belong to their respective states, who resigned their appointments after the tenth day of April, one thousand seven hundred and eighty or became supernumerary by the new arrangement in October, one thousand seven hundred and eighty."

(Section III, P. L.) Therefore, in compliance with the resolves of Congress aforesaid:

[Section I.] Be it enacted and it is hereby enacted by the Representatives of the Freemen of the Commonwealth of Pennsylvania in General Assembly met, and by the authority of the same, That all the officers, surgeons and surgeons' mates, non-commissioned officers and privates of the army of the United States in the line of this state, engaged to serve for three years or during the war, whose time of enlistment expired or who were honorably discharged since the said tenth day of April, one thousand seven hundred and eighty, and all officers in the late general hospital, who were inhabitants of or belonging to this state at the time of their entering into the service and who have resigned their appointments since the said tenth day of April, one thousand seven hundred and eighty, or who became supernumerary by the arrangement of October, one thousand seven hundred and eighty, and were not otherwise provided for by law, and no other persons whatever, shall be entitled to have the depreciation of their pay accounts adjusted and settled, making deduction therefrom of all enlargement of pay, subsistence money or other allowance, in lieu of loss occasioned by the depreciation of their original pay.

(Section IV, P. L.) And whereas, it appears by the resolves of Congress of March the fifteenth, one thousand seven hundred and seventy-nine, February the ninth, one thousand seven hundred and eighty, and October the third, one thousand seven hundred and eighty, that all detached corps, not originally of the line of the army, shall be credited to the states to which they respectively do belong, or were inhabitants of at the time of their entering into the service, and shall be provided for by the said states respectively, as those of equal rank in the line of the army:

Therefore:

[Section II.] (Section V, P. L.) Be it enacted by the authority aforesaid, That all officers, non-commissioned officers and privates of the artillery artificers, or other detached corps, who were inhabitants of this state at the time of their entering into the service of the United States, in any of the said corps or artillery artificers and who were enlisted to serve for three years or during the war, and who were in actual service on the said tenth day of April, one thousand seven hundred and eighty, and who have continued in the said service to this time or were honorably discharged since the said tenth day of April, shall be entitled to have the depreciation of their pay accounts settled and adjusted agreeable to the principles contained in the foregoing section.

(Section VI, P. L.) And whereas, by a resolve of Congress, dated the twenty-ninth day of March, one thousand seven hundred and eighty-one, the regiment of artillery artificers at Carlisle are reduced to two companies, under the command of Captains Wyly and Jordan, and agreeable to the resolves of Congress mentioned in the foregoing section, the said corps of artillery artificers are annexed to the line of this state:

Therefore:

[Section II.] (Section VII, P. L.) Be it enacted by the authority aforesaid, That the said Captains Wyly and Jordan, with the said corps of artillery artificers under their command, shall be entitled to all the benefits, emoluments and advantages granted, or proposed to be granted in future to officers of equal rank or privates in the said line, any law to the contrary hereof in anywise notwithstanding.

[Section IV.] (Section VIII, P. L.) And be it further enacted by the authority aforesaid, That the comptroller-general be and he is hereby directed to settle and adjust the depreciation of the pay accounts of the several officers and men in this act included.

[Section V.] (Section IX, P. L.) And be it further enacted by the authority aforesaid, That the supreme executive council be authorized to draw on the treasurer of this state for such sum or sums of the bills of credit emitted in pursuance of an act, entitled "An act for emitting the sum of five hundred thousand pounds in bills of credit for the support of the army and for establishing a fund for the redemption of the same, and for other purposes therein mentioned,"[1] as may from time to time appear by the report of the comptroller to be necessary and place the same into the hands of the said comptroller-general, who shall pay unto such persons as may apply for the same, one-third part of the sums found due on settlement in the bills aforesaid, and for the remaining two-thirds they shall receive certificates in like manner as other troops of this state.

Passed April 13, 1782. Recorded L. B. 514, etc.

CHAPTER CMLXXII.

AN ACT MORE EFFECTUALLY TO ENCOURAGE THE KILLING OF WOLVES.

(Section I, P. L.) Whereas the act, entitled "An act for killing wolves,[1] and such parts of the law, entitled "An act for raising of county rates and levies,"[2] and the several supplements to the same, as relate to the killing of wolves are found, by experience, to be defective, and inadequate to the good purposes for which they were intended:

[Section I.] (Section II, P. L.) Be it therefore enacted, and it is hereby enacted by the Representatives of the Freemen of the Commonwealth of Pennsylvania in General Assembly met, and by the authority of the same, That from and after the publication of this act the reward for killing of wolves shall be as

---
[1] Passed January 12, 1705-6, Chapter 146.
[2] Passed March 20, 1724-5, Chapter 284.

follows, That is to say: For every grown wolf, killed within the inhabited parts of this state, the sum of twenty-five shillings, good and current money of the state of Pennsylvania; and for every wolf puppy or whelp so killed in like manner, the sum of fifteen shillings like money.

[Section II.] (Section III, P. L.) And be it further enacted by the authority aforesaid, That any person or persons who kill any wolves shall bring the scalp or skin of the head of such wolf or wolves so killed, with the ears on it, to some justice of the peace for the county where they are killed, who is hereby empowered and required to examine the person or persons producing such scalp or skin with the ears, or, at the discretion of the said justice, to charge him or them upon oath or affirmation to declare that the wolf or wolves, whose scalps or skins are so produced, were killed in the same county, and by whom; and if it shall clearly appear to the satisfaction of such justice that the said scalp or scalps were taken from wolves so killed as aforesaid, then the said justice shall cause the said ears to be cut off such scalp or scalps, and then, and not before, shall grant an order upon the treasurer of the county where such wolf or wolves were killed, reciting therein the substance of the proof, and requiring the said treasurer to pay to the person or persons the respective sum or sums hereinbefore mentioned, and the said treasurer is hereby authorized to pay it out of the county rates and levies.

[Section III.] (Section IV, P. L.) And be it enacted by the authority aforesaid, That the said act, entitled "An act for the killing of wolves," and so much of the aforesaid act, entitled "An act for the raising of county rates and levies," and the several supplements to the same as relates to the killing of wolves, except the part thereof that mentions wolves killed by Indians and such as obliges the respective treasurers to make entries in books provided by them for that end, are hereby repealed and declared to be null and void.

Passed April 13, 1782. Recorded L. B. No. 1, p. 516. See the note to the Act of Assembly passed January 12, 1705-6, Chapter 146.

CHAPTER CMLXXIII.

AN ACT TO REDRESS CERTAIN GRIEVANCES, WITHIN THE COUNTIES
OF WESTMORELAND AND WASHINGTON.

(Section I, P. L.) Whereas, a number of the inhabitants of Westmoreland and Washington counties have represented to the general assembly that they labor under many inconveniences by reason that before the boundary was agreed to between the states of Virginia and Pennsylvania many of the inhabitants aforesaid, conceiving themselves under the jurisdiction of Virginia, which exercised judicial authority over them, had taken and subscribed the oath of allegiance and fidelity as prescribed by the laws and usages of the said state, are considered in many respects as not entitled to all the rights of free citizens of this state, and that for the reasons above mentioned, they have had no opportunity of entering or registering their slaves agreeable to the act of assembly of this state for the gradual abolition of slavery, and that a number of the records and papers containing the proceedings of the late counties of Youghiogheny, Monongahela and Ohio are now in the hands of the late clerks, who are not authorized to give exemplified copies thereof:

[Section I.] (Section II, P. L.) Be it therefore enacted by the Representatives of the Freemen of the Commonwealth of Pennsylvania in General Assembly met, and by the authority of the same, That all and every person or persons, inhabitants of the said counties of Westmoreland and Washington, whose names shall not be found in the records hereinafter mentioned, and who shall be possessed of certified copies of their having taken the oath of allegiance and fidelity as aforesaid, shall, within six months after the publication of this act, produce to the clerks of the general quarter sessions of the said counties respectively, the said certified copies or certificates of their having taken the oath of allegiance and fidelity to the state of Virginia before the said boundary was agreed to, shall be and they are hereby declared to be, to all intents and purposes, free citizens of this state.

[Section II.] (Section III, P. L.) And be it enacted by the authority aforesaid, That it shall and may be lawful for all such inhabitants of the said counties who were, on the twenty-third of September, one thousand seven hundred and eighty, possessed of negro or mulatto slaves or servants until the age of thirty-one years, to register such slaves or servants, agreeable to the directions of the act aforesaid, for the gradual abolition of slavery, on or before the first day of January next; and the said master or masters, owner or owners of such slaves or servants shall be entitled to his, her or their service as by the said act is directed, and the said slaves and servants shall be entitled to all the benefits and immunities in the said act contained and expressed.

[Section III.] (Section IV, P. L.) And be it further enacted by the authority aforesaid, That the clerks of the orphan courts, the registers for the probates of wills and granting letters of administration and the recorders of deeds for the respective counties of Westmoreland and Washington aforesaid, shall be authorized and empowered to call on the late clerks of the said counties of Youghiogheny, Monongahela and Ohio for all such papers and records in their custody or possession, which relate to or affect the taking of the oath or affirmation of allegiance, the probates of wills, granting letters of administration, and the recording of deeds or other indentures, bargain and sale of any of the inhabitants of the said counties of Westmoreland and Washington, and when they shall have received all or any part of the [said] papers and records as aforesaid, they shall be lodged within their respective offices, and become part of the records of the said counties and the said late clerks are hereby required and enjoined, on demand made as aforesaid, to deliver up entire and undefaced all such papers and records as aforesaid, and in case they, or either of them, shall refuse or neglect to deliver up the papers and records in manner and form aforesaid, they, or either of them, so neglecting or refusing shall forfeit and pay the sum of five hundred pounds, to be recovered by action of debt, in any court of common pleas within this commonwealth for the use of the same.

Passed April 13, 1782. Recorded L. B. No. 1, p. 516, etc.

CHAPTER CMLXXIV.

AN ACT TO ENCOURAGE THE APPREHENDING PRISONERS OF WAR, WHO HAVE OR HEREAFTER MAY ESCAPE FROM THE PLACE OF THEIR CONFINEMENT, AND TO DISCOURAGE HARBORING THEM IN THIS STATE.

(Section I, P. L.) Whereas, it has been found by experience that the lenity and indulgence extended to the British prisoners of war, confined in sundry places within the United States, have been abused by them to base and perfidious purposes, and [that] many of them, assuming the habit and profession of laborers, have effected their escape and joined our enemies within the British lines at New York:

For remedy whereof:

[Section I.] Be it enacted and it is hereby enacted by the Representatives of the Freemen of the Commonwealth of Pennsylvania in General Assembly met, and by the authority of the same, That it shall and may be lawful for any of the inhabitants of this state, as well as to the different officers, whether civil or military, in the same, and they are hereby strictly enjoined and required to make diligent inquiry after and take up all such prisoners of war as they may have reason to believe are either secreted or concealed under any habit or pretence whatsoever, and them forthwith to bring before the next justice of the peace for examination. And if, upon such examination, it shall appear that said person so brought is a prisoner of war, he shall be committed to the gaol of the county and notice immediately transmitted to the war office of the name and place of confinement of such offender, that proper measures may be taken to return him to the place of his confinement; but if he refuses to give a satisfactory account of himself, then he shall be committed to the gaol of the county where such person may be apprehended, there to remain until the next court of general quarter sessions of the peace, which court shall take order on the case of said prisoner.

(Section II, P. L.) And whereas, the honorable Congress of these United States has recommended to the states, respectively, to encourage the apprehending such prisoners, by giving a reward of eight dollars to any person or persons who shall apprehend any prisoner of war, escaping from the place of his confinement, and one-eighth of a dollar per mile for traveling charges to any gaol, together with five ninetieths of a dollar for the subsistence of each prisoner while he shall be confined, all such moneys to be repaid by the superintendent of finance for the United States as by the resolve is directed:

(Section III, P. L.) In compliance therefore with the said recommendation, and as an encouragement to those who may exert themselves in apprehending and securing such prisoners:

[Section II.] Be it further enacted by the authority aforesaid, That whenever any person or persons within this state shall apprehend any prisoner of war, who has escaped from the place of confinement, and shall bring him before any justice of the peace within this commonwealth as aforesaid, such justice shall and he is hereby required to give a certificate to the person or persons apprehending such prisoner to the following effect:

"I, A. B., one of the justices of the peace for the county of ——————, do hereby certify that C. D., on the —————— day of ——————, brought before me a person who, upon examination appears to be a prisoner of war, belonging to the regiment of ——————, in the service of the King of Great Britain, and who has escaped from the place of his confinement, and that the said C. D., on producing a receipt from the keeper of any prison within this state for the said prisoner, is entitled to the reward and expenses by law allowed in such cases, witness my hand and seal this —————— day of ——————, Anno Domini one thousand seven hundred and eighty——————."

Which certificate, together with a receipt from the keeper of any prison within this state for such prisoner, being delivered to the treasurer of any county in this state, it shall and may be lawful for such treasurer and he is hereby required and directed to pay the reward, mileage and subsistence money as by this act is hereafter directed and required, and the said certificate and receipt, together with a receipt for the money paid, shall be a sufficient voucher for the allowance thereof in his account.

[Section III.] (Section IV, P. L.) And be it further enacted by the authority aforesaid, That the reward to be paid for every prisoner so apprehended and secured shall be eight dollars, and that every person so apprehending such prisoner shall also be allowed one-eighth of a dollar per mile for traveling charges and five-ninetieth of a dollar per day for the subsistence of each prisoner, all which said sums agreeable to the said resolve of Congress are to be allowed and repaid by the superintendent of finance.

[Section IV.] (Section V, P. L.) And be it further enacted by the authority aforesaid, That if any dispute shall arise between the said treasurer and the party claiming such expenses and allowance, the same shall be settled and ascertained by any two of justices of the peace of the county where such prisoner shall be secured, whose certificate thereof shall be final and conclusive and be a sufficient voucher to such treasurer.

(Section VI, P. L.) And in order that due and punctual repayment may be made for all moneys thus advanced for the United States:

[Section V.] Be it enacted by the authority aforesaid, That the treasurer of every county, respectively, shall, once in every six months, transmit to the treasurer of the state the certificates and receipts taken as aforesaid, who, upon receipt thereof, shall adjust and settle the same with the superintendent of finance. And if any treasurer shall wilfully or negligently keep such certificates and receipts beyond the space of six months aforesaid, every such treasurer shall forfeit and lose the moneys by him paid, and no allowance shall be made therefor in the settlement of his account.

[Section VI.] (Section VII, P. L.) And be it further enacted by the authority aforesaid, That if any person suspected to be a prisoner of war escaped from his confinement shall be brought before any justice of [the] peace, and shall refuse to give any account of himself, it shall and may be lawful for such justice to grant a certificate upon the best information and evidence he can procure, which shall be as good and effectual for the recovery of the said reward and expenses as if the same had been granted on full conviction and acknowledgement made by such prisoner, anything hereinbefore contained to the contrary notwithstanding.

[Section VII.] (Section VIII, P. L.) And be it further enacted by the authority aforesaid, That if any keeper of any prison within this state shall wilfully or negligently suffer any prisoner of war committed to his custody to escape from the said prison, the keeper being convicted thereof in any court of record within this state shall forfeit and pay the sum of fifty pounds for every prisoner so escaping, with costs of suit, and be disabled from holding such office or place at any time thereafter.

(Section IX, P. L.) And in order the more effectually to deter all persons from the base and treacherous practice of aiding, abetting, concealing or assisting such prisoners of war:

[Section VIII.] Be it further enacted by the authority aforesaid, That whatsoever person shall be duly convicted in any court of quarter sessions of this state, either of concealing, aiding, abetting or otherwise assisting such prisoner of war in making his escape, shall forfeit, on such conviction, the sum of fifty pounds, one-half to the state and the other half to the person prosecuting for the same; but if the person so convicted shall be unable to pay he shall be publicly whipped with thirty-nine lashes; and this offense is hereby declared to be made inquireable in the court of quarter sessions, and the constables shall, on making their quarterly returns, answer on oath, touching their knowledge of any offense against this law.

[Section IX.] Provided always, That nothing in this act shall be meant, construed or intended to affect any persons who shall receive prisoners of war for the purposes of labor by any order from the war office or such officer whom they may authorize to grant such order. But such persons so receiving prisoners of war, are hereby required to enter the names of such prisoners with the next justice of the peace within one week after bringing them to the places of their respective residence.

Passed April 13, 1782. Recorded L. B. No. 1, p. 518, etc.

CHAPTER CMLXXV.

A SUPPLEMENT TO AN ACT, ENTITLED "AN ACT TO ALTER AND AMEND AN ACT, ENTITLED 'AN ACT FOR THE EFFECTUAL SUPPRESSION OF PUBLIC AUCTIONS AND VENDUES, AND TO PROHIBIT MALE PERSONS, CAPABLE OF BEARING ARMS, FROM BEING HAWKERS AND PEDLERS.'" [1]

(Section I, P. L.) Whereas the commissions or recompense allowed to the auctioneers for the city of Philadelphia, the Northern Liberties and the district of Southwark, respectively, for the services by them performed, by virtue of the act of assembly, entitled "An act to alter and amend an act, entitled 'An act for the effectual suppression of public auctions and vendues and to prohibit male persons capable of bearing arms from being hawkers and peddlers,'" [1] passed the twenty-third day of September, in the year one thousand seven hundred and eighty, have been remonstrated against by the merchants, traders and others residing within the said city, liberties and district, and are deemed more than adequate or necessary. And whereas, the exigencies of government require immediate additional funds for the support thereof:

[Section I.] (Section II, P. L.) Be it therefore enacted by the Representatives of the Freemen of the Commonwealth of Pennsylvania in General Assembly met, and by the authority of the same, That the auctioneers of the city of Philadelphia, the Northern Liberties and the district of Southwark, respectively may and shall, from and after the passing of this act,

---
[1] Passed September 23, 1780, Chapter 919.

have and receive for their expenses and trouble in selling any property at public auction, collecting the money and paying over the same without loss, the following allowance or reward and no more, That is to say: For houses, lands, tenements or real estates, and for ships or vessels, an half per centum; for wine, rum, sugar, coffee, tea and all other groceries, sold by the pipe, hogshead, tierce, barrel, bag, chest or box, one and a quarter per centum; and for horses, cattle and all other goods, wares and merchandises not before enumerated or sold in smaller quantities than before mentioned, two and an half per centum. Provided always, That any person or persons may contract and agree with any of the said auctioneers to pay them for their services in the premises any less reward which they may be willing to accept.

[Section II.] (Section III, P. L.) And be it further enacted by the authority aforesaid, That every of the said auctioneers, from and after the passing of this act, is hereby authorized, empowered and required to demand and receive, over and above the sum mentioned in the aforesaid act, to which this is a supplement, an additional one per centum of the gross amount of the sales by him made in pursuance of the said act, for the use of this commonwealth, except for ships or vessels, houses and lots, and shall account for and pay over the same to the state treasurer within the time and in the manner directed with respect to the one per centum imposed by the said act, under the penalty in the said act mentioned.

[Section III.] (Section IV, P. L.) And be it further enacted by the authority aforesaid, That the several bonds given by the said auctioneers to the president for the faithful performance of the duties of them required by the aforesaid act shall be a security for the payment of the one per centum imposed by this act.

[Section IV.] (Section V, P. L.) And be it further enacted by the authority aforesaid, That the revenue arising from the sales by auction in the city of Philadelphia, the Northern Liberties and the district of Southwark, from and after the passing of this act, shall be and the same is hereby appropriated to the support of government and the administration of justice within this commonwealth.

<blockquote>Passed April 13, 1782. Recorded L. B. No. 1, p. 521, etc. See the note to the Act of Assembly passed September 23, 1780, Chapter 917, and the Act of Assembly passed December 7, 1783, Chapter 1063.</blockquote>

CHAPTER CMLXXVI.

AN ACT TO REVIVE AND CONTINUE AN ACT, ENTITLED "AN ACT FOR OPENING AND KEEPING IN REPAIR THE PUBLIC ROADS AND HIGHWAYS IN THIS PROVINCE."[1]

(Section I, P. L.) Whereas, the act, entitled "An act for opening and keeping in repair the public roads and highways in this province,"[1] passed the twenty-first day of March, one thousand seven hundred and seventy-two, has expired by its own limitation, and whereas in its operation the said act hath proved beneficial and easy to the inhabitants and travelers in this state:

[Section I.] (Section II, P. L.) Be it therefore enacted by the Representatives of the Freemen of the Commonwealth of Pennsylvania in General Assembly met, and by the authority of the same, That the said act and every article, clause and thing therein contained, the clause for limitation only excepted, be and it is hereby declared to be revived and continued, and the same shall be and remain in full force and virtue for and during the term of five years from and after the passing of this act, and from thence to the end of the next sitting of assembly, and no longer.

<blockquote>Passed April 13, 1782. Recorded L. B. No. 1, p. 522, etc.,See the note to the Act of Assembly passed March 21, 1772, Chapter 653.</blockquote>

---

[1] Passed March 21, 1772, Chapter 653.

CHAPTER CMLXXVII.

AN ACT FOR ESTABLISHING FERRIES ON THE RIVERS MONONGAHELA AND YOUGHIOGHENY.

(Section I, P. L.) Whereas, great numbers of the inhabitants of Westmoreland and Washington counties have, by their petitions, humbly represented to the legislature of this state the great necessity there is of having ferries established on the rivers of Monongahela and Youghiogheny, and also praying that William Crawford be allowed the privilege of erecting a ferry over the said river of Youghiogheny, at Stuart's crossings, and John Devoir, executor of the estate of Jacobus Devoir, late of Westmoreland county, on behalf of the orphan children to whom the said estate belongs, and Joseph Parkinson, be also allowed the privilege of having a ferry erected over the said river of Monongahela, at the distance of about thirty perches below the mouth of Pigeon creek:

(Section II, P. L.) For the greater ease, conveniency and security of the [said] inhabitants and others passing and repassing the rivers aforesaid:

[Section I.] Be it enacted and it is hereby enacted by the Representatives of the Freemen of the Commonwealth of Pennsylvania in General Assembly met, and by the authority of the same, That the said William Crawford may at any time hereafter and at his own proper cost and charge, make, or cause to be made, a convenient landing on both sides of the said river Youghiogheny, and shall keep and maintain the same in good order and repair, fit for men, horses and carriages to pass and repass, and also shall provide and maintain a good, substantial boat or boats and capable ferrymen who shall duly and constantly attend as occasion may require.

[Section II.] (Section III, P. L.) And be it further enacted by the authority aforesaid, That the said John Devoir, for and on behalf of the said orphan children, and the said Joseph Parkinson, may each respectively make, or cause to be made, a convenient landing on that respective side of the said river of Monongahela on which he claims and shall keep and maintain the same in like good order and repair as aforesaid, and shall provide and maintain a good boat or boats and capable ferrymen, who shall duly and constantly attend, as occasion may require.

[Section III.] (Section IV, P. L.) And be it further enacted by the authority aforesaid, That the said rivers, so far up as they or either of them have been or can be made navigable for rafts, boats and canoes, and within the bounds and limits of this state, shall be and are hereby declared to be public highways.

Passed April 13, 1782. Recorded L. B. No. 1, p. 522, etc.

CHAPTER CMLXXVIII.

AN ACT TO ALTER AND REPEAL A PART OF THE ACT, ENTITLED "AN ACT FOR EMITTING THE SUM OF FIVE HUNDRED THOUSAND POUNDS IN BILLS OF CREDIT FOR THE SUPPORT OF THE ARMY, AND FOR ESTABLISHING A FUND FOR THE REDEMPTION THEREOF, AND FOR OTHER PURPOSES THEREIN MENTIONED."[1]

(Section I, P. L.. Whereas it is provided and declared in the fourteenth section of the act for emitting the sum of five hundred thousand pounds, passed the seventh of April, one thousand seven hundred and eighty-one, that no money be taken or received in the payment of taxes, after the first day of June, one thousand seven hundred and eighty-one, except gold or silver, or bills of credit by law equivalent thereto: And whereas, by the act for the repeal of so much of the laws as make bills of credit a legal tender, passed the twenty-first of June, one thousand seven hundred and eighty-one, no paper bills of credit (except in particular cases) are now equivalent to gold or silver: And whereas it is found that the said restrictions have prevented the payment of a sufficient sum of the old continental currency into the treasury, for the purpose of exchanging and sinking our quota of the same:

[1] Passed April 7, 1781, Chapter 939.

(Section II, P. L.) For remedy whereof:

[Section I.] Be it enacted by the Representatives of the Freemen of the Commonwealth of Pennsylvania in General Assembly met, and by the authority of the same, That so much of the said act as declares that no money, after the first of June, one thousand seven hundred and eighty-one, shall be received in taxes, other than gold or silver, or bills of credit by law equivalent thereto, is hereby repealed and made void; and the old continental bills of credit, the paper bills of credit, commonly called resolve money, emitted by the assembly of the late province of Pennsylvania, and the bills of credit called commonwealth money, emitted by act of general assembly, dated the twentieth day of March, one thousand seven hundred and seventy-seven, are hereby declared payable in all arrearages of taxes levied in continental bills of credit, for the use of the United States of America, from and after the twenty-seventh of March, one thousand seven hundred and seventy-eight. And the several collectors, county treasurers, and the state treasurer, are hereby authorized and required to receive the said several enumerated kinds of paper bills of credit at their nominal value, and the paper bills of credit emitted in pursuance of the resolve of Congress of the eighteenth of March, one thousand seven hundred and eighty, and the paper bills of credit emitted by the act for emitting the sum of five hundred thousand pounds, passed the seventh of April, one thousand seven hundred and eighty-one, at the rate of one dollar for seventy-five of the old continental currency, in the payment of the said taxes, anything in any law of this state to the contrary in anywise notwithstanding.

[Section II.] (Section III, P. L.) And be it further enacted by the authority aforesaid, That all sums of money heretofore received by collectors or county treasurers in any kind of paper money or that shall be received hereafter in consequence of this act, shall be paid into the treasury of this state in the same kind and at the same value at which they have or may receive the same on the oath or affirmation of such collector or county treasurer.

Passed April 13, 1782. Recorded L. B. No. 1, p. 523, etc.

CHAPTER CMLXXIX.

AN ACT FOR VESTING IN THE AMERICAN PHILOSOPHICAL SOCIETY HELD AT PHILADELPHIA FOR PROMOTING USEFUL KNOWLEDGE THE PROPERTY THEREIN MENTIONED UPON THE CONDITIONS THEREIN SPECIFIED.

(Section I, P. L.) Whereas, the American Philosophical Society, held at Philadelphia, for promoting useful knowledge, did, in the year one thousand seven hundred and seventy, set on foot a subscription to raise a fund for promoting the culture of silk in America, in consequence of which considerable sums were subscribed and collected and the business was commenced by forming a society for promoting the culture of silk in America:

And whereas, a former house of assembly were pleased to grant the sum of one thousand pounds to the said silk society for promoting the scheme they had undertaken:

And whereas, by the rules of the said silk society the managers and officers were to be annually chosen by the subscribers, which rules were to be in force for three years only:

And whereas, in consequence of the war the three years elapsed without any renewal of the constitution of the said silk society, since which time there hath no election been held nor any business done in the great purpose for which the subscribers originally associated:

And whereas, the stock of the said society, consisting of money, a quantity of raw silk and other articles, remain in the hands of the managers last appointed:

And whereas, it is not thought expedient to revive the prosecution of the said scheme at present and the said philosophical society having, by their petition, applied to this house for the money and other property remaining in the hands of the late managers of the said silk society:

[Section I.] (Section II, P. L.) Be it therefore enacted and it is hereby enacted by the Representatives of the Freemen of the Commonwealth of Pennsylvania in General Assembly met, and by the authority of the same, That the managers of the said silk society last appointed, or the survivors of them, shall and they are hereby directed to settle and adjust the accounts of the silk society and to collect and recover all sums of money due thereto. And as the silk remaining in their hands must sustain injury by remaining longer unwrought, they are hereby directed to make sale thereof, and the net proceeds, together with the other money in stock and the articles and utensils belonging to the said silk society, they shall pay and deliver unto the said philosophical society within four months after the publication of this act, whose receipt shall be a full discharge.

[Section II.] (Section III, P. L.) Provided always, and be it further enacted by the authority aforesaid, That if any subscriber of the said silk society shall, on or before the first day of October next ensuing, apply to the said philosophical society for reimbursement he shall be entitled to receive his proportional dividend of what may remain of the sum originally subscribed.

(Section IV, P. L.) And whereas, at a future day it may become expedient to revive the said silk society:

[Section III.] Be it enacted by the authority aforesaid, That the philosophical society shall be accountable for such sums of money and effects as shall remain in their hands unclaimed by the proprietors aforesaid, and shall redeliver to them such sum and implements whenever a majority of the subscribers shall, under their hands, request the same in order to revive the said institution.

Passed April 15, 1782. Recorded L. B. No. 1, p. 524, etc.

CHAPTER CMLXXX.

AN ACT TO AMEND AN ACT, ENTITLED "AN ACT TO ENABLE THE OWNERS OF SCHUYLKILL POINT MEADOW LAND, IN THE COUNTY OF PHILADELPHIA, TO KEEP THE BANKS, DAMS, SLUICES AND FLOODGATES IN REPAIR, AND TO RAISE A FUND TO DEFRAY THE EXPENSES THEREOF."[1]

(Section I, P. L.) Whereas, by an act, entitled "An act to enable the owners of Schuylkill Point meadow land, in the county of Philadelphia, to keep the banks, dams, sluices and floodgates in repair, and to raise a fund to defray the expenses thereof,"[1] it was, among other things, enacted, That Hough Roberts, Enoch Flower, Samuel Rhoads, Andrew Bankson, Joseph Johnson and John Smith, or any four of them, were thereby nominated, authorized and appointed, within two months after the publication of that act, to divide the banks which surrounded and included all that, the said tract or piece of marsh or meadow land, and allot and appoint how many perches of the said bank each owner or possessor of the said tract should make, repair, maintain and support in proportion to the number of acres of meadow he held therein, alloting the part and proportion so to be made, repaired, maintained and supported, as near and convenient as might be to the land of each respective owner thereof, beginning the allotments at the place of beginning in the said-recited act mentioned, all which said allotments so made and signified by an instrument in writing, under the hands and seals of any four of them, should be the proper shares, parts, proportions and quantities of bank for the several owners or possessors of the said meadow to make, repair and support at their own expense and charge, as in and by the said-recited act more fully appear:

(Section II, P. L.) And whereas, it is found by experience that the mode of supporting the said bank by individual allotments is attended with divers inconveniences:

[Section I.] Be it therefore enacted by the Representatives

---

[1] Passed September 26, 1761, Chapter 472.

of the Freemen of the Commonwealth of Pennsylvania in General Assembly met, and by the authority of the same, That from and after the publication of this act the several owners of meadow ground within the banks surrounding the said Schuylkill Point meadows shall be and they are hereby released and discharged from making, repairing, maintaining and supporting the several proper shares, parts, proportions and quantities of the said bank to them alloted, in pursuance of the said-recited act, at their own proper expense and charge and of and from all penalties and forfeitures by the said-recited act annexed to the neglect thereof.

[Section II.] (Section III, P. L.) And be it further enacted by the authority aforesaid, That immediately after the passing of this act it shall and may be lawful for the present managers of the said company to enter into and upon the said banks, and if, upon inspection it shall appear to them that any particular allotments thereof shall stand in immediate need of repair, then it shall be lawful for the said managers, without consulting the owners of the particular allotments which shall so require immediate repairs, to enter upon the adjoining grounds with such workmen, horses, carts, implements and tools as shall be necessary, and to dig and cast earth, or purchase other materials and cause the said allotments of bank to be repaired so as to put them all in order and repair as nearly as possible equal at the several expense and charge of each of the said owners of the said allotments which shall require such repair, and to levy, recover, collect and receive from each of them, respectively, the several amounts of the said respective expenses and charges, in the same manner and under the same penalties and forfeitures as the taxes for other purposes in the said-recited act mentioned are directed to be levied, recovered, collected and paid.

(Section IV, P. L.) And in order for the better and more certain and expeditious repairing and supporting the said bank in future, and for rendering the burden and expense thereof more equal upon all the said owners:

[Section III.] Be it enacted by the authority aforesaid, That from and after the publication of this act, it shall and may be lawful to and for the managers of the said Schuylkill Point meadows, elected and to be elected in pursuance of the before-recited act, and they are hereby enjoined and required to enter upon and inspect the said banks, drains and ditches, so often as they shall think necessary, but not less than four times in every year, and if, upon such inspection, it shall appear to them that any part of the said bank stands in need of repair, whether from gradual decay or a sudden irruption of the water, or otherwise, then and in such case it shall and may be lawful for the said managers, without consulting the owners of the particular place where such repairs are wanting, to enter upon the adjoining grounds with such workmen, horses, carts, implements and tools as shall be necessary, and there to dig and carry earth or purchase other materials for the repair and support of the said bank (in a good substantial and sufficient manner, according to the directions in the said-recited act contained), at the joint expense and charge of all the said owners.

(Section V, P. L.) And whereas, it may sometimes happen that great benefit may be derived to the general interest of the said company by making some additional works for the security of the said banks or draining the said meadows, but the great length of time necessary to procure the consent of all the said owners may prevent the same being done within due time:

[Section IV.] Be it therefore enacted by the authority aforesaid, That it shall and may be lawful for a board of the managers, at any time when they shall be of opinion that any such additional works (not herein nor by the act to which this is a supplement provided for) shall become necessary and expedient for the general benefit of all the said owners, to cause the same to be done and perfected at the joint expense and charge of all the said owners.

[Section V.] (Section VI, P. L.) And be it further enacted by the authority aforesaid, That it shall and may be lawful for the said managers, elected and to be elected as aforesaid, from time to time to lay such assessments and taxes on every acre of land within the said bank as they shall judge necessary for repairing, maintaining and supporting the same; and for the other purposes herein above mentioned, to be paid, collected and recovered in the same manner and under the same penalties and forfeitures as the taxes for other purposes in the said-recited act mentioned are thereby directed to be levied, recovered, collected and paid.

(Section VII, P. L.) And whereas, the penalty by the said-recited act annexed to the refusal or neglect of any owner of the said Schuylkill Point meadows to serve the office of a manager when thereto elected by the said company, is found to be insufficient to answer the ends thereby intended:

[Section VI.] Be it therefore enacted by the authority aforesaid, That from and after the publication of this act, whenever any owner or possessor of any of the said meadows shall be duly elected, in pursuance of the said-recited act, to serve as a manager to the said company, and shall neglect or refuse to take upon himself the burden of the said office, every such person so elected and neglecting or refusing, unless he shall have served the said office two successive years next before his said election, shall forfeit and pay to the treasurer of the said company for the time being the sum of five pounds, lawful money of this commonwealth for the public use of the said company, in lieu of such service, which said penalty shall be levied, collected, recovered and paid in the same manner, and under the same forfeitures, as other moneys payable to the treasurer of the said company are by the said-recited act directed to be recovered.

[Section VII.] (Section VIII, P. L.) And be it further enacted by the authority aforesaid, That so much of the said-recited act as is herein and hereby altered shall be and is hereby repealed and made null and void, but all and every other matter and thing therein contained shall be and remain in full force and virtue as if this act were never made.

Passed April 15, 1782. Recorded L. B. No. 1, p. 525, etc.

CHAPTER CMLXXXI.

AN ACT TO VEST A CERTAIN LOT OR LOTS OF GROUND IN THE DISTRICT OF SOUTHWARK, IN TRUSTEES FOR THE USE OF A PUBLIC LANDING UPON THE CONDITIONS HEREINAFTER MENTIONED AND OTHER PURPOSES.

(Section I, P. L.) Whereas the inhabitants of the district of Southwark have been long desirous to procure a commodious lot or lots of ground for the purpose of public landings and streets within the said district, and in pursuance of such desire, Luke Morris, Thomas Penrose and James Penrose did, in the year of our Lord one thousand seven hundred and sixty-eight, purchase of John Jekyl three lots of ground situate on the east side of Front street, in the said district, and extending from thence across Penn street and Water street into the river Delaware, which said lots were conveyed to them as joint tenants in fee, by indenture bearing date the twelfth day of May, Anno Domini one thousand seven hundred and sixty-eight. And whereas, the said Luke Morris, Thomas Penrose and James Penrose, by a certain deed poll under their hands and seals duly executed, bearing date the [said] twelfth day of May, in the same year, did declare and acknowledge that the said purchase, so as aforesaid by them made, was intended for public use, and did covenant and promise, that if the inhabitants of the said district should incline to take the same and should, within three years then next following, well and truly pay, or cause to be paid, to the said Luke Morris, Thomas Penrose and James Penrose, their heirs, executors, administrators or assigns, the full purchase money by them paid, together with lawful interest for the same and such reasonable costs and charges as should accrue to them upon the said purchase, then and in that case they, the said Luke Morris, Thomas Penrose and James Penrose, or the survivors or survivor [of them] would, by good and sufficient conveyance and assurance in the law, convey and assure the said lots of ground to trustees to be appointed for that purpose, to be held by them, their heirs and assigns forever, in trust for the public use as in and by the said indenture and deed poll recorded in the rolls office for the county of Philadelphia more fully appears. And whereas, divers attempts have been made by the inhabitants of the said district to fall upon some mode of raising money for those purposes, but hitherto the same have proved abortive. And whereas, the said inhabitants of Southwark aforesaid, have lately chosen and appointed Robert Knox, Joseph Blewer, Joseph Turner, John Brown, William Clifton and Isaac Penrose to be a committee to transact all business, touching and concerning the said lots, and to endeavor to raise moneys and procure a title to themselves for the said lots for public use, which committee having had several conferences with the said Luke Morris, Thomas Penrose and Abel James (guardian duly appointed of Clement Penrose, the only child of the said James Penrose, who is since dead) and have come to an agreement concerning the same:

[Section I.] (Section II, P. L.) Be it therefore enacted by the Representatives of the Freemen of the Commonwealth of Pennsylvania in General Assembly met, and by the authority of the same, That James Pemberton, Joseph Swift, Peter Knight, Henry Drinker and Richard Wells, or any three of them shall be and they are hereby appointed auditors to hear forthwith the said Luke Morris, Thomas Penrose and Abel James, and examine their accounts and vouchers and to settle the same agreeable to the original intent of the parties, and by deeds poll under their hands and seals to certify and ascertain the precise sum of money due to each of them, the said Luke Morris, Thomas Penrose and Clement Penrose, as the representative of the said James Penrose, for their respective shares of the principal, interest and costs of the said purchase, which certificates, so executed as aforesaid, shall be delivered to the said parties, and shall be and remain, conclusive evidence of the amount of the said respective sums due. And the said auditors shall have power to proceed upon the said examination and settlement of the accounts ex parte if any of the persons concerned shall neglect or refuse to attend them upon ten days' notice.

[Section II.] (Section III, P. L.) And be it further enacted by the authority aforesaid, That if the said Robert Knox, Joseph Blewer, Joseph Turner, John Brown, William Clifften and Isaac Penrose, or any of them, do and shall well and truly pay, or cause to be paid, to the said Luke Morris, Thomas Penrose and Clement Penrose, or to their heirs, executors, administrators and assigns or to the guardian of the said Clement Penrose, the several and respective debts or sums of money so as aforesaid to be certified and ascertained by the said auditors, with interest thereon from the date of the said deeds poll, within two years next after the passing of this act, and shall procure acknowledgments indorsed thereon and signed by the said Luke Morris, Thomas Penrose and Clement Penrose, respectively, or their heirs, executors, administrators or assigns, or the guardian of the said Clement Penrose (who are hereby [enjoined and] required to sign such acknowledgments upon receipt thereof) that such moneys are well and truly paid to them, then the said deeds poll and the acknowledgments indorsed (being proved or acknowledged by the parties in the manner and form that deeds of conveyance are usually proved or acknowledged) shall and may be recorded in the office for recording of deeds in and for the county of Philadelphia, and shall vest the estate of inheritance in fee simple of and in the said lots in them, the said Robert Knox, Joseph Blewer, Joseph Turner, John Brown, William Clifften and Isaac Penrose, as fully and effectually as the same could be vested in them by any feoffment or deed of conveyance whatsoever, in trust nevertheless to and for the uses, intents and purposes hereafter mentioned.

[Section III.] (Section IV, P. L.) And be it further enacted by the authority aforesaid, That if the said Robert Knox, Joseph Blewer, Joseph Turner, John Brown, William Clifften and Isaac Penrose shall neglect or refuse to pay to the said Luke Morris, Thomas Penrose and Clement Penrose, respectively, their heirs, executors, administrators or assigns, or to the guardian of the said Clement Penrose, the said several and respective sums of money so as aforesaid certified and ascertained by the said auditors to be due to them, with interest for the same, for the space of two years next after the passing of this act, then and from thenceforth all right, title, interest, claim and demand whatsoever, both at law and in equity, which the said trustees in behalf of the public have, or claim to have, of, in and to the said lots of ground shall cease, determine and become absolutely void and extinct, and the said Luke Morris, Thomas Penrose and Clement Penrose, and their heirs and assigns, shall and may have, hold and enjoy the same to their own proper use and behoof as tenants in common in equal shares and proportions in fee simple, without any further or other release or conveyance.

(Section V, P. L.) And whereas, it is intended to raise a sum of money by laying and collecting a tax upon the real and personal estates within the said district in yearly portions, sufficient within a reasonable number of years to reimburse the said trustees the whole principal and interest thereon which they shall advance for procuring the aforesaid title to them, and it is reasonable that they should be fully secured and indemnified from loss by paying their private moneys or engaging their private credit for public use:

[Section IV.] (Section VI, P. L.) Be it therefore enacted by the authority aforesaid, That so soon as the said trustees shall, by payment of the said purchase money, have procured a title to themselves, it shall and may be lawful for them, or the survivors of them, to lay out such parts of the said lots as they shall think necessary for the use of the public for streets and landings, and if any should be left, which in their judgment will not be necessary for public use, then they, or the survivors of them, shall and may sell all such unnecessary parts of the said lots by public sale for the best prices that can be obtained, and make good and perfect titles for the same, to the purchasers in fee simple, and apply the moneys arising from such sales towards the payment of themselves for the moneys they shall be in advance and that it shall and may be lawful for them, or the survivors of them, to borrow, on interest, any sum or sums of money not exceeding the amount which shall then be due to them, and to grant, bargain, sell, convey and assure to the lenders, in mortgage, all such parts of the said lots as shall be retained for public use, which deeds of mortgage shall be as good and valid in the law for securing the payment of the moneys borrowed as any mortgage made by a private person of his own estate now is.

[Section V.] (Section VII, P. L.) And be it further enacted by the authority aforesaid, That it shall and may be lawful for the said trustees and the survivors of them to demise, grant and to farm let to any person or persons whatsoever for any term of years not exceeding seven at one time, all the wharves, keys and landing places belonging to the said lots, as a public landing place, reserving such rents and conditions and establishing such rates and prices for the toll or wharfage of all kinds of articles which are usually brought to public landings as they shall think reasonable, and restraining the tenant from demanding higher rates and prices, and binding him in sufficient penalties in all things to abide by such rules, orders and regulations as the tenants of the public landings in the city [of] Philadelphia are bound to observe, and to receive the rents, issues, and profits thereof and to apply the same in discharge of the encumbrances on the said lots.

[Section VI.] (Section VIII, P. L.) And be it further enacted by the authority aforesaid, That so soon as a sufficient sum of money shall be raised by sale of part of the premises as aforesaid, by the rents, issues and profits of the residue, and by a public tax which is intended to be laid and collected within the said district, or by any other means sufficient to discharge all the encumbrances which the said lot shall be subject to, in manner aforesaid, then the said Robert Knox, Joseph Blewer, Joseph Turner, John Brown, William Cliffton and Isaac Penrose, or the survivors or survivor of them, or the heirs and assigns of the survivor, shall, by good and sufficient conveyance and assurance in the law, grant, release and confirm the said premises which shall be retained for public use as aforesaid to the supervisors of the highways in and for the said district of Southwark for the time being (who are hereby erected into and declared to be one body politic and corporate for this especial purpose, in deed and in law capable of holding the same, and of suing and being sued in all actions touching and concerning the same) by the name of the supervisors of the public landings and highways in the district of Southwark, and to their successors forever, in trust for the use of the public, in the manner hereinafter mentioned; that is to say, in trust that the said supervisors for the time being, or a majority of them, with the approbation of three justices of the peace of and for the said county, shall and may demise, grant and to farm let the same landings to any person or persons for any term of years not exceeding seven at one time upon such rents and conditions as they shall think proper, and shall and may make such rules, orders and regulations for the well governing as well the tenants thereof as the boat, flats, carts and wagons which shall frequent the same, and the owners, skippers and drivers thereof, and the prices or rates of toll or wharfage to be paid for all articles to be unladen thereon, and that the said supervisors shall receive the rents, issues and profits thereof and apply the same to make any improvements or buildings thereon, to pave any of the streets or to maintain and repair any of the highways or to any other public use within the said district which the said supervisors, or a majority of them, with the approbation of three justices of the said county as aforesaid shall order, direct and appoint.

Passed April 15, 1782. Recorded L. B. No. 1, p. 527, etc.

CHAPTER CMLXXXII.

AN ACT TO AMEND AND RENDER EFFECTUAL AN ACT, ENTITLED "AN ACT FOR REGULATING PARTY WALLS AND PARTITION FENCES IN THE CITY OF PHILADELPHIA," TO DECLARE DIVERS NEW STREETS AND WAYS, OPENED AND TO BE OPENED AND LAID OUT WITHIN THE SAID CITY, TO BE HIGHWAYS, AND ALSO TO DECLARE NUISANCES BY BUILDINGS WITHIN THE SAID STREETS REMOVABLE, AND FOR OTHER PURPOSES THEREIN MENTIONED.

(Section I, P. L.) Whereas an act of assembly, passed on the twenty-fourth day of February, which was in the year of our

Lord (according to the new style) one thousand seven hundred and twenty and one, entitled "An act for regulating party walls and partition fences in the city of Philadelphia,"[1] has, upon experience, been found to be an useful law, by preventing contentions concerning the boundaries of landed property within the said city, and by preserving the breadth and directness of the streets and alleys of the said city. And whereas, ever since the late revolution the said act, though revived with divers other laws of the late province of Pennsylvania, has been wholly dormant and inoperative, because of the dissolution of the late corporation of the mayor and commonalty of the said city, which corporation in and by the said act was authorized to appoint the surveyors and regulators in the said act mentioned and to receive and determine appeals from the said surveyors or regulators. And whereas divers amendments to the said act may be usefully made:

[Section I.] (Section II, P. L.) Be it therefore enacted by the Representatives of the Freemen of the Commonwealth of Pennsylvania in General Assembly met, and by the authority of the same, That any four or more of the justices of the peace who are or shall be commissioned for the city and county of Philadelphia, residing in said city, together with four or more of the commissioners for paving and cleansing the streets of the said city, shall appoint the surveyors or regulators aforesaid, as fully to all intents and purposes as they were formerly appointed by the mayor and commonalty of the said city in common council assembled; and in case of the death, removal, refusal to serve or misbehavior of any of the persons appointed by virtue of this act, the said justices and commissioners to appoint another or others in his or their room and stead.

[Section II.] (Section III, P. L.) And be it further enacted by the authority aforesaid, That all appeals hereafter made from the order, direction and award of the said regulators, in pursuance of the said act and of this act shall be taken and made and shall lie to the next court of common pleas to be holden for the county of Philadelphia, after the expiration of one calendar month from the time of making the order, direction or

---

[1] Passed February 24, 1721, Chapter 242.

award, appealed from, but not afterwards nor otherwise; whereupon the said court (upon security being entered by the party appealing for the payment of costs, as well his own as those of the party appellate in case he or she prevail not in his or her suit) shall direct a venire to the sheriff of the county, commanding him to summon a jury to try the matter in dispute, and shall proceed therein according to the course of the common law.

[Section II.] (Section IV, P. L.) And be it further enacted by the authority aforesaid, That if any person shall lay the foundation, or begin to lay the foundation of any party wall, or of any wall adjoining or upon the line of any public street, lane or alley, within the said city, before the line and boundaries of the lot or piece of land whereon the said foundation shall be so laid, or begun to be laid, shall be adjusted and marked out by the said regulators, or two of them, every such person, as well employer as master builder, shall forfeit the sum of ten pounds, one-half part thereof to the street commissioners for the time being, to be laid out towards making or amending the pavements of the public streets, and the other half thereof to the use of the informer, together with costs; provided the prosecution be commenced in the city of Philadelphia, and within twelve calendar months after the offense shall be committed.

[Section IV.] (Section V, P. L.) And be it further enacted by the authority aforesaid, That as soon as conveniently may be the northern line of Vine street and southern line of Cedar street shall be ascertained, regulated and marked out by the regulators of the city of Philadelphia, assisted by the regulators of the district of the Northern Liberties, so far as said district, that they are appointed for, is bounded on the said city, and assisted by the regulators of the district of Southwark, so far as the said district is bounded on said city, and the rest of the northern line of Vine street, and the rest of the southern line of Cedar street, respectively, shall be ascertained, adjusted and marked out by the regulators of the said city, which regulating and marking out of Vine and Cedar streets shall be performed and done at the joint proportionable expense of the said city, and districts, to be paid by the commissioners for paving and cleansing the streets, and by the regulators of the said districts, respectively, upon the certificate of the regulators of the said city and districts, who are hereby empowered to proportion the said expense.

[Section V.] (Section VI, P. L.) And be it further enacted by the authority aforesaid, That the regulators, so to be appointed as aforesaid for the said city, shall enter into a book all directions, orders and awards by them made in pursuance of said act, and of this act concerning the boundaries of any lot or land situated within the said city (such book to be provided for them, by the commissioners for paving and cleansing the streets of the said city) and every such order and award, if made with reasonable notice beforehand to the parties interested therein, shall conclude and bind all persons, unless the same be set aside upon appeal as aforesaid; and the said regulators of the said city shall in like manner enter in the same book all regulations, made by the [said] justices and themselves, of descents, watercourses, common sewers and all other their proceedings and actings in their office as regulators.

(Section VII, P. L.) Provided always, That no person under age, non compos mentis, covert, imprisoned or beyond sea, or any person who shall not have reasonable notice as aforesaid, shall be injured or affected by any proceeding, order, direction or award of the said regulators, so as the party and parties so disabled or not noticed enter and prosecute his, her and their appeal as aforesaid, within three years after coming to full age, sound memory, discoverture, return from beyond sea or if within the United States within one year after notice in writing shall be given of the order and award of the said regulators.

[Section VI.] (Section VIII, P. L.) And be it further enacted by the authority aforesaid, That the said regulators, for their trouble in regulating and setting out the lines of any lot or piece of land in pursuance of the said act and of this act, and for entering their order and award concerning the same as aforesaid, shall be paid by the parties interested therein, five shillings each, and no more; and for surveying, regulating and laying out any streets, water courses and common sewers the sum of ten shillings to each of them who shall be employed therein, for every day so employed; to be paid by the commissioners for paving and cleansing the streets of said city, by an order on their treasurer.

[Section VII.] (Section IX, P. L.) And be it further enacted by the authority aforesaid, That the regulators of said city, together with their necessary assistants, may at all seasonable hours enter into or upon any lot or land within the said city and survey and measure the same in order to perform the service and duty required of them by virtue of this act.

[Section VIII.] (Section X, P. L.) And be it further enacted by the authority aforesaid, That the streets, lanes and alleys within the said city heretofore opened for and dedicated to public use by private persons, and that all streets, lanes and alleys which have been directed and laid out by the supreme executive council for the accommodation of the purchasers of the public lots within the said city, that have been or shall be sold so far as the same are laid out through the said public lots for the redemption of the bills of credit of this commonwealth, dated the twenty-ninth day of April, one thousand seven hundred and eighty, shall be considered and deemed highways, according to the records thereof remaining in the surveyor-general's office, as fully, to all intents and purposes as any highways laid out by order of the court of quarter sessions of any county within this state.

(Section XI, P. L.) And whereas in time past, from inattention and otherwise, divers buildings and fences have been erected within the said city, in such manner as to stand partly on the public streets and alleys thereof, and these nuisances, from tenderness to the possessors or owners of the adjoining freeholds have been suffered to continue [for] many years, with design that when such buildings should decay, the public ways which were so obstructed might be properly opened and extended:

[Section IX.] Be it therefore enacted by the authority aforesaid, That no length of possession whatever of any part of any public street or way within the said city so encroached upon shall be available to bar or prevent the correction and removal of any nuisance by buildings, enclosure or otherwise which have been or hereafter may be erected or made within or upon any street, lane or alley in the said city.

(Section XII, P. L.) And whereas, trees growing in the public streets, lanes and alleys of the said city of Philadelphia do obstruct prospect and passage through the same and also disturb and disorder the watercourses and footways by the extending and increase of the roots thereof and must tend to spread fires when any break out within the said city:

[Section X.] Be it therefore enacted by the authority aforesaid, That all trees now growing or which shall hereafter grow or be planted within the streets, lanes and alleys of this city shall be removed out of the same by the said commissioners, and that if any person or persons shall obstruct or hinder the removal of any trees as aforesaid, every person so offending shall respectively forfeit the sum of ten pounds, to be recovered on indictment, with costs, in the city court, if the prosecution be commenced within six months after the offense, to the use of the said commissioners, to be by them applied to the paving and cleansing the streets of the said city.

(Section XIII, P. L.) And whereas, the grates in the public streets of the city of Philadelphia over vaults are become very dangerous by the manner of their constructions, and the owners neglecting to keep them in proper repair.

For remedy whereof:

[Section XI.] Be it enacted by the authority aforesaid, That within three calendar months after the passing this act, every owner or owners of vaults over which a grate or grates are placed, shall cause the said grate or grates to be made of good iron bars of one inch square, if eighteen inches long, and so in proportion to the length of the bar, the said bar to be [laid] crossways of the street, and the space between the bars not to exceed one inch and a quarter of an inch; and the said grate or grates shall be fixed in a frame of stone or good red cedar, the scantling of which to be at least six inches square for a bar of eighteen inches long and so in proportion for the length of the bar, the frame to be laid solid on the wall of the opening of the said vault and the upper side of the frame nearly level with the pavement; the wall of the opening, with the arch of the vault and the grate or grates, always to be kept in good repair. And every owner, if a resident within the said city, or tenant of a non-resident owner, who has or may have vaults under any of the public streets is hereby directed and enjoined to comply with the above regulations under the penalty of thirty shillings, to be paid to the commissioners for pitching, paving and cleansing the streets, and by them to be applied towards making, amending and cleansing the same. And the said commissioners are hereby directed to make and amend such vaults or grates which the owners neglect to repair agreeable to this act, out of the public money, and recover the expense thereof with the forfeiture of such resident owner or tenant of such non-resident owner, respectively, as the case may require in a summary way, as debts under five pounds are usually recovered.

[Section XII.] (Section XIV, P. L.) And be it enacted by the authority aforesaid, That if any tenant of a non-resident owner shall make or repair the vault, grate or grates agreeable to this act, it shall be allowed to him by the owner or landlord out of the rent then due or thereafter to become due. Provided nevertheless, That any grate or grates which may at present appear safe and substantial in the judgment of any two or more of the justices of the peace for the city with the said commissioners, or a majority of them, may be indulged therewith until they want repairing, or by the said justices [and] commissioners ordered otherwise.

[Section XIII.] (Section XV, P. L.) And be it enacted by the authority aforesaid, That no person or persons shall hereafter dig or cause to be dug any vault or vaults under any of the streets of the said city without first obtaining liberty of four of the justices of the peace for the city, with a majority of the regulators appointed by this act, who are hereby authorized to judge and determine on the necessity thereof and the distance to be dug under any of the streets, provided the same

[does] not exceed fifteen feet from the front wall of the dwelling before which such vault is intended to be dug.

<blockquote>
Passed April 15, 1782. Recorded L. B. No. 1, p. 531, etc. See the note to the Act of Assembly passed February 24, 1720-21, Chapter 242, and the Acts of Assembly passed March 11, 1789, Chapter 1394; April 2, 1790, Chapter 1509. The twelfth section of the Act in the text was repealed by the Act of Assembly passed September 20, 1782, Chapter 990.
</blockquote>

CHAPTER CMLXXXIII.

AN ACT TO ENABLE THE SUPREME EXECUTIVE COUNCIL TO NEGOTIATE SUCH LOANS, AS MAY BE NECESSARY TO PROCURE A SUFFICIENT SUM OF MONEY FOR THE DEFENSE OF THE FRONTIERS OF THIS STATE, AND THE SUPPORT OF CIVIL GOVERNMENT.

(Section I, P. L.) Whereas the several funds hereinafter mentioned cannot in their nature be so immediately productive as to answer the several exigencies of government depending thereon:

For remedy whereof:

[Section I.] Be it enacted by the Representatives of the Freemen of the Commonwealth of Pennsylvania in General Assembly met, and by the authority of the same, That the supreme executive council of this state be and they are hereby authorized and empowered to procure, on loan, such sum or sums of money as they may deem necessary for the purpose of defending the frontiers and for the other exigencies of government for the present year, not specially provided for by law. Provided always, That the said loan do not exceed the sum of thirty thousand pounds, and that the interest thereon do not exceed the rate of six per centum per annum.

[Section II.] (Section II, P. L.) And be it further enacted by the authority aforesaid, That the duties arising on spirituous liquors, the revenues that may arise on sales at vendues, the fines and forfeitures which have or may come into the naval and excise officers' hands and that may arise within the several courts of this state, the moneys arising from marriage, tavern and other licenses and the moneys due and that may be collected within the present year on mortgages in the loan office shall be and are hereby pledged as funds out of which the said loan or loans, with the interest and charges thereon, shall be discharged, satisfied and paid, and which the supreme executive council are hereby authorized and empowered from time to time to draw and apply to that purpose.

[Section III.] (Section III, P. L.) And be it further enacted by the authority aforesaid, That if it shall appear that the above-mentioned and appropriated funds will be inadequate and insufficient to discharge and pay off the said loan or loans, with interest and charges as aforesaid, the faith and honor of this state is hereby pledged that this house will, at their next sessions, take effectual and speedy measures to discharge and pay off the same.

Passed April 15, 1782. Recorded L. B. No. 1, p. 534, etc. The Act in the text was repealed by the Act of Assembly passed September 21, 1782, Chapter 995.

CHAPTER CMLXXXIV.

A SUPPLEMENT TO THE ACT, ENTITLED "AN ACT FOR GUARDING AND DEFENDING THE NAVIGATION IN THE BAY AND RIVER DELAWARE, AND FOR OTHER PURPOSES THEREIN MENTIONED."[1]

(Section I, P. L.) Whereas some doubts have arisen whether the commissioners appointed in and by the act, entitled "An act for guarding and defending the navigation in the bay and river Delaware, and for other purposes therein mentioned,"[1] are authorized by the said act to contract for, lay out and expend in the service therein directed, any greater or farther sum of money than twenty-five thousand pounds in the whole, whatever length of time it may be found requisite to continue the armament therein directed to be raised and supported, and

[1] Passed April 9, 1782, Chapter 965.

whereas, since the passing of the said act circumstances have arisen which evince the necessity of a larger armament than was at first proposed:

[Section I.] (Section II, P. L.) Be it enacted by the Representatives of the Freemen of the Commonwealth of Pennsylvania in General Assembly met, and by the authority of the same, That the said commissioners be and they are hereby authorized to procure, on the credit of the funds or revenues in the aforesaid act mentioned and on the terms therein expressed, such further sum and sums of money as shall be necessary from time to time so as the same shall not exceed the further sum of twenty thousand pounds, for the purpose of carrying the good intentions of the said act into execution, and the additional duties mentioned in the said act, together with the other duties and revenues assigned by the same, and the mortgage and pledge thereof shall be and are hereby continued till the expenses of the said armament and the debts contracted therefor shall be fully paid, though the same should exceed the said sum of twenty-five thousand pounds. Provided always, That whenever the said commissioners shall deem it necessary to make any addition to the said armament, beyond the ship Hyder Alley, already purchased, and her equipments and appurtenances, or to make other alterations in or to the said armament, they previously state in writing to the supreme executive council of this state a plan of the addition or alteration proposed, with an estimate of the probable expense thereof, and obtain the approbation of the council thereon, and such approbation shall be a sufficient warrant for the said commissioners to make such addition or alteration.

(Section III, P. L.) And whereas no appropriation is made of such prize money as may arise to the state by means of the said armaments, and it is reasonable and proper that the same should be added to the funds assigned for raising and supporting the same:

[Section II.] Be it enacted by the authority aforesaid, That whatever proportion of prize money shall become due to the state by means of captures made by the said armament, or any part thereof, shall be paid into the hands of the said commissioners, to be used and accounted for as they are directed to use and account for the other moneys appropriated to raise and support the said armament.

Passed April 15, 1782. Recorded L. B. No. 1, p. 534, etc.

CHAPTER CMLXXXV.

AN ACT TO EMPOWER ELIZABETH ALLEN, WIDOW OF JAMES ALLEN, ESQUIRE, DECEASED DURING THE MINORITY OF HER INFANT SON JAMES, TO GRANT AND CONVEY SUNDRY LOTS OF LAND IN THE TOWN OF NORTHAMPTON, IN THE COUNTY OF NORTHAMPTON, IN THIS STATE, TO SUCH PERSONS AS HAVE BUILT OR SHALL AGREE TO BUILD HOUSES ON THE SAME.

(Section I, P. L.) Whereas, James Allen, late owner of the town of Northampton, in his lifetime contracted with sundry persons to build houses in the said town, and that he or his heirs should grant to them and their heirs on certain fee farm rent, such lot or lots of land as they should build upon or improve:

And whereas, upon the faith of such contracts made with the said James Allen, sundry persons have built houses and others are willing and desirous to improve and build in the said town on the terms and conditions on which the other inhabitants thereof have built:

And whereas, the said James Allen, by his last will and testament did devise the tract of land on which the said town of Northampton is laid out unto his son James, now an infant about four years old, and the income of the said town to his wife Elizabeth, until the said James should arrive, at the age of sixteen years, but appointed no person who during the minority of his said son should confirm his contract with the inhabitants of the said town, and by deed grant to them the fee of the lands which they had improved agreeable to their contracts; and to make further contracts with the people for the improvement of the said town, by which omission the improvement and increase of a strong frontier town is stopped in its course and the interest as well of the said infant as of the good people who have bona fide built and improved on sundry of the town lots is likely to suffer:

And whereas the said Elizabeth Allen has humbly prayed the aid of the legislatures in the premises:

[Section I.] (Section II, P. L.) Be it therefore enacted and it is hereby enacted by the Representatives of the Freemen of the Commonwealth of Pennsylvania in General Assembly met and by the authority of the same, That from and after the passing of this act it shall be lawful to and for the said Elizabeth Allen, as guardian of the said infant, James Allen, and in case of her decease to and for such guardian and guardian as the orphans' court of the county of Philadelphia shall appoint for the said James during his minority, by deed under the hand and seal of the said Elizabeth Allen, or of such other guardian or guardians to be appointed as aforesaid, to grant, bargain and sell, release and confirm such lots of land in the said town of Northampton as have been heretofore disposed of by the said testator, James Allen, on condition to build on and to pay a yearly ground rent for the same unto the person and person to whom the said testator has disposed of such lot or lots and to his or their heirs and assigns forever, under the conditions and rents aforesaid. And also to contract with any other person or persons for the building on and improving of any such other lots in the said town of Northampton as have not been disposed of as aforesaid, and upon their compliance with the terms of their contract by such deed or deeds as aforesaid, to confirm to them and their heirs the fee simple and inheritance of the premises, always reserving a yearly ground rent not less than for any of the town lots of the like situation has been formerly reserved to and for the said James Allen, the son of the said Elizabeth, his heirs and assigns forever.

Passed August 30, 1782. Recorded L. B. No. 2, p. 1, etc.

raising, levying, collecting and paying the additional sum and sums of money hereby directed to be levied and paid as fully as if the said act was herein inserted; excepting only where the same is hereby altered, amended or supplied.

[Section IV.] (Section V. P. L.) Provided always, and be it further enacted by the authority aforesaid, That the paper bills of credit emitted in pursuance of an act entitled "An act for striking the sum of one hundred thousand pounds in bills of credit for the present support of the army, and for establishing a fund for the certain redemption of the same, and for other purposes therein mentioned,"[1] passed the twenty-fifth day of March, one thousand seven hundred and eighty, and the bills of credit emitted in pursuance of the resolutions of Congress of the eighteenth of March, one thousand seven hundred and eighty; and the bills of credit emitted in pursuance of the act entitled "An act for emitting the sum of five hundred thousand pounds in bills of credit, for the support of the army, and for establishing a fund for the redemption thereof, and for other purposes therein mentioned,"[2] passed the seventh day of April, one thousand seven hundred and eighty-one, ad gold and silver at their legal value, shall be received in payment of the said taxes, and no other money whatever.

(Section VI, P. L.) And whereas it is expedient that all unnecessary expenses be prevented in the levying and collecting the aforesaid taxes; therefore,

[Section V.] Be it enacted by the authority aforesaid, That the taxes hereby directed to be assessed, levied and collected, and the taxes to be assessed, levied and collected, by virtue of the aforesaid act entitled "A supplement to an act entitled An act for funding and redeeming the bills of credit of the United States of America, and for providing means to bring the present war to an happy conclusion,"[3] shall be assessed and levied on the returns of taxable persons and property made or to be made in pursuance of the directions of the act for raising effective supplies for the year one thousand

---

[1] Passed March 25, 1780, Chapter 907.
[2] Passed April 7, 1781, Chapter 939.
[3] Ante.

seven hundred and eighty-one, passed the twenty-first day of June, one thousand seven hundred and eighty-one, anything in the aforesaid acts to the contrary notwithstanding.

<small>Passed June 25, 1781. Recorded L. B. No. 1, page 450, etc.</small>

Laws enacted in the Fourth Sitting of the Fifth General Assembly of the Commonwealth of Pennsylvania, which commenced at Philadelphia, on Tuesday, the fourth day of September, A. D. 1781.

CHAPTER CMXLIX.

AN ACT TO INCORPORATE THE GERMAN SOCIETY CONTRIBUTING FOR THE RELIEF OF DISTRESSED GERMANS IN THE STATE OF PENNSYLVANIA.

(Section I, P. L.) Whereas the arrival of Germans from Europe, and the numerous settlements made by them in Pennsylvania, have greatly contributed to the present wealth and strength of this state; and the means of encouraging these foreigners to come and settle among us, by removing or lessening their distresses in a new country, have, on sundry occasions, deservedly engaged the attention of the former government of this country:

(Section II. P. L.) And wheras a number of German inhabitants of the city of Philadelphia and its neighborhood by their humble petition to the general assembly of this state, have represented and shown, that some time in the year of our Lord, one thousand seven hundred and sixty-four, some of the petitioners and divers other persons, all Germans by birth or descending from Germans who had settled in this state, moved by the sufferings of their countrymen then newly arrived, formed themselves into a charitable society, under the name of "The German Society of Philadelphia, in the province of Pennsylvania," and by voluntary subscriptions and stated contributions from time to time supplied the poor, the sick and otherwise distressed Germans brought to the city of Philadelphia, and have aided and assisted such passengers as for want of acquaintance with the language and laws of the country were in danger of being oppressed. Also, that some of the petitioners aforesaid have purchased two contiguous lots in the said city of Philadelphia, in order to build thereon for the reception and accommodation of their countrymen when need shall be. Also, that they have it in view to enlarge upon and further to extend the benefit of their first institution, by applying part of the fund of money in their hands, and which hereafter they may raise, for and towards other charitable purposes, such as to teach and improve poor children, both in the English and German languages, reading and writing thereof, and to procure for them such learning and education as will best suit their genius and capacities, and enable the proper objects to receive the finishing of their studies in the university established in the said city of Philadelphia; likewise to erect a library and to do any other matter or thing which, without any prejudice to other inhabitants of this state, in charity they might do for the relief and benefit of their own countrymen; wherefore, they have humbly prayed that they might be incorporated by a law for this purpose:

[Section I.] (Section II, P. L.) Be it therefore enacted and it is hereby enacted by the Representatives of the Freemen of the Commonwealth of Pennsylvania in General Assembly met, and by the authority of the same, That Henry Keppele, president; Lewis Weiss, vice-president; Lewis Farmer and Henry Leighthouser, secretaries; Christopher Ludwick, Peter Ozeas, Andrew Burckhart, John Fritz, Peter Kraft and Melchior Steiner, overseers; Michael Shubart, treasurer; Henry Kammerer, solicitor; and William Lehman, deacon; the present officers of the said German Society, elected and chosen at the last meeting of the members of that society, on the twenty-sixth day of December last past, and their successors in the respective offices and all persons who have subscribed and hereafter shall subscribe the rules and regulations of the said society, and have continued, and shall from time to time continue to contribute towards the aforesaid charitable purposes of the said society, be, and they are hereby made and constituted a corporation and body politic in law and in fact to have continuance forever by the name, style and title of The German Society contributing for the relief of distressed Germans in the state of Pennsylvania.

[Section II.] (Section IV, P. L.) And be it further enacted by the authority aforesaid, That the said corporation and their successors, by the name, style and title aforesaid, shall forever hereafter be persons able and capable in law, as well to take, receive and hold all and all manner of lands, tenements, rents, annuities, liberties, franchises and other hereditaments which at any time or times heretofore have been granted, bargained, sold, enfeoffed, released, devised or otherwise conveyed to the said German Society, or to any person or persons for their use or in trust for them; and the same lands, tenements, rents, annuities, liberties, franchises and other hereditaments are hereby vested and established in the said corporation and their successors forever. And the said corporation and their successors are hereby declared to be seized and possessed of such estate or estates therein as in and by the respective grants, bargains, sales, enfeoffments, releases, devises or other conveyances thereof is or are declared, limited and expressed; as, also, that the said corporation and their successors, at all times hereafter, shall be capable and able to purchase, have, receive, take, hold and enjoy in fee simple, or of any other lesser estate or estates, any lands, tenements, rents, annuities, liberties, franchises or other hereditaments by the gift, grant, bargain, sale, alienation, enfeoffment, release, confirmation or devise, of any person or persons, bodies politic and corporate, capable and able to make the same, and, further, that the said corporation and their successors may take and receive any sum or sums of money and any manner and portion of goods and chattels that shall be given and bequeathed to them by any person or persons, bodies corporate and politic, capable to make a gift or bequest thereof, such money, goods and chattels to be laid out by them in a purchase or purchases of lands, tenements, messuages, houses, rents, annuites or other hereditaments, to them and their successors forever, or the moneys lent on interest or otherwise disposed of according to the articles and by-laws of the said society and the intention of the donors.

[Section III.] (Section V, P. L.) And be it further enacted

by the authority aforesaid, That at every the four quarterly meetings of the said society. That is to say: On the twenty-sixth day of December, on the twenty-fifth day of March, on the twenty-fourth day of June and the twenty-ninth day of September in every year or when either of those days shall happen to be on a Sunday, then on the day following, each and every of the members of the said society, may propose any person or persons to be ballotted for as a member of the said society or corporation, and such person or persons, so proposed and balloted for, upon being elected by two-thirds in number of the members present, by ballot as aforesaid, and signing the articles of said society, and paying the entrance money, shall, from thenceforth become a member of the said corporation, and whilst he shall, from time to time, contribute towards the purposes aforesaid, shall remain a member of the said corporation, and not otherwise, making nevertheless proper and reasonable allowance of delay for his residence in the frontiers of this state, or his being engaged in the land or sea service of this state, or any of the United States, or a prisoner war, or beyond sea on a fair trade.

[Section IV.] (Section VI, P. L.) Provided always, and be it enacted by the authority aforesaid, That the members of the said society shall not at any time hereafter be less than seventy-five in number nor more than three hundred.

[Section V.] (Section VII, P. L.) And be it further enacted by the authority aforesaid, That the said corporation and their successors, or the majority of such as shall be convened at any of the four quarterly meetings of the said society, shall be authorized and empowered and they are hereby authorized and empowered, to make rules, by-laws and ordinances, and to do everything needful for the good government and support of the affairs of the said corporation. Provided always, That the said by-laws, rules and ordinances, or any of them, be not repugnant to the laws of this commonwealth, and that all their proceedings be fairly and regularly entered in a book to be kept for that purpose, which book and all papers and other documents of the said society shall at all times be liable to the inspection of the president and vice-president of the supreme executive council, the speaker of the general assembly and chief justice of the state for the time being, and that at the general meeting of the members of the said society or corporation on the days aforesaid, they, the said members, or a majority of such as shall be present, be authorized and empowered to elect and choose by ballot, one president, one vice-president, six overseers, a treasurer, two secretaries, one solicitor and one deacon; the said officers to be inhabitants of the said city of Philadelphia, and to remain in office until the next meeting of the said corporation on the twenty-sixth day of December then next following; and in case of death, removal or refusal to serve of any one or more of the officers so chosen, his or their place so dying, removing, or being removed or refusing, shall be supplied by an election in like manner at the next quarterly meeting and the person or persons so chosen shall remain in his said office by virtue of the said election until the next December meeting aforesaid.

[Section VI.] (Section VIII, P. L.) And be it further enacted by the authority aforesaid, That the rents, interest and profits arising from the said real and personal estate of the said corporation shall, by the officers of the said corporation and their successors, chosen and appointed in such manner and form as hereinbefore is directed and required, from time to time be applied for the relief and support of the poor, distressed Germans arriving in this state from parts beyond sea, for the erecting or supporting schools and seminaries of learning, and one or more library or libraries within this state, for the better educating and instructing the children and youth of the Germans and descendants of Germans, and in building, repairing and maintaining school houses, and other houses necessary for the purposes aforesaid, for salaries to schoolmasters and teachers and for such other charitable uses as are conformable to the true design and intent of the same society.

[Section VII.] (Section IX, P. L.) Provided always, and be it enacted by the authority aforesaid, That in the disposal and application of the public moneys of the said corporation, the aforesaid president, vice-president, overseers, secretaries, treasurer, solicitor and deacon, and their successors in office, or any seven of them, the said officers, may make orders and directions, for the relief of poor and distressed persons, and supporting scholars, schoolmasters and others, coming under their notice, and that upon emergent occasions, when immediate relief is wanted, an order signed by one of the presidents, and two of the overseers, directed to the treasurer, shall be a sufficient authority for the said treasurer to discharge and pay such order. Provided also, That neither of the said officers shall at any time during the execution of his office, or afterwards, be entitled to demand, sue for or recover any pay, reward or commission for his service in any of the said offices respectively.

[Section VIII.] (Section X, P. L.) And be it further enacted by the authority aforesaid, That the said corporation and their successors shall have full power and authority to make, have and use one common seal, with such device and inscription as they shall think proper and the same to break, alter and renew at their pleasure.

(Section IX, P. L.) And be it further enacted by the authority aforesaid, That the said corporation and their successors, by the name, style and title aforesaid, shall be able and capable in law to sue and be sued, plead and be impleaded in any court or courts, before any judge or judges, justice or justices, in all and all manner of suits, complaints, pleas, causes, matters and demands of whatever kind, nature and form they may be, and all and every matter or thing therein to do, in as full and effectual a manner as any other person or persons, bodies politic and corporate within this commonwealth may or can do.

[Section X.] (Section XII, P. L.) Provided always, and be it further enacted by the authority aforesaid, That the clear yearly value or income of the messuages, houses, lands, tenements, rents, annuities or other hereditaments, and real estate of the said corporation and interest of money lent, shall not exceed the sum of two thousand and five hundred pounds, lawful money of Pennsylvania, to be taken and esteemed exclusive of the moneys arising from annual or other stated subscriptions or payments, which said moneys shall be received by the treasurer of the said corporation, and disposed of by him upon the order of the other officers, or a majority of them, in the manner hereinbefore described, pursuant to a vote or votes of the members of the said society, appropriating the same at one of their quarterly meetings.

Passed September 20, 1781. Recorded L. B. No. 1, p. 452, etc.

CHAPTER CML.

AN ACT TO MAKE MORE EFFECTUAL PROVISION FOR THE DEFENSE OF THIS STATE.

(Section I, P. L.) Whereas the intelligence received of the preparations made by the enemy at New York indicate an invasion of the state, against which it is our duty to make every provision of defense which the circumstances of this commonwealth admit, and that the executive authority of the state be furnished with sufficient powers to draw forth the resources thereof with the utmost vigor and dispatch:

[Section I.] (Section II, P. L.) Be it therefore enacted and it is hereby enacted by the Representatives of the Freemen of the Commonwealth of Pennsylvania in General Assembly met, and by the authority of the same, That the president (or vice-president) in council be and is hereby authorized to call forth such and so many wagons as shall appear to them necessary for the transportation of the necessary baggage and stores of such troops, either continental or militia; as may be called forth into actual service on this emergency, or for the transportation of the records, books and papers, or other public property, either of the United States or of this state.

[Section II.] (Section III, P. L.) And be it further enacted by the authority aforesaid, That the late wagon-masters of the several counties in this state, and their deputies (or such other persons as shall be appointed by the supreme executive council) and the constables be empowered and are hereby required to do the several duties in the premises which were enjoined by the former wagon laws of this state, and that the owners of all such wagons be entitled to receive the sum of twenty-five shillings specie per diem for a wagon and four horses with suitable gears, and the sum of fifteen shillings specie per diem for a wagon and two horses with gears as aforesaid, they, the said owners, finding the driver and necessary forage for their respective teams.

[Section III.] (Section IV, P. L.) And be it further enacted by the authority aforesaid, That in case a sufficient number of wagons cannot be procured in the manner above mentioned, the president or vice-president in council be and hereby is authorized and empowered to direct his warrant, under his hand and seal, to such persons in the city or any county in this state as shall be deemed proper, authorizing such persons to seize and impress any wagons, horses and gears, boats, sloops or shallops for the transportation of the several articles above mentioned, and in the meantime to detain all wagons, horses, boats or other vessels which any persons may endeavor to remove.

[Section IV.] (Section V, P. L.) And be it further enacted by the authority aforesaid, That the president or vice-president in council be and hereby is in like manner authorized and empowered to seize and impress arms, ammuniton and military stores and provisions and forage of all kinds whatsoever, belonging to any private person or companies, and apply them, if need be, to the public use, such seizure to be certified and the value thereof [ascertained] as nearly as possible in specie.

[Section V.] (Section VI, P. L.) And be it further enacted by the authority aforesaid, That the president or vice-president in council be in like manner authorized and empowered to billet and quarter such troops as may be called together for the special defense of the state, in this emergency, upon any public houses, or in case of their insufficiency upon private houses, having due respect to the number and convenience of families.

(Section VII, P. L.) And whereas, the usual mode of calling out the militia by classes may be attended with fatal delay to the interests and property of the good people of this state:

[Section VI.] (Section VIII, P. L.) Be it therefore further enacted by the authority aforesaid, That the president or vice-president in council be and is hereby authorized and empowered (if the designs of the enemy shall, in their judgment, make it necessary) to call forth the whole of the militia without any respect to classes, and in that case every person now serving on a tour of militia duty shall repair to [and] join his own proper battalion, orders being first received therefor, and shall be allowed for the service already done.

[Section VII.] (Section IX, P. L.) And be it further enacted by the authority aforesaid, That if any person or persons called forth by the president or vice-president in council in manner aforesaid, shall refuse or neglect to perform a tour of militia duty, the person or persons so neglecting or refusing shall be subject to the same fines and penalties as in other cases when called forth in classes, by virtue of the law for regulating the militia of this state, anything in the said law to the contrary thereof notwithstanding.

[Section VIII.] (Section X, P. L.) And be it further enacted by the authority aforesaid, That the president or vice-president in council be authorized to draw upon the treasury for such money as may be necessary in the present emergency for repairing and procuring arms and ammunition and for other contingent expenses attending the present service.

[Section IX.] (Section XI, P. L.) And be it further enacted by the authority aforesaid, That the president or vice-president in council be authorized and empowered, when occasion shall require, to impress by warrant, under hand and seal, such and so many horses and wagons, with suitable gears, as he may judge necessary for the removal of the families and property of those inhabitants of the city of Philadelphia and the Northern Liberties and the district of Southwark, who may be in actual service against the enemy, and of such other citizens and persons who, in his opinion, may be entitled to and require the same, the hire of all such wagons and horses to be paid by the persons making use thereof: Provided nevertheless, That if any horses or wagons shall be impressed by virtue hereof and no use made thereof by the citizens [or persons] for whom they may be impressed, the expense thereof shall be paid by the state treasurer, upon the order of the president or vice-president in council.

[Section X.] (Section XII, P. L.) And be it further enacted by the authority aforesaid, That this act shall be and remain in force until ten days after the meeting of the next general assembly of this commonwealth, and no longer.

Passed September 28, 1781. Recorded L. B. No. 1, p. 455, etc.

CHAPTER CMLI.

AN ACT TO ALTER AND SUPPLY AN ACT ENTITLED "AN ACT FOR RECRUITING THE PENNSYLVANIA LINE IN THE ARMY OF THE UNITED STATES."[1]

(Section I, P. L.) Whereas a number of the classes have not procured recruits according to the directions of the act, entitled "An act for recruiting the Pennsylvania line in the army of the United States,"[1] which this act is intended to alter and supply, passed on the twenty-fifth day of June, one thousand seven hundred and eighty-one:

(Section II, P. L.) And whereas, it is absolutely necessary that money be procured from the delinquent classes and that the recruiting of the said line be carried on to effect in the most expeditious manner:

Therefore:

[Section I.] (Section III, P. L.) Be it enacted and it is hereby enacted by the Representatives of the Freemen of the Commonwealth of Pennsylvania in General Assembly met, and by the authority of the same, That the commissioners of the several counties within this state proceed, without delay, to levy the sum of twenty pounds specie on each of the delinquent classes within the city and the several counties, and cause the same to be collected and paid into the treasury of each county in the manner and under the pains and penalties directed in and by the act, entitled "An act to raise effective supplies for the year one thousand seven hundred and eighty-one."[2]

---

[1] Passed June 25, 1781, Chapter 946.
[2] Passed June 21, 1781, Chapter 944.

[Section II.] (Section IV, P. L.) And be it further enacted by the authority aforesaid, That all moneys brought into the treasury of each county in pursuance of this act shall be paid into the hands of the treasurer of the state by the treasurers of the several counties and remain there, subject to the orders of the supreme executive council of this state, for the sole purpose of recruiting the Pennsylvania line in the army of the United States.

[Section III.] (Section V, P. L.) And be it further enacted by the authority aforesaid, That all recruits who may or shall be enlisted in pursuance of this act shall be enlisted for a term not less than eighteen months from the date of their respective enlistments.

[Section IV.] (Section VI, P. L.) And be it further enacted by the authority aforesaid, That the supreme executive council of this state be and hereby is authorized and empowered to take such measures as to them may seem most expedient and effectual for enlisting the recruits necessary to complete the line of this state as directed by this act and the act which this act is intended to alter and supply.

[Section V.] (Section VII, P. L.) And be it further enacted by the authority aforesaid, That the act, entitled "An act for recruiting the Pennsylvania line in the army of the United States," passed the twenty-fifth day of June, one thousand seven hundred and eighty-one, and which this act is intended to alter and supply, and every clause, matter and thing contained therein, except what is herein altered or supplied shall be and continue in force and effect.

(Section VIII, P. L.) And whereas, it is absolutely necessary that some method be speedily taken more effectually to prevent desertion, Therefore,

[Section VII.] (Section IX, P. L.) Be it enacted by the authority aforesaid, That any person who shall, according to an act to discourage desertion, passed the twentieth day of February, one thousand seven hundred and seventy-seven, apprehend and deliver to the sheriff or jailor of the county a deserter from the line of this state, shall be exempted from his two next succeeding tours of militia duty, on producing the certificate of the sheriff or jailor of the county of his having delivered such deserter into his custody, to the lieutenant of the county, or such other officer or officers, whose duty it may be to superintend the appeals held on the calls of the militia when it would have been otherwise the turn of such person to have served.

Passed September 29, 1781.

CHAPTER CMLII.

AN ACT TO VEST THE TITLE OF A MESSUAGE AND LOT OF GROUND IN THE TOWN OF LISBURN IN JOHN RANKIN, ESQUIRE.

(Section I, P. L.) Whereas, John Rankin, esquire, of York county, hath presented a petition to this house, setting forth that a house and lot, in the town of Lisburn, in the county of Cumberland, was heretofore taken in execution as the estate of a certain Richard Carson, and in due form of law struck off and sold to James Rankin, and the consideration money by him paid to the sheriff; that the said Richard Carson held the possession of the said messuage and lot of ground, with the consent of the said James Rankin and afterwards paid and satisfied him for the money by him advanced to the sheriff; that the petitioner, with the knowledge and at the request of the said James Rankin, contracted verbally with the said Richard Carson for the premises, and afterwards paid him the full price agreed upon and obtained possession of the said premises. That soon after the petitioner, together with said James Rankin, went to Carlisle and employed a conveyancer to procure a sheriff's deed for the premises to the said John Rankin. That afterwards the said James Rankin joined the enemy at Philadelphia, and was thereupon attainted of high treason, previous to which the conveyancer aforesaid, had procured a sheriff's deed for the premises in the name of James Rankin, duly acknowledged in court and recorded, and thereupon prayed the house would permit him to bring in a bill to vest the title of the premises in the petitioner:

[Section I.] (Section II, P. L.) Be it therefore enacted and it is hereby enacted by the Representatives of the Freemen of the Commonwealth of Pennsylvania in General Assembly met, and by the authority of the same, That the lot of ground aforesaid, with the buildings and appurtenances, situate, lying and being in the town of Lisburn, in the county of Cumberland, containing, in front, on a street in the general plan of the said town, called Main street, one hundred and thirteen feet, and in depth on the westward side, three hundred and seventy-five feet to Yellow Breeches creek, and in depth on the eastward side two hundred and forty feet, be, and the same is hereby vested in the said John Rankin, his heirs and assigns, to be held by him, the said John Rankin, his heirs and assigns forever, subject to the same rents and conditions that the said Richard Carson formerly held the same, any law, custom or usage to the contrary thereof in anywise notwithstanding.

Passed September 29, 1781. Recorded L. B. No. 1, p. 458, etc.

CHAPTER CMLIII.

AN ACT TO GIVE RELIEF TO CERTAIN PERSONS TAKING REFUGE IN THIS STATE WITH RESPECT TO THEIR SLAVES.

(Section I, P. L.) Whereas many virtuous citizens of America and inhabitants of states that have been invaded are obliged, by the power of the enemy, to take refuge in this state:

And whereas, it is just and necessary that the property of such persons should be protected:

[Section I.] Be it therefore enacted and it is hereby enacted by the Representatives of the Freemen of the Commonwealth of Pennsylvania in General Assembly met, and by the authority of the same, That all and every person and persons, under the above description, now residing in this state, or who hereafter may be in like circumstances, shall retain, possess and hold their slaves, anything in the act for the gradual abolition of slavery passed the first day of March, one thousand seven hundred and eighty, to the contrary notwithstanding.

(Section III, P. L.) Provided always, That the owner or owners of such slaves, his or their lawful attorney, shall, in six months from the passing of this act, or in six months after their arrival in this state, as the case may be, register said slaves in manner and form directed in the fifth section of the act above mentioned for the gradual abolition of slavery. And be it further provided, That such slaves shall not be aliened or sold to any inhabitant nor retained in this state as slaves longer than six months after the conclusion of the present war with Great Britain.

[Section II.] (Section IV, P. L.) And be it also provided and declared, That nothing herein contained shall be deemed, construed or taken to enslave any person or persons who have been emancipated or freed under or by virtue of the act aforesaid.

Passed October 1, 1781. Recorded L. B. No. 1, p. 459, etc.

CHAPTER CMLIV.

AN ACT TO DISSOLVE THE MARRIAGE OF JACOB BILLMEYER WITH HIS WIFE MARY BILLMEYER LATE MARY EICHELBERGER.

(Section I, P. L.) Whereas, Jacob Billmeyer, of the town of York, in the state of Pennsylvania, conveyancer, hath presented a petition to this house, setting forth that his wife Mary, about eight years since, eloped from his bed and board, without any reasonable cause ,and ever since continued to absent herself from his bed and board; and that in the month of February, in the year of our Lord one thousand seven hundred and seventy-eight, she, the said Mary, became acquainted with a certain William Cole, with whom she intermarried and cohabited,

1718] *The Statutes at Large of Pennsylvania.* 513

with the supervisors of the highways for the time being, elected by the inhabitants of the said district, in pursuance of the act of assembly in such case provided, be and they are hereby appointed commissioners and, by and with the approbation of three of the justices of the peace of and for the county of Philadelphia, they are hereby authorized and empowered, for and in behalf of the inhabitants of the said district, and for their use, to purchase, or to take on ground rent, such lot or lots on the river Delaware within the said district, as they, the said commissioners, or a majority of them, shall think will be necessary for accommodating the said inhabitants with public landing places for such bulky articles as are hereinbefore mentioned, and to take one or more conveyances to them for the same, in fee simple, and thereupon to sink and erect proper and convenient wharves and quays, for the purposes aforesaid, and to borrow on interest from time to time, as the purchase moneys and expenses of improving the same shall grow due, such sum or sums of money as shall be sufficient to discharge their contracts, and to grant, bargain, sell, convey and assure to the lenders, in mortgage, all such lot or lots of ground; which deeds of mortgage, executed by the said commissioners, or their survivors, or a majority of them, shall be as good and valid in law for securing the payment of the moneys so borrowed as any mortgage made by a private person of his own estate now is.

[Section II.] (Section III, P. L.) And be it further enacted by the authority aforesaid, That whenever the said commissioners shall have purchased any lot or lots for the purposes aforesaid, they shall cause the same (or so much thereof as they shall think necessary) to be laid out for a landing or landings, and a street of sufficient breadth to give free access thereto, for public use; and if there shall be any overplus ground, then it shall and may be lawful for them, or a majority of them, or their survivors, to sell the said overplus ground by public or private sale, for the best prices that can be obtained, and make good and perfect titles for the same to the purchasers, in fee simple, and apply the moneys arising from such sales towards the payment of the first purchase money or the moneys they may have borrowed as aforesaid.

[Section III.] (Section IV, P. L.) And be it further enacted by the authority aforesaid, That it shall and may be lawful for the said commissioners, or a majority of them, to demise, grant and to farm let to any person or persons whatsoever, for any term of years not exceeding seven at one time, all the public wharves, quays and landing places, reserving such rents and conditions and establishing such rates and prices for the toll or wharfage of all kinds of articles which are usually brought to such landings, as they shall judge reasonable, and restraining the tenant from taking higher rates and prices and binding him in sufficient penalties in all things to abide by such rates, orders and regulations as the tenants of the public landings in the city of Philadelphia are bound to observe; and to receive the rents, issues and profits thereof, and to apply the same towards the discharge of the encumbrances on the said lots, until the whole of the encumbrances aforesaid are fully paid and discharged.

(Section V, P. L.) And in order to enable the said commissioners more speedily to pay off and discharge the debts which shall accrue by the purchase and improvement, as well of the said landing place in part agreed for with the said Luke Morris and others, as of any other land places hereafter to be purchased.

[Section IV.] Be it enacted by the authority aforesaid, That it shall and may be lawful for the said commissioners, or a majority of them or their survivors, together with the assessor and assistant freeholders of the said district, for the time being, to make or lay, yearly and every year, until the whole of the said debts and encumbrances shall be paid and discharged, one rate or assessment, not exceeding one shilling in the pound, of the clear yearly value of all the real and personal estates within the said district (over and above the rates and assessment which the said supervisors are directed to lay by the said act of assembly for the maintenance and repair of the streets and highways within the said district), and to appoint a collector for the same; which said assessment being fairly made, according to the best of their skill and judgment, having due regard to every man's estate within the said district, and without fear, favor or affection of or to any person, shall be fairly transcribed in a book to be kept by the said assessor and commissioners, and being approved by three justices of the peace of and for the said county, a fair transcript or duplicate thereof shall be delivered to the collector, by them to be appointed from among the inhabitants of the said district, who is hereby authorized, enjoined and required to receive, collect, levy and recover the said rate and assessment, in the same manner and form and by the same legal remedies which are by law appointed for recovering and collecting the county taxes in the said district; and, having received or collected the same, or any part of them, shall, at the end of every month from the time of his appointment (or when thereto required) account with and pay to one of the commissioners to be by them, or a majority of them, chosen as their treasurer, all such sums of money, part of the said assessment, which he shall so have collected during the preceding month, deducting only thereout six pence in the pound for his time and trouble.

[Section V.] (Section VI, P. L.) And be it further enacted by the authority aforesaid, That if any person by the said commissioners, or a majority of them, appointed to the office of collector aforesaid, shall refuse to take the same (not being disqualified nor entitled to an exemption therefrom, according to the customs in such cases used and approved) he shall forfeit and pay to the treasurer ten pounds, to be recovered by an action of debt, brought in the name of the treasurer for the time being, in any court of record within this commonwealth, wherein the plaintiff shall declare in general terms, that the defendant was duly appointed collector of the taxes imposed by the commissioners for the purchase of public landings for the district of Southwark, and that he refused to undertake the office, whereby action accrued, and the defendant shall plead the general issue, and shall be allowed to give this act and any special matter arising thereupon in evidence, but shall not be allowed wager of law, protection nor more than one imparlance, and if such person so appointed collector shall undertake the office but shall neglect or refuse, at the end of every month (or when thereto required), to account with and pay to the treasurer for the time being all such moneys as he shall have from time to time collected of the said assessment in manner aforesaid, then, upon complaint made to two justices of the peace of and for the said county, it shall and may be lawful for the said justices, and they are hereby required to issue their precept, directed to the sheriff of the said county, commanding him to take and bring the body of the said collector before them, to answer such complaint and if, upon his appearance and due examination had into the said complaint, it shall appear to them that the said collector has refused to account with and pay the said moneys to the said treasurer and shall before them neglect or refuse immediately so to do, then and in such case the said justices are hereby required, by warrant under their hands and seals, forthwith him to commit to the common gaol of the said county, there to remain without bail or mainprise until he shall so account for and pay the said moneys to the said treasurer, and in such case, or in case the person appointed to be collector shall refuse to undertake the office, it shall and may be lawful for the said commissioners to appoint another, under the penalties aforesaid, and so as often as there shall be occasion.

[Section VI.] (Section VII, P. L.) And be it further enacted by the authority aforesaid, That the treasurer of the said commissioners, before he undertakes his office, shall give a bond with two sufficient sureties, to the other commissioners, in the penalty of one thousand pounds, conditioned that he will well and faithfully execute his office, keep regular accounts of his receipts and disbursements, pay all the orders drawn on him by the said commissioners, or a majority of them, or their survivors, as soon as sufficient moneys shall come to his hands from any of the funds belonging to the commissioners; that he will, at least once in every year, settle and adjust with the said commissioners a full and just account, supported by proper vouchers, of all his receipts and payments during the preceding year; and that upon his death, or the appointment of another treasurer in his room (which the said commissioners, or a majority of them, or their survivors, are hereby authorized to do, whenever they see cause) he, his executors or administrators shall and will settle and adjust all his accounts with the said commissioners, and pay the remaining balance in his hands to his successor in office, charging no more than six pence in the pound on all the moneys by him received and paid.

[Section VII.] (Section VIII, P. L.) And be it further enacted by the authority aforesaid, That the said commissioners shall meet at some convenient place, by them to be fixed on, so often as the business under their care shall require, when two-thirds of their number being met shall constitute a board, a majority of whose voices shall be sufficient to determine any question that may arise or be made touching or concerning any of the matters or things hereby committed to their care.

[Section VIII.] (Section IX, P. L.) And be it further enacted by the authority aforesaid, That all and singular the powers and authorities hereby given to the said commissioners and the estate and estates which they shall acquire in any lots of ground by virtue of and in pursuance of this act, shall continue and remain in the said Robert Knox, Joseph Blewer, Joseph Turner, John Brown, William Clifton and Isaac Penrose, and the survivors of them, and the supervisors of the highways for the time being, until the said landings are purchased and improved and until the whole debts accrued by the purchase and improvement thereof are, by the sale of any parts of the grounds purchased, the rents and profits of the landings, and the rates and assessments hereby ordered to be laid and collected, or by some other means fully paid off and discharged, and until their accounts of and concerning the same are finally adjusted, and no longer; and then and from thenceforth the real estate of and in the same shall devolve upon and accrue to the supervisors of the highways in the said district, who are hereby erected into and declared to be one body politic and corporate (for this especial purpose) in deed and in law, capable of holding the same, and of suing and being sued in all actions touching and concerning the same, by the name of "The Supervisors of the public landings and highways in the district of Southwark, and to their successors forever, in trust for the use of the public, in the manner hereinafter mentioned, that is to say, in trust that the said supervisors for the time being, or a majority of them, with the approbation of three justices of the peace of and for the said county, shall and may grant, demise and to farm let the same landings to any person or persons for any term of years, not exceeding seven at one time, upon such rents and conditions as they shall think proper; and shall and may make such rules, orders and regulations for the well governing as well the tenants thereof as the boats, flats, carts and wagons which shall frequent the same, and the owners, skippers and drivers thereof, and the prices or rates of toll or wharfage to be paid for all articles to be unladen thereon; and that the said supervisors shall receive the rents, issues and profits thereof and apply the same to the making any improvements or buildings thereon, to the paving any of the streets or maintaining and repairing any of the highways or to any other public use within the said district, which the said supervisors, or a majority of them, by and with the approbation of three justices of the said county as aforesaid shall order and appoint.

(Section X, P. L.) And whereas, the number of supervisors within the said district directed to be chosen by the freeholders and inhabitants by the act of assembly in such case provided will be too small when this weighty trust shall wholly devolve on them:

[Section IX.] Be it therefore enacted by the authority aforesaid, That at the first election which shall be held for the said district, after the accounts of the said commissioners shall be finally adjusted, the freeholders and inhabitants of the said district shall elect six respectable freeholders to be the supervisors of the public landings and highways in the district of Southwark, in lieu of the three supervisors of the streets and highways by the said act directed to be chosen; which six freeholders, being duly elected according to the directions of the said act, shall have, hold, enjoy and exercise all the powers, authorities and estates by this act vested in the supervisors of the public landings and highways in the district of Southwark.

> Passed September 20, 1782. Recorded L. B. No. 2, p. 12, etc. See the Act of Assembly passed March 6, 1790. Chapter 1490.

CHAPTER CMXCII.

AN ACT FOR INCORPORATING THE PRESBYTERIAN CHURCH IN THE TOWNSHIP OF WARWICK, IN THE COUNTY OF BUCKS.

(Section I, P. L.) Whereas the minister, elders and members of the Presbyterian church in the township of Warwick, in the county of Bucks, have prayed that their said church may be incorporated and by law enabled, as a body corporate and politic, to receive and hold such charitable donations and bequests as may from time to time be made to their society, and vested with such powers and privileges as are enjoyed by the other religious societies who are incorporated in the state of Pennsylvania:

(Section II, P. L.) And whereas, it is just and right and also agreeable to the true spirit of the constitution that the prayer of their said petition be granted:

[Section I.] (Section III, P. L.) Be it therefore enacted and it is hereby enacted by the Representatives of the Freemen of the Commonwalth of Pennsylvania in General Assembly met, and by the authority of the same, That Richard Walker, Benjamin Snodgrass, William Scott, William Long, Nathan McKinstry, Gills Craven, William Walker, John Carr, Joseph Harb and their successors duly elected and appointed in such manner and form as hereinafter is directed be, and they are hereby made and constituted a corporation and body politic in law and in fact, to have continuance forever, by the name, style and title of "The Trustees of the Presbyterian Church in Warwick Township, in the county of Bucks."

[Section II.] (Section IV, P. L.) And be it further enacted

by the authority aforesaid, That the said corporation and their successors, by the name, style and title aforesaid, shall forever hereafter be persons able and capable in law as well to take, receive and hold all and all manner of lands, tenements, rents, annuities, franchises and other hereditaments which at any time or times heretofore have been granted, bargained, sold, enfeoffed, released, devised or otherwise conveyed to the said Presbyterian church in Warwick township and county aforesaid, or to the religious congregation worshipping therein, now under the pastoral charge and care of the Reverend Nathaniel Irvin, or to any other person or persons to their use or in trust for them, and the same lands, tenements, rents, annuities, liberties, franchises and other hereditaments are hereby vested and established in the said corporation and their successors forever, according to their original use and intention. And the said corporation and their successors are hereby declared to be seized and possessed of such estate and estates therein as in and by the respective grants, bargains, sales, enfeoffments, releases, devises or other conveyances thereof is or are declared, limited or expressed; as also that the said corporation and their successors aforesaid, at all times hereafter shall be capable and able to purchase, have, receive, take, hold and enjoy in fee simple, or of any lesser estate or estates, any lands, tenements, rents, annuities, liberties, franchises and other hereditaments by the gift, grant, bargain, sale, alienation, enfeoffment, release, confirmation or devise of any person or persons, bodies politic and corporate, capable and able to make the same; and, further, that the said corporation may take and receive any sum or sums of money and any manner or portion of goods and chattels that shall be given or bequeathed to them by any person or persons, bodies politic and corporate capable to make a bequest or gift thereof, such money, goods and chattels to be laid out by them in a purchase or purchases of lands, tenements, messuages, houses, rents, annuities or hereditaments to them and their successors forever; or moneys lent on interest or otherwise disposed of according to the intention of the donors.

[Section III.] (Section V, P. L.) And be it further enacted

by the authority aforesaid, That the rents, profits and interest of the said real and personal estate of the said church and corporation shall, by the said trustees and their successors from time to time, be applied for the maintenance and support of the pastor or pastors of the said church, for salaries to their clerk and sexton, in the maintenance and support of a school, and in repairing and maintaining their lot and house of public worship, burial ground, parsonage, house or houses, school house or houses and other tenements which now do or hereafter shall belong to the said church and corporation.

[Section IV.] (Section VI, P. L.) And be it further enacted by the authority aforesaid, That if hereafter the building for public worship or any other tenement belonging to the said church and corporation shall be burnt, endamaged or otherwise rendered unfit for use, or if hereafter the said house of public worship shall appear to be too small to accommodate the congregation, whereby it shall become necessary to rebuild or repair the same, that then and in such case it may be lawful for the said corporation and their successors to make sale or otherwise dispose of any part or parcel of said real or personal estate other than the site of the house of public worship, burial ground or grounds, parsonage house or houses, school house or houses, for the purposes aforementioned and not otherwise.

[Section V.] (Section VII, P. L.) Provided always, and be it further enacted by the authority aforesaid, That in the disposal and application of the public moneys of the said corporation, or in the making sale or disposition of any part or parcel of the real or personal estate of the said corporation for any of the purposes aforementioned, and public intimation of a meeting of the members of said church being given as hereinafter is directed, the consent and concurrence of the major part of the regular members of said church then met and qualified as hereinafter is directed, shall be had and obtained; and the votes hereinafter directed to be taken shall be by ballot, and also that the said trustees, in like manner qualified, shall be admitted to vote therein as members of said church.

[Section VI.] (Section VIII, P. L.) And be it further enacted by the authority aforesaid, That the said trustees and their successors shall not, by deed, fine [or] recovery, or by any other ways or means, grant, alien or otherwise dispose of any manors, messuages, lands, tenements or hereditaments in them or their successors vested, or hereafter to be vested, nor charge nor encumber the same to any person or persons whatsoever except as hereinbefore is excepted.

[Section VII.] (Section IX, P. L.) And be it further enacted by the authority aforesaid, That the said trustees, and their successors, or the majority of any five of them met, from time to time, after public intimation given the preceding Lord's day, commonly called Sunday, from the desk or pulpit of the said church, immediately after divine service before the congregation is dismissed, or after regular notice in writing left at the house of each trustee and the particular business having been mentioned at least one meeting before, be authorized and empowered, and they are hereby authorized and empowered to make rules, and by-laws, and ordinances and to do everything needful for the good government and support of the secular affairs of the said church.

(Section X, P. L.) Provided always, That the said by-laws, rules and ordinances, or any of them, be not repugnant to the laws of this commonwealth, and that all their proceedings be fairly and regularly entered into a church book, to be kept for that purpose; and also that the said trustees and their successors, by plurality of votes of any five or more of them met as aforesaid, after such intimation or notice as aforesaid, be authorized and empowered, and they are hereby authorized and empowered to elect and appoint from among themselves a president, and also to elect and appoint from among themselves or others, a treasurer and secretary, and the same president, treasurer and secretary, or any of them, at their pleasure to remove, change, alter or continue as to them, or a majority of any five of them or more so met as aforesaid, from time to time shall seem to be most for the benefit of the said church and corporation.

[Section VIII.] (Section XI, P. L.) And be it further enacted by the authority aforesaid, That the said corporation and their successors shall have full power and authority to make, have and use one common seal, with such device and inscription as they shall think proper, and the same to break, alter and renew at their pleasure.

[Section IX.] (Section XII, P. L.) And be it further enacted by the authority aforesaid, That the said corporation and their successors by the name of the trustees of the Presbyterian church in Warwick township, in Bucks county aforesaid, shall be able and capable in law to sue or be sued, plead and be impleaded, in any court or courts, before any judge or judges, justice or justices, in all and all manner of suits, complaints, pleas, causes, matters and demands of whatsoever kind, nature or form they may be, and all and every matter and thing therein in as full and effectual a manner as any other person or persons, bodies politic or corporate within this commonwealth may or can do.

[Section X.] (Section XIII, P. L.) And be it further enacted by the authority aforesaid, That the said corporation shall always consist of nine members, called and known by the name of "The Trustees of the Presbyterian Church in the Township of Warwick, in the county of Bucks," and the said members shall at all times hereafter be chosen by ballot, by a majority of such members met together of the said church or congregation as shall have been enrolled in the aforesaid book as stated worshippers with the said church, for not less than the space of one year, and shall have paid one year's pew rent or other annual sum of money, not less than ten shillings, for the support of the pastor or pastors and other officers of the said church, their house of public worship and lots and tenements belonging to the said church and corporation, and towards the other necessary expenses of the said church, and shall not at any time of voting be more than one-half year behind or in arrears for the same.

(Section XIV, P. L.) Provided always, That the pastor or pastors of the said church, for the time being, shall be entitled to vote equally with any member of the said church or congregation.

(Section XV, P. L.) And provided also, That all and every person or persons, qualified as aforesaid to vote and elect, shall and may be capable and able to be elected a trustee aforesaid, except in case of the said church having two pastors and one of them only to be eligible at the same time.

[Section XI.] (Section XVI, P. L.) And be it further enacted by the authority aforesaid, That the said Richard Walker, Benjamin Snodgrass, William Scott, William Long, Nathan McKinstry, Giles Craven, William Walker, John Carr [and] Joseph Hart, the first and present trustees hereby incorporated, shall be and continue trustees aforesaid until they be removed in manner following: That is to say, one-third part in number of the trustees aforesaid, being the third part herein first named and appointed, shall cease and discontinue, and their appointment determine on the second Monday in the month of May, which will be in the year of our Lord one thousand seven hundred and eighty-three, upon which day a new election shall be had and held of so many others in their stead and place, by a majority of the persons met and qualified agreeable to the purport, true intent and meaning of this act to vote and elect as aforesaid; and on the second Monday in the month of May, in the year following the second third part in number of the said trustees herein named shall, in like manner cease and discontinue, and their appointment determine, and a new election be had and held of so many in their place and stead, in like manner; and on the second Monday in May, in the year then next following, the last third part in number of the said trustees shall in like manner cease and discontinue, and their appointment determine, and a new election be had and held in like manner as hereinbefore is directed; and that in the same manner and by the like mode of rotation, one-third part in number of the said trustees shall cease, discontinue and their appointment determine, and a new election of said third part be had and held in manner aforesaid, and on the second Monday in the month of May in every year forever, so that no person or persons shall be or continue a trustee or trustees of said church for any longer time than three years together, without being re-elected.

(Section XVII, P. L.) Provided always, That the persons belonging to the said church who are in, and by this act authorized and empowered to elect, shall and may be at liberty to re-elect any one or more of the said trustees whose times shall have expired on the day of the annual election, whenever and so often as they shall think fit.

(Section XVIII, P. L.) Provided also, That whenever any vacancy happens by the death, refusal to serve, or removal of any one or more of the trustees aforesaid, pursuant to the directions of this act, an election shall be had of some fit person or persons, in his or their place and stead so dying, refusing or removing, as soon as conveniently can be done; and that the person or persons so elected shall be, remain and continue as a trustee or trustees aforesaid so long without a new election, as the person or persons in whose place and stead he or they shall have been so elected as aforesaid, would or might have remained and continued, and no longer, and that in all cases of a vacancy happening by the means in this act last mentioned, the remaining trustees shall be empowered to call a meeting of the electors for supplying the said vacancy, such meeting to be notified and published in like manner as hereinbefore is directed and appointed for notifying and publishing the meeting of the trustees.

[Section XII.] (Section XIX, P. L.) Provided always, and it is hereby enacted by the authority aforesaid, That the clear yearly value or income of the messuages, houses, lands, tenements, rents, annuities or other hereditaments and real estate of the said corporation shall not exceed the sum of one thousand pounds, lawful money of the state of Pennsylvania, to be taken and esteemed exclusive of the moneys arising from the letting of the pews and the contributions belonging to the said church, and also exclusive of the moneys arising from the opening the ground or burials, which said money shall be received by the said trustees and disposed of by them in the manner hereinbefore directed, pursuant to the votes of the members of the said church duly qualified to vote and elect as aforesaid.

Passed September 20, 1782. Recorded L. B. No. 2, p. 17, etc.

CHAPTER CMXCIII.

AN ACT FOR INCORPORATING THE DUTCH REFORMED CHURCH IN THE TOWNSHIPS OF NORTHAMPTON AND SOUTHAMPTON, IN THE COUNTY OF BUCKS.

(Section I, P. L.) Whereas, the minister, elders, deacons and members of the Dutch Protestant Reformed church, in the townships of Northampton and Southampton, in the county of Bucks, have prayed that some persons amongst them may be incorporated as trustees for the community, that they may receive and hold grants of lands and chattels, thereby to enable the petitioners to erect and repair public buildings for the worship of God, for school houses and for the maintenance of the ministry, and that the same trustees may plead and be impleaded in any suit touching the premises, and have perpetual success:

And whereas, it is just and right and also agreeable to the true spirit of the constitution that the prayer of their said petition be granted:

[Section I.] (Section II, P. L.) Be it therefore enacted and it is hereby enacted by the Representatives of the Freemen of the Commonwealth of Pennsylvania in General Assembly met, and by the authority of the same, That the Reverend Matthew Light, minister; Henry Kroesen, Gilliam Cornell, Henry Wynkoop, elders; William Bennet, Aart Lefferts and Daniel Hogeland, deacons of the Dutch Reformed congregation above named, in the county aforesaid, and their successors duly elected and nominated in their place and stead, be and they are hereby made and constituted a corporation and body politic in law and in fact, to have continuance forever, by the name, style and title of "The Trustees of the Dutch Reformed Church in Northampton and Southampton, in the county of Bucks."

[Section II.] (Section III, P. L.) And be it further enacted by the authority aforesaid, That the said corporation and their successors, by the name, style and title aforesaid, shall forever hereafter be persons able and capable in law to purchase, take, hold and enjoy any messuages, houses, buildings, lands, rents, tenements, annuities or any other hereditaments, in fee simple and forever, or for term of life or lives or in any other manner, so as the same exceed not at any time in the clear yearly value or income the sum of one thousand pounds, lawful money of the state of Pennsylvania, over and above all charges and reprizes; and, further, that the said corporation may take and receive any sum or sums of money and any manner or portion of goods and chattels that shall be given or bequeathed to them by any person or persons, bodies politis or corporate capable to make a bequest or gift thereof; and also that the said corporation and their successors shall and may give, grant, demise or otherwise dispose of all or any of the messuages, houses, buildings, lands, rents, tenements, annuities or any other hereditaments as to them shall seem meet.

[Section III.] (Section IV, P. L.) Provided always, and be it further enacted by the authority aforesaid, That in the making sale or disposition of any part or parcel of the real estate of the said corporation, the consent and concurrence of the major part of the regular members, who shall have been enrolled as stated worshippers with the said church for not less than the space of one year, and who shall have paid an annual sum of money not less than seven shillings and six pence for the support of the pastor or pastors and other officers of the said church, their houses of public worship and lots and tenements belonging to the said church and corporation, and towards the other necessary expenses of the said church, and who shall not at any time of voting be more than one-half year behind or in arrears for the same, shall be had and obtained.

[Section IV.] (Section V, P. L.) And be it further enacted by the authority aforesaid, That all and every such lands, tenements, hereditaments, money, goods and chattels, which at any time before or after the passing of this act have been or shall be devised, given or granted to the church above named, in the said county of Bucks, or to any person or persons in trust for them, shall be and remain and they are hereby declared to be vested in and shall remain in the peaceable and quiet possession of the corporation, according to the true intent and meaning of such devise or devises, gift or gifts, grant or grants.

[Section V.] (Section VI, P. L.) And be it further enacted by the authority aforesaid, that the said corporation, and their successors, by the name of "The Trustees of the Dutch Reformed Church in the townships of Northampton and Southampton, in the county of Bucks," shall be able and capable in law to sue and be sued, plead and be impleaded in any court or courts, before any judge or judges, justice or justices, in all and all manner of suits, complaints, causes, matters and demands of whatsoever kind, nature or form they may be, in as full and effectual a manner as any other person or persons, bodies politic and corporate in this commonwealth may or can do.

[Section VI.] (Section VII, P. L.) And be it further enacted by the authority aforesaid, That the said corporation, and their successors, shall have full power and authority to make, have and use one common seal, with such device or devices and inscription, as they shall think proper, and the same to break, alter and renew at their pleasure.

[Section VII.] (Section VIII, P. L.) And be it further enacted by the authority aforesaid, That the said trustees, and their successors, or a majority of them, met from time to time be authorized and empowered, and they are hereby authorized and empowered to make rules, by-laws and ordinances and to do everything needful for the good government and support of the secular affairs of said church. Provided always, That the said rules, by-laws and ordinances, or any of them, be consonant to the usages and customs of said church, and not repugnant to the laws of this commonwealth.

[Section VIII.] (Section IX, P. L.) And be it further enacted by the authority aforesaid, That the said Reverend Matthew Light, minister; Henry Kroesen, Gilliam Cornell, Henry Wynkoop, elders; William Bennet, Aart Lefferts, Daniel Hogeland, deacons, the first and present trustees hereby incorporated, shall be and continue trustees of the Dutch Reformed church, in the county aforesaid, until others shall be duly elected and confirmed, according to the manner, custom and method now in use in the said church, for electing the elders and deacons (the minister for the time being remaining a trustee), which persons so elected and confirmed as aforesaid shall have all the power and authorities of the above named trustees; and all and every such person or persons, so newly elected and confirmed as aforesaid, shall remain until other fit persons in like manner be elected and confirmed in their respective rooms and places.

[Section IX,] (Section X, P. L.) And be it further enacted by the authority aforesaid, That in case of the death or removal of a minister of the said congregation, and until another minister shall be duly appointed and approved for the said congregation agreeable to former method and usage, they, the said elders and deacons, shall have the same power and authorities as are hereinbefore vested in the whole corporation.

[Section X.] (Section XI, P. L.) And be it further enacted by the authority aforesaid, That the said trustees, and their successors be authorized and empowered, and they are hereby authorized and empowered to meet at such time or times, place or places as to them, or the major part of them, shall seem meet and convenient, and then and there, by plurality of votes to elect and appoint from among themselves a president, and also to elect and appoint a treasurer and secretary, which president so elected shall have the custody of the seal or seals of said corporation, and all books, charters, deeds and writings any way relating to the said corporation, and shall have power from time to time, and at all times hereafter, as occasion shall require, to call a meeting of the said trustees at such place as he shall think convenient, for the execution of all or any of the powers hereby given; and in case of sickness, removal or death of the president, all the powers hereby given to the president, shall remain in the senior elder, until the recovery of the president or until a new president shall be elected as aforesaid.

[Section XI.] (Section XII, P. L.) And be it further enacted by the authority aforesaid, That every act and order of the major part of the said trustees, consented or agreed to at such meeting as aforesaid, shall be good, valid and effectual, to all intents and purposes, as if the whole number of the said trustees had consented and agreed thereto; also, that all the proceedings of the said trustees, or a majority of them, shall, from time to time, be fairly entered in a book or books to be kept for the purpose by the president of the trustees for the time being, which book or books, together with the seal of the said corporation, and all charters, deeds and writings whatsoever, any way belonging to the said corporations shall be delivered over by the former president to the president of the said trustees newly elected, as such presidents shall hereafter successively from time to time be elected.

[Section XII.] (Section XIII, P. L.) And be it further enacted by the authority aforesaid, That all and every clause, sentence and article herein contained shall be, in all things, firm, valid, sufficient and effectual in law unto the said corporation and community and their successors forever, according to the true intent and meaning hereof; and that in all things it shall be construed, taken and expounded most benignly and for the greatest advantage and profit of the trustees of the said Dutch Reformed church of Northampton and Southampton, in the county of Bucks aforesaid, and their successors forever, notwithstanding any defect, default or imperfection may be found therein, or any other cause or thing whatsoever.

Passed September 20, 1782. Recorded L. B. No. 2, p. 21, etc.

CHAPTER CMXCIV.

AN ACT FOR PROCURING AN ESTIMATE OF THE DAMAGES, SUSTAINED BY THE INHABITANTS OF PENNSYLVANIA, FROM THE TROOPS AND ADHERENTS OF THE KING OF GREAT BRITAIN DURING THE PRESENT WAR.

(Section I, P. L.) Whereas great damages of the most wanton nature have been committed by the armies of the King of Great Britain, or their adherents, within the territory of the United States of North America, unwarranted by the practice of civilized nations, and only to be accounted for from the vindictive spirit of the said king and his officers:

And whereas, an accurate account and estimate of such damages, more especially the waste and destruction of property, may be very useful to the people of the United States of America in forming a future treaty of peace, and in the meantime may serve to exhibit in a true light to the nations of Europe the conduct of the said king, his ministers, officers and adherents:

(Section II, P. L.) To the end, therefore, that proper measures may be taken to ascertain the damages aforesaid, which have been done to the citizens and inhabitants of Pennsylvania in the course of the present war within this state:

[Section I.] Be it enacted by the Representatives of the Freemen of the Commonwealth of Pennsylvania in General Assembly met, and by the authority of the same, That every county within this state which has been invaded by the armies, soldiers or the adherents of the King of Great Britain, the commissioners of every such county, or any two of them, shall, without delay, meet together, each within their county, and issue directions to the assessors of the respective townships, wards or districts within such county where they have reason to believe any such damage hath been done, to notify the inhabitants thereof by at least three written notices, to furnish accounts and estimates of the damages, waste, spoil and destruction which hath been done and committed as aforesaid, upon the property, real or personal, within the same township, ward or district since the eighteenth day of April, which was in the year of our Lord one thousand seven hundred and seventy-five, and the same accounts and estimates to transmit to the said commissioners without delay. And if any person or persons shall refuse or neglect to make out such accounts and estimates, the said assessors of the township, ward or district shall, from their own knowledge and by any other reasonable and lawful methods, take and render such an account and estimate of all damage done or committed as aforesaid.

(Section III, P. L.) Provided always, That all such accounts and estimates to be made out and transmitted as aforesaid shall contain a narrative of the time and circumstances and, if in the power of the person aggrieved, the names of the general or other officer or adherent of the enemy by whom the damage in any case was done, or under whose orders the army, detachment, party or persons committing the same acted at that time, and also the name and addition of the person or persons whose property was so damaged or destroyed, and that all such accounts and estimates be made in current money, upon oath or affirmation of the sufferer, or of others having knowledge concerning the same; and that in every case it be set forth whether the party injured hath received any satisfaction for his loss and by whom the same was given.

[Section II.] (Section IV, P. L.) And be it further enacted by the authority aforesaid, That the said commissioners, having obtained the said accounts and estimates from the assessors of the several townships, wards and districts, shall proceed to inspect and register the same in a book to be provided for that purpose, distinguishing the district and townships, and entering those of each place together; and if any account and estimate be imperfect or not sufficiently verified and established, the said commissioners shall have power and they, or any two of them, are hereby authorized to summon and compel any person, whose evidence they shall think necessary, to appear before them at the day and place appointed, to be examined upon oath or affirmation concerning any damage [or] injury as aforesaid; and the said commissioners shall, upon registering as aforesaid, without delay, deliver over and transmit to the supreme executive council all and every of the original accounts, together with a copy of the register aforesaid.

[Section III.] (Section V, P. L.) And be it further enacted by the authority aforesaid, That all losses of servants, negro and mulatto slaves who have been deluded and carried away by the enemies of the United States, and which have not been recovered or recompensed, shall be comprehended within the accounts and estimates aforesaid; and that the commissioners and assessors of any county, which hath not been invaded as aforesaid, shall nevertheless inquire after and procure accounts and estimates of any damages suffered by the loss of such servants and slaves as is hereinbefore directed as to other property.

[Section IV.] (Section VI, P. L.) And be it further enacted by the authority of the aforesaid, That the charges and expenses of executing this act, as to the pay of the said commissioners and assessors shall be as in other cases, and that witnesses shall be rewarded for their loss of time and trouble, as witnesses summoned to appear in the courts of quarter sessions of the peace; and the said charges and expenses shall be defrayed by the commonwealth, but paid in the first instance out of the moneys in the hands of the treasurer of the county for county rates and levies upon orders drawn by the commissioners of the proper county.

Passed September 21, 1782. Recorded L. B. No. 2, p. 24, etc.

CHAPTER CMXCV.

AN ACT TO REPEAL THE ACT, ENTITLED "AN ACT TO ENABLE THE SUPREME EXECUTIVE COUNCIL TO NEGOTIATE SUCH LOANS, AS MAY BE NECESSARY TO PROCURE A SUFFICIENT SUM OF MONEY FOR THE DEFENSE OF THE FRNOTIERS OF THIS STATE AND THE SUPPORT OF CIVIL GOVERNMENT," AND FOR OTHER PURPOSES THEREIN MENTIONED.

(Section I, P. L.) Whereas the supreme executive council have not negotiated a loan of money by virtue of the act of assembly, entitled "An act to enable the supreme executive council to negotiate such loans, as may be necessary to procure a sufficient sum of money for the defense of the frontiers of this state and support of civil government,"[1] and it being inexpedient that the said act should any longer remain in force, the intention thereof being otherwise in part supplied by this house:

[Section I.] (Section II, P. L.) Be it therefore enacted by the Representatives of the Freemen of the Commonwealth of Pennsylvania in General Assembly met, and by the authority of the

---

[1] Passed April 15, 1782, Chapter 983.

same. That the said act, entitled "An act to enable the supreme executive council to negotiate such loans as may be necessary to procure a sufficient sum of money for the defense of the frontiers of this state, and the support of civil government,"[1] and every clause, matter and thing therein contained shall be and the same is hereby repealed and made void to all intents and purposes whatsoever.

(Section III, P. L.) And whereas, this house have negotiated a loan with the National Bank of North America for the sum of five thousand pounds, to be repaid in three months, with lawful interest, out of the money now due for interest in the loan office of this state:

[Section II.] Be it therefore enacted by the authority aforesaid, That all moneys now due for interest in the loan office of this state be and the same are hereby appropriated for the payment of the sum of five thousand pounds borrowed as aforesaid.

Passed September 21, 1782. Recorded L. B. No. 2, p. 26, etc.

INDEX.

A.

ABOLITION. See Slavery.

ACCOUNTS. See Pennsylvania Line, Public Accounts.

ACTION OF DEBT.
Penalties accruing under act for suppressing public actions to be recovered by, ... 17
Certificate of auditors appointed to settle public accounts to be conclusive evidence in, by the Commonwealth to recover amount due, ... 75
Certain penalties to be recovered by, ...137,294-295
Tenant compelled to pay taxes to recover same from landlord by, ... 141
Penalty imposed upon militia-lieutenants, etc., for neglecting or refusing to deliver up books, accounts, etc., to their successors in office to be recovered by bill, plaint, information, indictment or, ... 227
Penalties imposed on tax collectors in Southwark to be recovered by, ... 515

ACTIONS.
Pending in Westmoreland county against the inhabitants of newly erected county of Washington not to be stayed, ... 276

ACTS OF ASSEMBLY. See Private Acts.
Certain, repealed, ...9, 22, 37, 51, 52, 72, 73, 80, 96, 97, 105, 109, 139, 172, 175, 267, 287, 337, 378, 381, 405, 461, 505, 511, 533, 534
Certain, partly repealed, ...22, 31, 33, 113, 213, 220, 227, 267, 272, 284, 326, 405, 411, 438
Certain, repealed, after Oct. 1, 1781, 288

ACTS OF ASSEMBLY—Continued.
Certain, not repealed, ... 142
Certain, suspended, ...204, 266, 288
Certain, continued, 32, 182, 183, 227, 228, 288, 299, 352, 353
Certain, party continued, ...33, 225, 365
Certain, revived, ...115, 248, 470
Certain, revived and extended, 116, 283
Parts of certain, made perpetual, .. 405
Defects in certain, cured, ... 125
Certain altered and amended, ...81-82
Duration of certain, limited, ...9, 22, 116, 128, 218, 298, 364, 505
Certain, to be given in evidence in suits or prosecutions for things done under them, ...256, 319, 323, 515

ADMIRALTY. See High Court of Errors and Appeals.
Fees of the judge of, ... 41
Fees of the judge, register and marshall of the court of, to be paid in wheat, ... 40
Marshall of the court of, not to sell by public auction except prize ships, etc., and perishable goods, ...19-20
Marshall to make out an inventory of prizes and have them appraised, ... 20
Inventory and appraisement to be filed with the register of the court, ... 20
If no appeal be entered execution to issue upon entry of security, ... 20
Mode of distributing shares of prizes, 20
Compensation of marshall, ... 21
Compensation of appraisers, ... 21
High court of errors and appeals to be composed of the president of the supreme executive council, the judges of the supreme court, the judge of, and three persons of integrity and ability, ... 54
Appeals from the court of, to lie to the high court of errors and appeals,.. 54

(535)

Index

ADMIRALTY—Continued.

	Page
Judge of, not to sit in high court of errors and appeals on cases already heard and determined by him,	54-55
Compensation of judge of, for sitting in high court of errors and appeals,	58
Court of, established,	97
Supreme executive council to appoint a judge of,	97
Term of judge,	97
Jurisdiction of court of,	97
Prize causes, etc., to be judged by the law of nations and the acts of Congress,	97-98
Appeals in such cases to lie to Congress, upon security given,	98
Captains, etc., bringing into court captured vessels, etc., to exhibit to the judge of, within three days a libel in writing,	98
Libel to contain a full account of the time and manner of capture,	98
All books, papers, etc., found on captured vessel to be delivered to the register of the court of,	98
Penalty for neglect or refusal,	99
Register to give public notice in the newspapers of the day set for trial,	99
Owners to show cause why captured vessels should not be condemned as lawful prize,	99
Judge of, to appoint three appraisers if cargo be damaged or perishable,	99-100
And order the marshall to sell the same upon return of appraisement,	100
Marshall to keep money arising from such sales until the termination of trial,	100
Cost of appraisement and charges upon prize to be ascertained by the judge,	100
Appeals not to stay proceedings if appellees enter security,	100
Security to have effect as a statute staple,	100
Condemned vessels and cargoes to be sold at public auction for the benefit of the captors,	101
Marshall to file account of such sales with the register,	101

ADMIRALITY—Continued.

	Page
Negroes and mulattoes taken as prize not to be so sold,	101
To be appraised and delivered to captors,	101
Act not to interfere with act for suppression of public auctions,	101
Judge to appoint agents for absent persons,	102
Such agents to give security,	102-103
Unclaimed shares of prizes vested in the Pennsylvania Hospital,	103
Persons entitled may receive same if they apply within three years,	103
Ships, etc., belonging to foreigners not to be sold for three months,	103
Supreme executive council to appoint register of the court of,	103
Attestations of register to be received as evidence,	104
Supreme executive council to appoint a marshall of the court of,	104
Bond of marshall,	104
Traitors, pirates, felons, etc., offending upon the sea to be tried by grand and petit juries,	104
Trial to be had in court of oyer and terminer in Philadelphia,	105
Justices of the supreme court and judge of, constituted justices of oyer and terminer,	105
Judge of, to be president of oyer and terminer in chief justices absence,	105
Persons standing mute upon arraignment to be deemed to have pleaded not guilty,	105
Provision for trial of offences committed partly on land and partly at sea,	105
Proceedings in court of, liable to prohibition of the supreme court,	105
Prior act of assembly repealed,	105
Repeal not to prevent or stop any cause pending in court of,	105-106
A supplement to act regulating and establishing admiralty jurisdiction, passed,	220
Place and manner of trial of traitors, pirates, felons and criminals committing offences within the admiralty jurisdiction or upon the sea,	221

Index. 537

ADMIRALITY—Continued.
  Persons convicted of such crimes to suffer death without benefit of clergy, where the same is taken away for like offence committed on land, ... 221
  Trial and punishment of subjects of this State or any of the U. S. committing piracy, etc., under foreign colors, ... 222
  Persons betraying their trust at sea to be convicted and punished as pirates, ... 222
  Captains and masters of vessels harboring deserters to be fined 10,000£, 223
  Penalty to be recovered by distress, 223
  For want of sufficient distress such captain, etc., to suffer one years imprisonment without bail or mainprise, ... 223
  Prize money and wages of such deserters to be forfeited and applied for recruiting the Pennsylvania line in the federal army, ... 223
  Certain wills, powers of attorney, deeds of sale, etc., made by such deserters declared null and void, ... 223
  President and council to appoint persons to inspect muster roll of vessels in search of deserters, ... 223
  Penalty for obstructing search or refusing to deliver up deserters, ... 224
  Marshall upon notice, to pay prizes and wages due deserters to the state treasurer, ... 224
  The eleventh section of the act to which this is a supplement repealed, ... 224
  Marshall empowered to sell prize goods at public vendue, ... 224
  Mode of conducting sale and distributing proceeds, ... 224
  Distribution to be made within twenty days after end of sale, ... 224
  Penalty for neglect or refusal, ...224-225
  Vessels, goods, etc., sold by marshall and not paid for within three days to be resold, ... 225
  First purchaser to be liable for all loss occasioned thereby, ... 225
  Parts of prior act continued, ... 225

ADVERTISEMENTS. See Newspapers.
  Supreme executive council after February 1, 1781, to publish monthly in the Philadelphia English and German newspapers the rate of exchange between specie and continental money, ... 251
  Ten days' public notice to be given of the sale of goods condemned as contraband, if the value thereof be under, 50£, ... 502
  Like notice to be also inserted in one of the Philadelphia weekly newspapers, if the value exceeds 50£,... 503

AFFIRMATIONS. See Oaths.

ALLEGIANCE.
  Inhabitants of Westmoreland and Washington counties who produce certified copies of taking the oath of allegiance to the State of Virginia before the settlement of state boundary dispute declared to be free citizens of this state, ...462 463
  Such persons to register their slaves in accordance with act for the gradual abolition or slavery, ... 463

ALLEN, ELIZABETH.
  Empowered during the minority of her son to grant and convey sundry lots of land in the town of Northampton, county of Northampton, ... 496

ALMONER. See Militia.

ALMSHOUSES. See Poor; Workhouses.

AMERICAN PHILOSOPHICAL SOCIETY.
  Incorporated, ... 121
  Empowered to hold real estate not exceeding the yearly value of 10,000 bushels of wheat, ... 121
  Officers of, ... 121
  President of supreme executive council to be patron of, ... 121
  Annual election of officers, ...121-122
  Notice of annual elections to be given in the newspapers, ... 122
  Provision for the passing of by laws, regulations, etc., ... 123

AMERICAN PHILOSOPHICAL SO-
CIETY—Continued.
Empowered to correspond with enemys
in time of war on matters relating
merely to the business of the society, ...123-124
Such correspondence to be open to
the inspection of the supreme executive council, ... 124
Managers of silk society to adjust its
accounts, sell all silk remaining in
their hands, and pay over all net
proceeds to Philosophical Society,474-475
Subscribers of silk society entitled to
be reimbursed their proportional
dividend by applying for same on or
before October 1, 1783, ... 475
Philosophical society to keep all sums
unclaimed by such proprietors and
redeliver them when a majority of
the subscribers revive the said society, ... 475

AMIEL, JOHN.
Act for relief of, insolvent debtor, .. 421

AMNESTY.
Granted to all persons engaged in Wilson riots, ... 118

APPEAL. See High Court of Errors and
Appeals.
From supreme court, court of admiralty and register of wills to lie to the
high court of errors and appeals,.. 54
No such appeal to lie unless the matter in controversy exceed the value
of four hundred bushels of wheat, 55
Appellant to give security in double
the amount in dispute to prosecute
his appeal with effect, ... 55
Depositions taken before the register
of wills to be in writing and made
part of the record in such appeal,... 56
Facts decided by the verdict of a jury
in an issue directed to the common
pleas by the register not to be re-examined on appeal, ... 56

APPEAL—Continued.
Appeal from decree of register concerning the validity of a will, etc.,
not to act as a supersedeas where
executor gives security, ... 56
Appeals made before July 4, 1776 to
the king of Great Britain in council and not determined may be renewed in the high court of errors
and appeals, ... 56
Time of taking appeals to the high
court of errors and appeals limited
to twenty years, ... 57
Except where appellant is a minor,
feme covert, non compos mentis or
in prison, ... 57
Prize causes, etc., to be judged in admiralty by the law of nations and
the acts of Congress, ...97-98
Appeals in such cases to lie to Congress upon security given, ... 98
Not to stay proceedings where appellee enters security, ... 100
Party aggrieved by seizure of swine
found running at large in Passyunk,
etc., to have appeal to justice of the
peace, ... 117
Party appealing to forfeit 40s where
seizure is confirmed, ... 117
From assessment of county rates and
levies, etc., ...140-141
Party aggrieved by conviction for
violation of militia act to have, to
the common pleas, ... 160
Lieutenant and two freeholders to
hear appeals of parties aggrieved
by things done in pursuance of militia act, ... 163
Oath of freeholders, ... 163
From the order of regulators in Philadelphia to lie to the next court of
common pleas, ...486-487
Proceedings on appeal, ... 487
All orders and awards of regulators to
be conclusive unless set aside on appeal, ... 488
Not to lie from judgment of justices
condemning goods seized as contraband, ... 501
APPELLATE COURTS. See High Court
of Errors and Appeals.

Index. 539

APPRAISEMENT. See Appraisers.
Where imported goods, etc., remain in vessel ten days after arrival without duty being paid or secured, master to deliver same to naval officer to be warehoused and kept at owners risk and expense, ... 254
After three months naval officer to have all such goods appraised and sold at auction, ... 254

APPRAISERS. See Federal Army.
Amount of rent to be paid to owners of land occupied by the United States to be fixed by three, ... 46
Appointment of, ... 47
Appointment of, where cargo of captured vessel is damaged or perishable, ...99-100
Duties of, ... 100
Provisions seized for the use of the Federal Army to the paid for at rates fixed by two indifferent freeholders, ... 215
Appointment of, ... 215

APPRENTICES.
Masters, fathers, etc., to be accountable for the fines of minors and, under militia act, ... 159

ARMIES. See Armies of the United States; Federal Army; Pennsylvania Line; Public Defense.

ARMIES OF THE UNITED STATES. See Pensions; Pennsylvania Line, Public Defense.
Act preventing exports by sea for a limited time not to apply to provisions for the use of the, or their allies, ... 44
Militia while in service of the United States to be subject to the rules of the Federal Army, ... 159
Commissioners appointed to procure this states quota of provisions for 1780, ... 176
Commissioners to give security, ..176-177
Oath of commissioners, ... 177
Commissioners required to purchase wheat, flour, etc., at prices fixed by act, ... 177

ARMIES OF THE UNITED STATES
—Continued.
Where wheat, etc., cannot be bought commissioners to apply to justice of the peace, ... 177
Justice to issue warrant to the constable and two freeholders to seize the same, ... 177
Constable where necessary to break open doors, etc., in the daytime to make seizure, ...177-178
Tenant may tender amount received in payment to landlord, where wheat, etc., reserved for rent due is seized in his hands, ... 178
Such payment to be a good discharge for all such rent due, ... 178
Commissioners empowered to hire or seize mills for grinding and storehouses for keeping wheat and flour, etc., ... 178
And to impress horses, carriages, boats, etc., for transporting same, ...178-179
Commissioners empowered to seize wheat, etc., bought by quarter masters, etc., upon refunding advances made, ... 179
Provision for payment and disposition of same, ... 179
Price of provisions to be fixed by commissioner and party, ... 179
A third person to be called in where they cannot agree, ... 179
Provisions when collected by commissioners to be transported and delivered under the direction of the supreme executive council, ...179-180
Pay of wagoner for transporting same, ... 180
Commissioners to cease collecting provisions when ordered to do so by supreme executive council, ... 180
Commissioners to make monthly returns to supreme executive council, ... 180
Commissioners to annually settle their accounts before committee of assembly, ... 180
Commissioners not to deal in provisions, ... 180
Penalty for violation, ...180-181

540   Index.

ARMIES OF THE UNITED STATES —Continued.

	Page.
Commissioners in settling accounts to return to state treasurer identical money not used,	181
Compensation of commissioners,	181
Justices, sheriffs and civil officers to assist commissioners in carrying out provisions of act,	181
Quarter masters, foragemasters, etc., not to purchase provisions except for private use during continuance of act,	181
Penalty for violation,	181-182
Act for striking the sum of £100,000 for the support of the,	183
President to appoint commissioners to procure meat for the,	215
Commissioners to deliver same under directions of supreme executive council to the commissary general,	215
Commissary to give commissioners receipt for the same,	215
Cattle, sheep or salted provisions to be subject to seizure by the commissioners for the use of the,	215
Seized articles to be paid for at rates fixed by two indifferent freeholders,	215
Appointment of freeholders,	215
Commissioner to fix price where owner refuses to appoint appraiser,	215
Cattle, etc., not to be seized where owner takes oath that same are necessary for his private use,	216
Copy of oath to be served on persons seizing cattle, etc.,	216
Commissioners to make returns monthly to president of quantities and prices of meat, etc., seized or purchased and delivered to commissary general,	216
Penalty for neglect or refusal,	216
Voluntary sellers to commissioners to receive current prices for article sold,	216
Commissioners to give them certificate for same,	216
Tax collectors to receive such certificates in payment of all State taxes,	216
Certificates not transferrable,	216

ARMIES OF THE UNITED STATES —Continued.

	Page.
Where certificate exceeds tax, collector to endorse thereon the allowance made as so much of said certificate paid,	217
Collectors to keep registers of the names of the persons and the amounts so endorsed in credit,	217
To send copy thereof to county treasurer,	217
Copy to be a sufficient voucher,	217
Collector to take up certificate and return the same to county treasurer after crediting tax where certificate does not exceed tax demanded,	217
Faith and honor of the State pledged for payment of certificates not paid in for taxes, with 6 per cent. interest thereon,	217
Persons delivering a specified number of cattle and sheep to commissioners, to receive an order on the president in council for the price thereof,	217
Penalty for opposing commissioners in the performance of their duties,	217
Compensation of officers appointed by act,	218
Difficulty arising in execution of act to be referred to supreme executive council,	218
President empowered to suspend act when circumstances of the, admit thereof,	218
Duration of act limited,	218
2,700 men to be enlisted in the,	259
Proportionate share of each county,	259
Commissioners to direct assessors to meet at certain times and places, and in conjunction with them to class taxable persons and property in a certain manner,	260
Classes to be notified and to deliver one able bodied recruit within fifteen days thereafter,	260
Class delivering a deserter to be excused from furnishing a recruit,	260
Act not to authorize any one to enlist deserters from the British army or from the navy of the United States,	260-261

ARMIES OF THE UNITED STATES—Continued.

Commissioners and assessors to levy a tax of £15 on persons composing class where such class neglects or refuses to enlist recruit, ... 261

Such tax to be levied and collected in the usual manner, ... 261

Disputes about the payment of sums for enlistment of recruits to be adjusted, collected and paid in same manner as the collecting and payment of expenses of enlistment, .. 261

Supreme executive council to appoint officers to recruit and receive recruits, etc., ... 261

Recruits to be attested before a justice of the peace and delivered to the nearest officer, ... 262

Officer to give receipt in favor of class furnishing recruit, ... 262

Moneys paid under act by executors, guardians or others in legal trust to be allowed in the settlement of their accounts, ... 262

Recruits to receive one suit of clothes yearly and all other pay, etc., together with two hundred acres of land at the end of the war, ... 262

County commissioners neglecting to perform duty required by act to be liable to be fined £500 by the supreme executive council, ... 262

Assessors, collectors, etc., failing to perform duties required by act to be liable to be fined £100 by county commissioners, ... 262

Proceedings by collectors and commissioners to collect taxes under act where lands are unoccupied, ... 263

Tenants in possession to be accountable for sums charged on such lands, ... 263

Tenants to discount the same out of their rent, etc., ... 263

Compensation of persons appointed by commissioners to transmit and deliver to the several classes the tax duplicate, etc., ... 264

Act altering and supplying act for recruiting the Pennsylvania line in the, ... 364

ARMIES OF THE UNITED STATES—Continued.

Supreme executive council authorized to adopt expedient measures to recruit the Pennsylvania line, in the, 365

Act for recruiting the Pennsylvania line, in the, ... 365

Officers in the hospital and medical department of the, to receive the same benefits as military commissioned officers, etc., receive under prior acts, ... 370

All such officers to be liable to be called into actual service by the supreme executive council, ... 371

Their half pay to cease and determine upon their neglect or refusal to respond to such call, ... 371

Supreme executive council to determine claims of person claiming benefit of act and direct auditors to settle accounts, etc., of such officers, ... 371

Officers and privates of state regiments, etc., captured by the enemy entitled to full depreciation of their pay until the time of their exchange, 372

Widows and children of officers of State regiments killed in battle, etc., entitled to half pay of such officers, 372

ARMS. See Militia.

Penalty for buying or selling arms, etc., ... 163

ARMY. See Armies of the United States; Commissioners of Purchases; Federal Army; Pennsylvania Line.

ARTILLERY. See Militia.

ASPDEN, MATTHIAS.

A further time granted to, to render himself to a justice of the supreme court and stand trial for treason,.. 280

Attainder stayed upon condition that he does so on or before Dec. 31, 1781, 280

Upon failing to so render himself to be adjudged and attainted of high treason, ... 281

ASSEMBLY. See General Assembly.

ASSEMBLYMEN. See General Assembly.

ASSESSMENTS. See War Taxes.

542 Index.

Page.

ASSESSORS. See Carlisle, Borough of; City Assessors; County Commissioners; Philadelphia, City of; Wardens; War Taxes.
Fees of, to be paid in wheat, ...41,143

ASSOCIATORS. See Public Defense.

ATTAINDER. See Forfeited Estates.
House and lots on High, Minor and Sixth Sts., in Philadelphia, owned by Joseph Galloway before his, vested in the commonwealth, ...48-50
Of treason after peace with Great Britain not to disinherit heirs nor to prejudice any one except the offender, ... 112
A further time granted to Daniel Rundle and Matthias Aspden to render themselves to a justice of the supreme court and stand trial for treason, ... 280
Attainder stayed upon condition that they do so on or before Dec. 31, 1781, 280
Either party failing to so render himself to be adjudged and attainted of high treason, ... 281
Error in supplement to attainder act, cured, ... 125
The word March at foot of act to have like effect as April, ... 125

ATTORNEY GENERAL.
Fees of the, to be paid in wheat, ... 40

ATTORNEYS.
Fees of, to be paid in wheat, ... 40
The suspension for a limited time of certain acts of assembly making bills of credit of the U. S. legal tender, not to extend to sheriffs, executors, guardians, or, etc., ...204-205
Salary of, ... 377

AUCTIONEERS. See Public Auctions.
Damaged and shipwrecked goods may be sold by public auction, ... 81
Auctioneer in Philadelphia to first obtain a license from council, ... 82
President and council to appoint three, one for Philadelphia city, one for Northern Liberties and one for district of Southwark, ... 229

AUCTIONEERS—Continued.
Bond of, ...229-230
Authorized to sell by public outcry all kinds of real and personal property, except negro and mulatto slaves, 230
To pay 1 per cent. of gross receipts to state treasurer every three months, 230
Penalty for neglect or refusal, ... 230
Penalty for selling by auction without a license, ... 230
Application of penalty, ... 230
Offenders to give surety for good behavior, ... 231
Act not to hinder executors or administrators in selling lands, etc., of their respective testators or intestates, ... 231
Nor sheriffs, constables, etc., selling lands, etc., taken in execution, ... 231
Nor of selling goods, etc., distrained on for rent, ... 231
To keep a register of all horses sold, ...231-232
Register to be a public record and open for inspection, ... 232
Entitled to a fee of two dollars for every inspection of register and six dollars for every copy thereof, ... 232
Register to be given in evidence, upon trial respecting property of horses, etc., ... 232
Sale of stolen horses by, not to be deemed a public sale in market overt so as to change the property thereof, ... 232
Auctioneer not to exceed the limits of his district, ... 232
Fees of, ... 232
Fees of auctioneers in Philadelphia, Northern Liberties and Southwark, 469
Auctioneers to demand and receive an additional one per cent. for the use of the commonwealth, ... 469
Auctioneers bond to the president to be security for the proper application of the same, ... 469
Revenue arising from auctions in Philadelphia, Northern Liberties and Southwark appropriated to the support of government and the administration of justices, ... 469

AUCTIONS. See Public Auctions.

Index.

AUDITOR GENERAL. See Public Accounts.

AUDITORS. See Pennsylvania Line; Public Accounts.

Appointed to collect, audit and settle, etc., the accounts of late committee of safety, ... 75
And of the council of safety, ... 75
And of the accounts of all other persons entrusted with public money, 75
To direct public debtors to pay all debts to the state treasurer, ... 75
Certificate of, to be conclusive evidence in action of debt by the commonwealth to recover amount due, 75
No set off to be admitted, ... 75
To draw orders on state treasurer for balances found due creditors of the commonwealth, ... 75
To open an office in Philadelphia and employ accountants, ... 76
Compensation of accountants, ... 76
To give public notice of their appointment by advertisement in some newspaper printed in said city, ... 76
Like notices to be read in the courts of quarter sessions throughout the state, ... 76
Contents of notice, ... 76
Justices to cause this act to be read in the quarter sessions, ... 76
To prepare books, etc., and to call upon former auditors for their books etc., ... 76
Supreme executive council may direct, to attend at other places within the state, ... 77
Notice thereof to be first given, ... 77
Empowered to issue subpoenas and attachments, ... 77
And to commit for contempt, ... 77
Fees of witnesses, sheriffs, etc., to be the same as in the inferior courts, .. 78
To levy such costs and charges upon delinquents, ... 78
Empowered to issue an attachment upon the return of non est., ... 78
Defaulters upon summons to be barred of all set offs or deductions and to be liable for all the moneys advanced, ... 78-79

AUDITORS—Continued.
Proviso where extension is granted by, 79
To draw on state treasurer for necessary charges and expenses, ... 79
Filling vacancy in office of, ... 79
Compensation of, ...79-80
Supreme executive council to draw orders on state treasurer for payment of, ... 80
Certain accounts to be settled by committee of accounts, ... 80
Certain prior acts repealed, ... 80
Repeal not to affect settlements by former auditors or commissioners,.. 80
Debts and contracts entered into and made between January 1, 1777, and March 1, 1781, to be settled according to a scale of depreciation, ... 284
Mode of settlement where parties cannot agree, ... 285
Auditors to be appointed to hear and examine the parties and adjust the controversies, ... 285
Auditors not to reduce payments made in current money, ... 285
Where tender has been made creditor to be paid only the value of his claim reduced to specie at the time of tender, ... 285
Debtor prevented from paying by creditor absconding, etc., to have benefit of legal tender, ... 285
Auditors report to have the force of a verdict, etc., ... 286
Scale of depreciation, ... 286

B.

BAIL. See Mainprise.

Imprisonment without, or mainprise punishment for neglect or refusal of trustees of the University of Pennsylvania to comply with judgment of justices to deliver up books, records, etc., ... 29
Horse thieves not to be let out on, except by a judge of the supreme court, ... 113
Imprisonment without, or mainprise contingent punishment for captains and masters of vessels harboring deserters, ... 223

BAIL—Continued.
Upon second refusal of militia-lieutenant or sub-lieutenant to deliver up books, accounts, etc., offender to suffer six months imprisonment without, or mainprise, ... 227
Tax collector in Southwark neglecting or refusing to account for moneys received to be committed without, or mainprise, ... 516

BAKERS. See Bread.

BANK OF NORTH AMERICA.
Counterfeiting the common seal or any bank-bill or note of the, or uttering the same to be punished by death without benefit of clergy, ... 384
Embezzlement of any bill, note, bond, deed, money, or other effects from the, to be punished by death without benefit of clergy, ... 384
Incorporated, ... 406
Authorized to hold property to the amount of ten millions of dollars,.. 406
To sue and be sued, ... 407
Officers of the, ... 407
Powers of officers, ... 407
By-laws of the, ... 407
Seal of the, ... 408
Act of incorporation to be construed liberally in favor of the, ... 408
All moneys due for interest in the loan office appropriated to the payment of 5000 £ borrowed from the National Bank of North America, ... 534

BANK-NOTES. See Bank of North America.

BARRACKS.
Military, erected in the city of Philadelphia, and the Northern Liberties, vested in the commonwealth, ... 49

BAY WINDOWS. See Carlisle, Borough of; Nuisances.

BEDFORD COUNTY.
Act vesting court houses, jails, etc., throughout the state in the commonwealth not to extend to old temporary prison in, ... 50

BEDFORD COUNTY—Continued.
Act for the relief of the inhabitants of Northampton, Northumberland, Westmoreland, and, ... 114
County commissioners and assessors to lay state taxes by former returns, 114
Commissioners and assessors to exonerate from taxes persons driven off from their settlements by the enemy, ... 114
To transmit to the general assembly a list of the persons so exonerated,. 115
Deficiencies arising in raising quota of, to be made good out of state taxes, ... 115
Place of holding elections in townships of Air and Bethel, ... 220

BENEFICIAL SOCIETIES. See Society for the Relief of Masters of Ships.

BENEFIT OF CLERGY.
Not allowed to forgers or counterfeiters of continental loan office certificates or continental loan office bills of exchange, ... 14
Persons convicted of robbery to suffer death without, ... 110
Not allowed to persons convicted of counterfeiting, or uttering counterfeited bills of credit, ...189, 212, 307
Persons convicted of committing capital crimes upon the seas, to suffer death without, where the same is taken away for like offence committed on land, ... 221
Counterfeiting the common seal or any bank-bill or note of the Bank of North America or uttering the same to be punishable by death, without, 384
Embezzlement of any bill, note, bond, deed, money, or other effects from the Bank of North America to be punishable by death, without, ... 384

BILL.
Certain penalties to be recovered by, ...137, 294-295
Penalty imposed upon militia-lieutenants, etc., for neglecting or refusing to deliver up books, accounts, etc., to their successors in office to be recovered by indictment, plaint, information, action of debt, or, ... 227

Index. 545

BILLMEYER, JACOB.
Divorced from Mary Billmeyer, his wife, ... 369

BILLMEYER, MARY.
Divorced from Jacob Billmeyer, ... 369

BILLS OF CREDIT.
Counterfeiting, forging, or knowingly uttering forged or counterfeit, to be punished by death without benefit of clergy, ... 14
Raising of, or knowingly uttering, to be punished by fine, pillory and whipping, ... 15
Offender unable to pay fine to be sold into servitude, ... 15
To be emitted to the value of £100,000, 184
Commissioners appointed for the printing of certain, ... 184
Form of, ... 184
Denomination of, ...184-185
Signing of, ... 185
Oath of signers, ... 185
Mode of signing, ...185-186
Compensation of signers, ... 186
Compensation of commissioners, ... 186
Compensation of state treasurer for handling, ... 186
To be delivered to state treasurer as soon as signed, ... 186
To be applied to paying drafts of president, etc., ... 186
Legal value of, fixed, ... 186
Fund and mode of redemption, ... 186
Provisions for sinking, ... 187
To be used in purchasing wheat, etc., for the army, ... 187
Declaration in behalf of this state respecting continental bills of credit and loan-office certificates, ... 188
Penalty for counterfeiting, forging names of signers of or knowingly uttering forged or counterfeited, .. 189
Reward of informer, ... 189
Raising of, to be punished by fine, pillory and whipping, ... 189
Certain acts of assembly making bills of credit of the U. S. legal tender equal to gold and silver suspended for a limited time, ... 204
Act not to extend to any debt or con-

BILLS OF CREDIT—Continued.
tract made after November 1, 1779, upon which suit has actually been brought, ... 204
Nor to sheriffs, attorneys, executors, guardians, etc., ... 204
Monthly taxes levied under act for raising $2,500,000, etc., continued,209-210
Monthly taxes to redeem $25,000,000 for bills of credit of the U. S. also continued, ... 210
Received in payment of such monthly taxes not to be issued again, ... 210
Such bills to be kept by state treasurer to be cancelled and destroyed, 210
New bills of credit to bear interest at 5 per cent., ... 210
Provisions for sinking, ... 210
Proviso, ...210-211
Signing of, ... 211
Oath of signers, ... 211
Compensation of signers, ... 211
Penalty for counterfeiting, forging names of signers of, or knowingly uttering counterfeited, ...211-212
Reward of informer, ... 212
Raising of, to be punished by fine, pillory and whipping, ... 212
Reward of informer, ... 212
Offender unable to pay penalty, to be sold into servitude, ... 212
Act suspended so far as respects new bills of credit to be emitted by Congress until majority of states adopt resolves of Congress of March 18, 1780, ... 213
Parts of prior acts repealed, ... 213
Act to suspend laws making the bills of credit of the U. S. legal tender, in payment of debts equal to gold and silver, continued, ... 229
Duration of act, limited, ... 229
Act for funding and redeeming the, of the U. S., ... 238
93,640 £ 10s to be raised yearly for six years, by tax on estates, real and personal, ...238-239
Proportion of the city and counties, 239
To be destroyed under direction of general assembly, ... 239

35—X

546 — Index.

BILLS OF CREDIT—Continued.
Two acts for raising supplies for 1779 continued and extended to levying and collecting taxes under present act, ... 239
Single men over twenty-one and more than six months out of their apprenticeship or servitude to be taxed, ... 240
Emitted by Congress made legal tender, equal in value to gold and silver, ...241-242
Tender thereof to be good notwithstanding any contracts, etc., ... 242
Persons refusing to take, in payment of debts, etc., to be forever barred from suing for the same, ... 242
Persons refusing to take, in payment of necessaries, etc., to forfeit double the value of article, exposed to sale, 242
Application of penalty, ... 242
For second offense offender to be imprisoned and forfeit one-half of his or her property, ... 242
Informer to be a competent witness, ...242-243
Act suspending for a limited time the laws making, of the U. S. a legal tender, revived and continued, ... 248
Act extended to landlords and creditors who have distrained or brought suit for rents or debts due, ...248-249
Supplement to act for striking £150,000 in, for the support of the army, etc., ... 249
Made legal tender in all contracts, debts, etc., ... 249
Value of, compared with gold and silver, ...249-250
Persons refusing to accept, in payment of any debt, contract, etc., to be forever barred from suing for same, ... 250
Persons not to refuse to accept, equal in value to gold and silver for goods, etc., ... 250
Offenders to forfeit double the value of article so exposed to sale, ... 250
Application of penalty, ... 250
For second offense offender to suffer imprisonment and forfeit one-half of all his or her goods, etc., ... 250

BILLS OF CREDIT—Continued.
Informer against such offender to be a competent witness, ... 251
Received by public agents for any taxes or public dues, etc., to be accounted for at the same rate as received, ... 251
Rate of exchange between continental currency and bills of credit fixed,... 251
Such rate to be continued until February 1, 1781, ... 251
Supreme executive council to then publish monthly rate of exchange between specie and continental money, ... 251
Such rate to be the rate between continental money and, ... 251
Acts of assembly making bills of credit legal tender, suspended, ... 266
Act not to extend to sheriffs, attorneys, executors, etc., who have received money by legal authority in right of another, ... 266
Act not to prevent bills of credit, from being of the same value in payment of taxes, etc., as the bills of credit of the U. S. issued prior to March 1, 1780, ... 266
£500,000 to be emitted in, ... 301
Commissioners appointed for the printing of certain, ... 302
Form of, ... 302
Denomination of, ... 302
Signers of, appointed, ... 303
Mode of signing, ...303-304
Oath of signers, ... 304
Compensation of signers, ... 304
Compensation of state treasurer for handling, ... 304
To be delivered to state treasurer as soon as signed, ... 305
State treasurer to issue and pay the same according to the drafts of the general assembly, etc., for the public use, ... 305
Fund and mode of redemption, ... 305
Declared to be legal tender, ... 305
Persons refusing to receive such, at their legal value in payment of any debt, etc., to be barred from suing for same, ... 306

Index.   547

BILLS OF CREDIT—Continued.
Persons refusing to receive, in payment of live stock or other goods or chattels to forfeit five pounds, ... 306
Application of penalty, ... 306
Informer to be a competent witness against such offenders, ... 306
Counterfeiting, forging name of signers of, or knowingly uttering forged or counterfeit, to be punished by death without benefit of clergy, 307
Raising of, to be punished by fine, pillory and whipping, ... 307
Reward of informer, ... 307
Offender unable to pay penalty to be sold into servitude, ...307-308
All taxes after June 1, 1781, to be paid in gold, silver or, ... 308
State treasurer to set apart, £200,000 of the, for the purpose of exchanging old continental bills of credit, the commonwealth money emitted by act of March 20, 1777, and the money emitted by the resolves of the assembly, ... 308
County treasurers to be employed in exchanging, ... 308
President to set off and sell at public auction enough city lots to redeem residue of bills of credit dated April 29, 1780, ... 318
To take nothing but said bills of credit, Spanish milled dollars or gold and silver in payment, ... 318
Purchasers of such lots to have indefeasible estates in fee simple, ... 318
All laws declaring bills of credit to be legal tender, repealed, ... 337
Parts of such acts imposing penalties for refusal to accept, in payment of debts, etc., also repealed, ...337-338
Repeal not to extend to bills of credit emitted under acts of March 25, 1780 and April 7, 1781, ... 338
Such bills to be received in payment of all lands sold by the state excepting forfeited estates only, ... 338
Act not to affect any tender which has already been duly made, ... 338

BILLS OF CREDIT—Continued.
Debts, etc., contracted since January 1, 1777 and not satisfied or discharged to be paid in the particular money, etc., specified in the contract, ... 338
Rents, etc., contracted before January 1, 1777 to be sued for and judgment obtained and execution awarded for the interest, damages and costs, etc., ... 339
Execution not to issue for the principal for two years or until permission be given by act of assembly,... 339
Interest on such judgments to be paid annually, ... 340
Defendants not having sufficient real estate to satisfy judgment to give security for the same before departing from the commonwealth, ... 340
Upon neglect or refusal to give security court to award execution for the principal as well as the interest, etc., ... 340
Debts exceeding £50 contracted before January 1, 1777 not to be sued for in less than six months after passing of act, ... 340
Proviso where delay will cause creditor to lose debt, ... 340
Act not to extend to revived debts which were on January 1, 1776 barred by the act for the limitation of actions, ... 340
Debts, etc., not barred at that time not to be now barred until two years after passage of act, ... 341
Agents, factors, etc., receiving money and applying it to private use to account to their principal for as much gold and silver as the bills of credit so received were worth at the time of application, ... 341
Agents, factors, etc., to render an account under oath of the profit or loss made on such moneys, ... 342
Principal to obtain benefit of profit,.. 342
Agents, etc., refusing to make such oath, to account for money the same as if applied to private use, ... 342
Fees of officers and fines incurred under act to be paid in gold and silver, 342

548 *Index.*

BILLS OF CREDIT—Continued.
 All fines imposed by acts of assembly to be recovered in gold, etc., ... 343
 All debts and contracts entered into after March 1, 1781 to be discharged according to their nature, ... 343
 Contracts for old continental currency, however, to be liquidated and paid at specie value, ... 343
 Act not to prevent new continental bills of credit from being received in payment of taxes laid under act of December 18, 1780, ... 344
 Of certain emissions to be received in payment of war taxes, ... 353
 Different emissions of paper money declared payable in arrearages of taxes, ... 473
 Received by tax collectors or county treasurers to be paid into state treasury at the same value as received, ... 473

BLUBBER. See Oil.

BOARD OF PROPERTY.
 President, secretary of the land office, receiver-general, surveyor-general, and a member of the supreme executive council constituted a board of property, ...408-409
 Board to determine all cases of irregularity, etc., touching escheats, imperfect titles, etc., ... 409
 Secretary of the land office to receive caveats and with advice of President appoint days of hearing and grant citations in all such cases, 409
 No action of board to prevent either of parties from bringing their action at law for the recovery of possession or for damages for waste or trespass, ... 409
 Time for payment of purchase money, under act for establishing a Land Office, for office rights issued before September 10, 1776, extended for two years, ...409-410
 Surveyor-general to receive returns from late deputy-surveyors, ... 410
 Fees of receiver-general, ...410-411
 Parts of prior act repealed, ... 411

BOLTERS. See Flour.

BONDS.
 Of appellant in cases of appeal to high court of errors and appeals, ... 55
 Of marshall of court of admiralty, .. 104
 Of auctioneers, ...229-230
 Masters of ships, etc., to give bonds for faithful compliance with provisions of act permitting the exportation of flour by sea, under certain restrictions, ... 245
 All suits on such bonds to be brought within two years, ... 245
 Burden of proof in actions on such bonds to lie upon the obligees, ...245-246
 Of naval officer, ... 257
 Sureties thereon to be approved of by the president and council, ...257-258
 To be filed and recorded with the secretary of the supreme executive council, ... 258
 Of collector of excise of Washington county, ... 277
 Of sheriff of Washington county, ... 278
 To be entered in the office for recording of deeds, ... 278
 Of treasurer of Washington county,.. 278
 Of officers of the land office, ... 310
 Of comptroller general, ... 456
 Of treasurer of commissioners appointed to secure public landing places in Southwark, ... 516

BOUNDARIES. See Washington County.
 Of the borough of Carlisle, ... 424
 Of Washington County defined, ... 272

BOUNTY.
 Act to encourage the killing of wolves, 460
 Reward for killing wolves, ...460-461
 Prior act repealed, ... 461

BRANDING.
 Punishment for horse stealing, second offence, ... 113

BRAND MARKS. See Bread; Flour.

BRANDY. See Excise.

BREAD.
 Certain acts preventing the exportation of bread and flour not merchantable, repealed, after October 1, 1781, ... 288

Index. 549

BREAD—Continued.
- Millers and bolters allowed until then to dispose of, for exportation, their flour in barrels of any dimension, .. 289
- Size of casks used in exporting, regulated, ... 289
- Casks to be of three distinct sizes, .. 289
- Millers, bolters and bakers to provide brand marks and enter them with the clerk of the quarter sessions with their names and places of abode, ... 289
- Penalty for violation, ... 289
- Millers, bolters or bakers to brand each cask of flour or bread before removing same from place where bolted or baked, ... 289
- Miller or bolter to brand every cask of flour according to the respective diameters, and weight, ... 289
- Penalty for violation, ... 290
- Quantity of flour to be put in the respective casks, ... 290
- Penalty for violation, ... 290
- Flour bolted for exportation to be of due fineness, ... 290
- Casks of bread to be weighed and tare marked thereon, ... 290
- Penalty for putting a false tare on any cask of bread, ... 290
- Powers of bread-inspectors and their deputies, ... 290
- Bakers of bread for exportation to deliver an invoice of contents with the bread, with brand mark and name, etc., ... 291
- Penalty for violation, ... 291
- Bakers to forfeit bread and casks falsely invoiced, ... 291
- Wagons, etc., conveying flour and bread from mill, etc., to place of exportation, etc., to have a covering, etc., ... 291
- Flour not to be left at any landing place except it be in a sheltered position, ... 291
- Flour or bread not to be carried from mill, etc., to place of exportation, etc., in open boats, etc., without a covering, ... 291
- Carrier of bread or flour to forfeit one shilling per cask where the same gets wet or damaged through his negligence, ... 291

BREAD—Continued.
- Flour intended for exportation to be inspected, ... 291
- Penalty for loading uninspected flour, 291
- Merchantable flour to be branded with the state arms, etc., ... 292
- Compensation of inspector, ... 292
- Owner of unmerchantable flour to pay inspectors fees, ... 292
- Fees to be recovered by action of debt where owner refuses to pay, ... 292
- Flour attempted to be exported without being branded to be forfeited, .. 292
- Manner of proceeding in cases of dispute respecting the fineness, etc., of flour, etc., ... 292
- Masters of ships, etc., to set forth in their manifest, etc., the number of barrels of flour shipped, and the persons shipping the same, ... 293
- Penalty for failure to make return of manifest to naval officer, ... 293
- Inspectors to have the power to enter on board vessels to search for flour intended to be illegally exported, .. 294
- Penalty for hindering or preventing inspector from so doing, ... 294
- Penalty for counterfeiting brand marks, ... 294
- Inspectors not to trade in flour, ... 294
- Penalty for violation, ... 294
- Penalty, how recoverable, ... 294
- Application of penalty, ... 294
- Inspectors empowered to appoint deputies, ... 294
- Oath of deputy, ... 295
- Oath to be administered by a justice of the peace, ... 295
- Fines and forfeitures arising under act, how recoverable, ... 295
- Application of, ... 295
- Inspectors appointed throughout the different counties, ... 295
- Term of office of inspector, ... 295
- Vacancies, how filled, ...295-296
- Supplement to act preventing the exportation of unmerchantable bread and flour, ... 379
- Offering flour for sale packed in unseasoned casks, etc., prohibited, ... 379
- Penalty for violation, ... 379

BREAD—Continued.
　Penalty on bolters, etc., for not entering their respective brands, ...379-80
　Penalty for deficiency of weight of flour casks, etc., ... 380
　Casks for exportation to be stamped with the letters SP, ... 380
　Casks not so stamped to be forfeited if offered for exportation, ... 380
　Middlings for exportation to be branded as such, ... 380
　Fines and penalties under act, how recoverable, ... 380
　Parts of prior act altered and repealed, ... 381

BREAKING DOORS.
　Constable where necessary empowered to break open doors, etc., in the day time in serving warrant for seizing provisions for the army, ...177-178

BRISTOL TOWNSHIP.
　Act to prevent trespassing upon unenclosed grounds in Passyunk, Moyamensing, Northern Liberties and Germantown, extended to, ... 116
　Penalty for suffering beasts to run at large in, ... 116
　Running at large of swine in, prohibited, ... 116
　Such swine to be forfeited, ... 116
　Disposition of forfeiture, ...116-117
　Person aggrieved by seizure of swine to have appeal to justice of the peace, ... 117
　Party appealing to forfeit 40s where seizure is confirmed, ... 117
　Act to prevent the trespassing upon the unenclosed grounds of Passyunk, Moyamensing, Northern Liberties, Germantown and, revived, ... 283

BRITISH TROOPS.
　Act for procuring an estimate of the damages sustained by the inhabitants of this State from the British troops, ... 530
　County commissioners of every county invaded by British troops to direct assessors to notify inhabitants to furnish accounts of damages, etc., done thereby and transmit the same to commissioners, ... 531

BRITISH TROOPS—Continued.
　Assessors to render such accounts where inhabitants refuse, ... 531
　Contents of account, ...531-532
　Commissioners to transmit accounts to supreme executive council, ... 532
　Servants, nego and mulatto slaves deluded and carried away by British troops to be included in accounts,.. 532
　Charges and expenses of executing act to be defrayed by the commonwealth, ... 533

BRUSH NETS.
　Not to be used for the purpose of catching fish in the Schuylkill river, 271
　Penalty for violation, ... 271
　All brush nets in the Schuylkill river to be removed and destroyed, ... 271
　Penalty for hindering or obstructing persons removing or destroying, .. 271

BUCKS COUNTY.
　The Trustees of the Presbyterian Church in Warwick township, in county of Bucks, incorporated, ... 519
　The Trustees of the Dutch Reformed Church in Northampton and Southampton, in the county of Bucks, incorporated, ... 526

BURDEN OF PROOF.
　To be upon obligees in actions on bonds given by masters, etc., of ships for faithful compliance with provisions of act permitting exportation of flour by sea under certain restrictions, ...245-246

BURGESSES. See Carlisle, Borough of.

C.

CAPITAL CRIMES. See Crimes.

CARLISLE, BOROUGH OF.
　Erected, ... 423
　Boundaries of, ... 424
　Burgesses appointed, ... 425
　High constable and town clerk appointed, ... 425
　Style, power and privileges of the borough of, ... 426
　Time, place and maner of electing burgesses, town clerk and constable, ...426-427

Index. 551

CARLISLE, BOROUGH OF—Continued.
Burgesses to be conservators of the peace and to remove all nuisances in highways, etc., ... 427
Other powers and duties of burgesses, ...427-428
Oath of office of burgess, constable and town clerk, ... 428
Burgesses, etc., to have and keep two markets in each week and two fairs in each year, ... 428
Clerk of the market appointed, ... 429
Penalties for refusal or neglect of persons elected burgess, etc., to serve, ... 429
Fine for such offense not to exceed 10 £, ... 429
Penalty, how recoverable, ... 429
Filling of vacancy, ... 429
Burgess, high constable and assistants to hold town meetings and make rules and ordinances, ...429-430
Buildings heretofore erected that encroach on highways, etc., not to be deemed nuisances, ... 430
Owners not to rebuild on highways, etc., so encroached on, ... 430
Offenders upon conviction to forfeit and pay 20 £ to supervisors, ... 430
Foundation of party walls, etc., not to be laid before obtaining consent of regulators to do so, ... 431
Surveyors and regulators to be appointed by burgess and assistants,. 431
Builder of party wall to be reimbursed one moiety of the cost thereof before next builder breaks into same, ... 431
Persons laying foundation of party wall before viewed by regulators to forfeit 5 £, ...431-432
Application of penalty, ... 432
Party aggrieved by order of regulators to have appeal to quarter sessions, ... 432
Costs of appeal to be paid as court directs, ... 432
Compensation of regulators, ... 432
Regulators empowered to regulate partition fences, ... 432
Time, manner and place of electing supervisors and assessors, ... 433

CARLISLE, BOROUGH OF—Continued.
Persons so elected to be fined 10 £ upon their neglect or refusal to serve, ... 433
Application of penalty, ... 433
Five days' notice to be given of the election of assessors and supervisors, ... 433
Supervisors and assessors to levy tax for repairing roads, etc., not exceeding 1s. in the pound, ... 433
Oath of supervisors and assessors, .. 434
Oath to be administered by the burgess, or justice of the peace, ... 434
Filling of vacancy, ... 434
Compensation of supervisors and assessors, ... 435
Supervisors before collecting tax to have the same allowed of by the burgesses, ... 435
Upon neglect or refusal to pay, taxes to be collected by distress, ... 435
Aggrieved taxpayers to have appeal to quarter sessions, ...435-436
Goods of tenants, etc., to be liable to distress for taxes, ... 436
Tenants to deduct such tax from their rent or recover it by action, ... 436
Act not to alter any contract between any landlord and tenant respecting the payment of road tax, ... 436
Supervisors to keep streets, etc., clean and in repair, ... 436
Supervisors empowered to enter upon adjoining lands to cut drains or ditches for carrying off the water, etc., ... 437
Penalty on owners for filling up such drains, ditches, etc., ... 437
Application of penalty, ... 437
Penalty for supervisors misfeasance or non-feasance in office, ... 437
Aggrieved supervisors to have appeal to quarter sessions, ...437-438
Supervisors to annually account to burgesses and assistants, ... 438
Burgesses and assistants to adjust and settle accounts of supervisors, ... 438
Aggrieved supervisor to have appeal to quarter sessions, ... 439
Delinquent supervisors to be committed, ... 439

CARLISLE, BOROUGH OF—Continued.
Borough of Carlisle declared to be one
distinct district for general elections, ... 439
Justices of the peace empowered to
act in all matters appertaining to
their office, etc., ... 440
Act not to authorize justice to act in
determining appeals to the quarter
sessions of matters relating to the
borough, ... 440
Persons not to cast dirt, earth, etc.,
from their improvements into the
public streets without removing the
same, ... 440
Penalty for violation, ... 441
Persons not to cast shavings, ashes,
dung, etc., on any pavement without
removing the same, ... 441
Penalty for violation, ... 441
Persons not to cast rubbish, etc., in
any public street, ... 441
Penalty for violation, ... 441
Distillers, soap-boilers, and tallow-
chandlers not to discharge foul li-
quor so as to run through the
streets, etc., nor to collect and keep
putrid fat, etc., ...441-442
Penalty for violation, ... 442
Butchers not to keep garbage or filth
at or near slaughter-house, ... 442
Penalty for violation, ... 442
Carrion, filth, etc., not to be left on
unenclosed ground, ... 442
Penalty for violation, ... 442
Common sewers not to be obstructed, 442
Penalty for violation, ... 442
Pavements or foot-ways, etc., not to
be made contrary to the directions
of regulators, ... 443
Penalty for violation, ... 443
Regulation relating to encroachments
in streets, etc., by cellar-doors, bay-
windows, etc., ... 443
Penalty for refusing to remove same
upon notice from regulators, ... 444
Owners of porches, etc., extending
into streets to be assessed till the
same be reduced or taken away, ... 444
Water-spouts on houses to be fixed so
as not to incommode persons walk-
ing along the streets, etc., ... 444

CARLISLE, BOROUGH OF—Continued.
Penalty for removing or injuring pub-
lic water pipes or trunks, ...444-445
Not more than 25 lbs. of gun-powder
to be kept in one house, ... 444
Penalty for violation, ... 445
Buildings erected on commons, etc.,
declared to be nuisances, ...445-446
To be torn down by burgesses, etc., .. 446
Penalty for erecting buildings, etc.,
on the commons after publication
of act, ... 446
Penalty for digging holes, ditches or
quarries on the commons, ...446-447
Manner and mode of collecting fines,
penalties, and forfeitures under act, 447
General road act of March 21, 1772 not
to extend to the, ...437-438
Said act repealed so far as it relates
to the, ... 438
Persons sued under act may plead the
general issue and give act and
special matter in evidence, ... 448
Defendant to have treble costs if
plaintiff becomes non-suit, suffers a
discontinuance, or has verdict pass
against him, ... 448

CATTLE. See Federal Army.
Cattle, sheep or salted provisions to
be subject to seizure for the use of
the federal army, ... 215

CARRIAGES. See Wagons.

CEDAR STREET.
Northern line of Vine street and
southern line of Cedar street to be
marked out by regulators of Philadelphia City assisted by regulators
of the Northern Liberties, ... 487
Expense thereof to be borne proportionately by the said city and district, ...487-488

CELLAR DOORS. See Carlisle, Borough
of; Nuisances.

CHAPLAINS. See Pennsylvania Line.
And surgeons to receive same emoluments and benefits as commissioned
officers, ...314-315
Entitled also to the half pay of a
captain for life, ... 315

Index.

CHAPLAINS—Continued.
To be liable to be called into service by the supreme executive council at any time, ... 315
Penalty for neglect or refusal to obey such call, ... 315

CHESTER COUNTY.
Persons appointed to build new court house and prison in, ... 143
Old court house and prison to be sold at public vendue, ... 143
Moneys arising therefrom to be used in paying for new court house and prison, ... 143-144
County commissioners and assessors to levy the necessary money by tax, 144

CHIEF JUSTICE.
Salary of, ... 377

CHIMNEYS. See Chimney Sweepers.

CHIMNEY SWEEPERS.
In Philadelphia city, Southwark, and the Northern Liberties to register and obtain a certificate, ... 5-6
Penalty for neglect or refusal, ... 6
Fee of officer for granting certificate, 6
To wear the number contained in their certificate on the front of their caps, ... 6
Penalty for neglect or refusal, ... 6
To sweep chimneys within 48 hours after application, ... 7
Penalty for neglect or refusal, ... 7
Rates allowed, for sweeping chimneys, ... 7
Penalty on persons whose unswept chimneys take fire and blaze out at the top, ... 7
Penalty imposed upon, where chimneys take fire and blaze out at the top within one month from the sweeping, ... 7
Each, to pay officer for granting certificate, etc., 10s. per day, ... 7
Three justices of the peace and wardens of the city to appoint officer for granting certificates, etc., to, ... 8
Justices of the peace to regulate and fix prices for sweeping chimneys,.. 8

CHIMNEY SWEEPERS—Continued.
Rates to be published in the newspapers, ... 8
Penalties arising under act to be paid equally to overseers of the poor and officer for granting certificates, ... 8
Penalties, how recoverable, ... 8
Provisions of act, limited to within one mile of Philadelphia city, ... 8
Certain acts of assembly repealed,.. 9
Duration of act limited, ... 9

CHURCHES.
Charter of the German Lutheran Congregation in Philadelphia confirmed and amended, ... 83
The Trustees of the Presbyterian Church in Warwick township, in county of Bucks, incorporated, ... 519
The Trustees of the Dutch Reformed Church in Northampton and Southampton, in the county of Bucks, incorporated, ... 526
Charter of the Second Presbyterian Church in Philadelphia, continued and confirmed, ... 89

CITY ASSESSORS.
Office of, abolished, ... 241
Duties to be performed by city commissioners, ... 241
Commissioners to meet annually on the first Tuesday of August to issue warrants, ... 241

CITY COMMISSIONERS.
Duties of city assessors to be performed by, ... 241
Commissioners to meet annually on the first Tuesday of August to issue warrants, ... 241

CITY LOTS. See Lands.

CIVIL OFFICERS.
Justices, sheriffs and, to assist commissioners in carrying out provisions of act for procuring army supplies for 1780, ... 181

CLERK OF THE ESTREATS. See Estreats.

CLERK OF THE MARKET. See Carlisle, Borough of.

554 *Index.*

CLERKS OF THE ASSEMBLY.
Wages of, ... 378
Mileage of, ... 378
To collect rent from market-houses, etc., and pay the same over to the treasurer of the wardens and assessors, ... 201
Compensation of the, ... 201
Penalty for neglect or refusal, ... 202

COLLECTOR OF EXCISE.
Act for making the excise on wine, rum, brandy, etc., continued, ... 299
Retailers to still take permits from the, and give him security, ... 299
Additional, excise to be raised for the support of the government, ... 299
Manner and mode of collecting, ... 300
Compensation of, ... 300
State treasurer to pay money arising under act as directed by act or order of assembly, ... 300
No other excise to be paid than imposed by act, ... 301

COLLEGE AND ACADEMY OF PHILADELPHIA.
Former by-law narrowing original plan of, declared void, ... 24
Supreme executive council to reserve confiscated estates not sold and create a fund for the maintenance of the provost, etc., of, ... 24
Such income not to exceed 1,500 £ per annum, ... 24
Such reservation to be laid before the general assembly for confirmation, 24
Confirming of such estate not to extend to establishing estates in original trustees, etc., ... 25
Superintendents and trust to be vested in certain named persons, ...24-25
Such persons to be styled "The Trustees of the University of Pennsylvania," 26
Powers of trustees, ... 26
Filling of vacancy where trustees neglect or refuse to act, ... 26
Selection to meet with approval of general assembly, ... 26
Former oath of trustees, etc., superseded, ...26-27

COLLEGE AND ACADEMY OF PHILADELPHIA—Continued.
Clauses in former charters directing trustees to make rules, ordinances and statutes not repugnant to laws of great Britain, etc., repealed, ... 27
Trustees to review old rules, etc., and frame new ones consistent with the constitution and laws of this state, 27
Business of corporation to be transacted and determined by a majority of seven of the trustees, ... 28
Certain matters to require a majority of eleven of the trustees, ... 28
Clause in first charter limiting trustees to inhabitants of Pennsylvania residing within five miles of the, declared void, ... 28
Trustees to have power to sue and be sued, ... 28
Former trustees to deliver up books, records, etc., ... 29
Penalty for neglect or refusal, ... 29
Trustees declared to be a body politic and corporate, ...29-30
To have power to make a common seal, rules, etc., and to alter and amend them, ... 30
Name, style and title of officers of the University of the State of Pennsylvania, ... 30
Trustees to submit accounts to visitors from the general assembly, 30
Trustees to meet annually on first Wednesday in December, ... 30
Defect in prior act cured, ... 125
The word college in section 16 to be construed university, ... 125

COLORS. See Foreign Colors.

COMMANDER IN CHIEF.
Salary of, ... 377

COMMERCE. See Bread; Contraband Embargo; Exports; Flour; Impost; Tariff.
Supplement to act regulating navigation and trade, ... 418
No goods, wares, or merchandise produced or manufactured by Great Britain to be imported into this state, ... 419
All such goods to be confiscated, ... 419

COMMERCE—Continued.

One-half to go to informer and the other half to the commonwealth, .. 419
All actions under act against importers to be brought within six months, ... 419
Proviso as to goods, wares, merchandise taken as prize, ... 419
Such goods, wares and merchandise not to be imported from neutral ports, ... 420
Captain, etc., of vessels to certify that imported goods from neutral ports are not the growth, product, etc., of Great Britain, ... 420
Such goods to be confiscated if captain neglects to produce certificate, ...420-421
Part of prior act regulating navigation and trade repealed, ... 421
All subjects of His Most Christian Majesty entitled to the rights and privileges stipulated in their behalf by the 11th article of the treaty of amity and commerce concluded between him and the U. S. of America, 510
Act to take effect as of February 6th, 1778, ... 510

COMMISSIONERS OF PURCHASES.

To appoint a place and person in each township to receive wheat, flour, etc., for the army, ... 198
To notify county treasurer of such appointment, ... 198
Wheat, flour, etc., to be received by such persons in payment of taxes,.. 198

COMMISSARY GENERAL. See Federal Army.

COMMITTEE OF SAFETY.

Auditors appointed to collect, audit and settle, etc., the accounts of the late, ... 75

COMMON LABOR. See Labor.

COMMON LANDS. See Lands.

Act preserving the common lands appurtenant to the city of Philadelphia and other towns from unwarrantable encroachment, ... 317

COMMON PLEAS.

Fees of the justices of the, to be paid in wheat, ... 40
Fees of the clerks of the, to be paid in wheat, ... 40
To have jurisdiction in actions of debt over fifty pounds by tenants against their landlord for taxes, ... 141
Parties convicted under militia act to have appeal to the, ... 160
Verdict of, to be conclusive, ... 160
To have jurisdiction to recover penalties for unlawfully hawking or peddling where the amount is over 50£, 21
Plaintiffs or defendants in actions brought in the supreme or common pleas courts for debts in case of their sudden departure upon giving security may apply for special courts and have their cases determined at once, ... 417
Defendants in supreme court entitled to same benefits as defendants in common pleas, ... 418
Act not to prevent plaintiff or defendant from being allowed a reasonable time to procure testimony, ... 418
Appeals from the orders of regulators in Philadelphia to lie to the next court of, ...486-487
Proceedings on appeal, ... 487

COMMONS.

Buildings erected on commons in Carlisle declared to be nuisances, ...445-446
No holes, ditches, or quarries to be dug on the Carlisle commons without consent of regulators, ...446-447

COMPTROLLER GENERAL. See Public Accounts.

Office for auditing, liquidating and adjusting the accounts of the commonwealth instituted, ...448-449
Office to be styled, "the Comptroller-General's office," 449
Powers and duty of comptroller general, ... 449
All public accounts to be rendered into the comptroller general's office and when settled transmitted to the president and council, ... 449

COMPTROLLER GENERAL—Continued.
President, etc., to draw warrant on State Treasurer for any balance due by the commonwealth, ... 450
Comptroller general to enter warrant in his books, indorse and deliver it to the party entitled, ... 450
Comptroller general to recover any balance found due and owing to the state, ... 450
Comptroller general to form abstracts of the names, etc., of the persons who have received money of the commonwealth for which they have not properly accounted, ... 450
And to direct the prothonotary of the county wherein such persons reside to issue process against such persons, ... 451
Persons so summoned neglecting or refusing to exhibit their accounts to be liable to pay the full value of all money or public affects which have come into their hands, ... 451
Auditors or other persons refusing to deliver up public books or papers upon demand of comptroller general to be liable to a thousand pounds penalty, ... 452
Method of recovering balances due and owing to the state, ... 452
Mo..ey so recovered to be paid to the state treasurer, ... 452
No rccounts to be deemed settled until they be audited by the comptroller general, ... 453
Comptroller general authorized to revise, etc., accounts settled by the auditors, commissioners or committees of assembly, and report substantial errors to the general assembly, ... 453
Comptroller general authorized to summon witnesses and commit delinquents for contempts, ... 453
Fees and mileage of sheriff, coroner or of process server and witnesses, 454
Comptroller general to issue attachment for absent witnesses, ... 454

COMPTROLLER GENERAL—Continued.
Secretary of the supreme executive council to enter into comptroller general's office all marriage, tavern and other licenses, ... 454
Comptroller general to debit the respective prothonotaries therewith,.. 454
Prothonotaries to settle their accounts with comptroller general once in every three months, ... 454
Comptroller general to select such parts of accounts as are properly chargeable against the United States and institute an account between the United States and this state, 454-455
State treasurer not to issue or pay any monies without a warrant from the president entered and certified by the comptroller general, ... 455
Exceptions, ... 455
Books, papers, etc., of comptroller general to be opened to the inspection of the committees of account,.. 455
And copies thereof be furnished to the legislature and president when required, ...455 456
Salary of comptroller general, ... 456
Bond of comptroller general, ... 456
Oath of comptroller general, ... 456
Prior acts relating to public accounts repealed, ... 456
Act to be publicly read in every court of oyer and terminer and quarter sessions, ... 456
John Nicholson appointed comptroller general, ... 457
Comptroller general directed to settle depreciation of the pay accounts of the officers, etc., of the Pennsylvania line, ... 460
Supreme executive council to draw on state treasurer and turn over to the comptroller general all necessary sums for so doing, ... 460
Comptroller general in settling sums due to pay one-third thereof in bills of credit and two-thirds in certificates, ... 460
Powers of, extended to embrace the duties of the former auditors, ... 508
His certificate to be as valid as those issued by them, ... 508

Index. 557

CONFISCATION. See Attainder; Forfeited Estates; Proprietary Estates.

CONGRESS.
Prize causes, etc., to be judged in admiralty by the law of nations, and the acts of, ...97-98
Appeals in such cases to lie to, upon security given, ... 98
Appeals not to stay proceedings where appellees enter security, ... 100
Authorized to levy a five per cent. ad valorem duty on imports, ... 297
Arms, ammunition, clothing, wool cards, cotton cards and wire for making them, and salt excepted,... 297
Authorized to levy a like duty on prizes and prize goods condemned by the admiralty court, ... 297
To appoint collectors for collecting same, ... 298
Moneys arising from such duties to be appropriated in payment of debts, contracted on the faith of the U. S. for support of the present war, ... 298
Act to continue in force until such debts are fully and finally discharged, ... 298

CONSTABLES. See Carlisle, borough of.
Fees of, to be paid in wheat, ... 40
Sheriffs, coroners and, may be compelled to attend sessions of High Court of errors and appeals, ... 57
Where necessary empowered to break open doors, etc., in the day time in serving warrant for seizing provisions for the army, ...177-178

CONTINENTAL BILLS OF CREDIT. See Bills of Credit.
State treasurer to set apart £200,000 in bills of credit for the purpose of exchanging old continental bills of credit, etc., ... 308

CONTINENTAL CURRENCY. See Bills of Credit; Legal Tender.
Counterfeiting, forging, or knowingly uttering forged or counterfeit, to be punished by death without the benefit of clergy, ... 14
Raising of, or knowingly uttering, to be punished by fine, pillory and whipping, ... 15

CONTINENTAL CURRENCY—Continued.
Offender unable to pay fine to be sold into servitude, ... 15
Rate of exchange between continental currency and bills of credit fixed, .. 251
Such rate to be continued, until February 1, 1781, ... 251
Supreme executive council to then publish rate of exchange between specie and continental money monthly, ... 251
Such rate to be the rate between continental money and bills of credit,.. 251

CONTRABAND.
All goods, etc., of the growth, product or manufacture of Great Britain, or of any country under the dominion thereof, or any goods coming from countries held by the forces thereof, to be considered as contraband, ... 497
All contraband to be liable to seizure, condemnation and confiscation, ... 497
Goods, etc., taken as prize upon water and condemned as such in a court of admiralty of the U. S. excepted, .497-498
Salt, salt petre, gunpowder, lead, etc., also excepted, ... 498
Clothing for prisoners of war also excepted, ... 498
Goods, etc., imported from France, Spain, or the United Provinces not to be treated as contraband, ... 498
Any person authorized to seize goods, etc., in or moving through the state which he believes to be contraband, ...498-499
Proceedings upon seizure, ...499-501
Persons desiring to defend property seized to first enter security, ... 501
No carriage, beast, boat or vessel to be condemned unless the goods connected therewith exceed 10 £, ... 501
No replevin to lie for goods seized, .. 501
Proceedings before justice to be final, ...501-502
Goods, etc., seized and condemned as contraband to be forthwith advertised and sold at public auction by sheriff under warrant of justice, ... 502

558 Index.

CONTRABAND—Continued.
Ten days' public notice in writing to be given thereof, if the value be under 50 £, ... 502
Where value of goods exceed 50 £, like notice to be also inserted in one of the Philadelphia weekly newspapers, ... 503
After sale justice to deduct all expenses and order sheriff, etc., to pay one-half of residue to plaintiff and the other half to county treasurer, .. 503
County treasurer to transmit the same to state treasurer, ... 503
Fees of county treasurer for so doing, 503
Costs of proceedings, ... 503
All suits for things done in pursuance of act to be brought within six months, ... 503
Defendant to recover treble costs if plaintiff wilfully delays, discontinues or has verdict or judgment passed against him, ...503-504
Persons convicted of trading with subjects of King of Great Britain to forfeit one-third of the value of goods seized besides the goods so seized or suffer three months imprisonment, ... 504
Prosecutions therefor to be made in any court of quarter sessions or oyer and terminer, ... 504
All persons coming out of the line of the enemy into this state without a license from the president, etc., to be imprisoned by any justice of the peace, ... 504
All such intruders to be fined, ... 504
No person to go out of the state into the lines of the enemy without proper authority, ... 504
Penalty for so doing, ... 504
Disposition of penalty, ...504-505
Act not to affect persons furnished with a pass from any of the other states, if same be approved by president, etc., ... 505
Certain act of assembly repealed, ... 505
Duration of act limited until close of war, ... 505

CONTRACTS. See Debts.
Between supreme executive council and quarter-master general of the U. S. for the passage of men, etc., not annulled by the further supplement to act regulating nightly watch, etc., ... 203

CORONERS.
Fees of, to be paid in wheat, ... 40
Sheriffs, constables and, may be compelled to attend sessions of the high court of errors and appeals, ... 57
Fees of, for attending before auditors appointed to settle public accounts, 78
Of Westmoreland county to act in Washington county until one be there chosen, ... 278

CORPORATIONS. See College and Academy of Philadelphia; University of the State of Pennsylvania.
University of the state of Pennsylvania incorporated, ...29-30
German Lutheran Congregation in Philadelphia, incorporated, ... 83
Second Presbyterian Church in Philadelphia, incorporated, ... 89
Society for the Relief for the Masters of Ships, incorporated, ...91-92
American Philosophical society, incorporated, ... 121
The German society contributing for the relief of distressed Germans in the state of Pennsylvania, incorporated, ...256-257
Bank of North America, incorporated, ... 406
The Trustees of the Presbyterian Church in Warwick township, in the county of Bucks, incorporated, 519
The Trustees of the Dutch Reformed Church in Northampton and Southampton, in the county of Bucks, incorporated, ... 526

COSTS.
Appellee to have double costs where judgment is affirmed by the high court of errors and appeals, ... 55
Each party to pay their own costs where judgment is reversed, ... 55
To be recovered in certain actions, .. 137

Index. 559

COUNCIL OF SAFETY.
  Auditors appointed to collect, audit, settle, etc., the accounts of the, .. 75

COUNTERFEITING.
  Penalty for, continental loan-office certificates, the continental loan-office bills of exchange or the paper money of the U. S., ... 14
  Of bills of credit to be punished by death, ...189,212,294,307
  Penalty for, the common seal or any bank bill or notes of the Bank of North America, ... 384
  Penalty for uttering the same, ... 384
  Offenders to suffer death without benefit of clergy, ... 384

COUNTY ASSESSORS. See County Commissioners.
  Office of, abolished, ... 241
  Duties of, to be performed by county commissioners, ... 241
  Commissioners to meet annually on first Tuesday of August to issue warrants, ... 241

COUNTY COMMISSIONERS.
  Powers and duties of the several and respective, in collecting the monthly tax of $2,500,000 for the use of the United States, ...10-11
  Compensation of, and assessors, to be satisfied in wheat, ...41,142
  And assessors to appoint tax collectors in case of vacancy, or refusal to serve, etc., ... 197
  Duties of county assessors to be performed by, ... 241
  Commissioners to meet annually on first Tuesday of August to issue warrants, ... 241
  £200,000 to be raised, levied and collected during 1781, ...326-327
  Proportionate share of the different cities and counties, ... 327
  County commissioners to meet on or before the first Tuesday in July and issue their warrants to the assessors requiring them to make returns of all taxable persons and their property, ...327-328
  Assessors to administer an oath or affirmation to each taxable as to the truth of his return, ... 328

COUNTY COMMISSIONERS—Continued.
  Form of oath, ... 328
  Penalty for taxables refusing to make returns or to swear to the truth thereof, ... 328
  Assessors to find out and return property refused to be returned, ... 328
  Lands not returned to be charged with all such taxes in the next assessment, ... 329
  In case of vacancy in office of assessor county commissioners to appoint others, ... 329
  Upon receipt of assessors returns commissioners to quota the districts, etc., ... 329
  And within six days thereafter furnish the assessors with a transcript of the quota charged upon the township, etc., to which the assessor belongs, ...329-330
  Assessors and two freeholders to levy and assess the quota of each township, etc., on the persons and their estates therein, ... 330
  List of the different kinds of property subject to taxation under act, ... 330
  Such enumerated articles to be rated at what they are bona fide worth,... 330
  Single freemen over twenty-one and more than six months out of their apprenticeship to pay a sum not over £6 nor under 45s, ...330-331
  Trades, professions, etc., to be rated at the discretion of the assessors and freeholders, ... 331
  Goods of tenants, etc., liable to be distrained for such taxes, ... 331
  Tenant to deduct taxes from rent where he is compelled to pay the same, ... 331
  Or recover the same by action at law, 331
  Act not to alter any contract made between landlord and tenant concerning the payment of taxes, ... 331
  Oath of county commissioners, ... 332
  Oath of assessors, ... 332
  County commissioners to appoint a tax collector for each township, ward and district, ... 332
  Commissioners to prefix a warrant to collectors duplicate, etc., ... 332
  Contents of warrant, ... 332

Index.

COUNTY COMMISSIONERS—Continued.
  Assessors and collectors to notify commissioners in writing within two days of their election or appointment as to their intention to serve or decline the office, ...332-333
  Failure to do so to be considered as a refusal to serve, ... 333
  Penalty for neglect or refusal of assessors and collectors to serve, ... 333
  Where owner of goods distrained on for taxes refuses to receive the overplus collector to pay the same to the county treasurer, ... 333
  County treasurer to deduct 1 per cent. and give notice thereof to the county commissioners within twenty days, 333
  Owner to have the remainder discounted out of any future tax, ..333-334
  Receipt of treasurer to exonerate collector, ... 334
  Collectors to make out accounts of their seizures, etc., and settle the same with commissioners, ... 334
  Compensation of collectors, ... 334
  Commissioners empowered to proceed against delinquent collectors, ... 334
  Collectors to pay the tax charged in their duplicate within thirty days after the day of appeal, ... 334
  Proviso as to cases where he has been obliged to make distress, etc., ... 334
  Respective county treasurers to make payments to the state treasurer within certain specified times after receiving the same from collector,334-335
  Commissioners to transmit copies of the assessment to state treasurer within thirty days after day of appeal, ... 335
  Compensation of county commissioners and assessors, ... 335
  Compensation of collectors, ... 335
  Taxes to be paid in gold or silver only, 335
  Proviso as to persons who have taken the oath of allegiance to this state, ...335-336
  Penalty for neglect or refusal of commissioners to do their duty under act, ... 336
  Penalty, how recoverable, ... 336
  Act for raising supplies for 1779, extended and continued, ... 336

COUNTY RATES AND LEVIES.
  To be laid and assessed according to state tax, ... 140
  Act not to extend to state tax on ready money, ... 140
  Nor to prevent appeals or alter mode of collecting same, ... 140
  Nor to alter mode of taxation in counties where state tax has not been laid within twelve months, ... 140
  Proceedings on appeal from, ...140-141
  Tax on real estate transferred to be charged to buyers, ...140-141
  Compensation of county and city assessors, ... 141
  Goods of tenant of non-resident owner subject to distress for, ... 141
  Distress to be deducted from rent, .. 141
  Or be recovered by action of debt,.. 141
  Act not to affect existing contracts between landlord and tenant as to payment of, ... 142
  Nor to repeal act for raising additional sum of $5,700,000, ... 142
  Compensation of county commissioners and assessors to be satisfied in wheat, ... 142

COUNTY TREASURER.
  To receive one-half of net proceeds from the sale of contraband goods, 503
  To turn the same over to state treasurer, ... 503
  Fees of, for so doing, ... 503

COURT CLERKS.
  Fees of, for registering slaves, ... 70

COURT CRIER.
  Fees of, to be paid in wheat, ... 40

COURT HOUSES. See Chester County; Washington County.
  Jails, prisons, workhouses and, throughout the state vested in the commonwealth, ... 50
  Act not to extend to old temporary prison in Bedford, ... 50
  Nor to old jail and workhouse at 3d and High Sts., Philadelphia, ... 50
  Supreme executive council to sell old jail and workhouse in Philadelphia for benefit of said city and county,. 51

Index. 561

COURT HOUSES—Continued.
Certain prior acts of assembly repealed, ... 52
Persons appointed to build new court house and prison in Chester county, 143
Old court house and prison to be sold at public vendue, ... 143
Moneys arising therefrom to be used in paying for new court house and prison, ...143-144
County commissioners and assessors to levy the necessary money by tax, 144
Court house and prison to be erected in Washington county, ...275-276
Certain persons authorized to select and purchase site for, in Washington county, ...275-276
Taxes not exceeding a certain amount to be levied to defray expenses of erecting, ... 276

COURT MARTIAL. See Militia.
Make up of general court martial, ... 167
Make up of regimental court martial, ... 167
Convictions to be had on two-thirds vote, ... 167
Witnesses to be examined on oath by president of, ... 168
Oath of members of, ... 168
By whom administered, ... 168
Members of the militia called as witnesses and refusing to give evidence to be censured or fined, ... 168
Officer or private charged with transgressing rules to be relieved until trial, ... 168
Officer or private aggrieved by commanding officer to complain to lieutenant, ... 168
Lieutenant to summon regimental court martial, ... 168
Punishment by, limited to, degrading, cashiering or fining, ... 168
Inferior officer or private injured by captain, etc., to complain to commanding officer, ... 168
Commanding officer to summon regimental court martial, ... 168
Commanding officer empowered to pardon persons court martialed, ... 169

36—X

COURTS. See Admiralty; Common Pleas; High Court of Errors and Appeals; Oyer and Terminer; Quarter Sessions; Supreme Court.

CRIMES. See Counterfeiting; Forgery; Horse Stealing; Misprison of Treason; Raising; Robbery, Treason; Uttering.
Place and manner of trial of traitors, pirates, felons and criminals committing offences within the admiralty jurisdiction or upon the sea, 221
Persons convicted of such crimes to suffer death without benefit of clergy, where the same is taken away, for like offence committed on land, ... 221
Trial and punishment of subjects of this state or any of the U. S. committing piracy, etc., under foreign colors, ... 222
Persons betraying their trust at sea to be convicted and punished as pirates, ... 222
Captains and masters of vessels harboring deserters to be fined 10,000£, 223
Penalty to be recovered by distress, .. 223
For want of sufficient distress such captain, etc., to suffer one year's imprisonment without bail or mainprise, ... 223
President and council to appoint persons to inspect muster roll of vessels in search of deserters, ... 223
Penalty for obstructing search or refusing to deliver up deserters, ... 224

CUMBERLAND COUNTY.
Place of holding general elections in, 219

D.

DAMAGES.
Persons convicted of counterfeiting, raising or knowingly uttering counterfeited or raised bills of credit, loan office certificates or bills of exchange, to be multced in double, .. 15

DAMS. See Schuylkill Point Meadows; State Island.

DEATH.
Without benefit of clergy, penalty for forging or counterfeiting continental loan office certificates, or bills of exchange, ... 14

Index.

DEATH—Continued.
  Without benefit of clergy, punishment for robbery, ... 110
  Without benefit of clergy, punishment for forging or counterfeiting certain bills of credit, ... 189
  Punishment for counterfeiting bills of credit, ... 212
  Punishment for forging or counterfeiting or knowingly uttering forged or counterfeited bills of credit, ... 307

DEBTS. See Legal Tender; Public Debt.
  Act to suspend laws making the bills of credit of the U. S. legal tender, in payment of debts equal to gold and silver, continued, ... 229
  Duration of act limited, ... 229
  Debts and contracts entered into and made between January 1, 1777, and March 1, 1781, to be settled according to a scale of depreciation, ... 284
  Proviso clauses in suspension acts of May 31, 1780, Sept. 22, 1780, and Feb. 20, 1781, repealed, ... 284
  Mode of settlement where parties cannot agree, ... 285
  Auditors to be appointed to hear and examine the parties and adjust the controversies, ... 285
  Auditors not to reduce payments made in current money, ... 285
  Where tender has been made the creditor to be paid only the value of his debt reduced to specie at the time of tender, ... 285
  Debtor prevented from paying by creditor absconding, etc., to have benefit of legal tender, ... 285
  Auditors report to have the force of a verdict, etc., ... 286
  Scale of depreciation, ... 286
  Supplement to act for the more easy recovery of small debts, repealed,. 287
  Act for limitation of actions suspended during the close of courts of justice and the time of any suspension acts, ... 288
  All laws declaring bills of credit to be legal tender, repealed, ... 337
  Parts of such acts imposing penalties for refusal to accept bills of credit in payment of, etc., also repealed, 337-338

DEBTS—Continued.
  Repeal not to extend to bills of credit emitted under acts of March 25, 1780, and April 7, 1781, ... 338
  Such bills to be received in payment of all lands sold by the state excepting forfeited estates only, ... 336
  Act not to affect any tender which has already been duly made, ... 338
  Debts, etc., contracted since January 1, 1777 and not satisfied or discharged to be paid in the particular money, etc., specified in the contract, ... 338
  Rents, etc., contracted before January 1, 1777 to be sued for and judgment obtained and execution awarded for the interest, damages and costs, etc., ... 339
  Execution not to issue for the principal for two years or until permission be given by act of assembly, ... 339
  Interest on such judgments to be paid annually, ... 340
  Defendants not having sufficient real estate to satisfy judgment to give security for the same before departing from the commonwealth, ... 340
  Upon neglect or refusal to give security court to award execution for the principal as well as the interest, etc., ... 340
  Debts exceeding £50 contracted before January 1, 1777 not to be sued for in less than six months after passing of act, ... 340
  Proviso where delay will cause creditor to lose debt, ... 340
  Act not to extend to revived debts which were on January 1, 1776 barred by the act for the limitation of actions, ... 340
  Debts, etc., not barred at the time not to be now barred until two years after passage of act, ... 341
  Agents, factors, etc., receiving money and applying it to private use to account to their principal for as much gold and silver as the bills of credit so received were worth at the time of application, ... 341

Index. 563

DEBTS—Continued.
Agents, factors, etc., to render an account under oath of the profit or loss made on such moneys, ... 342
Principal to obtain benefit of profit,.. 342
Agents, etc., refusing to make such oath to account for money the same as if applied to private use, ... 342
Fees of officers and fines incurred under act to be paid in gold and silver, ... 342
All fines imposed by acts of assembly to be recovered in gold, etc., ... 343
All debts and contracts entered into after March 1, 1781 to be discharged according to their nature, ... 343
Contracts for old continental currency, however, to be liquidated and paid at specie value, ... 343
Act not to prevent new continental bills of credit from being received in payment of taxes laid under act of December 18, 1780, ... 344

DEFENCE. See Frontiers.
Act providing for the, of this state, 361
President to call out enough wagons to transport baggage and stores of troops called out for the defense of the state, ... 361
County wagon masters and constables to perform same duties as required under former wagon laws, ... 361
Compensation of wagon masters, ... 362
President to seize and impress wagons, etc., if sufficient number cannot be procured in manner prescribed by act, ... 362
President to seize and impress arms, ammunition, stores, etc., when necessary and apply the same to public use, ... 362
Seizure to be certified and the value to be ascertained in specie, ... 362
President to billet and quarter troops upon public or private houses, ... 362
President authorized to call out all of the militia without respect to classes, ... 363
Person neglecting or refusing to perform tour of militia duty on call of president to be fined, ... 363

DEFENCE—Continued.
President authorized to draw upon the treasury for necessary money to procure arms, ammunition, etc., ... 363
President authorized to impress horses and wagons, etc., for the removal of families and property of inhabitants of Philadelphia, Northern Liberties, and Southwark who are in actual service against the enemy, ... 363
Duration of act limited, ... 364
Act for guarding and defending the navigation in the Delaware river, ...411
Commissioners appointed to procure vessels, etc., for the defense of the navigation in the Delaware river, .. 412
Supreme executive council to commission officers for such vessels, ... 412
Oath of commissioners, ... 412
Commissioners to report to and lay their accounts before the Supreme executive council, ...412-413
Moneys arising under certain prior acts appropriated for the uses of this act, ... 413
Duties laid on imports for purpose of raising revenue to carry out provisions of act, ... 414
Provisions for collecting same, ... 414
Commissioners empowered to borrow money not to exceed 25,000£, ...414-415
Provisions for repayment of same,.... 415
Rate of interest on such borrowed money limited to 6 per cent., ... 415
Disposition of prize money arising from captures made by vessels commissioned under act, ...415-416
Act to enable the supreme executive council to negotiate loans, etc., for the defence of the frontiers and support of government, repealed, ... 534

DEFENDANTS.
To have treble costs where plaintiff becomes nonsuit, discontinues or has judgment pass against him in certain actions, ...171,256,257,324,448
To recover treble costs, if plaintiff in suits to condemn certain goods as contraband, wilfully delay, discontinue, or have verdict passed against them, ...503-504

Index.

DEFENDANTS—Continued.
Plaintiffs or defendants in actions brought in the supreme or common pleas courts for debts in case of their sudden departure upon giving security may apply for special courts and have their cases determined at once, ... 417
Defendants in supreme court entitled to same benefits as defendants in common pleas, ... 418
Act not to prevent plaintiff or defendant from being allowed a reasonable time to procure testimony, ... 418
Defendant in certain actions allowed to plead the general issue and give act and special matter in evidence, 515

DELAWARE BAY. See Delaware River.
Act for guarding and defending the navigation in the, ... 411
Commissioners appointed to procure vessels, etc., for the defense of the navigation in the, ... 412
Commissioners to report to supreme executive council every vessel procured and equipped, ... 412
Supreme executive council to commission officers for such vessels, .. 412
Oath of commissioners, ... 412
Commissioners to report to and lay their accounts before the supreme executive council, ...412-413
Moneys arising under certain prior acts appropriated for the uses of this act, ... 413
Duties laid on imports for purpose of raising revenue to carry out provisions of act, ... 414
Provisions for collecting same, ... 414
Commissioners empowered to borrow money not to exceed 25,000 £, ...414-415
Provisions for repayment of same, .. 415
Rate of interest on such borrowed money limited to 6 per cent., ... 415
Disposition of prize money arising from captures made by vessels commissioned under act, ...415-416

DELAWARE RIVER.
Philadelphia wardens empowered to purchase a lot on north side of Sassafras street along, for a public wharf 203

DELAWARE RIVER—Continued.
Act for guarding and defending the navigation in the, ... 411
Commissioners appointed to procure vessels, etc., for the defense of the navigation in the, ... 412
Commissioners to report to supreme executive council every vessel procured and equipped, ... 412
Supreme executive council to commission officers, for such vessels, ... 412
Oath of commissioners, ... 412
Commissioners to report to and lay their accounts before the supreme executive council, ...412-413
Monies arising under certain prior acts appropriated for the uses of this act, ... 413
Duties laid on imports for purpose of raising revenue to carry out provisions of act, ... 414
Provisions for collecting same, ... 414
Commissioners empowered to borrow money not to exceed 25,000 £, ...414-415
Provisions for repayment of same,... 415
Rate of interest on such borrowed money limited to 6 per cent., ... 415
Disposition of prize money arising from captures made by vessels commissioned under act, ...415-416
Supplement to act for guarding and defending the navigation in the Delaware river and bay, ... 493
Commissioners appointed under prior act authorized to borrow 20,000 £ additional for carrying it into execution, ... 494
State share of prize money appropriated for raising and supporting armament for the defense of the navigation in the Delaware river, etc., ...494-495

DEPRECIATION CERTIFICATES.
Supreme executive council to appoint auditors to settle the depreciation of pay accounts of officers and privates of the Pennsylvania line, ... 233
Auditors to estimate in specie all pay received by such officers and privates, ... 233

Index.

DEPRECIATION CERTIFICATES—Continued.
Auditors to give officers and privates certificates for the sums due in specie, ...233-234
Confiscated estates to be sold on or before July 1, 1781 by the proper agents and specie certificates, etc., received in payment, ... 234
Certificates of privates not to be transferred unless attested by commanding officer, ... 234
Certificates to be received in payment for unlocated lands, etc., ... 234
Auditors to settle the accounts of all officers and privates who have died in the service, etc., ... 235
Widows and children of such officers and privates entitled to certificates, 235
Officers and privates of the navy in actual service entitled to all benefits extended to the Pennsylvania line by act, ... 235
Officers and privates of this state made prisoners in actual service, also entitled to benefits of act, ... 235
Oath of auditors, ... 235
Assembly may call in certificates and pay off the same, ...235-236
Moneys received from sale of confiscated estates to be reserved for redeeming certificates, ... 236
All such certificates so received by state treasurer to be kept by him and cancelled by order of assembly, 236
Scale of depreciation for guidance of auditors, ...236-237
Pay of auditors, ... 237
Certificates to be provided by supreme executive council and delivered to the said auditors, ... 238
Supreme executive council to draw on state treasurer for sums to pay off part of the certificates granted to the officers and soldiers of the Pennsylvania line, ... 316
Commissioners appointed by the supreme executive council, to take up old certificates and grant new ones, 316
New certificates to be interest bearing and negotiable, ... 316

DEPRECIATION CERTIFICATES—Continued.
Old certificates not taken up also to bear interest and be negotiable, ... 316
State Treasurer on demand to pay holders thereof one-third of face value and grant new certificates for the balance, ... 316
Officers and privates of state regiments, etc., captured by the enemy entitled to full depreciation of their pay until the time of their exchange, 272
Officers of the Pennsylvania line entitled to, enumerated, ... 458
Artillery officers, etc., and privates of the artillery artificers or detached corpse, inhabitants of this state also entitled to, ... 459
Comptroller general directed to settle depreciation of the pay accounts of the officers, etc., of the Pennsylvania line, ... 460
Supreme executive council to draw on state treasurer and turn over to the comptroller general all necessary sums for so doing, ... 460
Comptroller general in settling sums due to pay one-third thereof in bills of credit and two-thirds in certificates., ... 460

DESERTERS. See Militia; Pennsylvania Volunteers.
From the enemy not to be enrolled,.. 164
Nor to be subject to fine for not serving in the militia, ... 164
Provision for proceeding against, .. 170
Not to be enlisted in the Pennsylvania Volunteers, ... 191
Penalty for harboring or concealing, from the allies of the U. S., ... 214
Reward for apprehending, ... 214
Captains and masters of vessels harboring, to be fined 10,000 £, ... 223
Penalty to be recovered by distress,.. 223
For want of sufficient distress such captain, etc., to suffer one year's imprisonment without bail or mainprise, ... 223
Prize money and wages of, to be forfeited and applied for recruiting the Pennsylvania line in the federal army, ... 223

Index

DESERTERS—Continued.
Certain wills, powers of attorney, deeds of sale, etc., made by, declared null and void, ... 223
President and council to appoint persons to inspect muster roll of vessels in search of, ... 223
Penalty for obstructing search for or refusing to deliver up, ... 224
Marshall upon notice, to pay prizes and wages due deserters to the state treasurer, ... 224

DESERTION. See Deserters.

DETINUE.
Imported goods together with the casks, etc., to vest in the commonwealth where naval officer tenders to importer the value of such goods with 10 per cent. increase, ... 253
Commonwealth to recover possession thereof by action of trover and conversion, replevin or, ... 253

DISCONTINUANCE.
Defendant to recover treble costs in certain cases where plaintiff becomes nonsuit, suffers a, or has judgment pass against him, 256-257-324-448
Defendant to recover treble costs in suits for the condemnation of goods as contraband, if plaintiff wilfully delays, discontinues, or has judgment pass against him, ...503-504

DISCOVERER.
Of raising bills of credit, loan office certificates or bills of exchange to receive one-half of the penalties,.. 15
Reward of, in case penalty be not paid, ... 15
Of raising bills of credit, to receive one-half of penalty, ... 189

DISTILLERS. See Nuisances.
Act to permit making of whiskey, etc., from rye, etc., under certain restrictions, etc., repealed, ...175-176

DISTRESS. See Landlord and Tenant.
Penalty imposed upon captains and masters of vessels, for harboring deserters to be recovered by, ... 223
Fines under militia act to be recovered by, ... 171

DISTRICT ASSESSORS. See County Commissioners; War Taxes.

DITCHES. See Lancaster, Borough of; State Island.

DIVORCE.
Of Giles Hicks and Hester Hicks, ... 268
Giles Hicks authorized and empowered to remarry, ... 269
Of Jacob Billmeyer and Mary Billmeyer, ... 367

DOUBLE TAXES.
So much of act for making more equal the burden of the public defense as imposes, repealed, ... 31

DOOR-KEEPER.
Of the assembly, wages of, ... 378
Mileage of, ... 378

DRAFT. See Federal Army.

DUTCH REFORMED CHURCH.
The Trustees of the Dutch Reformed Church in Northampton and Southampton, in the county of Bucks, incorporated, ... 526

DUTIES. See Impost; Excise; Tariff.
United States authorized to levy a five per cent. ad valorem duty on imports, ... 297
Arms, ammunition, clothing, wool cards, cotton cards and wire for making them, and salt excepted,.. 297
Authorities to levy a like duty on prizes and prize goods condemned by the admiralty court, ... 297
Congress to appoint collectors for collecting same, ... 298
Moneys arising from such duties to be appropriated in payment of

Index 567

DUTIES—Continued.
debts, contracted on the faith of the U. S. for support of the present war, 298
Act to continue in force until such debts are fully and finally discharged, ... 298

DUTY. See Impost; Tariff.

E.

EARS.
Lopping of, part punishment for counterfeiting or raising bills of credit, loan-office certificates or bills of exchange, ... 15
Lopping of, part punishment for horse stealing, first offence, ... 113
Lopping of, part punishment for raising or knowingly uttering raised bills of credit, ...189,212,307

EDUCATION. See College and Academy of Philadelphia; University of the State of Pennsylvania.

ELECTIONS. See Carlisle, Borough of.
Places of holding elections in Cumberland and Bedford counties, ..219-220
Place and manner of holding elections in Washington county, ... 273
Time, place and manner of electing burgesses, town clerks, and constable in the borough of Carlisle,.426-427
Time, place and manner of electing supervisors and assessors in Carlisle, ... 433
Borough of Carlisle declared to be one distinct district for general elections, ... 439

ELECTION DISTRICTS.
Borough of Carlisle declared to be one distinct district for general elections, ... 439

EMBARGO. See Contraband; Flour; Exports.
Laid for a limited time on all exports by sea, ... 43
Act not to prevent vessels taking on board provisions necessary for voyage, ...43-44.
Nor to extend to provisions for the use of the armies or ships of the United States or their allies, ... 44

EMBARGO—Continued.
To be suspended by supreme executive council upon its becoming unnecessary, ... 44
Exports attempted to be shipped in violation of act to be forfeited, ... 44
Disposition of forfeited exports, ... 44
Claim for seized ship, etc., not to be admitted unless security be entered, 45
All actions against officers or persons making seizure to be brought within three months, ... 45
Act laying an embargo on the exportation of provisions by sea, continued, ... 228
Flour of wheat permitted to be exported by sea under certain limitations and restrictions, ... 244
Act not to limit power of president and council to lay embargoes whenever necessary, ... 247
Act to revive and continue act for laying an embargo on the exportation of provisions, etc., repealed,.. 267
Supplement to act regulating navigation and trade, ... 418
No goods, wares or merchandise, produced or manufactured by Great Britain to be imported into this state, ... 419
All such goods to be confiscated, ... 419
One-half to go to informer and the other half to the commonwealth,.. 419
All actions under act against importers to be brought within six months, ... 419
Proviso as to goods, wares, merchandise taken as prize, ... 419
Such goods, wares and merchandise not to be imported from neutral ports, ... 420
Captain, etc., of vessels to certify that imported goods from neutral ports are not the growth, product, etc., of Great Britain, ... 420
Such goods to be confiscated if captain neglects to produce certificate, ...420-421
Part of prior act regulating navigation and trade repealed, ... 421

EMBEZZLEMENT.
Of any bill, note, bond, deed, money, or other effects from the bank of North America to be punished by death without benefit of clergy, .. 384

ESCUTCHEONS. See Bills of Credit.

ESSOIN.
Not allowed, ...137, 295

ESTATES.
Elizabeth Allen empowered during the minority of her son to grant and convey sundry lots of land in the town of Northampton, county of Northampton, ... 496

ESTREATS.
All fines, etc., to be estreated into the supreme court every April and September, ... 134
Penalty for violation, ...134-135
Schedules to be delivered yearly to sheriffs and prothonotary of the supreme court, by clerks of the peace, 135
Penalty for violation, ... 135
Justices of the supreme court to award process for levying fines, etc., ... 135
Estreats to be returned upon oath,... 136
Form of oath, ... 136
Penalty for fraudulently concealing fines, etc., ,........................136-137
Penalty for failing to make estreat of fines, etc., ... 137
Justices of the supreme court to view estreats and cause prothonotary to enroll them, ... 137
Justices to hear complaints concerning immoderate fines, etc., estreated, ... 137
Justices to appoint a clerk of the estreats, ... 137
Duties of clerk, ... 137
Moneys recovered through act to be paid to the state treasurer, ... 138
Compensation for state treasurer for receiving and handling, ... 138
Compensation of the clerk of estreats, ... 138
Secretary of supreme executive council to certify duties arising from tavern and other licenses, ... 138
Penalty for neglect or refusal, ... 138

ESTREATS—Continued.
Former act for recovery of fines, etc., repealed, ... 139

EVIDENCE.
Certificate of auditors appointed to settle public accounts to be conclusive in action of debt by the commonwealth to recover amount due,.. 75
No set off in such case to be admitted, ... 75
Attestations of the register of the court of admiralty to be received as, ... 104
Defendants in actions under militia act may plead general issue and give act and special matter in, ...170-171
Persons sued under act for impost on goods, etc., may plead the general issue and give act and special matter in evidence, ... 256
Grantees under act for the better support of the public credit by an immediate sale of the lands, etc., to plead the general issue and give act in, in suits brought for the recovery of such lands, ... 319
Such evidence to be final and conclusive against any such claimant, 319
Defendants in actions brought against them for doing anything in pursuance of act to plead the general issue and give act and special matter in evidence, ... 323
Persons sued under act incorporating the borough of Carlisle may plead the general issue and give act and special matter in evidence, ... 448
Defendant in certain actions to plead the general issue and give act and special matter in evidence, ... 515

EXCHANGE. See Bills of Credit.
Rate of, between continental currency and bills of credit fixed, ... 251
Such rate to be continued until February 1, 1781, ... 251
Supreme executive council to then publish rate of, between specie and continental money monthly, ... 251
Such rate to be the rate between continental money and bills of credit, 251

Index. 569

EXCHANGE.
Rate of exchange at which the receiver general is to receive the £5 sterling for every 100 acres of land, fixed, ... 350

EXCISE.
To be levied and collected during remainder of ten years prescribed in former act, ... 130
After May 1, 1780 to be levied and paid in wheat as fees of officers, ... 130
Act for making the excise on wine, rum, brandy, etc., continued, ... 299
Retailers to still take permits from the collector of the, and give him security, ... 299
Additional, to be raised for the support of the government, ... 299
Manner and mode of collecting, ... 300
Compensation of collector of, ... 300
State treasurer to pay money arising under act as directed by act on order of assembly, ... 300
No other excise to be paid than imposed by act, ... 301

EXECUTION.
Outstanding public accounts to be collected by, ... 196
For want of sufficient distress defendant to be imprisoned until sums due and costs be paid, ... 196
Rents, etc., contracted before January 1, 1777 to be sued for and judgment obtained and execution awarded for the interest, damages and costs, etc., ... 339
Execution not to issue for the principal for two years or until permission be given by act of assembly,. 339
Interest on such judgments to be paid annually, ... 340
Defendants not having sufficient real estate to satisfy judgment to give security for the same before departing from the commonwealth, ... 340
Upon neglect or refusal to give security court to award execution for the principal as well as the interest, etc., ... 340

EXECUTORS AND ADMINISTRATORS.
Not affected in the discharge of their duties by act suppressing public auctions, ... 17
The suspension for a limited time of certain acts of assembly making bills of credit of the U. S. legal tender, not to extend to sheriffs, attorneys, guardians, or, etc., ...204-205

EXPORTS. See Bread; Flour.
Embargo laid for a limited time on all exports by sea, ... 43
Act not to prevent vessels taking on board provisions necessary for voyage, ...43-44
Nor extend to provisions for the use of the armies or ships of the United States or their allies, ... 44
Embargo to be suspended by supreme executive council as soon as it becomes unnecessary, ... 44
Attempted to be shipped in violation of act to be forfeited, ... 44
Disposition of forfeited exports, ... 44
Claim for seized ship not to be admitted unless security be entered,. 45
All actions against officers or persons for making seizure to be brought within three months, ... 45
Act laying embargo on exportation of provisions by sea, continued, ... 228
Flour of wheat permitted to be exported by sea under certain limitations and restrictions, ... 244
Act to revive and continue act for laying an embargo on the exportation of provisions. etc., repealed,.. 267
Act to permit the exportation of flour of wheat, partly repealed, ... 267
Supplement to act preventing the exportation of unmerchantable bread and flour, ... 379
Offering flour for sale packed in unseasoned casks, etc., prohibited, ... 379
Penalty for violation, ... 379
Penalty on bolters, etc., for not entering their respective brands,..379-380
Penalty for deficiency of weight of flour casks, etc., ... 380
Casks for exportation to be stamped with the letters S. P., ... 380

570   *Index.*

EXPORTS—Continued.
    Casks not so stamped to be forfeited if offered for exportation, ... 380
    Middlings for exportation to be branded as such, ... 380
    Fines and penalties under act, how recoverable, ... 380
    Parts of prior act altered and repealed, ... 381
    Parts of act to permit the exportation of flour of wheat, etc., repealed, ... 326

F.

FAIR DEALING.
    Act for the encouragement of, repealed, ... 175-176

FAIRS.
    Burgesses, etc., of Carlisle, to have and keep two markets in each week and two fairs in each year, ... 428

FEDERAL ARMY. See Armies of the United States.

FEES.
    Of officer appointed for granting certificates to chimney sweepers in Philadelphia, etc., ... 7
    Of certain officers of the state to be satisfied in wheat, ... 39-40
    Payment of fees to be also made in lawful money of this state or of the United States in sums proportioned to value of wheat, ... 40
    Offices to which payment of fees in wheat shall extend, enumerated,...40-41
    Act not to extend to fees rated by the £ or £100, ... 41
    Of clerk and register of the high court of errors and appeals, ... 57
    Of judge of admiralty and three extra associate judges for sitting in the high court of errors and appeals, .. 58
    Of court clerk for registering slaves, 70
    Of witnesses, sheriffs, etc., attending before auditors appointed to settle public accounts, ... 78
    To be paid by delinquents, ... 78
    Of auditors appointed to settle public accounts, ... 79-80

FEES—Continued.
    Of auctioneers, ... 232
    Of naval officer. 257
    Of signers of bills of credit, ... 304
    Of secretary of the land office, ... 309
    Of receiver-general, ... 310
    Of surveyor-general, ... 310
    Of county commissioners and assessors, ... 335
    Of tax collectors, ... 335
    Of receiver-general, ...410-411
    And mileage of sheriff, coroner, or other process server and witnesses, 454
    Of regulators, ... 488

FELONY. See Crimes.

FERGUSON, ELIZABETH.
    Forfeited estate of Henry Hugh Ferguson, traitor, vested in, his wife, 282

FERGUSON, HENRY HUGH.
    Forfeited estate of, traitor, vested in Elizabeth Ferguson, his wife, ... 282

FERRIES.
    Wardens of Philadelphia to let market-houses, wharves, public landing places and, ... 201
    Treasurer of wardens and assessors to receive rents from market-houses, wharves, public landing places and, ... 201
    Owners of wharves, public landing places and, to pay their rents to the treasurer of the wardens and assessors, ... 202
    The further supplement to act regulating nightly watch, etc., not to extend to the estate and interest of the city of Philadelphia to the middle ferry on Schuylkill from May 1, 1780 to May 1, 1781, ... 203
    Unless wardens agree with president in council to keep such bridge in repair, etc., ... 203
    Established on the Youghiogheny River, ... 471
    Established on the Monongahela River, ...471-472
    Certain rivers declared to be public highways, ... 472

FIDUCIARIES.

Agents, factors, etc., receiving money and applying it to private use to account to their principal for as much gold and silver as the bills of credit so received were worth at the time of application, ... 341
Agents, factors, etc., to render an account under oath of the profit or loss made on such moneys, ... 342
Principal to obtain benefit of profit, 342
Agents, etc., refusing to make such oath to account for money the same as if applied to private use, ... 342
Moneys paid by executors, guardians and other, in pursuance of act for recruiting the Pennsylvania Line, etc., to be allowed in the settlement of their accounts, ... 347

FINES AND PENALTIES.

For chimney sweepers in Philadelphia, etc., neglecting or refusing to obtain certificates, ... 6
For chimney sweepers neglecting or refusing to wear number contained in certificates on the front of their by action of debt, ... 17
For chimney sweepers neglect or refusal to sweep chimneys within 48 hours after application, ... 7
For persons whose unswept chimneys take fire and blaze out at the top,... 7
On chimney sweepers where chimneys take fire and blaze out at the top within one month from sweeping,... 7
Arising under act regulating chimney sweepers, in Philadelphia, etc., to be recoverable before justices of the peace, ... 8
Accruing under act for the suppressing of public auction to be recovered by action of debt, ... 17
Disposition of, ... 17
Imposed upon trustees of the University of Pennsylvania for neglect or refusal to deliver up books, records, etc., to successors, ... 29
How recoverable, ... 29
Punishment for officers of land office, etc., refusing to deliver up books, papers, etc., on demand of president of supreme executive counsel, ... 38

FINES AND PENALTIES—Continued.

To be computed and satisfied in wheat, ... 41
For neglect or refusal to deliver up books, papers, etc., found on captured vessels, ... 99
Act to restore and ascertain the value of divers fines and penalties, ... 106
To be computed, levied and satisfied in same manner as fees are computed under act for support of certain officers, etc., ... 107
Certain prior acts repealed, ...108-109
For suffering beasts to run at large in Passyunk, Moyamensing, Northern Liberties, and Germantown, increased, ... 116
Penalty for committing trespass or waste on unoccupied lands, etc., .. 127
All fines, etc., to be estreated into the supreme court every April and September, ... 134
Penalty for violation, ...134-135
Schedules to be delivered yearly to sheriffs and prothonotary of the supreme court, by clerks of the peace, 135
Penalty for violation, ... 135
Justices of the supreme court to award process for levying, ... 135
Estreats to be returned upon oath,... 136
Form of oath, ... 136
Penalty for fraudulently concealing, etc., ...136-137
Penalty for failure to make estreat of, etc., ... 137
Justices of the supreme court to view estreat and cause prothonotary to enroll them, ... 137
Justices to hear complaints concerning immoderate fines, etc., estreated, ... 137
Justices to appoint a clerk of the estreats, ... 137
Duties of clerk, ... 137
Moneys recovered through act to be paid to the state treasurer, ... 138
Compensation for state treasurer for receiving and handling, ... 138
Compensation of the clerk of estreats, 138
Secretary of supreme executive council to certify duties arising from tavern and other licenses, ... 138

FINES AND PENALTIES—Continued.

Penalty for neglect or refusal, ... 138
Former act for recovery of fines, etc., repealed, ... 139
Penalty for militia men failing to meet on days of exercise, ... 154-155
How recoverable, ... 155
Disposition of, ... 156
Penalty for refusing to perform tour of militia duty, ... 158
Masters, fathers, etc., to be accountable for the fines of minors and apprentices, ... 159
Imposed under militia act, how recoverable, ... 169
Penalty for raising bills of credit,... 189
On delinquent tax collectors increased, ... 196-197
Penalty for neglect or refusal to collect militia fines, ... 197-198
For neglect or refusal of clerk of the market to collect rent from markethouses, etc., and properly pay over the same, ... 202
On owners, etc., of ferries, etc., neglecting to pay their rents to the treasurer of the wardens and assessors, ... 202
For raising or knowingly uttering raised bills of credit, ... 212
For harboring or concealing deserters from the allies of the U. S., ... 214
On captains and masters of vessels harboring deserters, ... 223
Penalty for obstructing search for, or refusing to deliver up deserters, .. 224
Penalty for neglect or refusal of marshall to distribute proceeds of prize sale within twenty days, ... 224-225
Fines and penalties for neglect of militia duty to be ascertained and determined by price of labor as fixed by the general assembly, ... 226
Act not to be construed to alter, mitigate or discharge any fine or penalty already accrued, ... 226
Lieutenants or sub-lieutenants of militia neglecting or refusing to deliver up to their successors in office books, accounts, etc., to forfeit 10,000 £, ... 227
For selling at public auction without a license, ... 230

FINES AND PENALTIES—Continued.

Application of, ... 230
Penalty for neglect or refusal of county commissioners to perform duties under act for recruiting the Pennsylvania Line, etc., ... 247-248
Penalty for neglect or refusal of assessors or collectors to perform duties under same act, ... 248
Penalty imposed on millers, bolters and bakers for neglect or refusal to provide brand marks and enter the same with the clerk of the quarter sessions, ... 289
Penalty for putting a false tare on any cask of bread, ... 290
Penalty for failure of bakers of bread for exportation or failure to deliver an invoice of contents of casks of bread, etc., ... 291
Penalty for loading for exportation uninspected flour, ... 291
Penalty for hindering or preventing inspectors of flour from entering vessels to search for flour intended to be illegally exported, ... 294
Penalty for counterfeiting brand marks, first offence, ... 294
Arising under act for an impost on goods, etc., imported into this state, how recoverable, ... 256
County commissioners neglecting to perform duties required by act for completing the quota of the federal army to be subject to a £500 fine,.. 262
Assessors, collectors, etc., failing to perform duties under same act to be subject to a £100 fine, ... 262
For catching fish with brush nets in the Schuylkill river, ... 271
For hindering or obstructing persons removing or obstructing brush nets in the Schuylkill river, ... 271
For raising or knowingly uttering raised bills of credit, ... 307
Penalty on surveyor-general for neglect or refusal to make returns of certain lands within a limited time, 312
How recoverable,, ... 312
Application of, ... 312
Penalty on assessors and tax collectors for neglect or refusal to serve, ... 333

FINES AND PENALTIES—Continued.

On county commissioners for neglect or refusal to perform duties under act for raising supplies for 1781, .. 336
How recoverable, ... 336
Parts of acts imposing, for refusal to accept bills of credit in payments of debts, etc., repealed, ...337-338
All, imposed by acts of assembly to be recovered in gold and silver, ... 343
For offering for sale flour packed in unseasoned casks, etc., ... 379
On bolters, etc., for not entering their respective brands, ... 380
Fines and penalties under supplement to act to prevent the exportation of bread and flour not merchantable, how recoverable, ... 380
Penalty for concealing property, etc., in order to escape the payment of war taxes, ... 388
Penalty for neglect or refusal of assessors and collectors to perform duties under act for raising supplies for 1782, ... 393
Manner and mode of collecting fines, penalties and forfeitures under act incorporating the borough of Carlisle, ... 447
For prison keepers wilfully or negligently suffering prisoners of war to escape, ... 467
For concealing, aiding or assisting prisoners of war to escape, ... 467
For laying foundation walls in Philadelphia before they are adjusted and marked by the regulators, ... 487
For obstructing commissioners in Philadelphia in removing trees growing in streets, ... 490
Penalty for members of the general assembly neglecting or refusing to attend the meetings thereof, on the date fixed by the Constitution, etc., 506
general assembly empowered to remit any such fines, ... 507
Penalties imposed on tax collectors in Southwark to be recovered by, action of debt, ... 515

FISH. See Schuylkill River.
Not to be caught in the Schuylkill river with brush nets, etc., ... 271

FISH—Continued.
Penalty for violation, ... 271
Penalty, how recoverable, ... 271
Application of penalty, ... 271
Limitations and restrictions respecting the catching of shad by seines or nets in the Schuylkill river, ... 271

FLOOD GATES. Schuylkill Point Meadows; State Island.

FLOUR.
Wheat flour, etc., to be received in payment of taxes, ... 198
Flour of wheat permitted to be exported by sea under certain limitations and restrictions, ... 244
Not to be laden on board any vessel until master of such vessel deliver to naval officer a memorial in writing, ... 245
Memorial to contain the design, name, kind, size or tonnage of vessel, name of owner, etc., and number and size of guns with which she is armed together with quantity of flour to be laden, ... 245
Naval officer to take bond in double the value of flour to be shipped for faithful compliance of master with provisions of act, ... 245
Naval officer then to grant permit for lading of same, ... 245
All flour to be laden within forty days within date of permit in the day time and at some unenclosed wharf, 245
All suits on above bonds to be brought within two years, ... 245
Burden of proof in actions on such bonds to lie upon the obligees, ..245-246
Ship containing, not to be cleared until master produce to naval officer a certificate from the proper officer acknowledging the receipt or tender of flour at market price for the public use equal to one-third of cargo, ... 246
Supreme executive council empowered to take off such restriction when expedient, ... 246
Act not to discharge master of ship from delivering to naval officer a true manifest of the lading thereof, 246

FLOUR—Continued.
Or from performing any requirement under act for regulation of navigation and trade of this state, ... 246
Neglect of master to perform such requirements to be a forfeiture of his bond, ... 247
Fines, penalties, etc., under prior act to be imposed unless all conditions of this act, etc., have been complied with, ... 247
Act not to limit power of president and council, to lay embargoes whenever necessary, ... 247
Act to permit the exportation of flour of wheat, partly repealed, ... 267
Certain acts preventing the exportation of bread and flour not merchantable, repealed, after Oct. 1, 1781, ... 289
Millers and bolters allowed until then to dispose of, for exportation their flour in barrels in any dimension,... 283
Size of casks used in exporting, regulated, ... 289
Casks to be of three distinct sizes, .. 289
Millers, bolters and bakers to provide brand marks and enter them with the clerk of the quarter sessions with their names and places of abode, ... 289
Penalty for violation, ... 289
Millers, bolters or bakers to brand each cask of flour or bread before removing same from place where bolted or baked, ... 289
Miller or bolter to brand each cask of flour according to the respective diameters, and weight, ... 289
Penalty for violation, ... 290
Flour bolted for exportation to be of due fineness, ... 290
Casks of flour to be weighed and tare marked thereon, ... 290
Penalty for putting a false tare on any cask of bread, ... 290
Powers of bread inspectors and their deputies, ... 290
Bakers of bread for exportation to deliver an invoice of contents with the bread, with brand mark and name, etc., ... 291
Penalty for violation, ... 291

FLOUR—Continued.
Bakers to forfeit bread and casks falsely invoiced, ... 291
Wagons, etc., conveying flour and bread from mill, etc., to place of exportation, etc., to have a covering, etc., ... 291
Flour not to be left at any landing place except it be in a sheltered position, ... 291
Flour or bread not to be carried from mill, etc., to place of exportation, etc., in open boats, etc., without a covering, ... 291
Carrier of bread and flour to forfeit one shilling per cask where the same gets wet or damaged through his negligence, ... 291
Flour intended for exportation to be inspected, ... 291
Penalty for loading uninspected flour, 291
Merchantable flour to be branded with the states' arms, etc., ... 292
Compensation of inspector, ... 292
Owner of unmerchantable flour to pay inspectors' fees, ... 292
Fees to be recovered by action of debt where owner refuses to pay, ... 292
Flour attempted to be exported without being branded to be forfeited,.. 292
Manner of proceeding in cases of dispute respecting the fineness, etc., of flour, etc., ... 292
Masters of ships, etc., to set forth in their manifest, etc., the number of barrels of flour shipped, and the persons shipping the same, ... 293
Penalty for failure to make return of manifest to naval officer, ... 293
Inspectors to have the power to enter on board vessels to search for flour intended to be illegally exported, .. 294
Penalty for hindering or preventing inspector from so doing, ... 294
Penalty for counterfeiting brand marks, ... 294
Inspectors not to trade in flour, ... 294
Penalty for violation, ... 294
Penalty, how recoverable, ... 294
Application of penalty, ... 294
Inspectors empowered to appoint deputies, ... 294
Oath of deputy, ... 294

Index. 575

FLOUR—Continued.
  Oath of deputy, ... 295
  Oath to be administered by a justice of the peace, ... 295
  Fines and forfeitures arising under act, how recoverable, ... 295
  Application of, ... 295
  Inspectors appointed throughout the different counties, ... 295
  Term of office of inspector, ... 295
  Vacancies, how filled, ...295-296
  Parts of act to permit the exportation of flour of wheat, etc., repealed, ... 326
  Supplement to act preventing the exportation of unmerchantable bread and flour, ... 379
  Offering flour for sale packed in unseasoned casks, etc., prohibited,... 379
  Penalty for violation, ... 379
  Penalty on bolters, etc., for not entering their respective brands, ...379-380
  Penalty for deficiency of weight of flour casks, etc., ... 380
  Casks for exportation to be stamped with the letters S. P., ... 380
  Casks not so stamped to be forfeited if offered for exportation, ... 380
  Middlings for exportation to be branded as such, ... 380
  Fines and penalties under act, how recoverable, ... 380
  Parts of prior act altered and repealed, ... 381

FOREIGN COLORS.
  Trial and punishment of subjects of this state or any of the U. S. committing piracy, etc., under foreign colors, ... 222

FORFEITED ESTATES.
  Of Henry Hugh Ferguson traitor, vested in Elizabeth Ferguson, his wife, ... 282
  Supreme executive council to order sale of all estates forfeited under act to adjust the accounts of the Pennsylvania troops, etc., ... 317
  Such sales to be made on or before May 10, 1781, ... 317
  Money arising therefrom to be applied to the uses and purposes specified in act, ... 317

FORFEITED LANDS. See Forfeited Estates.

FORFEITURE.
  Part punishment for counterfeiting, raising or knowingly uttering counterfeited or raised, bills of credit, loan-office certificates or bills of exchange, ... 15
  Penalty for unlawfully hawking or peddling, ... 21
  All ships unlawfully laden with exports to be seized and forfeited, ... 44
  Penalty for neglect or refusal to deliver up books, papers, etc., found on captured vessel, ... 99
  Swine found running at large in Passyunk, Moyamensing, Northern Liberties, Germantown and Bristol, to be forfeited, ... 116
  Disposition of, ...116-117
  Penalty for quartermasters, foragemasters, etc., purchasing wheat, etc., in violation of act, ... 182
  Part punishment for counterfeiting, raising or knowingly uttering counterfeit or raised bills of credit, .. 212
  Part punishment for counterfeiting, raising or knowingly uttering raised bills of credit, ... 189
  Penalty for refusing to take bills of credit, in payment of goods, etc.,... 242
  Persons refusing to accept bills of credit equal in value to gold and silver for goods, etc., to forfeit double the value of the article so exposed to sale, ... 250
  For second offense offender to suffer imprisonment and forfeit one-half of all his or her goods, etc., ... 250
  Penalty imposed on masters of ships unloading imported goods without a permit, ... 255
  Penalty imposed on master of ship for refusing to exhibit the manifest of his cargo, ... 256
  Part punishment for counterfeiting, forging, raising, or knowingly uttering counterfeited, forged or raised bills of credit, ... 307
  Flour casks not stamped with the letters S. P. to be forfeited if offered for exportation, ... 380

FORFEITURE—Continued.

Penalty for importing goods, wares, merchandise produced or manufactured by Great Britain, ... 419

Manner and mode of collecting fines, penalties and forfeitures under act incorporating the borough of Carlisle, 447

FORESTALLING.

Act for preventing repealed, ...175-176

FORGERY.

Penalty for counterfeiting or forging continental loan office certificates, continental loan office bills of exchange or paper money of the United States, ...15-16

Of bills of credit to be punished by death, ...189, 212, 307

FRANCE.

Goods, etc., imported from France, Spain, or the United Provinces, not to be treated as contraband, ... 498

All Subjects of His Most Christian Majesty entitled to the rights and privileges stipulated in their behalf by the 11th Article of the treaty of amity and commerce concluded between him and the U. S. of America, 510

Act to take effect as of February 6th, 1778, ... 510

FREEDOM DUES.

Negro and mulatto children born after March 1, 1780, of slaves to be entitled to, upon attaining the age of 28, ... 69

FRONTIERS. See Militia.

One extra company of the militia to be raised for the defense of the frontiers of the state, ... 373

To be clothed, etc., by and be under the direction of the supreme executive council, ... 373

Supreme executive council to appoint and commission the officers of said company, ... 373

Officers to be taken from those of the Pennsylvania line who are on half pay, ... 374

Compensation of recruits, ... 374

FRONTIERS—Continued.

Inhabitants waylaying and annoying the enemy in their incursions and depredations to be entitled to militia pay and rations, ... 374

Supreme executive council to draw on the treasury for such necessary sums, ... 374

Forces raised under act to be bound by the rules and regulations of the army of the United States, ...374-375

Supreme executive council empowered to order all of troops or any expedition against the savages or other enemies on the frontiers of the state, 375

Taxes due by persons driven from their homes to be levied proportionately on the other parts of the counties, ... 375

County commissioners authorized to exonerate from taxation inhabitants who have been so driven off and distressed by the enemy, ... 375

Also to exonerate those inhabitants who stay on the frontiers for the purpose of its defense, ... 376

Commissioners to transmit to general assembly a list of the names, etc., of the persons so exonerated, ... 376

Supreme executive council authorized to borrow enough to defend the frontiers and for the other exigencies of government, ... 492

Loan not to exceed 30,000 £, ... 492

Interest thereon not to exceed 6 per cent. per annum, ... 492

Duties arising on liquors, revenues from sales at vendues, fines and penalties from naval and excise officers, and moneys arising from marriage, tavern and other licenses pledged as funds for the payment thereof, ... 493

Supreme executive council empowered to apply the same to that purpose, ... 493

Faith and honor of the state pledged to make up and pay off any deficiency, ... 493

Act to enable the supreme executive council to negotiate loans, etc., for the defence of the frontiers and support of government, repealed, ... 534

Index.   577

G.

GALLOWAY, JOSEPH.
House and lots on High, Minor and Sixth Sts., Philadelphia owned by, before his attainder, vested in the commonwealth, ...48-50

GAOL DELIVERY.
Courts of, to be held in Washington county in like manner as elsewhere, 274

GENERAL ASSEMBLY.
Fees of representatives to be paid in wheat, ... 41
Fees of clerk of, to be paid in wheat, 41
Washington county to have two representatives in the, ... 273
Members neglecting or refusing to attend on the date fixed by the Constitution, etc., to be fined 15£, ... 506
Members duly elected who give written notice of their refusal to serve within 15 days after receiving notice of their election excepted, ... 506
Members of the, after 15 days, to make out a list of delinquents, and transmit it to the supreme executive council, ... 507
Supreme executive council to require attorney general to sue for and recover from delinquents the fines prescribed by act, ... 507
Empowered to remit any fines recovered under act, ... 507

GENERAL ISSUE.
Defendants in action under militia act may plead, and give act and special matter in evidence, ...170-171
May be pleaded in actions under act for an impost on goods, ... 256
Grantees under act for the better support of the public credit by an immediate sale of such lands, etc., to plead the, and give act in evidence in suits brought for the recovery of such lands, ... 319
In suits brought under said act defendant may plead the, and give act and special matter in evidence, ... 323
Persons sued under act incorporating the borough of Carlisle may plead the general issue and give act and special matter in evidence, ... 448

37—X

GERMAN LUTHERN CONGREGATION.
Charter of, confirmed and amended,. 83
Fundamental articles of, confirmed,.. 83
Clause in former charter requiring rules and by-laws, etc., not to be repugnant to laws of Great Britain, annulled, ...83-84
Present officers of the, enumerated,... 84
Office of rector abolished, ... 84
Elections of officers, etc., ...84-85
Filling of vacancy, ... 86
Minors under 18 not entitled to vote, 86
Elections to be by ballot, ... 86
Members only, entitled, ... 87
To elect president, secretary and treasurer, ... 87
Two-thirds of members to be a quorum, ... 87
Empowered to erect additional church and hold other real estate, ...87-88

GERMAN SOCIETY.
For the relief of distressed Germans in the state of Pennsylvania, incorporated, ...356-357
Name, style and title of, ... 357
Powers, franchises, etc., of, ... 357
To hold estates heretofore granted to the society, ... 357
And the acquired additional property, etc., ... 357
Quarterly meetings of the, ... 358
Election of new members, ... 358
Membership of the, not to be less than 75 nor more than 300, ... 358
Empowered to make rules, by laws, etc., ... 358
Rules, by laws, etc., not to be repugnant to laws of the state, ... 358
To keep minutes of all proceedings, .. 358
Minute book to be open to the inspection, etc., ...358-359
Officers of the, to be elected annually, 359
Filling of vacancy, ... 359
Application of rents, interest and profits, etc., belonging to the, ... 359
Proviso regarding the disposal of money, etc., ...359-360
Officers of the, to serve without pay, 360
To have a common seal, ... 360
Empowered to sue and be sued, etc., 360

GERMAN SOCIETY—Continued.
Yearly value of real estate and interest on money exclusive of stated subscriptions, limited to £2,500 annually, ... 360

GERMANTOWN.
Act to prevent trespassing upon unenclosed grounds in Moyamensing, Northern Liberties, Passyunk, and, revived, ... 116
Penalty for suffering beasts to run at large in, increased, ... 116
Running at large of swine in, prohibited, ... 116
Such swine to be forfeited, ... 116
Disposition of forfeiture, ...116-117
Person aggrieved by seizure of swine to have appeal to justice of the peace, ... 117
Party appealing to forfeit 40s. where seizure is confirmed, ... 117
Act not to extend to any part of, northwestward of Livezey's lane,.. 117
Act to prevent the trespassing upon the unenclosed grounds of Passyunk, Moyamensing, Northern Liberties, Bristol and, revived, ... 283

GOLD. See Bills of Credit.
Certain acts of assembly making bills of credit of the U. S. legal tender equal to gold and silver suspended for a limited time, ... 204
Act not to extend to any debt or contract made after November 1, 1779, upon which suit has actually been brought, ... 204
Nor to sheriffs, attorneys, executors, guardians, etc., ... 204
Act to suspend laws, making the bills of credit of the U. S. legal tender, in payment of debts, equal to, and silver, continued, ... 229
Duration of act limited, ... 229
Value of bills of credit compared with gold and silver, ...249-250
Duties under act for an impost on goods, etc., to be paid in, or silver as they passed in 1775 or other money equivalent, ... 257
Certain war taxes to be paid in, or silver only, ... 335

GOLD—Continued.
Proviso as to persons who have taken the oath of allegiance to this state, ...335-336
All fines imposed by acts of assembly to be recovered in, or silver, etc.,.. 343
Certain war taxes to be paid in gold and silver only, ... 399

GOVERNMENT.
Act for the support of the, making excise on wine, rum, etc., more equal, amended and continued, ... 299
Act for the support of the, ... 376
Supreme executive council authorized to borrow enough to defend the frontiers, and for the other exigencies of government, ... 492
Loan not to exceed 30,000 £, ... 492
Interest thereon not to exceed 6 per cent. per annum, ... 492
Duties arising on liquors, revenues from sales at vendues, fines and penalties from naval and excise officers, and moneys arising from marriage, tavern and other licenses, pledged as funds for the payment thereof, ... 493
Supreme executive council empowered to apply the same to that purpose, ... 493
Faith and honor of the state pledged to make up and pay off any deficiency, ... 493
Act to enable the supreme executive council to negotiate loans, etc., for the defence of the frontiers and support of government, repealed,.. 534

GRAEME PARK.
In Harsham township, Philadelphia, county, forfeited by Henry Hugh Ferguson, traitor, vested in Elizabeth, his wife, ...281-282

GRAIN. See Exports; Flour.

GREAT MUD ISLAND.
Vested in the commonwealth, ... 49

GUARDIANS.
The suspension for a limited time of certain acts of assembly making bills of credit of the U. S. legal tender, not to extend to attorneys, executors, sheriffs, or, etc., ...204-205

Index.

GUARDIANS OF THE POOR. See Overseers of the Poor; Poor.

GUEST, HENRY.
Given sole right for five years of manufacturing oil and blubber from materials discovered by him, ... 132
All other persons prohibited, ... 132
Penalty for violation, ... 132
To lodge a sample of materials used with the clerk of assembly, ... 133
And also to publish the same, ... 133

GUN POWDER.
Not more than 25 lbs. to be kept stored in one house in Carlisle, ... 444

H.

HAWKERS.
Male persons capable of bearing arms not to be, or pedlars, ... 21
Penalty for violation, ... 21
Disposition of penalty, ... 22
Prior act repealed, ... 22

HEALTH OFFICER.
Fees of, to be paid in wheat, ... 41

HICKS, GILES.
Divorce of Giles Hicks and Hester Hicks, ... 268
Authorized and empowered to remarry, ... 269

HIGH COURT OF ERRORS AND APPEALS.
Established, ... 52
Jurisdiction of, ...53-54
To be composed of the president of the supreme executive council, the judges of the supreme court, the judge of admiralty and three persons of integrity and ability, ... 54
Appeals from supreme court, court of admiralty and register of wills to lie to, ... 54
Justices of the supreme court or judge of admiralty not to sit in cases heard and determined by them, ...54-55
No appeal to lie to the, unless the matter in controversy exceed the value of four hundred bushels of wheat, ... 55

HIGH COURT OF ERRORS AND APPEALS—Continued.
Appellant to give security in double the amount in dispute, to prosecute his appeal with effect, ... 55
Appellee to have double costs where judgment is affirmed, ... 55
Each party to pay their own costs where the judgment is reversed, .. 55
Depositions taken before the register of wills to be in writing and made part of the record in appeals to the, 56
Where register sends an issue to the common pleas, the facts decided by the verdict of a jury not to be reexamined on appeal, ... 56
Appeal from decree of register concerning validity of a will, etc., not to act as a supersedeas where executor gives security, ... 56
Appeals made before July 4, 1776 to the king of Great Britain in council and not determined may be renewed in the, ... 56
Time and place of holding, ... 57
May compel the attendance of sheriffs, coroners and constables, etc., ... 57
Appointment of clerk and register of, 57
Fees of clerk and register of, ... 57
Time of taking appeals limited to twenty years, ... 57
Except where appellant is a minor, feme covert, non compos mentis or in prison, ... 57
Compensation of judge of admiralty and three extra associate judges,... 58

HIGH SEAS. See Admiralty.

HIGHWAYS. See Public Highways; Streets.
Palmer's Lane in the Northern Liberties, vacated, ... 174
Northern line of Vine street and southern line of Cedar street to be marked out by regulators of Philadelphia City assisted by regulators of the Northern Liberties, ... 487
Expense thereof to be borne proportionately by the said city and district, ...487-488
All streets, etc., in Philadelphia dedicated to public use declared to be highways, ... 489

HIGHWAYS—Continued.

All streets laid out by supreme executive council declared to be highways, ... 489
No length of time to bar the removal of nuisances from public streets,.489-490
Commissioners to remove trees growing in the streets, ... 490
Penalty for obstructing them in so doing, ... 490
Regulations respecting grates over vaults in streets, ... 491

HIGHWAY TAXES.

To be laid and assessed according to state tax, ... 140
Act not to extend to state tax on ready money, ... 140
Nor to prevent appeals or alter mode of collecting same, ... 140
Nor to alter mode of taxation in counties where state tax has not been laid within twelve months, ... 140
Proceedings of appeal from, ...140-141
Tax on real estate transferred to be charged to buyers, ...140-141
Goods of tenant of non-resident owner subject to distress for, ... 141
Distress to be deducted from rent, .. 141
Act not to affect existing contracts between landlord and tenant as to payment of, ... 142
Nor to repeal act for raising additional sum of $5,700,000, ... 142
Compensation of county commissioners and assessors to be satisfied in wheat, ... 142

HORSES.

Auctioneers to keep a register of all horses sold, ... 231-232
Register to be a public record and open for inspection, ... 232
Auctioneers entitled to a fee of two dollars for every inspection of register and six dollars for every copy thereof, ... 232
Register to be given in evidence upon trial respecting property of horse, etc., ... 232
Sale of stolen horses by auctioneers not to be deemed a public sale in market overt so as to change the property thereof, ... 232

HORSE STEALING.

Defined, ... 113
Penalty for first offence, ... 113
Penalty for second offence, ... 113
Horse thief not to be bailed unless by a judge of the supreme court, ... 113
Certain prior acts repealed, ... 113

HORSE THIEF. See Horse Stealing.

HOUSEHOLDERS.

Removing from one township to another not prevented from selling household goods, etc., by public auction, ... 17

I.

IMPARLANCE.

More than one, not allowed, ...137,295,515

IMPORTS. See Tariff.

Supplement to act regulating navigation and trade, ... 418
No goods, wares, merchandise produced or manufactured by Great Britain to be imported into this state, ... 419
All such goods to be confiscated, ... 419
One-half to go to informer and the other half to the commonwealth, .. 419
All actions under act against importers to be brought within six months, ... 419
Proviso as to goods, wares, merchandise taken as prize, ... 419
Such goods, wares and merchandise not to be imported from neutral ports, ... 420
Captain, etc., of vessels to certify that imported goods from neutral ports are not the growth, product, etc., of Great Britain, ... 420
Such goods to be confiscated if captain neglects to produce certificate, ...420-421
Part of prior act regulating navigation and trade repealed, ... 421

IMPOSTS. See Excise.

Duties on imported goods, etc., ... 253
Imported goods together with the casks, etc., to vest in the commonwealth, where naval officer tenders to importer the value of goods and 10 per cent. increase, ... 253

Index. 581

IMPOSTS—Continued.

Importer liable for freight, etc., accruing previous to landing, etc., ... 253

Commonwealth to recover possession of such goods by action of detinue, trover and conversion, or replevin, 253

Naval officer upon due entry of goods, etc., and payment of or securing the duties imposed by act to grant a permit for landing, ...253-254

Where goods, etc., remain in vessel ten days after the arrival thereof, without the duty being paid or secured, master to deliver same to naval officer to be warehoused and kept at owner's risk and expense,.. 254

Naval officer to keep all such goods except they be perishable for three months and then have them appraised and sold at auction, ... 254

Moneys arising therefrom after payment of duty and charges to be lodged with state treasurer for use of owner, ... 254

Masters of ships not to unload without permit, ... 254

Penalty for violation, ... 255

Naval officer, his deputy and assistants to enter vessels and suspected houses in search of concealed goods liable to duty, ... 255

In case of opposition or refusal naval officer to obtain a writ of assistance from two justices of the supreme court or of the peace and break open doors, etc., ... 255

No search to be made of any dwelling until due cause of suspicion be shown to satisfaction of a justice either of the supreme court or of the peace,.. 255

Persons trading in the Delaware and coming into port with goods in vessels liable to duties to comply with provisions of act, ... 255

River vessels not required to pay more than two shillings for exhibiting a manifest of goods liable to duty, .. 255

Master refusing to exhibit manifest to forfeit £1,000, ... 256

Fines, penalties and forfeitures incurred under act, how recoverable, 256

Application of, ... 256

IMPOSTS—Continued.

In actions against goods seized, burden of proof to lie upon claimant instead of prosecutor, ... 256

Claimant to enter security for costs before instituting action, ... 256

Naval officer or person sued under act may plead the general issue and give act and special matter in evidence, 256

Defendant to have treble costs where plaintiff becomes nonsuit, discontinues or has judgment pass against him, ... 256-257

All suits under act to be brought within one year from time of injury, ... 257

Naval officer to keep fair accounts, etc., and pay over balance monthly to state treasurer, ... 257

Naval officer to submit all his books and papers to the inspection of the president and council, ... 257

Naval officer to annually settle his accounts with the auditors of the public accounts, ... 257

Compensation of naval officer, ... 257

Duties to be paid in gold or silver as they passed in 1775 or other money equivalent, ... 257

Fines, penalties, etc., to be levied, satisfied and paid accordingly, ... 257

Bond of naval officer, ... 257

Sureties on such bonds to be approved of by the president and council, .257-258

Bond to be filed and recorded with the secretary of the supreme executive council, ... 258

Naval officer to appoint a deputy,.... 258

Act not to give authority to collect duty on common salt, gunpowder, etc., ... 258

Amount of loans negotiated under resolutions of May 29, 1780 to be set apart in hands of state treasurer subject to orders of supreme executive council for the purpose of discharging such loans together with interest thereon, ... 258

United States authorized to levy five per cent. ad valorem duty on imports, ... 297

Arms, ammunition, clothing, wool cards, cotton cards and wire for making them, and salt, excepted,.. 297

IMPOSTS—Continued.
    Authorities to levy a like duty on prizes and prize goods condemned by the admiralty court, ... 297
    Congress to appoint collectors for collecting same, ... 298
    Moneys arising from such duties to be appropriated in payment of debts, contracted on the faith of the U. S. for the support of the present war,... 298
    Act to continue in force until such debts are fully and finally discharged, ... 298

IMPRISONMENT.
    Penalty for counterfeiting continental loan office certificates, continental bills of exchange or paper money of the United States, ... 16
    Without bail or mainprise, punishment for trustees of the University of Pennsylvania neglect or refusal to comply with judgment of justices to deliver up books, records, etc., to successors, ... 29
    Officers of land office, etc., persisting in refusal to deliver up books, etc., after being convicted in oyer and terminer to suffer, ... 39
    Punishment for contempt before auditors appointed to settle public accounts, ... 77
    Without bail or mainprise, contingent punishment for captains and masters of vessels harboring deserters, ... 223
    Six months, without bail or mainprise, additional penalty imposed upon militia-lieutenant or sub-lieutenant for refusal to deliver up books, to successor, ... 227
    Penalty for second offence in refusing to take bills of credit in payment of necessaries, goods, etc., ... 242
    Persons refusing to accept bills of credit equal in value to gold and silver for goods, etc., for second offence to suffer imprisonment and forfeit one-half of all his or her goods, etc., ... 250
    Part punishment for third offence of counterfeiting brand marks on any cask of flour, ... 294
    Certain insolvents relieved from, ... 421

IMPRISONMENT—Continued.
    Tax collectors in Southwark failing to account for moneys received to be committed without bail or mainprise, ... 516

INDEMNITY.
    Act for procuring an estimate of the damages sustained by the inhabitants of this state from the British troops, ... 530
    County commissioners of every county invaded by British troops to direct assessors to notify inhabitants to furnish accounts of damages, etc., done thereby and transmit the same to commissioners, ... 531
    Assessors to render such accounts where inhabitants refuse, ... 531
    Contents of account, ...531-532
    Commissioners to transmit accounts to supreme executive council, ... 532
    Servants, negroes and mulatto slaves deluded and carried away by British troops to be included in accounts, .. 532
    Charges and expenses of executing act to be defrayed by the commonwealth, ... 533

INDIAN PURCHASE. See Land Office.

INDICTMENT.
    Penalty imposed upon militia-lieutenants, etc., for neglecting or refusing to deliver up books, accounts, etc., to their successors in office to be recovered by bill, plaint, information, action of debt, or, ... 227
    Penalty imposed on surveyor-general for neglect or refusal to make returns of certain lands within a limited time to be recovered by, ... 312

INFORMATION.
    Fines under act for recovering fines, etc., to be recovered by, ... 137
    Certain penalties to be recovered by, ...294-295
    Penalty imposed upon militia-lieutenants, etc., for neglecting or refusing to deliver up books, accounts, etc., to their successors in office to be recovered by indictment, plaint, bill, action of debt, indictment, or, 227

Index.

INFORMATION—Continued.
Penalty imposed on surveyor-general for neglect or refusal to make returns of certain lands within a limited time to be recovered by, .. 312

INFORMER.
Reward of, concerning counterfeiting, etc., of bills of credit, loan office certificates or bills of exchange, ... 15
To receive one-third of seized goods attempted to be unlawfully exported, ... 44
Against quartermaster, foragemaster, etc., purchasing wheat, etc., in violation of act to receive one-half the penalty, ... 182
To be a competent witness in such case, ... 182
Reward of, concerning counterfeiting, etc., of bills of credit, ... 189
To receive one-half the penalty for refusing to take bills of credit in payment of necessaries, goods, etc., 242
To be a competent witness against parties refusing to take bills of credit in payment of necessaries, goods, etc., ... 242
To receive one-half the penalty imposed on persons refusing to accept bills of credit equal in value to gold and silver for goods, etc., ... 250
To be a competent witness in the trial of such cases, ... 251
To receive one-half the penalty imposed for catching fish in the Schuylkill river with brush nets, .. 271
To recover one-half the penalty imposed upon inspectors of flour for trading in flour, ... 294
To receive one-half the penalty for raising or knowingly uttering raised bills of credit, ... 307
To receive one-half the penalty imposed on persons refusing to receive bills of credit in payment of live stock, etc., ... 306
To be a competent witness against such offender, ... 306
To receive one-half the penalty, imposed on surveyor general for neglect or refusal to make returns of certain lands within a limited time, 312

INFORMER—Continued.
To receive one-half of confiscated goods attempted to be imported from Great Britain, ... 419
Informer to receive one-half of penalty for laying party walls in Philadelphia before they are adjusted and marked by the regulators, ... 487

INSOLVENTS.
Certain insolvent debtors relieved from imprisonment by act of assembly,... 421

INSPECTORS OF BREAD. See Bread.
Powers of, ... 290

INSPECTORS OF FLOUR. See Flour.
Fees of, to be paid in wheat, ... 41
Duties of, ... 291
Compensation of, ... 292
Owner of unmerchantable flour to pay fees of, ... 292
To have power to enter on board vessels to search for flour intended to be illegally exported, ... 294
Not to be hindered or prevented from so doing, ... 294
Penalty for violation, ... 294
Not to trade in flour, ... 294
Penalty for violation, ... 294
Penalty, how recoverable, ... 294
Application of penalty, ... 294
Empowered to appoint deputies, ... 294
Oath of deputy, ... 295
Oath to be administered by a justice of the peace, ... 295
Certain persons appointed throughout the different counties, ... 295
Term of office of, ... 295
Vacancies, how filled, ...295-296

INTERNAL REVENUE. See Excise.

INVASIONS. See Militia.

J.

JAILS.
Jails throughout the state vested in the commonwealth, ... 50
Act not to extend to old temporary prison in Bedford, ... 50
Nor to the old jail and workhouse at 3rd and High Sts., Philadelphia, .. 50

JAILS—Continued.
Supreme executive council to sell old jail and workhouse in Philadelphia for benefit of said city and county, 51
Certain prior acts of assembly repealed, ... 52

JUDGMENT.
Defendant to recover treble costs in certain cases where plaintiff becomes nonsuit, suffers a discontinuance or has, pass against him, ...256-7, 324
Plaintiff to be mulcted in treble costs if he wilfully delays, discontinues or has judgment or verdict passed against him, in suits to condemn certain goods as contraband, ...503-504

JUDICIAL NOTICE.
Courts to take, of act pardoning persons engaged in the Wilson riots,... 119

JURORS.
Fees of, to be paid in wheat, ... 40

JUSTICES OF THE PEACE. See Carlisle, Borough of.
Three, and wardens of the city to appoint officer for granting certificates to chimney sweepers in Philadelphia, etc., ... 8
To regulate and fix prices for sweeping chimneys in Philadelphia, etc., 8
To have jurisdiction in cases to recover penalties arising under acts regulating chimney sweepers in Philadelphia, etc., ... 8
To have jurisdiction to recover penalties for unlawfully hawking or peddling where the amount is under 50 £, ... 21
To have jurisdiction of cases to compel trustees of the University of Pennsylvania to deliver up books, records, etc., to successor, ... 29
Any two, upon complaint of the overseers of the poor to levy a tax not exceeding 7s 6d in the £ for the relief of the poor, ... 33
Fees of the, to be paid in wheat, ... 40

JUSTICES OF THE PEACE—Continued.
Where runaway slaves are brought back proof of the absconding to be made before two, ... 72
Party aggrieved by seizure of swine found running at large in Passyunk, etc., to have appeal to, ... 117
Party appealing to forfeit 40s where seizure is confirmed, ... 117
To have jurisdiction in actions of debt under fifty pounds by tenants against their landlord for taxes, ... 141
To issue warrant to constable and two freeholders, to seize provisions where owners refuse to sell the same for the use of the army, ... 177
Justices, sheriffs and civil officers to assist commissioners in carrying out provisions of act for procuring army supplies for 1780, ... 181
Penalty for catching fish with brush nets in the Schuylkill river to be recovered before two, ... 271
Freeholders in each township in Washington county to elect two,.. 274
Of Washington county to hold courts of general quarter sessions, gaol delivery and county courts for holding of pleas, ... 275
To administer oath to deputy flour inspector, ... 295
Scalp of wolves killed for bounty to be taken before, ... 461
Justice upon proof that wolves are killed in same county to grant an order for the bounty on the county treasurer, ... 461
Persons suspected of being escaped prisoners of war to be taken before, 464
Justice to commit guilty party to county jail, and immediately notify the war office, ... 464
To commit persons so arrested where they refuse to give a satisfactory account of themselves until the next quarter sessions, ... 465
To give certificates to persons who apprehend prisoners of war, ... 465

JUSTICES OF THE SUPREME COURT.
See Supreme Court.
Salary of, ... 377

Index. 585

JUT WINDOWS. See Carlisle, Borough of; Nuisances.

LABOR.
Price of day labor to be fixed by general assembly, ... 226
Fines and penalties for neglect of militia duty, and militia bounty to be ascertained and determined for a limited time by such rate, ... 226

LAMPS. See Philadelphia, City of.

LANCASTER, BOROUGH OF.
Military barracks erected in, vested in the commonwealth, ...49-50
The public storehouse and magazine in, vested in the commonwealth, ..49-50

LANDLORD AND TENANT.
Goods of tenant of non-resident owner subject to distress for taxes, ... 141
Distress to be deducted from rent, ... 141
Or be recovered by action of debt, ... 141
Act not to affect existing contracts between, as to payment of taxes, .. 142
Nor to repeal act for raising additional sum of, $5,700,000, ... 142
Tenant where wheat, etc., reserved for rent due is seized in his hands by army commissioners may tender amount received in payment to landlord, ... 178
Such payment to be a good discharge for all rent due, ... 178
Goods and chattels of tenant to be distrained on for war taxes, etc., as well as the owners lands, etc., ... 240
Tenants paying such taxes to reserve them out of rent, etc., or recover the same by action of debt, ... 240
Eighteenth section of act for raising $5,700,000 obliging tenants to pay taxes over and above their rent not extended to taxes under act, ... 241
Tenants to be accountable for sums charged on lands in their possession under act for completing the quota of the federal army, ... 263
Tenants to discount the same out of their rent, etc., ... 263

LANDLORD AND TENANT—Continued.
Goods of tenants, etc., to be subject to distraint for war taxes, ... 331
Tenant to deduct taxes from rent, where he is compelled to pay the same, ... 331
Or recover the same by action at law, 331
Act not to alter any contract between, concerning the payment of taxes, .. 331
Rents, etc., contracted since January 1, 1777, to be sued for and judgment obtained and execution awarded for the interest, damages and costs, etc., ... 339
Tenant in possession to pay certain taxes and deduct the same out of rent, ... 349
Goods of tenant, etc., liable to be distrained for war taxes, ... 391
Tenant to deduct taxes from rent where he is compelled to pay same, 391
Or recover the same by action at law, 391
Act not to alter any contract between, after the payment of taxes, . 391
Goods of tenant, etc., in Carlisle to be liable to distress for taxes, ... 436
Tenants to deduct such tax from their rent or recover it by action, ... 436
Act not to alter any contract between any landlord and tenant respecting the payment of road tax, ... 436

LAND OFFICE.
Established, ... 309
To consist of three persons known as the secretary of the land-office, receiver-general and surveyor-general, 309
Where to be kept, ... 309
Records of the former offices to be removed into and kept by the, ... 309
Officers of the, to be appointed by the general assembly and commissioned by the president, ... 309
Term of office of officers, ... 309
Fees of officers, ...309-310
Officers to appoint deputies, ... 310
Bond of officers, ... 310
Persons entitled to lands within the Indian purchase to have patents on payment of purchase money and interest, etc., ... 310

586 Index.

LAND OFFICE—Continued.
Where surveys have not been returned to the former office an order of survey and patent may be obtained on certain conditions, ... 310-311
Purchase money to be paid to the receiver-general, ... 311
Times of payment, ... 311
Manner and mode of proceeding in case of refusal to pay, ... 311
List of delinquents to be transmitted by the officers of the, to the county commissioners, ... 312
Returns of certain lands to be made within a limited time, ... 312
Penalty on surveyor-general for neglect or refusal to do so, ... 312
Penalty, how recoverable, ... 312
Application of penalty, ... 312
Form of patent, ... 312-313
Patent to be recorded in the rolls office, ... 313
Lands granted to be clear of all reservations and restrictions, etc., ... 313
Act not to extend to grants, etc., issued after July 4, 1776, for lands within ten miles of Philadelphia or within three miles of any county town, ... 313
Nor to any warrant, etc., for more than five hundred acres in one tract, 313
Nor to any lands not within the Indian purchase, ... 313-314
Supplement to act for establishing, .. 349
The word "location" in prior act defined, ... 350
President, etc., to sign warrants of acceptance, re-survey and partition, ... 350
Receiver general to pay all moneys received to the state treasurer once in every month, ... 350
Rate of exchange at which the receiver general is to receive the £5 sterling for every 100 acres of land, fixed, ... 350
President, secretary of the land office, receiver-general, surveyor-general and a member of the supreme executive council constituted a board of property, ... 408-409

LAND OFFICE—Continued.
Board to determine all cases of irregularity, etc., touching escheats, imperfect titles, etc., ... 409
Secretary of the land office to receive caveats and with advice of president appoint days of hearing and grant citations in all such cases, .. 409
No action of board to prevent either of parties from bringing their action at law for the recovery of possession or for damages for waste or trespass, ... 409
Time for payment of purchase money, under act for establishing a land office for office rights, issued before September 10, 1776, extended for two years, ... 409-410
Surveyor-general to receive returns from late deputy-surveyors, ... 410
Fees of receiver-general, ... 410-411
Parts of prior act repealed, ... 411

LAND PATENTS. See Land Office; Patents.

LANDS. See Attainder; Forfeited Estates; Proprietary Estates.
President to set off and sell at public auction enough city lots to redeem residue of bills of credit dated April 29, 1780, ... 318
To take nothing but said bills of credit Spanish milled dollars or gold and silver in payment, ... 318
Purchasers of such lots to have indefeasible estates in fee simple, ... 318
Grantees to plead general issue and give act in evidence in any suits brought for such lands, ... 319
Such evidence to be final and conclusive against any such claimant, .. 319
Just claimants claiming under William Penn, etc., to receive a full equivalent for all lots so sold, ... 319
Proceedings by claimants to secure rights, etc., prescribed, ... 319
Costs to be paid by the state where claimant proves the justness of his cause, ... 320

LANDS—Continued.

Claimants to secure a writ from the prothonotary of the supreme court and have unappropriated lots assigned to them by a jury, ... 320
All claims against the commonwealth to be commenced and prosecuted within a limited time, ... 321
Proviso as to infants, feme coverts, persons non compos mentis, imprisoned or beyond the seas, ... 321
Manner and mode of taking care of city lots and certain lots appurtenant to other towns, etc., prescribed, ... 322
Manner of proceeding where lots are in the possession of private persons, etc., ...322-323
All sums against persons for doing anything in pursuance to act, to be brought within twelve months, ... 323
Defendants in such cases to plead the general issue and give act and special matter in evidence, ... 323
Defendants in such actions to recover treble costs where plaintiff becomes non-suit suffers a discontinuance or has judgment pass against him, .. 324
Penalty for neglect or refusal to perform duties required by act, ... 324
Penalty, how recoverable, ... 324
Application of penalty, ... 324
Certain lands having public buildings erected thereon vested in the United States during the war, ... 46
Act not to justify the taking of lands without consent of owner from and after January 1, 1779, ... 46
United States authorized to remove its buildings from such lands, ... 46
All title and interest of the United States in and to the land to cease and determine, upon removal of buildings, ... 46
Owners of land temporarily vested in and occupied by the United States to be paid a reasonable rent for same, ... 46
Rent to be fixed by three appraisers, 46-47
Appointment of appraisers, ... 47
Upon termination of war United States to remove or pull down and sell all its public buildings which it no longer requires, ... 47

LANDS—Continued.

United States empowered to purchase, hold or convey lands, etc., for maintaining public buildings, ... 47
All such lands, etc., to be subject to the disposition and appropriation of Congress, ... 47
All surveys made of, without license of president and council declared to be void, ... 127
All surveys, made since July 4, 1776 to be filed in the office of the secretary of the supreme executive council or be void, ... 127
Time of filing surveys limited, ...127-128
Time of filing surveys, limited, ... 128
Duration of act, limited, ... 128

LAND TITLES See Proprietary Estates.

House and lots of High, Minor and Sixth Sts., Philadelphia, formerly belonging to Joseph Galloway, traitor, vested in the commonwealth, ...48-50
Certain persons appointed to purchase land and build new court house and prison in Chester county, ... 143
Old court house and prison to be sold at public vendue, ... 143
Certain persons empowered to execute the assurances therefore, ... 143
Messuage and lot of ground in the town of Lisburn, Cumberland county, vested in John Rankin, ... 367
Elizabeth Allen, widow of James Allen, empowered during the minority of her son to grant and convey sundry lots of land in the town of Northampton, county of Northampton, ... 496

LAW OF NATIONS.

Prize causes, etc., to be judged in admiralty by the, and the acts of congress, ...97-98

LEGAL TENDER.

Certain acts of assembly making bills of credit of the U. S. legal tender equal to gold and silver suspended for a limited time, ... 204

Index

LEGAL TENDER—Continued.

	Page
Act not to extend to any debt or contract made after November 1, 1779, upon which suit has actually been brought,	204
Nor to sheriffs, attorneys, executors, guardians, etc.,	204
Act to suspend laws making the bills of credit of the U. S. legal tender, in payment of debts equal to gold and silver, continued,	229
Duration of act limited,	229
Bills of credit emitted by Congress made, equal in value to gold and silver,	241-242
Tender thereof to be good notwithstanding any contracts, etc.,	242
Persons refusing to take bills of credit in payment of debts, etc., to be forever barred from suing for the same,	242
Persons refusing to take bills of credit in payment of goods, etc., to forfeit double the value of article exposed to sale,	242
Application of penalty,	242
For second offence, offender to be imprisoned and forfeit one-half of his or her property,	242
Informer to be a competent witness,	242-243
Act suspending for a limited time the laws making, of the U. S. a legal tender, revived and continued,	248
Act extended to landlords and debtors who have distrained or brought suit for rents or debts due,	248-249
Supplement to act for striking £150,000 in bills of credit for the support of the army, etc.,	249
Bills of credit made, in all contracts, debts, etc.,	249
Value of bills of credit, compared with gold and silver,	249-250
Persons refusing to accept bills of credit in payment of any debt, contract, etc., to be forever barred from suing for same,	250
Persons not to refuse to accept bills of credit equal in value to gold and silver for goods, etc.,	250
Offenders to forfeit double the value of article so exposed to sale,	250
Application of penalty,	250

LEGAL TENDER—Continued.

	Page
For second offence offender to suffer imprisonment and forfeit one-half of all his or her goods, etc.,	250
Informer against such offender to be a competent witness,	251
Bills of credit received by public agents for any taxes or public dues, etc., to be accounted for at the same rate as received,	251
Rate of exchange between continental currency and bills of credit fixed,	251
Such rate to be continued until February 1, 1781,	251
Supreme executive council to then publish rate of exchange between specie and continental money monthly,	251
Such rate to be the rate between continental money and bills of credit,	251
Acts of assembly making bills of credit, suspended,	266
Act not to extend to sheriffs, attorneys, executors, etc., who have received money in legal authority in right of another,	266
Act not to prevent bills of credit from being of the same value in payment of taxes, etc., as the bills of credit of the U. S. issued prior to March 1, 1780,	266
Debts and contracts entered into and made between January 1, 1777 and March 1, 1781, to be settled according to a scale of depreciation,	284
Proviso clauses in suspension acts of May 31, 1780, Sept. 22, 1780, and Feb. 20, 1781, repealed,	284
Mode of settlement where parties cannot agree,	285
Auditors to be appointed to hear and examine the parties and adjust the controversies,	285
Auditors not to reduce payments made in current money,	285
Where tender has been made the credit or to be paid only the value of his debt reduced to specie at the time of tender,	285
Debtor prevented from paying by creditor absconding, etc., to have benefit of legal tender,	285

Index. 589

LEGAL TENDER—Continued.
Auditors report to have the force of a verdict, etc., ... 286
Scale of depreciation, ... 286
Supplement to act for the more easy recovery of small debts, repealed,... 287
Act for limitation of actions suspended during the close of courts of justice and the time of any suspension acts, ... 286
Certain war taxes to be paid in gold or silver only, ... 335
Proviso as to persons who have taken the oath of allegiance to this state, 335-336
Certain bills of credit declared to be,... 305
All laws declaring bills of credit to be legal tender, repealed, ... 337
Parts of such acts imposing penalties for refusal to accept bills of credit in payment of debts, etc., repealed, 337-338
Repeal not to extend to bills of credit emitted under acts of March 25, 1780, and April 7, 1781, ... 338
Such bills to be received in payment of all lands sold by the state excepting forfeited estates only, ... 336
Act not to affect any tender which has already been duly made, ... 338
Debts, etc., contracted since January 1, 1777 and not satisfied or discharged to be paid in the particular money, etc., specified in the contract, ... 338
Rents, etc., contracted before January 1, 1777 to be sued for and judgment obtained and execution awarded for the interest, damages and costs, etc., ... 339
Execution not to issue for the principal for two years or until permission be given by act of assembly,... 339
Interest on such judgments to be paid annually, ... 340
Defendants not having sufficient real estate to satisfy judgment to give security for the same before departing from the commonwealth, ... 340
Upon neglect or refusal to give security court to award execution for the principal as well as the interest, etc., ... 340

LEGAL TENDER—Continued.
Debts exceeding £50 contracted before January 1, 1777 not to be sued for in less than six months after passing of act, ... 340
Proviso where delay will cause creditor to lose debt, ... 340
Act not to extend to revived debts which were on January 1, 1776 barred by the act for the limitation of actions, ... 340
Debts, etc., not barred at the time not to be now barred until two years after passage of act, ... 341
Agents, factors, etc., receiving money and applying it to private use to account to their principal for as much gold and silver as the bills of credit so received were worth at the time of application, ... 341
Agents, factors, etc., to render an account under oath of the profit or loss made on such moneys, ... 342
Principal to obtain benefit of profit,... 342
Agents, etc., refusing to make such oath to account for money the same as if applied to private use, ... 342
Fees of officers and fines incurred under act to be paid in gold and silver, ... 342
All fines imposed by acts of assembly to be recovered in gold, etc., ... 343
All debts and contracts entered into after March 1, 1781 to be discharged according to their nature, ... 343
Contracts for old continental currency, however, to be liquidated and paid at specie value, ... 343
Act not to prevent new continental bills of credit from being received in payment of taxes laid under act of December 18, 1780, ... 344
Certain war taxes to be paid in gold or silver only, ... 399

LEVIES. See County Rates and Levies.

LICENSES. See Tavern Licenses.
Of auctioneer in Philadelphia to sell damaged and shipwrecked goods, .. 82

LIEUTENANTS. See Militia; Pennsylvania Volunteers.

Index.

LIGHTING. See Philadelphia, City of.

LIGHT HORSE. See Militia.

LIMITATION OF ACTIONS.
Suits against persons making seizure of vessels laden with exports to be brought within three months, ... 45
Suits on bonds, given by masters of ships, etc., for faithful compliance with provisions of act permitting the exportation of flour by sea under certain restrictions to be brought within two years, ... 245
All suits under act for an impost on goods, etc., to be brought within one year from time of injury, ... 257
Act for, suspended for a limited time, 288
All claims against the commonwealth for things done under act for the better support of the public credit by an immediate sale of the lands, etc., to be commenced within a limited time, ... 321
All suits against persons for doing anything in pursuance to act to be brought within twelve months, ... 323
Debts exceeding £50 contracted before January 1, 1777 not to be sued for in less than six months after passing of act, ... 340
Proviso where delay will cause creditor to lose debt, ... 340
Act not to extend to revived debts which were on January 1, 1776, barred by the act for the, ... 340
Debts, etc., not barred at that time not to be now barred until two years after passage of act, ... 341
All actions against the importers for importing goods from Great Britain to be brought within six months, .. 419
All prosecutions for laying foundations of party walls in Philadelphia before the adjustment and marking of the regulators to be brought within one year, ... 487
All suits for things done in pursuance of act for the more effectual suppression of all intercourse and commerce with the enemies of the U. S. to brought within six months, ... 503

LIQUORS. See Excise.
Excise on, after May 1, 1780 to be paid in wheat in like manner as fees of officers, ... 130
Act to permit making of whiskey, etc., from rye, etc., under certain restrictions, etc., repealed, ... 175-176

LISBURN.
Messuage and lot of ground in the town of, Cumberland county, vested in John Rankin, ... 367

LOAN OFFICE.
Penalty for counterfeiting or forging, etc., the certificates of the, ... 15-16
Mortgages to be discharged by one trustee of the, ... 109

LOAN OFFICE CERTIFICATES.
Declaration in behalf of this state respecting continental bills of credit, and, ... 188

LOYALISTS. See Forfeited Estates.

M.

MAINPRISE. See Bail.

MANSLAUGHTER.
Forfeiture for, removed, ... 111
Imprisonment and fine added, ... 111

MANUFACTURES.
Act to permit making of, whiskey, etc., from rye, etc., under certain restrictions, etc., repealed, ... 175-176

MARKET-HOUSES.
Wardens of Philadelphia to let ferries, wharves, public landing places and, ... 201
Treasurer of wardens and assessors to receive rents from ferries, wharves, public landing places and, ... 201
Clerk of the market to collect rent from market-houses, etc., and pay the same over to the treasurer of the wardens and assessors, ... 201

MARKET OVERT.
Sale of stolen horses by auctioneers not to be deemed a public sale in, so as to change the property thereof, 232

Index. 591

MARKETS.
Burgesses, etc., of Carlisle, to have and keep two markets in each week and two fairs in each year, ... 428

MARINERS.
And seamen not to be subject to penalties under militia act, ... 159

MARSHALL. See Admiralty.
Of the court of admiralty not to sell by public auction except prize ships, etc., and perishable goods, ...19-20
To make out an inventory of prizes and have them appraised, ... 20
Inventory and appraisement to be filed with the register of the court of admiralty, ... 20
If no appeal be entered execution to issue upon entry of security, ... 20
Mode of distributing shares of prizes, 20
Compensation of marshall, ... 21
Compensation of appraisers, ... 21

MARSH LANDS. See Schuylkill Point Meadows.

MASTER OF THE ROLLS.
Fees of the, to be paid in wheat, ... 40

MEADOW LANDS. See Schuylkill Point Meadows; State Island.

MEMBERS OF ASSEMBLY. See General Assembly.
Wages of, ... 378
Mileage of, ... 378

MEMBERS OF CONGRESS.
Wages of, ... 377
Mileage of, ... 378

MEMBERS OF SUPREME EXECUTIVE COUNCIL.
Wages of, ... 377
Mileage of, ... 378

MIDDLE FERRY ON SCHUYLKILL. See Ferries.

MIDDLINGS.
Intended for exportation to be branded as such, ... 380

MILEAGE.
Mileage of members of congress, ... 377
Of members of the supreme executive council, ... 377

MILEAGE—Continued.
Of speaker of the house, ... 377
Of members of the assembly, ... 378
Of clerks of the assembly, ... 378
Of sergeant at arms of the assembly, 378
Of door-keeper, ... 378
Fees and, of sheriff, coroner or other process server and witnesses, ... 454
Of persons apprehending prisoners of war, ... 466

MILITIA. See Pensions; Pennsylvania Line.
Act for making more equal the burden of the public defence and for filling the quota of troops, etc., partly repealed, ... 31
President in council to appoint a lieutenant in each county, ... 145
Also sub-lieutenants, ... 145
Lieutenants to give bond in the sum of 20,000 £ for faithful discharge of duties, ... 145
Lieutenant by warrant to commanding officer to annually secure a list of all male white inhabitants between 18 and 53, ... 146
Delegates in Congress, etc., excepted, 146
Militia to be divided and classed by the lieutenants, ...146-147
Of Northern Liberties, Southwark, Moyamensing and Passyunk united to city of Philadelphia, ... 147
Of Philadelphia to form a battalion of artillery, ...147-148
Lieutenants of each county to form a corps of light horse, ... 148
Light horse troop of Philadelphia city limited to 50 privates, ... 148
Light horseman appointed a commissioned officer to vacate his place in the horse, ... 149
All horses to be appraised before going into actual service, ... 149
Owner to recover value where horses killed, etc., ... 149
Election of commanding officers of the, 149
Qualification of officers, ... 150
Names of persons elected to be sent to president and council, ... 150
Elections for officers in the light horse to be made in same manner as in the infantry, ... 150

Index.

MILITIA—Continued.
   Lieutenant to appoint commanding officers where battalion, etc., neglects or refuses to elect, ... 150
   Appointment to be approved by the supreme executive council, ... 150
   Three sergeants, three corporals, one drummer and fifer to be appointed by commissioned officers of each company, ... 151
   Officers, etc., not reelected to deliver up arms, etc., ... 151
   One chaplain, one quartermaster, one sergeant, one adjutant, one quartermaster sergeant, one sergeant major and one drum and fife major to be appointed by field officers of each battalion, ... 151
   Pay of adjutant, quartermaster sergeant, drummer and fifer, ... 151
   Lieutenants to reimburse captains, etc., for moneys paid to drummers and fifers, ... 152
   Commissioned officers of each company to appoint an almoner, ... 152
   Almoner to provide for families of poor militia men, ... 152
   Lieutenants and sub-lieutenants to render accounts and make returns to supreme executive council, ... 152
   Penalty for neglect, ... 153
   Rank and precedence of the officers of the city and several counties, ... 153
   Exercise days of the, and duties connected therewith, ... 153-154
   Absentees to be noted and fined, ...154-155
   Fines, how recoverable, ... 155
   Fines to be paid to state treasurer and kept as a fund, ... 156
   Fund to be used in relieving suffering in the, ... 156
   Fines to be kept separate, ... 156
   Calling out of, in case of invasion or rebellion, ... 156
   Order of calling out the different classes, ... 156
   Time of service, ... 157
   Pay of private to be equal to a day's labor, ... 158
   Price of day's labor to be fixed by quarter sessions and become the rate for payments of fines, ... 158

MILITIA—Continued.
   Justices of quarter sessions to send certificate of price fixed to the lieutenants, ... 158
   Militia men to receive three days written notice of their being called out, 158
   Penalty for refusing to perform tour of duty, ... 158
   Masters, fathers ,etc., to be accountable for the fines of minors and apprentices, ... 159
   Mariners and seamen not to be subject to penalties prescribed by act, 159
   While in service of the United States to be subject to the rules of the Federal Army, ... 159
   Offences, however, to be tried by court martial of this state, ... 159
   President of the supreme executive council empowered to pardon, etc., person convicted under act, ... 159
   Fine for non-attendance, how recoverable, ...159-160
   Aggrieved party to have appeal to the common pleas, ... 160
   Verdict of common pleas to be conclusive, ... 160
   Deed for all real estate so sold to be made by sheriff, ... 160
   No militia man to leave his company, 160
   Penalty for violation, ... 160
   Militia man removing from one battalion to another to obtain certificate of discharge and produce it to the commanding officer where he next settles, ...160-161
   Penalty for neglect or refusal, ... 161
   Enrolled militia men to prove their age, ... 161
   Persons having estates to pay 15s in every £100 over and above their other fines for non-attendance, ... 161
   Provision for ascertaining amount of such estates, ... 162
   Pay of lieutenants and sub-lieutenant, ... 162
   Provision for the hiring of substitutes, 162
   Lieutenant and two free-holders to hear appeals of parties aggrieved by things done in pursuance of act, .. 163
   Oath of freeholders, ... 163

MILITIA—Continued.

Penalty for buying or selling arms, etc., 163
Deserters from the enemy not to be enrolled, ... 164
Nor to be subject to fine for not serving in the, ... 164
Civil process not to be served on officers or privates while going to or returning from review, ... 164
Moneys arising from act to be used for relief of disabled militia men, their widows and children, ...164-165
Provision for support of families of militia men killed in service, ...165-166
Relief not to exceed half pay of deceased officer or private, ... 166
Penalty for misbehavior of officers while on parade, ... 166
Penalty for officers neglecting to give orders for assemblying battalion, or company, ...166-167
Penalty for captains neglecting to make out a list of persons noticed to perform tour of duty, ... 167
Rules and regulations, ...167-169
Makeup of general court martial, ... 167
Make up of regimental court martial, 167
Convictions to be had on two-thirds vote, ... 167
Witnesses to be examined on oath by president of court martial, ... 168
Oath of members of court martial, .. 168
By whom administered, ... 168
Members of the, called as witnesses and refusing to give evidence to be censured or fined, ... 168
Officer or private charged with transgressing rules to be relieved until trial, ... 168
Officer or private aggrieved by commanding officer to complain to lieutenant, ... 168
Lieutenant to summon regimental court martial, ... 168
Punishment by court martial limited to, degrading, cashiering or fining, 168
Inferior officer or private injured by captain, etc., to complain to commanding officer, ... 168

38—X

MILITIA—Continued.

Commanding officer to summon regimental court martial, ... 168
Commanding officer empowered to pardon persons court martialed, ... 169
Militia in exercising not to be kept under arms more than six hours per day, ... 169
Not to meet at taverns on days of exercise, ... 169
Fines, how recoverable, ... 169
Payment for services where no special recompense is provided, ... 170
To assist in collecting fines when necessary, ... 170
Penalty for neglect or refusal, ... 170
Provision for proceedings against deserters, ... 170
All suits under act to be brought in the county where the offence is committed, ... 170
Defendants may plead general issue and give act and special matter in evidence, ...170-171
Defendant to have treble costs where plaintiff becomes nonsuit, discontinues or has judgment pass against him, ... 171
Fines, how recoverable, ... 171
To be collected by distress, ... 171
Aggrieved parties to have appeal to common pleas, ... 171
Verdict of common pleas to be conclusive, ... 172
Former acts of assembly repealed,... 172
Repeal not to alter powers, etc., of present lieutenant, etc., ... 172
Retiring lieutenant to deliver to successor under oath an account of all outstanding fines, etc., ... 173
Each company of the, to furnish one man for the formation of the Pennsylvania Volunteers, ... 191
Proceedings where militia company fails or neglects to furnish volunteer, ... 193
Captains of militia companies to notify companies to meet and carry act into effect, ... 193
Penalty for neglect or refusal, ... 193

MILITIA—Continued. Page.
  Penalty for lieutenant or sub-lieutenant neglecting to perform duty required by act, ... 194
  Each company to furnish two men for the Pennsylvania Volunteers instead of one, ... 195
  Penalty for neglect or refusal to collect militia fines, ... 197-198
  Supplement to act for the regulation of the, ... 225
  Price of day labor to be fixed by general assembly, ... 226
  Fines and penalties for neglect of militia duty, and militia bounty to be determined for a limited time by such rate, ... 226
  Act not to be construed to alter, mitigate or discharge any fine or penalty already accrued, ... 226
  Authority of the quarter sessions under prior act, continued, ... 226
  Lieutenant or sub-lieutenant neglecting or refusing to deliver up, to their successors in office, books, accounts, etc., to forfeit 10,000 £, ... 227
  Forfeiture to be recovered by indictment, bill, plaint, information or account of debt, ... 227
  Application of the penalty, ... 227
  Upon second refusal offender to suffer additional penalty of six months imprisonment without bail or mainprise, ... 227
  Parts of prior act repealed, ... 227
  Act providing for the present defense of this state, ... 361
  President to call out enough wagons to transport baggage and stores of troops called out for the defense of the state, ... 61
  County wagon masters and constables to perform same duties as required under former wagon laws, ... 361
  Compensation of wagon masters, ... 362
  President to seize and impress wagons, etc., if sufficient number cannot be procured in manner prescribed by act, ... 362
  President to seize and impress arms, ammunition, stores, etc., when necessary and apply the same to public use, ... 362

MILITIA—Continued. Page
  Seizure to be certified and the value to be ascertained specie, ... 362
  President to billet and quarter troops upon public or private houses, ... 362
  President authorized to call out all of the militia without respect to classes, ... 363
  Person neglecting or refusing to perform tour of militia duty on call of president to be fined, ... 363
  President authorized to draw upon the treasury for necessary money to procure arms and ammunition, etc., .. 363
  President authorized to impress horses and wagons, etc., for the removal of families and property of inhabitants of Philadelphia, Northern Liberties, and Southwark who are in actual service against the enemy, ... 363
  Duration of act limited, ... 364
  One extra company of the, to be raised for the defense of the frontiers of the state, ... 373
  To be clothed, etc., by and be under the direction of the supreme executive council, ... 373
  Supreme executive council to appoint and commission the officers of said company, ... 373
  Officers to be taken from those of the Pennsylvania line who are on half pay, ... 374
  Compensation of recruits, ... 374
  Inhabitants waylaying and annoying the enemy in their incursions and depredations to be entitled to militia pay and rations, ... 374
  Supreme executive council to draw on the treasury for such necessary sums, ... 374
  Forces raised under act to be bound by the rules and regulations of the army of the United States, ...374-375
  Supreme executive council empowered to order all of troops or any expedition against the savages or other enemies on the frontiers of the state, 375
  Taxes due by persons driven from their homes to be levied proportionately on the other parts of the counties, ... 375

MILITIA—Continued.

County commissioners authorized to exonerate from taxation inhabitants who have been so driven off and distressed by the enemy, ... 375
Also to exonerate those inhabitants who stay on the frontiers for the purpose of its defence, ... 376
Commissioners to transmit to general Assembly a list of the names, etc., of the persons so exonerated, ... 376

MILLERS. See Flour.

MONONGAHELA RIVER.

Ferries established on, ... 471
Declared to be a public highway, ... 472

MONOPOLIES.

Henry Guest given sole right for 5 years of manufacturing oil and blubber in manner discovered by him, .. 132
All other persons prohibited, ... 132
Penalty for violation, ... 132
Sample of materials used to be lodged with clerk of assembly, ... 133
Same to be also published, ... 133

MOYAMENSING.

Act to prevent trespassing upon unenclosed grounds in, Passyunk, Northern Liberties, Germantown, and, revived, ... 116
Penalty for suffering beasts to run at large in, increased, ... 116
Running at large of swine in, prohibited, ... 116
Such swine to be forfeited, ... 116
Disposition of forfeiture, ...116-117
Person aggrieved by seizure of swine to have appeal to justice of the peace, ... 117
Party appealing to forfeit 40s where seizure is confirmed, ... 117
Militia of Southwark, Passyunk, The Northern Liberties and, united to the city of Philadelphia, ... 147
Act to prevent the trespassing upon the unenclosed grounds of Passyunk, Northern Liberties, Germantown, Bristol, and, revived, ... 283

MOYAMENSING—Continued.

Corporation of contributors, etc., neglecting to meet annually and choose 12 managers, overseers of the poor of Philadelphia, Southwark, Moyamensing and the Northern Liberties to be vested with their powers, etc., 402
Overseers of the Poor incorporated under the name of "The Guardians of the Poor of the City of Philadelphia," 402
To appoint half-yearly six of their number to superintend the almshouse and house of employment, etc., ... 403
Such six overseers to be exempt from all other duties as overseers, ... 403
Any overseer with the consent of one justice of the peace to afford relief to the sudden necessity of any poor person not exceeding 3£ in three months, ... 403
One-half of overseers not to continue in office more than six months and their successors to be appointed half-yearly, ... 403
Penalty for neglect of overseers to serve, ... 404
Overseers with the approbation of two justices of the peace to bind out poor disorderly persons, ... 404
Persons over forty years or married exempted, ... 404
Term of binding not to exceed 3 years, ...404-405
Part of prior act for the relief of the poor made perpetual, ... 405
Authority of mayor, recorder and aldermen of Philadelphia under such act vested in the justices of the peace of said city, ... 405
Act for the better relief of the poor, etc., repealed, ... 405
Act for the relief of the poor repealed, 405
Act for the better employment of the poor incorporating Passyunk with Philadelphia, Southwark, Moyamensing and Northern Liberties repealed, ...405-406

MULATTOES. See Slavery.

And negroes taken as prize upon the sea not to be sold, ... 101

MULATTOES—Continued.
To be appraised and delivered to captors, ... 101

MUTILATION.
Part punishment for raising or knowingly uttering raised bills of credit, 307

N.

NAVAL OFFICER.
Fees of, to be paid in wheat, ... 40
To receive one-third of seized goods attempted to be unlawfully exported, 44
Flour of wheat not to be laden on board any vessel until master of such vessel delivers to, a memorial in writing, ... 245
Contents of memorial, ... 245
Naval officer to take bond in double the value of flour to be shipped for faithful compliance of master with provisions of act, ... 245
To then grant permit for lading of same, ... 245
Ship containing flour not to be cleared until master produce to naval officer a certificate from the proper officer acknowledging the receipt or tender of flour for the public use equal to one-third of cargo, ... 246
Act not to discharge master of ship from delivering to naval officer a true manifest of the lading thereof,. 246
Duties on imported goods, etc., ... 253
Imported goods together with the casks, etc., to vest in the commonwealth where naval officer tenders to importer the value of the goods and 10 per cent. increase, ... 253
Importer liable for freight, etc., accruing previous to landing, etc., ... 253
Commonwealth to recover possession of such goods, by action of detinue, trover and conversion, or replevin, 253
Naval officer upon due entry of goods, etc., and payment of or securing the duties imposed by act to grant a permit for landing, ...253-254
Where goods, etc., remain in vessel ten days after the arrival thereof, without the duty being paid or secured, master to deliver same to naval officer to be warehoused and kept at owner's risk and expense, .. 254

NAVAL OFFICER—Continued.
Moneys arising therefrom after payment of duty and charges to be lodged with state treasurer for use of owner, ... 254
Masters of ships not to unload without permit, ... 254
Penalty for violation, ... 255
Naval officer his deputy and assistants, to enter vessels and suspected houses in search of concealed goods liable to duty, ... 255
In case of opposition or refusal naval officer to obtain a writ of assistance from two justices of the supreme court and break open doors, etc.,.. 255
Persons trading in the Delaware and coming into port with goods in vessels liable to duties to comply with provisions of act, ... 255
River vessels not required to pay more than two shillings for exhibiting a manifest of goods liable to duty, .. 255
Master refusing to exhibit manifest to forfeit £1,000, ... 256
Fines, penalties and forfeitures incurred under act, how recoverable, 256
Application of, ... 256
In actions against goods seized, burden of proof to lie upon claimant instead of prosecutor, ... 256
Claimant to enter security for costs before instituting action, ... 256
Naval officer or person sued under act may plead the general issue and give act and special matter in evidence, 256
Defendant to have treble costs where plaintiff becomes nonsuit, discontinued or has judgment pass against him, ...256-257
All suits under act to be brought within one year from time of injury, ... 257
To keep fair accounts, etc., and pay over balance monthly to state treasurer, ... 257
To submit all books and papers to the inspection of the president and council, ... 257
To annually settle his accounts with the auditors of the public accounts, 257
Compensation of, ... 257

Index. 597

NAVAL OFFICER—Continued.
  Duties to be paid in gold or silver as they passed in 1775 or other money equivalent, ... 257
  Fines, penalties, etc., to be levied, satisfied and paid accordingly, ... 257
  Bond of, ... 257
  Sureties on such bond to be approved of by the president and council, ... 258
  Bond to be filed, and recorded with the secretary of the supreme executive council, ... 258
  To appoint a deputy, ... 258
  Act not to give authority to collect duty on common salt, gunpowder, etc., ... 258
  Amount of loans negotiated under resolutions of May 29, 1780, to be set apart in hands of state treasurer subject to orders of supreme executive council, for the purpose of discharging such loans with interest thereon, ... 258

NAVIGATION. See Delaware River; Delaware Bay.
  Supplement to act regulating navigation and trade, ... 418
  No goods, wares, merchandise produced or manufactured by Great Britain to be imported into this state,.. 419
  All such goods to be confiscated, ... 419
  One-half to go to informer and the other half to the commonwealth, .. 419
  All actions under act against importers to be brought within six months, ... 419
  Proviso as to goods, wares, merchandise taken as prize, ... 419
  Such goods, wares and merchandise not to be imported from neutral ports, ... 420
  Captain, etc., of vessels to certify that imported goods from neutral ports are not the growth, product, etc., of Great Britain, ... 420
  Such goods to be confiscated if captain neglects to produce certificate, ...420-421
  Part of prior act regulating navigation and trade repealed, ... 421

NAVIGATION—Continued.
  Supplement to act for guarding and defending the navigation in the Delaware river and bay, ... 493
  Commissioners appointed under prior act authorized to borrow 20,000 £ additional for carrying it into execution, ... 494
  State share of prize money appropriated for raising and supporting armament for the defense of the navigation in the Delaware river, etc., ...494-495

NAVY. See Pensions.
  Officers, seamen and marines to receive like allowances of pensions as the army, ...63-64
  Widows of officers of the, etc., also entitled, ... 64

NEGROES. See Slaves.
  And mulattoes taken as prize upon the sea not to be sold, ... 101
  To be appraised and delivered to captors, ... 101

NETS. See Brush Nets.
  Limitations and restrictions respecting the catching of shad by seines or nets in the Schuylkill river, ... 271

NEWSPAPERS.
  Rates for sweeping chimneys in Philadelphia, etc., to be published in one or more, ... 8
  Auditors appointed to settle public accounts to give public notice of their appointment by advertisement in some newspaper printed in Philadelphia, ... 76
  Contents of such notice, ... 76
  Register of admiralty to give notice in the, of the day set for trial of prize causes, etc., ... 99
  Supreme executive council after February 1, 1781, to publish monthly in the Philadelphia English and German, the rate of exchange between specie and continental money, ... 251
  Ten days' public notice to be given of the sale of goods condemned as contraband, if the value thereof be under 50 £, ... 502

598 *Index.*

NEWSPAPERS—Continued.
Like notice to be also inserted in one of the Philadelphia weekly newspapers, if the value exceeds 50£, .. 503

NIGHTLY WATCH. See Philadelphia, City of.

NON OBSTANTE CLAUSE.
Use of, ...172, 243, 269

NON-SUIT.
Defendant to have treble costs in certain suits, if plaintiff becomes, suffers a discontinuance, or has judgment passed against him,.256, 257, 324, 448

NORTHAMPTON COUNTY.
Act for relief of the inhabitants of Bedford, Northumberland, Westmoreland and, ... 114
County commissioners and assessors to lay state taxes by former returns, 114
Commissioners and assessors to exonerate from taxes persons driven off from their settlements by the enemy, ... 114
To transmit to the general assembly a list of the persons so exonerated,. 115
Deficiencies arising in raising quota of, to be made good out of state taxes, ... 115
Elizabeth Allen, widow of James Allen, empowered during the minority of her son to grant and convey sundry lots of land in the town of Northampton, county of Northampton, ... 496

NORTHAMPTON TOWNSHIP.
The Trustees of the Dutch Reformed Church in Northampton and Southampton, in the county of Bucks, incorporated, ... 526

NORTHERN LIBERTIES.
Chimney sweepers in, to register and obtain a certificate, ... 5-6
Penalty for neglect or refusal, ... 6
To wear the number contained in their certificate on the front of their caps, 6
Penalty for neglect or refusal, ... 6
Chimney sweepers in, to sweep chimneys within 48 hours after application, ... 7

NORTHERN LIBERTIES—Continued.
Penalty for neglect or refusal, ... 7
Rates allowed for sweeping chimneys, 7
Penalty on persons whose unswept chimneys in, take fire and blaze out at the top, ... 7
Penalty where chimneys take fire and blaze out at the top within one month from sweeping, ... 7
Chimney sweepers in, to pay officer 10s per day for granting certificate, etc., ... 7
Officer for granting certificates to chimney sweepers in, to be appointed by warden and three justices, .. 8
Rates for sweeping chimneys in, to be regulated and fixed by justices of the peace, ... 8
Rates to be published in one or more newspapers, ... 8
Penalties arising under act to be paid equally to overseers of the poor and officer for granting certificates, ... 8
Provisions of act limited to within one mile of the bounds of Philadelphia city, ... 8
Military barracks erected in the city of Philadelphia and the, vested in the commonwealth, ... 49
Act to prevent trespassing upon unenclosed grounds in Moyamensing, Passyunk, Germantown, and, revived, ... 116
Penalty for suffering beasts to run at large in, increased, ... 116
Running at large of swine in, prohibited, ... 116
Such swine to be forfeited, ... 116
Disposition of forfeiture, ...116-117
Person aggrieved by seizure of swine to have appeal to justice of the peace, ... 117
Party appealing to forfeit 40s where seizure is confirmed, ... 117
Militia of Southwark, Moyamensing, Passyunk, and the, united to the city of Philadelphia, ... 147
Palmer's Lane in the, vacated, ... 174
Act to prevent the trespassing upon the unenclosed grounds of Passyunk, Moyamensing, Germantown, Bristol and, revived, ... 283

NORTHERN LIBERTIES—Continued.

Corporation of contributors, etc., neglecting to meet annually and choose 12 managers; overseers of the poor of Philadelphia, Southwark, Moyamensing and the Northern Liberties to be vested with their powers, etc., 402

Overseers of the poor incorporated under the name of "The Guardians of the Poor of the City of Philadelphia," 402

To appoint half-yearly six of their number to superintendent the almshouse and house of employment, etc., 403

Such six overseers to be exempt from all other duties as overseers, ... 403

Any overseer with the consent of one justice of the peace to afford relief to the sudden necessity of any poor person not exceeding £2 in three months, ... 403

One-half of overseers not to continue in office more than six months and their successors to be appointed half-yearly, ... 403

Penalty for neglect of overseers to serve, ... 404

Overseers with the approbation of two justices of the peace to bind out poor disorderly persons, ... 404

Persons over forty years or married exempted, ... 404

Term of binding not to exceed 3 years, ...404-405

Part of prior act for the relief of the poor made perpetual, ... 405

Authority of mayor, recorder and aldermen of Philadelphia under such act vested in the justices of the peace of said city, ... 405

Act for the better relief of the poor, etc., repealed, ... 405

Act for the relief of the poor repealed,, 405

Act for the better employment of the poor incorporating Passyunk with Philadelphia, Southwark, Moyamensing and Northern Liberties repealed, ...405-406

Fees of auctioneers in Philadelphia, Northern Liberties and Southwark, 468,469

NORTHERN LIBERTIES—Continued.

Auctioneers to demand and receive an additional 1 per cent. for the use of the commonwealth, ... 469

Auctioneers bond to the president to be security for the proper application of the same, ... 469

Revenue arising from auctions in Philadelphia, Northern Liberties and Southwark appropriated to the support of government and the administration of justice, ...469,470

NORTHUMBERLAND COUNTY.

Act for the relief of the inhabitants of Northampton, Bedford, Westmoreland and, ... 114

County commissioners and assessors to lay state taxes by former returns, 114

Commissioners and assessors to exonerate from taxes persons driven off from their settlements by the enemy, ... 114

To transmit to the general assembly a list of the persons so exonerated,.. 115

Deficiencies arising in raising quota of, to be made good out of state taxes, ... 115

NOTARY PUBLIC.

Fees of, to be paid in wheat, ... 41

NUISANCES. See Carlisle, Borough of.

Burgesses of Carlisle to remove all nuisances in highways, etc., ... 427

Buildings erected encroaching on highways in Carlisle prior to its incorporation as a borough not to be deemed nuisances, ... 430

Persons in Carlisle not to cast dirt, earth, etc., from their improvements into the public streets without removing same, ... 440

Nor to cast shavings, ashes, etc., on any pavement or into any public street, ... 441

Distillers, soap-boilers and tallowchandlers not to discharge foul liquor so as to run through the streets of Carlisle, nor to collect and keep putrid fat, etc., ...441-442

Butchers in Carlisle not to keep garbage or filth at or near Carlisle, ... 442

Carrion, filth, etc., not to be left on unenclosed ground, ... 442

NUISANCES—Continued.
 No length of time to bar the removal of nuisances from public streets in Philadelphia, ...489-490
 Commissioners to remove trees growing in the streets, ... 490
 Penalty for obstructing them in so doing, ... 490
 Regulations respecting grates over vaults in the streets of Philadelphia, ... 491
 Part of act directing the removal of trees out of the streets, etc., of Philadelphia, repealed, ... 511

O.

OATHS.
 Of the trustees, etc., of the University of the state of Pennsylvania,...26-27
 Form of in returning estreats, ... 136
 Of members of court martial, ... 168
 By whom administered, ... 168
 Of commissioners appointed to procure this state's quota of army provisions for 1780, ... 177
 Of election officers in Washington county, ... 275
 Of deputy flour inspector, ... 295
 To be administered by a justice of the peace, ... 295
 Of signers of bills of credit, ... 304
 Of county commissioners, ... 332
 Of assessors, ... 332
 Of office of burgess, constable and town clerk of the borough of Carlisle, ... 428
 Of comptroller general, ... 456

OFFICERS. See Militia; Pennsylvania Line; Pennsylvania Volunteers.
 Serving in the Pennsylvania Volunteers to receive same pay as troops in the Federal Army, ... 193
 Exempted from taxation during term of service, ... 194

OIL.
 Henry Guest given sole right for 5 years of manufacturing, and blubber from materials discovered by him,... 132
 All other persons prohibited, ... 132
 Penalty for violation, ... 132
 Sample of materials used to be lodged with the clerk of assembly, ... 133
 Same to be also published, ... 133

ONUS PROBANDI. See Burden of Proof.

ORPHANS' COURT.
 Fees of the justices of the, to be paid in wheat, ... 40
 Fees of the clerks of the, to be paid in wheat, ... 40
 Widows claiming pensions to produce to the, a certificate of husband's death and his commission, ...60-61
 When satisfied of the justice of the claim to ascertain the same by way of annuity, ... 61
 And to make an order on the county treasurer for the payment thereof,.. 61
 To examine the records of annuities every three months and send list of widows entitled to county treasurer, 61
 Clerk of, to transmit a copy of such list to the secretary of the supreme executive council, ... 61

OVERSEERS OF THE POOR.
 One-half of fines arising under act regulating chimney sweepers in Philadelphia, etc., to be paid to, ... 8
 One-half of penalties accruing under act for the suppression of public auctions to go to, ... 17
 Two justices of the peace upon complaint of the, to levy a tax not exceeding 7s 6d in the pound for the relief of the poor, ... 33
 To bind out negro and mulatto children born of slaves where they are abandoned by persons entitled to them, ... 69
 To receive one-half of forfeited swine found running at large in Passyunk, Moyamensing, Northern Liberties, Germantown and Bristol, ... 117
 One-half of all fines, forfeitures and charges imposed under act to prevent the exportation of bread and flour not merchantable, etc., to go to the, ... 295
 Corporation of contributors, etc., neglecting to meet annually and choose 12 managers; overseers of the poor of Philadelphia, Southwark, Moyamensing and the Northern Liberties to be vested with their powers, etc., 402

OVERSEERS OF THE POOR—Continued.

Overseers of the poor incorporated under the name of "The Guardians of the Poor of the City of Philadelphia," 402

To appoint half-yearly six of their number to superintend the almshouse and house of employment, etc., ... 403

Such six overseers to be exempt from all other duties as overseers, ... 403

Any overseer with the consent of one justice of the peace to afford relief to the sudden necessity of any poor person not exceeding 2£ in three months, ... 403

One-half of overseers not to continue in office more than six months and their successors to be appointed half-yearly, ... 403

Penalty for neglect of overseers to serve, ... 404

Overseers with the approbation of two justices of the peace to bind out poor disorderly persons, ... 404

Persons over forty years or married exempted, ... 404

Term of binding not to exceed 3 years, ...404-405

Part of prior act for the relief of the poor made perpetual, ... 405

OYER AND TERMINER.

To have jurisdiction of offenses where officers of land office, etc., neglect or refuse to deliver up books, papers, etc., ... 38

Traitors, pirates, felons, etc., offending upon the sea to be tried by grand and petit juries, ... 104

Trial to be had in Philadelphia court house, ... 105

Justices of the supreme court and judge of admiralty constituted justices of, ... 105

Judge of admiralty to be present of, in chief justices absence, ... 105

Persons standing mute upon arraignment to be deemed to have pleaded not guilty, ... 105

OYER AND TERMINER—Continued.

Provision for trial of offences committed partly on land and partly at sea, ... 105

P.

PALMER'S LANE.

In the Northern Liberties, vacated, .. 174

PAPER MONEY. See Bank of North America; Bills of Credit.

Penalty for counterfeiting or forging, of the U. S., ...15-16

Different emissions of paper money declared payable in arrearages of taxes, ... 473

Received by tax collectors or county treasurers to be paid into state treasury at the same value as received, ... 473

PARDONS.

Supreme executive council empowered to pardon persons convicted of treason or other felony on condition of their leaving the United States, .. 111

Such pardons to be void if such persons return, ... 111

Of all persons engaged in Wilson Riots, ... 118

To be construed beneficially as to persons charged, ... 118

President of supreme executive council empowered to pardon, etc., persons convicted under militia act, ... 159

Commanding officer empowered to grant pardons to persons court martialed, ... 169

PARENT AND CHILD.

Fathers, masters, etc., to be accountable for the fines of minors and apprentices under militia act, ... 159

PARTY WALLS. See Carlisle, Borough of.

Foundation of, in Carlisle not to be laid before obtaining consent of regulators to do so, ... 431

Builder thereof to be reimbursed one moiety of the cost before next builder breaks into same, ... 431

Person laying foundation of, before viewed by regulators, to forfeit 5£, 432

PARTY WALLS—Continued.
  No foundations of, to be laid in Philadelphia until the same be adjusted and marked by the regulators, ... 487
  Penalty for violation, ... 487
  Disposition of penalty, ... 487
  All prosecution to be commenced within one year from the date of offence, 487

PASSYUNK.
  Act to prevent trespassing upon unenclosed grounds in Moyamensing, Northern Liberties, Germantown, and, revived, ... 116
  Penalty for suffering beasts to run at large in, increased, ... 116
  Running at large of swine in, prohibited, ... 116
  Such swine to be forfeited, ... 116
  Disposition of forfeiture, ...116-117
  Person aggrieved by seizure of swine to have apeal to justices of the peace, ... 117
  Party appealing to forfeit 40s where seizure is confirmed, ... 117
  Militia of Moyamensing, Southwark, the Northern Liberties and, united to the city of Philadelphia, ... 147
  Act to prevent the trespassing upon the unenclosed grounds of, Moyamensing, Northern Liberties, Germantown, Bristol and, revived, ... 283
  Act for the better employment of the poor incorporating Passyunk with Philadelphia, Southwark, Moyamensing and Northern Liberties, repealed, ... 405-406

PAUPERS. See Overseers of the Poor; Poor.

PATENTS. See Land Office.
  Persons entitled to lands within the Indian purchase to receive patents on payment of purchase money and interest, etc., ... 310
  Where surveys have not been returned to the former land office an order of survey and patent may be obtained under certain conditions, .310-311
  Form of, ...312-313
  To be recorded in the rolls office, ... 313

PATENTS—Continued.
  Henry Guest given sole right for 5 years of manufacturing oil and blubber from materials discovered by him, ... 132
  All other persons prohibited, ... 132
  Penalty for violation, ... 132
  Sample of materials used to be lodged with clerk of assembly, ... 133
  Same to be also published, ... 133

PEDLARS.
  Male persons capable of bearing arms not to be hawkers or, ... 21
  Penalty for violation, ... 21
  Disposition of penalty, ... 22
  Prior act repealed, ... 22

PENALTIES.
  Persons having estates to pay 15s in every £100 over and above their other fines for non-attendance in militia, ... 161
  Provision for ascertaining amount of such estates, ... 162
  For quartermasters, foragemasters, etc., purchasing wheat, etc., in violation of act, ... 182
  Of commissioners appointed to secure provisions for the federal army for failure to make monthly returns to president of the quantities, etc., delivered to commissary general, ... 216
  Manner and mode of collecting fines, penalties and forfeitures under act incorporating the borough of Carlisle, ... 447

PENNSYLVANIA LINE. See Public Defence.
  Half pay allowed by Congress for seven years to commissioned officers of this state in the service of the United States, continued for life, .. 59
  Rules regulating the application and payment thereof, ...59-60
  Widows of such officers to receive half pay during widowhood, ... 60
  Widow to produce to the orphans' court a certificate of husbands' death and his commission, ...60-61
  Orphans' court satisfied of the justice of the claim to ascertain same by way of annuity, ... 61

Index.   603

PENNSYLVANIA LINE—Continued.
 And make an order on the county treasurer for the payment thereof,.. 61
 County treasurer to pay the same out of state moneys, ... 61
 Orphans' court to examine the records of annuities every three months, and send list of widows entitled to county treasurer, ... 61
 Clerk of such court to transmit a copy of such list to the secretary of the supreme executive council, ... 61
 Lands granted to officers and soldiers to be exempt from taxation, ... 61
 Officers to receive a complete uniform suit of clothes annually, ...61-62
 Prices to be paid by officers and soldiers of the state for provisions, fixed, ... 63
 Supreme executive council to defray expense of procuring and distributing such provisions, ... 63
 Officers and soldiers entitled only while on actual duty, ... 63
 Officers not entitled to a proportion of clothing or stores for more than one commission, ... 63
 Officers, seamen and marines to receive like allowances with the army, ...63-64
 Widows of officers of the navy, etc., also entitled, ... 64
 Provisions made for children, etc., of such officers, ... 64
 And also for the invalids from the,..64-65
 Troops entitled to benefits of act, enumerated, ... 65
 Persons refusing to conform to arrangements and regulations as may be made by Congress or the supreme executive council to forfeit benefits of act, ... 66
 Disputes concerning persons entitled to be adjusted by the supreme executive council, ... 66
 Supreme executive council to appoint auditors to settle the depreciation of pay accounts of officers and privates of the, ... 233
 Auditors to estimate in specie all pay received by such officers and privates, ... 233

PENNSYLVANIA LINE—Continued.
 Auditors to give officers and privates certificates for the sums due in specie, ...233-234
 Confiscated estates to be sold on or before July 1, 1781 by the proper agents and specie certificates, etc., received in payment, ... 234
 Certificates of privates not to be transferred unless attested by commanding officer, ... 234
 Certificates to be received in payment for unlocated lands, etc., ... 234
 Auditors to settle the accounts of all officers and privates who have died in the service, etc., ... 235
 Widows and children of such officers and privates entitled to certificates, 235
 Officers and privates of the navy in actual service entitled to all benefits extended to the, by act, ... 235
 Officers and privates of this state made prisoners in actual service, also entitled to benefits of act, ... 235
 Oath of auditors, ... 235
 Assembly may call in certificates and pay off the same, ...235-236
 Moneys received from sale of confiscated estates to be reserved for redeeming certificates, ... 236
 All such certificates so received by state treasurer to be kept by him and cancelled by order of assembly, 236
 Scale of depreciation for guidance of auditors, ...236-237
 Pay of auditors, ... 237
 Certificates to be provided by supreme executive council and delivered to the said auditors, ... 238
 Chaplains and surgeons to receive same emoluments and benefits as commissioned officers, ...314-315
 To be entitled also to half pay of a captain for life, ... 315
 Commissioned officers, chaplains and surgeons to be liable to be called into service by the supreme executive council at any time, ... 315
 Penalty for neglect or refusal to obey such call, ... 315

604 Index.

PENNSYLVANIA LINE—Continued.
- Additional auditors for settling the accounts of the, to be appointed by the supreme executive council, ... 315
- Powers, authority and compensation of auditors, ... 315
- Supreme executive council to draw on state treasurer for sums to pay off part of certificates granted to the officers and soldiers of the, ... 316
- Commissioners appointed by supreme executive council, to take up old certificates and grant new ones, ... 316
- New certificates to be interest bearing and negotiable, ... 316
- Old certificates not taken up to also bear interest and be negotiable, ... 316
- State treasurer on demand to pay holders thereof one-third of face value and grant new certificates for the balance, ... 316
- Supreme executive council to order sale of all estates forfeited under act to adjust the accounts of the, etc., 317
- Such sales to be made on or before May 10, 1781, ... 317
- Money arising therefrom to be applied to the uses and purposes specified in act, ... 317
- Act for recruiting the, in the army of the U. S., ... 344
- 2,700 men to be raised to serve in the, for 18 months, ... 344
- Proportionate quota of each county, 344-345
- County commissioners to transmit to the several classes under act of December 23, 1780 an order with duplicate annexed, ... 345
- Order to contain the names of each and every person containing such class and require each class to deliver one able bodied recruit within fifteen days, ... 345
- Commissioners or assessors empowered to enlist for delinquent classes,... 345
- Such classes to pay the costs and expenses thereof, ... 345
- Commissioners to keep a book in which to enter in numerical order the several delinquent classes, etc., ... 346

PENNSYLVANIA LINE—Continued.
- And enlist recruits for the delinquent classes according to their respective numbers, ... 346
- Oath of commissioners and assessors, 346
- Persons enlisting recruits to be exempted from militia duty, ... 346
- Pay of recruits, ...346-347
- Provisions for adjusting disputes between delinquent classes and persons furnishing recruits as to the amount which such delinquents ought to pay, ... 347
- Supreme executive council to appoint officers to inspect and take recruits in charge, ... 347
- Recruits to be attested before some justice of the peace and if accepted delivered by the proper class to the nearest officer, ... 347
- Officer to give a receipt in favor of class furnishing such recruit, ... 347
- Moneys paid by executors, guardians, etc., in pursuance of act to be allowed in the settlement of their accounts, ... 347
- Penalty for neglect or refusal of county commissioners to perform duties under act, ...347-348
- Penalty for neglect or refusal of assessors or collectors to perform duties required by act, ... 348
- Manner of collecting taxes on property owned by non-residents, ...348-349
- Tenant in possession to pay taxes and deduct the same out of rent, ... 349
- Lands to be sold where one year's rent is insufficient to pay such taxes, 349
- Compensation of persons appointed to deliver orders to the several classes, 349
- Act altering and supplying act for recruiting the, in the army of the United States, ... 364
- County commissioners to levy £20 on delinquent classes and cause the same to be collected and paid into the treasury, ... 364
- County treasurers to pay the same over to state treasurer, ... 365
- State treasurer to hold the same subject to orders of the supreme executive council for the purpose of recruiting the, ... 365

Index. 605

PENNSYLVANIA LINE—Continued.

Recruits enlisted in pursuance of act to serve at least eighteen months,... 265
Supreme executive council authorized to adopt expedient measures to recruit the, ... 365
Act for recruiting the, continued, ... 365
Persons apprehending deserters to be excused from two tours of militia duty, ...365-366
Officers in the hospital and medical department of the, to receive the same benefits as military commissioned officers, etc., receive under prior acts, ... 370
All such officers to be liable to be called into actual service by the supreme executive council, ... 371
Their half pay cease and determine upon their neglect or refusal to respond to such call, ... 371
Supreme executive council to determine claims of person claiming benefit of act and direct auditors to settle accounts, etc., of such officers, 371
Officers and privates of state regiments, etc., captured by the enemy entitled to full depreciation of their pay up until the time of their exchange, ... 372
Widows and children of officers of state regiments killed in battle, etc., entitled to half pay of such officers, 372
Officers of the Pennsylvania line entitled to depreciation certificates, enumerated, ... 458
Artillery officers, etc., and privates of the artillery artificers or detached corps, inhabitants of this state also entitled to depreciation certificates,. 459
Comptroller general directed to settle depreciation of the pay accounts of the officers, etc., of the Pennsylvania line, ... 460
Supreme executive council to draw on state treasurer and turn over to the comptroller general all necessary sum for so doing, ... 460
Comptroller general in settling sums due to pay one-third thereof in bills of credit and two-thirds in certificates, ... 460

PENNSYLVANIA HOSPITAL.

Unclaimed shares of prizes awarded in admiralty vested in the, ... 103
Persons entitled to receive same if they apply within three years, ... 103

PENNSYLVANIA VOLUNTEERS. See Militia.

Each company of militia to furnish one man for the formation of the,.. 191
Deserters not to be enlisted in the, ... 191
Terms and continuance of enlistment, 192
Persons enrolled in the, neglecting to serve to procure substitutes, ... 192
Proceedings to procure substitute where such person refuses to do so, 192
Proceedings where militia company fails or neglects to furnish volunteer, ... 193
To be formed by the president into one or more regiments, ... 193
Officers of the, to be appointed and commissioned by the President, ... 193
Officers and privates to receive same pay as troops in the Federal Army, 193
Captains of militia companies to notify companies to meet and carry act into effect, ... 193
Penalty for neglect or refusal, ... 193
Volunteers neglecting or refusing to perform service or being guilty of desertion, etc., to be subject to same punishments as are inflicted for like offences in the federal army, ... 194
Penalty for lieutenant or sub-lieutenant neglecting to perform duties required by act, ... 194
President to issue orders to commissioners of purchase for necessary supplies for the, ... 194
Persons engaged in the, exempted from taxation during term of service, ... 194
May be discharged by the president before the expiration of the term of enlistment, ... 194
Each militia company to furnish two volunteers instead of one, ... 195

PENSIONS.

Widows and children of officers of state regiments killed in battle, etc., entitled to half pay of such officers, 372

	Page.
PENSIONS—Continued.	
Chaplains and surgeons serving throughout the war to receive half pay of a captain for life,	315
Provision for support of families of militiamen killed in service,	165-166
Moneys arising from militia act to be used for relief of disabled militia men, their widows and children,	164-165
Relief not to exceed half pay of deceased officer or private,	166
Half pay allowed by Congress for seven years to commissioned officers of this state in the service of the United States, continued for life,	59
Rules regulating the application and payment thereof,	59-60
Widows of such officers to receive half pay during widowhood,	60
Widow to produce to the orphans' court a certificate of husband's death and his commission,	60-61
Orphans' court satisfied of the justice of the claim to ascertain same by way of annuity,	61
And make an order on the county treasurer for the payment thereof,	61
County treasurer to pay the same out of state moneys,	61
Orphans' court to examine the records of annuities every three months, and send list of widows entitled to county treasurer,	61
Clerk of such court to transmit a copy of such list to the secretary of the supreme executive council,	61
Lands granted to officers and soldiers to be exempt from taxation,	61
Officers to receive a complete uniform suit of clothes annually,	61-62
Prices to be paid by officers and soldiers of the state for provisions, fixed,	63
Supreme executive council to defray expense of procuring and distributing such provisions,	63
Officers and soldiers entitled only while on actual duty,	63
Officer not entitled to a proportion of clothing or stores for more than one commission,	63

	Page.
PENSIONS—Continued.	
Officers, seamen and marines to receive like allowances with the army,	63-64
Widows of officers of the navy, etc., also entitled,	64
Provision made for such officers, etc., children,	64
And also for the invalids from the Pennsylvania line,	64-65
Troops entitled to benefits of act, enumerated,	65
Persons refusing to conform to arrangements and regulations as may be made by Congress or the supreme executive council to forfeit benefits of act,	66
Disputes concerning persons entitled to be adjusted by the supreme executive council,	66

PHILADELPHIA, CITY OF. See German Society.

Chimney sweepers in, to register and obtain a certificate,	5-6
Penalty for neglect or refusal,	6
To wear the number contained in their certificate on the front of their caps,	6
Penalty for neglect or refusal,	6
Chimney sweepers in, to sweep chimneys within 48 hours after application,	7
Penalty for neglect or refusal,	7
Rates allowed for sweeping chimneys,	7
Penalty on persons whose unswept chimneys in, take fire and blaze out at the top,	7
Penalty where chimneys take fire and blaze out at the top within one month from sweeping,	7
Chimney sweepers in, to pay officer 10s per day for granting certificate, etc.,	7
Officer for granting certificates to chimney sweepers in, to be appointed by wardens and three justices,	8
Rates for sweeping chimneys in, to be regulated and fixed by justices of the peace,	8
Rates to be published in one or more newspapers,	8

Index. 607

PHILADELPHIA, CITY OF—Continued.
Penalties arising under act to be paid equally to overseers of the poor and officer for granting certificates, ... 8
Provisions of act limited to within one mile of the bounds of, ... 8
Supreme executive counsel to commission auctioneer for holding public auctions in, ... 19
State House at 6th and Chestnut Sts. in, vested in the commonwealth, ... 48
Military barracks erected in the, and the Northern Liberties vested in the commonwealth, ... 49
Act vesting court houses, jails, etc., throughout the state in the commonwealth not to extend to old jail and workhouse at 3rd and High Sts., in, 50
Supreme executive council to sell said jail and workhouse for the benefit of, and county, ... 51
Certain acts of assembly repealed,..51-52
Charter of the Second Presbyterian church in, continued and confirmed, 89
Charter of the German Lutheran Congregation in, confirmed and amended, ... 83
Society for the Relief of Masters of Ships, incorporated, ...91-92
The American Philosophical society held at, incorporated, ... 121
Taxes in, for opening, etc., roads, supporting nightly watch, lamps and pumps, and for pitching, etc., streets, etc., and for regulating, etc., the water courses and sewers, to be laid and assessed according to state tax, ... 140
Wardens of the, to let market-houses, ferries, wharves and public landing places, ... 201
Wardens with assessors to levy an additional rate not exceeding six pence in the pound, ... 201
Said rate to be collected in the usual manner, ... 201
Treasurer of wardens to receive rents from market-houses, etc., ... 201
And all other income, fines, etc., which were formerly received by the treasurer or the mayor of the, ... 201

PHILADELPHIA, CITY OF—Continued.
Clerk of the market to collect rent from market-houses, etc., and pay the same over to the treasurer of the wardens, and assessors, ... 201
Penalty for neglect or refusal, ... 202
Owners, etc., of ferries, etc., in, to pay their rents to the treasurer of the wardens and assessors, ... 202
Penalty for neglect or refusal, ... 202
Penalty for persons receiving money under act and not paying the same over to the treasurer of the wardens and assessors, ... 202
Moneys received under act to be used by wardens for purposes specified in act regulating nightly watch, etc.,. 202
Wardens empowered to purchase a lot on the north side of Sassafras street along Delaware river for a public wharf, ... 203
Act not to extend to the estate and interest of the, in the middle ferry on Schuylkill from May 1, 1780 to May 1, 1781, ... 203
Unless wardens agree with president in council to keep such bridge in repair, etc., ... 203
Act not to annul contracts made by supreme executive council with quarter-master general of the U. S. for passage of men, etc., ... 203
President to set off and sell at public auction enough city lots to redeem residue of bills of credit dated April 29, 1780, ... 318
To take nothing but said bills of credit, Spanish milled dollars or gold and silver in payment, ... 318
Purchasers of such lots to have indefeasible estates in fee simple, ... 318
Grantees to plead general issue and give act in evidence in any suits brought for such lands, ... 319
Such evidence to be final and conclusive against any such claimant, .. 319
Just claimants claiming under William Penn, etc., to receive a full equivalent for all lots so sold, ... 319
Proceedings by claimants to secure rights, etc., prescribed, ...319-320

PHILADELPHIA, CITY OF—Continued.
Costs to be paid by the state where claimant proves the justness of his cause, ... 320
Claimants to secure a writ from the prothonotary of the supreme court and have unappropriated lots assigned to them by a jury, ... 320
All claims against the commonwealth to be commenced and prosecuted within a limited time, ... 321
Proviso as to infants, feme coverts, persons non compos mentis, imprisoned or beyond the seas, ... 321
Manner and mode of taking care of city lots and certain lots appurtenant to other towns, etc., prescribed, ... 322
Manner of proceeding where lots are in the possession of private persons, etc., ...322-323
All suits against persons for doing anything in pursuance to act to be brought within twelve months, .. 323
Defendants in such cases to plead the general issue and give act and special matter in evidence, ... 323
Defendants in such actions to recover treble costs where plaintiff becomes non-suit, suffers a discontinuance or has judgment pass against him, .. 324
Penalty for neglect or refusal to perform duties required by act, ... 324
Penalty, how recoverable, ... 324
Application of penalty, ... 324
Corporation of contributors, etc., neglecting to meet annually and choose 12 managers; overseers of the poor of Philadelphia, Southwark, Moyamensing and the Northern Liberties to be vested with their powers, etc., 402
Overseers of the Poor incorporated under the name of "The Guardians of the Poor of the City of Philadelphia," 402
To appoint half-yearly six of their number to superintend the almshouse and house of employment,. etc., ... 403
Such six overseers to be exempt from all other duties as overseers, ... 403

PHILADELPHIA, CITY OF—Continued.
Any overseer with the consent of one justice of the peace to afford relief to the sudden necessity of any poor person not exceeding 3.£ in three months, ... 403
One-half of overseers not to continue in office more than six months and their successors to be appointed half-yearly, ... 403
Penalty on neglect of overseers to serve, ... 404
Overseers with the approbation of two justices of the peace to bind out poor disorderly persons, ... 404
Persons over forty years or married exempted, ... 404
Term of binding not to exceed 3 years, ...404-405
Part of prior act for the relief of the poor made perpetual, ... 405
Authority of mayor, recorder and aldermen of Philadelphia under such act vested in the justices of the peace of said city, ... 405
Act for the better relief of the poor, etc., repealed, ... 405
Act for the relief of the poor repealed, 405
Act for the better employment of the poor incorporating Passyunk with Philadelphia, Southwark, Moyamensing and Northern Liberties repealed, ...405-406
Regulators to be appointed in Philadelphia by 4 justices together with 4 street commissioners, ... 486
Filling of vacancies, ... 486
Appeals from the orders of regulators to lie to the next court of common pleas, ...486-487
Proceedings on appeal, ... 487
Foundations of party walls not to be laid until same be adjusted and marked by the regulators, ... 487
Penalty for violation, ... 487
One-half of penalty to go to street commissioners and the other half to the informer, ... 487
All prosecutions for such violation to be commenced within one year from date of offence, ... 487

Index. 609

PHILADELPHIA, CITY OF—Continued.
Northern line of Vine street and southern line of Cedar street to be marked out by regulators of Philadelphia City assisted by regulators of the Northern Liberties, ... 487
Expense thereof to be borne proportionately by the said city and district, ...487-488
Regulators to enter in a book to be provided for the purpose all their directions, orders and awards concerning boundaries of land, ... 488
All such orders and awards upon notice to parties interested, to be conclusive unless appealed from, ... 488
Regulators to enter in same book all regulations made by justices and themselves of descents, water courses and other official business,.. 488
Awards not to bind minors, persons non compos mentis, covert, imprisoned or beyond sea, or other persons without notice, ... 488
Fees of regulators, ... 488
Regulators empowered to enter upon any lot or land in order to survey and measure it, ... 489
All streets, etc., dedicated to public use declared to be public highways, 489
All streets laid out by supreme executive council declared to be public highways, ... 489
No length of time to bar the removal of nuisances from public streets,489-490
Commissioners to remove trees growing in the streets, ... 490
Penalty for obstructing them in so doing, ... 490
Penalty, how recoverable, ... 490
Disposition of penalty, ... 490
Regulations respecting grates over vaults in streets, ... 491
Fees of auctioneers in Philadelphia, Northern Liberties and Southwark, 468-69
Auctioneers to demand and receive an additional 1 per cent. for the use of the commonwealth, ... 469
Auctioneers bond to the president to be security for the proper application of the same, ... 469

PHILADELPHIA, CITY OF—Continued.
Revenue arising from auctions in Philadelphia, Northern Liberties and Southwark appropriated to the support of government and the administration of justice, ... 469
Part of act directing the removal of trees out of the streets of Philadelphia, repealed, ... 511

PHILADELPHIA COUNTY.
Palmer's Lane in the Northern Liberties, in, vacated, ... 174

PHILADELPHIA, PORT OF. See Naval Officer.

PILLORY.
Part punishment for counterfeiting or raising bills of credit, loan-office certificates or bills of exchange, ... 15
Part punishment for horse stealing, for first offence, ... 113
Part punishment for raising or knowingly uttering raised bills of credit 189,212,307
Part punishment for third offence of counterfeiting brand marks on any cask of flour, ... 294

PIRATES. See Admiralty.
Traitors, felons, etc., offending upon the sea to be tried by grand and petit juries, ... 104
Trial to be had in Philadelphia court house, ... 105
Justices of the supreme court and judge of admiralty constituted justices of, ... 105
Judges of admiralty to be president of, in chief justices absence, ... 105
Persons standing mute upon arraignment to be deemed to have pleaded not guilty, ... 105
Provision for trial of offences committed partly on land and partly at sea, ... 105
Trial and punishment of subjects of this state or any of the U. S. committing piracy, etc., under foreign colors, ... 222
Persons betraying their trust at sea to be convicted and punished as pirates, ... 222

39—X

PLAINT.

Penalty imposed upon militia-lieutenants, etc., for neglecting or refusing to deliver up books, accounts, etc., to their successors in office to be recovered by bill, information, action of debt, indictment, or, ... 227

Certain penalties to be recovered by, ... 294-295

PLAINTIFF.

To be mulcted in treble costs in certain suits if he becomes non-suit suffers a discontinuance or has judgment passed against him,.256-257,324,448

To be mulcted in treble costs, where he becomes non-suit, discontinues or has judgment pass against him in actions under militia act, ... 171

To be mulcted in treble costs if he wilfully delays, discontinues or has judgment or verdict passed against him, in suits to condemn certain goods as contraband, ... 503-504

Plaintiffs or defendants in actions brought in the supreme or common pleas courts for debts in care of their sudden departure upon giving security may apply for special courts and have their cases determined at once, ... 417

Defendants in supreme court entitled to same benefits as defendants in common pleas, ... 418

PLEADING.

Persons sued under act for impost on goods, etc., may plead the general issue and give act and special matter in evidence, ... 256

Defendant in certain actions to plead the general issue and give act and special matter in evidence, ... 515

POLICE. See Philadelphia, City of.

POOR.

Two justices of the peace upon complaint of the overseers of the poor to levy a tax not exceeding 7s 6d in the £ for the use of the, ... 33

Prior act, partly continued, ... 33

Fines for selling by public auction without a license, to be applied to the use of the, ... 230

POOR—Continued.

One-half of penalty for refusing to take bills of credit in payment of necessaries, goods, etc., to go to the, ... 242

One-half the penalty imposed on persons refusing to accept bills of credit equal in value to gold and silver for goods, etc., to go to the, ... 250

One-half of penalty for catching fish in the Schuylkill river with brush nets to go to the, ... 271

To receive one-half the penalty imposed on persons for refusing to sell live stock, etc., for bills of credit,.. 306

Authority of mayor, recorder and aldermen of Philadelphia under such act vested in the Justices of the Peace of said city, ... 405

Act for the better relief of the poor, etc., repealed, ... 405

Act for the relief of the poor repealed, 405

Incorporation of Passyunk with Philadelphia, etc., annulled, ... 405-406

Corporation of contributors, etc., neglecting to meet annually and choose 12 managers; overseers of the poor of Philadelphia, Southwark, Moyamensing and the Northern Liberties to be vested with their powers, etc., 402

Overseers of the poor incorporated under the name of "The Guardians of the Poor of the City of Philadelphia, ... 402

To appoint half-yearly six of their number to superintend the almshouse and house of employment, etc., ... 403

Such six overseers to be exempt from all other duties as overseers, ... 403

Any overseer with the consent of one justice of the peace to afford relief to the sudden necessity of any poor person not exceeding 3£ in three months, ... 403

One-half of overseers not to continue in office more than six months and their successors to be appointed half-yearly, ... 403

Penalty or neglect of overseers to serve, ... 404

Index. 611

POOR—Continued.
Overseers with the approbation of two justices of the peace to find out poor disorderly persons, ... 404
Persons over forty years or married exempted, ... 404
Term of binding not to exceed 3 years, ...404-405
Part of prior act for the relief of the poor made perpetual, ... 405

POOR TAX.
To be laid and assessed according to state tax, ... 140
Act not to extend to state tax on ready money, ... 140
Nor to prevent appeals or alter mode of collecting same, ... 140
Nor to alter mode of taxation in counties where state tax has not been laid within twelve months, ... 140
Proceedings on appeal from, ...140-141
Tax on real estate transferred to be charged to buyers, ...140-141
Compensation of county and city assessors, ... 141
Goods of tenant of non-resident owner subject to distress for, ... 141
Distress to be deducted from rent, .. 141
Act not to affect existing contracts between landlord and tenant as to payment of, ... 142
Nor to repeal act for raising additional sum of $5,700,000, ... 142
Compensation of county commissioners and assessors, to be satisfied in wheat, ... 142

PORCHES. See Carlisle, Borough of; Nuisances.

PRACTICE.
Plaintiffs or defendants in actions brought in the supreme or common pleas courts for debts in case of their sudden departure upon giving security may apply for special courts and have their cases determined at once, ... 417
Defendants in supreme court entitled to same benefits as defendants in common pleas, ... 418
Act not to prevent plaintiff or defendant from being allowed a reasonable time to procure testimony,.. 418

PRACTICE—Continued.
Persons sued under act incorporating the borough of Carlisle may plead the general issue and give act and special matter in evidence, ... 448
In cases of seizure of goods claimed to be contraband, ...499-501

PRESBYTERIAN CHURCHES. See Second Presbyterian Church.

PRESIDENT OF THE SUPREME EXECUTIVE COUNCIL. See Board of Property; Federal Army; Supreme Executive Council.
The judges of the supreme court, the judge of admiralty, three persons of integrity and ability and the, to compose the high court of errors and appeals, ... 54
To form the Pennsylvania Volunteers into one or more regiments, etc.,... 193
To appoint and commission officers of the Pennsylvania Volunteers, ... 193
To issue orders to the commissioners of purchase for necessary supplies for the Pennsylvania Volunteers, .. 194
To discharge Pennsylvania Volunteers before the end of the term of enlistment if expedient, ... 194
To appoint commissioners, to procure ment for the federal army, ... 215
Empowered to suspend act for procuring an immediate supply of provisions for the federal army when circumstances of the army admit thereof, ... 218
And council to appoint persons to appoint muster roll of vessels in search of deserters, ... 223
To call out enough wagons to transport baggage and stores of troops called out in defense of the state,.. 361
To seize and impress wagons, etc., where sufficient number cannot be procured in manner prescribed by act, 362
To seize and impress arms, ammunition, when necessary and apply the same to public use, ... 362
To billet and quarter troops in public or private houses, ... 362
To call out all the militia without respect to classes, ... 363

PRESIDENT OF THE SUPREME EXECUTIVE COUNCIL—Continued.
　Penalty to neglect or refuse to obey call of the president, ... 363
　To draw upon the treasury for necessary money to procure arms, ammunition, etc., ... 363
　Authorized to impress horses and wagons, etc., for the removal of the families and property of inhabitants of Philadelphia, Northern Liberties, and Southwark who are in actual service against the enemy, ... 363
　Salary of, ... 377
　To be one of the members of the board of property, ...408-409
　Naval officer to submit all his books and papers to the inspection of the, and council, ... 257
　Sureties on bond of naval officer to be approved of by the, and council, 257-258

PRISONERS OF WAR.
　Inhabitants enjoined to inquire after and take suspected persons before justices of the peace, ... 464
　Justice to commit guilty party to county jail and immediately notify the war office, ... 464
　Person arrested refusing to give a satisfactory account of himself to be committed until the next quarter sessions, ... 465
　Justice to give certificate to persons who apprehend, ... 465
　County treasurer, upon receiving certificate and receipt from keeper of prison, to pay to such persons their reward, mileage and subsistence money, ... 466
　Persons apprehending, to receive eight dollars reward and be allowed one-eighth dollar per mile mileage and 5-90 of a dollar per day subsistence money, ... 466
　Disputes concerning payment of same between treasurer and claimant to be settled by two justices of the peace, ... 466
　County treasurer to transmit state treasurer all certificates and receipts so taken once in every six months, 466

PRISONERS OF WAR—Continued.
　State treasurer, upon receipt thereof, to settle the same with the superintendent of finance, ... 466
　Penalty for treasurer keeping certificates beyond the space of six months, ... 466
　Penalty for keeper of prison wilfully or negligently suffering, to escape, 467
　Penalty for concealing, aiding or assisting, to escape, ... 467
　Penalty to be divided equally between state and prosecutor, ... 467
　Guilty parties unable to pay penalty to be publicly whipped, ... 467
　Act not to affect persons who receive prisoners of war for labor from the war office, ... 467
　Persons so receiving prisoners to enter their names with the next justice of the peace within one week, ... 468

PRISON KEEPERS.
　Penalty for negligently or wilfully suffering prisoners of war to escape, .. 467

PRISONS. See Chester County; Jails; Washington County.

PRISON. See Washington County.
　And courthouse to be erected in Washington county, ... 275
　Certain persons authorized to select and purchase sight for, in Washington county, ...275-276
　Taxes not exceeding a certain amount to be levied to defray expenses of erecting, ... 276

PRIVATES. See Militia; Pennsylvania Line; Pennsylvania Volunteers.
　Serving in the Pennsylvania Volunteers to receive same pay as troops in the Federal Army, ... 193
　Exempted from taxation during term of service, ... 194

PRIZE GOODS. See Prizes.

PRIZES. See Admiralty.
　And prize goods condemned by the admiralty court to be subject to the five per cent. ad valorem duty levied by Congress, ... 297

Index.

PROPRIETARY ESTATES.
Vested in the commonwealth, ... 35
To be disposed of by the legislature,... 35
Estates, etc., granted by a proprietary to other persons prior to July 4, 1776, excepted, ...35-36
Private estates, etc., of proprietaries, confirmed, ... 36
Proprietary tenths or manors surveyed and returned to land office prior to July 4, 1776, together with the quit rents reserved thereout, also confirmed, ... 36
Other quit rents abolished, ... 36
Arrears of purchase money for land purchased of late proprietaries to be paid to the commonwealth, ... 37
Former acts of assembly granting powers and privileges to proprietaries, repealed, ... 37
130,000 £ donated to late proprietaries, 37
Time of payment of same, prescribed, 38
Officer to deliver up books, papers, etc., on demand of president of supreme executive counsel, ... 38
Penalty for neglect or refusal, ... 38

PROSECUTOR.
To receive one-half of fines accruing under act for recovering fines, etc., 137
To receive one-half of penalty on person convicted of assisting prisoners of war to escape, ... 467
To receive one-half of forfeited swine found running at large in Passyunk, Moyamensing, Northern Liberties, Germantown and Bristol, ... 117
To receive one-half of penalty for violation of act for suppression of public auctions, ...17,19
Reward of, concerning counterfeiting, etc., of bills of exchange, loan office certificates or bills of exchange, .. 15

PROTECTION OF LAW. See Wager of Law.
Not allowed, ...295,515

PROVINCE ISLAND. See State Island.
Vested in the commonwealth, ... 49
General assembly to appoint trustees for the management of, ... 51

PROVISIONS. See Army of the United States; Bread; Exports; Flour; Pennsylvania Line.
Prices to be paid by officers and soldiers in the Pennsylvania Line for provisions, fixed, ... 63
Supreme executive council to defray expense of procuring and distributing such provisions, ... 63
Officers and soldiers entitled only while on actual duty, ... 63
Act for procuring immediate supply of provisions for the federal army, .. 214
Act laying an embargo on the exportation of, by sea, continued, ... 228
Act to revive and continue act for laying an embargo on the exportation of provisions, etc., repealed, ... 267
Part of act to permit the exportation of flour of wheat, etc., repealed,.... 326

PUBLIC ACCOUNTS.
Act to compel the settlement of the,... 73
Auditors appointed to collect, audit and settle, etc., the accounts of late committee of safety, ... 75
And of the council of safety, ... 75
And of the accounts of all other persons entrusted with public money, 75
Auditors to direct public debtors to pay all debts to the state treasurer, 75
Certificate of auditors to be conclusive evidence in action of debt by the commonwealth to recover amount due, ... 75
No set off to be admitted, ... 75
Auditors to draw orders on state treasurer for balances found due creditors of commonwealth, ... 75
Auditors to open an office in Philadelphia and employ accountants, ... 76
Compensation of accountants, ... 76
Auditors to give public notice of their appointment by advertisement in some newspaper printed in said city, 76
Like notices to be read in the courts of quarter sessions throughout the state, ... 76
Contents of notice, ... 76
Justices to cause this act to be read in the quarter sessions, ... 76

PUBLIC ACCOUNTS—Continued.
Auditors to prepare books, etc., and to call upon former auditors for their books, etc., ... 76
Supreme executive council may direct auditors to attend at other places within the state, ... 77
Notice thereof to be first given, ... 77
Auditors empowered to issue subpoenas and attachments, ... 77
And to commit for contempt, ... 77
Fees of witnesses, sheriffs, etc., to be the same as in the inferior courts, 78
Auditors to levy such costs and charges upon delinquents, ... 78
Auditors empowered to issue an attachment upon the return of non est, ... 78
Defaulters upon summons to be barred of all set offs or deductions and to be liable for all the moneys advanced, ...78-79
Proviso where auditors grant extension, ... 79
Auditors to draw on state treasurer for necessary charges and expenses, 79
Filling vacancy in office of auditor, .. 79
Compensation of auditor, ...79-80
Supreme executive council to draw orders on state treasurer for payment of auditors, ... 80
Certain accounts to be settled by committee of accounts, ... 80
Certain prior acts repealed, ... 80
Repeal not to affect settlements by former auditors or commissioners, 80
Auditors to grant execution to collect outstanding, ... 196
For want of sufficient distress defendant to be imprisoned until sums due and costs be paid, ... 196
Fines on delinquent tax collectors increased, ...196-197
County commissioners and assessors to appoint other collectors in the place of delinquents, ... 197
Pay of county treasurers increased,.. 197
Pay of tax collectors increased, ... 197
Penalty for neglect or refusal to collect militia fines, ...197-198

PUBLIC ACCOUNTS—Continued.
Commissioners of purchases to appoint a place and person in each township to receive wheat flour, etc., for the army, ... 198
To notify county treasurer of such appointment, ... 198
Wheat flour, etc., to be received by such persons in payment of taxes,.. 198
Receipts therefor to be received by tax collector in discharge of taxes, 198
County treasurers to receive such receipts in payment from collector,... 199
Where certificate exceeds amount of taxes due, collectors to give receipt for the surplus, ... 199
Treasurer to keep a record of all sums over and above amount of taxes charged against persons holding receipts, ... 199
And discount the surplus with interest to collector of next state tax,.. 199
State treasurer to receive such certificates from county treasurers and deliver them to principal of the respective departments from whom the payment is due, ...199-200
To take receipts from such principals and lodge the same with the board of treasury, ... 200
Office for auditing, liquidating and adjusting the accounts of the commonwealth instituted, ...448-449
Office to be styled, "the Comptroller-General's office,", ... 449
Powers and duty of comptroller-general, ... 449
All public accounts to be rendered into the comptroller general's office and when settled, transmitted to the president and council, ... 449
President, etc., to draw warrant on state treasurer for any balance due by the commonwealth, ... 450
Comptroller general to enter warrant in his books, indorse and deliver it to the party entitled, ... 450
Comptroller general to recover any balance found due and owing to the state, ... 450

Index. 615

PUBLIC ACCOUNTS—Continued.
  Comptroller general to form abstracts of the names, etc., of the persons who have received money of the commonwealth for which they have not properly accounted, ... 450
  And to direct the prothonotary of the county wherein such persons reside to issue process against such persons, ... 451
  Persons so summoned neglecting or refusing to exhibit their accounts to be liable to pay the full value of all money or public effects which have come into their hands, ... 451
  Auditors or other persons refusing to deliver up public books or papers upon demand of comptroller general to be liable to a thousand pounds penalty, ... 452
  Method of recovering balances due and owing to the state, ... 452
  Money so recovered to be paid to the state treasurer, ... 452
  No accounts to be deemed settled until they be audited by the comptroller general, ... 453
  Comptroller general authorized to revise, etc., accounts settled by the auditors, commissioners or committees of assembly and report substantial errors to the general assembly, ... 453
  Comptroller general authorized to summon witnesses and commit delinquents for contempt, ... 453
  Fees and mileage of sheriff, coroner or other process server and witnesses, ... 454
  Comptroller general to issue attachment for absent witnesses, ... 454
  Secretary of the supreme executive council to enter into comptroller general's office all marriage, tavern and other licenses, ... 454
  Comptroller general to debit the respective prothonotaries therewith,... 454
  Prothonotaries to settle their accounts with comptroller general once in every three months, ... 454

PUBLIC ACCOUNTS—Continued.
  Comptroller general to select such parts of accounts as are properly chargeable against the United States and institute an account between the United States and this state, ...454-455
  State treasurer not to issue or pay any moneys without a warrant from the president entered and certified by the comptroller general, ... 455
  Exceptions, ... 455
  Books, papers, etc., of comptroller general to be opened to the inspection of the committees of account, 455
  And copies thereof be furnished to the legislature and president when required, ...455-456
  Salary of comptroller general, ... 456
  Bond of comptroller general, ... 456
  Oath of comptroller general, ... 456
  Prior acts relating to public accounts repealed, ... 456
  Act to be publicly read in every court of oyer and terminer and quarter sesisons, ... 456
  John Nicholson appointed comptroller general, ... 457

PUBLIC ACT.
  Act pardoning all persons engaged in Wilson riots to be deemed a, ... 118

PUBLIC AUCTIONS. See Auctioneers; Public Vendue.
  No goods or other property to be sold by public auction, vendue or outcry, ... 17
  Exceptions, ... 17
  Penalty for violation, ... 17
  Penalty, how recoverable, ... 17
  Disposition of, ... 17
  Act not to prevent such sales by sheriffs, executors or administrators or householders removing from a district, ... 17
  Public auctions allowed by act to be carried on in Philadelphia by a person commissioned for that purpose, 18
  The auctioneer of the city of Philadelphia to be appointed by supreme executive counsel, ... 18
  Penalty for other persons holding, in Philadelphia, ... 18

Index.

PUBLIC AUCTIONS—Continued.
 Auctioneer to inquire into offences against acts and inform against offenders, ... 19
 Auctioneer to recover penalties provided by acts, ... 19
 Prosecutor may also sue for penalties under act, ... 19
 Bond of auctioneer, ... 19
 Oath of auctioneer, ... 19
 Compensation of auctioneer, ... 19
 Marshall of the court of admiralty not to sell by, except prize ships, etc., and perishable goods, ...19-20
 Marshall to make out an inventory of prizes and have them appraised, .. 20
 Penalty for printing or advertising prohibited sales, ... 21
 Prior act, repealed, ... 22
 Duration of act, limited, ... 22
 Damaged and shipwrecked goods may be sold by, ... 81
 Auctioneer in Philadelphia to first obtain a license from council, ... 82
 Condemned vessels and cargoes to be sold by marshall at, for the benefit of the captors, ... 101
 Marshall to file account of such sales with the register, ... 101
 Negroes and mulattoes taken as prize not to be sold, ... 101
 To be appraised and delivered to captors, ... 101
 Act not to interfere with act for suppression of, ... 101
 Where imported goods, etc., remain in vessel ten days after arrival without duty being paid or secured, master to deliver same to naval officer to be warehoused and kept at owner's risk and expense, ... 254
 After three months naval officer to have all such goods appraised and sold at auction, ... 254
 Fees of auctioneers in Philadelphia, Northern Liberties and Southwark, ...468-469
 Auctioneers to demand and receive an additional 1 per cent. for the use of the commonwealth, ... 469
 Auctioneers bond to the president to be security for the proper application of the same, ... 469

PUBLIC AUCTIONS—Continued.
 Revenue arising from auctions in Philadelphia, Northern Liberties and Southwark appropriated to the support of government and the administration of justice, ...469-470
 Goods, etc., seized and condemned as contraband to be forthwith advertised and sold at, ... 502

PUBLIC CREDIT.
 Act for the better support of the, by an immediate sale of the lands therein mentioned, ... 317

PUBLIC DEBT.
 Supreme executive council authorized to borrow enough to defend the frontiers and for the other exigencies of government, ... 492
 Loan not to exceed 30,000 £, ... 492
 Interest thereon not to exceed 6 per cent. per annum, ... 492
 Duties arising on liquors, revenues from sales at vendues, fines and penalties from naval and excise officers, and moneys arising from marriage, tavern and other licenses pledged as funds for the payment thereof, ... 493
 Supreme executive council empowered to apply the same to that purpose, ... 493
 Faith and honor of the state pledged to make up and pay off any deficiency, ... 493
 Act to enable the supreme executive council to negotiate loans, etc., for the defence of the frontiers and support of government, repealed, ... 534
 All moneys due for interest in the loan office appropriated to the payment of 5,000 £ borrowed from the National Bank of North America, ... 534

PUBLIC DEFENSE.
 Act for making more equal the burden of the, partly repealed, ... 31

PUBLIC HIGHWAYS.
 Act for opening and repairing public roads and highways revived and continued for 5 years, ... 470

PUBLIC HOUSES. See Taverns.

PUBLIC LANDINGS. See Southwark; Wharves.
Wardens of Philadelphia to let market-houses, ferries, wharves, and,. 201
Treasurer of wardens and assessors to receive rents from market-houses, wharves and, ... 201
Owners of ferries, wharves and, to pay their rents to the treasurer of the wardens and assessors, ... 202

PUBLIC NOTICES.
Auditors appointed to settle public accounts to give, of appointment by advertisement in some newspaper printed in Philadelphia, ... 76
Like notices to be read in the courts of quarter sessions throughout the state, ... 76
Contents of notice, ... 76

PUBLIC ROADS.
Act for opening and keeping in repair the, revived and continued for 5 years, ... 470

PUBLIC VENDUE. See Auctioneers; Public Auction.
Old court house and prison in Chester county to be sold at, ... 143
Marshall empowered to sell prize goods at, ... 224
Mode of conducting sale and distributing proceeds, ... 224
Distribution to be made within twenty days after end of sale, ... 224
Penalty for neglect or refusal, ...224-225
Vessels, goods, etc., sold by marshall and not paid for within three days to be resold, ... 225
First purchaser to be liable for all loss occasioned thereby, ... 225

PUMPS. See Philadelphia, City of.

Q.

QUARTER-MASTER GENERAL.
Contracts made between supreme executive council and the, of the U. S. for passage of men, etc., not annulled by the further supplement to act regulating nightly watch, etc., ... 203

QUARTER SESSIONS. See Militia.
Fees of the clerks of the, to be paid in wheat, ... 40

QUARTER SESSIONS—Continued.
Act to compel settlement of public accounts to be read in the, ... 76
Public notice of appointment of auditors under above act to be read in the, ... 76
Price of days labor to be fixed by, and become the rate for payment of fines under militia act, ... 158
Justices to send certificate of price fixed to the lieutenants, ... 158
Millers, bolters and bakers to provide brand marks and enter them with the clerk of the, with their names and places of abode, ... 289
Penalty for violation, ... 289
Fees of clerk for making such entries, 289

QUAYS. See Southwark; Wharves.

QUIT RENTS. See Proprietary Estates.
Quit rents reserved out of proprietary tenths, etc., returned, etc., to land office prior to July 4, 1776, not confiscated, ... 36
Other quit rents abolished, ... 36

R.

RANKIN, JOHN.
Messuage and lot of ground in the town of Lisburn, Cumberland county vested in, ... 367

RAISING.
Punishment for, bills of credit, ...189,307

REBELLIONS. See Militia.

RECEIVER-GENERAL. See Board of Property; Land-Office.
To be one of the members of the board of property, ...408-409
Fees of, ...410-411

To pay all moneys received to the state treasurer once in every month, ... 350
Rate of exchange at which the receiver general is to receive the £5 sterling for every 100 acres of land, fixed, ... 350

RECORDER OF DEEDS.
Fees of, to be paid in wheat, ... 40

RECRUITS. See Federal Army.

REGISTER OF WILLS.

	Page.
To receive like fees as were formerly due to register general,	40
Fees of the, to be paid in wheat,	40
Appeals from, to lie to high court of errors and appeals,	54
Depositions taken before the register to be in writing and made part of the record in such appeals,	56
Facts decided by the verdict of a jury in an issue directed to the common pleas by the register not to be re-examined on appeal,	56
Appeal from decree of register concerning validity of a will, etc., not to act as a supersedeas where executor gives security,	56

REGULATORS.

Fees of, to be paid in wheat,	41
To be appointed in Philadelphia by 4 justices together with 4 street commissioners,	486
Filling of vacancies,	486
Apeals from the orders of regulators to lie to the next court of common pleas,	486-487
Proceedings on appeal,	487
Foundations of party walls not to be laid until same be adjusted and marked by the regulators,	487
Penalty for violation,	487
One-half of penalty to go to street commissioners and the other half to the informer,	487
All prosecutions for such violation to be commenced within one year from date of offence,	487
Northern line of Vine street and southern line of Cedar street to be marked out by regulators of Philadelphia City assisted by regulators of the Northern Liberties,	487
Expense thereof to be borne proportionately by the said city and district,	487-488
Regulators to enter in a book to be provided for the purpose all their directions, orders and awards concerning boundaries of land,	488
All such orders and awards upon notice to parties interested, to be conclusive unless appealed from,	488

REGULATORS—Continued.

	Page.
Regulators to enter in same book all regulations made by justices and themselves of descents, water courses and other official business,	488
Awards not to bind minors, persons non compos mentis, covert, imprisoned or beyond sea, or other persons without notice,	488
Fees of regulators,	488
Regulators empowered to enter upon any lot or land in order to survey and measure it,	489
All streets, etc., dedicated to public use declared to be public highways,	489
All streets laid out by supreme executive council declared to be public highways,	489
No length of time to bar the removal of nuisances from public streets,	489-490
Commissioners to remove trees growing in the streets,	490
Penalty for obstructing them in so doing,	490
Penalty, how recoverable,	490
Disposition of penalty,	490
Regulations respecting grates over vaults, in streets,	491
Tenants of non-resident owners repairing grates, etc., to deduct the cost thereof out of his rent,	491
No new vaults to be dug without the consent of 4 justices of the peace and the majority of the regulators,	491-492

REGRATING.

Act for preventing, repealed,	175-176

REPEAL. See Acts of Assembly.

Of laws, declaring bills of credit to be legal tender,	337
Not to extend to bills of credit emitted under acts of March 25, 1780 and April 7, 1781,	338

RENT.

Treasurer of wardens and assessors to receive rents from market-houses, etc.,	201
Clerk of the market to collect rent from market-houses, etc., and pay the same over to the treasurer of the wardens and assessors,	201
Penalty for neglect or refusal,	202

Index. 619

RENT—Continued.
  Owners, etc., of ferries, etc., in Philadelphia, to pay their rents to the treasurer of the wardens and assessors, ... 202
  Rents, etc., contracted before January 1, 1777 to be sued for and judgment obtained and execution awarded for the interest, damages and costs, etc., ... 339

REPLEVIN.
  Imported goods together with casks, etc., to vest in the commonwealth where naval officer tenders to importer the value of such goods with 10 per cent. increase, ... 253
  Commonwealth to recover possession thereof by action of trover and conversion, detinue or, ... 253
  Not to lie for good seized as contraband, ... 501

RESOLVE MONEY.
  Different emissions of paper money declared payable in arrearages of taxes, ... 473
  Received by tax collectors or county treasurers to be paid into state treasury at the same value as received, ... 473

REWARD.
  Of informer concerning counterfeiting, etc., bills of credit, loan office certificates or bills of exchange, .. 15
  For prosecuting to conviction counterfeiters, etc., of continental loan office certificates, bills of exchange or paper money of the United States, 16
  To be paid by state treasurer upon production of certificate from trial judge, ... 16
  For capturing runaway slaves to be the same as for white servants bound for years, ... 71
  Of informer against quartermaster, foragemaster, etc., purchasing wheat, etc., in violation of act, .. 182
  Of informer concerning counterfeiting, etc., bills of credit, ... 189
  Of informer of offense of forging, counterfeiting, raising or knowingly uttering counterfeit or raised bills of credit, ... 212

REWARD—Continued.
  For apprehending deserters, ... 214
  Informer to receive one-half of confiscated goods attempted to be imported from Great Britain, ... 419
  Of informer against persons refusing to take bills of credit in payment of goods, etc., ... 242
  Of informer on persons refusing to accept bills of credit equal in value to gold and silver for goods, etc.,... 250
  Of informer against persons catching fish in the Schuylkill river with brush nets, ... 271
  Persons apprehending prisoners of war to receive eight dollars and be allowed mileage and subsistence money, ... 466
  Disputes concerning payment of same between claimant and county treasurer to be settled by two justices of the peace, ... 466
  Informer to receive one-half of penalty for laying party walls in Philadelphia before they are adjusted and marked by the regulators, ... 487

RIOTS.
  All persons engaged in Wilson, pardoned, ... 118

RIVER BANKS. See Schuylkill Point Meadows; State Island.

RIVERS. See Delaware River.
  Ferries established on the Youghiogheny river, ... 471
  Ferries established on the Monongahela river, ...471-472
  Said rivers declared to be public highways, ... 472

ROADS. See Carlisle, Borough of.
  Palmer's Lane in the Northern Liberties, vacated, ... 174
  General road act revived and continued for 5 years, ... 470

  General road act of March 21, 1772 not to extend to the borough of Carlisle, ...437-438

ROAD TAXES. See Highway Taxes.

ROBBERY.
Defined, ... 110
Punishment of, ... 110
ROLLS OFFICE.
Land patents to be recorded in the,... 313
RUM. See Excise.
RUNDLE, DANIEL.
A further time granted to, to render himself to a justice of the supreme court and stand trial for treason,.... 280
Attainder stayed upon condition that he does so on or before Dec. 31, 1781, 280
Upon failing to do so to be adjudged and attainted of high treason, ... 281

S.

SALARY. See Fees; Wages.
Of president of the supreme executive council, ... 376
Of commander in chief, ... 377
Of vice presidents, ... 377
Of chief justice, ... 377
Of justices of the supreme court, ... 377
Of attorney general, ... 377
Of secretary of supreme executive council, ... 377
Prior acts of assembly fixing salaries of government officers repealed, .. 378
Of comptroller general, ... 456
SALTED PROVISIONS. See Federal Army.
Cattle, sheep or, to be subject to seizure for the use of the federal army, ... 215
SASSAFRAS STREET.
Philadelphia wardens empowered to purchase a lot on the north side of, along Delaware river for a public wharf, ... 203
SCHUYLKILL POINT. See Schuylkill Point Meadows.

SCHUYLKILL POINT MEADOWS.
Owners released from making, repairing, etc., of the banks of, at own expense and charge, ... 477
Managers thereof to make present needed repairs at the several expense and charge of the owners of the banks repaired, ... 477
Managers to inspect banks, etc., at least every three months, ... 478

SCHUYLKILL POINT MEADOWS—Continued.
Managers to enter upon its adjoining lands when necessary to make repairs and obtain earth and other materials at the joint expense of all the owners, ... 478
Managers, when they deem it necessary, to make new banks and dig new ditches at the joint expense and charge of the owners, ... 478
Managers to levy taxes for repairing banks, etc., ... 478
Penalty for neglect or refusal of manager to serve after being duly elected, ... 479
Part of prior act repealed, ... 479

SCHUYLKILL RIVER.
The further supplement to act regulating nightly watch, etc., not to extend to the estate and interest of the city of Philadelphia to the middle ferry on Schuylkill from May 1, 1780 to May 1, 1781, ... 203
Unless wardens agree with president in council to keep such bridge in repair, etc., ... 203
Commissioners appointed for clearing, etc., and putting in execution former acts relating thereto, ... 270
To have the same powers and to perform the same duties as commissioners under former acts, ... 270
Surviving commissioners under former act to turn over to commissioners appointed by this act all unappropriated money, books, papers, tools, etc., ... 270
Fish not to be caught with brush nets, etc., ... 271
Penalty for violation, ... 271
Penalty to be recovered before two justices of the peace, ... 271
Application of penalty, ... 271
All brush nets in the, to be removed and destroyed, ... 271
Penalty for hindering or obstructing persons removing or destroying brush nets, ... 271
Application of penalty, ... 271

Index.

SCHUYLKILL RIVER—Continued.
Limitations and restrictions respecting the catching of shad by seines or nets, in the, ... 271
Part of prior act relating to the appointment of commissioners, repealed, ... 272

SECOND PRESBYTERIAN CHURCH.
Charter of the in Philadelphia, continued and confirmed, ... 89
Trustees, reinstated, ... 89-90
Elections of trustees, ... 90
Annual elections to be held on first Monday of May, ... 90
Nine trustees to be a quorem, ... 90
Empowered to hold real estate not exceeding the yearly value of 1,000 bushels of wheat for each house of worship, ... 90

SECRETARY OF THE LAND OFFICE.
See Board of Property; Land Office.
To be one of the members of the board of property, ... 408-409

SECRETARY OF SUPREME EXECUTIVE COUNCIL.
Salary of, ... 377
Fees appertaining to the office of the, to be paid to state treasurer quarterly, ... 377

SEINES. See Brush Nets.
Limitations and restrictions respecting the catching of shad by seines or nets in the Schuylkill river, ... 271

SERGEANT AT ARMS OF THE ASSEMBLY.
Wages of, ... 378
Mileage of, ... 378

SERVICE OF PROCESS.
Civil process not to be served on officers or privates while attending, going to or returning from militia review, etc., ... 164

SERVITUDE. See Slavery.
Contingent punishment for counterfeiting, raising or knowingly uttering raised or counterfeited bills of credit, ... 15
Not to exceed seven years, ..15,189-213,307

SEWERS. See Philadelphia, City of.
Not to be obstructed in the borough of Carlisle, ... 442
Penalty for violation, ... 442

SHAD.
Limitations and restrictions respecting the catching of, by seines or nets in the Schuylkill river, ... 272

SHEEP. See Federal Army.
Cattle, sheep or salted provisions to be subject to seizure, for the use of the federal army, ... 215

SHERIFFS.
Not affected in the discharge of their duties by act suppressing public auctions, ... 17
Fees of, to be paid in wheat, ... 40
Coroners, constables and, may be compelled to attend sessions of high court of errors and appeals, ... 57
Fees, for attending before auditors appointed to settle public accounts,. 78
Justices, civil officers and, to assist commissioners in carrying out provisions of act for procuring army supplies for 1780, ... 181
The suspension for a limited time of certain acts of assembly making bills of credit of the U. S. legal tender, not to extend to attorneys, executors, guardians or, etc., ...204-205
Of Westmoreland county to act in Washington county until one be there chosen, ... 278

SILK SOCIETY.
Managers of, to adjust its accounts, sell all silk remaining in their hands, and pay over all net proceeds to Philosophical Society, ...474-475
Subscribers of silk society entitled to be reimbursed their proportional dividend by applying for same on or before Oct. 1, 1783, ... 475
Philosophical Society to keep all sums unclaimed by such proprietors and redeliver them when a majority of the subscribers revive the said society, ... 475

SINGLE MEN. See War Taxes.
Over twenty-one and more than six months out of their apprenticeship to pay a war tax not over six pounds nor under 45s, ...330-331
Over twenty-one and more than six months out of their apprenticeship or servitude to be subject to certain taxation, ... 240

SINKING FUND. See Bills of Credit.

SILVER.
Certain acts of assembly making bills of credit of the U. S. legal tender equal to gold and silver suspended for a limited time, ... 204
Act not to extend to any debt or contract made after November 1, 1779, upon which suit has actually been brought, ... 204
Nor to sheriffs, attorneys, executors, guardians, etc., ... 204
Act to suspend laws making the bills of credit of the U. S., legal tender, in payment of debts equal to gold and, continued, ... 229
Duration of act limited, ... 229
Value of bills of credit compared with gold and silver, ...249-250
Duties under act for an impost on goods, etc., to be paid in gold or, as they passed in 1775 or other money equivalent, ... 257
Certain war taxes to be paid in gold or, only, ... 335
Proviso as to persons who have taken the oath of allegiance to this state, ...335-336
Certain war taxes to be paid in gold and silver only, ... 399
All fines imposed by acts of assembly to be recovered in gold, or, etc., ... 343

SLAVERY. See Slaves.
Act for gradual abolition of, ... 67
No children born after March 1, 1780, to be slaves, ... 68
Such negro and mulatto children to be servants until 28 years of age,... 69
To be liable to correction and punishment and entitled to relief and freedom dues, the same as bond servants, ... 69

SLAVERY—Continued.
Overseers of the poor to bind out such children where they are abandoned by persons entitled to them, ... 69
All slaves to be registered before November 1, 1780, ...69-70
Negroes or mulattoes not registered to be deemed no longer slaves, ... 70
Fees of clerk of court for registering slaves, ... 70
Owner of slaves not registered to be liable for their support, ... 70
Unless by deed of record such slaves are freed by him before attaining the age of 28, ... 70
Slaves to be tried for criminal offences like other inhabitants, ... 70
Slaves not to be admitted as witnesses against freemen, ... 70
Jury to value slaves in case of sentence of death, ... 71
State treasurer in case of execution to pay owner such value and costs of prosecution, ... 71
Reward for capturing runaway slaves to be the same as for white servants bound for years, ... 71
No persons to be deemed slaves except those registered as above directed, ... 71
Domestics attending delegates in Congress, etc., also excepted, ... 71
Act not to give relief to runaway slaves from other states, ...71-72
Runaway slaves, etc., from this state may be brought back and registered, ... 72
Proof of absconding, etc., to be made before two justices of the peace within 5 years, ... 72
Negroes or mulattoes, other than infants not to be bound out for more than seven years, ... 72
Prior acts of assembly repealed, ...72-73

SLAVES. See Slavery.
Negro and mulatto children born after March 1, 1780 not to be, ... 68
Such negro and mulatto children to be servants until 28 years of age, ... 69
To be liable to correction and punishment and entitled to relief and freedom dues, the same as bond servants, 69

Index. 623

SLAVES—Continued.
  Overseers of the poor to bind out such children where they are abandoned by persons entitled to them, ... 69
  All, to be registered before November 1, 1780, ...69-70
  Negroes and mulattoes not registered to be deemed no longer slaves, ... 70
  Fees of clerk of court for registering, 70
  Owners of, not registered to be liable for their support, ... 70
  Unless by deed of record such slaves are freed by him before they attain the age of 28, ... 70
  To be tried for criminal offenses like other inhabitants, ... 70
  Not to be admitted as witnesses against freemen, ... 70
  Jury to value slaves in case of sentence of death, ... 71
  State treasurer in case of execution to pay such value and costs of prosecution to owner, ... 71
  Reward for capturing runaway slaves to be the same as for white servants bound for years, ... 71
  No persons to be deemed, except those registered as above directed,. 71
  Domestics attending delegates in Congress, etc., also excepted, ... 71
  Act not to give relief to runaway, from other states, ...71-72
  Runaway slaves, etc., from this state may be brought back and registered, 72
  Proof of absconding, etc., to be made before two justices of the peace within five years, ... 72
  Negroes and mulattoes other than infants not to be bound out for more than seven years, ... 72
  Prior acts of assembly repealed, ...72-73
  Person taking refuge in this state authorized to retain their slaves, ...367-368
  Owners to register such slaves within six months after their arrival, ... 368
  Such slaves not to be sold nor retained in Pennsylvania more than six months after end of war, ... 368
  Act not to enslave any person who has been freed under previous act for the gradual abolition of slavery, 368

SLAVES—Continued.
  Inhabitants of Westmoreland and Washington Counties who claimed to be residents of Virginia before settlement of state boundary dispute to register their slaves in accordance with act for the gradual abolition of slavery, on or before January 21, 1784, ... 463

SLUICES. See Schuylkill Point Meadows; State Island.

SOAP BOILERS. See Carlisle, Borough of; Nuisances.

SOCIETY FOR THE RELIEF OF MASTERS OF SHIPS.
  Incorporated, ...91-92
  Present managers continued, ... 93
  Powers and duties of managers, ... 93
  Moneys at interest and donations, etc., to be considered as capital stock, ... 93
  Contributions and annual payments to be estimated at 10s for a bushel of wheat, ... 94
  General and special meetings of contributors, ... 94
  Notice of special meetings to be published in Philadelphia newspapers,. 94
  Majority of contributors empowered to adopt by-laws, etc., ... 94
  12 managers and a treasurer to be annually elected, ...94-95
  Treasurer to give security, ... 95
  Powers and duties of treasurer, ... 95
  Security of treasurer to be recorded in recorder of deeds office in Philadelphia, ... 96
  Time and place om meeting of managers, ... 96
  To keep fair minutes and publish and lay their accounts before a committee of assembly, ... 96
  Former act of assembly repealed, ..96-97

SOLDIERS. See Pennsylvania Line.
  Lands granted to officers and, exempted from taxation, ... 61

SOUTHAMPTON TOWNSHIP.
  The Trustees of the Dutch Reformed Church in Northampton and Southampton, in the county of Bucks, incorporated, ... 526

SOUTHWARK.

Entry	Page
Chimney sweepers in, to register and obtain a certificate,	5-6
Penalty for neglect or refusal,	6
To wear the number contained in their certificate on the front of their caps,	6
Penalty for neglect or refusal,	6
Chimney sweepers in to sweep chimneys within 48 hours after application,	7
Penalty for neglect or refusal,	7
Rates allowed for sweeping chimneys,	7
Penalty on persons whose unswept chimneys in, take fire and blaze out at the top,	7
Penalty where chimneys take fire and blaze out at the top within one month from sweeping,	7
Chimney sweepers in, to pay officer 10s per day for granting certificate, etc.,	7
Officer for granting certificates to chimney sweepers in, to be appointed by warden and three justices,	8
Rates for sweeping chimneys in, to be regulated and fixed by justices of the peace,	8
Rates to be published in one or more newspapers,	8
Penalties arising under act to be paid equally to overseer of the poor and officer for granting certificates,	8
Provisions of act limited to within one mile of the bounds of Philadelphia city,	8
Militia of Moyamensing, Passyunk, The Northern Liberties and, united to the city of Philadelphia,	147
Corporation of contributors, etc., neglecting to meet annually and choose 12 managers, overseers of the poor of Philadelphia, Southwark, Moyamensing and the Northern Liberties to be vested with their powers, etc.,	402
Overseers of the Poor incorporated under the name of 'The Guardians of the Poor of the City of Philadelphia,"	402
To appoint half-yearly six of their number to superintend the almshouse and house of employment, etc.,	403

SOUTHWARK—Continued.

Entry	Page
Such six overseers to be exempt from all other duties as overseers,	403
Any overseer with the consent of one justice of the peace to afford relief to the sudden necessity of any poor person not exceeding 3£ in three months,	403
One-half of overseers not to continue in office more than six months and their successors to be appointed half-yearly,	403
Penalty for neglect of overseers to serve,	404
Overseers with the approbation of two justices of the peace to bind out poor disorderly persons,	404
Persons over forty years or married exempted,	404
Term of binding not to exceed 3 years,	404-405
Part of prior act for the relief of the poor made perpetual,	405
Authority of mayor, recorder and aldermen of Philadelphia under such act vested in the justices of the peace of said city,	405
Act for the better relief of the poor, etc., repealed,	405
Act for the relief of the poor repealed,	405
Act for the better employment of the poor incorporating Passyunk with Philadelphia, Southwark, Moyamensing and Northern Liberties repealed,	405-406
Fees of auctioneers in Philadelphia, Northern Liberties and Southwark,	468-69
Auctioneers to demand and receive an additional 1 per cent. for the use of the commonwealth,	469
Auctioneers' bond to the president to be security for the proper application of the same,	469
Revenue arising from auctions in Philadelphia, Northern Liberties and Southwark appropriated to the support of government and the administration of justice,	469-70

SOUTHWARK—Continued.
Auditors appointed to examine and settle the accounts and certify that the sums due to Luke Morris, Thomas Penrose and Abel James for the purchase of lots for the use of a public landing, ... 481
On payment of sums so certified the fee simple to said lots to vest in certain trustees, ... 482
Trustees not to obtain any rights to said lots unless they pay sums certified by auditor within two years,.. 483
Upon procuring title trustees to lay out streets and landings, ... 483
Trustees to dispose of unnecessary parts of lots at public sale, ... 483
Trustees to mortgage the parts retained for public use, ... 484
Trustees to let out wharves, quays and landing places for terms not exceeding 7 years, ... 484
Trustees to establish rates and prices for wharfage, ... 484
And bind all tenants to observe the same rules and regulations as tenants of public landings in Philadelphia are bound to observe, ... 484
Trustees to pay off incumbrances as soon as they have sufficient means and convey the premises to the supervisors of the highways, ...484-485
Commissioners appointed to purchase with the approbation of three justices a lot or lots for the accommodation of Southwark with public landing places, ... 513
Commissioners to erect wharves and quays thereon, ... 513
And if necessary to mortgage such lots in order to do so, ... 513
Commissioners to lay out landing places, ... 513
And dispose of any over-plus at either public or private sale, ...512-514
Commissioners to let out the wharves, etc., establish the rates of toll, and receive the rents, etc., ... 514
To apply the same towards discharging all incumbrances on said lots, .. 514

SOUTHWARK—Continued.
Commissioners together with assessors and freeholders, to levy a yearly assessment not exceeding 1 shilling in the S, ... 514
To appoint a collector to collect the same, ... 514
Powers of collector, ... 515
Duties of collector, ... 515
Fees of collector, ... 515
Penalty on persons appointed collectors refusing to serve, ... 515
Penalty, how recoverable, ... 515
Defendant in such action to plead the general issue and give act and special matter in evidence, ... 515
But not allowed protection or wager of law nor more than one imparlance, ... 515
Collector failing to account for moneys received to be committed, without bail or mainprise, ... 516
Filling of vacancy in office of collector, 516
Bond of treasurer of commissioners, 516
Two-thirds of commissioners to constitute a board, ... 517
Estate in lots secure under act vested in the commissioners until all incumbrances are discharged, ... 517
Such lots to then devolve upon the supervisors of the highways who are erected into a corporation for the purposes of the trust. 517-518
Three additional supervisors to be elected at the first election after the final adjustment of the commissioners accounts, ... 518

SPAIN.
Goods, etc., imported from France, Spain, or the United Provinces, not to be treated as contraband, ... 498

SPEAKER OF THE HOUSE.
Wages of, ... 377
Mileage of, ... 377

SPECIAL MATTER. See Evidence.
Defendants in actions under militia act may plead general issue and give act and, in evidence, ...170-171

SPECIAL MATTER—Continued.

Persons sued under act for impost on goods, etc., may plead the general issue and give act and special matter in evidence, ... 256

Persons sued under act incorporating the borough of Carlisle may plead the general issue and give act and special matter in evidence, ... 448

Defendant in certain actions allowed to plead the general issue and give act and special matter in evidence, 515

STATE ARMS. See Flour.

Merchantable flour intended for exportation to be branded with the, ... 292

STATE HOUSE.

In the city of Philadelphia, vested in the commonwealth, ... 48

STATE ISLAND.

Act for better repairing banks, dams, ditches, sluices, flood-gates, ... 381

Manager and treasurer appointed,... 381

Election of managers and treasurer, ... 381-382

Managers to repair banks, dams, ditches, and flood-gates and make new ones, etc., ... 382

Costs of repairs to be born proportionately, ... 382

Penalty for neglect or refusal of owners to pay their share of costs assessed against them, ... 382

Managers either to restrain or sue for the same, ... 382-383

Managers to be styled the Managers of State Island, ... 383

Treasurer to be styled the Treasurer of State Island, ... 383

Treasurer to give security, ... 383

Treasurer to hand over to successor all money remaining in his hands, under penalty of £100, ... 383

STATE TAXES. See Federal Army.

Inhabitants of Bedford, Northampton, Northumberland and Westmoreland counties driven off and disabled by the enemy to be exonerated from,.. 114

STATE TAXES—Continued.

County rates and levies, etc., to be laid and assessed according to, ... 140

Act not to extend to state tax on ready money, ... 140

Nor to alter mode of taxation in counties where, has not been laid within twelve months, ... 140

Tax collectors to receive in payment of state taxes certificates granted to persons, for provisions furnished to federal army, ... 217

STATE TREASURER.

Amount of loans negotiated under resolutions of May 29, 1780, to be set apart in hands of the, subject to orders of supreme executive council for the purpose of discharging such loans together with interest thereon, ... 258

To pay reward to party entitled to prosecuting counterfeiters, etc., upon his producing a certificate to that effect from the trial judge, ... 16

Moneys recovered through act for recovering fines, etc., to be paid to,.. 138

Compensation of for receiving and handling same, ... 138

Compensation of for handling bills of credit, ... 186

Auctioneers to pay 1 per cent. of gross receipts to, every three months, ... 230

Compensation of for handling bills of credit, ... 304

To issue bills of credit and pay the same according to the drafts of the general assembly, etc., for the public use, ... 305

To set apart £200,000 in bills of credit for the purpose of exchanging old continental bills if credit, etc., ... 308

STREETS. See Philadelphia, City of.

Northern line of Vine street and southern line of Cedar street to be marked out by regulators of Philadelphia city assisted by regulators of the Northern Liberties, ... 487

Expense thereof to be borne proportionately by the said city and district, ... 487-488

Index. 627

STREETS—Continued. Page.
All streets, etc., in Philadelphia dedicated to public use declared to be highways, ... 489
All streets laid out by supreme executive council declared to be highways, ... 489
No length of time to bar the removal of nuisances from public streets,489-490
Commissioners to remove trees growing in the streets, ... 490
Penalty for obstructing them in so doing, ... 490
Regulations respecting grates over vaults in streets, ... 491
Part of act directing the removal of trees out of the streets of Philadelphia, repealed, ... 511

SUBSISTENCE MONEY.
Of persons apprehending prisoners of war, ... 466

SUBSTITUTES. See Militia; Pennsylvania Volunteers.
To be procured by persons enrolled in the Pennsylvania Volunteers and neglecting or refusing to serve, ... 192
Proceedings to procure, where such person refuses to serve or get one,.. 192

SUPERVISORS. See Carlisle, Borough of.
Premises containing public wharves in Southwark to be conveyed to the supervisors as soon as they are cleared of all insumbrances, ...484-485
Lots purchased by commissioners for public landing places in Southwark to devolve upon the supervisors of the highways as soon as they are, cleared of all incumbrances, ...517-518
Three additional supervisors to be elected in the district of Southwark, 518

SUPPLIES. See War Taxes.
Act for raising, for 1781, ... 326
Act for raising, for 1782, ... 385
Act for raising additional, for 1781,.. 351
Act not to prevent plaintiff or defendant from being allowed a reasonable time to procure testimony, ... 418

Page.
SUPREME COURT. See High Court of Errors and Appeals.
Act empowering supreme executive council and justices of the, to apprehend suspected persons, continued, ... 31
Fees of the prothonotary of the, to be paid in wheat, ... 40
High court of errors and appeals to be composed of the president of the supreme executive council, the judge of admiralty and three persons of integrity and ability, ... 54
Appeals from the, court of admiralty and register of wills to lie to the high court of errors and appeals, ... 54
Justices of the, or judge of admiralty not to sit in high court of errors and appeals in cases already heard and determined by them, ...54-55
Horse thieves not to be let out on bail except by a judge of the, ... 113
All fines, etc., to be estreated into the, every April and September, ... 134
Penalty for violation, ...134-135
Schedules to be delivered yearly to sheriffs and prothonotary of the, by clerks of the peace, ... 135
Penalty for violation, ... 135
Justices to award process for levying fines, etc., ... 135
Estreats into, to be returned upon oath, ... 136
Form of oath, ... 136
Justices to view estreats and cause prothonotary to enroll them, ... 137
To hear complaints of immoderate fines, etc., estreated, ... 137
To appoint a clerk of the estreats, .. 137
Duties of clerk, ... 137
Secretary of supreme executive council to certify duties arising from tavern and other licenses, ... 138
Act empowering supreme executive council and justices of the, to apprehend suspected persons, etc., continued, ...182-183
Jurisdiction of the justices of the, to be the same in Washington county as in other counties, ... 274

SUPREME COURT—Continued.

	Page.
Plaintiffs or defendants in actions brought in the supreme or common pleas courts for debts in case of their sudden departure upon giving security may apply for special courts and have their cases determined at once,	417
Defendants in supreme court entitled to same benefits as defendants in common pleas,	418

SUPREME EXECUTIVE COUNCIL. See Board of Property.

To appoint and commission an auctioneer for holding public auctions in Philadelphia,	19
To reserve confiscated estates not sold and create a fund for the maintenance of the provost, etc., of the University of Pennsylvania,	24
Such income limited to 1,500£ per annum,	24
Act empowering justices of the supreme court and the, to apprehend suspected persons, etc., continued,	31
Officers of land office, etc., to deliver up books, papers, etc., on demand of president of,	38
Fees of the secretary of the, to be paid in wheat,	40
Wages and mileage of members of the to be the same as wages and mileage of members of assembly under late government,	41
To suspend act preventing exports by sea for a limited time as soon as it becomes unnecessary,	44
To sell old jail and workhouse in Philadelphia for benefit of said city and county,	51
House and lots on High, Minor and Sixth Sts., in Philadelphia formerly belonging to Joseph Galloway, traitor, and appropriated by prior act to the use of the president of the, vested in the commonwealth,	48-50
To defray expense of procuring and distributing provisions for the officers and soldiers in the Pennsylvania Line, at certain prices,	63
Disputes concerning eligibility of persons claiming pensions to be adjusted by the,	66

SUPREME EXECUTIVE COUNCIL—Continued.

	Page.
May direct auditors appointed under act for settlement of public accounts to attend to other places in the state than Philadelphia,	77
To draw orders on state treasurer for payment of auditors,	80
To appoint a judge of the court of admiralty,	97
To appoint a register of the court of admiralty,	103
To appoint a marshall of the court of admiralty,	104
Empowered to pardon persons convicted of treason or other felony on condition of their departing the United States,	111
Such pardons to be void if such persons return,	111
Secretary of the to certify duties arising from tavern and other licenses to the supreme court,	138
Penalty for neglect or refusal,	138
Commissioned lieutenants, etc., to render accounts and make returns to,	152
President of the, to have the power to pardon, etc., persons convicted under militia act,	159
Army provisions when collected by commissioners to be transported and delivered under the direction of,	179-180
Commissioners to cease collecting army provisions when ordered to do so by the,	180
Monthly returns, to be made by army commissioners to the,	180
Act empowering justices of the supreme court and the, to apprehend suspected persons, etc., continued,	182-183
Contracts between the quarter-master general of the U. S. and the, for the passage of men, etc., not annulled by the further supplement to act regulating nightly watch, etc.,	203
Commissioners appointed to procure provisions for the federal army to deliver same under directions of the, to the commissary general,	215

SUPREME EXECUTIVE COUNCIL—Continued.

Difficulties arising in execution of act for procuring provisions for federal army to be referred to the, ... 218

After February 1, 1881, to publish monthly rate of exchange between specie and continental money, ... 251

Bond of naval officer to be filed and recorded with the secretary of the, 258

Amount of loans negotiated under resolutions of May 29, 1780 to be set apart in hands of state treasurer subject to orders of, for the purpose of discharging such loan together with interest thereon, ... 258

To appoint officers to recruit and receive recruits, etc., under act for completing the quota of the federal army, ... 261

Empowered to call the commissioned officers, chaplains and surgeons of the Pennsylvania Line into service at any time, ... 315

To appoint additional auditors for settling the accounts of the Pennsylvania Line, ... 315

To draw on state treasurer for sums to pay off part of certificates granted to the officers and soldiers of the Pennsylvania Line, ... 316

To appoint commissioners to take up old certificates and grant new ones, 316

To order sale of all forfeited estates on or before May 10, 1781, ... 317

Authorized to adopt expedient measures in order to recruit the Pennsylvania line in the army of the United States, ... 365

One extra company of the militia to be raised for the defense of the frontiers of the state, ... 373

To be clothed, etc., by and be under the direction of the supreme executive council, ... 373

Supreme executive council to appoint and commission the officers of said company, ... 373

Officers to be taken from those of the Pennsylvania line who are on half pay, ... 374

Compensation of recruits, ... 374

SUPREME EXECUTIVE COUNCIL—Continued.

Inhabitants waylaying and annoying the enemy in their incursions and depredations to be entitled to militia pay and rations, ... 374

Supreme executive council to draw on the treasury for such necessary sums, 374

Forces raised under act to be bound by the rules and regulations of the army of the United States, ...374-375

Supreme executive council empowered to order all troops on any expedition against the savages or other enemies on the frontiers of the state, 375

Taxes due by persons driven from their homes to be levied proportionately on the other parts of the counties, ... 375

County commissioners authorized to exonerate from taxation inhabitants who have been so driven off and distressed by the enemy, ... 375

Also to exonerate those inhabitants who stay on the frontiers for the purpose of its defense, ... 376

Commissioners to transmit to general assembly a list of the names, etc., of the person so exonerated,.. 376

Supreme executive council authorized to borrow enough to defend the frontiers, and for the other exigencies of government,, ... 492

Loan not to exceed 30,000 £, ... 492

Interest thereon not to exceed 6 per cent. per annum, ... 492

Duties arising on liquors, revenues from sales at vendues, fines and penalties from naval and excise officers, and moneys arising from marriage, tavern and other licenses, pledged as funds for the payment thereof, ... 493

Supreme executive council empowered to apply the same to that purpose, ... 493

Faith and honor of the state pledged to make up and pay off any deficiency, ... 493

SUPREME EXECUTIVE COUNCIL—
Continued.
  Members of the general assembly, after 15 days, to make out a list of delinquent assemblymen and transmit it to the, ... 507
  To require attorney general to sue for and recover from such delinquents the fines prescribed by act,.. 507
  Act to enable the supreme executive council to negotiate loans, etc., for the defense of the frontiers and support of government, repealed, ... 534

SURGEONS. See Pennsylvania Line.
  And chaplains to receive same emoluments and benefits as commissioned officers, ...314-315
  Entitled also to the half-pay of a captain for life, ... 315
  To be liable to be called into service by the supreme executive council at any time, ... 315
  Penalty for neglect or refusal to obey such call, ... 315

SURVEYOR-GENERAL. See Board of Property; Land Office.
  To be one of the members of the board of property, ...408-409
  To receive returns from late deputy-surveyors, ... 410

SURVEYORS AND REGULATORS. See Carlisle, Borough of; Regulators.

SURVEYS.
  Made without license of president and council declared to be void, ... 127
  All, made since July 4, 1776, to be filed in the office of the secretary of the supreme executive council or be void, ... 127
  Time of filing, limited, ...127-128
  Filing not to give relief to which party was not entitled before passing of act, ... 128
  Duration of act, limited, ... 128

SUSPECTED PERSONS.
  Act empowering supreme executive council and justices of the supreme court to apprehend, etc., continued, ...182-183

SWINE.
  Prohibited from running at large in Passyunk, Moyamensing, Northern Liberties, Germantown and Bristol, 116
  Such swine to be forfeited, ... 116
  Disposition of forfeiture, ...116-117
  Person aggrieved by seizure of swine to have appeal to justice of the peace, 117
  Party appealing to forfeit 40s where such seizure is confirmed, ... 117
  Act to prevent swine from running at large within Passyunk, Moyamensing, Northern Liberties, Germantown and Bristol, revived, ... 283

T.

TALLOW CHANDLERS. See Carlisle, Borough of; Nuisances.

TARE. See Bread.

TARIFF.
  On imported goods, etc., ... 253
  Imported goods together with the casks, etc., to vest in the commonwealth where naval officer tenders to importer the value of goods and 10 per cent. increase, ... 253
  Importer liable for freight, etc., accruing previous to landing, etc., ... 253
  Commonwealth to recover possession of such goods by action of detinue, trover and conversion, or replevin, 253
  Naval officer upon due entry of goods, etc., and payment of or securing the duties imposed by act to grant a permit for landing, ...253-254
  Where goods, etc., remain in vessel ten days after the arrival thereof, without the duty being paid or secured, master to deliver same to naval officer to be warehoused and kept at owners' risk and expense,.. 254
  Moneys arising therefrom after payment of duty and charges to be lodged with state treasurer for use of owner, ... 254
  Masters of ships not to unload without permit, ... 254
  Penalty for violation, ... 255
  Naval officer, his deputy and assistants to enter vessels and suspected houses in search of concealed goods liable to duty, ... 255

Index. 631

TARIFF—Continued.
  In case of opposition or refusal naval officer to obtain a writ of assistance from two justices of the supreme court and break open doors, etc., .. 255
  Persons trading in the Delaware and coming into port with goods in vessels liable to duties to comply with provisions of act, ... 255
  River vessels not required to pay more than two shillings for exhibiting a manifest of goods liable to duty, ... 255
  Master refusing to exhibit manifest to forfeit £1,000, ... 256
  Fines, penalties and forfeitures incurred under act, how recoverable, 256
  Application of, ... 256
  In actions against goods seized, burden of proof to lie upon claimant instead of prosecutor, ... 256
  Claimant to enter security for cost before instituting action, ... 256
  Naval officer or person sued under act may plead the general issue and give act and special matter in evidence, 256
  Defendant to have treble costs where plaintiff becomes nonsuit, discontinues or has judgment pass against him, ...256-257
  All suits under act to be brought within one year from time of injury, .. 257
  Naval officer to keep fair accounts, etc., and pay over balance monthly to state treasurer, ... 257
  Naval officer to submit all his books and papers to the inspection of the president and council, ... 257
  Naval officer to annually settle his accounts with the auditors of the public accounts, ... 257
  Compensation of naval officer, ... 257
  Duties to be paid in gold or silver as they passed in 1775 or other money equivalent, ... 257
  Fines, penalties, etc., to be levied, satisfied and paid accordingly, ... 257
  Bond of naval officer, ... 257
  Sureties on such bonds to be approved of by the president and council, ..257-258
  Bond to be filed, and recorded with the secretary of the supreme executive council, ... 258

TARIFF—Continued.
  Naval officer to appoint a deputy, ... 258
  Act not to give authority to collect duty on common salt, gunpowder, etc., ... 258
  Amount of loans negotiated under resolutions of May 29, 1780, to be set apart in hands of state treasurer subject to orders of supreme executive council, for the purpose of discharging such loans together with interest thereon, ... 258

TAVERN LICENSES.
  Fees for, after August 9, 1780 to be paid in wheat in like manner as fees of officers, ...130-131
  Security to be given in the same manner, ... 131
  Act increasing fees on, partly repealed, ... 131

TAVERNS. See Tavern Licenses.
  Militia not to meet at, on days of exercise, ... 169

TAXATION.
  Pennsylvania Volunteers exempted from, during term of service, ... 194

TAX COLLECTORS. See County Commissioners; War Taxes.
  Fines on delinquent, increased, ...196-197
  Penalty for neglect or refusal to collect militia fines, ...197,198
  County commissioners and assessors to appoint other collectors in the place of delinquents, ... 197
  Receipts for wheat flour, etc., delivered to commissioners of purchases, etc., to be received by, in discharge of taxes, ... 198
  County treasurers to receive such receipts in payment from, ... 199
  Where certificate exceeds amount of taxes due collector to give receipt for the surplus, ... 199
  Treasurer to keep a record of all sums over and above amount of taxes charged against persons holding receipts, ... 199
  And discount the surplus with interest to collector or next state tax, ... 199

Index

TAX COLLECTORS—Continued.
  State treasurer to receive such certificates from county treasurers and deliver them to principal of the respective departments from whom the payment is due, ...199-200
  To take receipts from such principals and lodge the same with the board of treasury, ... 200
  To receive in payment of state taxes certificates granted to persons for provisions furnished to federal army, ... 217

TAXES.
  Not exceeding 1s in the £ annually to be levied in Southwark in order to discharge incumbrances against the public landing places, etc., ... 514
  Tax collector to be appointed to collect the same, ... 514
  Powers and duty of collector, ... 515
  Fees of collector, ... 515
  Penalty for tax collector refusing or neglecting to serve, ... 515
  Penalty, how recoverable, ... 515
  Collector failing to account for moneys received to be committed without bail or mainprize, ... 516

TAXES. See County Rates and Levies; Excise; Military Taxes; Pennsylvania Line; State Taxes; War Tax.
  $2,500,000 in, to be raised monthly for the use of the United States, ... 10
  Duties of the several and respective commissioners, collectors and treasurers of the different counties in collecting the same, ...10-11
  Powers of commissioners, collectors and treasurers, ... 11
  Not paid in the months they become due to be collected as soon after as they may be, ...11-12
  Collector to give receipt and discharge for monthly assessments paid in advance, ... 12
  Lands granted to officers and soldiers exempted from, ... 61
  Inhabitants of Bedford, Northampton, Northumberland and Westmoreland counties driven off and disabled by the enemy to be exonerated from, ... 114

TAXES—Continued.
  Pennsylvania Volunteers exempted from, during term of service, ... 194
  Wheat flour, etc., to be received in payment of, by persons appointed by commissioners of purchases, ... 198
  Receipts therefor to be received by tax collector in discharge of taxes,. 198
  County treasurers to receive such receipts in payment from collectors,. 199
  Where certificate exceeds amount of taxes due collector to give receipt for the surplus, ... 199
  Treasurer to keep a record of all sums over and above amount of taxes charged against persons holding receipts, ... 199
  And discount the surplus with interest to collector of next state tax,... 199
  State treasurer to receive such certificates from county treasurers and deliver them to principal of the respective departments from whom the payment is due, ...199-200
  To take receipts from such principals and lodge the same with the board of treasury, ... 200
  Monthly taxes levied under act for raising $2,500,000, etc., continued,209-210
  Monthly taxes to redeem $25,000,000 of bills of credit of the U. S., also continued, ... 210
  Bills of credit received in payment of such monthly taxes not to be issued again, ... 210
  Such bills to be kept by state treasurer to be cancelled and destroyed, 210
  New bills of credit to bear interest at 5 per cent., ... 210
  Bills of credit received by public agents for any taxes or public dues, etc., to be accounted for at the same rate as received, ... 251
  After June 1, 1781, to be paid in gold, silver or bills of credit, ... 308
  Not exceeding 1s in the £ annually to be levied in Southwark in order to discharge incumbrances against the public landing places, etc., ... 514
  Tax collector to be appointed to collect the same, ... 514
  Powers and duty of collector, ... 515

TAXES—Continued.

Fees of collector, ... 515
Penalty for tax collector refusing or neglecting to serve, ... 515
Penalty, how recoverable, ... 515
Collector failing to account for moneys received to be committed without bail or mainprize, ... 516

TORIES. See Loyalists.

TOWNSHIP ASSESSORS. See County Commissioners; War Taxes.

TOWN CLERK. See Carlisle, Borough of.

TRADE. See Bread; Contraband; Embargo; Exports; Flour.

Part of act to permit the exportation of flour of wheat, etc., repealed, ... 326
Supplement to act regulating navigation and trade, ... 418
No goods, wares, merchandise produced or manufactured by Great Britain to be imported into this state, ... 419
All such goods to be confiscated, ... 419
One-half to go to informer and the other half to the commonwealth,... 419
All actions under act against importers to be brought within six months, ... 419
Proviso as to goods, wares, merchandise taken as prize, ... 419
Such goods, wares and merchandise not to be imported from neutral ports, ... 420
Captain, etc., of vessels to certify that imported goods from neutral ports are not the growth, product, etc., of Great Britain, ... 420
Such goods to be confiscated if captain neglects to produce certificate, ...420-421
Part of prior act regulating navigation and trade repealed, ... 421

TREASON.

Attainder of, after peace with Great Britain not to disinherit heirs nor to prejudice any one except the offender, ... 112
Persons charged with, may be proceeded against as for misdemeanor, 112

TREASON—Continued.

A further time granted to Daniel Rundle and Matthias Aspden to render themselves to a justice of the supreme court and stand trial for,.. 280
Attainder stayed upon condition that they do so on or before Dec. 31, 1781, 280
Either party failing to so render himself to be adjudged and attainted of high, ... 281

TREATY.

All subjects of His Most Christian Majesty entitled to the rights and privileges stipulated in their behalf by the 11th article of the treaty of amity and commerce concluded between him and the U. S. of America, ... 510
Act to take effect as of February 6th, 1778, ... 510

TREBLE COSTS.

Defendant to have, where plaintiff becomes nonsuit, discontinues or has judgment pass against him in actions under militia act, ... 171
Defendant to recover, in certain cases where plaintiff becomes nonsuit, suffers a discontinuance or has judgment pass against him, ...256-57,324,448
Defendant to recover treble costs in suits for the condemnation of goods as contraband, if plaintiff wilfully delays, discontinues, or has judgpassed against him, ... 503-504

TREES.

Growing in the streets of Philadelphia to be removed by the commissioners, 490
Penalty for obstructing them in so doing, ... 490
Penalty, how recoverable, ... 490
Part of act directing the removal of trees out of the streets, etc., of Philadelphia, repealed, ... 511

TRESPASS.

United States authorized to bring actions of, to protect its property, ... 46
Act to prevent trespassing upon unenclosed grounds in Passyunk, Moyamensing, Northern Liberties and Germantown revived and extended to Bristol township, ... 116

634   Index.

TRESPASS—Continued.
  Persons guilty of committing, on lands of absentees, etc., to pay treble damages, ... 127
  May be fined and imprisoned upon conviction thereof, ... 127
  Duration of act limited, ... 127
  Act to prevent the trespassing upon the unenclosed grounds of Passyunk, Moyamensing, Northern Liberties, Germantown and Bristol, revived, ... 283

TROOPS. See Militia; Pennsylvania Line; War.

TROVER.
  Imported goods together with the casks, etc., to vest in the commonwealth where naval officer tenders to importer the value of such goods with 10 per cent. increase, ... 253
  Commonwealth to recover possession thereof by action of detinue, replevin or, ... 253

TUMULTS.
  All persons charged with engaging in Walnut street tumult on October 4, 1779, near James Wilson's house, pardoned, ... 118
  Act pardoning such persons to be deemed a public act, ...118-119

U.

UNIFORMS. See Pennsylvania Line.

UNITED PROVINCES.
  Goods, etc., imported from France, Spain, or the United Provinces, not to be treated as contraband, ... 498

UNITED STATES. See Pennsylvania Line.
  $2,500,000 to be raised monthly by taxation, for the use of the, ... 10
  Duties of the several and respective county commissioners, collectors and treasurers in collecting the same, ..10-11
  Powers of commissioners, collectors and treasurers, ... 11

UNITED STATES—Continued.
  Sums not paid in the months they become due to be collected as soon after as may be, ...11-12
  Collector to give receipt and discharge for monthly assessments paid in advance, ... 12
  Penalty for counterfeiting or forging the paper money of the, ...15-16
  Certain public property vested in the, during the war, ... 46
  Empowered to sue trespassers, etc., .. 46
  Act not to justify the taking of lands without consent of owner from and after January 1, 1779, ... 46
  Authorized to remove its buildings from such lands, ... 46
  Upon removal of buildings all title and interest of the, in and to the lands whereon the buildings were erected to cease, ... 46
  Owners of land temporarily vested in and occupied by the, to be paid a reasonable rent for same, ... 46
  Rent to be fixed by three appraisers,46-47
  Appointment of appraisers, ... 47
  Upon termination of war to remove or pull down and sell all such buildings which it no longer requires, ... 47
  Empowered to purchase, hold or convey lands, etc., for maintaining public buildings, ... 47
  All such lands, etc., to be subject to the disposition and appropriation of Congress, ... 47
  Certain acts of assembly making bills of credit of the U. S. legal tender equal to gold and silver suspended for a limited time, ... 204
  Act not to extend to any debt or contract made after November 1, 1779, upon which suit has actually been brought, ... 204
  Nor to sheriffs, attorneys, executors, guardians, etc., ... 204
  Act for funding and redeeming the bills of credit of the, ... 205
  Monthly taxes to redeem $25,000,000 of bills of credit of the United States continued, ... 210

Index.

635

UNITED STATES—Continued.
Act suspended so far as respects new bills of credit, to be emitted by Congress until majority of states adopt resolves of Congress of March 18, 1780, ... 213
Act to suspend laws making the bills of credit of the, legal tender, in payment of debts equal to gold and silver, continued, ... 229
Duration of act, limited, ... 229
Authorized to levy a five per cent. ad valorem duty on imports, ... 297
Arms, ammunition, clothing, wool cards, cotton cards and wire for making them, and salt excepted, .. 297
Authorized to levy a like duty on prizes and prize goods condemned by the admiralty court, ... 297
To appoint collectors for collecting same, ... 298
Moneys arising from such duties to be appropriated in payment of debts, contracted on the faith of the, for support of the present war, ... 298
Act to continue in force until such debts are fully and finally discharged, ... 298
All Subjects of His Most Christian Majesty entitled to the rights and privileges stipulated in their behalf by the 11th Article of the treaty of amity and commerce concluded between him and the U. S. of America, 510
Act to take effect as of February 6th, 1778, ... 510

UNITED STATES BILLS OF CREDIT.
See Bills of Credit.

UNIVERSITY OF THE STATE OF PENNSYLVANIA.
Former by law narrowing original plan of the college, academy and charitable school of Philadelphia declared void, ... 24
Supreme executive council to reserve confiscated estates not sold and create a fund for the maintenance of the provost, etc., ... 24
Such income not to exceed 1,500£ per annum, ... 24

UNIVERSITY OF THE STATE OF PENNSYLVANIA—Continued.
Such reservation to be laid before the general assembly for confirmation, 24
Confirming of such estates not to extend to establishing estates in original trustees, etc., ... 25
Superintendents and trust to be vested in certain named persons, ...24-25
Such persons to be styled "The trustees of the University of Pennsylvania," 26
Powers of trustees, ... 26
Filling vacancy where trustee neglects or refuses to act, ... 26
Selection to meet with approval of general assembly, ... 26
Former oath of trustees, etc., superseded, ...26-27
Clauses in former charters directing trustees to make rules, ordinances and statutes not repugnant to laws of Great Britain, etc., repealed, ... 27
Trustees to review old rules, etc., and frame new ones consistent with the constitution and the laws of this state, ... 27
Business of corporation to be transacted and determined by a majority of seven of the trustees, ... 28
Certain matters to require a majority of eleven of the trustees, ... 28
Clause in first charter limiting trustees to inhabitants of Pennsylvania residing within five miles of the college and academy of Philadelphia, declared void, ... 28
Trustees to have power to sue and to be sued, ... 28
Former trustees to deliver up books, records, etc., ... 29
Penalty for neglect or refusal, ... 29
Trustees declared to be a body, politic and corporate, ...29-30
To have power to make a common seal, rules, etc., and to alter and amend them, ... 30
Name style and title of officers of the University of the state of Pennsylvania, ... 30
Trustees to submit accounts to visitors from the general assembly, ... 30

UNIVERSITY OF THE STATE OF PENNSYLVANIA—Continued.
   Trustees to meet annually on first Wednesday in December, ... 30
   Defect in prior act confirming estates, etc., in the, cured, ... 125
   The word college in section 16 to be construed university, ... 125

UTTERING.
   Punishment for knowingly uttering counterfeit or raised bills of credit, loan office certificates or bills of exchange, ... 15
   Punishment for uttering forged, counterfeited or raised bills of credit, 139, 212, 307

V.

VENDUE. See Public Vendue.

VERDICT.
   Defendant to have treble cost in certain cases where plaintiff becomes non-suit, suffers a discontinuance, or has verdict passed against him, 448
   Defendant to recover treble costs, if plaintiff in suits to condemn certain goods as contraband, wilfully delays, discontinues or has judgment verdict pass against him, ...503-504

VICE-PRESIDENTS.
   Salary of, ... 377

VINE STREET.
   Northern line of Vine street and southern line of Cedar street to be marked out by regulators of Philadelphia City assisted by regulators of the Northern Liberties, ... 487
   Expense thereof to be borne proportionately by the said city and district, ...487-488

W.

WAGER OF LAW.
   Not allowed, ...137, 295, 515

WAGES. See Militia.
   Price of day's labor to be fixed by quarter sessions and become the rate for payment of fines under militia act, ... 158

WAGES—Continued.
   Of members of congress, ... 377
   Of members of the supreme executive council, ... 377
   Of speaker of the house, ... 377
   Of members of the assembly, ... 378
   Of clerks of the assembly, ... 378
   Of sergeant at arms of the assembly, 378
   Of door-keeper of the assembly, ... 378
   Prior acts fixing wages of government officers repealed, ... 378

WAGONERS. See Militia; Pennsylvania Volunteers.
   In actual service not to be enlisted in the Pennsylvania Volunteers, ... 191

WAGON MASTERS. See Wagons.
   Duties of, ... 361
   Compensation of, ... 362

WAGONS. See Defence; Militia; War.
   President to call out enough wagons to transport baggage and stores of troops called out for defense of state, 361
   County wagon masters and constables to perform same duties as required under former wagon laws, ... 361
   Compensation of wagon masters, ... 362
   President to seize and impress wagons, etc., if sufficient cannot be procured in manner prescribed by act, ... 362

WAR. See Army of the United States; Militia; Pensions; Pennsylvania Line; Prisoners of War; United States; War Tax.
   Act providing for the present defense of this state, ... 361
   President to call out enough wagons to transport baggage and stores of troops called out for the defense of the state, ... 361
   County wagon masters and constables to perform same duties as required under former wagon laws, ... 361
   Compensation of wagon masters, ... 362
   President to seize and impress wagons, etc., if sufficient number cannot be procured in manner prescribed by act, ... 362

Index. 637

WAR—Continued.
President to seize and impress arms, ammunition, stores, etc., when necessary and apply the same to public use, ... 362
Seizure to be certified and the value to be ascertained specie, ... 362
President to billet and quarter troops upon public or private houses, ... 362
President authorized to call out all of the militia without respect to classes, 363
Person neglecting or refusing to perform tour of militia duty on call of president to be fined, ... 363
President authorized to draw upon the treasury for necessary money to procure arms and ammunition, etc., .. 363
President authorized to impress horses and wagons, etc., for the removal of families and property of inhabitants of Philadelphia, Northern Liberties, and Southwark who are in actual service against the enemy,... 363
Duration of act limited, ... 364
All goods, etc., of the growth, product or manufacture of Great Britain, or of any country under the dominion thereof, or any goods coming from countries held by the forces thereof, to be considered as contraband, .. 497
All contraband to be liable to seizure, condemnation and confiscation, ... 497
Goods, etc., taken as prize upon water and condemned as such in a court of admiralty of the U. S. excepted,...497-498
Salt, salt petre, gunpowder, lead, etc., also excepted, ... 498
Clothing for prisoners of war also excepted, ... 498
Goods, etc., imported from France, Spain, or the United Provinces not to be treated as contraband, ... 498
Any person finding goods, etc., in or moving through the state which he believes to be contraband, to seize the same, ...498-499
Proceedings upon seizure, ...499-500-501
Persons desiring to defend property seized to first enter security, ... 501
No carriage, beast, boat or vessel to be condemned unless the goods connected therewith exceed 10£, ... 501
No replevin to lie for goods seized, .. 501

WAR—Continued.
Proceedings before justice to be final, ...501-502
Goods, etc., seized and condemned as contraband to be forthwith advertised and sold at public auction by sheriff under warrant of justice, .. 502
Ten days' public notice in writing to be given therefor, if the value be under 50£, ... 502
Where value of goods exceed 50£, like notice to be also inserted in one of the Philadelphia weekly newspapers, 503
After sale justice to deduct all expenses and order sheriff, etc., to pay one-half of residue to plaintiff and the other half to county treasurer, 503
County treasurer to transmit the same to state treasurer, ... 503
Fees of county treasurer so doing,... 503
Costs of proceeding, ... 503
All suits for things done in pursuance of act to be brought within six months, ... 503
Defendant to recover treble costs if plaintiff wilfully delay, discontinue, or have verdict or judgment passed against him, ...503-504
Persons convicted of trading with subjects of King of Great Britain to forfeit 1-3 of the value of goods seized besides the goods so seized or suffer three months imprisonment, ... 504
Prosecutions therefor to be made in any court of quarter sessions or oyer and terminer, ... 504
All persons coming out of the line of the enemy into this state without a license from the president, etc., to be imprisoned by any justice of the peace, ... 504
All such intruders to be fined, ... 504
No person to go out of the state into the lines of the enemy without proper authority, ... 504
Penalty for so doing, ... 504
Disposition of penalty, ...504-505
Act not to affect persons furnished with a pass from any of the other states, if same be approved by president, etc., ... 505

WAR—Continued.

- Certain act of assembly repealed, .. 505
- Duration of act limited until close of war, ... 505
- Act for procuring an estimate of the damages sustained by the inhabitants of this state from the British troops, ... 530
- County commissioners of every county invaded by British troops to direct assessors to notify inhabitants to furnish accounts of damages, etc., done thereby and transmit the same to commissioners, ... 531
- Assessors to render such accounts where inhabitants refuse, ... 531
- Contents of account, ...531-532
- Commissioners to transmit accounts to supreme executive council, ... 532
- Servants, negroes and mulatto slaves deluded and carried away by British troops to be included in accounts,.. 532
- Charges and expenses of executing act to be defrayed by the commonwealth, ... 533

WARDENS.

- Of Philadelphia city to let market-houses, ferries, wharves and public landing places, ... 201
- With assessors to levy an additional rate not exceeding 6d in the £, ... 201
- Said rate to be collected in the usual manner, ... 201
- To authorize treasurer to receive rents from market-houses, etc., ... 201
- Clerk of the market to collect rents from market-houses, etc., and pay the same over to the treasurer of the, ... 201
- Penalty for neglect or refusal, ... 202
- Owners, etc., of ferries, etc., in Philadelphia to pay their rents to the treasurer of the, ... 202
- Penalty for neglect or refusal, ... 202
- Penalty for persons receiving money under act and not paying the same over to the treasurer of the, ... 202
- Moneys received under act to be used by wardens for purposes specified in act regulating nightly watch, etc., ... 202

WARDENS—Continued.

- Empowered to purchase a lot on north side of Sassafras street along Delaware river for a public wharf, ... 203
- Act not to extend to the interest held by the city of Philadelphia to the middle ferry on Schuylkill from May 1, 1780 to May 1, 1781, ... 203
- Unless wardens agree with the president in council to keep such bridge in repair, etc., ... 203
- Act not to annul contracts made by supreme executive council with quarter-master general of the U. S. for passage of men, etc., ... 203

WAR TAX.

- £93,640, 10s to be raised yearly for six years, by tax on estates real and personal, ...238-239
- Proportion of the city and counties, .. 239
- Provisions of act for raising supplies for 1779 continued and extended to levying and collecting taxes under act, ... 239
- Single men over twenty-one and more than six months out of their apprenticeship or servitude to be taxed,.. 240
- Goods and chattels of tenant to be liable to be distrained on for war taxes, etc., as well as the owners of lands, etc., ... 240
- Tenants paying such taxes to reserve them out of rent, etc., or recover the same by action of debt, ... 240
- Eighteenth section of act for raising $5,700,000 obliging tenants to pay taxes over and above their rent not extended to taxes under act, ... 241
- £200,000 to be raised, levied and collected during 1781, ...326-327
- Proportionate share of the different cities and counties, ... 327
- County commissioners to meet on or before the first Tuesday in July and issue their warrants to the assessors requiring them to make returns of all taxable persons and their property, ...327-328
- Assessors to administer an oath or affirmation to each taxable as to the truth of his return, ... 328
- Form of oath, ... 328

WAR TAX—Continued.
Penalty for taxables refusing to make returns or to swear to the truth thereof, ... 328
Assessors to find out and return property refused to be returned, ... 328
Lands not returned to be charged with all such taxes in the next assessment, ... 329
In case of vacancy in office of assessor county commissioners to appoint,... 329
Upon receipt of assessors returns commissioners to quota the districts, etc., ... 329
And within six days thereafter furnish the assessors with a transcript of the quota charged upon the township, etc., to which the assessor belongs, ...329-330
Assessors and two freeholders to levy and assess the quota of each township, etc., on the persons and their estates therein, ... 330
List of the different kinds of property subject to taxation under act, ... 330
Such enumerated articles to be rated at what they are bona fide worth... 330
Single freemen over twenty-one and more than six months out of their apprenticeship to pay a sum not over £6 nor under 45s, ...330-331
Trades, professions, etc., to be rated at the discretion of the assessors and freeholders, ... 331
Goods of tenants, etc., liable to be distrained for such taxes, ... 331
Tenant to deduct tax from rent where he is compelled to pay the same, .. 331
Or recover the same by action at law, 331
Act not to alter any contract between landlord and tenant as to the payment of taxes, ... 331
Oath of county commissioners, ... 332
Oath of assessors, ... 332
County commissioners to appoint a tax collector for each township, ward and district, ... 332
Commissioners to prefix a warrant to collectors duplicate, etc., ... 332
Contents of warrant, ... 332

WAR TAX—Continued.
Assessors and collectors to notify commissioners in writing within two days of their election or appointment as to their intention to serve or decline the office, ...332-333
Failure to do so to be considered as a refusal to serve, ... 333
Penalty for neglect or refusal of assessors and collectors to serve, ... 333
Where owner of goods distrained on for taxes refuses to receive the overplus collector to pay the same to the county treasurer, ... 333
County treasurer to deduct 1 per cent. and give notice thereof to the county commissioners within twenty days,. 333
Owner to have the remainder discounted out of any future tax,..333-334
Receipt of treasurer to exonerate collector, ... 334
Collectors to make out accounts of their seizures, etc., and settle the same with commissioners, ... 334
Compensation of collectors, ... 334
Commissioners empowered to proceed against delinquent collectors, ... 334
Collectors to pay the tax charged in their duplicate within thirty days after the day of appeal, ... 334
Proviso as to cases where he has been obliged to make distress, ... 334
Respective county treasurers to make payments to the state treasurer within certain specified times after receiving the same from collector,334-335
Commissioners to transmit copies of the assessment to state treasurer within thirty days after day of appeal, ... 335
Compensation of county commissioners and assessors, ... 335
Compensation of collectors, ... 335
Taxes to be paid in gold or silver only, 335
Proviso to persons who have taken the oath of allegiance to this state, ...335-336
Penalty for neglect or refusal of commissioners to do their duty under act, 336
Penalty, how recoverable, ... 336
Act for raising supplies for 1779, extended and continued, ... 336

WAR TAX—Continued.
£80,000 to be raised, levied and collected during 1781, ... 351
Proportionate share of the different counties, ...351-352
To be raised, levied and collected in same manner as provided for in supplement to act for funding and redeeming the bills of credit of the U. S., etc., ... 352
Said act continued until present supplies are raised, ...352-353
Bills of credit of certain emissions to be received in payment of, ... 353
To be assessed on the returns made or to be made in pursuance of act for raising £200,000 for year 1781,353-354
420,297£, 15s to be raised for the year 1782 by a tax on estates real and personal, ... 385
Proportionate share of the cities and counties, ...385-386
County commissioners to meet on or before April 15th, and issue their warrants to the assessors requiring them to make returns of all taxable persons and their property, ... 386
Each township, board or district to elect two free-holders to assist assessors in levying taxes, etc., ... 386
Assessors to demand returns of property and make returns to the commissioners, etc., ...385-386
Penalty for refusal or neglect to give returns, ... 387
Assessors, etc., to search records to discover concealed property, ... 387
Lands not returned to be charged with all such taxes in the next assessment, ... 388
Penalty for concealing property, etc., 388
Upon receipt of assessors' returns commissioners to quota the districts,.. 388
And within six days thereafter furnish the assessors with a transcript of the quota charged upon the township, etc., to which the assessor belongs, ...388-389
Assessor and two free-holders to levy and assess the quota of each township, etc., on the person and their estates therein, ... 389

WAR TAX—Continued.
List of the different kinds of property subject to taxation under act, ... 389
Such enumerated articles to be rated at what they are bona fide worth,.. 390
Sums raised not to be deemed the exact proportion of the city and counties until the same be correctly and finally adjusted by the legislature, 390
Single freemen to be taxed not more than 6£ or less than 3£, ... 390
Trades, professions, etc., to be rated at the discretion of the assessors and freeholders, ... 390
Assessors may demand security from single freemen, ... 390
Single freemen failing to give security to be committed for one month or until he enters security or pays the tax, ... 390
House-holders upon demand of assessor to furnish names and occupations of inmates, ... 391
Penalty for neglect or refusal, ... 391
Disposition of penalty, ... 391
Goods of tenants, etc., liable to be distrained for such taxes, ... 391
Tenant to deduct tax from rent where he is compelled to pay same, ... 391
Or recover the same by action at law, 391
Act not to alter any contract between landlord and tenant as to the payment of taxes, ... 391
Oath of county commissioners, ...391-392
Oath of assessors, ... 392
County commissioners to appoint a collector for each township, ward, and district, ... 392
Commissioners to prefix a warrant to collector's duplicate, etc., ... 392
Contents of warrants, ... 392
Penalties, how recoverable, ... 392
Assessors and collectors to notify commissioners in writing within two days of their election as to their intention to serve or not, ... 393
Failure to do so to be considered as a refusal to serve, ... 393
Penalty for neglect or refusal of assessors and collectors to serve, ... 393
Penalties, how recoverable, ... 393

Index.

WAR TAX—Continued.
Persons aggrieved by assessment to appeal to county commissioners, ... 394
Proceedings on appeal, ... 394
Upon refusal to pay tax collector to distrain for same, ... 394
Collector authorized to break open in the day-time any house, trunk, etc., in order to make distress, ... 394
Collector to return the over-plus after deducting charges to owner, ... 395
For want of sufficient distress taxable to be committed, ... 395
Collectors collector to pay to the county treasurer the whole tax charged in duplicate within thirty days, ... 395
Time extended in cases where distress is necessary, ... 395
Commissioners to issue warrants to the sheriff, etc., requiring him to seize the bodies and estates of delinquents, ... 396
Proceedings upon such seizures, ... 396
Commissioners may sell land, etc., where owners neglect or refuse to pay the taxes assessed thereon within thirty days after the day of appeal, ... 397
Where owner of goods distrained on for taxes refused to receive the over-plus, collector to pay the same to the county treasurer, ... 398
County treasurer to deduct one per cent. and give notice thereof to the county commissioners within twenty days, ... 398
Owner to have the remainder discounted out of any future tax, ... 398
Receipt of treasurer to exonerate collector, ... 398
Collectors to make out accounts of their seizures, etc., and settle the same with commissioners, ... 398
Respective county treasurers to make payment to the state treasurer within certain specified time after receiving the same from collectors, .. 398
Compensation of county commissioners, ... 399
Compensation of collectors, ... 399
All taxes to be paid in gold or silver only, ... 399

WAR TAX—Continued.
Commissioners neglecting to perform duty under act to be fined by the supreme executive council, ... 400
Compensation of county treasurer,.. 400
Compensation of state treasurer, ... 400
Commissioners to lay a bare transcript of the returns of property together with a pound rate and sums quota before the assembly, ... 400
Commissioners empowered to employ clerks, ... 400

WARWICK TOWNSHIP.
The Trustees of the Presbyterian Church in Warwick township, in county of Bucks, incorporated, ... 519

WARWICK PRESBYTERIAN CHURCH.
The Trustees of the Presbyterian Church in Warwick township, in county of Bucks, incorporated, ... 519

WASHINGTON COUNTY.
Erected, ... 272
Boundaries of, ... 272
Privileges, etc., of the inhabitants to be the same as those of other counties, ... 273
To be divided into townships, ... 273
Inhabitants to choose inspectors, ... 273
Place and manner of conducting elections in, ... 273
To have two representatives in the general assembly, ... 273
Inhabitants to elect one counsellor, two sheriffs, two coroners and three commissioners, ... 273
Justices of the supreme court to have like powers and jurisdictions in, as in other counties, ... 274
Jail deliveries to be made in, in like manner as elsewhere, ... 274
Freeholders of each township in, to elect two justices of the peace, ... 274
Election of judges of elections and inspectors, ... 274
Duties of election officers, ... 274
Oath of judge of elections, ... 275
Oath of inspector, ... 275
Jurisdiction of justices of the peace, 275
Justices to hold courts of general quarter sessions, jail delivery, and county courts for holding of pleas, 275

Index

WASHINGTON COUNTY—Continued.
    Time of holding said courts, ... 275
    Courts to be held at court house when erected, ... 275
    Certain persons authorized to select and purchase site for court house and prison, ...275-276
    To cause court house and prison to be erected thereon, ... 276
    Tax not exceeding £1,000 to be levied to defray expenses of building courthouse and prison in, ... 276
    Actions pending in Westmoreland county against inhabitants of, not to be discontinued by reason of act, 276
    Justices of Westmoreland county authorized to issue process in such suits to sheriff, ... 276
    Sheriff directed to obey such writs and return them to justices of Westmoreland county, ... 276
    A collector of the excise of, appointed, 277
    Powers and duties of said collector, .. 277
    Collector to obtain from collector of excise of Westmoreland county a list of the arrearages within, ... 277
    Bond of collector of excise, ... 277
    Fees and perquisites of said collector, 278
    Sheriff and coroner of Westmoreland county to discharge their duties within, until a sheriff and coroner shall be there chosen, ... 278
    Bond of sheriff, ... 278
    Bond to be entered in the office for the recording of deeds, ... 278
    Treasurer appointed for receiving state taxes to give security, ... 278
    Treasurer appointed for receiving county levies to give security, ... 278
    Such persons to register their slaves in accordance with act for the gradual abolition of slavery, ... 463
    Orphans' court clerks, register of wills and recorders of deeds of Westmoreland and Washington counties to receive from late Clerks of Youghiogheny, Monongahela and Ohio counties all public papers, records, etc., ... 463

WASHINGTON COUNTY—Continued.
    Inhabitants of Westmoreland and Washington counties who produce certified copies of taking the oath of allegiance to the state of Virginia before the settlement of state boundary dispute declared to be free citizens of this state, ...462-463

WASTE.
    United States authorized to bring actions for, to protect its property, .. 46
    Persons guilty of committing, on lands of absentees, etc., to pay treble damages, ... 127
    May be fined and imprisoned upon conviction thereof, ... 127
    Duration of act limited, ... 127

WATCH. See Philadelphia, City of.

WATCHMEN. See Philadelphia, City of.

WATER COURSES. See Philadelphia City of.

WATER SPOUTS. See Carlisle, Borough of; Nuisances.

WESTMORELAND COUNTY.
    Act for the relief of the inhabitants of Northumberland, Bedford, Northampton and, ... 114
    County commissioners and assessors to lay state taxes by former returns, 114
    Commissioners and assessors to exonerate from taxes persons driven off from their settlements by the enemy, ... 114
    To transmit to the general assembly a list of the persons so exonerated,.. 115
    Deficiencies arising in raising quota of, to be made good out of state taxes, ... 115
    Inhabitants of Westmoreland county and Washington county who produce certified copies of taking the oath of allegiance to the state of Virginia before the settlement of state boundary dispute declared to be free citizens of this state, ...462-463

Index.

WESTMORELAND COUNTY—Continued.

	Page.
Such persons to register their slaves in accordance with act for the gradual abolition of slavery,	463
Orphans' court clerks, register of wills and recorders of deeds of Westmoreland and Washington counties to receive from late clerks of Youghiogheny, Monongahela and Ohio counties all public papers, records, etc.,	463

WHARVES.

	Page.
Wardens of Philadelphia to let market-houses, ferries and public landing places and,	201
Treasurer of wardens and assessors to receive rents from market-houses, ferries and public landing places and,	201
Owners of ferries and public landing places and, to pay their rents to the treasurer of the wardens and assessors,	202
Philadelphia wardens empowered to purchase a lot on north side of Sassafras street along Delaware river for a public wharf,	303
Commissioners appointed to purchase with the approbation of three justices a lot or lots for the accommodation of Southwark with public landing places,	513
Commissioners to erect wharves and quays thereon,	513
And if necessary to mortgage such lots in order to do so,	513
Commissioners to lay out landing places,	513
And dispose of any over-plus at either public or private sale,	513-514
Commissioners to let out the wharves, etc., establish the rates of toll, and receive the rents, etc.,	514
To apply the same towards discharging all incumbrances on said lots,	514
Commissioners together with assessors and freeholders, to levy a yearly assessment not exceeding 1 shilling in the £,	514
To appoint a collector to collect the same,	514

WHARVES—Continued.

	Page.
Powers of collector,	515
Duties of collector,	515
Fees of collector,	515
Penalty on persons appointed collectors refusing to serve,	515
Penalty, how recoverable,	515
Defendant in such action allowed to plead the general issue and give act and special matter in evidence,	515
But not allowed protection or wager of law nor more than one imparlance,	515
Collector failing to account for moneys received to be committed, without bail or mainprize,	516
Filling of vacancy in office of collector,	516
Bond of treasurer of commissioners,	516
Two-thirds of commissioners to constitute a board,	517
Estate in lots secure under act vested in the commissioners until all incumbrances are discharged,	517
Such lots to then devolve upon the supervisors of the highways who are erected into a corporation for the purposes of the trust,	517-518
Three additional supervisors to be elected at the first election after the final adjustment of the commissioners accounts,	518
Auditors appointed to examine and settle the accounts and certify that the sums due to Luke Morris, Thomas Penrose and Abel James for the purchase of lots for the use of a public landing,	481
On payment of sums so certified the fee simple to said lots to vest in certain trustees,	482
Trustees not to obtain any rights to said lots unless they pay sums certified by auditors within two years,	482
Upon procuring title trustees to lay out streets and landings,	483
Trustees to dispose of unnecessary parts of lots at public sale,	483
Trustees to mortgage the parts retained for public use,	484
Trustees to let out wharves, quays and landing places for terms not exceeding 7 years,	484

Index.

WHARVES—Continued.
Trustees to establish rates and prices for wharfage, ... 484
And bind all tenants to observe the same rules and regulations as tenants of public landings in Philadelphia are bound to observe, ... 484
Trustees to pay off incumbrances as soon as they have sufficient means and convey the premises to the supervisors of the highways, ... 484-485

WHEAT. See Flour.
Fees of certain officers to be estimated and paid in wheat, ... 39-40
Payment to be also made in lawful money of this state or of the United States in sums proportioned to value of wheat, ... 40
Offices to which payment of fees in wheat shall extend, enumerated, ..40-41
Act not to extend to fees rated by the £ or £100, ... 41
Compensation of county commissioners and assessors to be satisfied in, 142
Wheat flour, etc., to be received in payment of taxes, ... 198
Act to permit the exportation of flour of wheat, partly repealed, ... 267
Parts of act to permit the exportation of flour of wheat, etc., repealed, .. 326

WHIPPING.
Part punishment for counterfeiting or raising bills of credit, loan-office certificates or bills of exchange, ... 15
Part punishment for horse stealing, for first offence, ... 113
Part punishment for counterfeiting, raising or knowingly uttering raised bills of credit, ... 189
Part punishment for knowingly uttering raised bills of credit, ... 212
Part punishment for raising or knowingly uttering raised bills of credit, 307
Persons convicted of assisting prisoners of war to escape and unable to pay fines to be publicly whipped, .. 467

WHISKEY.
Act to permit making of, etc., from rye, etc., under certain restrictions, etc., repealed, ... 175-176

WILSON RIOTS.
All persons engaged in, pardoned by act of assembly, ... 118
Act to be deemed a public act, ... 119

WINES. See Excise.
Excise on, after May 1, 1780 to be paid in wheat in like manner as fees of officers, ... 130

WITNESSES.
Fees of, to be paid in wheat, ... 40
Slaves not to be admitted as witnesses against freemen, ... 70
Fees of, for attending before auditors appointed to settle public accounts, 78
Informers against, quartermasters, foragemasters, etc., purchasing wheat, etc., in violation of act to be admitted as, ... 182
In court martial proceedings to be examined on oath by the president, .. 168
Members of militia called as, and refusing to give evidence to be censured or fined, ... 168
Informer against person refusing to take bills of credit in payment of necessaries of life to be a competent witness, ...242-243
Informer to be a competent witness against persons refusing to accept bills of credit equal in value to gold and silver for goods, etc., ... 250
Fees and mileage of, ... 454

WOLVES.
Act to encourage the killing of, ... 460
Reward for killing, ... 460
Persons killing, to bring scalps with ears on to a justice of the peace and make proof of their right to reward, 461
Prior act repealed, ... 461

WORKHOUSES.
Court houses, jails, prisons and, throughout the state vested in the commonwealth, ... 50
Act not to extend to old temporary prison in Bedford, ... 50
Nor to old jail and workhouse at 3d and High Sts., Philadelphia, ... 50

WORKHOUSES—Continued.
Supreme executive council to sell old jail and workhouse in Philadelphia for the benefit of said city and county, ... 51
Certain prior acts of assembly repealed, ... 52

WRITS OF ASSISTANCE.
Naval officer, his deputy and assistants to enter vessels and suspected houses in search of concealed goods liable to duty, ... 255

WRITS OF ASSISTANCE—Continued.
In case of opposition or refusal naval officer to obtain a, from two justices of the supreme court or of the peace, and break open doors, etc., 255
No search to be made of any dwelling until due cause of suspicion be shown to satisfaction of the justice either of the supreme court or of the peace, ... 255

Y.

YOUGHIOGHENY RIVER.
Ferries established on, ... 471
Declared to be a public highway, ... 472

Milton Keynes UK
Ingram Content Group UK Ltd.
UKHW040058180324
439604UK00007B/1105